Benjamin Britten

PAUL KILDEA

Benjamin Britten

A Life in the Twentieth Century

ALLEN LANE
an imprint of
PENGUIN BOOKS

ALLEN LANE

Published by the Penguin Group

Penguin Books Ltd, 80 Strand, London WC2R ORL, England

Penguin Group (USA) Inc., 375 Hudson Street, New York, New York 10014, USA

Penguin Group (Canada), 90 Eglinton Avenue East, Suite 700, Toronto, Ontario, Canada M4P 2Y3
(a division of Pearson Canada Inc.)

Penguin Ireland, 25 St Stephen's Green, Dublin 2, Ireland (a division of Penguin Books Ltd)

Penguin Group (Australia), 707 Collins Street, Melbourne, Victoria 3008, Australia
(a division of Pearson Australia Group Pty Ltd)

Penguin Books India Pvt Ltd, 11 Community Centre, Panchsheel Park, New Delhi – 110 017, India

Penguin Group (NZ), 67 Apollo Drive, Rosedale, Auckland 0632, New Zealand
(a division of Pearson New Zealand Ltd)

Penguin Books (South Africa) (Pty) Ltd, Block D, Rosebank Office Park,
181 Jan Smuts Avenue, Parktown North, Gauteng 2193, South Africa

Penguin Books Ltd, Registered Offices: 80 Strand, London WC2R ORL, England

www.penguin.com

First published 2013
001

Set in 10.2/13.87pt Sabon LT Std
Typeset by Jouve (UK), Milton Keynes
Printed in Great Britain by Clays Ltd, St Ives plc

ISBN: 978–1–846–14232–1

ALWAYS LEARNING   **PEARSON**

For two teachers,
Malcolm and Keith

Contents

Illustrations

Acknowledgements

I am grateful to the many people who gave generously of their time and scholarship, including Michael Berkeley, Peter Biggs, Kate Bucknell, Michael Burden, John Carey, Christopher Chowrimootoo, John Copley, Neil Dalrymple, Tony Fell, Paul Fitzsimon, Malcolm Gillies, Carolyn Hart, David Hewett, Jennifer Higgie, Graham Johnson, Mark Kruger, Hermione Lee, Judith LeGrove, Stephen Lock, Ian Munro, Bayan Northcott, Michael Petch, David Price, Basil Reeve, Peter Roennfeldt, Tom Rosenthal, Brian Soloman, Alan Swerdlow and David Wheatley.

Friends and colleagues to have offered ideas and encouragement include Warwick Anderson, Chris Bornet, Penny Bradfield, Jon Canter, Maria Crealey, Felicity Ehrlich, Tom Hamilton, Simon Hewett, Lindy Hume, Simon Kenway, Margaret and Tony Kidd, Sue Kildea, Peter and Ruth Kraus, Sue Kruske, Belinda Matthews, Helen Napper, David Pear, Lee Primer, Jonathan Reekie, Patrick Summers, Jack Turner, Benjamin Waters, Andrew Watts, Mark Williams, Jonathan Wright and David Wroe.

John Allison commissioned from me for Glyndebourne a number of long articles on different Britten operas, variants of which make their way into these pages. The same can be said of Michael Pederson at Opera Australia, Philip Reed at English National Opera, and Jane Billingham at Aldeburgh Music. John Fuller was very helpful on Auden and his poetry, and I reproduce some of his thoughts with his permission.

Rosamund Strode was unfailingly kind and informative, as was Rita Thomson – two remarkable women whom Britten trusted implicitly. I am grateful to both for their permission to quote from interviews with them. I had the great privilege of working at Aldeburgh with the scholar Jennifer Doctor who was ever generous with her thoughts and expertise. Tom Sutcliffe, Walter Sutcliffe and Simon Butteriss were helpful on postwar English opera production. I am grateful to Bob Shingleton for alerting me to Britten's unexpected connection with the folk singer and activist Pete Seeger. I am also grateful to Susie Walton for her account of Britten's final hours. Many years ago Eric Crozier was incredibly generous with his time, giving me among other things a copy of his unpublished 'After

Long Pursuit' and 'Notes on Benjamin Britten', the latter a rich mine (but also potentially dangerous minefield) of information. I thank him, posthumously, for his thoughts and words and for permission to reproduce them. Muki Fairchild shared with me her grandmother Elizabeth Mayer's diary, and I reproduce excerpts here with her permission. Excerpts from an interview with her mother, Beata Sauerlander, and uncle, Michael Mayer, are reproduced with permission. I thank Bridget Kitley for permission to reproduce her mother Enid Slater's photograph of Wulff Scherchen. Clarissa Lewis kindly granted permission to reproduce excerpts from interviews with her parents, John and Myfanwy Piper, and, on behalf of the estate of John Piper, also generously allowed us to use *Interior of St Mark's, Venice* as the book's endpapers. Permission to quote from other interviews was granted by the Sydney Nolan Trust, the Holst Foundation, the estate of Joan Cross, the estate of Tanya Moiseiwitsch, the estate of Stephen and Natasha Spender, the estate of Stephen Reiss, Will Kerley, Humphrey Maud, Colin Matthews and David Matthews. Excerpts from the Lord Chamberlain's Papers are copyright © British Library Board and HM the Queen, and are reproduced by kind permission of the British Library. I have made every attempt to track down copyright holders; any omissions will be addressed in future editions if brought to the publisher's attention.

Hywel and Lucette Davies were unfailingly generous with their time, hospitality and expertise. The staff at the Red House, Aldeburgh, could not have been more helpful, namely Thomas Barnes, Jude Brimmer, Nick Clark, Kevin Gosling, Chris Grogan, Caroline Harding, Jon Manton, Judith Ratcliffe, Carol Scopes, Anne Surfling, Lucy Walker and Pam Wheeler. Nicolas Bell at the British Library supplied the photograph of the opening page of Britten's *A Midsummer Night's Dream* manuscript (BL Add. MS 60605), which is copyright © 1960 by Hawkes & Son (London) Ltd. Reproduced by permission of Boosey & Hawkes Music Publishers Ltd., courtesy of The British Library. I thank Andy Chan in this context.

I thank Jon Stallworthy for permission to reproduce excerpts from Wilfred Owen's poems. Stallworthy's two-volume critical edition of Owen's *Complete Poems and Fragments* (1983) supersedes the edition Britten worked from and outlines different readings of the poems, from which I profited. The standard texts of Owen's poems are to be found in Stallworthy's *Wilfred Owen: The War Poems* (London, Chatto & Windus, 1994). Extract from 'Still Falls the Rain' from *Collected Poems* by Edith Sitwell reprinted by permission of Peters Fraser & Dunlop (www.petersfraserdunlop.com) on behalf of the Estate of Edith Sitwell. Extract from 'Praise we Great Men' from *The Outcast* by Edith Sitwell reprinted by permission of Peters Fraser & Dunlop on behalf of the Estate of Edith Sitwell.

The Britten–Pears Foundation was supportive of the project from its inception, notably Richard Jarman, Colin Matthews, Donald Mitchell, Janis Susskind and Marion Thorpe. Colin particularly was insightful and helpful, as he is to the many scholars and composers he talks to when he really should be in his study composing. This book could not have been written without the groundbreaking Britten letters project, edited by Donald Mitchell, Philip Reed and Mervyn Cooke. Michael Richards at Boydell & Brewer allowed me to see volumes 5 and 6 prior to publication and I am grateful to Philip and to Jill Burrows for facilitating this. The letters and all other writings by Benjamin Britten and Peter Pears and reproductions of the composer's manuscripts are © Britten–Pears Foundation.

Parts or the whole of the manuscript were read by Michael Black, John Bridcut, Paul Broussard, Sue Hackett, Colin Matthews, Helen Moody, David Oldham, Anne Surfling and Pam Wheeler, all of whom gave invaluable comments and criticisms. Graeme Honner brought his stern if inspiring sub-editing eye to the task. Any errors are mine alone. This book was written between gigs, many of them featuring Britten's music, and I thank the musicians, directors and designers I have worked with over the years. In addition to the two teachers to whom this book is dedicated, Malcolm Gillies and Keith Radford, I had the great privilege of studying as a postgraduate with Cyril Ehrlich, Brian Trowell and Arnold Whittall, with whom my thoughts on Britten and English culture and history were first formulated.

I thank my agent David Godwin for pushing me towards this subject when my eye was elsewhere, as I do his team at DGA: Charlotte Knight, Anna Watkins, Caitlin Ingham and Kirsty Mclachlan.

It was a huge privilege to be edited by Stuart Proffitt, who made the book much better. I was also extremely well served by Elizabeth Stratford (whose knowledge of Hardy came in handy, in addition to her eagle-eyed copy editing), Shan Vahidy, Richard Duguid and Pen Vogler. I thank Christopher Phipps for his index.

Though it is almost impossible to calculate accurately the worth of money in one year versus another, I have converted Britten's earnings to today's approximate value via the Bank of England's inflation calculator (http://www.bankofengland.co.uk/education/Pages/inflation/calculator/index1.aspx).

Benjamin Britten's East Anglia

North Sea

N
W   E
S

The Wash

Holt •

NORFOLK

Norwich •

Lowestoft •

Southwold •
Blythburgh •
Horham •
Yoxford •
(Dunwich) •

CAMBRIDGESHIRE

Saxmundham •
Snape
R. Alde
Thorpeness •
Aldeburgh •

SUFFOLK

• Cambridge

Ufford •
Bentwaters airbase
Orford •

Long Melford •

Ipswich •

R. Stour

Felixstowe •

ESSEX

London, 100 miles
from Aldeburgh

0   10   20 miles
0   10   20   30 kilometres

Prologue: The Art of Dissent

I

All art is a kind of confession, more or less oblique. All artists,
if they are to survive, are forced, at last, to tell the whole story,
to vomit the anguish up. All of it, the literal and the fanciful.

James Baldwin, 1960

In early summer 1940, a little over a week after the final evacuations
from the French port of Dunkirk, German troops prepared to march
into a shaken Paris. One of the few foreign war correspondents still in
the capital on 13 June, the eve of the occupation, described it as a 'city
of the dead'. The government had fled to Bordeaux, the army somewhere south; shops, hotels and restaurants were shuttered, newspaper
presses silent, the Champs-Elysées deserted bar a smattering of Americans searching vainly for passage.

News of this improbable French ghost town and imminent occupation transfixed London. An unsteady mixture of celebration and
trepidation had existed in Britain since the German invasion of France
and the Low Countries a month earlier, replacing the monotonous
uncertainty of the phoney war. Churchill picked up on the mood a few
days later, in arguably the most iconic speech of his career, when he told
the House of Commons that, were the British Empire and Commonwealth to last a thousand years, the defeat of Hitler would still be
remembered as 'their finest hour'. But a day before the occupation it
was the turn of Conservative MP Major Sir Jocelyn Lucas. He rose in
his seat, this veteran of Ypres and younger brother of a fallen soldier,
and asked the House 'whether British citizens of military age, such as
Mr W. H. Auden and Mr Christopher Isherwood, who have gone to the

United States and expressed their determination not to return to this country until war is over, will be summoned back for registration and calling up, in view of the fact that they are seeking refuge abroad?' His Eton and Sandhurst accent filled the chamber, his temper up. His contempt for these writers exemplified one of the extreme ideological clashes of 1930s England, a distillation of the conflict between the Establishment and its critics that had grown out of war, the Depression and the disillusionment and decadence of the 1920s. 'Is my hon. Friend aware of the indignation caused by young men leaving the country and saying that they will not fight? If they are not registered as conscientious objectors will he see that they lose their citizenship?'

Benjamin Britten was one of the young men inspiring Lucas's indignation. He had travelled to America in spring the previous year with no real plan, just the conviction that Europe was somehow finished and his future was in the New World, not the Old. He was not running away: war was likely but not certain, and, if ever it came, his pacifism would keep him from the fight. Yet his absence angered patriotic Britons. Not even his return to England in 1942, aged twenty-eight, his belief in the great American Dream diminished, dampened the hostility. Thin-skinned at the best of times, he found himself impossibly exposed in London, convinced that his pacifism and civvies marked him out for special animus. The conscientious objector retreated to the Suffolk mill he had converted just before the war to write the opera that effected his rehabilitation.

2

Peter Grimes did save his reputation, but so too did it end up a sort of disguise, as people began to mistake Britten for the character he created. Peter Pears, the first Grimes, initiated the conflation. A year after the premiere, which announced to the world the artistic primacy of the two young Englishmen, Pears said of the central character: 'He is very much of an ordinary weak person who, being at odds with the society in which he finds himself, tries to overcome it and, in doing so, offends against the conventional code, is classed by society as a criminal, and destroyed as such.' It is not much, but this one phrase, *at odds with the society in which he finds himself*, soon became the widely accepted shorthand for both the character Peter Grimes and his creator.

Britten seemed happy enough with the confusion. Two years later he followed Pears's lead in an interview for *Time*, lending his gently lined, thoughtful face to the cover of an issue marking the Metropolitan Opera's new production of *Grimes*. He volunteered that the story was 'a subject very close to my heart – the struggle of the individual against the masses. The more vicious the society, the more vicious the individual'. It sounds a little like the George Orwell of *The Road to Wigan Pier* who proposed that in England 'a middle-class child is taught almost simultaneously to wash his neck, to be ready to die for his country, and to despise the "lower classes"' – except that Britten seems not to have read Orwell by 1948 (and probably never did).

By the time he returned to the theme fifteen years later, this notion of being at odds with society was a recognized, entrenched motif of Britten's great opera, and a motif of his life too. Britten duly obliged Murray Schafer in a 1963 interview, claiming a thread of nobility in Grimes's character where Pears had earlier emphasized weakness, and finally gave name to the source of this social isolation.

> A central feeling for us was that of the individual against the crowd, with ironic overtones for our own situation. As conscientious objectors we were out of it. We couldn't say we suffered physically, but naturally we experienced tremendous tension. I think it was partly this feeling which led us to make Grimes a character of vision and conflict, the tortured idealist he is, rather than the villain he was in Crabbe.

But by 1963 the world had changed, and Britten was living in an era of Cold War posturing and fashionable campaigns for nuclear disarmament. It was thirteen years since North Korea's invasion of South Korea, seven since the Soviet incursion into Hungary, and only a year since the potentially disastrous brinkmanship in Cuba. Joe McCarthy's vicious pettifoggery in the US Senate had changed the culture of American politics and provided the 1950s with a disturbing backdrop. Pacifism had become an entirely respectable form of dissent, and Britten found himself in the unusual if welcome position of naming and claiming the moral high ground he had long trod.

He was a little slow in doing so, for in the interim others had made hay with the whispers of the previous decades, with the fisherman and his maker. Émigré Hans Keller, a swashbuckling Viennese musicologist and Britten champion who looked a little like Groucho Marx and spoke a lot like Sigmund Freud (and who found himself, as a consequence, slightly out of place in the gentler English climate following the *Anschluss*), identified in the composer the thread of 'heavily repressed sadism [that] underlies pacifistic attitudes'. 'What distinguishes Britten's musical personality is the violent repressive counter-force against his sadism.' Such psychosexual analysis later influenced critic Andrew Porter, who wrote what others after Keller had merely hinted at: that the pacifism Britten spoke of to explain why he felt like an outsider in wartime England was a cipher for another form of social isolation. 'It has often been suggested (though seldom in print) that Grimes's inner struggle (like Claggart's and perhaps Captain Vere's) is against a homosexuality that neither he nor, for that matter, his creator is consciously aware of.'

It was a short but logical step from Porter's trio of repressed, gay operatic characters to the 'horrifying sextet' identified in 1983 by scholar Philip Brett, drawing on a lifetime of Britten's operas – Grimes, Vere, Claggart, Quint, Oberon and Aschenbach – each representative of the composer's 'predominantly negative "homosexual vision"'. Brett was certain that Britten was aware of Grimes's homosexuality, libretto drafts and correspondence between Pears and Britten at the time supporting his view. 'The more I hear of it,' Pears told Britten in March 1944 as *Peter Grimes* slowly took shape, 'the more I feel that the queerness is unimportant & doesn't really exist in the music (or at any rate obtrude) so it mustn't do so in the words.' Brett was not interested in stepping gingerly through real minefields, past the shells and detritus of actual wars and the civilian dissent they inspired. His goal was to strip the operas of their veils, to recognize that whatever pacifistic ideals shaped certain works and Britten's outlook, much of the composer's inspiration was to be found in his sexuality and his or society's troubled, oppressive response to it. Brett argued that the horrifying sextet would not exist without this creative impetus.

Brett was rightly dismissive of those who thought sexuality the only motivating force, as he was of those who could find no connection between composer and fisherman – conductor Colin Davis and tenor Jon Vickers being two such figures; in the 1970s the latter brutalized Grimes's personality, took liberties with text and tempo, and robbed his voice of the dreamy lyricism Britten had in mind for the role. He was almost equally dismissive of the polite and hypocritical mien too often adopted by British critics when dealing with one of their culture's most distinguished practitioners, too keen to take him at his word when he spoke of conscientious objection and its overtones rather than what then remained more morally troubling themes.

3

At odds with the society in which he finds himself. It is an attractive point of entry into someone's life, and biographers have explored it fully, not least Humphrey Carpenter in 1992, who was also fond of its near corollary, the destruction of childhood innocence. It is not a wholly accurate shorthand for the man, yet it has come to dominate our contemporary image of Britten at the expense of more nuanced readings.

To all appearances Britten was an enthusiastic subscriber to the upper-middle-class life he created for himself after the war. He spoke in a voice indebted more to public school, the Auden crowd and RP (received pronunciation) than to a childhood in Lowestoft. He lived in large houses and drove fast cars. And he accepted a host of awards, from his appointment as Freeman of Lowestoft in 1951 to a seat in the House of Lords twenty-five years later. These were hardly symbols of dissent. He went to tea parties and suppers with the Queen and her mother and took holidays with her cousin. And in his own scores he distanced himself from the more extreme experimentations in English music in the 1960s and 1970s. His friend and fellow composer Michael Tippett had the good grace all his life to dress like an artist; his clothes affirmed the times, never more so than in the 1960s and 1970s. Britten dressed conservatively, in tweed jackets and knitted ties. He preferred rural life, rejecting the opportunity to hide in a big city. He liked the pace and space of country living, which allowed him to think clearly and use his time fruitfully. He valued also his proximity to the sea that pulses through a handful of his important works and which gave him a narrative link to a childhood spent overlooking the Suffolk coast.

There was no filial schism, either. Despite political differences in the mid-1930s, as Britten flexed his newly toned intellectual muscle, mother and son maintained a loving, mutually admiring relationship until her death in 1937. It was much the same with his father, a more distant figure (a characteristic no doubt compounded by his sinister silent-film-villain physiognomy) who nonetheless retained Britten's love and respect while alive, an attitude possibly revised after his death. He remained close to his two sisters all his life and maintained a cordial if unsympathetic relationship with his brother, who shared his father's hooded eyes, aloofness and values.

His relationship with Peter Pears was illegal until 1967, but otherwise conventional in the manner of the day. The tall, handsome singer, with his thickset frame, aquiline profile and light lyric voice, first met the composer in 1937 when so much of what we now know about Britten was still nebulous. Two years later, with more of his character in place, they embarked on the relationship that absorbed them both until Britten's death in 1976.

Britten had no taste for bohemian living or counter-culture; had there been the slightest instinct in this direction before the war it was cured in the filth and chaos of the communal house in Brooklyn he shared during it with W. H. Auden, Carson McCullers, Paul and Jane Bowles, Gypsy Rose Lee and a revolving guest list of lovers, artists (including Salvador Dalí), circus animals and their trainers. Britten's life and vision thrived on order and discipline, not Romantic notions of artists living and working outside the pulls of conventional society. He ran his life as he would have run a farm or small business.

This is not to say that he cared much for conventional society, at least not for the way it operated. And in this context he was at odds with society – not through a dark stain at the core of his own heart, but because of one he perceived to be at the heart of humanity. Thus his first grand opera is wholly representative of his psyche, but for reasons distinct from those usually given.

Britten disclosed as much in January 1958 when Covent Garden revived its eleven-year-old production of *Peter Grimes*. He was mealy-mouthed about Tyrone Guthrie's staging first time round, disliking its tilt towards abstractness where the original production had opted for cluttered realism. Yet in 1958 he was moved to write to his friend Princess Margaret of Hesse and the Rhine, 'It is a funny old piece, but it has more of me, of the sea, of Suffolk, of the worry of 20th century life, than perhaps anything I've ever done.' 'The worry of 20th century life' is no hard-nosed political manifesto, too coy by half to link the middle-aged composer with his younger, socialist self, yet the phrase hints at the dysfunction Britten identified in contemporary society and speaks to the universal themes he saw in the century's poverty and inhumanity.

This is also how American writer and literary critic Edmund Wilson characterized *Grimes* in its original June 1945 season.

> By the time you are done with the opera – or by the time it is done with you – you have decided that Peter Grimes is the whole of bombing, machine-gunning, mining, torpedoing, ambushing humanity, which talks about a guaranteed standard of living yet does nothing but wreck its own works, degrade or pervert its own moral life and reduce itself to starvation. You feel, during the final scenes, that the indignant shouting trampling mob which comes to punish Peter Grimes is just as sadistic as he. And when Balstrode gets to him first and sends him out to sink himself in his boat, you feel that you are in the same boat as Grimes.

Wilson's take could not be further from the solipsistic view of the opera and composer that has been in currency in England since Pears first wrote about the work. He saw Britten as a Goya-like figure, able to make 'eloquent and morally urgent art out of human disaster', as Robert Hughes said of the creator of *Los Desastres de la Guerra* (The Disasters of War), prints depicting the Spanish attempt to break free of Napoleon's yoke, a series awash with blood and random acts of great viciousness. Another parallel is with the Picasso of *Guernica* onwards, who captured the horror of industrialized war. Such comparisons should prompt us to realize that Britten was a far more complex man than the picture that emerged from the biographical dust storm Pears initiated in 1946, one which Britten, among many others, perpetuated. 'It's an encouraging sign', Britten continued in his letter to Princess Margaret of Hesse, 'to find that even when the individual isn't particularly attractive, or guiltless, how the sympathy of the audience goes to *him* rather than to the man-hunting crowd . . .'

4

Through such characterization and commentary about his aims, Britten encouraged the public personification and victimhood initiated by Pears, though the identification with his operatic creation became a burden once he experienced true fame. It was all too easy for the outside world to conclude that Britten's outwardly normal demeanour was a disguise for some sort of depravity, the clues to which could be found in his operas.

Yet if this simple-minded correlation between composer and his characters was all the outside world had to go on, even those who knew Britten well found it hard to come to any sort of agreement about him. 'Very warm-hearted and full of fun and impishness and sort of childishness, this sort of nice childlike nature seemed to bubble out of him,' his friend from the 1940s John Lindsay said. Ronald Duncan, a friend in the same decade and the one before, and later the wayward librettist of *The Rape of Lucretia*, only partially agreed, taking Hans Keller's cue. 'No man had more charm, could be more generous or kind – as I should know; but behind that mask was another person, a sadist, psychologically crippled and bent. Perhaps that's what we all are, but with less power, and with less charm to attract others to us, we do less harm and cause less pain then he.' 'A mother's boy', thought another librettist and friend, Eric Crozier. A later and younger friend, Humphrey Maud, enjoyed the sense of impishness identified by Lindsay, yet also noticed 'that he could be quite petulant and waspish and bad tempered'.

Stephen Spender thought much the same of the older Britten and the environment he created for himself. 'The atmosphere of Aldeburgh was always rather unfortunate . . . if you were an old friend . . . it was rather like a sort of school and . . . you wonder whether the head boy is going to speak to you that morning and if you meet him in the street whether he'll recognize you.' But Christopher Isherwood, describing Britten in the 1930s, had seen a different person. 'Well Ben is like water in our hands. Ben is a very weak character and Wystan [Auden] and I can do anything we like with him.'

Mezzo-soprano Janet Baker saw Spender's school analogy and raised it to a royal court. 'To be with him was a bit like being with the Queen: in those circumstances you're never quite natural. I suppose it's almost like the sensation of being in love.' Tippett thought the same. 'I think that all of us who were close to Ben had for him something dangerously near to love.' Tenor Robert Tear also viewed Aldeburgh in terms of a royal court (from before Henry VIII's break with Rome), identifying there a 'Pope, King, a couple of sycophantic academics and perhaps a handmaiden or two strewing palms'. Tear disliked what he identified as the reverence of Aldeburgh and its festival, 'an atmosphere laden with waspishness, bitterness, cold, hard eyes, with cabalistic meetings under the Cherry Tree with Pimms, with the inscrutability of the elite. It was an atmosphere of secrecy.' Tear still considered Britten the greatest musician he ever met, the greatest conductor he ever worked with and a peerless pianist. He saw no contradiction between these wildly divergent points of view.

Joan Cross, who created the role of Ellen Orford and other important Britten characters, though she could not claim a close friendship, nonetheless retained 'a lasting memory of a man of great charm and a glorious sense of humour, given to occasional and sudden bursts of fury (which he often regretted later) and of course total dedication'. Swiss conductor Ernest Ansermet, who liked and respected Britten, found no such humour in him, confiding in a Glyndebourne colleague, in idiosyncratic English, that all he needed was 'a little joke then and now. Yes, very sometimes.'

Crozier, an intimate friend and collaborator in the 1940s and early 1950s, saw at close hand the sort of ruptures that permeated the reminiscences of Tear and Duncan. Watching Britten unwrap a Christmas present in the late 1940s and enquiring who sent it, Crozier was handed a handsomely framed sixteenth- or seventeenth-century map of Suffolk, Britten's face a mixture of distaste and embarrassment. '"Monty Slater," he replied. "One of my 'corpses'." Then, with a queer kind of pleasure, he went on: "You'll be one, too, one day."' Crozier's recollection dates from 1966 when their friendship was over, and much of the document in which it is contained reads as if written by a spurned lover bent on revenge. The phrase 'Britten's corpses', however, lived on, not least because of the good run given it by Humphrey Carpenter, to whom Crozier presented his extensive unpublished notes and who returned his generosity by taking them at their word.

Crozier did have a good eye for detail, and he retained a robust and precise memory until the end of his life, the time I came to know him. There is no reason to doubt his assertion that a few years before meeting Britten he dined with a 'future Professor of Music at Cambridge' who on hearing Britten's name exploded, 'What? That hateful little Jewboy!' (This was probably the composer Patrick Hadley, who assumed the chair in 1946.) His outburst was an encapsulation of the era's casual anti-Semitism, not an accurate genealogy, yet it adds another perspective to the emerging picture of Britten the man and the strong reactions he provoked in others (often embittered composers).

Even if the perpetuation of the term 'corpse' was partly Crozier's work, the concept does seem to have been Britten's. 'He has sometimes told me, jokingly, that one day I would join the ranks of his "corpses,"' Crozier told his fiancée Nancy Evans in mid-1949, 'and I have always recognized that any ordinary person must soon outlive his usefulness to such a great creative artist as Ben.' Marion Thorpe, a lifelong friend, confirmed the offhandedness towards friends and colleagues, adding it was 'obviously very hard for the people who suddenly felt themselves pushed away into the cold but – it's difficult to explain why and how each individual case happened – but I think it was again a sort of self-protection . . . he didn't want to get any nearer, or he'd had all he could out of that particular relationship'. Yet in her personal experience, which amounted to more than thirty years of friendship and occasional mutual domicile, he was always 'wonderful to be with because he was such fun', with his 'tremendous sense of humour – quite a sort of school-boy sense of humour', though she recognized 'a lot of people *were* deeply hurt' by his behaviour.

On the other hand, the remarkable Rosamund Strode, who took over from Imogen Holst as Britten's assistant in 1964, thought such emotions a little too self-regarding. 'He needed people who knew the business, who would do what he asked them to do and get on with it' – a succinct, no-nonsense indication of how she viewed her role at the Red House, Britten's home from 1957. The equally remarkable woman she replaced had her own unique perspective, which filled her diary between 1952 and 1954. Britten 'came in looking *so* beautiful that my heart turned over so that it was thumping when he embraced me but I explained that I'd run down the hill too fast,' she wrote in one representative entry. And Donald Mitchell – scholar, publisher and friend – is also sceptical of Crozier's corpses. 'I must say people used to talk endlessly about the whole Britten climate and the Britten circle and what Ben was up to and all those sorts of things, but I never was aware of hostility or doubts or anxieties about friends or betrayals or not being loyal.'

Crozier's rejoinder to Mitchell would be that for evidence of Britten's mendacity we should take the way he spoke. 'For public utterance, he adopted a plummy, pedantic, schoolmasterly voice which gave a false impression of his normal speech and at the same time seemed to reveal something hidden in the depths of his personality – an unpleasant sense of his own superiority.' ('It sounds a bit prissy, even, doesn't it?' said

Marion Thorpe independently.) If deaf to his voice, then perhaps look to his appearance, Crozier said, startling in its ugliness in middle age. 'His neck is thicker, his features coarser, and when his face is in repose his expression seems to be largely compounded of arrogance, impatience and hostility.'

5

Loving, spontaneous, loyal, corrupt, humorous, humourless, soulless, courageous, weak, abnormal, flawed, beautiful, ugly, petulant, secretive, wonderful, crippled, sadistic, charming, great, hateful. To those who knew him, and knew him well, Benjamin Britten displayed all these characteristics, and more besides. Is it possible for one person to be a bundle of such violent contradictions?

The problem, in part, is Britten's fame during his lifetime and the sheer scale of the documentation project in place since his death. Even so, the number of epithets suggests that, to those who knew him, Britten was a difficult man to pin down. And those without the privilege of either access or acquaintance (and many with both) have traditionally been happy to play Freud or Holmes with the composer and the characters that populate his great operas, usually with a measure of comic ineptitude.

'Did you know Ben?' locals asked on my visits to Aldeburgh in the mid-1990s when I first started thinking and writing about him. 'No, alas,' I'd reply primly, too young by half; not the man, but definitely the music, which I had come to know in fits and starts. I played his *Night Piece (Notturno)* in an exam, one of his small handful of mature works for piano. I forgot about this first brush with his music until years later, rehearsing its half-sister, Britten's setting of Goethe's 'Um Mitternacht' with the incomparable mezzo-soprano Ann Murray, when the memory of it rushed back. There was not much Britten performed where and when I grew up. I remember seeing *Noye's Fludde* when I was eighteen or so, but two years of biology at my Catholic senior school with the formidable Mrs Dawson, a smart, plain-speaking Darwinist, had left me largely unsympathetic to the plot.

There are certain things I regret in not having known Britten. I remain sad that I never heard him play the piano, with his spider-like fingers and unerring sense of legato and harmony. 'It always seemed to me that music sprang out of his fingers when he played the piano,' Tippett wrote in his obituary of Britten. Listening to his recordings today I am still struck by the magical world of nuance and musicality he constructs. Mischievously, I am disappointed not to have been at the inaugural concert at Snape Maltings in 1967, sitting where I could see his face when the choir under his baton entered the fray of his new and difficult work, *The Building of the House*, a full semitone too high ('Except the Lord the house doth make'), staying there until the cavalry arrived. I wish we could have talked about the end of *King Lear*, where the old, blind monarch stumbles yowling onto stage, Cordelia dead in his arms. 'Howl, howl, howl, howl! O, ye are men of stone. / Had I your tongues and eyes, I'd use them so / That heaven's vault should crack. – Oh she is gone forever!' Had your operatic adaptation not been scuppered, how would you have set this scene, Mr Britten?

There are other questions, too – about his youthful hatred of conductor Adrian Boult (easy to comprehend and fun to ask), and his adult hatred of Brahms (ditto). But perhaps I would have been too worried about which version of the composer I was about to encounter to ask him anything. None of this matters, since my interest is in treating Britten not solely as a great composer, or performer, or a serial hurter of people's feelings, or a buttoned-up artiste with a penchant for pre-adolescent boys, but as a significant historical figure, firmly rooted in the long, dark twentieth century. It is doing him no more courtesy than that now extended to Arthur Miller, or (perhaps more aptly) the homosexual Tennessee Williams – the former two years younger than Britten, the latter two years older. The works of both playwrights are acknowledged as prisms through which to view the social history of twentieth-century America. These men, these plays, not only commented on American culture and society; they shaped it as well.

Considering Britten in this light, it is important to look dispassionately at the relationship between the man and his music, before looking once more at the relationship between these two elements and the Britain in which he lived during four decades or so. It is a matrix Britten biographers have tended to misread – though Tippett got it just right in his obituary. 'It seems to me that certain obsessions belonged naturally to the works of art which he produced. I don't think it matters at all that they may not in any way have belonged to his personality. I refer to a deep sense of cruelty, cruelty upon people, cruelty as suffering. A sense, I think, also of the fragility of all existence, leading him to a sense of death.' This is both a summation and a warning. Writing about Britten in those exceptionally charged days following (or, more likely, anticipating) his death, some years before the revival in Britten's reputation, Tippett articulated a way of viewing his friend – part Baldwin (art as personal confession), part Tear (the need to separate distaste for the man from love of the music), part Wilson (art as social commentary) – that has too often been ignored.

6

'The artist ought not to judge his characters or what they say, but be only an unbiased witness,' Chekhov wrote. Britten strayed far from this dictum in *Grimes*, for his control over our emotional response to the characters is absolute. Yet he stuck closely to it in subsequent works. From 1945 onwards he concealed the dark themes and social critiques explicit in *Grimes* beneath layers of extraordinarily beguiling surface matter. Perhaps he was suspicious of *Grimes*'s success, doubtful that a work lauded so fully by the public had hit its target. Whatever his reason, he became a much more subtle social commentator, careful not to judge his characters publicly, leaving such things to the audience.

One vignette illustrates this evolution. Rosamund Strode told me of an argument she had with Britten and Pears in the early 1970s over the opera *Billy Budd*, a sort of Christian parable based on the novella by Herman Melville, first performed six years after *Peter Grimes*. In it Captain Vere, a wise, philosophically inclined father figure dispensing Plutarch and port wine, must decide whether to follow his conscience or maritime law when sitting in judgement on the goodly, young, handsome sailor Billy Budd, who has struck out and killed the malevolent master-at-arms when falsely accused by him of mutiny. Vere refuses to intervene, and Billy is hanged from the yardarm, sent on his way by the Articles of War and a ditty bag of other naval statutes. Rosamund stood by the decision – Vere's, Melville's and Britten's. Yet on this occasion both Britten and Pears, the original Vere, argued that he should have intervened at some point to save Billy; good ought to have triumphed over evil. It was Britten's private judgement twenty years after writing the opera; his public decision when composing the piece, rooted in the laws of drama and human nature, was to let Billy hang.

Perhaps Edmund Wilson would have found the works after *Grimes* too oblique, to use James Baldwin's word. Another American had no problem seeing through the careful layers of disguise: the great all-rounder Leonard Bernstein, a colleague but never a friend of Britten's (there were too many overlaps in talent, too few in temperament), said following his death, 'When you hear Britten's music, if you really hear it, not just listen to it superficially you become aware of something very dark. There are gears that are grinding and not quite meshing, and they make a great pain.'

Bernstein described a darkness audible, taking his cue from Milton. Certainly, gears grind and never quite mesh beneath the surface of the great bulk of Britten's operas – an anthology of some of the twentieth century's greatest obsessions as much as they are a collection of damaged, complex, repressed yet often glorious male characters. The pain Britten felt was for the failures of society, as he saw them; the darkness was that of the bloody twentieth century, with no plausible end in sight.

Part seer, part Fool, part fugitive from his class and upbringing, Britten spent forty years vomiting up the anguish he felt about the world, as Baldwin suggested artists must, creating a body of mainstream works out of minority causes: pacifism, homosexuality, socialism, Christian hypocrisy, modernism. He had wildly poked a stick at some of these themes in the 1930s; from 1945, famous and a much better composer than he had been in the 1930s, this wolf in tweed clothing set to work to challenge the politics and values of contemporary British society while his country held him firmly and for the most part fondly in its heart. 'Britten's artistic effort was an attempt to disrupt the centre that it occupied with the marginality that it expressed,' said Philip Brett. If in these works Britten refused to stick his fangs into the heart, it was only because he thought dramatic ambiguity was a stronger force than didacticism or finger-pointing. His response to Captain Vere shows he could keep his own counsel when required.

Britten's life story is not solely about composition. Throughout the storm of new works and ideas he was also chipping away at the self-regarding English approach to music-making. One or two institutions aside, Britten rejected it as crudely amateur: the badly performed symphony concerts or seasonal operas presided over by feeble English conductor knights or second-rate European autocrats; the Jane Austen drawing-room feel to chamber-music performances; the watery recital debuts in London sponsored by a rich, indulgent father or an ear-less entrepreneur; the parading and promenading at the expense of serious performances of serious music. And in a country barely off its knees after war with Germany, Britten did it carefully, without drawing attention to the debt these new practices had to Britain's recent enemy. England had never before seen his kind. He was a Wagner, a Mahler, a Strauss: a composer-executant-entrepreneur of ferocious talent and achievement. And he left English music and English musical life transformed.

Who was this man? And what was it in the twentieth century that both defined and repelled him?

Early

I

Boyhood

Suffolk, 1913–1930

I

'Suffolk, the birthplace and inspiration of Constable and Gainsborough, the loveliest of English painters; the home of Crabbe, that most English of poets; Suffolk, with its rolling, intimate countryside; its heavenly Gothic churches, big and small; its marshes, with those wild sea-birds; its grand ports and its little fishing villages. I am firmly rooted in this glorious county.'

With as much pomp and ritual as he could muster, in late July 1951 the mayor of Lowestoft stood on stage at the Sparrow's Nest Theatre and granted Honorary Freedom of the Borough to the town's most famous son, Benjamin Britten, who was born in Lowestoft thirty-seven years earlier, living in Suffolk for all but eight of them, which is why he could speak so passionately of the county when accepting the award.

It was not Britten's first time in the Sparrow's Nest. In his speech, which touched on other charmed Suffolk ambassadors besides Constable and Crabbe – his refined voice incongruous in the small-town setting – and which demonstrated an ease and fluency often absent in addresses by such a reluctant public speaker, Britten recalled his earlier appearance. 'Some of you may remember, more than thirty years ago, a very small boy, dressed in skin-coloured tights, with madly curly hair, trying desperately to remember the lines spoken by Tom the water-baby, sitting on the lap of Mrs Do-as-you-would-be-done-by (played on this occasion by his own mother) – *on this very stage.*'

At one point in rehearsals for Kingsley's fable the cast had assembled outside for a photograph. In it Britten, aged five or six, replicates his onstage pose, sitting on the lap of his mother, a pre-Raphaelite beauty then in her mid-forties who could easily pass for a Rossetti model. The boy's hair is itself a sparrow's nest, which is why as an adult he wore it, unwaveringly, in a close crop. He has fins by his shoulders, fins by his toes, and, as in so many Renaissance paintings of the Christ child, his face is not that of a small boy; his eyes are piercing, his expression serious and adult.

Notwithstanding Britten's reference to the great Suffolk artist in his speech, Lowestoft is some distance north of the heart of Constable country. In Constable's now impossibly familiar painting of 1821, *The Hay Wain*, a black-hatted farmer, looking for all the world like a scarecrow or a pilgrim, steers his horses and cart through the River Stour where it straddles the counties of Suffolk and Essex. The river-bank traced by the farmer (owned by the Constables and their neighbour) is in Suffolk, yet most of the land in the painting is in Essex, as are the distant harvesters and their crop.

There are nonetheless Constable scenes that Britten would have encountered in the countryside near Lowestoft, close to the Norfolk border. More than two dozen Constable landscapes include Dedham church somewhere in the frame, with its handsome Perpendicular design and imposing square tower. Dedham is also in Essex, but such towers are characteristic of the imposing English Gothic 'wool churches' dotted around north-east Suffolk, a legacy of a prosperous medieval wool trade and God-fearing age. There is a magnificent example in Blythburgh, thirteen miles by road from Lowestoft, which dominates the surrounding landscape, its hulking, flinty shell a sharp counterpoint to the low surrounding fields. This is one of the 'heavenly Gothic churches' Britten spoke of in Lowestoft in 1951, one that has played host to extraordinary musicians since the early years of the Aldeburgh Festival.

George Crabbe's Suffolk is much closer to the Sparrow's Nest Theatre than Constable's, in location and temperament. The Georgian poet's bleak descriptions of life on the isolated strip of coast at his birthplace Aldeburgh, hemmed in by the North Sea on one side and the River Alde on the other, form a chilly contrast to the country idylls Constable was then painting. Crabbe's was rough, unforgiving country, its people beholden to a fickle sea for their livelihood and safety.

Hark! to those sounds, they're from Distress at Sea!
How quick they come! What terrors may there be!
Yes, 'tis a driven Vessel: I discern
Lights, signs of terror, gleaming from the Stern;
Others behold them too, and from the Town,
In various parties Seamen hurry down;
Their Wives pursue, and damsels urg'd by dread,
Lest Men so dear be into danger led;
Their head the gown has hooded, and their call
In this sad night, is piercing like the squall;
They feel their kinds of power, and when they meet,
Chide, fondle, weep, dare, threaten or entreat.

E. M. Forster admired the way Crabbe refused to idealize his surroundings and the poor people living in them. 'When he started writing,' Forster suggested in the *Listener* in 1941, 'it was the fashion to pretend that they were happy shepherds and shepherdesses, who were always dancing, or anyhow had hearts of gold. But Crabbe knew the local almshouses and hospital and prison, and the sort of people who drift into them; he read, in the parish registers, the deaths of the unsuccessful, the marriages of the incompetent, and the births of the illegitimate.' It is Crabbe as an East Anglian Hogarth, the poet's black pen-sketches of Aldeburgh in the nineteenth century equal to anything the clear-eyed artist produced of London in the eighteenth.

2

Lowestoft, twenty-five miles up the coast from Aldeburgh, was in 1913 larger and less isolated than Crabbe's birthplace. It had also benefited in the nineteenth century from the sort of investment in civic infrastructure that centuries earlier had left Suffolk brimful of churches. Postcards and photographs of the town at the time Britten was a boy show wide boardwalks and a bustling seafront; military bands on the grand South Pier, watched by formally dressed promenaders; and busy streets with tramlines past impressive Victorian façades. There are churches and gardens and a wooden pier with shimmering glass enclosures that stretches 400 yards out into the water. There are terraces overlooking the sea, minutes away from the large house, 21 Kirkley Cliff Road, where the Britten family lived. The terraces gradually disappeared as the cliff eroded, snatched one at a time. Much later Britten vividly recalled a childhood coloured by fierce storms that ate away at the neighbouring cliffs and beached ships with reckless ease.

There are vessels of every kind in the photographs: moored drifters used by herring fishermen; pleasure steamers paddling on the harbour; larger ships arriving from London and disembarking at Claremont Pier, now a ghostly wreck; a lifeboat ready to launch immediately a maroon explodes in alarm; steam trawlers catching cod, plaice and other white fish; tugboats and crew waiting for calm days, when their services will be required. These pictures show a seaside town in its heyday, full of straw boaters and sleek motors. It seems totally incongruous now, but chic art deco advertising was as at home here as it was in the resort towns that fared rather better in the long term than Lowestoft.

The town owed its original Victorian prosperity and lingering wealth to the fishing industry and its busy ports. Once the railway arrived in Lowestoft midway through the nineteenth century, Britain had easy sea passage to northern Europe from its easternmost point, and Lowestoft luxuriated in the attention. It was not only heavy freight: trains brought holiday-makers into Lowestoft and took out of it herring in varying stages of preservation. Before its collapse in the 1950s from overfishing, the herring industry thrived along this part of the coast, in Lowestoft in particular, as it did round much of the North Sea.

The herring season dictated a particular rhythm, fleets slowly moving down the east coast of Britain from late spring through winter, which Lowestoft fell in with in November and December. Hundreds of barrels were stacked high in preparation for the catch. Drifters brought in the fish, some of which was sold at the market to local merchants, cooks and picklers. Nets were stretched out to dry ('Where hang at open doors, the Net and Cork, / While squalid Sea-Dames mend the meshy work', as Crabbe described the scene) – huge silk walls to be picked at by fat gulls. The more demonstrative of the predatory fish tracking the herring shoals into the waters off Lowestoft unwittingly provided entertainment for those on the boardwalk or pier ('Th'unwieldy Porpoise through the day before, / Had roll'd in view of boding men on shore'). And the splendidly named Consolidated Steam Fishing & Ice Co., whose large fleet of trawlers used the port's resources, was a constant reminder of how industrialized the simple profession had become.

On his pilgrimage through East Suffolk in 1992, the lugubrious writer W. G. Sebald encountered a constellation of ghost towns, the history and past achievements of each only just traceable in the streets and ruins. Those towns facing east were hostage to the harsh climate and centuries of coastal erosion. 'Especially at the time when the continent of America was being colonized, it was noticeable that the townships spread to the west even as their eastern districts were falling apart.' Britten knew the area, and this aspect of it, well. Forty years or so before Sebald's wanderings he walked in Suffolk with the schoolboy David Spenser, the first Harry in his 1947 opera *Albert Herring*, telling him of the coastal villages that had drowned long before and the ghostly church bells that could be heard on still nights. He was thinking of the port town of Dunwich that had formerly stood eight miles up the coast from Aldeburgh, whose churches of St Michael, St Bartholemew, St Leonard, St Nicholas and a host of other saints, obscure and renowned, were claimed by the sea over the centuries.

Even the towns facing west retained traces of long-dead industries, never to be replaced. Nowhere was Sebald more despondent than in Lowestoft, where he found 'rows of run-down houses with mean little front gardens', and a town centre made up of 'nothing but amusement arcades, bingo halls, betting shops, video stores, pubs that emit a sour reek of beer from their dark doorways, cheap markets, and seedy bed-and-breakfast establishments with names like Ocean Dawn'. EU money has improved things since, yet it arrived too late to prevent the tramlines being dug up or boards being placed over the Victorian shop windows. The bones of Lowestoft's heyday remain visible, but most of the flesh has long decomposed.

The postcard images of Lowestoft, then, are from a lost world. Yet it was the world that those living at 21 Kirkley Cliff Road in the first four decades of the century experienced and fondly recalled. 'When the drifters arrived,' Britten's sister Beth wrote much later, 'so did the Scots girls, who followed the boats.' They stayed for two months, these working-class girls in their colourful shawls and scarves, with their singsong accents and intriguing habit of knitting as they walked about town, a strong smell of fish in the air.

Benjamin loved this aspect of his childhood, the poetic mixture of poverty, class and seasonal routine. It remained with him, at least into early adulthood. The violinist Remo Lauricella, a friend and fellow student at the Royal College of Music (RCM), stayed at the Britten family house in late 1935 following a joint recital in town. Britten dragged him out of bed at 4 a.m. to watch the drifters return to harbour with their catch, the young composer's excitement not quite assuaging his friend's numbness from the cold. If they had followed the catch into the warehouse they would have encountered merchants, apprentice boys, a bobby or two, and oilskin-clad fishermen standing knee-deep in herring. Later they would have seen the Scottish fisher-girls in their aprons, their hair pulled back in scarves, gutting, cleaning and packing the fish into brine and barrels, 'singing their lovely, lilting Highland tunes' as they went about the arduous work. Ten years later, when composing his first grand opera, Britten evoked these scenes with a sure hand, re-enacting the perennially combative relationship between humans and the sea, a drama of Melvillian proportions.

3

Robert Victor and Edith Rhoda Britten (née Hockey) moved into their seafront house in 1908, a year before Charlotte Elizabeth (Beth) was born. There were older children too: Robert Harry Marsh, born in 1907 (known as Bobby to differentiate him from his father), and Edith Barbara, known by her second name, born in Ipswich in 1902, almost nine months to the day after her parents' September wedding at St John's, Smith Square, London.

There were skeletons rattling around in closets on both sides of the union. Edith's father was a bastard, her mother a drunk – 'admitted periodically to a home for inebriates', Beth recalled. Edith's brother Henry (Willie), an abstemious organist with a post in Ipswich, also succumbed to drink, though not before establishing kinship with young Benjamin, encouraging him in his music, presenting him with books and scores. There was alcoholism among Robert's siblings, too, a brood of ten children born to silk mercer and general draper Thomas Britten and his wife; one brother eventually died of it. For all that, the waft of Temperance in the Britten household – sickly evangelicalism mixed with a fear of booze – was propagated by Edith alone; Robert Victor had none of his wife's instincts towards either religion or alcohol.

Their children's names were picked mostly from low-lying branches of the family tree. The youngest was christened Edward Benjamin soon after his birth on 22 November 1913, though from the outset no one seems to have used his first name. Britten employed it in childhood and adolescence as a sort of stage name, signing early compositions 'E. B. Britten' as though a Victorian lady novelist; but this habit fell away in his late teens, a few years after he started composing music of interest and originality. (He later told conductor Albert Goldberg somewhat archly that he dropped Edward because it took him so much longer to sign cheques.) His second name, according to Beth, was a reference to the youngest child of Jacob, scripture's fecund centenarian polygamist, grandson of Abraham, father of twelve, patriarch of all Israelites, chosen by Britten's parents in the hope that, as with Jacob and Rachel, Benjamin would be their last child. Beth was coy on whether more interventionist methods of birth control were thereafter practised.

To others in the house, the youngest son was known as Benny. Once Britten learned to write, this came out as Beni, prefiguring the erratic hold on spelling he demonstrated all his life. Public school effected the abbreviation Ben, which stuck – though Auden and Isherwood pre-ferred the more intimate and juvenile Benji (sometimes Benjie or Bengi in letters), which they borrowed from Britten's teacher and his wife, Frank and Ethel Bridge.

Robert Victor has had some damning things written about him, from accusations of drunkenness (including a finger or two of whisky for daily elevenses) to suggestions by Humphrey Carpenter of homosexual-ity and paedophilia, with Britten as a sort of Artful Dodger rounding up young boys to be pressed into service of the criminal adult. The first is possible though hardly scandalous, the second 'utterly absurd' accord-ing to Basil Reeve, Britten's childhood friend, his elder by a year. Reeve's recollections were razor sharp if occasionally incautious, and in this instance, based on the memories and observations of other contempor-aries, he was surely right.

Robert was certainly an unusual-looking man. Eric Crozier captured him well – at least, his appearance in photographs, which is all Crozier ever knew. He was 'attractively ugly, provincial, and very much like the face of Barbara (Ben's elder sister) in its squareness, its slightly puzzled frown, and the nervousness of its smile'. Of course by the time Crozier wrote these notes everyone in the family, bar Edith, was unattractive in one way or another.* Crozier had an ally in Robert's daughter-in-law, however, who described her first meeting with him in 1928 in similar terms. 'I took an instantaneous dislike to him, partly because he frightened me. It was his eyes – they were sort of hooded – that made me think there was something funny about him. I can't explain it, but here was this extraordinary father who gave me the creeps.'

Appearance aside, and despite the charm Beth identified in her father, Robert was a loner. Another of Britten's childhood friends, John Pounder, thought him severe and old-fashioned ('He was rather a hard man, I'd say; but a good person'), a view corroborated by Reeve. Both credited him for how hard he worked in his dental practice, situated on the ground floor of the family home. (Upstairs he referred to as 'heaven', a view the whole family shared.) His hours were long and his habits – drinking aside – ascetic. He visited patients on Sunday mornings, and in the afternoon allowed himself his one hot bath for the week, a habit he passed on to his youngest son. He was involved in the local Masonic lodge, but to what extent it is impossible to say.

Friends remembered clearly delineated roles within the home: Mr Britten as provider, Mrs Britten responsible for keeping house and rearing the children, aided by a small team of domestic help as their class and era required. Yet Beth contradicted this characterization, suggesting her father was closely involved in the education of his children, deferring to his wife only in the matter of Benjamin's musical training.

It is difficult to get a clear picture of Robert Britten, given these circumstances and how much of Benjamin's energies were poured into his relationship with his mother. Moreover, Crozier asserted that around the time of *Peter Grimes* Britten removed a photograph of Robert from the foot of the staircase in his home, having heard from Barbara 'that his father had never really believed in him or had any confidence in his future success as a musician'. 'His father,' Crozier continued, 'I think, Ben did not like – maybe this was his reaction to the belief that his

---

* For example, Crozier wrote that Beth, 'like Robert and Barbara, had something a little ugly and unfinished in her appearance – or rather in her expression, for it was not so much an ugliness of features as the reflection of an inner disharmony'.

father did not wholly like him.' Britten possibly did re-evaluate his father posthumously along the lines Crozier described, yet this says nothing about the nature of their relationship when he was alive.

Reeve thought the lack of belief obvious at the time. 'He never thought that Ben could do a thing, musically. In a sense, he didn't see how anyone could make a living at it.' Yet Ben's was a world about which Robert knew nothing; he relied on outsiders for advice and counsel, musicians and non-musicians alike. One such was Captain Thomas Sewell, headmaster of South Lodge preparatory school, which Britten attended between 1923 and 1928. A talented mathematician, Sewell advised Robert and Edith of other possibilities for their son, given that 'security in the world of music was not so assured, even for a genius'. He later told the successful composer he was impressed by Mr Britten's rejection of the advice. 'Personally I thought that he was absolutely right, but some men would have played for safety.'

Apart from such implicit encouragement and the natural desire to safeguard Britten's future, there are signs of a genuinely close relationship between father and son. There were frequent walks with Pop, often over the bridge to the fish markets. As a young boy he relished the Dickens stories read to him by his father, a task not automatically relegated to Nanny Walker. And writing to Britten in 1933 after the successful first run-through of the quixotic *A Boy was Born*, Robert evinced warmth and approval:

My dear Son Benjamin.

Hearty congratulations! over and over again and also envy & jealousy.

Oh! Ben my boy what does it feel like to hear your own creation? Didn't you want to get up and shout – It's mine! It's mine! I understand your feeling that – 'you don't care a cuss whether they do it or not *now*.'

What a break to get a crowd who could really do it as you want it. I want to cry!

Thanks for letting us know so soon we were all on edge to hear.

Go on my son

Your very loving & admiring
Pop
R. V. Britten

4

'The mother was very much softer and gentler,' thought Pounder, protective of her youngest, slightly delicate child. 'I liked her very much,' Britten's childhood friend John Alston said. 'She was a charming person; but I can't remember very much except that.' Reeve thought her driven and demanding: 'she ran both our lives', he stated with some vehemence, seventy years after she had allegedly done so. It was Reeve who asserted Edith was determined from the earliest days that her son would become the 'fourth B' – after Bach, Beethoven and Brahms – yet this strikes an odd note. When Beth was asked about it after her brother's death she dismissed the idea as too hubristic for their household. 'I don't believe it; because if my father had ever heard this, he'd have pooh-poohed it, he'd have said "This is ridiculous".' Her wording allows Reeve some wriggle room, yet Edith's phrase was probably nothing more than a self-conscious play on what cousins and relations called the Britten children: the four Bs.*

This is not to suggest that Edith did not recognize her son's talents and was not ambitious for him as a result. Beth recalled a train journey in which her mother said from nowhere, 'It's very odd you know, but it's never happened before in the middle classes,' which Beth took to mean that genius was only ever found in the aristocracy or the lower classes – an absurd if apparently heartfelt belief. Pears later stressed that Britten did not consider himself anything of the sort. 'He certainly didn't think of himself as a great composer, absolutely not. To him a great composer was Mozart, Bach, Purcell, Schubert. But, as time went on, he realized I think eventually that he was a rather lone voice.'

Crozier found it difficult to form an impression of Edith from what her children said, though he noted their great affection for her. Reeve told a striking story of meeting Britten in Aspen in 1964 when he was collecting a prize and where the two of them reminisced about their childhoods. 'You know,' said Britten, 'I can't remember anything about my mother.' To Reeve, a medical doctor, this was a symptom of Britten's development as an adult, his need to escape the inhibiting emotional

---

* Or else it was no more than the curse of most composers since Brahms with a surname beginning with B; the mantle was claimed for Bartók, for example.

hold of his mother. Reeve also remembered Britten daily playing Wagner's *Siegfried Idyll* to his mother after lunch – she reclining on the sitting-room couch as though posing for a mid-nineteenth-century portraitist. Beth remembered her mother tackling Captain Sewell when she felt her son was being overworked or not given time to practise the piano and write his music.

However, her endearing magpie correspondence, her passionate interest in music, her low-church evangelism (overseen by Reeve's father, William, the vicar of St John's, a grand Victorian church in Lowestoft, from 1925 to 1936), which she buttressed late in life with the hokum claims of Christian Science (to the extent of resenting the interfering 'chest specialist' who came to see her sick husband a month before his death), hint at a more benign figure. The nuances of her character would not matter much had her overall aims not set in train a particular and unfortunate Freudian version of Britten's childhood: a young boy driven by his dominating mother who structured his life's every aspect and coddled him to the detriment of his latent masculinity. 'I suspect this is why he became a homosexual,' said Reeve, much as one might become a lion tamer or an astronaut, notwithstanding more convincing studies of human sexuality.

This view – with its clumsy inference about the origins of Britten's sexuality – has, to varying degrees, shaped five important biographical studies since Reeve first articulated it in 1986. In none is a note of caution sounded; each perpetuates the notion of a driven Mrs Britten, unceasing in her quest to create the 'fourth B'. Reeve's recollections are important, but he also held strong views on how history should treat his boyhood friend, which he combined with an intrinsic distaste for homosexuality and Britten's choice of partner, the 'unpleasant' Peter Pears. When Donald Mitchell pressed John Alston on Mrs Britten's 'dominating', 'string-pulling' character two years after hearing about it from Reeve, Alston replied: 'I never felt that, no. I never felt that. I've heard that said, but I never felt it myself . . . She was just a nice mother all the time. I thought kind and caring.' Mitchell was cautious in his use of Reeve's perspective in the long and insightful introduction to the first volume of Britten's letters and diaries (1991).

Here was a loving mother, an amateur musician active in the Lowestoft Musical Society, who had an extremely close bond with her son, encouraging his evident musical talent, seeking outside help when it developed beyond her, even though it served to dilute her influence and control over him. Fundamentally, Edith took her son seriously. She allowed him to think of himself as a composer from a young age, where someone less perceptive might have missed the signs or misinterpreted their value. She assembled a team of musicians of similar mind: Miss Ethel Astle for piano, sight-reading and theory; Uncle Willie as a professional mentor; Mrs Audrey Alston for viola lessons; Frank Bridge for composition; Harold Samuel for piano. It is a glorious list, and even if some of it came about through happenstance – geographical and filial – it is no less impressive for that.

5

Britten was comfortable on stage at an early age, an irony given his nervousness before performances later in life, assuaged only by a hefty glug – or more – of brandy in the dressing room immediately before he walked out. Miss Ethel programmed small concerts, while at the musical soirées she hosted at home Edith sang and young Benny played. Britten fondly remembered their repertory many years later: Schubert's 'Who is Sylvia?', with an accompaniment that putters along like an early motor engine, and 'Hark! hark! the lark' – both in clunky English retranslations; and Roger Quilter's setting of 'Now sleeps the crimson petal', a poem by Tennyson to which Britten later turned.

These were not the family's first domestic entertainments. Throughout their childhoods all four children were involved in theatrical productions of increasing ambition and sophistication. A pole was rigged up in the nursery, from which hung an improvised stage curtain. Nanny Walker prepared the scripts, as she did the costumes; both were beautifully tailored to the participants. Beth included a photograph of the cast of *Cinderella* in her memoir of her brother. With his elfin skullcap and star-shaped collar, the three-year-old Britten looks little like the royal page he was playing. But the rest of the cast – eleven in total, clumped around the young page – are splendidly adorned. In their pose and fine clothing, in the formality of the setting and the serious expressions on their faces, the children are a fairy-tale parody of Edith and Robert's wedding party, the formal photograph of which Beth reproduced a few pages earlier.

The wedding photograph, Quilter's sentimental song (so popular following its publication in 1904 and championship by the tenor Gervase Elwes), the amateur theatricals, and the relative independence enjoyed by the Britten children all point to an Edwardian sensibility. It is as if life in Kirkley Cliff Road was frozen in that idyllic period between Queen Victoria's death and the outbreak of the Great War. There was a touch of J. M. Barrie to the household: the rocking-horse and cod liver oil; the smocks and sailor suits; the sixpenny editions of the 'nice bugaler' A. J. Raffles (as Britten spelled him); Cook stoning raisins or baking fudge; the Saturday afternoon bag of sweets, bought by Pop and carefully rationed until the arrival of its replacement; the Sunday morning kippers; the bedtime stories, often read by one parent or other; the domestic music-making in lieu of the gramophone Mr Britten refused to purchase lest it discourage his children's musical talents; the consequent piano duets with Mummy (Wagner and Beethoven at this stage, Mozart much later) after rich Sunday lunches of sirloin; and Nanny bathing the brilliant young boy, his nose in a book all the while. 'Lift your leg, dear; now the other one. Now get out and I will dry you.'

The idea of life being played out in the nursery touched Britten long after he left it. Home for Christmas in 1933, his father ill with the disease that would kill him only months later, Britten plucked from a shelf Barrie's *The Little White Bird*, which he judged a 'little wonder'. It was in this book, published in 1902, that Barrie introduced the character of Peter Pan and his friends, the fairies in Kensington Garden, who two years later were given a more commanding platform. *Peter Pan: or, The Boy Who Wouldn't Grow Up* is a sort of secular *Water Babies* and in many ways epitomizes the Edwardian era. The 1902 version depicts the friendship between a young working-class boy and a retired soldier, a friendship that strengthens as they embark on a series of adventures together. Characters such as Barrie's were then creeping into British fiction and consciousness, far from Victorian depictions of working-class children in the age of industrialization, whose lack of hygiene, schooling, money, food, good health and teeth was both a rebuke and a threat to middle-class society. It is far away, too, from what Virginia Woolf termed 'the rules and demands of Victorian society': distant parents and repressive fathers; strict social hierarchies; children raised nearly exclusively by the downstairs help; polite deference to elderly relatives at formal tea parties. Barrie's children were given a voice and a certain stature within their families and society. This, too, was Britten's childhood.

It was a childhood dominated by women. In addition to Nanny Walker, the household ran to a cook, other maids, and a string of secretaries over time for Robert. For the first seven years of his life, women fed and dressed Benny, cleaned up after him, nursed him through illnesses (including the pneumonia that almost carried him off when he was three months old, Edith expressing milk and feeding him through a fountain-pen filler), taught him how to read and write and play the piano, and partnered him in informal musical performances. The Astle sisters ran Southolme, the pre-preparatory school he attended, one of whom gave him his first formal music lessons. There were the close friends of his sociable mother who fussed over the blue-eyed, curly headed little boy, and from this constituency his viola teacher emerged. Because both parents came from large families, there were plenty of aunts in his life and a handful of female cousins. A number of the aunts were maiden, including Aunt Queenie, Edith's youngest sister, a talented artist with melancholic habits and an unstable grip on her religious beliefs; her true and gently impressionistic miniature watercolour of Britten aged seven or so, with its evident debts to late-Victorian art-school tuition, is in the collection of the National Portrait Gallery. A slight competitiveness with his brother, in addition to their differences in temperament, helped cement Britten's close relationship with his sisters, especially Beth. Even Barbara, eleven years Britten's senior, did her bit in this regard, taking a woman as her lifelong companion.

The war, which made such feminine bonds all too common in 1920s England, played no role here. Robert Victor was thirty-seven at the start of hostilities and vulnerable to conscription under the Military Service Acts of 1916. Yet doctors, dentists and vets could apply to a Special Tribunal for exemption from military service, which is probably what happened here, for Robert never served. Edith's youngest brother had no such armour and died in 1916 on the Somme.

During the war, Lowestoft's port and proximity to Europe now made it vulnerable to Zeppelin attacks. Robert fortified the cellar, stocked it with rations and spare clothing, an axe and some spades, and the family sheltered there when the dumb, sluggish beasts flew overhead at night, en route to increasingly ambitious targets. Beth remembered a number of them exploding over the sea or nearby towns – startling, almost mythical immolations, Prometheus brought low by Zeus, stolen fire in his hands.

Beth also remembered the German navy coming to town, a month before its engagement with the Grand Fleet at Jutland on 31 May 1916. Most of the damage from bombardments occurred away from Kirkley Cliff Road, though one shell exploded in the field opposite the Brittens' house, carving a huge crater. Benny was too young to recall much of what went on during the war, though he remembered this terrifying event and waking up to the 'threatening roar of an explosion'.

The war's legacy was evident in other ways: pacifism in Britten's adolescence, socialism in his twenties, and a distrust and dislike of politicians thereafter. Then there were key works such as *War Requiem* of 1962, full not with the imagery of the recent Second World War, but of the more distant First – the monstrous guns, wailing shells, bugle calls, green thick odour of poison gas, trenches and soldiers who died like cattle.

Britten's parents worked hard to keep the household ticking over normally, a privilege of their class. War notwithstanding, teeth still needed mending and children educating (Britten's two eldest siblings boarded). Successive hikes in income tax to pay for armaments – the standard rate of six per cent in 1914 increased fivefold during the war – must have impacted on household expenditure and Robert's work ethic, as would rising costs of food and coal, and (to a lesser extent) the increase in tax on beer. Yet there were no real privations. Even the number of domestic staff remained stable, against the wartime trend in middle-class households throughout the country.

In such details can the Brittens' extended Edwardian idyll be found. In 1909 the influential journalist, politician and reformer Charles Masterman characterized the three understood classes of Edwardian society – upper, middle and working class – as conquerors, suburbans and the multitude (with a subset, the prisoners). A year later, in his troubling excursion through Edwardian England, *Howards End*, E. M. Forster gave these categories family names: the Wilcoxes, the Schlegels and the Basts. The Brittens remained contented members of this second group, the suburbans (Schlegels), long after the Armistice when Masterman's categories no longer held up so well, and were generous and respectful in their dealings with the third. (Britten would later propel himself into the first.)

6

Britten later plundered his childhood memories for his composition. Though set in a house far grander than that on Kirkley Cliff Road, Britten's opera for children *The Little Sweep* (1949) is a sharp snapshot of his boyhood. Everything takes place in a well-appointed nursery. 'There is a toy-cupboard at one side of the fireplace, an armchair and a rocking-horse,' the score specifies. The year is 1810 (it needed to be set before 1840 when Parliament made it illegal for chimney sweeps to use boy apprentices), yet the middle-class children who plot to save the sweep-boy Sammy from his indenture, and the nursemaid who aids them, are straight from Britten's childhood. Inspiration for the opera came from Blake's two poems entitled 'The Chimney Sweeper', one of which Britten returned to in his 1965 cycle *Songs and Proverbs of William Blake*.

> A little black thing among the snow,
> Crying 'weep 'weep in notes of woe!
> Where are thy father & mother? say?
> They are both gone up to the church to pray.

Britten's setting of this poem in his song cycle forms a pessimistic counterpart to the easy-going charm (and happy ending) of *The Little Sweep*. Though a rocking lullaby with distinct, brilliant fanfare-like interjections – perhaps the song of a winter robin, companion to the little black thing in the snow – it sounds at once martial and comforting (a combination Mahler never achieved), and skewers the hypocritical mixture of religion, false piety and brutishness of the sweep-boy's parents and their society. By 1965 Britten held no illusions about the cruelty adults inflict on children; Blake, in industrial Britain at the end of the eighteenth century, with its systemic neglect and abuse of children, thought no differently.

Britten wrote other, more innocent recollections of childhood: the songs in *Tit for Tat*, which he knitted together in 1968 from the many settings he made in the late 1920s and early 1930s of Walter de la Mare, the near-official spokesman for children. Most of the poems he set come from *Peacock Pie*, de la Mare's collection of rhymes first published the year Britten was born, and a 1921 reprint of which he owned. It is a world of poachers laying snares in the woods, fireplaces and well-read books, moonlight enveloping sleeping dogs and motionless fish in its silvery sheen, bucolic folk rhythms, and, in one instance, of a breathless treatment of the death of a child and the lasting impact of the event on the mother. 'I do feel that the boy's vision has a simplicity and clarity which might have given a little pleasure to the great poet, with his unique insight into a child's mind,' he wrote of the settings.

As with the de la Mare songs, Britten's *Simple Symphony* (1934) is a literal plundering of childhood. Much as Elgar had done in 1907 for his *Wand of Youth* suites, Britten raided his manuscript cupboard and fashioned the bounty – unruly songs and piano works from the mid-1920s – into a four-movement string symphony, complete with alliterative titles ('Boisterous Bourrée', 'Playful Pizzicato', etc.), a great sense of fun, and an adult eye for the potential and errors of youth.

Works such as *A Ceremony of Carols* (1942) and Britten's setting of Christopher Smart's asylum poetry, *Rejoice in the Lamb* (1943), look back to the institutional church of his boyhood – only here made much better; this is the type of music he wished he had encountered when growing up, instead of the low-church gloominess of St John's, the music-less curriculum of prep school, and the starchy high-church flavour of public school. The same is true of *Saint Nicolas* (1948), in which the holy protagonist is part mystic adventurer, part Medici ruler, part conjurer; and *Noye's Fludde* (1958), in which Britten stuck to the script. Even amid the nuanced tale of war, court jealousies and emotional trickery in his coronation opera *Gloriana* (1953), Britten included a rabble of boys – boisterous rebels siding with the disgraced Earl of Essex, singing of their allegiance in youthful, truncated phrases and in the chesty voices Britten liked. Working as Britten's assistant at the time, Imogen Holst complimented his realistic touch, to which he replied: 'It's because I'm still 13.'

The same boisterousness is required of the boys' choir in *Spring Symphony* (1949). 'The driving boy' in the symphony's first part is nothing so much as a John Singer Sargent canvas set to music: 'Strawberries swimming in the cream, / And schoolboys playing in the stream'. In the final movement the boys move from country to town, and, employing a trick he used so exhilaratingly four years earlier in the finale of *The Young Person's Guide to the Orchestra*, the theme playing itself out in duple time against an accompaniment in triple time, Britten created for these youths a bucolic riot. And the boys disport themselves well, bursting into the centre of town, a rabble equal to anything that marched on Essex's behalf, crashing the Mayday celebrations under way – an ecstatic carousel waltz provided by a stage full of adults singing and playing for all they are worth. Refusing to conform, the boys bray over the top the duple-time medieval canon 'Soomer is icoomen in, / Loode sing cuckoo'.

It is not solely the boyishness that is germane here: the whole piece is a paean to the Suffolk countryside of Britten's childhood, inspired by 'a lovely tree-bordered meadow somewhere between Snape and Ufford', he told Crozier. It is a work full of the county's spring light and a landscape that defies interruption by any mere hill. It was Britten's version of Constable painting and repainting the same scenery around the watermill in Flatford where he spent his boyhood.

It was not only in his music that childhood was evoked. Once Britten settled on the seafront in Aldeburgh in 1947, certain routines emerged. There were walks, and swims, and nursery games at night: Happy Families, draughts, jigsaws – anything to help him switch his mind off the day's work. There were puns and word games and jokes that were never of high sophistication. Even his diet could be interpreted as a nod to the food of his upbringing – simple fare with nursery and public-school resonances.

Yet his diet also serves as a warning about seeing everything in the adult Britten's life as childhood recreated; this is just how people of a certain class in England ate at the time. English cuisine was not at all adventurous then, while rationing only came to an end in 1954, the year Elizabeth David released her call to arms, *Italian Food*, with such *fioritura*. David noted that her reason for writing the book was that, although the English were good at cakes, jams, jellies, pastries, preserves and roasted meat, during the 'last twelve years or so we have been obliged to exercise ingenuity and patience to the utmost limit, but we have perhaps become too accustomed to accepting third-rate travesties of good food'. She was uninterested in the post-war nostalgia for nursery food – the mutton, watery vegetables and singed rice pudding.

With her list of successful indigenous foods, David could have been describing the grand May Day celebrations in *Albert Herring* (set in 1900). There the village children feast on jelly and pink blancmange, iced seedy-cake, 'sausagey' rolls, treacle tart and trifle, cheesey straws, chicken and ham, marzipan – all of it washed down with fruit punch. The excitement of the scene stems from the fact that rarely have these working-class children encountered such middle-class staples of the nursery. To Britten it was familiar fare.

Britten's boyhood was thus a happy time in the adult composer's memory.* Even so, all sunny depictions of childhood in his work are not necessarily autobiographical, nor are the dark ones – the tense psychological battle at the heart of *The Turn of the Screw* (1954), or the bleak, ultimately hopeless pilgrimage undertaken by the war-made orphans in *Children's Crusade* (1969) – either disinterested social observations or representative of a deep, dark secret. 'I do not hold with the belief become so prevalent these days', noted Britten's contemporary, English writer Sybille Bedford in her pitch-perfect evocation of European manners and values in the first half of the twentieth century, 'that any traumatic or so-called incident in childhood exercises a fatal hold on future life.' The same must be said of Britten. His childhood was a rich vein, which he mined throughout his life, but he also fossicked far from it to hypnotic effect.

7

Britten was well served by his pre-preparatory education at Southolme. In *Great Expectations* Dickens has good sport with such dame-schools, one of which is run by Mr Wopsle's great-aunt: 'she was a ridiculous old woman of limited means and unlimited infirmity, who used to go to sleep from six to seven every evening, in the society of youth who paid twopence per week each, for the improving opportunity of seeing her do it.' Reforms to English education policy in the last decades of the nineteenth century and the first decade of the next put an end to such institutions, and they were replaced by registered preparatory schools. Some schools retained the old label, but they were now carefully regulated. Britten remained appreciative all his life of the musical grounding he received between the ages of seven and nine at the Miss Astles' establishment. 'I can never say enough how much I personally benefited from

---

* Film director Wes Anderson returned the compliment in his 2012 film *Moonrise Kingdom*, set in 1965, in which the young protagonists Suzy and Sam meet at a performance of *Noye's Fludde* (Suzy in raven costume), a work Anderson remembers fondly from his childhood. 'It is the colour of the movie in a way,' he said after the Cannes screening. Other Britten works are on the soundtrack, including *The Young Person's Guide to the Orchestra*.

your teaching, & knowing you all those years,' he wrote to Miss Ethel in 1942. 'I often remember things you used to tell me!'

Yet if there were no Dickensian aspects to Britten's earliest schooling, his prep school conformed more readily to a particular literary stereotype. 'The [prep] school has not to discover the career for which its individual members are best suited,' wrote Alec Waugh in 1922. 'It has merely to decide which of them are good enough to be trained specially for scholarships.' So it was at South Lodge, a small prep school of only thirty students, most of whom boarded, which Britten entered a year after Waugh's book appeared. A bright boy with an aptitude for mathematics, Britten fulfilled Waugh's scholarship criterion perfectly and soon came to the attention of the headmaster, a passionate mathematician and Greek scholar determined to groom his young charge.

Captain Sewell also had a taste for corporal punishment, which he inflicted with little provocation. For serious misdemeanours the whole school was assembled and the miscreant paraded before it, which shocked young Britten. Much later he spoke of this culture of punishment and retribution, and the imprint it made. 'I can remember the first time – I think it was the very first day that I was in a school – that I heard a boy being beaten, and I can remember my absolute astonishment that people didn't immediately rush to help him.' Britten was, on the whole, spared the experience ('his contacts with the cane or the slipper were happily rare', he wrote of himself in 1955), yet it is hardly fanciful to attribute his burgeoning aversion to cruelty and violence to what he witnessed here.

It is easy enough now to turn Sewell into a pantomime villain; he has been cast as far more in a number of Britten biographies, a brother-in-arms to the unreformed pederast, bigamist and drunkard Captain Grimes in Evelyn Waugh's *Decline and Fall*. Yet in so far as this might have been true, it needs qualification: Sewell's regime was common to many prep and public schools at the time. His son Donald was later horrified at the level of punishment at South Lodge, but respected his father nonetheless. 'He wasn't a vindictive person at all. It was just that this was how discipline was exerted in those days.'

And there were good things to balance the bad. Britten discovered a love of cricket – captaining the school team in his final years – and from it learned the patience, restraint and sense of team spirit Alec Waugh saw as the point of the game (its reinforcement of homosocial society a bonus). Britten excelled in mathematics but did less well with history and Latin. His early school reports ranked him in the middle of his class (having come bottom in his first term), though Sewell took pride in his external musical achievements, commenting on them in various editions of the scrappy school magazine. He made friends easily and learned how to pace himself through the long days, which ran from 7.30 a.m. (early work) to 8 p.m. (prayers). He dressed in a double-buttoned grey flannel suit, with an oversized white collar, a soft hat perched somewhat precariously on his wiry hair in winter, a straw hat in summer, or in cricketing whites – a boldly striped blazer serving him well off the pitch. In his own words, 'he worked his way up the school slowly and steadily, until at the age of thirteen he reached that pinnacle of importance and grandeur never to be quite equalled in later days: the head of the Sixth, head-prefect, and Victor Ludorum [the winner of games]'.

It is not so clear the other ways in which South Lodge influenced Britten, whether it was anything more than Waugh's scholarship breeding ground. Because he was a day-boy there were no letters home, while the diary that now tells us so much (and so little) about Britten's teenage years was begun only in his last terms. We know almost nothing about the books he read, or what ideas were discussed, whether there were debates, or how religious he found the environment, what skills other than mathematics or sports he acquired. We do know that in his final term he spoke out against bullying, bringing the full weight of his head-prefecture to the issue, and that his response to an end-of-term essay on animals was an impassioned tirade against hunting, cruelty and war, which earned him a zero score and the opprobrium of his teachers. (Though even this tale, recounted by Imogen Holst in her biography of Britten, sounds apocryphal in its retelling: 'Such a thing had never been known to happen, and he left South Lodge under a cloud of disapproval.')

We know a lot about him as a musician in these years – the parallel existence to the life at South Lodge Edith forced Sewell and other masters to accommodate. From the personal library of study scores he started in 1925 we know the large-scale music he was devouring: Beethoven symphonies (nos. 3, 5 and 6 in his first year); an unlikely early appearance of Stravinsky's suite from *The Firebird* (catalogued as 'No. 4' in his collection); the expected Wagner overtures and preludes, as well as *Siegfried Idyll* and *Tannhäuser* in late 1926 ('Edward Benjamin

Britten with best wishes for his 13th birthday from Mum & Daddy Nov 22 – 26'); overtures to Mozart's *Le nozze di Figaro* and *Die Zauberflöte* in the same year, alongside an occasional Mozart symphony; more Beethoven symphonies, drip-fed into his collection, as well as a handful of his string quartets and concertos; Tchaikovsky's Symphony No. 6 in July 1928. By the time he went to public school in September 1928 he had accumulated a library of sixty-four scores. His fifteenth birthday brought a bumper crop: ten celebrated Mozart string quartets and the Piano Concerto in C minor, K. 491; and two more Beethoven symphonies, nos. 7 and 8.

Since he had almost no opportunity to listen to these works, either on gramophone or in concert, it is evident he heard them perfectly well in his head even at this young age. 'I have always found reading music easier than reading books,' he said in 1962. 'Even at school I can remember clearly the vocal and energetic surprise with which the other small boys caught me reading orchestral scores in bed.' He was like a synesthete, who involuntarily sees colours when listening to sounds, except he happily heard music when looking at scores. It is a particular talent, by no means common to all composers. (William Walton begrudgingly admired the skill: 'I do envy Ben Britten his – not facility, but being able to do it all in his head, like Mozart or Rossini.')

From the songs Britten wrote we know the poets he read: Kipling (from *The Jungle Book*), Longfellow, Byron, Burns and Tennyson (*The Foresters*, his dramatization of the Robin Hood legend), Walter Scott, Wordsworth, John Masefield, Shakespeare, Shelley, Robert Louis Stevenson, Matthew Arnold, Sir John Suckling and Philip James Bailey. He poached their poems from a handful of sources – though surprisingly not Sir Arthur Quiller-Couch's ubiquitous *Oxford Book of English Verse*. There are Bible passages, a number lifted from the Book of Samuel, a complicated and fanciful story concerning Philistine depravity, yet one more routing of the Israelites, and the fate of the Ark of the Covenant. And there is the magazine poet 'Chanticleer', a nom de plume G. F. Joy borrowed from the polygamous rooster in Chaucer's *The Canterbury Tales* whose nightmare of being devoured almost comes true. Writing against type, 'Chanticleer' produced poems about bunnies and lambs ('Little Persian Lambkin, frolicsome and sweet! / Dearly would I love thee ever we should meet'), which were well matched by young Britten's simple, pastoral music.

From the compositions in these years we can also determine what Britten was playing. 'Between the ages of thirteen and sixteen I knew every note of Beethoven and Brahms,' he later wrote, though his infatuation with the former evidently predated his teen years. Britten's 'sonata fantasti', written in April 1923, is covered in Beethoven's fingerprints: fast, chordal fanfares; right-hand arpeggios acting as cadenzas; left-hand arpeggios spelled out for harmony; an occasional diminished chord; sudden changes of mood. It could have been written under the sway of any number of Beethoven's middle-period piano sonatas, perhaps most obviously Op. 31. It is unlikely he was learning such pieces for his Associated Board exams, however; a few months later he would sit for his Higher Division certificate, which demanded less difficult works.

The same can be said of an untitled piece for piano in E flat, from some time in 1924, which has heavy debts to Beethoven's Sonata, Op. 53 ('Waldstein'). Britten's harmonic language in these pieces is basic; there is some modulation and use of secondary chords – essentially portals to other tonalities – but no sooner does he employ such techniques than he generally loses his footing and the piece ignobly crashes. Or if he keeps his footing, the work may conclude without warning, since Britten held the economical view that all pieces should finish at the bottom-right corner of a sheet of manuscript. His 'Fantasie improptu' (*sic*; *c*. 1922) steams its way more successfully through several modulations, staying on track while doing so. It too makes no attempt to disguise its debts: the opening theme is a straight lift from his mother's afternoon music of choice, Wagner's *Siegfried Idyll*.

None of the music was very good. It is little more than the sort of exercises any diligent student would write when learning harmony (counterpoint was still some years off) – much as a child learns cursive writing. There is an Edwardian parlour feeling to some of the songs, appropriate given their destination. On his ninth birthday Britten received Stainer and Barrett's *A Dictionary of Musical Terms* (first published in 1876, a gold-embossed St Cecilia on its cover), a present from Uncle Willie. He devoured it as though it were a detective novel, and his scores were instantly more prescriptive. In 1923 he revised his setting of Longfellow's 'Beware!' from the previous November, adding a tempo marking ('Allegro ma non troppo') and a direction for the voice in the final bars ('Sotto voce'), Stainer and Barrett's work well applied.

There was something intriguing about a child wanting to commit to paper his thoughts and piano improvisations, though Britten later suggested this had less to do with the sounds in his head than the way music looked on paper.

> I remember the first time I tried composing, I was an extremely small boy. The result looked rather like the Forth Bridge, in other words – hundreds of dots all over the page connected by long lines all joined together in beautiful curves. I am afraid it was the pattern on the paper which interested me and when I asked my mother to play it, her look of horror upset me considerably.

Even once he learned how to connect the written notes with his conception of sound, he was not so different from a young child showing some talent for drawing; it was too soon to see if it indicated originality.

He progressed quickly, however. His attempts at writing in imitation – a tentative and quickly abandoned fughetta – are evident in one of his Book of Samuel pieces (c. 1923–4), which is suitably hymnic and demonstrates the positive influence of the harmony lessons he had recently begun with Audrey Alston. Such influence is further evident in his first named fugue (c. November 1924); in the 'Walztes' (sic) he brushed down and published in 1970, two of which are from 1924 and which emulate the gentle swirl of Chopin; and in 'A Dirge' from 1926. It is not solely his harmonic language that has developed in 'A Dirge'; with its armoury of suspensions and resolutions, diminished and chromatic chords, it is an evocative setting of Shelley's moaning and wailing for the world's wrongs. 'Rough wind that moanest loud / Grief too sad for song; / Wild wind when sullen cloud / Knells all the night long.' The short setting illustrates two key stages in Britten's development: he had learned how to choose a poem that resonated with his physical if not emotional environment, and he was beginning to learn how to evoke mood in music.

8

Robert sent his son's orchestral 'Ouverture' to the British Broadcasting Company, a submission for the infant broadcaster's 1926 Autumn Musical Festival Prize Competition. The accompanying letter provides a glimpse of life, music and relationships in the Britten household.

Having established that the overture was written by a twelve-year-old in only nine days, snatching time from the routine of prep school ('in the very early mornings for instance'), Mr Britten gives his own (or more probably his wife's) assessment of his son's progress. 'He has only an elementary knowledge of harmony. Has had no instruction of any kind in orchestration or counterpoint; a little in form. It is quite an original copy; no piano score written before. We thought it worth sending, if only for advice.' The letter displays a touching faith in the vision and expertise of the new company, then only four years old and an unknown quantity.

No response from the BBC survives, though a few months later Charles Macpherson, a professor at the Royal Academy of Music and organist at St Paul's, gave his reaction to scores sent to him by a friend of Mrs Britten's. 'The outlook is founded on the simpler classical; there is no counterpoint, or feeling in that direction. The work is of course remarkable for one so young, but there is as yet not much sign of individual outlook, or certainty in treatment. If unduly flattered I should say the spark would be quenched.' It was a fair assessment.

Two works illustrate Britten's development in these years, each dedicated to his parents. The first is the tone poem 'Chaos and Cosmos', completed in early September 1927, just in time for Edith and Robert's twenty-sixth wedding anniversary; the second is *Quatre chansons françaises*, finished a few days before their twenty-seventh. What a difference this year made! The tone poem, one of five composed during 1926–7, is for a fantastically large orchestra of triple winds; its scale, spirit and title demonstrate Britten was by then working his way through late-Romantic scores ('although I fear I was not really sure what the words [of the title] meant', he later admitted), but it is of modest accomplishment.

The songs are a different matter altogether. Settings of Verlaine and Hugo – two poems each, extracted from *The Oxford Book of French Verse* (1924) – they are delicate, thoughtful songs for soprano and small orchestra that employ an entirely new palette of colours, some borrowed from Debussy, others from Wagner. One of the songs, 'L'Enfance', incorporates a nursery rhyme sung by a young child – the sort of song Britten was writing himself only a few years earlier – here used as a backdrop to the death of the infant's mother. It is a Mahlerian conceit, some years before Britten's first encounter with the great Viennese composer. Another, 'Sagesse', see-saws between black and white keys, unable to put down roots, while it paints the bleak repercussions of wisdom gained. Still another, 'Les Nuits de Juin', is full of summer perfume, with an opening that juxtaposes two tonalities separated by a semitone – much as Britten over twenty years later would begin his opera *Billy Budd* – and an overall chromatic harmonic language inconceivable in the composer of 'Chaos and Cosmos'. The final song, 'Chanson d'automne', pays homage to the slow-pulsed, serene ending to Wagner's *Tristan und Isolde*. For all their evident debts, the songs offer a startling riposte to the bourgeois, predictable musical journey Britten was on previously. What had happened between late 1927 and 1928?

9

As a child I heard little music outside my own home. There were the local choral society concerts and the very occasional chamber concert, but the main event was the Norwich Triennial Festival. There in 1924, when I was 10, I heard Frank Bridge conduct his suite 'The Sea,' and was knocked sideways.

It turned out that my viola teacher, Audrey Alston, was an old friend of Bridge's. He always stayed with her, and when the success of 'The Sea' brought him to Norwich again in 1927 with a specially written work called 'Enter Spring,' I was taken to meet him.

We got on splendidly, and I spent the next morning with him going over some of my music (I'd been writing music since I was about five). From that moment I used to go regularly to him, staying with him in Eastbourne or in London, in the holidays from my prep school.

Frank Bridge and his music are largely forgotten today, yet here was a fortuitous meeting of minds. A left-leaning pacifist and consummate craftsman, performer and conductor, Bridge was a living, walking, performing example of what a British composer could be. He was not a professor at one of the London colleges or Oxford or Cambridge. Nor was he a composer-conductor in the manner of Mahler or Strauss: despite his occasional Prom concerts and guest appearances with fledgling opera companies and orchestras, England could not then sustain such a model. He made his living not from one musical activity or another but from many – performing, composing, conducting – which made him desperately difficult to categorize. And despite his pre-war compositions, which *sound* English (*The Sea* included, which Britten came to think of as a little crude), his interest in Continental modernism was genuine and increasingly influential on his own aesthetic in the period in which Britten worked with him.

In her biography of Britten, Imogen Holst relates three anecdotes about the way in which those around the young composer viewed his musical talent and aspirations. There was his first day as a boarder at Gresham's in Holt, Norfolk, fifty miles from Lowestoft, on 20 September 1928, where he was greeted by the music master with the words, 'So *you* are the little boy who likes Stravinsky!' There was the tennis party in Lowestoft, after Gresham's, where he was asked what career he intended to pursue, and having replied, 'a composer', the astonished tennis player responded, 'Oh, but what *else*?' And there was the remark made by one of the adjudicators for his Royal College of Music scholarship examination: 'What is an English public schoolboy doing writing music of this kind?' To Britten each of these comments was emblematic of the particular brand of English cultural philistinism he experienced growing up.

It was understandable that he thought this way: from jingoistic wartime programming of the major performance organizations, to the status of English music and musicians, to the lack of performance infrastructure in the first decades of the twentieth century and the low standards at the London music colleges, England presented an ignominious comparison to other European countries. Britten was contending 'not only with the Englishman's innate lack of seriousness in his attitude towards the arts', as his post-war friend the Earl of Harewood put it, 'but also with the determined amateurism fostered in the public schools, and supported by every form of pressure, social and moral, at their command'. There is a lot to be said for Harewood's frankness, yet before the inception of the British Broadcasting Company in 1922 and its more ambitious successor five years later, the British Broadcasting Corporation, before the gramophone's growth spurt in the same era, and before the many other changes in Britain's cultural infrastructure following the First World War, it is more accurate to think of the comments directed at the boy Britten as provincial rather than philistine.

'The English seemed entirely preoccupied with Empire Exhibitions, the Royal Jubilee of 1937 [*recte* 1935], and sport,' wrote Spender at the end of his life. 'What happened on the Continent, they seemed to feel, was none of their business.' It was the land of Mapp and Lucia, E. F. Benson's comic creations, cooking Lobster *à la Riseholme*, dropping Italian phrases into conversations to imply untested fluency, and hosting musical soirées where the sole offering was the slow movement of Beethoven's 'Moonlight' Sonata. Britain just didn't know any better.

Exactly what Bridge must have made of the boy with his suitcase bulging with manuscripts, his Advanced Level exam (honours) at the Associated Board almost two years behind him, can only be imagined. But one thing is certain: Bridge knew better than those around him, knew he should take Britten seriously. With introductions completed, the adolescent composer embarked a few months later on a remarkable course of study with the older musician.

The lessons with Bridge were frequent and arduous. Britten and his mother would travel to London, sometimes staying overnight to have a second lesson the following morning. 'I remember one that started at half past ten,' Britten later wrote, 'and at tea-time Mrs Bridge came in and said, "Really, you must give the boy a break."' There were tears (from exhaustion) and relatively little laughter; composing was a serious business, not an amateur pastime. A composer must find himself, his voice, and be true to what he finds, taught Bridge; this was only possible with scrupulous attention to good technique, learning how to say in music exactly what was on one's mind.

Vitally, the lessons with Bridge also allowed Britten to peek into the life of an artist. 'I heard conversations which centred round the arts; I heard the latest poems discussed, and the latest trends in painting and sculpture.' When the hard work was over for a day or weekend, Britten relaxed with the Bridges and their circle of cultured friends. Bridge was an excitable character (according to sister Beth) who talked a lot – about pacifism and politics, the Queen's Hall concerts they all attended or knew of, about new books and poets and ecclesiastical architecture. There were tennis matches and shrimping parties, and fast drives in the narrow lanes branching through the Sussex countryside. There were introductions to other eminent musicians – Schoenberg backstage at Queen's Hall, neither his severe countenance nor his Op. 31 *Variations* making much of an impression on Britten, which was curious given it was the most radical score and composer he had yet encountered.

Photographs of Bridge and his circle show the older composer wearing his hair long and trousers high, his expression benevolent; Mrs Bridge, a square-framed mother figure, fussing over Frank or their guests; a group shot with the Catalan violinist Antonio Brosa (who would later give the premiere of Britten's Violin Concerto in Carnegie Hall), the Bridges' neighbour and close friend Marjorie Fass (an amateur artist), Audrey Alston's son Christopher, and a serious-looking Britten in the background. This was a different milieu for the sheltered boy from Suffolk. Beth recognized Bridge was the antithesis of her father, and it was Bridge, not Robert Victor, who ultimately had the greater impact. Bridge, with his highly refined artistic sensibility and ability to bring Britten on, knew how to nurture talent, not just recognize it. And it was the influence of this improbable English bohemian that separated 'Chaos and Cosmos' from *Quatre chansons françaises*.

10

Bridge had been a force in his life for nine months or so by the time Britten arrived at Gresham's school. Britten resented being there: his enrolment was the result of a compromise deal thrashed out by his older siblings and his parents, the former arguing that School Certificate (the precursor of O Levels/GCSE) was the bare minimum their brother should acquire before embarking on so uncertain a profession, the latter tending towards Bridge's advice that his pupil lodge in London with his friend the pianist Harold Samuel and pursue private tuition in piano and composition from them both.

With such mentors, it is understandable that Britten's response to the Gresham's music master was so uncharitable: he described the man and his playing variously as 'awful', 'lacking in sanity', 'abominable'. Writing to Edith, Britten was uncharacteristically droll: 'Mr Greatorex, who played the organ, does not play well. I am sure it is bad never to play 2 notes together.' But his temper was up from the beginning. Greatorex told him he had a 'flimsy technick', that it was quite hopeless for a boy of his age to play later Beethoven, and that it 'would be no good whatsoever for me to go into the musical profession. Music in this school is now finished for me!' One month out from beginning his lessons with Samuel, Britten viewed the master's comments as much a criticism of

Miss Astle and his mother as they were of him. (Late Beethoven remained for young pianists top-shelf material way beyond the 1920s.)

W. H. Auden, who was at the school from 1920 to 1925, was more generous about the music master. 'I owe [Greatorex] not only such knowledge of music as I possess, but my first friendship with a grown up person, with all that that means.' So was Stephen Spender. 'Is Greatorex the eighth or the ninth greatest musician in England? A great king, why has he come down among us?' Yet Britten remembered only antipathy and hostility between them. Perhaps, as Beth suggested, Greatorex resented this brilliant student taking lessons outside school. Even so, it is possible to read Greatorex's initial greeting of his young charge with reference to Stravinsky as encouragement rather than rebuke, though Britten would have been too sensitive to do so. And one of Greatorex's final gestures to his student was to programme his 'Bagatelle' in a school concert and then sit at the piano with the composer (on viola) and another staff member (on violin) for the performance. Britten completed the trio only six weeks earlier, a fact *The Gresham* implicitly acknowledged in its description of it as a work in the 'modern idiom'. Britten's aggressive view aside, Greatorex was an encouraging teacher.

He was also probably homosexual, though this would have made little impression on Britten. Unlike the sexually precocious if prim Auden, Britten's time at Gresham's coincided with only a dim awareness of his emerging sexuality, the first squeaks of which had been evident at South Lodge. There he formed a number of close friendships with slightly younger boys, whom he continued to see after he moved on to public school; together they took tea, swam at the beach, and had sleepovers. His childhood friend John Pounder recognized something stronger than mere friendship in these bonds, later asserting that Britten's relationship with two such boys, Francis Barton and Michael Halliday, made him identify Britten's sexuality. To what limited extent Britten was coming to the same conclusion is unknown; none of his other friends could recall a conversation on the topic. None was homosexual either, which doubtless did nothing to advance Britten's sexual development. There were communal showers at public school, of course, where Spender first encountered pubescent nakedness outside his family, to some effect. But the diary that Britten began just before entering Gresham's is unrevealing on such matters, tilting instead towards a bloodless *Tom Brown's Schooldays* approach to his experiences and feelings. 'Go and see some boys off,' he wrote on his last day at South Lodge. 'I am frightfully sorry to say good-bye to them. Francis Barton especially. He has been a ripping boy.' With such language and sentiment did Britten chart his attachment to this string of boys, an aspect of his personality he found impossible to lose.

One of the most startling revelations in the embittered Crozier notes of 1966 is a specific allegation about Britten's schooling and sexuality: 'He told me he had been raped by a master at his school, as if his sexual deviation had stemmed from that one incident.' Crozier's assertion – unconfirmed by any other document or friend, Pears included – was given prominence by Humphrey Carpenter, who pointed a speculative finger at Captain Sewell. (Crozier did not in fact specify whether the alleged crime occurred at prep school or at public school.) It is strong language – not for Crozier the weak euphemism 'abuse' – but it is an unstable prosecution, pressed into the service of his hostile theory that 'having been corrupted as a boy, he seemed to be under a compulsion to corrupt other small boys'.

This motif has hijacked our understanding of the composer for two decades, presenting a troubling and erroneous insinuation. In any circumstance, these are treacherous waters psychologically, and because of what has been said about Britten since his death they require careful navigation. There is nothing in his diaries from this time to suggest he was even aware of homosexuality as a concept, not even in its romanticized public-schoolboy manifestation. Later, in 1940, with a temperature of 103 °F, Britten addressed the creeping awareness of his sexuality in adolescence, yet the friend by his side in that moment, Beata Mayer, could subsequently recall only the broad brushstrokes of his fevered ravings. 'He talked about his schooldays and how it came about and how he found out about his sexuality. And my recollection is that the schooldays were not exactly happy.'

Gresham's should have been the ideal place for him to discover such things about himself. It pursued a liberal curriculum, a progressive social agenda, all within spacious modern buildings. Britten's house, Farfield, was built only two years before his birth, while the stone chapel – a bold riposte to the redbrick buildings around it – was completed just three years after it. The headmaster in Britten's time, J. R. Eccles, condemned corporal punishment – not least in the pages of *The Times* – and oversaw a policy whereby, unusually, membership of the

Officers' Training Corps was voluntary (Britten did not join). There were scholarships for music (Britten unsurprisingly won one, worth £30), an active Debating Society, and summer plays in the garden – *A Midsummer Night's Dream*, with fairies dressed in short smocks and dragonfly wings; or *As You Like It*, with stern-looking nobles in high boots, holding wooden swords; or in one special year *The Tempest*, with Auden as Caliban. A few years after Britten left Gresham's, the Debating Soc. tabled the notion, 'In the opinion of this House a Fascist Dictatorship is preferable to Socialism', which was carried ninety-nine votes to fifty-four, an indication of the free-spirited privilege and rebellion of the pupils. Its curriculum favoured sciences, while its languages were German and French rather than the more traditional Latin (a little) and Greek (none at all). Boys were allowed to wander unsupervised in the surrounding countryside as long as they respected the school timetable, a freedom Auden used to his advantage.

Britten was later churlish about the place. 'Well I went on to Gresham's School at Holt which was chosen because they didn't actively hate music, as so many other public schools did.' He thought it a waste of his time when all he wanted to do was become a musician ('I didn't even play the piano there,' he exaggerated). Yet Spender greatly valued his instruction at Gresham's on Romantic poets and the good example they set – rule-breakers and iconoclasts to a man, diving deep into their creative imaginations to fetch pearls, which they polished and displayed. And Britten must have appreciated certain aspects of the school, given his attempts in the 1950s to send the young David Hemmings there. Perhaps in doing so he was remembering the liberal education and discouragement of the cult of the athlete, progressive rejoinders to traditional nineteenth-century public-school life.

Yet for all its academic liberalism, Gresham's was a strangely puritan place. There was an honour system operating, whereby boys pledged not to smoke, swear or behave indecently. So far, so Baden-Powell. But they were also honour-bound to intervene if they encountered such behaviour in others. The tub-thumping Eccles sermonized to terrified young boys on the dangers of masturbation.

Auden found the system ridiculous. 'I believe no more potent engine for turning them into neurotic innocents, for perpetuating those very faults of character which it was intended to cure, was ever devised.' He flew in the face of it, courtesy of a number of chaste but loving relationships with other boys, among them Robert Medley, subsequently a successful artist whom Britten would encounter through his work in the mid-1930s for the Group Theatre. 'It meant', Auden wrote in 1934, 'that the whole of our moral life was based on fear, on fear of the community, not to mention the temptation it offered to the natural informer, and fear is not a healthy basis. It makes one furtive and dishonest and unadventurous. The best reason I have for opposing Fascism is that at school I lived in a Fascist state.' Any boy less intellectually robust than Auden would not have found Gresham's the best environment in which to discover his sexuality.

Britten wrote in his diary his own dramatic reaction to the system, which chimes with Auden's mature reflection.

> I think that the 'Honour System' is a positive failure in Farfield. If Eccles new what happens he would either disbelieve it or have 10 blue fits. Atrocious bullying on all sides, vulgarity & swearing. It is no good trying the Honour System on boys who have no honour. Boys, small & rather weak are turned into sour & bitter boys, & ruined for life.

His letters home were more circumspect, full instead of requests for jam, manuscript paper and parental visits; details of his lessons in London; grateful acknowledgement of biscuits, cakes, honey, eggs, socks, Kolynos toothpaste and other public-school rations ('I have just finished the grapes, darling, which were absolutely ripping; You *were* an angel'); and news of radio broadcasts, films, school concerts and hockey games. His mother is addressed variously as 'little one', 'angel of my heart', 'darling' or 'darling pet', and letters are signed off with 'tons of love', much adoration and gratitude, and the occasional protestation of worship.

Whatever the school's faults and fantasies, Britten was made to work hard. At the end of his time at Gresham's he sat School Certificate in geography, history, German, French, mathematics, European history, précis writing, general knowledge and English literature ('The Pardoner's Tale' and 'The Nun's Priest's Tale' from *The Canterbury Tales*, home to Chanticleer the rooster). Between studies, lessons in London and Sussex, games and composition, Britten was developing the discipline and work ethic he would retain all his life.

He also composed an extraordinary amount, scribbling ideas down on paper whenever an opportunity arose. 'All the time I am writing on odd sheets of writing-paper etc, scraps of new quartets and things. All that is possible.' Many of these late scribbles are works of astonishing accomplishment for such a young composer, a number of which are still performed today. He started revising his compositions too, working at second or third drafts in an attempt to get his ideas on paper exactly as he wanted them, as per Bridge's instruction. 'A poem is never finished, only abandoned,' Auden would later say to anyone who listened, borrowing the words of French poet and philosopher Paul Valéry. Yet at the time, as Britten chipped away at various drafts before inking a fair copy, he would have found the aphorism unsatisfactory. It was the composer's job to finish a work, to perfect an idea.

For the first time in his life he had ready access to gramophone recordings and radio broadcasts and was going to concerts more than ever before, usually on his trips to London. In his diary he wrote of 'a marvellous performance of Hiawatha at Albert Hall' (19 June 1930); a 'topping concert at Queen's H. with Mummy. Backhaus was simply ideal; I enjoyed the Bax [Symphony No. 2] but didn't understand it' (14 March 1930); a 'marvellous Schönberg concert on the Billison's wireless', featuring his Chamber Symphony, Suite, Op. 25, for piano, and the alluring, austere sound world of *Pierrot lunaire* (7 April 1930). The new sounds, ideas and composers he encountered, together with Bridge's tutelage, revolutionized his compositions. Each of the influences made him consider music in relationship to its environment and heritage. 'I am thinking much about modernism in art,' he wrote in his diary in November 1929. 'Debating whether Impressionism, Expressionism, Classicism etc. are right. I have half-decided on Schönberg. I adore Picassos's pictures.' It was a glorious checklist in a febrile time; much of the adult Britten's knowledge and personality – his taste in art and music in particular – was unlocked in these years.

Britten's *Quartettino* for string quartet, composed in the first months of 1930, affirms his November diary entry: he really *was* thinking about sound and form, in a manner inconceivable only a year earlier. Not even *Rhapsody* for string quartet of 1929 skates so close to the Continental modernism of *Quartettino*. Key signatures have been ditched in favour of a five-note row, which Britten spells out under the title as though it were a crossword clue, and then sets to work on it with great fire and skill. Every detail in the score is specified – a battery of harmonics, *portamenti*, chromatic acrobatics, dance gestures and skittish tonality. The work was not played at the time, nor does the manuscript contain Bridge's usual corrections. In preparing the work for publication in 1983, Britten's one-time assistant Colin Matthews wondered if Britten had perhaps been unwilling to show it to his teacher because he had borrowed so much from his mentor's idiom but then had the nerve to take it even further. Significantly, having crafted the piece with such care, in the following years Britten stepped back from the brink of atonality it implied.

Nor were the revelations to be found only in modernism. *A Hymn to the Virgin* (1930) extended Britten's reach backwards by a few centuries, its antiphonal writing reminiscent of Allegri or Vittoria, its doleful melody similar to the one he later borrowed from Dowland for *Lachrymae,* its variation treatment anticipating that in *A Boy was Born* by only a few years, and its mixture of English poetry and Latin prayer prefiguring the same idea, writ large, in *War Requiem.* If its veneration of the mother of Christ sits uneasily with a low-church Anglican, perhaps the inspiration was to be found closer to home. Its first performance by the Lowestoft Musical Society at his mother's church in early January 1931 undoubtedly gave Edith much pleasure.

Other works contain such veneration of the matriarch. 'The Birds' is a beautiful short song, written 'For my Mother' in 1929 and revised over the following years.* With its dry, lute-like accompaniment, 'The Birds' would later serve as a funeral march for his mother and as nuptial music for his sister Beth; it remains much performed today. It was not all jewels, as his setting of Tennyson's 'Lilian' in the same year demonstrates. No doubt intended for his mother to sing (it is in her range), the song tells of flirty, cruel Lilian who mocks the narrator for loving her, and whose probable fate is to be crushed like a rose leaf by the spurned lover, a victim of his cold, psychopathic revenge. Britten somehow overreached: his setting strives for harmonic and rhetorical purpose, yet sounds only forced and clumsy – a gilded, giddy waltz, and an odd bedfellow of 'The Birds'. For whatever reason, 'Lilian' is only one of a sequence of poems stressing the fickleness and inconstancy of women that caught Britten's eye in the decade.

---

* 'I had a terrible struggle with this before finding what has been called "the right ending in the wrong key",' Britten wrote of 'The Birds' and Bridge's critique of the modulation in the final line, 'And bring my soul to Paradise'. But Britten's decision was inspired, a sudden musical elevation to relay a spiritual one.

11

Harold Samuel was a brilliant musician, whom Barnum would have invented in slightly earlier times. He carried in his head the entire Bach keyboard oeuvre, which he performed in large chunks or small concertos in the 1920s when the composer was much in vogue. Samuel became Britten's teacher in November 1928 and helped his pupil develop the instrumental technique that would later have a huge impact on British piano playing, song accompaniment in particular. 'If I never again hear playing such as this I shall die happy,' Britten wrote in August 1930 after hearing Samuel play Bach's keyboard concerto in D minor. Recordings from the time explain his enthusiasm: Samuel has a clean, powder-dry, unsentimental approach to Bach, with careful voicing and a sense of intimacy, in happy contrast to the billowing performances of Bach that were then more common. There are certain similarities between these recordings and Britten's mature playing, particularly in the long phrasing and the way harmony is employed rhetorically.

The school chaplain wrote an account of Britten's contribution to a concert at Gresham's in Lent Term 1930 (while he was a Samuel student). Having witnessed such concerts in more than twenty-four years at the school, calibrating the contribution of some fine musicians, the chaplain concluded that 'it is no slight to any of them to place Britten above them all'.

> The interpretation of Raff's *Fileuse* alone was enough to establish him as a past-master of delicate workmanship, but the *Polichinelle* of Rachmaninoff held one bewildered, spellbound. Two thoughts arose: 1. How on earth could anyone have written it? 2. How on earth could anyone play it? The effect was devastating. The more the fire and fury, or the leaping and plunging increased, the more rapturously I could have shouted for joy . . . of course Britten was encored.

Raff's musical portrait of a spinning maid is no longer played much, coming across like those Liszt transcriptions of Schubert songs, the melody presented simply, the accompaniment busy, decorous, delicate. It is not flashily difficult, yet once the spinning-wheel ornamentation begins it does not let up. (Had Britten heard the acoustic gramophone recording by the brilliant, eccentric Pachmann made in 1909?) In style it is a complete antidote to the red-blooded works Britten had previously been playing, and the memory of it must have returned to him with a jolt when in 1942 he set a French folk song of the same name.* By contrast, Rachmaninov's *Polichinelle* sounds less like a *commedia dell'arte* character study than the accompaniment to a cavalry scene in a silent movie. (Did Britten know the composer's own whimsical piano-roll performance of 1919?) It is potentially a show-stopper, as it appears to have been on this occasion.

It is odd now to think of Britten playing this virtuoso repertory and the works to come: Franck's *Variations symphoniques*, Walton's *Sinfonia concertante*, Debussy's *L'Île joyeuse*, Tchaikovsky's and Brahms's Piano Concerto No. 1, Brahms's *Variations on a Hungarian Song*, etc. His discography is modest in this area, more handmaiden than alpha male. Yet for all his compositional aspirations, a career as a pianist – with all its precariousness and hardships – was at this stage more likely. Moreover, once out of school his view of himself as a musician was pointedly Romantic. He needed this repertory, the meaty and the ornamental alike.

He found such qualities in Ravel's *Miroirs*, which he studied through the Easter holidays in 1930, following the Gresham's concert. A fine pianist, Ravel was a good example of composer-executant, a common enough figure in the previous century, yet one now unfashionable or in short supply in England. Moreover, Ravel was engaging with modernist ideas, creating his own personal sound-world, rooted in colour and unflashy virtuosity. His influence as a composer was felt immediately in the compositions of his young admirer. It may be Skryabin who infuses the first of Britten's *Three Character Pieces* for piano of late 1930, yet the final two are steeped in Ravel's language; the third is an almost self-conscious homage to 'Noctuelles' from *Miroirs*, a score of which his mother had given him two years earlier. (He wrote self-deprecatingly and unconvincingly about the last of these *Character Pieces*: 'it is terribly hard, & I simply haven't the technique', though he never composed piano works or accompaniments technically beyond him.) Britten dedicated each piece to a young Lowestoft friend, the character of whom he

---

* In Britten's version an old woman hunches over her spinning wheel and recalls her fancy-free youth as a shepherdess in the mountains, being wooed by a shepherd lad, and the accompaniment owes as much to Raff's old spinner as it does to Schubert's Gretchen, another woman from the same parlour.

attempted to capture in music, much as Elgar had done so successfully in his *Enigma Variations*.

Ravel's influence aside, the development these pieces represents is remarkable. In the space of two years Britten had transformed himself from a cosseted, precious boy, with hazy notions of his voice as a composer and future as a pianist, into an adolescent of startling achievement. It is this fast-maturing boy whom Basil Reeve remembers – the fluent score-reading; the two of them busking through sonatas for violin or viola, or piano trios in the company of another friend; the trips to Morlings, the music shop in town, where together they played two-piano music (on more than one occasion Britten's arrangement of Brahms's Symphony No. 4) or listened to gramophone recordings shipped into Lowestoft like bootleg; the invitations they inveigled from neighbours to hear radio broadcasts; the conversations they had about their futures, Britten's in particular.

Reeve may have thought Edith kept her son on too tight a leash. 'Everything was absolutely controlled before; the length of time that we two could be together, what we could do together – absolutely controlled . . . [it] might have been a Communist state.' Yet in reality she had already lost him to a cosmopolitan world of ideas and music she could scarcely have recognized, one Britten would never have encountered in his cosy life at 21 Kirkley Cliff Road.

Britten began his School Certificate exams on 14 July 1930, only three weeks after he was awarded an open scholarship to the Royal College of Music (RCM) in London, the result of a scrambled application in late May and last-minute summons to London on 19 June for examination and interview. He passed his School Certificate with five credits, a perfectly good result which caught him by surprise. Whatever his misgivings about the school, it had served him well academically. In his English notebook for Lent Term 1929 he recorded a Gresham's resolution, 'That everyone shall be able to argue, to debate, to read aloud, and to lecture'. Auden had left the school a few years earlier armed with the same aspiration, and was soon to make it the guiding principle of 1930s literary England. This was not part of Britten's character as he stood on the cusp of adulthood. He was serious, driven and musically confident, this father of the man, but hardly a loquacious or domineering figure. And he would soon need every one of the skills contained in the Gresham's resolution to survive the suffocating embrace of Auden's friendship.

He left Gresham's with a swag of prizes – scores of Schoenberg's *Pierrot lunaire*, Rimsky-Korsakov's suite from *The Golden Cockerel*, Strauss's *Don Quixote* and five orchestral songs, plays by John Drinkwater, and the inevitable *Oxford Book of English Verse* – and with so many of the pieces of the Britten puzzle in place, a few conspicuous by their absence. In an unconscious reflection of his departure from South Lodge two years earlier, he wrote of his school friends, 'I am terribly sorry to leave such boys as these . . .' The coming years in London would help him understand the true nature of these feelings.

2

Apprenticeship

London, Suffolk, 1930–1939

I

He arrived in London in September 1930 like Tom Rakewell, the callow protagonist of Stravinsky's opera, kitbag over his shoulder, in the capital to garner experience and make his fortune. Britten's relationship with London, while more fortunate than Tom's, was never easy. He distrusted the city and felt oppressed by its attempts at order and the sprawling evidence of its failure. 'I've lived on and off in London for quite a few years,' he said much later, 'but I don't feel happy there. Essentially I like living in small communities.' When asked in his fiftieth year what he thought of cities, London in particular, he was more candid. 'I hate them! When I come up for a day to London to do the usual boring things, I rush about and in the end get terribly behind and utterly exhausted. Probably I don't appreciate London.' Auden would have teased from him something more revealing: while fleshing out Hogarth's dystopic sequence of images as the libretto for Stravinsky's *The Rake's Progress* he proposed that a city's filth, corruption and lawlessness, its failure to protect the most vulnerable, were metaphors for the darkest aspects of humanity.

The metaphors were not lost on Britten. For the first time he saw how the physical hierarchies of a great city mirrored those of its population, how the stratification of housing and urban planning reflected and reinforced the layers of society itself. In any direction from his boarding house on Prince's Square, Bayswater, he encountered evidence of the rapid expansion of the capital, made possible by tube trains and sewers, and saw the scars and rewards of more than a hundred years of industrialization. He saw the most extraordinary montage of architectural styles

58

and conditions, from elegant town houses near the major parks to slum clearances in Paddington. Walking through Kensington Gardens to the RCM next to the Royal Albert Hall he passed liveried nannies pushing large prams in small convoys; in town it was telegraph boys in their smart black uniforms topped off with webbing and peaked caps. Queuing for *Lohengrin* tickets at Edward Barry's grand opera house in Covent Garden he saw society figures walking past dirty barrow boys and aproned fruiterers, the women in furs, the men in black tie. (Foreign visitors were known to observe sniffily that the 'Royal Opera stands in the middle of a vegetable market', their memories of Berlin and Vienna strong.) For this was a city of crippling poverty and unimagined wealth, juxtaposed with no fanfare, a jumble of images equal to anything in *The Rake's Progress*. As the decade advanced, as the strikes and protest marches into London increased in number, so too this sense of scale and inequality loomed large in Britten's imagination and work.

His boarding house was in a cluttered row of terraces not far from the Bridges' place in Kensington, with five or six floors occupied by tenants straight from an Agatha Christie mystery: numerous old ladies; two 'foreign men'; the private secretary to a famous violin dealer; a woman called Tumpty and her callous sister; and the sixteen-year-old Britten. They were overseen by a Miss Thurlow Prior, whom Britten referred to as Miss Monday-Tuesday, for no discernible reason. His room was small, nestled into the eaves, into which he squeezed an upright piano, taking care not to play after ten at night. Despite initial protestations of misery, he adapted well enough to his new domestic environment. A few days after arrival he wrote home full of news and cheer, and concluded his letter with touching gratitude: 'Thank you very much for letting me come.' They could, after all, have insisted on two more years of schooling.

Britten was later as scathing about the RCM as he was about Gresham's. 'I was rather a failure as a student,' he said in 1959. 'The trouble was, I had been studying with Bridge since I was a young boy. Bridge's approach was that of the highly professional international musician. The attitude of most of the R.C.M. students was amateurish and folksy. That made me feel highly intolerant.' As with Gresham's, caveats are required. It is true he found the students mediocre, but, as cultural and economic historian Cyril Ehrlich has shown, the London colleges were all underfunded – hostage to dilettante pupils and the need for poorly paid teachers to scrap for work elsewhere. The 'conservatory dignitary, dispensing medals and certificates throughout the provinces, and occa-sionally the Empire', with a house in Hampstead and his boys at public school, was a rare exception. George Dyson, appointed a professor at the RCM in 1921 and the college's director seventeen years later, recalled the atmosphere in the 1920s, when students enrolled in great numbers with 'little more than a school-child's accomplishment and a natural desire to follow an attractive and favourite hobby'. There were exceptions in Britten's time. Remo Lauricella was one, whom Britten befriended and accompanied in these early London years; cellist Ber-nard Richards was another, with whom he and Lauricella performed piano trios (and who would later work with Britten as principal cellist of the English Chamber Orchestra). Yet pickings were slim.

Britten only infrequently wrote about the student concerts he attended because he did not involve himself much in the musical life of the col-lege, such as it was. With opera and concerts on his doorstep, he saw little point in throwing away nights on bad student performances and consequent rages. It is impossible to say whether the small number of friends he made and saw at the RCM was more due to his shyness or his distaste for the low level of the music-making.

Later in life Britten happily fuelled the perception he found the teaching as poor as the students. Ralph Vaughan Williams, then a Titan of English music and teacher of composition at the RCM, defin-itely aroused Britten's suspicions. He disliked the influence he thought Vaughan Williams wielded, perpetuating a clumsy amateurishness to upcoming generations of composers. (Much later he changed his mind, saying in 1952 that 'he can be *imitated* but he hasn't influenced', which was not a huge advance.) 'My struggle all the time was to develop a consciously controlled professional technique,' he recalled. 'It was a struggle away from everything Vaughan Williams seemed to stand for.' And Sir Hugh Allen, the RCM director, was no better, representing all that Britten detested in 'academic musicians', unfairly in this instance.

Vaughan Williams may or may not have said the critical things attrib-uted to him – including the remark, 'very clever but beastly music', reputedly in response to Britten being awarded the Farrar Composition Prize at the end of his first year – and the thin-skinned Britten may or may not have taken genuine offence. Yet Allen wrote to Britten's parents in August to tell them 'how highly [Vaughan Williams] thought of your boy's work'. Moreover, Vaughan Williams later sent Britten's *Two Psalms* to Sir Ivor Atkins, organist at Worcester Cathedral and director of the Three Choirs Festival, proposing them for performance. He also alerted composer and impresario Anne Macnaghten to this bright talent at the RCM, an intervention that led to a number of premieres in the new Macnaghten–Lemare concert series, including Britten's *Sinfonietta* at London's Mercury Theatre in January 1933. So the malevolence of the old guard towards this Young Turk's music has been overblown – not least by Britten himself, whose dislike for V.W.'s music – not universal but nonetheless heartfelt – clouded his judgement about the great man's fiefdom and his favourites at court.

There were reasons for his disappointment with the RCM, however. No provision was made for this exceptionally gifted musician, who had to spend his class time in elementary dictation lessons alongside hobbyists learning their craft, while at the same time trying half-heartedly and unsuccessfully to get the RCM interested in performing his music. (He was exempted from the second term.) Never in his short life had he been treated as just another student. On the one hand, Bridge did not help: Britten was still working closely with him, seeing him more frequently than before, and the comparison between his approach to music and that of the college was invidious. On the other hand, Bridge did occasionally *try* to help, intervening on behalf of his private pupil when the college shrugged its shoulders at Britten choral works – probably *A Hymn to the Virgin* and what is now known as the carol *The Sycamore Tree*. Vaughan Williams told Bridge that the singers were not up to it, to which he replied that it was the college's responsibility to enrol some who were. By the time he left the RCM in July 1933, Britten had heard only two of his works in college concerts – his *Phantasy* in F minor (1932) and *Sinfonietta* (1932), which had already received its premiere elsewhere. 'Without aural experience it was difficult to link notes and sounds,' Britten later forlornly commented, his near empty slate of performances at college compounding his resentment.

2

Britten liked his piano teacher, however. Twenty years his senior, with a handsome, contained face, Arthur Benjamin was an Australian composer and pianist who swerved between the two disciplines without ever making a real fist of either, a few popular compositions aside. Britten enjoyed his lessons and had positive things to say about Benjamin's one-act opera *The Devil Take Her*, which he saw in sketch form and then on stage at the college early in his second year. Benjamin told Britten in his first lesson that he was to practise four hours a day if he wished to take performing seriously, and on a good day he managed three. At the end of his first year Britten joined his teacher for tea at his house, and three years later dedicated *Holiday Diary* to him, though it is unclear whether Benjamin ever played it. Like Greatorex before him, Benjamin was discreetly if comfortably gay, yet again Britten seems not to have realized.

His relationship with his composition teacher, John Ireland, was less easy. Ireland, fifty-one when he met Britten, was a former organist and choirmaster, and was then considered one of England's leading composers. He was an alumnus of the RCM, having studied composition under Sir Charles Villiers Stanford at the turn of the century, where he overlapped with Bridge. Less prolific than his student, Ireland would visibly wilt when Britten arrived each week with a stack of manuscripts, getting through only one or two, the pile magically replenished in the following week. What he offered was far from Bridge's marathon lessons in which each new piece was carefully analysed and assessed, ideas tossed around and resisted, with occasional notes, corrections and queries added. But Bridge had only one composition pupil; Ireland was responsible for a whole string and was distracted by the urgency and difficulty of making a living. Bridge, with his Kensington residence and house in the country, and with financial support from American heiress and philanthropist Elizabeth Sprague Coolidge, had a more congenial life than his old friend.

Britten was also put off by Ireland's louche behaviour. He was occasionally still in bed at his chaotic home when Britten arrived for a morning lesson, hung-over from the previous night's excesses, dirty milk bottles cluttering the doorstep. At one evening lesson Britten found him 'quite drunk most of the time – foully so'. Ireland's sexuality was never quite pegged down either, despite an attempt at marriage and its public failure, which no doubt unsettled his pupil. Ireland was discreet about this part of his life, writing only to his friend the Revd Kenneth Thompson of his feelings for young men, hinting at unresolved homosexual inclinations. Britten later told a number of friends – Pears included –

that Ireland made a pass at him. It is possible, for it is otherwise an odd detail to invent, and, given Britten was only sixteen when he first met his teacher, he fitted the fantasy. The Ireland scholar Bruce Phillips doubts the story, noting that, though Ireland evidently worshipped adolescent youths, he was not interested in sexual relations with them, a fine line Britten himself would later tread. And anyway, the naive young Britten would have recognized only the most explicit signs or behaviour, which does not sound like Ireland.

Ireland was undoubtedly a melancholic figure; in photographs he looks sad, almost deflated – a Trollopian vicar without a parish. Britten later said that he possessed a strong personality but a weak character. As Britten noticed, he was drinking a lot at this time, a leaky refuge from his disastrous marriage. Much of his music must have seemed to Britten a poor substitute for Bridge's, which in the late 1920s was exploring ideas and sounds more modern than the French Impressionism to which Ireland was drawn. It was Bridge, however, who had strongly recommended Ireland as a teacher, convincing his pupil that he was a far better bet than the academic R. O. Morris, Harold Samuel's suggestion. 'If I were a young man I should plump for a live composer whose activities are part of the present-day outlook with a heavy leaning towards tomorrow's!'

Sure enough, Britten began lessons only ten days before the first performance of Ireland's Piano Concerto in October 1930. It was Ireland's attempt to take on Prokofiev and Ravel at their own game, and in this he was largely successful: Clifford Curzon, Eileen Joyce, Artur Rubinstein, Gina Bachauer and Moura Lympany (née Mary Gertrude Johnstone) all took it up, as did its dedicatee, the young Helen Perkin.

All of this could have translated into capital in a young or impressionable student's eyes: the teacher as living artist rather than cloistered academic. Britten was impressed by the premiere broadcast, describing the concerto as 'very beautiful', though by the time he returned to it in September the following year he thought it 'very loosely put together'. Part of the problem at this second hearing was that Britten had discovered Walton's Viola Concerto, broadcast two weeks previously, buying the score in preparation, excitedly playing it through with Basil Reeve. No music of that generation could compare, he wrote in his diary, implicitly dismissing Ireland, telling Walton in 1963 that it was a great turning point in his musical life. It is not that Britten did not like any of his new teacher's music; he described Ireland's symphonic rhapsody *Mai-Dun* (1920–21) as 'magnificent', where more commonly he would have remained silent. But it was not even or impressive or new enough. And it is not that he did not find many of Ireland's lessons 'interesting' or 'frightfully instructive'. It was simply that on matters musical and moral Ireland seemed to fall below Britten's aspirations for himself, and by extension, his teachers as well.

Britten's sour characterization of the college and of Ireland stemmed from his dislike of being told what to do, a trait of the adult Britten already firmly in place as a teenager. 'He is *terribly* critical and enough to take the heart out of any one!' Britten wrote in his diary after his first proper lesson. Yet Ireland was determined to give him some technical backbone, which he thought lacking in this inspired, brilliant musician – 'so talented that it's indecent', as Lauricella remembered him saying. So was Bridge. 'I think you may have to do a certain amount of work to sharpen up your technique,' Bridge wrote a month or so before term began, 'which may appear to you, at first, as being a retrograde step, but you know that this will be the first moment when serious study is to monopolize your daily life, & possibly – il faut reculer pour mieux sauter!' So Britten found himself on a diet of harmony, counterpoint, Bach fugues, choral writing and Palestrina voice-leading – very much the German pedagogic model, but here just a bit duller. Ireland's argument was that to write the truly great music of the future one must understand that of the past. Art students with a taste for large abstract canvases must first learn cross-hatching, in the same way that e. e. cummings cut his teeth writing sonnets. Such training, important in a performer, is vital in a composer. Ireland understood this far more than his pupil, and deflected any potential criticism for his didactic ways with the assurance that once Britten had mastered the techniques, he was happy to 'let him loose, so to speak, to go his own way'.

3

Ireland's tuition had no immediate impact on Britten's music. The third of Britten's *Three Character Pieces* was composed after his first term with Ireland, Ravel at his shoulder, a riot of colour and intricate fingerwork, far from the Germanic order and discipline Ireland was hoping to impress on him. In it Britten quotes from 'Ragamuffin', the second of Ireland's *London Pieces* (1917–20), but the tribute is intended for Ravel.

Yet soon Britten's college exercises spilled over into his compositions. *Christ's Nativity* (January–March 1931) is an unsettling hybrid of Britten's own harmonic language, which had been evolving under Bridge's supervision (chromatic tonality cased in standard forms), and the exercises Ireland set him: there are fugues at the third, fourth and sixth degrees of the scale, and the opening melody is soon elongated and employed as a sort of Palestrinian cantus firmus (the technique in which a pre-existing tune is pressed into service), here jumping from part to part. The piece has a disorientating feel, though it is by no means unaccomplished. Immediately afterwards Britten composed a short Fugue in A for solo piano, though this was probably only ever intended as an exercise, its publication posthumous. His String Quartet in D of May–June 1931 is infused with the language of the madrigals he was then singing and studying, finishing off with a fugal treatment of the movement's opening theme. (He would revisit this piece in 1974.) *Simple Symphony* (1934), though based on music written when he was a child with no mastery of the form, uses imitative writing and short fugal episodes as if to say, 'look what I can do now'.

Ireland's technical instruction, fugue in particular, far outlasted Britten's student days. The finale to *Variations on a Theme of Frank Bridge* (1937) contains a fugue ('I feel rather proud of my 11 part fugue with Canto written straight into score in ink!' he said in July), as does that of his first numbered string quartet of 1942 – exactly the type he'd write with such seat-of-the-pants excitement three years later in *The Young Person's Guide to the Orchestra*. His Prelude and Fugue for string orchestra of 1943 does just what the title suggests, while in Act 1 Scene 1 of *Peter Grimes* fugal voices warn that 'A high tide now will eat the land', to great effect. There are many other instances of strict fugal writing, right up to the early 1970s.

When Britten's fugal writing is good it is very good, but when it is bad it sounds grafted onto the piece, a section tossed off with the fluency and muscle memory of youth, a deadline looming, a test to pass. Having mastered Ireland's curriculum, Britten was able to press it into action without much thought – a fallback in dry times, not necessarily sympathetic to the context. Such occasions include the 'Quam olim Abrahae' section of *War Requiem* and the 'Serve the Faith and spurn His enemies' fugue in *Saint Nicolas*. Even the energetic fugal introduction to the lesson scene in *The Turn of the Screw*, intended to underline the learned atmosphere of a classroom, grates a little. In their surroundings these sections startle the listener – much like the unexpected fugue in Liszt's Piano Sonata, the gesture of a great exhibitionist. 'Sometimes he seems over impressed with the look of his notes on paper, as in the fugue,' wrote the *New York Times* critic of Britten's *Variations on a Theme of Frank Bridge* at the decade's tail, calling him on his conceit.

Britten's music is full of old forms and techniques: waltzes, scherzos and variations by the cart-load; a cortège-worth of funeral marches; a tarantella here and a sarabande there; much pastiche and parody. In each case the old form is remodelled by the sheer power of Britten's imagination and musical language, his cap tipped to his ancestors. Fugue was different, however: it locked him into tonal thinking in a way the other forms did not, at a particular time in his own development and that of modern music, when tonality was a seemingly precarious language. Other contemporary composers used fugue, if infrequently: the expressionist Berg in the second act of *Wozzeck* (1917–22) and the neo-classicist Stravinsky in the second movement of *Symphony of Psalms* (1930). Doubtless these pieces encouraged Britten as he dipped his toes in the same waters, since both composers – both works, in fact – exerted a strong influence on him. Berg and Stravinsky disguised the bare bones of their fugues more skilfully than Britten often managed, however, and Britten never quite shook the habit, where his elders most certainly did.

Fugue and variation form were stock-in-trade for the Romantic composer-pianists: Brahms, Beethoven, Chopin and Liszt (each an organist as well as pianist) all improvised their way through the nineteenth century with glorious insouciance, pressing fugue into action as the ultimate circus trick, variations as seduction or tribute. If inspiration ran dry, it was possible to write down these 'improvised' thoughts beforehand, which they all did. Chopin mostly preferred wisps of imitative writing in his works to full fugues; the organic, contrapuntal writing in his fourth Ballade is only one example. Yet the others loved the badge of club membership. Even though people were no longer listening to music contrapuntally, audiences still loved a showman.

This is the model to which Britten turned. When in December 1930 Benjamin told Britten he did not see him as a solo pianist – a fate of his temperament, perhaps, or build, or musical taste – Britten responded predictably, working hard at his technique and learning big

Romantic repertory. Piano was part of how he saw his future. Four years after leaving college, his status as a composer more assured, he did what any self-respecting Romantic would do: he wrote himself a virtuosic piano concerto, which he played at a Promenade concert in August 1938, announcing to popular society his claims as a composer-pianist in the nineteenth-century tradition. Regardless, then, of Britten's smouldering memories of Ireland's teaching, it was clearly effective. The moody old stick achieved what he set out to do: instil some order in his gifted, headstrong pupil.

If there was a problem with Ireland's teaching, it was less the booze, the scruffy demeanour and the missed lessons, far less the possible sexual advance, and more that he encouraged the Romantic language of the nineteenth-century professional model at the expense of some of the untamed and modernist individuality Britten had already exhibited. Ireland would have laughed (or sighed) at the idea: 'I do not think he was influenced in matters of style by either Bridge or myself.' But if it was not style, it was definitely technique, strong traces of which survived the decade.

Bridge originally thought Britten might have followed in Auden's steps from Gresham's to Oxford, continuing his lessons with his mentor all the while; Bobby later thought his brother regretted not having done so. This would have been less than ten years after the Brideshead generation matriculated, when Oxford was a playground for both truly brilliant thinkers and not-terribly-bright scions of aristocratic families, a place full of heady intellectual traditions, excessive dining clubs, particular fashions advertising allegiance to club or class, and romantic fraternal friendships that effortlessly spilled over into homosexual relationships. ('Everyone was queer at Oxford in those days,' John Betjeman later said.) Had Britten gone to Oxford he would have become a different composer, but this is less an indictment of Ireland than recognition that Britten would also have become a different person.

4

London in the 1930s was chock-full of pleasures for a cultured young man about town. Apart from practice and lessons and the constant grind of composition, Britten's life was demarcated by broadcasts, suppers in his digs with Beth or Barbara, teas at Selfridges, dinners with the Bridges, concerts, walks, gramophone recordings, tennis matches and sitting in the stands for games at Wimbledon, pitchers of lemonade, rehearsals, theatre outings and rehearsals of the English Madrigal Society, in which he sang a reedy bass. Even so, his life was built mostly around music, as Bridge predicted. He was immersed in it, from the moment he rose to the moment he went to sleep (often with a score by his pillow). His diary entry for 9 February 1931 charts a random yet typical day:

> Practise & write as usual. [Albert] Sammons is practising & writing in the room next to mine in the afternoon. I go to Queen's Hall to get tickets, & Augeners to get my Brahms picture framed after tea. Practise viola after supper, & then as I settle down to write, I notice in Radio Times that Brahms quartet 3 is going to be broadcast by Hungarian S. Q. So I borrow Miss Prior's wireless, & have marvellous ½ hr listening to the purest music in the purest of possible forms. What a marvellous craze for the viola Brahms had! What a humorous theme the last movement has!

Britten's diaries give no sense of his interior life. It is as though he took his cue from Thomas Mann's diary, but noticed only the entries about lamb cutlets and white beans, not the politics and homoeroticism. Britten never wrote about whether he was lonely, or analysed why he had so few friends at college. He recorded nothing of what was said in his lessons or his thoughts on girls or boys. He had nothing to say about Britain's abandonment of the gold standard or the Great Depression playing out daily around him. He was barely engaged politically, mentioning a by-election in his district in 1930 almost in passing (though it did flush out his 'Bolshy' hostility towards the diehard Conservatives with whom he shared the house in Prince's Square). He read André Maurois's biography of Disraeli, the Conservative politician, dandy, imperialist, novelist and embodiment of the Victorian age, yet had nothing to say in response other than how marvellous it was. And though his diary suggests disappointment at the October 1931 general election results as they unfolded on the radio ('so far only a long list of Conservative successes'), there is no sense of engagement with what Ramsay MacDonald was trying to achieve with his proposed coalition government. Britten listed church services high and low, overseen by a whole communion of saints – James, Matthew, Mark, Stephen and Jude – but gave no indication of whether he thought their claim on his time legitimate. On paper he comes across in these years as naive, still in thrall to the culture and costume of public school.

There are other accounts to help round out our picture of the student Britten. Lauricella remembered pronounced left-wing political views when he was at the RCM, and his distress over Spain. Francis Barton, Britten's friend from South Lodge, experienced the same. 'Ben can't talk about *anything* but the Spanish war!' he complained to his sister in 1936. Both recollections postdate Britten's time at the RCM, though he was already a committed pacifist by the time he got there. 'I had been, for instance, already a pacifist at school ... and although he [Bridge] didn't encourage me to take a stand for the sake of a stand, he did make me argue and argue and argue. His own pacifism was not aggressive, but typically gentle.' A fellow bass in the madrigal society, Paul Wright, recalled him improvising brilliantly in his digs on popular tunes, on snippets from here and there, and on one occasion on the carol 'Unto us is born a son'. But Wright was aware even then that there were some things 'one didn't joke about with Ben', particularly anything that 'touched on his deepest musicality and musical instinct'. Quietly charismatic when needed, and in many ways young for his age, leading an emotionally cloistered life, Britten was still capable of expressing extreme disapproval if someone transgressed certain standards.

The pianist and composer Howard Ferguson, five years Britten's senior, recalled only one side of Wright's characterization: he found the young Britten a 'cold fish' who carefully built walls between himself and those around him. Perhaps Britten simply did not like Ferguson, or his coldness was an instinctive reaction to Ferguson's homosexuality: as self-awareness slowly dawned, Britten used distance to help pretend that this was not his own fate or inclination.

The compensation for Britten's guardedness on personal matters is a wonderful openness about the music and performances he was hearing, which, for all his brilliance, he dissected with a fairly blunt knife. His adolescent love of Brahms remained, though was not to last much longer; the break-up, when it came, was painless and final. ('Now, do you think that's good music, Charles?' he would later ask conductor Charles Mackerras of Brahms's Symphony No. 4, having sung him the opening phrases in brutal caricature.) He got the measure of earnest Adrian Boult (*'terrible execrable* conductor'), and thought the show-man Malcolm Sargent ridiculous. He dismissed some Ethel Smyth songs as 'despicable' and Rachmaninov's Piano Concerto No. 2 as 'terrible – vulgar, old-fashioned'. He primly labelled a performance of Beethoven's Symphony No. 7 as 'unscholastic' under that 'worst of all conductors (?) Adrian Boult', and implied the same thing about Boult's performance of Haydn and Mozart – 'both played with over 60 strings!!' He was hard on Ravel's Piano Concerto in G on its first performance in England ('I cannot take [it] seriously') and was correct about the composer's con-ducting of it, which he dismissed as 'inefficient' (even Ravel's close friends thought him a bad conductor). He labelled Richard Strauss's interpretation of a Mozart symphony 'dull and annoying' and his *Symphonia domestica* as 'amusing, & annoying by turns; but with some lovely bits'. He described Henry Wood as an 'absolute vandal', decrying his 'usual exaggeration and lack of detail' whenever the opportunity arose. 'Henry J. Wood is ~~becoming~~ a public menace – & ought to be shot quickly, before he does much more murdering of classics ancient & modern.' He dismissed playboy Thomas Beecham as 'disgraceful' for his conducting of the first act of *Tristan und Isolde*, and listed his objec-tions to a Stravinsky broadcast under him: 'Listen to a faked perf. of Petroushka by Beecham – within an inch of a collapse all the time.' He returned to the theme five years later, describing Beecham as 'irrespon-sible' and a 'vandal'.

These carve-ups are all hugely entertaining: but there is a serious aspect to them – for even at this young age Britten found the way in which music was conceived and performed in England unsatisfactory. The skel-etal economic model Henry Wood had established for his Queen's Hall concerts in the 1890s – one rehearsal, working from carefully marked-up orchestral parts, followed by the performance – did more than any other twentieth-century initiative or intervention to entrench the reckless Eng-lish reputation for sight-reading. Undoubtedly the founding of the BBC Symphony Orchestra in 1930 and the London Philharmonic Orchestra two years later represented a watershed in English orchestral standards. ('Famous genius conducts London Philharmonic's masterly rehearsal at Queen's Hall', trumpeted a British Movietone News film as an introduc-tion to the latter and its conductor, Beecham.) Even so, both orchestras were up against player complacency, impatience and vanity.

Britten thought there was a feebleness to symphonic England – under-rehearsed orchestras, mixed bags of soloists, stylistic incongruities and bad conductors, for whom he saved most of his ammunition. Boult, Sargent, Beecham and Wood each created new ensembles and opportunities for audiences and players alike, each learned a great number of works on the fly, still often managing to perform from memory, and each passionately advocated a broad range of composers, foreign and home-grown, new and old. Yet none was profoundly musical in the way Britten would later demonstrate in performances of his own works and those of his gods, in which phrasing and harmony were carefully tended and where works sounded logical and unforced. The available time and talent frequently conspired against them in performance, and they often came across as tin men of the podium, vainly searching for their hearts in great orchestral scores. They represented the bumbling amateurism Britten identified in English music-making at the time and which his post-war career would turn on its head. The RCM was, to his mind, little more than a feeder-school to this scrappy industry.

The many variations of Britten's dismissive assessment of Boult were a partial consequence of his support for Bridge, whom he considered a far superior conductor and thought should have been appointed inaugural chief of the new BBC Symphony Orchestra in Boult's place. This was not unthinking partisanship: Bridge *was* a much better conductor. He lacked Wood's sheer endurance and Beecham's easy charm and music-hall patter, but he worked orchestras hard, polishing tiny details that were overlooked in Sargent's broad brushstrokes, discussing with his players string sound and articulation, gesture and harmony. 'When F.B. conducts the chief advantage is to be able to listen to the music without bothering about the interpretation,' Britten enthused in January 1935. 'The shows are always "just right".' Making the music speak for itself is not an easy trick; Bridge understood this better than most.

Britten learned much from watching Bridge conduct, connecting his teacher's physicality with the sound he produced. These thoughts and observations were carried over into the late-night suppers after each concert, where conversation flowed with the wine. Usually it was a studio performance at Maida Vale with the BBC Symphony Orchestra, but even his direction of the low-key Chapman Orchestra earned Britten's admiration. 'F.B. conducts the most marvellous musical thrill of my life yet,' he wrote in his diary in February 1932. 'The strings (all amateurs!) were the best I have *ever* heard . . . The Beethoven overtures were electric; but as for the 9th Symph. – !!'

It would take a trip to Vienna in 1934 to verify these instincts. At the decade's beginning Britten was working out how he would do things differently, with the disparate examples of Bridge and the four conductor-knights (current and future) before him. Writing about a performance of Strauss's *Don Quixote* at a 1932 BBC concert under Wood, he noted, 'This work is too diff. for performance under modern conditions. 20 rehearsals are needed'. It was an exaggeration, even when the piece was still relatively young, a long way from being under the players' fingers, but the reference to 'modern conditions' was nothing if not a shot across Wood's bow. His derisory comment about playing Mozart and Haydn with a body of sixty strings – the number an orchestra today wields for thumping great works by Bruckner and Strauss – was similarly laced, showing an awareness of what would become known as performance practice some decades before it was fashionable.

There is one final point to Britten's observations. In this decade, long before Britten morphed into a composer-conductor in the model of Strauss or Mahler, before he had even expressed an interest in that direction, his detailed criticisms of conductors isolated him from the cultural mainstream; British audiences did not think about an orchestral performance in terms of who was conducting it. Or perhaps more accurately, the maestro was not so much a factor where *British* conductors were concerned. Visitors such as Austro-Hungarian Arthur Nikisch could boast of a cult following in the early decades of the century. Or Wilhelm Furtwängler, visiting London in 1927 with the Berlin Philharmonic, showing up the natives. Wood's dominance at the Proms – night after night slogging through orchestral repertory good and bad – emphasized to the broad, populist audience the notion of the piece, not the interpretation. The concept of interpretation as we understand it today – each individual performance calibrated against hundreds of others recorded or written about or remembered – would not take hold until after the war, in an age of easy air travel, LP recordings, the BBC's Third Programme, and when Leonard Bernstein and Herbert von Karajan helped foster the post-war cult of the conductor. Before then, British audiences looked on most conductors as shepherds, guiding their charges through sometimes inhospitable terrain that did not belong to them, tenants not landlords. Unlike singers, star fiddle players and a handful of great pianists, the conductor's time in the sun was still to come.

5

The patterns of Britten's first year at college continued in the final two. Britten the musician was confident, accomplished, focused, extremely hard-working and producing works and exercises at a furious pace. Britten the individual was not much more formed than when he first arrived in London. He took refuge in his pre-London habits: much time with the Bridges and their friends; meals and amusements with his sisters, before beating a hasty retreat to Kirkley Cliff Road the minute term was over. He moved from Prince's Square to a boarding house on Cromwell Road, where Beth joined him while she studied at the grandly named Paris Academy of Dressmaking and Design in Bond Street. In his lodgings Britten had room for a single bed, a piano, a desk, a bedside table and a chair. In a photograph of him in bed (probably Beth's handiwork), the shade of the standard lamp tilted to bathe him in light, he looks impossibly boyish. And fairly miserable, too, but perhaps it was just tiredness.

Beth helped him broaden his London experiences and to nudge him occasionally away from his work and into the warm embrace of popular culture. American films were flooding into England, and Britten developed a taste for the Marx Brothers, Disney and Charlie Chaplin. He laughed his way through *A Night at the Opera*, particularly the scene at the theatre, which begins with a speech from Groucho ('Ladies and Gentlemen – I guess that takes in most of you') before the arrival of the conductor, who taps his stand with his baton in readiness, Harpo and Chico noisily following suit. 'It's none of my business,' Groucho loudly tells a bejewelled and mortified Margaret Dumont, 'but I think there's a brace of woodpeckers in the orchestra.' This was exactly Britten's humour.

The siblings went for long Sunday walks after church, meandering through parts of the city Britten would normally have no cause to visit, before making their own version of a Lowestoft Sunday lunch at Cromwell Road. They went to almost all of the West End theatres at one time or another, arriving early enough to book camp stools in the queue at sixpence each, after which they would find a chophouse close by, returning half an hour before the theatre doors opened to retrieve their place. Buskers entertained while they waited, unsuccessfully pressing them for a coin at the end of the routine, until they were at last granted entry to the theatre gallery. It was cheap enough: 1s. 3d. for a gallery seat. (A seat in the stalls, at 3s. 6d., was too luxurious.)

Britten's theatrical taste was mostly highbrow: the anti-war play *The Plough and the Stars* by socialist Irish playwright Sean O'Casey; *The Cherry Orchard* (directed by his later collaborator Tyrone Guthrie); Ernest Temple Thurston's *The Wandering Jew*; *Twelfth Night*. Cinema was more mixed: the romantic comedy *Sunshine Susie*; the farce *Thark*; Garbo's *Mata Hari* ('She is most attractive, I suppose, but what slop!'); the touching French drama *Poil de Carotte*; the comedy of morals *Strictly Dishonorable*; the German children's film that so captured his imagination, *Emil und die Detektive*, and another German film, *Kameradschaft* (Comradeship), set in the Ruhr between Germany and France, German workers rescuing French miners trapped underground following a tragic accident. Britten saw it twice and thought it a 'marvellous but terrible film'; only a few years later he would work on similar projects, Montagu Slater's 1936 play for the Left Theatre, *Stay down Miner*, among them.

Last thing at night, and often first thing in the morning, he would have his nose in a book. In 1932 he read *Barnaby Rudge* and *David Copperfield* (a second or third time), George Bernard Shaw's royal intrigue *The Apple Cart*, Dorothy Wynne Willson's *Early Closing* ('the best school book I've ever read'), H. A. Vachell's *The Hill*, with its two Harrow boys rather boldly competing for the love of a third ('v. good, if too full of Harrow & Sentimentality'), George Gissing's *New Grub Street*, and *Good-bye to All That*, Robert Graves's excoriating 1929 memoir of the First World War and the Edwardian period leading to it. His taste in literature swerved from the sentimental to the classic; the overt politics and graphic imagery of Graves's book – with its tales of military incompetence, of German POWs murdered by British troops for revenge, of wartime souveniring and descriptions of stinking, bloated German corpses, black blood dripping from the nose and beard – were new for him and no doubt helped cement his childhood pacifism.

Money was tight. Britten's open scholarship at the RCM was worth

£40 per year, supplemented by a small grant for tuition fees. His father gave him a modest allowance, and he pocketed the rewards of various composition prizes: the Farrar Prize in 1931 and 1933 (around £4, most of which, first time round, he spent on a tennis racket); the Sullivan Prize in 1932 (£10); the Cobbett Prize in 1932, an award given for a single-movement chamber work, which Britten received for his *Phantasy* for string quintet, the proceeds of which (thirteen guineas) he spent on a new suit and a study score of Manuel de Falla's *El Amor brujo*. Bridge had scooped the same prize several times earlier in the century with *Phantasies* of his own.

There was the occasional disappointment. The panel judging his submission to the inter-college Mendelssohn Scholarship in 1932 thought his technique undeveloped, so he lost out to Ivor Walsworth from the Royal Academy of Music, who went on to a minor career as a composer. Britten was granted a maintenance grant of £50 in consolation ('so as not to discourage me in composing!!!!!!'), which the Mendelssohn Foundation repeated for the 1933–4 academic year, during which he was a student for only one term. This was as much a fence-sitting assessment of his potential as it was recognition of his achievements. When the foundation attempted the same deal in September 1935, offering this time £100 for six months, Britten declined; he was either to be appointed Mendelssohn Scholar, with the appropriate kudos and remuneration, or he would take nothing at all.

In the late 1920s in England a doctor earned on average £723 a year, a postman £160. In Britten's field, rank-and-file players of the new BBC Symphony Orchestra received in 1930 a salary of £11 per week, in addition to provisions for holidays and sick leave. It cost Britten £3. 3s. per term to hire a piano, and rent at Cromwell Road was around £8 per quarter. Music was not cheap: piano scores set him back as much as 10s. 5d. (Rachmaninov's *Preludes*, Op. 32), while a full-score could cost 24s. (Stravinsky). A gramophone record was anywhere between 1s. 6d. and 2s. 6d, while the Marconi Model 291, 'The radio-gram par excellence', would have cost him around fifty guineas had he been in the market for one; the powerful Wolseley Hornet his father set out to buy in 1932 was slightly over three times this amount. Britten was careful with the little money he had, a habit he retained once wealthy.

Whether through pique, opportunity or necessity (or a combination of the three), he dipped his toe into the choppy waters of the English music industry long before he left the RCM. The Macnaghten–Lemare series was his first foray, and Anne Macnaghten's advocacy of this unknown composer deserves acknowledgement – a view Britten himself did not actually hold. ('Anne did her best with my "Go Play, Boy, Play" – but again, I want 1st class instrumentalists besides enthusiasm.') It was through his relationship with publisher Hubert Foss of Oxford University Press, however, that Britten first laid claims to the label 'professional composer'.

Foss was a bilingual ex-soldier, competent pianist, a composer of sorts, an enthusiastic writer on contemporary music, a lover of English church music and, later, the author of books on Vaughan Williams and Mussorgsky. Britten would have dismissed him as a typically English amateur had Foss been a lesser person. In 1925, when only twenty-six, Foss drew some of his talents together and founded OUP's music publishing division, signing up Vaughan Williams and Walton. By 1931 he had bagged a number of important British composers and works. Bridge did not bring Britten and Foss together; he was published by Stainer & Bell and later, following the spectacularly prescient merger in 1930 of two old family firms, by Boosey & Hawkes. In February 1932 Foss and Britten had lunch together at Amen House, OUP's London office, where the composer presented a handful of his works. Foss held on to the *Three Two-part Songs*, which Britten had finished that morning, partly at Ireland's behest.

Well crafted as it all was, Britten had not yet composed much of startling originality; his own true voice was unformed. 'I remember him telling me very clearly that he had such facility in imitating the other composers that he didn't know which way to turn,' his school friend David Layton later said. *Sinfonietta* was still some months away, *Phantasy*, Op. 2, further still. He had only days earlier completed his *Phantasy* for string quintet, which would in the coming months be distinguished by a RCM performance and prize, the Macnaghten–Lemare outing, and a BBC regional broadcast. Britten would have shown it to Foss, but it is not a great piece: it has a few motific ideas, which Britten explores somewhat obviously in the opening pages and spreads a little thinly in subsequent ones. Yet it has a central section of brooding melodiousness, which hints at the mature composer. Britten also had the String Quartet in D to hand – which two weeks after his lunch with Foss would receive its first performance in a private run-through – as well as choral works such as *A Wealden Trio* and *A Hymn to the Virgin*, his *Two Portraits* for string orchestra and *Christ's Nativity*.

It would be easy to accuse Foss of undue caution, selecting a single commercially viable work instead of publishing Britten's entire output, but he was trying to pick front-line winners for OUP's bold new adventure; nurturing young composers was then, as now, a luxury. Moreover, each of the works he rejected (*A Hymn to the Virgin* aside) is uneven in one way or another. Foss knew OUP's existing markets, knew the schools and amateur choirs that bought up the Oxford Choral Songs in quantity; Britten's *Three Two-part Songs* was a perfectly legitimate start to their dealings. After some minor revisions – simplifications in the piano part and the transposition of two songs – the short collection was accepted, appearing late in the year. In 1933 Robert Britten was able to write proudly to Bobby of his brother's first royalty cheque (15s.), representing the 1,000 copies of the songs sold in Britain and America in four months or so. With this modest success, Britten and Foss were now primed to develop their relationship during the composer's final year at college.

6

In the 1930s all young composers were working in the giant shadow of Igor Stravinsky. Thirty-one years older than Britten, Stravinsky had announced himself as an original and immensely powerful voice with his ballet *The Firebird*, premiered at the Paris Opéra in 1910. He had three quick follow-ups before war intervened: *Petrushka* (1911), *Le Sacre du printemps* (1913) and *Le Rossignol* (1914). It was sinewy, visceral music – whether in the primitiveness of *Le Sacre* (which caused a riot, possibly carefully staged, at its premiere in France, six months before Britten was born) or the ecstasy of the radiant *Firebird*. Britten probably knew no more of Stravinsky's music than this last work when Greatorex first welcomed him at Gresham's, boisterously linking their names, yet early in his second term at the RCM he fell under its spell.

First there was a radio broadcast of an all-Stravinsky programme in January 1931, given by the BBC Symphony Orchestra under Ernest Ansermet. 'Remarkable, puzzling. I quite enjoyed the pft. Concerto. Sacre, – bewildering & terrifying. I didn't really enjoy it, but I think it's incredibly marvellous & arresting.' It was bewildering and terrifying music to those raised on plainer English fare – Elgar and Bax symphonies, Vaughan Williams songs, Greatorex hymn tunes (including 'Woodlands') – as Britten was. Thereafter he took every opportunity to hear Stravinsky's music, slowly working at overcoming the sheer terror of it. He bought gramophone records of one of the few living composers to pioneer the new electric technology, listened to broadcasts from Maida Vale or Queen's Hall, and asked for miniature scores for Christmas and 78s for his birthday. By September 1932 Britten had conquered his fear. *Le Sacre* was 'the World's Wonder', which he listened to obsessively, hypnotized by its sheer daring, its brazen rule-breaking. And by 1936 he was grappling stiffly with Stravinsky in print – in his first published article, a subtly critical piece for *World Film News* on the occasion of a BBC broadcast of *Oedipus rex*, Stravinsky's opera-oratorio of 1927. '*Oedipus Rex* demonstrated Stravinsky's remarkable sense of style in drawing inspiration from every age of music and in leaving the whole a perfect shape, satisfying every aesthetic and emotional demand.' This was to become Britten's manifesto in the following years.

Vaughan Williams detected Stravinsky's influence on the *Two Psalms* he sent Ivor Atkins. 'Of course it wd never have been written except for the "Symphonie des Psaumes" but it is no worse for that.' Britten first heard the piece with Frank Bridge in January 1932 when it was near new, Bridge insisting that Stravinsky's neo-classical excursion was a masterpiece where others were more doubtful. Britten's later relationship with Stravinsky was not always particularly dignified on either side – jealousy and mistrust informed both their outlooks – but at this stage of his development Stravinsky was a figure of phenomenal importance. Britten and his contemporaries were left reeling from his power, in thrall to the hobgoblin wizard spreading magic and mischief in equal measure. It was not so much that British composers started writing ballets, though some did, Britten included.* Nor was it that local composers aped the master's neo-classicism. Instead, it was much as Debussy wrote two weeks after Britten was born, acknowledging Stravinsky's gift of the score of *Le Sacre du printemps*: 'It is a special satisfaction to tell you

---

* Two months after seeing *Petrushka* performed by a breakaway troupe from the defunct Ballets Russes, Britten commenced *Plymouth Town*, a quayside morality tale to a scenario by folk-dance authority Violet Alford.

how much you have enlarged the boundaries of the permissible in the empire of sound.'

Stravinsky forced Britten to sweep out the stables, to think in new forms and subjects, to consider more extreme instrumental colours. Britten never lost himself in the mists of Stravinsky's music, nor in its earthy primitivism, but Stravinsky allowed him to rebel musically in a way he was not yet ready to do with his sexuality – arguably retarding his personal development since he could tell himself that musical sophistication equalled emotional growth. Bridge occasionally rejected aspects of his pupil's work as inauthentic, too much composed under the influence. 'At about 18 or 19, perhaps naturally, I began to rebel. When Bridge played questionable chords across the room at me and asked if that was what I meant, I would retort, "Yes it is." He'd grunt back, "Well it oughtn't to be."'

Perhaps hints of the wariness that would characterize Britten and Stravinsky's later relationship were by then already in place, for at the end of 1933, with a travelling scholarship under his belt (£100, enough to sustain a young student on the Continent for six months, Britten calculated), it was not the composer of 'the World's Wonder' Britten aspired to for lessons. He asked instead to study with Alban Berg.

Berg had had nowhere near the same impact on Britten as Stravinsky in the early 1930s, regardless of how he later showed his hand. Britten knew little of his music, notwithstanding his careful enthusiasm for Berg's teacher and mentor Schoenberg. Early in 1933 he heard Berg's 'astounding' *Lyric Suite* and *Three Pieces* from *Wozzeck* ('thoroughly sincere & moving music'), which he possibly already knew from score; and he surely stayed to hear Helen Perkin play Berg's finely crafted Piano Sonata in the same concert in which his own *Phantasy*, Op. 2, was given its first public performance. Yet this concert was as late as 21 November 1933, by which time he would have submitted his study proposal to college authorities. Bridge is likely to have hatched the Berg plan: he had for some years been skating around the edges of atonality, much like Berg in his early pieces, and now more than ever thought Britten should 'leave England and experience a different musical climate'. It was an inspired idea. Berg began lessons with Arnold Schoenberg in 1904 with plenty of raw talent but no real technique. Schoenberg – a sort of revolutionary Charles Villiers Stanford figure to a generation of German and Austrian composers – grounded him in harmony, counterpoint and theory, before moving on to composition. Once Berg emerged from his own rigorous apprenticeship he straddled the Romantic and modernist eras with brilliance and imagination; language differences aside, there would have been much for Berg and Britten to talk about.

The RCM – probably even Sir Hugh Allen himself – decided otherwise. 'I *am* going to study with Berg, aren't I?' he asked his mother in the holidays. 'No dear,' she replied. 'He's not a good influence.' 'The insinuation seemed to be that he was unsuitable on more than just musical grounds,' Britten later said. The nineteen-year-old was still dependent on the support of his elders, who equated Berg's supposedly lawless, degenerate music with equivalent morality and behaviour. Bobby Britten said much later that his parents were aware of and concerned about their youngest son's latent homosexuality, and were determined to keep him out of harm's way. Thus the RCM, aided by Britten's mother, committed its final, ignoble, ironic act: the resoundingly heterosexual Berg, who fathered his first child by a kitchen maid at seventeen, did not become Britten's teacher. It was not to happen on the college's coin. He died two years later.

It was unlikely anyway: Berg was busy composing his opera *Lulu*, and with the ascent of the Nazis in January 1933 performances of his music quickly dried up. Students did not plug the gap in this unsettled epilogue to his life. Britten came to think lessons with him would not have changed anything of substance – except in one area: 'It might have taught me how to unlock gates I did in fact have to climb over.'

Britten's apprenticeship by rights ended in 1932, the year he composed his *Sinfonietta*, Op. 1. A composer's first opus number is a public statement about the conclusion of his training. He has emerged from the shadow of his teacher or mentor (though this is rarely clear-cut) and is now producing worthy and substantial works. Thus Beethoven, a recent student of Haydn's, with his first piano trios, composed in his mid-twenties, published on subscription in Vienna, a signal that this rough German émigré was setting up his stall at the centre of Viennese high society. Thus Brahms with his hulking Piano Sonata, Op. 1, with its strong flavours of Beethoven's 'Hammerklavier' and a middle movement that trills with German folk song. And thus Rachmaninov in his fully formed Piano Concerto No. 1, as with Berg and Prokofiev in their first piano sonatas. Britten now had a calling card he could slap down on the table when asked by his elders what he did for a living or confronted by those sceptical ghosts from his youth. It owes much of its scale and sonority to Schoenberg's first *Kammersymphonie*, yet the influence does not detract from what is an assured and personal work.

But of course his apprenticeship lingered beyond *Sinfonietta*, which Britten himself recognized. When in 1936 he finished his orchestral cycle *Our Hunting Fathers*, Op. 8, he wrote, 'it's my op. 1 alright.' (He said the same of his later *Les Illuminations*, Op. 18.) Partly this spoke to the orchestral cycle's political agenda, partly to Britten's more settled and mature character. Yet it is also true that *Our Hunting Fathers* represented a considerable musical advance on the pieces of the early 1930s. And this is where Berg might have helped. Together they could have worked on large-scale form, something of which Britten was still shy – much of the early music is episodic. And perhaps Berg would have fired Britten's operatic imagination, though once the tuition was over he would be returning to a country with a malnourished operatic culture, and without any opportunities for him to ply his trade. But the most important lesson Berg would have taught him was how to be a modernist composer in an essentially lyrical and tonal language. Britten was already learning this without Berg's direct instruction, but supervision from the Viennese master would have quickened the process.

7

Britten passed his exam for Associate of the Royal College of Music (ARCM) on 13 December 1933. He was later impossibly self-deprecating about his playing, recalling in 1957, 'I did stagger through the ARCM for solo piano . . . I had very gentle examiners.' This was the time in his life in which he did the most work on his playing. Anyone who has had to rely on a technique refined in student days, but tended only occasionally thereafter, remains grateful for the initial investment. So it was with Britten. When critic John Amis asked him in 1964 whether he ever practised the piano, he replied, 'No; not really. There are certain bits which I jolly well *have* to look at if I've got to play. But I wish I *did*, and it's not a recommendation. I think it's very, very dangerous to play as little as I do, and I find it catches me out seriously if I'm nervous.'

It is evident from countless commercial and off-air recordings that

Britten accumulated a good deal of performing capital as a student. It is also evident that as an adult he chose to play a particular type of music; the Romantic repertory to which he cleaved in his youth did not last much beyond his Piano Concerto of 1938. This vein of repertory was partly a matter of taste: after the war he was busy foraging through piles of nineteenth-century lieder, and songs from earlier periods, which mostly eschewed virtuosic display for musical substance. Partly it came about because Britten's post-war collaborations were more an expression of his desire to work with particular artists than to play particular pieces.

The performing capital manifested itself in a number of ways. Peter Pears put it well when he said that Britten 'had an extraordinary perception between his brain and his heart and the tips of his fingers. You could watch Ben holding his hands over the piano preparatory to playing a slow movement, a soft, soft chord – and you could see his fingers alert, alive, really sometimes even quivering with intensity . . . it was amazing what colours he could get.' It is all there in archival footage of Britten and Sviatoslav Richter playing Mozart piano duets: Richter, the stern, Slavic, old-school virtuoso is cajoled by a smiling Britten who displays few signs of rehearsal or nerves and every indication of a musician performing on pure instinct and old sinew. He almost *accompanies* Richter, who responds with great freedom and daring. They are intoxicating performances.

Around the time Britten met Richter he distilled his thoughts on the responsibilities of performing.

> This magic comes only with the sounding of the music, with the turning of the written note into sound – and it only comes (or comes most intensely) when the listener is one with the composer, either as a performer himself, or as a listener in active sympathy. Simply to read a score in one's armchair is not enough for evoking this quality. Indeed, this magic can be said to consist of just the music which is *not* in the score. Sometimes one can be quite daunted when one opens the *Winterreise* – there seems to be nothing on the page. One must not exaggerate – the shape of the music in Schubert is clearly visible. What *cannot* be indicated on the printed page are the innumerable small variants of rhythm and phrasing which make up the performer's contribution. In the *Winterreise*,

it was not possible for Schubert to indicate exactly the length of rests and pauses, or the colour of the singer's voice or the clarity or smoothness of consonants. This is the responsibility of each individual performer, and at each performance he will make modifications. The composer expects him to; he would be foolish if he did not. For a musical experience needs three human beings at least. It requires a composer, a performer, and a listener; and unless these three take part together there is no musical experience.

This was the most articulate passage he ever wrote on the subject.

For all his accomplishment, Britten could not have graduated at a worse time. The Depression left unemployment high, and the music industry had its own unique problems: talkies arrived late the previous decade and cinema orchestras collapsed in their wake, with considerable knock-on effects. Broadcasting provoked in many observers and musicians dire predictions about the future of music in England. The showman Beecham prophesied in 1934 that in twenty years time 'there will not be a single musical institution left in this country, except possibly organizations providing music inside a cellar in London. You will depend for every kind of music on the radio and musical reproduction by mechanical devices.' Britten was inured to Beecham's speakeasy imagery, the industry flux ultimately working to his advantage. He was talented and adaptable enough in the 1930s and 1940s to put his imprint on the near-blank slate.

In July 1933 he packed up the cramped room on Cromwell Road, dispatched the piano to J. B. Cramer & Co., and returned to Lowestoft. He had business cards printed in a dizzy, cursive font, listing his new professional address:

Mr Benjamin Britten.
21 Kirkley Cliff Road,
Lowestoft.

Anyone else might have found it dispiriting to be returning home after three years in London, but Britten was delighted. 'You were glad to see the end of your student days?' he was asked in 1959. 'I only started enjoying myself as a human being after I left college and got down to real work,' he replied.

8

Britten's father was dying. Everyone hoped otherwise, jumping on the slightest sign of progress, no matter how unconvincing, but his luck had left him. There had been the odd portent: he missed Bobby's wedding in 1931 and in May the following year was too sick to leave his bed for a time. Robert Victor's decline threads its way through Britten's 1933–4 diaries: the morphine and chest pains; the talks about Britten's future and finances; the full-time nurse and daily visits from the doctor towards the end. 'Let us see whether 1934 can give us back what seems to us the impossible – Pop's health,' Britten wrote at the end of 1933, though he was under no illusion. He distracted himself with work: the broadcast of *A Boy was Born* was slated for February, and he was planning a trip to the International Society for Contemporary Music (ISCM) in Florence a month later for a performance of his *Phantasy*, Op. 2. Yet he was helpless about his father.

A Boy was Born is a terrific piece. Composed for unaccompanied eight-part choir plus boys' choir descant, it took Britten almost six months to compose, beginning in late November 1932. Rummaging through *Ancient English Christmas Carols* and the *Oxford Book of Carols*, he found a handful of settings of poems by different writers that cumulatively narrate the story of Christ's birth – from the simple church-door announcement of his arrival, through Herod's machinations and the flight from Jerusalem they inspired, to the visitation of the Kings and a hearty fifteenth-century welcome ode: 'For every man, both old and ying, / Is glad of your coming'.

Britten had attempted this anthology technique, with similar iconography, in *Christ's Nativity*. But this time he got everything right. He uses variation form here not so much as a sign of virtuosity but as glue: the different poems are pruned (and in one notable instance, Variation V, juxtaposed one on top of the other), and a way sought to make the picture cohesive. He begins with an ancient-sounding chorale (shades of the Madrigal Society) built on a four-note motif, the source of the subsequent variations. But what happens thereafter is so inventive, so touching and difficult, it is hard to believe it was composed only eighteen months or so after *Christ's Nativity*. The virtuosic finale, which canters along perilously close to the cliff edge for some minutes, includes an audacious hold-up: the opening theme is fleshed out into a longer, beautiful melody, a simple chorale sung by the boys' choir. The women provide a sparse accompaniment for the boys that sounds like a four-finger organ part played on a wheezy harmonium in some damp old church. The rest of the choir picks up this chorale to finish the work. It is like the monstrances of Catholic churches that house the Eucharistic host: the host itself is just plain wafer – egg whites, flour and water, nothing more – while the casing is ornate, bejewelled, wonderful.

Britten would use this technique of gradual revelation again and again, of putting horse behind cart, no doubt chuckling at his cleverness as he did so. It is such a simple idea, but highly effective in practice. His *Lachrymae* of 1950 for viola and piano (later string orchestra), subtitled 'Reflections on a Song of John Dowland', concludes with a statement of the lute song 'If my complaints could passions move', snippets of which can be picked up in the previous pages by the acute listener like distant sounds travelling over water. He does something similar in *Variations on a Theme of Frank Bridge* of 1937: though the theme is played in the work's opening section, it is done so rather whimsically, and it is only at the end of the piece that it is spelled out with weight and clarity. When it arrives it makes sense of everything that has gone before it, demanding that we start again from the beginning, hearing the work once more, this time with our ears alert. He uses the same device in the original slow movement of the Piano Concerto (1938) and in his other Dowland tribute, *Nocturnal after John Dowland* (1963) for guitar, in which the theme finally emerges from the belly of a melancholic passacaglia. The same idea governs his Third Suite for Cello (1971), a work spun from four Russian tunes that are played in their entirety only at the end of the piece.

It was the informal run-through of *A Boy was Born* to which Robert Victor referred in his warm letter to his son of July 1933: 'Ben my boy what does it feel like to hear your own creation?' As it happens, many thousands had the opportunity: *A Boy was Born* was broadcast as part of a BBC Concert of Contemporary Music on 23 February 1934, the day Elgar died. (Britten's father, the dedicatee, was probably too ill to listen.) Britten's first experience with broadcasting was in February the previous year, when the International String Quartet performed his *Phantasy* in F minor as part of the same BBC series. Then, on 6 August, three members of the quartet joined with distinguished oboist Leon Goossens in a relay of Britten's *Phantasy*, Op. 2, while the next day his

Sinfonietta went out on Radio Strasbourg – all this for someone who began listening to the radio regularly only a few years earlier.

It is easy to mock the BBC's director-general John Reith as something between a dictator and a zealot. Many have done so, for there was a near religious mania to his mission, a determination to improve the minds and lives of his listeners, much as Victorian biographers sought to do with their readers. Yet his aspiration for his country and culture was heartfelt and visionary. Those who could afford to buy or hire a receiver and the 10s. for a licence fee suddenly found themselves exposed to a world of political talks and ideas, radio plays, philosophical lectures, the latest art music and the hippest big-bands. The BBC cut across class and revolutionized both the provision and consumption of culture. Between 1927 and 1935 licence fees generated just under £18 million; the BBC took more than half of this for its programming, staff and orchestras. Reith was famously determined that the BBC would provide its audiences with something rather better than they thought they wanted. 'He who prides himself on giving what he thinks the public wants is often creating a fictitious demand for lower standards which he himself will then satisfy,' he thundered. In just a few years the BBC transformed British culture.

From his earliest dealing with the BBC, Britten grasped its power and potential regarding his own music. He told OUP's Foss of the BBC's interest in his music in almost the same breath that he told the BBC about his new publisher, gently playing one against the other. (He used them both in his ongoing struggles with the Mendelssohn Foundation.) The BBC was not an unwilling participant in such games; in Britten it had the perfect encapsulation of Reith's high aspirations for British culture.

Bureaucracies are cumbersome, and already the BBC was becoming one: by the mid-1930s there were assessment committees and sub-committees, panels, minutes and recommendations. Good people fell through the cracks, and naturally there was potential for those in charge of policy to perpetuate the amateurishness Britten decried in contemporary British music. Yet from Britten's student days onwards the BBC kept a paternal eye on the young composer. There were projects discussed, works assessed and performed, commissions undertaken. After *A Boy was Born* these mostly occurred without the troubling bureaucratic layers to which most other young composers were subject. Partly this was due to the powerful BBC programme-maker Edward Clark, an adventurous and knowledgeable musical buccaneer (later husband of composer Elisabeth Lutyens) with a taste for the Continental music he plundered for his various projects. But more orthodox characters also identified Britten's potential. The minor composer, academic and BBC apparatchik Victor Hely-Hutchinson assessed *A Boy was Born* from Britten's play-through and reported to Boult, 'I do whole-heartedly subscribe to the general opinion that Mr Britten is the most interesting new arrival since Walton, and I feel that we should watch his work very carefully.' Meanwhile, the worst predictions about the effect of broadcasting on music were discounted one by one. The Performing Right Society (PRS), founded in 1914 to measure musical performances in the new electronic age and recompense composers for their work with a performance royalty, in 1935 received thirty-nine per cent of its total annual revenue from the BBC; five years later it was fifty-four per cent.

In addition to new audiences for his music ('I have had a large number of letters,' Britten wrote after the performance of *A Boy was Born*), broadcasting brought him a whole new slew of critics. The *Daily Telegraph, Morning Post, News Chronicle* and *Musical Opinion* all reviewed his choral variations and there was a preview in the *Radio Times*. The critic in the *Telegraph* astutely noted: 'Here modern harmony comes to a fine point, and hints at possibilities that are, as yet, unexplored.' Yet even this sort of prescient analysis was unlikely to placate the touchy composer, who was already adopting the aggressive position he would maintain against critics all his life.

Britten later pinpointed the origins of this attitude to the first performance of his *Three Two-part Songs*.

> The only written criticism of this performance damned them entirely – as being obvious copies of Walton's three Façade Songs. Now anyone who is interested can see for himself that this is silly nonsense. The Walton Songs are brilliant and sophisticated in the extreme – mine could scarcely have been more childlike and naive, with not a trace of parody throughout. It is easy to imagine the damping effect of this first notice on a young composer. I was furious and dismayed because I could see there was not a word of truth in it. I was also considerably discouraged. No friendliness – no word of encouragement – no perception. Was this the critical treatment which one was to expect all one's life? A gloomy outlook.

His solution was simple. 'I decided to avoid reading critics from that day onwards,' he lied.

His critics dealt with, Britten was able to appreciate what broadcasting's connection to a wide audience gave him: currency. Broadcasting as a public service was much discussed in the 1930s – by Reith, politicians, and other media, which were caught out by the BBC's appearance and quick ascendency. The debate was similar in essence to, and helped shape, Britten's post-war ideas on the function of music in society, his determination never to be an 'ivory tower' composer writing for his own edification rather than that of his audiences. 'The B.B.C. has in fact aimed at providing a service somewhat ahead of what the public would demand were it possible for such demand to be made articulate and intelligible,' the broadcaster stated in 1935 in its submission to the Ullswater Committee, charged with renewal of its charter, ten years after Reith had said much the same. Certainly there were numerous institutions after the war exploring this Matthew Arnoldian notion that the state should be responsible for the protection and promotion of culture, the Arts Council chief among them. The BBC was there first, however, and the corporation had a lasting impact on the way Britten approached his music; he too would view his post-war career in terms of public service.

This correlation between the BBC's public service ethic and his own was not one Britten himself drew; in fact, he was later rather rude about broadcasting. In 1964 he was awarded the first Aspen Award ('To Benjamin Britten, who, as a brilliant composer, performer, and interpreter through music of human feelings, moods, and thoughts, has truly inspired man to understand, clarify and appreciate more fully his own nature, purpose and destiny'). In his speech he decried electronic reproduction. 'If I say the loudspeaker is the principal enemy of music, I don't mean that I am not grateful to it as a means of education or study, or as an evoker of memories. But it is not part of true musical *experience*. Regarded as such it is simply a substitute, and dangerous because deluding.' Yet in the 1930s he viewed the BBC wholly as an ally, its function unambiguously good.

9

Paris was his first foreign city. With his new passport in his pocket (Height: 5′ 11″; Eyes: blue; Hair: brown) and his friend John Pounder at his side, Britten set off from Victoria station on 28 March 1934, bound for the ISCM festival in Florence. He crossed the Channel at Newhaven, keeping his sea legs when those around him did not, and en route to Gare de Lyon did a lightning tour through the centre of town: the Place de la Concorde, the Eiffel Tower and Notre Dame quickly ticked off his list, seen much the way Impressionists depicted them, colours dabbed and edges blurred, nothing more precise. He pleased himself with his Gresham's French, ordering dinner from a waitress (who took his order almost in her stride), and then boarded a train to Turin, Pisa and finally Florence. In Florence he had a few days before the performance on 5 April, which he filled with concerts and meanderings through the city. He caught the Good Friday procession in Grassina and a day later was at the Duomo to see *Lo scoppio del Carno*, the medieval Easter pageant in which a mechanical dove improbably ignites a cart filled with small explosives, as though in a Disney cartoon, to the delight of the large and occasionally devout crowd in the piazza. He wandered through the Uffizi, rooting himself in front of any painting by Botticelli. He visited the Ponte Vecchio at night, admiring the swatch of moonlight on the murky Arno. One of the concerts he dismissed as a showcase for 'Italian Parrys & Stanfords', a terrifying prospect. But there was plenty else to hear, not least an early performance of Ravel's Piano Concerto for the Left Hand, a showpiece for the one-armed pianist Paul Wittgenstein, who would later commission just such a work from Britten. A friend of Pounder's, Allan Pearce, joined them in Florence and later remembered Britten as a retiring young man, happiest when lodged at a piano rather than engaging in conversation, in contrast to the extrovert Pounder. This was Britten's character just now: confortable with his intimates, confident with his musical peers, but socially shy, watching from the sidelines or hiding behind a piano.

The ISCM was, and remains, an august body, born in 1922 of the prevalent idealism and distrust of nationalism in Europe following the First World War. Works were selected for performance at the annual festival regardless of 'aesthetic trends', according to the aims of the founders; unsurprisingly, Czech, Austrian and German members fought for a more avant-garde agenda than that pursued by Britain – until Hitler put paid to such degenerate notions.

The 1934 festival enjoyed the patronage of Benito Mussolini, and among some of the delegates there was talk of the worsening political situation in Italy and Germany. The German branch had been put on notice the previous year, and the uncertainty of its fate filtered through the conference. In his opening address, musicologist and ISCM president Edward J. Dent spoke of the 'dangers of nationalism and the necessity of free thought and speech for the artist', fully aware that no Italian would dare say the same in public in these unsettled times. Once more Britten seemed to have been untouched by political events around him.

A few of the composers sharing Britten's concert were not heard of again. Others were schooled in the serialism of Schoenberg and Webern, not least Leopold Spinner, a pupil of Webern's, who ended up as a quietly spoken editor at Boosey & Hawkes, where his name was once more linked with Britten's. The programme's outer works have had more of a life – Britten's *Phantasy*, Op. 2, for oboe and string trio, and Lars Erik Larsson's *Sinfonietta*, lyrical contrasts to the works they sandwiched.

Like its namesake, the *Phantasy* for string quintet, the *Phantasy* quartet is not a strong piece. For all his life – from the quiet ecstasy of the *Quatre chansons françaises* (1928) to the slow, dignified suicide at the end of *Phaedra* (1975) – Britten was a melodic Rumpelstiltskin, spinning gold from straw. But in *Phantasy*, Op. 2, the melodic material is not as imaginative as the loose palindromic structure encasing it, while the first third might just as well have been written for string quartet for all the notice it takes of the oboe's idiom.* Yet there is a central section of still beauty, one of Britten's early nocturnal wanderings, where the oboe retreats into a white sound before darting around the compass with dexterity and long lines. Perhaps this section helped Britten feel comfortable with the instrument and its potential (and who knows what the master musician Goossens told him in rehearsals), for

---

* *The Times* thought otherwise: 'Its colloquies between the oboe and the strings stamp it as music which belongs inherently to the instruments for which it is scored.'

when he returned to the oboe four years later in his *Temporal Variations*, he was able to concoct a far more idiomatic and impressive piece.

The work was well received, but this was in some ways incidental to the purpose of the visit, which was to hear the latest in Continental contemporary music and to meet other composers and important industry figures, among them the paternal Dent and the BBC's Edward Clark. He also met the somewhat wild and free-spirited conductor Hermann Scherchen, a Schoenberg intimate, who was already well on his way towards his final tally of five wives. Scherchen's son Wulff, thirteen at the time, was with his father and would a few years later become an important part of Britten's life. Scherchen *père* arranged an excursion for his orchestra to Siena, and Britten tagged along. It rained all day, which made their visit to the cathedral crowded and their lunch with the mayor welcome. Scherchen *fils* shared Britten's raincoat, each of them wearing one sleeve, and they made their way through the streets of Siena like a lumbering mythological creature.

Wulff later snapped a photograph of Britten holding the score of *A Boy was Born*, intended for the older Scherchen. Sixty years later Wulff described its subject. 'Look at his face in that photo – it's the face of a young boy, just come out of the egg, not of a grown-up young man. I didn't feel he was seven years older than me. I thought we were much closer in age than that. We were boys together.' Britten does look young in the photo, a public schoolboy on exeat, an impression compounded by his fusty double-breasted suit, a cut favoured by his father. There are numerous photographs of Britten from this time in which he appears impossibly boyish; in others he already looks old beyond his years, his eyes guarded and sad.

On the day he was splashing his way through Siena, enjoying the companionship of the young Scherchen, Robert Victor Britten died of a cerebral haemorrhage, the unexpected coda to his long battle with lymphoma. Britten knew nothing of this until the following day, when after a morning walk with Wulff he received a telegram: 'Come today, Pop not so well.' Robert was already dead, as Britten discovered on his arrival in Lowestoft two days later, following an upsetting, uncertain journey. The funeral was held on the afternoon of 11 April, overseen by Basil Reeve's father and Britten's uncle, Sheldon Painter. Benjamin and Bobby chose the music: 'Jesu, as Thou art our Saviour' – the touching, homophonic third variation of *A Boy was Born*, its dedicatee lying in the casket – and the glorious final chorus of Bach's *St Matthew Passion*: 'We sit down in tears / And call to you in the grave: / Rest softly, softly rest!'

In a drawer, next to the morphine pills Robert had squirrelled away during the previous months, insurance against his ever becoming a burden, was a letter addressed to the four Bs. 'Goodbye my four, my love to you all. So glad to have known you and had your love. Comfort Mum.' They did their best. Soon after the funeral Britten took her to stay for a few weeks at the prep school in North Wales run by Bobby. They helped her deal with Robert's will and then, the following year, looked with her for a smaller house in Frinton, the seaside town in Essex recommended by a fellow Christian Scientist. They sold off the heavy furniture, as they did Pop's business, and bought lighter pieces for the new cottage. Robert Britten bequeathed an estate worth £15,000* to his wife, £100 to each of his children, and £50 to his first grandchild, Bobby's son John. 'A great man – with one of the finest brains I have ever come across,' Britten wrote stiltedly, self-consciously, in his diary, a little over a year before he would meet a poet with stronger claims on this description, '& what a father!'

I O

The impact of Hitler's émigrés on post-war British culture and intellectual life was disproportionate to their number. Publisher and philanthropist George Weidenfeld, academic and statistician Claus Moser, philosopher Karl Popper, writers Arthur Koestler and Elias Canetti, graphic designer Berthold Wolpe, three members of the Amadeus Quartet, art critic Ernst Gombrich and music critic Hans Keller were all children of prescient Jews who watched Hitler's rise with alarm and who immediately made Britain, London in particular, their home. Yet the impact of Nazism on Britain was also felt before the war, when slightly older men in portable professions slipped into important roles in British universities and industry, bringing with them a new sensibility, outlook and book of contacts. Opera at Glyndebourne would have been inconceivable without Fritz Busch, Carl Ebert and Rudolf Bing – a

* Around £900,000 today.

triumvirate of cultured men of the theatre, steeped in German operatic traditions and contemptuous of Nazi thuggery. But in the main, it was London that benefited and the capital became a carnival-mirror image of Berlin and Vienna in the 1930s.

Never was this more obvious than in the operations of the music publisher Boosey & Hawkes. Following the annexation of Austria in 1938, the firm became home to a distinguished roster of composers and publishing figures: Kodály and Bartók came over from the nazified Universal Edition, as did publisher Ernst Roth, a smart lawyer and musician of Czech birth, who in his early thirties was made head of publications at U.E. and who at Boosey & Hawkes from 1938 was instrumental in signing up the old man Strauss and the middle-aged radical Stravinsky. Another U.E. refugee, Schoenberg pupil and friend of Mahler's, Erwin Stein, joined the company's editorial team and would soon assume a vital place in Britten's life. Bohuslav Martinů was another pre-war signing, while the post-war acquisition of Serge Koussevitzky's Editions Russe de Musique brought in significant (and lucrative) works by Rachmaninov and Prokofiev, as well as the big Stravinsky ballets. A major British music publisher was now engaging with European culture, Continental modernism in particular.

Although the recently merged company was ostensibly a meeting of equals – instrument makers and publisher of band music Hawkes & Son and publisher and concert promoter Boosey & Co. – it was Ralph Hawkes who oversaw the more daring acquisitions and signings. Though untrained as a musician, Hawkes possessed a good nose for business. He was debonair and charismatic – a Clark Gable figure, replete with thin moustache and love of yachting, to Leslie Boosey's retired colonel. None of this vision and expansion, none of these lucrative foreign signings, seemed likely when the two firms united in 1930. Boosey and Hawkes met on the board of the PRS in the 1920s and, having sized each other up, their competitive hackles raised, opted instead for a merger. 'He was the engine, I was the brakes,' as Boosey put it. The rest came about, almost literally, with chutzpah.

It was Hawkes's commitment to the PRS that eventually enticed Britten into his stable. Foss was philosophically opposed to it and the specific royalty it collected. He considered it against a publisher's interests, arguing that a performer should not have to pay a composer a royalty in addition to a fee for the sale or hire of his music. It was at the time easy enough to come down on this side of the argument: faced with a choice, conductors and concert societies selected modern works outside the PRS's jurisdiction. 'The general opinion seems to be that a charge of £3–3–0, in excess of cost of purchase of score & parts, for performing right is an avoidable burden which the exigencies of concert giving today do not warrant our undertaking,' conductor Wilfred Ridgway told Foss regarding Britten's *Simple Symphony*. It was a blow to protectionism – like employers turning to scab labour to thwart striking union workers. Such thinking governed Foss's advice to Britten to lend, without fee, the score and parts of his *Sinfonietta* to Scherchen for the performance in Strasbourg in 1933.

'I incline to accepting this in order to keep Britten. I believe it will get much performed,' Foss wrote in a memo concerning *Simple Symphony*. But he was simultaneously glum about the prospects for the *Phantasy* quartet, and Britten was left frustrated by this hot-cold relationship. More damaging was Foss's cynicism, exemplified by a memo he sent Humphrey Milford in June 1933 about Britten, in which he stated that 'it may be worth while to let Boosey waste some money on him so long as we can keep his more remunerative efforts'.

Where Foss saw only the pitfalls in Britten's uneven oeuvre, Hawkes saw the potential, buoyed by the young man's self-belief. Though he probably shared his rival's thoughts about their commercial viability, Hawkes took over the *Two Part-Songs* (texts by George Wither and Robert Graves, composed in 1932 and revised the following year), *Sinfonietta* and the *Phantasy*, Op. 2. This was the sort of trust Britten expected between composer and publisher, and so in September 1934 he was elected a member of the PRS and in early January 1936 would sign an exclusive agreement with Boosey & Hawkes, with a weekly allowance of £3, an advance against future royalties, and casual work vetting scores (Shostakovich's *Lady Macbeth of the Mtsensk District* included).

Foss did teach Britten one important lesson. When he accepted his *Three Two-part Songs* for publication, he broached a subject Britten had never before considered. 'I am afraid that you have chosen rather unfortunate poems for de la Mare always charges a high figure for permission to reprint, usually 2 to 3 guineas each in advance of a 5% royalty. I fear this will mean that we should have to offer you a very small royalty as clearly we have to publish the works at a low price, if we do them at all.' Britain's 1911 Copyright Act extended the protection of a literary work to fifty years after the author's death; of Britten's seventy-odd songs and scraps with identifiable authors composed before 1932, almost two-thirds of texts were still in copyright. From 1934 onwards, however, for a period of twenty years, Britten published only four settings of copyright texts, in addition to those by friends. A number of other completed settings were not published in his lifetime because of the fees involved; still others were declined permission by the author's estate or publisher. In the last twenty or so years of his life he made more settings of contemporary poetry, but by then he had the money, reputation and publisher's goodwill to do much as he pleased. Before the mid-1950s, he watched his pennies and channelled the inspiration he felt reading much older poets.

Britten was proud of his *Simple Symphony*, partly because it was well put together, partly because it allowed him to underline what an unusual boy he had been, writing manuscripts by the barrow-load which subsequently clogged up a cupboard in the family home. He wrote it in the six weeks following Christmas 1933, his father slowly dying in his bed. In such circumstances there was understandably an element of Britten revisiting a happy childhood; but there was also a gifted melodist foraging through early manuscripts, determined not to squander precious material. Britten put it well in his sleeve-note for the 1955 Decca recording: 'When Benjamin Britten, a proud young composer of twenty (who'd already had a work broadcast), came along and looked in this cupboard, he found some of them not too uninteresting; and so, rescoring them for strings, changing bits here and there, and making them more fit for general consumption, he turned them into a SIMPLE SYMPHONY.'

II

Some of these tangles with publishers were still occurring when in October 1934 Britten set off for Europe. His plan to work with Berg scotched, Britten opted to spend his travelling scholarship experiencing the music and culture of important European cities, his mother at his side. They visited Basle, Salzburg, Vienna, Munich and Paris, returning to London six weeks later. Edith was disorientated by Robert's death, as was her son: the year that began so promisingly with the broadcast of *A Boy was Born* was largely unproductive. It was Britten's first stretch as a professional composer and despite the performances and foreign trips, the business cards and contracts, he was a little unsure what to do next. He tinkered a little – revising 'The Birds' once more – and composed two liturgical pieces, *Jubilate Deo* and *Te Deum* in C, for the Choir of St Mark's, North Audley Street, which had supplied the boys for the broadcast of *A Boy was Born*. But these were minor works, unperformed by the choir. (*Jubilate* had to wait fifty years for publication, an unworthy fate for such an unambiguously joyous work, with its false ending and skittish organ writing.)

Holiday Diary, the suite he completed before his travels (and dedicated to Arthur Benjamin) is more substantial. When Clifford Curzon was performing it ten years later, Britten told him he intended it to be a series of impressions of a boy's pre-war seaside holiday – nostalgia for a time he never knew. There is no commercial disc of Curzon performing the suite, but he did record Britten's curious *Introduction and Rondo alla Burlesca* and *Mazurka Elegiaca* in the 1940s, with the composer on second piano, and these pressings suggest a lost opportunity. Britten and Curzon ape each other, two artists performing mirror work. Their sound is dry but warm, occasionally self-consciously virtuosic, mostly contained and fluid. It would have been an illuminating experience to hear the great Mozartian Curzon play *Holiday Diary*, especially the motionless 'Night' movement, which expertly gives the impression of sound travelling more slowly, as it does on cool evenings, with its associated refractory effects.

The European travels found him more relaxed than on the previous trip. Perhaps it was Edith's presence, perhaps it was the relatively slow pace at which they moved from one city to the next by train, a form of transport he loved. (They flew once, from Paris to London, not so many years since commercial pilots navigated their way from Dover to the capital by tracing the railway tracks.) Or perhaps it was just that he was determined to put behind him the year's terrible event, to stop worrying about his meagre output and Foss's inconstancy, and steeled himself to have a good time. There was food he had never tried: finicky hors d'oeuvres that, once gulped, left him sated, unable to touch the soufflés and *bombes glacés* that followed. There was scenery to admire: mountains and glaciers along the border of Switzerland and the Tyrol region, which they saw on their way to Salzburg and then Vienna; countryside around Basle, which they explored in motor cars supplied by friends and contacts; and more museums and palaces than Britten found strictly necessary.

Touchingly, he invented reasons to speak his schoolboy German – going into shops to ask the price of goods he would have neither cause nor money to buy – and became quite proficient as a consequence, though untouched by native cadence. (Later in life Britten often slipped into his second language, most famously with cellist Mstislav Rostropovich, whose German was that of a Soviet merchant seaman on shore leave, his English far worse.) And he felt privileged to trace Mozart's footsteps in Salzburg. He met two of Boosey & Hawkes's later émigrés, Hans Heinsheimer and Erwin Stein. And he spent time with the conductor Felix Weingartner, whom he thought nice but uninterested in contemporary music. Nor was Weingartner able to furnish him with the sort of entrée to cultured European society he and Edith hoped for. Mother and son were puzzled by the foreign currency (thirteen marks to the pound) and how expensive things were. He heard lots of opera, swooning over soprano Elisabeth Schumann and the various orchestras he encountered. ('I felt so sorry for you with those London orchestras!' he wrote to Grace Williams.) He also sharpened his sword on a number of European conductors for a change, including a 'BAD' performance by Willem Mengelberg and a 'VERY BAD' one by Weingartner. He was dimly aware of tensions in Vienna, as the left and right slugged it out on the streets.

Though his spirits remained high, the trip did not provide an immediate compositional fillip. In Vienna he began his violin Suite, Op. 6, which would include a postcard Viennese waltz ('Don't be surprised if I write nothing but Vienna Waltzes from now onwards!' he told Arthur Benjamin), and in Basle commenced another part of his liturgical triptych, a *Magnificat* for boys alone, which he never completed. He thought he was working a lot, yet ended up with little to show for it; the Suite is a strangely impersonal work exploring the instrument but nothing more. In fact, he would have little to show for the next eighteen months.

Something hugely valuable did occur on the trip, for amid the performances of *Salome*, *Carmen*, *Die Fledermaus*, *Cavalleria rusticana* and *I pagliacci*, and *Falstaff* (a 'glorious score – humour, tenderness abounding, & the glorious fugue to end', the applause lasting for fifteen minutes), the conductors (good and bad) and the orchestras (marvellous),

Britten corroborated his instincts about English music and the industry back home: something was fundamentally lacking there. The Vienna Philharmonic played 'as if it *wanted* to play', he told Grace Williams, thrilled by the sound and precision of the performances. 'Much as I want to like them [the London orchestras], & do admire alot of their playing – it's *nothing* like this. However you know it already.' (Williams had spent time in Vienna earlier in the decade studying with Egon Wellesz.) Even Beecham thought British orchestras gave concerts of 'prodigious sight reading', little more. This idea of cultural and musical disparity stayed with Britten. Following a broadcast two months after his return of Vaughan Williams sloppily conducting his own music and that of R. O. Morris, Robin Milford and Grace Williams herself, he wrote again to his friend.

> R.V.W. I know is a very nice man, but he shouldn't conduct. It was *hope-less*. The concert came over quite well; it wasn't the wireless's fault. But, oh, the ragged entries, the half-hearted & doubtful playing – and the beastly tone . . . I have never felt more depressed for English music than after that programme – putting your effort aside – especially when I felt that that is what the public – no, *not* the public, the critics love and praise.

His comparison was for the most part fair. Slick and full of promise as it was, the BBC Symphony Orchestra was then so young, without history or infrastructure on its side; the London Philharmonic Orchestra was younger still. Britten was not the only one to find fault with the BBC's roster of conductors. In 1932 *Manchester Guardian* critic Neville Cardus described the orchestra as a 'beautiful music machine . . . usually wasted for want of a great conductor'. Quite apart from his limitations as a performer, Boult was also music director of the BBC as a whole, responsible for overseeing or initiating programming and policy. He was a good delegator with an organized mind, yet his treacly musical influence was felt everywhere. Moreover, those to whom he delegated, as some critics at the time observed, all seemed to be variants of the 'enthusiastic English amateur' model. The BBC responded defensively and exaggeratedly to accusations of musical amateurism. 'All five [administrators] are composers whose works have had public performance; two are also concert pianists; three have been conductors . . .' The response only underlined the criticism's validity.

Of course there were great performances in London – concerts with fine English soloists, or (on a good day) indigenous conductors, or when there was a Continental charabanc in town inspiring the natives.* There was something exciting about being in London just as the capital went about assembling a music back catalogue, discovering a nineteenth-century music history that other great European cities took for granted. Even so, the orchestral culture and traditions were completely different from Berlin or Vienna, as were the way players trained and conductors served their apprenticeships. (Many of these differences remain to this day.) Nor was there an ingrained opera culture providing opportunities for these poorly trained young singers and conductors. Covent Garden then was a permanently pitched circus tent, into which paraded a long and not always scrupulously programmed string of artists and dancing bears, their impresarios cheering them on with greedy eyes. The musical infrastructure that even minor German cities took for granted simply did not exist.

Music is frequently described as a subjective art form, yet so much of a performance is not subjective at all: so much of it is about an artist hearing and speaking the harmonic language of a particular composer, and doing so with grace and fluency. Harmony has its own rhetoric, as does any language; some artists use it well, others remain stubbornly deaf to it. Britten's time in Vienna confirmed his instincts about performance and about all those poor musicians he had dismissed as a teenager. It was an opportunity to hear for himself what Bridge had long muttered about and Britten tried to express in his diary working from instinct alone. The experience confirmed his suspicion of the figures running England's music institutions. His trip was therefore an ideal use of his travelling scholarship, and an ideal response to Bridge's original suggestion that he experience a different musical climate on the Continent. After the war he would keep these sounds, experiences and suspicions in mind as he strove to do things differently in England, playing his hand with great assuredness. First he needed a job.

---

* Britten was thrilled by the Wagner season at Covent Garden in May 1935 starring Frida Leider and Lauritz Melchior. He was more even-handed about the conductor: 'Beecham wasn't bad, but not good enough.'

12

Two-thirds of the way into Evelyn Waugh's black comedy *Vile Bodies* (1930) is a razor-sharp vignette of the infant British film industry. A director-impresario pitches an idea to the anti-hero Adam Symes, hoping he'll stump up some cash. He hands Symes his business card, the company's name scratched out, a new one written above (The Wonderfilm Company of Great Britain), and launches into his spiel. 'It is the most important All-Talkie super-religious film to be produced solely in this country by British artists and management and by British capital. It has been directed throughout regardless of difficulty and expense, and supervised by a staff of expert historians and theologians.' It is all there – the burgeoning industry, new technology, fly-by-night companies and their crooked overlords, the uniquely British marriage of history, entertainment and education, the whole venture run on a wing and a shoestring.

An offshoot of the chaotic young industry was a film company formed early in the same year Waugh's book appeared by brilliant director John Grierson with Stephen Tallents, an official at the Empire Marketing Board, on the back of Grierson's short silent film *Drifters*. Grierson was a creature of his times: a visionary Scot with a strong Calvinist upbringing (John Reith was cut from similar hessian), piercing eyes and the great energy and tough manners of a fundamentalist preacher. His was not a shallow undertaking: Grierson was convinced that education was the cornerstone of any successful democracy, and the new technology suited his purpose admirably – as it did Lenin and Mussolini, who of course had different aspirations for it. Britten appears not to have seen *Drifters* following its 1929 release, despite its resonance with his childhood, a poetic exploration of a herring fleet and the associated industry, indebted to Soviet cinema of the 1920s (Eisenstein and the like), but still much the product of a new and vibrant cinematic voice. There is one standout image, of a school of buckling phosphorus herring, magnificent and textured, like a swatch of fine silk.

Grierson gradually put together a team of like-minded, recent university graduates. Each had a background similar to Britten's, though most had a more urgent sense of political engagement. Together they set about informing the British public on subjects as diverse as lumberjacks, salmon fishing, the agrarian evolution of North America. Early films were made through cobbling together existing footage gleaned from all parts of the Empire, but soon they were shooting their own film, pointing their cameras into the dark corners of 1930s British society.

Part of Grierson and Tallents' cinematic revolution was a dignified portrayal of working-class Britain. The seething masses had not been well treated in literature in the first three decades of the century, and there was no reason to believe cinema would take a different approach. Yet both men felt differently. Another part was distribution: Grierson sought out unusual venues to screen the films – stores and railway stations – hoping to cast his net over a much wider audience than his background or product normally achieved. It was art as politics, a sharp reflection of the Zeitgeist. Artist and director William Coldstream later called the films 'leftwing propaganda', though he was merely stating a general perception. When the Empire Marketing Board closed down in 1933, Tallents (now Sir Stephen) went over to the General Post Office as its new public relations officer, taking Grierson and his team with him. The GPO thus found itself with a Film Unit, something it had never anticipated.

It was this group that in April 1935 sought a composer. They were making a documentary film about the design and production of a postage stamp to commemorate King George V's Silver Jubilee, which the whole country would celebrate on 6 May. Despite its short history, the GPO Film Unit already had a reputation for tackling far more than was suggested in any single title sequence. 'It was something altogether new to be looking at ordinary things as if they were extraordinary,' Grierson observed. Accordingly, this modest film about a postage stamp was more accurately concerned with social reform in the wake of the 1840 introduction of the penny black and twopenny blue.

Bridge had been pestering Edward Clark for some time on behalf of his impecunious pupil. In February, and again in April, Britten sat down with some of those English gentlemen in the BBC he so disdained, a full-time position with the corporation on the table. No such grim scenario was tested, for almost from nowhere, at the end of April, Clark's secretary phoned and invited Britten to contact 'a certain film impresario, M. Cavalcanti' who invited him to lunch that day. Waugh could not have scripted it better. The lunch was congenial: Alberto

Cavalcanti was Grierson's sound technician, though he was quickly acquiring additional responsibilities, and they were joined by Coldstream, only six years Britten's senior. A few days later Britten put his business cards in a drawer, moved back into the boarding house on Cromwell Road and began work for the GPO Film Unit.

Composing for film requires specific skills, none of which Britten had ever thought about before, let alone acquired. His job was to enhance or emulate images on screen, timing his music to the second, working with a tiny budget and instrumental team. Film scores were far more episodic then than now. When Garbo pulls a gun on Lionel Barrymore's General Shubin in *Mata Hari*, the film that attracted Britten's derision in 1932, there is no underscoring, no music to heighten the visual or narrative tension. Nor is there when Ramon Novarro as Lieutenant Rosanoff attempts to seduce her – until she sits at the piano and, with much exaggerated movement of the shoulders, plays a soupy pastiche of Tchaikovsky, the *echt* tragic-Romantic icon. In the 1930s many of the big studios had their own music libraries: scores were literally on the shelf, where they were filed and selected according to mood, recorded (often by orchestras made up of Hollywood's émigrés), and used in isolation at appropriate points in the film.

Britten was later rude about the art form – 'I don't take film music seriously qua music' – but he also recalled positive aspects about writing for cinema, ones that informed his serious compositions. 'I had to work quickly, to force myself to work when I didn't want to, and to get used to working in all kinds of circumstances . . . It was also extremely good practice for me as a young composer to take exact instructions from the directors and producers of those plays and to try to please them.'

He thought he made a poor fist of it on his first day. With a stopwatch in one hand and a pencil in the other, he scribbled ideas for a small ensemble (flute, clarinet, percussion and two pianos), working from a script marked with 'precise' timings, which would shift in the editing suite. 'I spend the whole blessed day . . . trying to make what little ideas I have (& they are precious few on this God-forsaken subject) syncronize with the Seconds . . . I slog away until abt. 11.0 at night – trying to concoct *some* rubbish about a Jubilee Stamp.' No masterpiece, the score nonetheless does the trick: the large printing press clickety-clacks away, pushing out half a million stamps an hour, accompanied by Britten's repetitive industrial music.

What endeared Britten to this talented group was less his conspicuous skill and the speed at which he worked, more that he was an easy colleague. As his association with the Film Unit continued, Britten rolled up his sleeves and mucked in, as all of them did: he rigged lights, held cameras, cut films, fixed sound effects and attended script meetings. Coldstream later described his young collaborator as naive, unsophisticated, charming – 'an ordinary schoolboy', without intellectual pretensions – yet he also identified something special in him. They worked on three films together: *The King's Stamp*, *Coal Face* (1935) and *God's Chillun* (1936). For *Coal Face* Grierson and Cavalcanti brought on board writer Montagu Slater and poet W. H. Auden, two men who would assume vital roles in Britten's life. The 1930s now really began for him.

13

So much has been written of Auden in this decade and his hold on English imagination that it is sometimes difficult to picture what he must really have been like. In 1934 he described his boyhood self as 'mentally precocious, physically backward, short-sighted, a rabbit at all games, very untidy and grubby, a nail-biter, a physical coward, dishonest, sentimental, with no community sense whatever, in fact a typical little highbrow and difficult child'. Christopher Isherwood sketched something similar of the adult Auden, detailing in his 1936 diary the stubby, nail-bitten, nicotine-stained fingers sticking out the end of sleeves with holes at the elbow; the small yellow eyes, too close together by half; the cups of tea all day and the hot bath every night; the ravenous appetite; the mess he left in his wake; the bed piled with every conceivable cover to stave out the cold, real or imagined – blankets, overcoats, rugs, anything to hand.

Britten's new GPO colleague, director Harry Watt, pithily captured Auden's physicality: 'He looked exactly like a half-witted Swedish deckhand.' But he was more a scarecrow savant – with twiggy hands, ill-fitted clothing in bad repair and messy straw-blond hair. None of these characteristics was unique to the Auden of the 1930s; they were with him for life. Only his face seemed to change with age, over time bearing the brunt of Touraine-Solente-Golé syndrome, an inherited medical condition. ('If his face looks like this,' wondered David Hockney in 1968 while sketching him, 'what on earth must his balls look like?') The endless flow of conversation was a permanent characteristic too, the ideas, images and analogies pouring from him as he held forth on art, literature, politics, music, the church, philosophy, Latin and sex. He was, in turn, witty, didactic, stern, moralistic. He would rarely pause in conversation, instead simply change stream, minnow-like. 'I've never thought about that' was a sentence he found no cause to employ.

Auden was twenty-eight when he first worked for the GPO Film Unit, the author of four books (the first published privately by Stephen Spender), a compilation volume and, with Isherwood, the play *The Dog beneath the Skin*. He was cheer-leader to a generation of brilliant writers, his reputation already considerable.

'It may well be that it was Wystan who first awoke Ben's real imaginative and emotional life,' said Basil Wright in 1948, himself a GPO Film Unit director and friend of both men. However much of the jigsaw puzzle was in place by the time Britten had left Gresham's and the RCM, key pieces were still missing. If he thought about sex, he kept it to himself. If he was worried about Europe's long, slow dance towards another war, he did not write about it in his diaries or letters. There is no reason to doubt his pacifist beliefs, yet other than in his schoolboy decision not to join Gresham's OTC and his distribution of League of Nations ballots in Lowestoft in early 1935 (pushing disarmament, the prohibition of arms sales and the use of sanctions against aggressor nations), it remained a mostly private conviction. In conversation and correspondence his mother flitted from topic to topic with endearing ease; Britten, like his father, was more reserved. His 1939 orchestral song cycle *Les Illuminations* is headed with a musical epigraph, which turns up twice more in the piece: 'I alone hold the key to this savage parade'. This was Auden – not just that it was he who introduced Britten to the bisexual boy-poet Rimbaud, whose words he set in the cycle with such empathy and insight. Auden was the one holding the key. He unlocked doors, bullied and cajoled his new friend, pushed him to experience life as he did. And he came into Britten's life not a moment too soon.

Britten's private post-war memories of Auden were tinged with sadness, regret, disappointment, frustration and even anger. Spender remembered Auden in the early 1950s, by then the librettist of *The Rake's Progress*, writing Britten a criticism of *Gloriana*, which was returned to him in its original envelope, ripped into tiny pieces. But there was love and gratitude too, whatever transpired in the seven years following their first meeting. 'I think it was really that he was such a large personality,' Britten said in 1964, 'a whirlwind one, if you like, and, of course, I was swept away by his poetry. He was incredibly intelligent, very, very vocal; he talked marvellously well, he was very engaging and sympathetic and deeply interested in people.' Britten was thrilled with the poets and writers he discovered through his friend: Rimbaud, Donne and Smart whom he acknowledged, Hölderlin, Melville, Blake, Mann and many others whom he did not. The real sadness, of course, was that he made these grateful comments to other people – journalists, friends, Pears, academics – not to Auden himself.

They met on 5 July 1935, two months to the day since Britten had grudgingly draped Union Jacks on the family house in preparation for the next day's Jubilee celebrations. With Wright he drove to Downs School in Colwall, Malvern, where Auden was a schoolmaster. ('A prep-school master teaching Games, / Maths, French, Divinity, / Harsh hand-bells hurried me from sleep / For thirty pounds a term and keep' – John Betjeman's words, but very much Auden's experience.) Auden had written to Wright earlier in the year asking for work. 'Don't be a fool, fetch him,' Grierson responded when Wright hesitated, perhaps wondering if his friend was such a good fit. In Colwall they discussed the poet's first contribution to a GPO project, an epilogue to a film already in production. 'Auden is the most amazing man,' Britten wrote after their meeting, 'a very brilliant & attractive personality.'

For all Britten's subsequent protestations of intellectual inadequacy in Auden's company, which lasted for many years, the positive impact of the friendship was quickly evident. There is one telling example, a BBC Symphony Orchestra concert they attended in late October, which included the first UK performance of Berg's arrangement for strings of three movements from his *Lyric Suite*. Britten's prose was always rather plain (it became even plainer post-war), yet in the letter he wrote to Marjorie Fass after the concert the language is new. In place of the usual boyish, literal descriptions and recitations, the rages and petty gripes, there is lightness, metaphor and imagery. Instead of picking at Boult as he normally did, as though shooting fish in a barrel, Britten got inside his mind.

Of course the performance was execrable – it seemed to me as if A.B. had said to himself (if he were capable of forming opinions of anything) 'This is a clever work, but perhaps a little too free – after all one doesn't talk of or mention these things in public, does one? One must make it as decent & clean as possible!' And he did, didn't he? Practically every speed was wrong – the Estatico too slow, by half, the Adagio too fast – to prevent it becoming too sensuous – no doubt. What would he do with Tristan, I wonder!!

It is the conversation Britten and Auden had as they spilled out of Queen's Hall at the interval, talking over each other, interjecting details here, contradicting others there, Britten grabbing the opportunity to demonstrate that he was not, after all, intellectually inadequate in Auden's presence. This was his turf. In his diary following the performance he wrote that Boult gave 'a Kensington drawing room apology' for the work, which was also new language for him – a class-based insult, no less, from the same stable as the aspersion he lobbed at Elgar's Symphony No. 1 a month earlier: 'I swear that only in Imperialist England would such a work be tolerated.' It is a striking change.

There are other indications of a shift. Britten mentions political ideologies in his diary for the first time, and in early August this newly minted Communist sympathizer attempted to strike an accord with the Christian Scientist in his life. 'Letters after dinner, & try to talk communism with Mum, but it is impossible to say anything to anyone brought up in the old order without severe ruptions.' He read Communist journalist R. Palme Dutt's *Fascism and Social Revolution* ('Fascism is antithetical to everything of substance within the liberal tradition', its thesis), a volume of some impact in this topsy-turvy decade. With Dutt and Auden peering over his shoulder Britten advised Fass that every serious person, every artist especially, should be soaked in politics, exhibiting 'strong opposition in every direction to Facism, which of course restricts all freedom of thought'. In October he wrote his response to Italy's attack on Abyssinia, with updates every few days, and by March 1936 he extended his reach even further:

The International situation now is ludicrously complicated – Germany now discards Locarno & Versailles & occupies Rhine territory – Italian successes on Abyssinian front continue in spite of financial difficulties – Japan owing to the shooting of her statesmen in last week's revolt is more

milataristic than ever – & Russia is pressed on the other side as well by
Germany & Poland. Central Europe is a hot-bed of intrigue – and our
re-armament plans mount up & up.

A few months later it was capitalism's turn for a swipe, Britten having
played Monopoly with friends – 'a grand new American game (showing
up incidently the fatal attractions & hopeless fatuity of Capitalism – but
nevertheless very good game)'.

With a click of Auden's fingers Britten had been transformed from a
political neophyte into a polite student activist. All of what followed
between them must be viewed in the context of the unexpected intimacy: the mutual infatuation; the collaborations, weak and strong;
Isherwood's assertion that Britten during this decade was water in his and
Auden's hands; the modulation of Britten's personality through his diet
of Rabelais, Marx and Swift; the perhaps inevitable estrangement. Britten did his best to keep up with this extraordinary man and his circle.
He read more and thought more. He learned the difference between
blackshirts, brownshirts and blueshirts. He could do little about the
physical impression he made on friends – the pale boyish face, curly
fairish hair, slim build and shy manner – but the refined accent we know
from the adult Britten is further evidence of his attempts to fit in with
his smart Oxbridge crowd, notwithstanding what Gresham's and London had already chiselled from his flat Lowestoft vowels.

Keeping up was rarely easy. Time and again he concluded his was a
second-rate mind in first-rate company. 'I always feel very young &
stupid when with these brains – I mostly sit silent when they hold forth
about subjects in general,' he wrote a few months after meeting Auden.
Partly it was shyness, partly it was that the RCM was no Oxford or
Cambridge; he had never thought about many of the things being
discussed and found himself scrambling. Moreover, he had spent his
childhood as a sort of dauphin figure, reigning over those in his household with steely benevolence, leaving them in no doubt of his status. It
was a shock to find this privileged upbringing did not translate into
anything similar in his new life.

There was another aspect to Britten's response to the Auden crowd,
something he touched on later in life: 'I do not easily think in words,
because words are not my medium.' He often hoisted up this flag of surrender when he had a speech or interview to give, and though it sounded

pat and was difficult to believe in someone so sensitive to poetry, it was genuine. 'I am a very bad speaker,' he said in 1950. 'I always think of what I wanted to say afterwards.' Or seven years earlier, to Imogen Holst, 'I have no aptitude at all for expressing myself in words.' Such comments were a rationalization for all the times he sat mute in the corner while his brilliant friends danced around him with lambent words and ideas. See, Auden? I'm the composer, you're the poet, he seemed to be saying, I wasn't even *meant* to talk. Perhaps this is the reason Britten could not sustain the friendship longer than he did; their minds worked in such different ways, which he found exhausting and Auden found good sport. But for a while it worked and the ride was fast and fun.

14

Their first collaboration was on the film *Coal Face*, for which Auden wrote a noble-savage lyric about miners at work. 'O lurcher-loving collier, black as night / Follow your love across the smokeless hill.' (A lurcher is a mongrel dog, favoured by hunters and poachers.) It offers an odd marriage of proletarian and high cultures (there are echoes of Shakespeare's Petruchio) and, courtesy of a murky recording, it is fair to say that ambition outstripped achievement. Yet the film itself is hugely innovative, full of montage, clever scoring, soundtracks played backwards, other natural sounds recorded and put to good use, and some pointed dialogue. Britten made instruments out of raw materials close at hand – much as he would later do in *Noye's Fludde*, slinging teacups on string and instructing children to hit them with wooden spoons to replicate the sounds of fat, plopping raindrops. For all its innovation, *Coal Face* is an aesthetically cohesive film in which the workers are treated with dignity, the dangers of their industry emphasized through stark words and images. The production team was a *Who's Who* of the documentary film industry: Grierson (production), Cavalcanti (script and sound), Watt (photography), Coldstream (editing and sound), Slater (script and commentary), Humphrey Jennings (photography), Stuart Legg (sound).*

* Grierson and Slater returned to the coalmines in their 1952 feature film *The Brave Don't Cry*, a depiction of an underground disaster.

Quite apart from the personnel involved, the medium itself influenced Britten. When asked in 1963 about electronic reproduction, foreshadowing his Aspen speech of a year later, he responded: 'Gramophone, radio and TV are for me like a photograph of a painting, simply a very convenient reminder. My reactions to the film, even, are quite different from my reactions to the other arts. More immediate, perhaps, but less profound.' This was evidently his belief, but by the time of the interview certain cinematic techniques had crept into his operas. The end of *Billy Budd* contains a cinematic fade from one scene and era to another: the suddenly older Captain Vere is left alone on stage, memories and ghosts swirling around him. *Gloriana* does the same, where the fast decline in Queen Elizabeth's health is marked by a series of cinematic flashbacks, literally underscored.

So Britten was happy to take what he could from the genre. Nor was the traffic one-way: he introduced to his incidental scores techniques from opera, such as Wagnerian leitmotifs, which produced cohesion. The spill from one genre to another concerned Virginia Woolf. In her 1926 essay 'The Cinema' she derided the simple literalism of a genre that was then rapaciously preying on books for subject matter. A kiss equals love, she scoffed. A broken cup means jealousy, a grin happiness, a hearse death. It was literature's job to explore the inner world of a character, she argued, not reduce a story to a series of ciphers. Film was trespassing on modern literature's property, damaging it. Worse, she thought, was modern literature's attempt to keep up with the pace and jumble of film. She was talking about silent film, of course, which relied on such visual cues. Sound changed all that and helped make films subtler; but it further broke down the distinction between genres. This Britten understood. As the 1930s progressed, there was considerable overlap in his music for film, theatre, radio and concert hall.

A handful of films followed *Coal Face* in quick succession. Each new release, with incidental or title music by Britten, embraced Grierson's credo of looking at ordinary things as if they were extraordinary: gas supply, savings banks, telegraphs, telephones and telegrams were all worthy subjects. Partly it was that technology in these areas was new and needed explanation – there is no other way to account for the Britten–Auden song 'When you're feeling like expressing your affection', an explication of international telephoning, in which, with neither embarrassment nor credit, Auden lifts the rhyme 'Moscow' and 'kiosk

O' from a Francis Mahony poem. But still their strongest motivation was the desire to excavate hidden, suppressed, working-class Britain – much as George Orwell would do early the following year, travelling to industrial Wigan and writing about his experiences in angry, unbelieving prose.

In September Auden joined the Film Unit full time, drawing a weekly salary of £3, all the while thrusting spikes into Grierson's smoothly spinning wheels. Auden and Britten sketched ideas for a film with the working title 'Negroes', a study of the slave trade in the West Indies. Coldstream was right: this film script was little more than left-wing propaganda, its principal target empire, a stale old biscuit, thought Auden. 'Acts of injustice done / Between the setting and the rising sun / In history lie like bones, each one . . . But between the day and night / The choice is free to all; and light / Falls equally on black and white.' After difficult birthing pains the film was released two years later as *God's Chillun*, long after Auden had left the unit and some time since he had shoehorned the stark lyric into his play with Isherwood, *The Ascent of F6*.

Britten and Auden hit their stride in the next project together, which remains an iconic work of art from the 1930s. *Night Mail* (January 1936) is a more conventional film than *Coal Face*, but is nonetheless distinguished by innovative ideas, not least the celebrated finale. Both documentaries occupy common territory. The coal miners of the earlier film were scrubbed down and put into clean uniforms, but *Night Mail* is still an attempt to illustrate how invisible workers grease the cogs of industrialized middle-class Britain. Real people, not actors, speak dialogue either written for, or coaxed from, them by Grierson, Wright and Watt; it is charmingly stilted. ('Take it away, sonny boy,' one old hand chirrups. 'Right-O, handsome,' comes the reply.) Workers for the new shift are picked up at the border and gallantly take leave of their tea and waitresses, as though heading out on a troop train. The photography is striking, from the near-abstract close-ups of the postal train's features – couplers, smokestack, furnace and whistle – to shots of vast, inky panoramas. There is lovely footage of clerks in the hours before dawn sorting the one hundred tons of mail intended for Glasgow and the industrial north – including Orwell's 'mines of Wigan', mention of which Britten accompanies with a wailing shift siren. And the sheer camaraderie and industry of these workers in their travelling office, as they fling mail-filled leather satchels from the train at various junctures and, using a sort of giant lacrosse stick, snare other satchels positioned by the tracks, is a joy to watch.

A similar sense of camaraderie is evident between composer and poet, particularly in the film's final sequence. The lyric here sounds as though it took Auden no more than a few hours one wet Sunday afternoon, and Britten's music leaves no greater impression. But together they evoke the machine world and grand narrative scope of the mail train. Taking his tempo from earlier footage of the train rattling along tracks, Britten made a simple bed for Auden's words: 'This is the night mail crossing the border, / bringing the cheque and the postal order.' The ending is full of semitone clashes and breathless woodwind flourishes, punctuated with trumpet fanfares that (incongruously) invoke an old-fashioned post horn.

> Asleep in working Glasgow, asleep in well-set Edinburgh,
> Asleep in granite Aberdeen,
> They continue their dreams,
> But shall wake soon and long for letters,
> And none will hear the postman's knock
> Without a quickening of the heart.
> For who can bear to feel himself forgotten?

It is not solely the trumpet tootling that brings to mind Schubert's setting of Wilhelm Müller's 'Die Post' in *Winterreise*, the most beautiful miniature ever devised on the subject. Each is brilliantly evocative of the transport system of the day – horses' hoofs on cobblestones in the earlier lied, a steam engine clacking along tracks in the film – and each brilliantly captures the Romantic iconography and expectations of mail, heart beating hard in anticipation or potentially broken upon receipt. 'From the street a post-horn sounds. / What is it that makes you leap so, / My heart?'

Ultimately Auden could not stomach the Romantic depiction of the worker *Night Mail* represents. 'It is doubtful whether an artist can ever deal more than superficially (and cinema is not a superficial art) with characters outside his own class, and most British documentary directors are upper middle,' he muttered soon after completing the film, not wholly convincingly. Or perhaps he started to suspect his own motives, that his lionizing of working-class men was more erotic than political, more Forster than Marx. These convictions spoiled his relationship with Grierson, and *Night Mail* was his last project with them. At the end of 1936 Auden teamed up once more with Britten for a documentary about the electrification of the London–Portsmouth railway line, *The Way to the Sea*, though this was for another company. There is a final sequence heavily indebted to that of *Night Mail*, and though the director Paul Rotha introduced a visual warning against English rearmament (a sudden and foreboding shot of artillery), there is nothing in Auden's text to support it. His disgruntlement with 'socialist art' remained and this view characterized his future collaborations with Britten, with one notable exception – the orchestral song cycle *Our Hunting Fathers*.

The short duration of Auden's film career coincided with Britten's first steps as a collaborative artist. *A Boy was Born* demonstrated his capacity in assembling a neat narrative arc out of existing texts, but is something very different from working with a living poet on a new piece. He did surprisingly well for someone so used to having his own way, revelling in the fusion of talents. He helped decide which sequences needed music, was consulted on the shape of the script, and occasionally found himself in the luxurious position of recording the soundtrack first, watching the film cut to match. This was his operatic apprenticeship, though it provided no sense of the sort of hands-on collaborator he would become post-war. In awe of Auden, he mostly just set what the poet sent his way.

If this superman Auden never managed to get the serious young Britten to laugh at himself, did he at least tease out some humour? After *Grimes*, his responsibilities onerous, Britten possessed what was frequently described as a 'schoolboy' sense of humour – all puns and word games in which he found relief from his work and adult life. But numerous things changed in the glow of *Grimes* and humour may have been one of them. Soprano Sophie Wyss, who worked with Britten in the 1930s, recalled his face often lit by a charming laugh (a view unsupported by photographic evidence). He loved comic films and admired Chaplin and the Marx Brothers and their slapstick, but in letters and contemporaneous descriptions there is little to suggest a sparkling wit. Again it was Grace Williams who best encouraged him. Writing to her in 1935, Britten said of a broadcast of Vaughan Williams's *Five Mystical Songs* that 'The fifteen biblical songs of R.V.W. finished me entirely'. Yet even here it is not clear whether the exaggeration was intended as wit or as a sober assessment of V.W.'s foggy choral songs.

There was certainly no humour in his music before Auden. Composition was a serious business, as Bridge taught him, one he was unwilling or unable to dilute for comic effect, whatever that may have meant at the time. Yet from the beginning of the 1930s Auden had been using a whole bag of tricks – pastiche, parody, word play – to entertain, pay homage and educate. Observing this in one of England's most brilliant young artists, Britten relaxed, dipped into this bag and learned how to do the same in his music.

15

In November 1935 Britten and Beth moved into a two-bedroom flat in London's West Hampstead, he a film composer, she a dressmaker. The family home was now empty and their respective careers were progressing: it was time to put down shallow roots in something other than a boarding house. 'It was a mews flat over a garage,' Britten later said, 'the coldest in London, built on top of nothing, with nothing on either side of it.' They furnished it cheaply, bought a leaky ten-year-old two-seater Lagonda for £5 – all right-angles on wheels, a child's drawing of a car – and set about living as adults. On Sundays they motored down to visit the Bridges in Friston in east Sussex, or mother in Frinton; Monday morning Britten was back in the Blackheath studio, stopwatch and pencil to hand. Regardless of Auden's disaffection with the unit, the GPO was now paying Britten a generous £5 for a four-day week.

He nonetheless had little money. No doubt the subject came up in Britten's negotiations with Hawkes in the final months of 1935, but it was January 1936 before contract and advance were settled. So he took work where he could find it – mostly in left-leaning arts organizations, his entrée stage-managed by Auden. Britten tried his hand at commercial cinema, too, discussing with a mysterious Mr Lortorov and his 'firm of obvious film crooks' a possible feature flick, which came to nothing. There was music to write for the Group Theatre and Left Theatre late in the year, none of it substantial or particularly imaginative, but a helpful experience in other ways. Left Theatre's production of *Easter 1916* was Britten's first collaboration with Montagu Slater, following their separate contributions to *Coal Face*, and the play brought him face to face with a Communist's take on the pitiful Easter Rising in Ireland

and Britain's heavy-handed response – ground which Yeats trod in his poem of the same name. The disillusionment Britten began to feel with English politics and society in the following years – the recurring Conservative governments of jack-in-the-box Stanley Baldwin part of it – stems from such films and plays and the conversations that swirled around them.

The Group Theatre was a vital part of Britten's apprenticeship. It was the brainchild of actor Ormerod Greenwood, a young Cambridge graduate who, together with dancer and choreographer Rupert Doone, founded the company in 1932. The concept, which they drafted in an early statement, was simple yet unusual for the time: 'by continually playing together and by using its own producers, playwrights, painters, musicians, technicians, etc., to produce a company which will work like a well-trained orchestra'. Borrowing liberally from the philosophies of Brecht, Cocteau, Compagnie des Quinze and Diaghilev's Ballets Russes (with which Doone had for a short time been a *premier danseur*, a rare distinction for an Englishman), they forged collaborations with some of the greatest artistic minds of the time, many of whom would later be important figures in Britten's creative life: Auden, Isherwood, Spender, Eliot, Yeats, director Tyrone Guthrie, painter John Piper, poet and playwright Louis MacNeice and his later wife, singer Hedli Anderson.

Doone was an infuriating, tyrannical, haphazard figure and his direction swung between chaos and despotism. But there was no denying his determination and hypnotic power. Auden joined him a few months after the group's formation, no doubt as a consequence of his friendship with designer Robert Medley, who was now Doone's boyfriend. Medley later recalled his first encounter with Britten, 'a slim young man, unobtrusively dressed in sports jacket and grey flannel bags, with irregular features and crinkly hair, and wearing a pair of slightly owlish spectacles, which emphasized his watchful reticence'. (He wore his reading glasses only reluctantly in public.)

The literary critic Michael Sidnell suggests the conflation of left-wing politics, pacifism and homosexuality characteristic of Britten's post-war life was a currency of the Group Theatre. Cyril Connolly later identified the 'authentic rallying cries of homo-communism' in one of the group's productions, while later still Philip Brett talked of the alliance of the 'thirties homosexual/pacifist sensibility of Britten and Pears with the Marxist left'. In cast lists of early productions there are as many gay members as there are Communist sympathizers (frequently one and the same person), an unofficial left-wing gay brotherhood. Isherwood later remembered a review of his second novel, *The Memorial*, in which the critic remarked 'that he had at first thought the novel contained a disproportionately large number of homosexual characters but had decided, on further reflection, that there *were* a lot more homosexuals about, nowadays'. So it was in the Group Theatre, but this in no way diminished its left-leaning politics, which trickled into its thinking and infrastructure. Artists were in charge of their lives and work, they argued, free to go in whatever direction they wanted. Patronage belonged to the aristocracy or the Church and had no valid place in modern Britain – a view that left the group scrambling for more democratic subscriptions, which they extracted from 'participating spectators'.

Britten's music for the group's production of Shakespeare's *Timon of Athens* in November 1935 is mostly generic – fanfares and banquet music, which he would take to a new level eighteen years later in *Gloriana* – but it does include an atmospheric funeral march, a sign of many Mahlerian things to come. Trevor Howard, Britten's exact contemporary, played Lucullus, ten years before *Brief Encounter* made him a star. John Moody, later a distinguished theatre and opera director, was Lucilius. Film and television actor Peter Copley was Lucius, while Frederick Piper was Flavius, six years before the release of the hit film *49th Parallel* in which he played a small role, underpinned by Vaughan Williams's lush score.

A year earlier Britten had been holed up in Lowestoft, wondering how he would earn a living; now he was part of a vibrant milieu, meeting and collaborating with some of the country's most prominent artistic voices. Frank Bridge was pushed to the sidelines as a consequence. He remained important to Britten, but more as a father figure and tennis partner than teacher. Britten's busy days at the GPO and Group Theatre left him with few moments to himself and fewer ideas for his own work; nothing of substance or scale was written. In a letter to Marjorie Fass he revealed his thoughts on Bridge when Berg died at Christmas. 'I feel it is a real & terrible tragedy – one from which the world will take long to recover from. The real musicians are so few & far between, arn't they? Apart from the Bergs, Stravinskys, Schönbergs & Bridges one is a bit stumped for names, isn't one?' If Bridge's star today shines less brightly than those of the other composers, it is neither a comment on the quality of his music nor the esteem in which Britten held it.

16

It is telling that Britten did not turn to his mother for an allowance, begging her indulgence so he could free himself from paid work and focus on his own compositions. The inheritance had left her well off and she would have been sympathetic, but Britten had a strong work ethic and instead churned through everything the GPO threw at him. And he enjoyed himself hugely, grasping the opportunity to accumulate further evidence of his professional status, and recognizing the fact he was at last growing up.

'1936 finds me infinitely better off in all ways than did the beginning of 1935,' he wrote to ring in the New Year, before listing the many reasons why: a salary of £5 per week from the GPO, with potential for it to rise to £10; an advance against royalties from his new, exclusive publisher, Boosey & Hawkes; a steadily growing reputation; peers such as Auden, Wright and Coldstream, regardless of how inferior they made him feel; friends like the Bridges, Henry Boys, Reeve, and two young ex-pupils of South Lodge, Francis Barton and Piers Dunkerley.

Dunkerley was an impossibly handsome boy, seven and a half years Britten's junior, whose good looks stayed with him into adulthood. They met in Lowestoft in March 1934 – casually, in town, Britten walking with his sister – and thereafter maintained a steady correspondence and increasingly close friendship. Much has been written about Britten's relationships with such boys, not least by Auden. Britten himself characterized his role as a sort of father-confessor, and there was an element of this, but the model closest to hand was that of head prefect or school captain, someone to whom the boys could turn as they navigated adolescence. On a deeper level the friendships contained the same sublimated sexuality that characterized many such public-school relationships between prefect and junior. In his New Year diary Dunkerley's name is appended with the words 'tell it not in Gath', a phrase from the Book of Samuel that Britten so admired as a child, in which the love between David and Jonathan is detailed. Colloquially it means 'keep this quiet', but here the context is unambiguously sexual, the first frisson of such feelings to emerge, undisguised, in his diary. Britten very properly counselled Dunkerley on the sexual advances being made to him at school ('it makes one sick that they can't leave a nice lad like Piers alone – but it is understandable – good heavens!') and could tell himself that, though he was extremely fond of Piers, the attraction was not sexual. 'I am getting to such a condition that I am lost without some children (of either sex) near me.' It is not a terribly convincing line, but it was one he would tread for the remainder of his life, propriety mostly trumping sexual desire.

It is impossible to say how much the mentoring would have changed had one of the young boys in Britten's life shared his sexual orientation, had identified some of Britten's sublimated desire and reciprocated it. It is significant that Britten did not actively seek out boys he may have thought homosexually inclined, then or later. Most he befriended were good-looking. Some came from troubled backgrounds; the majority were free-spirited, bright and independent, untroubled by sexual crises of their own.

Auden thought the friendships with schoolboys were evidence of Britten fumbling round the edges. It was not so much the age difference that concerned him; a few years earlier, aged twenty-six, he had fallen in love with thirteen-year-old Micheal Yates, writing him a string of poems before the infatuation petered out. It was more that Britten seemed unable to open himself to the potential and dangers of an adult sexual relationship, focusing instead on boys who were constitutionally unable to view him as anything other than mentor or older brother. Auden tackled the matter in a poem, which he dedicated to its target:

> Underneath the abject willow,
> Lover, sulk no more;
> Act from thought should quickly follow:
> What is thinking for?
> Your unique and moping station
> Proves you cold;
> Stand up and fold
> Your map of desolation.

Britten's problem was that in his early twenties he barely had the thoughts Auden alluded to, clamping down hard on nascent feelings. Auden saw through this, and no doubt the gay flavour of the Group Theatre and impressive parade of Auden's and Isherwood's young lovers helped bring on the emergence of Britten's sexuality. It still took time and bravery, but the fact that he was gradually able to identify his desire was a step forward. Throughout 1936 this repression began to melt away and Britten found himself open to the idea posed in the final lines of Auden's poem: 'Coldest love will warm to action, / Walk then, come, / No longer numb / Into your satisfaction.'

Britten's religious beliefs were also falling away as the decade progressed. He retained a sentimental or cultural attachment to Christianity all his life, but the diary entries of only two years earlier, detailing Sunday services at a handful of London churches, are in 1936 conspicuous by their absence. When in Frinton on a Sunday he would argue with his mother against his going to communion. And following the death of an acquaintance in an aeroplane crash in April 1937, Britten found himself arguing against religion with a deeply Catholic friend of them both. 'A thing like that does make me cling desperately to such religious faith as I have,' the friend countered, before urging the vacillating Britten to 'reconsider all that – it does matter so terribly'. Though Auden would soon balance his rediscovered faith and his long-practised sexuality with aplomb, Britten was not so minded. He found it more difficult to reconcile childhood beliefs and adult sexuality, and one dropped away as the other emerged.

17

The composition drought continued for all of 1936, broken only once by a powerful, original orchestral song cycle devised by Britten and Auden, their first collaboration outside film and theatre. They discussed it over dinner at the beginning of the year in the cold West Hampstead flat, Britten probably arranging for Beth or their housekeeper to rustle up some food: he never learned to cook even simple dishes. 'We talk amongst many things of a new Song Cycle (probably on Animals) that I may write.' They were working on *Night Mail* at the time, and, though Auden was soon to extract himself from documentary production, his eye remained on a disintegrating Europe and the iniquity of the English class system – the housekeeper aside. Both themes informed the new piece.

Anthology in music can end up a mess. A poem is given new meaning through its juxtaposition with another and can easily slip its moorings as a result. Britten had already demonstrated skill as an anthologist, knitting together poems from different eras and sources, uniting them in narrative cohesion. Yet *A Boy was Born* was a retelling of the most famous story of all time: it did not need the skills of an Orson Welles. The much more obscure tale Auden was brewing, which would use metaphors inherent in the relationship between animals and humans to skewer his targets, was altogether more complex.

Though Auden was clearly in charge, Britten had his own well-developed love and understanding of poetry. When asked many years later about the origins of this passion, he dated it to his boyhood. 'I had always read poetry. I find it, in a way, easier to read than prose.' In any case, Auden served him some gems. There is the anonymous 'Rats Away!' in which the narrator – a cross between the Pied Piper and a holy visionary – orders rodents from the town's dwellings, calling on an impressive cast of Apostles, saints, archangels and deities to this end. The anonymous 'Messalina' depicts the spoilt, promiscuous, treacherous Roman Empress, grieving over her dying monkey, as mad as Ophelia. Thomas Ravenscroft's 'Hawking for the Partridge' is a paean to falconry, those 'murdering kites' scouting for prey. Auden strung the three poems together between his own prologue and epilogue, and even if the thicket in these bookends is a little dense, they introduced Britten to a framing mechanism he would return to time and again in his operas. 'Our hunting fathers told the story / Of the sadness of the creatures, / Pitied the limits and the lack / set in their finished features.' Humankind had no such limits, such lack. Humans had developed reason, but with it came invented gods and vicious wars. Did this really represent an advance?

Britten's politics had evolved considerably in the eighteen months he had known Auden. They were less sophisticated than the poet's, but less changeable as a consequence. When forced to start thinking about politics, he took a sort of package deal – a left-wing cocktail of anti-fascism, pacifism (from his teenage years), pro-socialism, anti-capitalism, anti-aristocracy, anti-imperialism and anti-monarchy. (When George V was slowly dying in January 1936 and updates were announced every fifteen minutes on the BBC by an increasingly quavery Stuart Hibberd – 'The King's life is moving peacefully towards its close' – Britten snapped unsympathetically in his diary: 'Really this King *won't* die.')

Many of these ideas would be exercised in the coming months, as Spain sank under the weight of civil war. Some of them are behind

Rotha's short film *Peace of Britain* ('Demand peace by reason', it implores), for which Britten in March 1936 wrote music, and over which the British Board of Film Censors initially executed its power of veto. And some of them are threaded through *Our Hunting Fathers*, Op. 8, which attacks the rituals and values of the hunting set, with its easy cruelty and gluttonous lunches of oysters and pâté and steak-and-kidney pudding, washed down with glasses of kümmel. The cycle is also an attack on religious zealotry and a commentary on human primitiveness, for all its advances over the poor animals we snare, pet and eat. It even contains a line by Lenin's wife, Nadezhda Krupskaya, on her husband's early revolutionary fight: 'To live illegally, to go hungry, and remain totally anonymous was quite different from speaking at crowded meetings without any risk at all.' Auden stumbled across this sentence in a 1933 biography of Lenin, published by Gollancz, and lifted it for the poem that ends the cycle: 'To hunger, work illegally, / And be anonymous?'

There are great musical ideas, too: Messalina's mad scene, prefiguring Grimes's by nine years; the unhinged 'Dance of Death', encasing the Ravenscroft, with its wink at Stravinsky's *Symphony of Psalms*, as macabre as anything Holbein came up with in his woodcuts of the same name; the slow funeral march ending the piece, a nod in Mahler's direction; the untrammelled vocal writing, full of extreme leaps and dynamics, wrested from the opera stage, so different from anything he had previously written for voice. The influence of film montage in the final movement's fragmentary repetition of motives from earlier parts of the work is strong, the sudden juxtaposition of conflicting or complementary images a mark of the times. In fact, the whole piece is startlingly visual and this too is a departure.

Britten conducted the premiere in September 1936 in the Norwich Triennial Festival, which commissioned the work. The first rehearsal with Beecham's orchestra, the LPO – in which he had to ignore the bad behaviour of the musicians and their snickering at his difficult music – was traumatic for the inexperienced conductor, the players' philistinism greatly distressing him. Worse, he suffered the ignominy of Vaughan Williams, of all people, intervening to reprove them for their attitude and manners. Sophie Wyss, with her strong features and dark eyes, and possessing the sort of even, lyric soprano voice Britten loved and used all his life, did her best with the solo part, but the audience had no idea what to make of it. Its dedicatee, Ralph Hawkes, was no better equipped, though he recognized a full press contingent when he saw one. Later it became evident that Britten's great mentor did not rate the work, perhaps fearing his pupil had crossed a bridge and then set it on fire. The reviews were mostly imbecilic: 'if it is just a stage to be got through, we wish him safely and quickly through it' (*The Times*); 'Benjamin Britten, lightly unburdening himself of dire nonsense' (*Observer*); 'The general impression is a kind of orchestral prank in which the instruments lead a distracted human voice into one embarrassing position after another' (*Daily Telegraph*); and so forth.

There was more and more of this cloth-eared pontificating on the worth of Britten's music as his reputation grew; the early comparison between his part-songs and Walton's *Façade* was mild compared to the things he had to read about his scores in the late 1930s. Although published quibbles with Britten's music dated back to 1932, the eminent critic J. A. Westrup initiated the really intemperate language in early 1936 when reviewing the premiere of Britten's *Three Divertimenti* at Wigmore Hall. 'As in some other works from the same pen, there was much play with technical devices, but little solid matter to justify the escapades. Mr Britten will have proved his worth as a composer when he succeeds in writing music that relies less on superficial effect.'

Westrup was right here: the piece *is* too reliant on superficial effect, almost as though Britten was test-driving the quartet genre. Westrup was not to know that *Three Divertimenti* is a reworking of Britten's 'Go, play, boy, play' suite of 1933, written when he was much in sway to the technical tricks Ireland was teaching him. Had he been less thin-skinned, Britten might even have conceded Westrup's point: following the performance (but before the next morning's *Telegraph*) he admitted the piece needed 'a little more boiling'. Yet somehow the notion of a facile youngster, all show and no substance, now became the critical meme, passed from one commentator to the next. Because he was so sensitive, Britten was reduced to raging sulks, not sober contemplation, and there would be no talking him down over the following forty years. 'I feel so depressed,' he fumed in his diary after reading Westrup's review. 'I feel like a spanked school-boy – exactly as I used to feel after a jaw [reprimand].' For *Three Divertimenti* to be treated in this way was one thing; when such criticism was applied to works of substance like *Our Hunting Fathers*, he was inconsolable.

The cycle was broadcast in April the following year, under Boult ('he doesn't really grasp the work – tho' he is marvellously painstaking'), and then lay unperformed for thirteen years, when it was exhumed by Pears and Norman Del Mar. Even then it did not catch on. Most people missed that it was his real Op. 1, a bold modernist experiment, a shadowy look into his future. Britten, hearing a large orchestral canvas of his own making for the first time in his life, knew for certain it was.

18

Quite apart from this major outing on the podium in Norwich, he was also playing a little more in 1936, supplementing his income with broadcast fees, surprising himself with how little the process unnerved him, how inured he was to the psychological power of the studio's red light. (Years later he told record producer John Culshaw about the loneliness and emptiness he felt when the red light went off at the end of a take and nothing was heard from the control room.) More than ever he relied on his student-honed technique. 'It isn't that I don't know what to do,' he wrote in March 1936 during rehearsals with Antonio Brosa for a broadcast of his violin Suite, 'but with so little time to practise, my fingers simply won't do what I want.' A month later they were in Barcelona for the annual ISCM Festival, the Suite an official selection.

What a difference between Britten in Barcelona and Britten in Florence two years earlier. This time he flew, travelling via Paris, Lyons and Marseilles, making the last leg on a small flying boat. Once there he wandered freely through the city, intoxicated by the smells, sounds and tastes. 'It is difficult not to believe in the supernatural when in a place like this,' he wrote after hearing Vittoria performed in the monastery at Montserrat in the mountains outside Barcelona, gorgeous polyphony echoing round the semi-darkness. He was smitten by Gaudí's sandcastle architecture, describing the Basílica of the Sagrada Família as 'a disbanded Holywood set', its creator clearly 'a religious maniac'. He loved the native music and Catalan dances, which he rifled the following year for the *Mont Juic* suite, and was stunned by Berg's new Violin Concerto, conducted by Scherchen on a day's notice, which straddles old and new worlds so confidently. He ate seven-course banquets at meals lasting hours. With his instant new friends, the composer Lennox Berkeley and the gifted young critic Peter Burra, Britten set off down the stinking, narrow streets of the Chino, stepping past bums and pimps, to visit a seedy nightclub, jam-packed with pickpocketing harlots and cross-dressing men, all straight out of a song by Brecht. The visit led nowhere, but Britten was at least now thinking of himself as a sexual being. In the coming months he and Burra would skate delicately around each other, each reticent about acting on the attraction he felt.

It is possible Auden was in love with Britten, though if so he was uncharacteristically silent on the subject. Isherwood thought nothing happened between the two (just as nothing happened between him and Britten). Auden's beautiful poem 'Night covers up the rigid land', which he dedicated to Britten, includes one stanza that hints at both attraction and rejection: 'For each love to its aim is true, / And all kinds seek their own; / You love your life and I love you, / So I must lie alone.' Regardless of whether it was directed at Britten (the Auden scholar and poet John Fuller thinks this is by no means certain), the implicit suggestion that Britten was able to talk about such things represents a huge advance. He was still unsure what to do, however. Back home he went for long walks, thrashing it out in his mind, solving nothing. 'Life is a pretty hefty struggle these days – sexually as well,' he wrote in his diary in June 1936. 'Decisions are so hard to make, & its difficult to look unprejudised on apparently abnormal things.' He was changing, but slowly, a prisoner of his upbringing and social censure.

The following month, when Lennox Berkeley visited Britten on his composition sabbatical in Cornwall, the two swam and sunbathed, laughed their way through study scores of Vaughan Williams and Walton symphonies, deriding the composers' clumsy efforts, and talked Mozart and Mahler. They disagreed over a few things – religion one of them (it was Berkeley who wrote to Britten about the need for faith in the face of tragedy) – but it was a harmonious and sympathetic friendship. Yet even with the evident spark between them and with Berkeley's 'avowed sexual weakness for young men of my age & form' (he was ten years older than Britten), no sustained sexual relationship developed. Britten was far keener on Piers Dunkerley, now fifteen, whom he took to the cinema, invited to tea and treated as though they were courting.

It has often been suggested that it was only with the death of his mother that Britten was released from his bind and was finally free to explore his sexuality. There is some truth in this, and the assertion is certainly not contradicted by chronology. When Ben and Bobby were sorting

out their mother's affairs in April 1937, the younger brother confided in
the older about his 'queerness', to which Bobby responded sympathetically. Yet Edith was not a Freudian puppeteer, controlling her son's every
movement. Given the circles in which Britten moved, it is unlikely he would
not have come to terms with his sexuality regardless of his mother's
probable disapproval. By mid-1936 the problem was less realizing the
nature of his sexuality, more finding an appropriate outlet for it.

Edith's death was sudden and unexpected. In October 1936 Britten
and Beth moved from the bleak West Hampstead flat to Finchley Road.
Their mother kitted out a room for herself, somewhere she could stay
when visiting Beth or attending Benny's London concerts. In January
the following year there was a severe influenza epidemic in England, to
which Beth succumbed. At Britten's prompting, Edith came to London
to care for her, only to fall ill herself. Britten moved out of the house
and on daily visits charted his mother's course through delirium, high
temperatures, incoherence and occasional lucid patches, as well as his
sister's slow return from critical status. ('Christian Scientists were busy
working on my recovery, but neglecting mum,' Beth later said, before
conceding sulpha drugs probably did the trick.) Early on 31 January
1937 Britten was summoned to the house and, on arrival, discovered his
mother had died only minutes earlier, a heart attack punctuating her
bronchial pneumonia. Britten and Barbara attempted to save Beth from
the moment of truth, acting out the macabre charade that their mother
was still alive, recovering in the room next door. But Beth soon grew
suspicious and the doctor told her the tragic news.*

Edith Britten was the most important figure in her son's life to that
point. She was the first to recognize his enormous gifts and thereafter
remained unwavering in her love and support. From their informal performances together, to the works he dedicated to her, to the loving letters
he sent from his earliest days at Gresham's through to his busy professional years in London, she was always in his thoughts. The Frinton house
was sold and each child received almost £2,000† from the estate, which
Britten soon used to put down roots, once more, in Suffolk.

---

* Chekhov rehearsed this exact scenario in his short story 'Typhus' (1886). A young soldier
contracts the disease and quickly spirals into fever and delirium, cared for by his aunt and
sister. On recovery he learns that his beloved sister caught the disease from him and died
soon after.
† Over £110,000 today.

19

He was left distraught by Edith's death. 'I lose the grandest mother a person could possibly have – & I only hope she realised that I felt like it. Nothing one can do eases the terrible ache that one feels . . .' Enid Slater, who was close to Britten in the late 1930s, thought he did not know how to fill the gap. He threw himself into work, composing for Auden and Isherwood's play *The Ascent of F6* incidental music that ended up being anything but. Isherwood was never the same influence on Britten as Auden, but there was nonetheless something appealing about this handsome, posh writer completely at ease with his sexuality, who took one look at the repressed young composer and decided to make him a project as much as a friend. 'We were extraordinarily interfering in this respect,' Isherwood later said about his and Auden's determination to make Britten confront his sexuality, 'as bossy as a pair of self-assured young psychiatrists – [Auden] wasn't a doctor's son and I wasn't an ex-medical student for nothing!'

The Ascent of F6 is noteworthy, not least for its first scene, in which the mountain-climbing hero Michael Ransom (inspired by T. E. Lawrence) is depicted reading Dante, a prototype Britten returned to in *Billy Budd*. At the government's pleading he agrees to undertake an expedition to the peak of F6, but dies in his haste to beat a team from another, hostile country. In its implicit criticism of empire and light-handed sketch of homosexual love or potential, and in its portrayal of cynical politicians using the expedition to their own ends, the play provides an accurate temperature of its creators and the decade. Britten wrote an effective score – some of it singled out in press dispatches for dishonourable mention following performances at London's Mercury Theatre – including the show-stopping Auden lyric 'Funeral Blues', which Hedli Anderson belted out as she would a Brechtian torch song, which in many ways it is. 'Stop all the clocks, cut off the telephone, / Prevent the dog from barking with a juicy bone, / Silence the pianos and with muffled drum / Bring out the coffin, let the mourners come.'*

Over the following two years Britten wrote a number of songs in the

---

* The poem became popular following its inclusion in the film *Four Weddings and a Funeral* (1994).

vein of 'Funeral Blues', each infused with the dark, smoky mood of the Berlin cabarets Auden and Isherwood knew well from the late 1920s, but which Britten had never experienced. (His closest encounters were at the Trocadero Grillroom on Piccadilly Circus, and in Paris just before his mother died where, in between visits to the Louvre, an unsuccessful attempt to find Oscar Wilde's grave and an inadvertent but traumatizing visit to a bordello, Britten and his companions took in a show at the Folies Bergères.) There is a lightness to these settings – not just the three other miniatures that, along with the brooding 'Funeral March', form his posthumously published *Cabaret Songs*, but to other Auden lyrics from these years. Auden would scribble a poem over breakfast, which often Britten took as a challenge to knock out a song from it by lunch. And composer was now more than a match for poet in terms of affectionate parody and pastiche: in 'Johnny' of 1937, a parable of unrequited love, Britten conjures first a matinee ball, then a grand opera, and then a slow, romantic waltz – all well realized. Each verse concludes with the same sullen refrain, 'But he frowned like thunder and went away', and it is difficult to hear the piece without picturing a young gay man, trapped in repeated social encounters with an enraptured woman, unable to extract himself with a courageous disclosure.

Almost thirty years later Auden spoke of his mood in 1937. '*F6* was the end. I knew I must leave [England] when I wrote it . . . I knew it because I knew then that if I stayed, I would inevitably become a member of the British establishment' – exactly the Establishment the play attacks. Spender thought this a danger for them all, writing in 1938, the year after Auden had picked up the King's Medal for poetry, that the 'English ruling classes are cleverer than any other at absorbing their opponents by a process of tolerance, invitations, and sharing out places'. (This observation would have further resonance in the 1950s.) For all these young men, the late 1930s was a time when they were forced to balance aspirations with conscience. Yet the government's censor, the Lord Chamberlain, merely tinkered with Auden and Isherwood's plays rather than rejecting them wholesale: their social critiques were heavily cloaked. Auden knew this, so while *The Ascent of F6* was still in rehearsal, he headed off to the Spanish Civil War, offering his services as an ambulance driver. 'I am not one of those who believe that poetry need or even should be directly political,' he told a friend a little before he left, 'but in a critical period such as ours, I do believe that the poet must have direct knowledge of the major political events.'

The deteriorating situation in Spain is a recurring theme in Britten's letters and diaries at this time, further evidence of his politicization under the influence of his friends. Spender outlined what he identified as the key dilemma of his political class: 'It is really simply a question of whether in the process of absorption the Left absorbs the representatives of the ruling classes, or whether they absorb the Left.' This was not Britten's dilemma before the war, though it would become so after it; in 1937 it would not have occurred to Britten to join Auden on his quixotic quest. 'Wystan can do more good back here than out there,' he told Pounder. On 8 January 1937, a day before Auden's departure, the two met in a Lyons Corner House in Tottenham Court Road – all wooden floors, studded leather chairs and art deco lighting in the brasserie, white-clothed tables and gorgeous glass-leaf sconces in the café – and made their peace over the poet's decision. 'It is terribly sad & I feel ghastly about it,' Britten wrote, 'tho' I feel it is perhaps the logical thing for him to do – being such a direct person. Anyhow it's phenomenally brave.' For his part, Auden scribbled the poem 'It's farewell to the drawing-room's civilised cry' on the published score of Britten's *Sinfonietta*, which the composer had to hand, a fitting testimony to the era. Later that year Britten made a still, intimate setting of it with slow-moving harmonies, a clock chiming throughout.

Where Spender spoke in generalities, Orwell was specific about what the Spanish Civil War meant to this generation of left-leaning artists. 'The Spanish war and other events in 1936–37 turned the scale and thereafter I knew where I stood. Every line of serious work that I have written since 1936 has been written, directly or indirectly, *against* totalitarianism and *for* democratic socialism, as I understand it.' One might expect Auden to have held an identical view, but his thoughts on the role of art as society's conscience had been zigzagging between political and apolitical stances. Spender thought the war 'offered the twentieth century an 1848', an opportunity for those with revolution on their minds to bring down the old guard.

Britten was nowhere near as extreme as Spender, managing an unexpectedly sympathetic response to King Edward VIII as the abdication crisis played out in December 1936 ('It would have been good politically to unite England & U.S.A. – she would have been an excellent Queen'). He viewed Spain as an indictment of capitalism, religion and empire, however, and thought it the role of the artist to criticize; the sleep of reason brings forth monsters, as Goya said about another Spanish war. 'However with this religious war upon one', he wrote in his diary on New Year's Day 1937, 'one only prays for courage enough to give one's life to the most useful & necessary cause, & for guidance in that direction.' His stance was close to that of his future collaborator, Communist writer Randall Swingler, who wrote a severe editorial in the *Left Review* in April 1938 arguing that the European crisis was a direct consequence of British foreign policy – 'the logical conclusion of Toryism, a Government loathed by the people, pursuing a policy odious to the people, to an outcome which could only be calamitous for the people'.

Britten reconciled his pacifism with his support for the republican cause by thinking that republicans were simultaneously underdogs and in the right. Fascism was the decade's virus and the Spanish war an attempt to find either a cure for, or an inoculation against, the German strain of the disease. Tales of Fascist brutality made their way to England. 'But what about the fascists lining up all the little Popular Front boys against a wall & putting the machine guns on them?' Britten asked his mother in July 1936, soon after the beginning of hostilities. This had to be stopped somehow.

Yet there were key differences in his response to this war and its immediate successor. The coming world war would involve him and his country in ways the Spanish war did not, and his default pacifism would be made manifest. Moreover, his ideological response to Auden's decision about Spain had its limits: 'It is also sickening as I have lots of work planned with him . . .' Or perhaps the outburst merely underlined Britten's conviction that Auden could do more for the cause in England than in Spain, where he was vulnerable to a rough martyrdom.

20

Britten contributed from England, collaborating on *Pacifist March* with writer Ronald Duncan, whom he had met in Cornwall. It is a curious little piece, jarringly martial in tone, a paradox neither man seemed to mind. Its roots are in the early-twentieth-century protest songs composed for any number of causes: women's suffrage, labour and union movements, anti-war groups. It has a whiff of proletarian uprising about it. 'In our heart we've no hate but complaint against the chain-store state; / We will build peace for earth's plenty. / March, stride to resist, strong with force not with fist.' *Advance Democracy* of 1938 is a gentler piece than *Pacifist March* but from the same mould. It is a setting for double chorus of a Swingler poem, employing the technique of seamless, meandering accompaniment, passed from voice to voice, that characterizes the fourth variation of *A Boy was Born*. The work is not subtle, but subtlety was hardly the point; Britten and Swingler were aiming to shake people from their complacency. 'Ah there's a roar of war in the factories, / And idle hands on the street, / And Europe held in nightmare / By the thud of marching feet.'

Many people thought Europe was marching blindly towards another war. Virginia Woolf dreaded its imminence: following Hitler's invasion of Austria she forecast the humiliation war would bring to an unprepared Britain, the primitive exaltation of men in uniform it would promote, the suicides to come, the refugees refused entry at Newhaven, the aeroplanes droning overhead. She would have found no argument from Britten with any of this, yet *Advance Democracy* is another awkwardly martial work.* Time to arise, Democracy, as the poem puts it – but arise for what? Gentle conversation? Polite national disagreements?

In addition to Paul Rotha's film *Peace of Britain*, plays such as Slater's *Pageant of Empire* and *Spain*, and Britten's *Russian Funeral* (a Shostakovichian march for brass and percussion) were part of a wider political response to the darkening clouds over Europe. In 1935 the charismatic, ailing Canon Dick Sheppard more or less nailed his pacifist theses to the doors of London's Royal Albert Hall, through which thousands came to join him in protest against future wars. He had roused them with an article in the *Manchester Guardian*, asking readers to send him a postcard pledging to renounce war and never again support or sanction hostilities. More than 130,000 people made the pledge. Britten was not one of them, but he did become a sponsor of the Peace Pledge Union in 1945 and remained so until his death. Sheppard edited a

* Britten later wrote music for a film of the same name, weaving a number of left-wing anthems into the end-title music, including 'The Red Flag' and the 'Internationale'. There is no musical material common to film and chorus, though both share a common purpose.

collection of essays in 1937, capturing the mood of the times in the title: *Let Us Honour Peace*, an inversion of Victor Hugo's *cri de cœur*, 'Let us dishonour war'.

The major Britten work to emerge from this increasingly febrile atmosphere, which would not appear until early 1939, was *Ballad of Heroes*. It is now rarely performed, but there is much to admire in it, beginning with the opening funeral march that gives way to a jabbing, accusatory setting of a Swingler poem, 'You who stand at your doors'. The poem is a version of Sheppard's determination to recognize and respect the Unknown Soldier by making his death mean something. 'For they have restored your power and pride, / Your life is yours, for which they died.' Then follows Britten's setting of one of the poems Auden wrote out for him when they met in the Lyons Corner House, 'It's farewell to the drawing-room's civilised cry'. Britten transformed this into a mad, skirmishing *danse macabre*, a portent of what was to come if humans stood at their doors, wiping their hands on their aprons, shrugging their shoulders at the descent into war. A return to the musical and poetical themes of the first movement closes the piece. Structurally and politically it is a dress rehearsal for *Sinfonia da Requiem* of the following year; though it is in many respects naive, and rooted in the decade in which it was composed, the characteristics of Britten's mature full-orchestral sound and his rhetorical technique were now much in evidence.

The use of funeral marches was not always political. Originally they served a function in funerals or memorial services – Mozart's *Maurerische Trauermusik*, composed in memory of two Masonic brethren, or Purcell's funeral music for Queen Mary. But these were actual events: it took Handel to make the funeral march popular in the theatre and concert hall, which then gave it more currency on the street.* Britten sometimes considered the march a political statement, sometimes not. Between 1936 and 1941, between *Russian Funeral* and *Scottish Ballad*, he composed seven 'serious' pieces with funeral marches. Additionally there were a few incidental scores, including the classic 'Funeral Blues'

---

* When news of the warrior king's death reaches Israel in Handel's oratorio *Saul*, a solemn Dead March plays; this same march later became a staple of English royal funerals – literally music fit for a king. Beethoven's Symphony No. 3 'Eroica', written as a tribute to Napoleon, contains a majestically poised march. (Nelson, who died routing Napoleon's navy at Trafalgar, had to make do with the Handel.) Chopin turned the genre into key Romantic imagery, which Berlioz and Mahler then developed.

and the 'Lament' movement of his collaboration with Berkeley, *Mont Juic* (subtitled 'Barcelona, July 1936'). Here was an ideal marriage between form and function, the inspiration political, not personal. Yet in the late 1930s Britten was devouring as much of Mahler's music as he could – unusual since Mahler's rehabilitation was still some years away – and began emulating certain of his practices. His touching 'Funeral March for a Boy' in the cantata *The Company of Heaven* (1937) is the purest Mahler.

It was not just the form of Mahler's music that appealed, but also its inherent sad beauty. Writing to his friend Henry Boys in June 1937 Britten addressed the influence of the great composer on his music, in particular the final movement – 'Der Abschied' (Farewell) – of *Das Lied von der Erde*. It is the most open and personal thing Britten ever wrote about music, and it points to the confusion and yearning he then felt, this young man determined to be old.

> It is cruel, you know, that music should be so beautiful. It has the beauty of loneliness & of pain: of strength & freedom. The beauty of disappointment & never-satisfied love. The cruel beauty of nature, and everlasting beauty of monotony.
>
> And the essentially 'pretty' colours of the normal orchestral palette are used to paint this extraordinary picture of loneliness. And there is nothing morbid about it. The same harmonic progressions that Wagner used to colour his essentially morbid love-scenes (his 'Liebes' is naturally followed by 'Tod') are used here to paint a serenity literally supernatural. I cannot understand it – it passes over me like a tidal wave – and that matters not a jot either, because it goes on for ever, even if it is never performed again – that final chord is printed on the atmosphere.

Mahler could be both ambiguous and mischievous about the programmatic meaning of his works and came to regret the way speculation overtook certain symphonies, imbuing them in the public imagination with meanings he did not intend. Britten tended not to comment on his own musical purposes. Only *Sinfonia da Requiem* has a specific Mahlerian programme: it is a memorial to his parents, in particular his mother, whose passing 'had an especially powerful emotional effect on me and set me, in self-defence, analysing my feelings in regard to suffering and death. To this personal tragedy were soon added the more general world tragedies of the Spanish and the present wars.' So even when Britten protested otherwise, the backdrop to these marches suggests a lament for his times, one which would be played out, both internationally and personally, in 1939.

2 1

Though Bridge was less of an immediate presence in Britten's life in these pre-war years, his pupil made up for it with an extraordinarily bold and mature work, *Variations on a Theme of Frank Bridge*. In May 1937 the one-time naval officer and doctor Boyd Neel, who, five years previously (in a very English way), had formed his own orchestra, was invited to bring his band to the Salzburg Festival that August on the proviso that he give the premiere of a new English work. Neel had conducted the first broadcast of Britten's *Simple Symphony* in May 1935 and worked with him again the following year on the Ann Harding and Basil Rathbone thriller *Love from a Stranger* (for which Britten earned £200 – ten months' salary at the GPO). Neel was struck each time by Britten's speed and creativity and turned to him for the Salzburg piece. In under two weeks Britten dutifully arrived at Neel's house with the work fully sketched; four weeks later it was fully scored. The fair copy went to Boosey & Hawkes, and days later the orchestra was rehearsing. Suddenly the small marches and incidental scores of the previous twelve months were embarrassing trifles: here was an audacious and substantial new work.

Britten considered Elgar's *Enigma Variations* cloying – too thick, inflexible and prone to triteness. 'I listened with an open mind, but cannot say that I was less annoyed by them than usual,' he wrote of a Queen's Hall performance of the piece in 1931. 'I suppose it's my fault, and there is something lacking in me, that I am absolutely incapable of enjoying Elgar, for more than 2 minutes.' But he was happy to filch the work's guiding principle (as he had done in his youthful *Two Portraits* and *Three Character Pieces*): a composer's friends portrayed musically, here in variation form. Britten went one better: he created a portrait of just one person, capturing his mentor's different attributes in a series of variations – 'His integrity', 'His wit', 'His skill', etc. Britten took the theme from the second of Bridge's early *Three Idylls* for string quartet (1906) and set about sketching the man in music. He relied on a number of commonplace styles or forms: a wistful Viennese waltz, a careering *moto perpetuo*, a strumming *aria Italiana*. It too contains a funeral march and, to be expected, a fugue ('His skill'). The piece is at once insouciant, touching and assured. There are hints of Berg, but the colossal personalities here are Britten and Bridge, the latter's seriousness, humour and vitality captured well.

Britten dedicated the work 'To F.B. A tribute with affection and admiration.' Bridge responded, 'Thank you & thank you, Benjie. What a great pleasure! And "ain't I glad" I love the work itself? I like to think of you just forging ahead & perhaps the most pleasant reflection is that you should have come into my life just when you did. Of course I should say *our* lives because Ethel & I are united in our devotion to you.' It was reparation from both parties after the disappointment of *Our Hunting Fathers*. Neel described the concert premiere on 27 August as a 'major sensation' with the conservative Salzburg audience, a view reflected in press reports. Work commitments prevented Britten from attending the premiere, but a new friend, Peter Pears, was in the audience and echoed Neel's line: 'I think there can be no doubt about it that the Variations were a great success, as indeed the orchestra was and Boyd Neel.'

In a photograph of the schoolboy Pears, taken in 1927 or thereabouts, he is seated at the piano, surrounded by fellow members of the Lancing Chamber Music Society – a grand title for such an unprepossessing gypsy band. He has Rupert Brooke's hypnotic, questioning eyes. One of his boxer's paws rests on his knee. His fellow student Peter Burra stands behind him, violin in hand. The photograph captures so well the Pears of the coming decade – the mixture of confidence and uncertainty, handsome looks and slightly ungainly body – and Burra as guardian angel.

Unlike Britten's family background, the sheep in Pears's lineage were mostly white: an academic turned priest; an army man turned educator; a string of merchants, home and abroad; still more army officers, still more clergy. Pears's father was a director of Burma Railways, and, until he retired in 1923 when Pears turned thirteen, he was rarely in England. Pears's mother was often with her husband in India and Burma, hence the boarding schools, Pears's hazy memories of his father in his early life and his complicated relationship with both parents later.

At Lancing he was a musical but ungifted pianist and a poor bassoonist. His apprenticeship came about because he was drunk on

Christianity, gaining a taste of his future trade by singing in the chapel choir at twice daily services, three times on Sunday. He was comfortable in his homosexuality, though possibly had not yet acted on it. He had a knockabout charm and an ordinary intellect, which got him entry to Oxford to read music, but no further: he came down after two terms, having failed Mods. Thereafter, like Auden, he took a job in a prep school, where he remained until the end of 1933. In the last months of his final year as a schoolmaster, he combined teaching with studies at the RCM. This was Britten's final term at college, though the two did not meet. A successful audition for the BBC's Wireless Vocal Octet (later the BBC Singers) initiated Pears's departure from the RCM in 1934 after only a year of study. At the time he did not have a particularly large or secure voice, nor was it yet resolutely a tenor.

Burra, having met Britten in Barcelona and written to Pears about him, brought the two together. Following his sudden death in an aeroplane accident in late April 1937, Britten offered to help Pears with the sad ritual of sorting out their friend's belongings, removing any sexually incriminating materials (a cache of photographs of young blond men in summer clothing, as it turned out). Thereafter, Pears (or, tellingly, 'Piers') turns up frequently in Britten's diary. 'He's a dear – & I'm glad I'm going to live with him,' Britten wrote on 8 September, foreshadowing the apartment they would take together the following March. At this stage it was only friendship; regardless of how intimate their rapport, this large-framed, slightly older man could not have been more different from the whippet-thin boys who then caught Britten's eye.

One such boy was Harry Morris, a thirteen-year-old from a poor London family whom Barbara knew through her work. He was good-looking, musical and responded warmly to Britten's attention and treats, one of which was a holiday in Cornwall in August 1937. Auden and Isherwood were just then acting as something between confessors and sirens in the twenty-three-year-old Britten's life. 'He gives me sound advice about many things,' Britten wrote after a long dinner with Isherwood in June, '& he being a grand person I shall possibly take it.' It was not all talk: Isherwood followed up his advice a week later by taking Britten to a notorious Turkish bath in Jermyn Street, an Aladdin's cave of treasures and pleasures, a literal hotbed of male homosexual potential and excess. 'Very pleasant sensations – completely sensuous, but very healthy. It is extraordinary to find one's resistance to anything gradually weakening.'

Given these experiences, it would be surprising if Britten's thoughts on his role as mentor to young Harry did not conflict with his sexual tastes.

Morris thought they did, telling first his mother on his early return from the holiday, and then much later his wife and son, that Britten made a sexual advance towards him, Morris repelling him with a scream and a chair. The cry brought Beth running into the room, where she quickly sized up the situation. John Bridcut wonders whether Britten would have seen Harry for tea after the holiday, or visited his family to offer advice about his education, had a clumsy attempt at seduction occurred. Yet Harry was adamant all his life that he had not misread Britten's intentions and remained distressed by the memory.

The London flat Britten was to share with Pears was an obvious necessity; all his work was centred on the capital. But Britten's heart was in Suffolk, and just before the Cornwall holiday he bought an old mill and adjoining cottage in Snape, a small village six miles from Crabbe's Aldeburgh, right on the River Alde. It was a slightly eccentric, free-spirited purchase: Snape was isolated and the mill far from ready for occupation. There was much structural and cosmetic work to be done, and for this he turned to Arthur Welford, father of Beth's fiancé Christopher (Kit), an architect and a generous man who offered to undertake the project for no fee. Moreover, Welford's large house in Peasenhall became Britten's Suffolk bolthole while the contracts were drawn up and the renovations getting under way. Together they discussed ideas and sketched plans: the round mill house would be converted into a studio with a spiral staircase up to the bedroom. A balcony would be added to a third of the mill's circumference, offering uninterrupted views across the adjoining marshes and fields. A single-storey corridor, housing various rooms, would join cottage and mill, while a granary already connected to the cottage would have windows and a fireplace added. It was a young man's house and an impulsive decision, but it established a pattern of living that Britten retained all his life.

2 2

He remained under the spell of Auden's poetry, dipping into the collection *Look, Stranger!* (1936) for a series of modest, uneven yet affecting songs. Some of these he published as *On This Island*; others he wrote for a potential second volume that never appeared. The published songs, which display a neat understanding of Auden's mood, if not always meaning – a mixture of love, desire and politics – were premiered by Britten and Wyss in a BBC broadcast on 19 November 1937. It was an obvious home for them, given Britten's ongoing relationship with different departments of the sprawling Corporation – religion, features, music. It was also one of the last of Britten's works to be looked at by Bridge, whose involvement in the collection underlines how much their relationship had shifted. Bridge had strong views on the opening of the first song, 'Let the florid music praise!', which in an early draft began with a downward piano glissando. 'Bridge hated that, and said I was trying to make a side-drum or something non-tonal out of the instrument.' It was not as benign as that. Marjorie Fass saw Bridge emerging from the particular lesson, muttering to her that 'never again wld he try & help Benjy over his work, as some of the things he pointed out, the boy simply wldn't alter, so why waste his time & energy'. 'But they're *my* songs,' Britten exploded at Fass when she remonstrated with him, only later guiltily changing the song's opening bars into the Handelian fanfare we know today.

Fass blamed Britten's truculence on Auden and Isherwood, not for the last time. 'The thing that is bad for him is that he's meeting brilliant people who are not brilliant in *his* sphere, but their own, & so make a mutual admiration society . . .' It was a fair observation, though one informed by a tinge of regret or jealousy that the artistic and intellectual environment at Friston was being sidelined. It can be read both ways – the Friston crowd's sadness at losing brilliant, 'spoilt young Benjy', or Britten's impatience for those around him to recognize that his musical apprenticeship was over. 'I know he is in a mental muddle abt a great deal & dreads the future,' continued Fass. 'He really hates growing up & away from a very happy childhood that ended only with his Mother's death last Christmas.'

The BBC reinforced Britten's view of himself and his crowd, and the radio commissions were more elaborate than anything he wrote for theatre or film, far closer in spirit and structure to his concert works. Some were a little creaky – D. G. Bridson's *King Arthur*, for example, or *The Company of Heaven* and *The World of the Spirit*, the last two programmes of text and music settings devised by the literary critic Richard Ellis Roberts, one eye on the afterlife. They nonetheless hint at future pieces. Both of the religious scores incorporate re-harmonized hymn tunes – something both Auden and Britten enjoyed doing at the piano when in their cups – a practice to which Britten returned so affectingly in *Saint Nicolas* and *Noye's Fludde*. The BBC Chorus sang in *The Company of Heaven*, and Britten obliged his new friend Pears with a short yet ecstatic solo ('he makes it sound charming. He is a good singer & a first-rate musician').

Creaky or not, the works paid well: a big job such as *The Company of Heaven* earned Britten just over £50. With such commissions, Britten's gross income in 1937–8 was £364,* the lion's share of it from royalties and BBC fees. He was hardly affluent: a journalist then earned £10 to £15 per week; in the late 1920s Virginia Woolf famously suggested that £500 was the minimum income a woman required, in addition to a room of one's own, if she were to be free to write. Britten had the room, but not yet the income. This all soon changed: a year later, no longer writing for the GPO, Britten's gross income was a few shillings shy of £600, his PRS income and broadcast fees having increased in multiples.

The extra money did not change Britten much; his habits remained ascetic, his work ethic strong. It allowed him a more stylish car (a Lea Francis saloon, which he crashed and replaced with a modest Morris Eight), and it gave him more confidence in his future. It also allowed him nicer homes. After much hunting, in March 1938 Britten and Pears moved into a flat in Earls Court, in a square of imposing terraces overlooking a gated garden. A month later the Old Mill in Snape was ready, which he was to share with Lennox Berkeley.

Neither Berkeley nor Pears managed to transform his intensifying friendship with Britten into anything more lasting or intimate during 1937–8. Berkeley had given it a good shot as early as April 1937, Britten gently turning him down: 'he is a dear & I am very, very fond of him; nevertheless, it is a comfort that we can arrange sexual matters to at least *my* satisfaction', his diary as opaque as ever. Pears shared some of Britten's sexual reticence. From Glyndebourne, singing in the chorus for *Don Pasquale* and *Macbeth* (remarkably, its first professional production in England), he told his new friend in June 1938 he was 'running mildly after a sweet tough Stage Hand but as usual I can't come to the

---

* A little over £20,000 today.

point!!' But so too was it his hesitation at entering a fully fledged relationship, for whatever reason.

There was an enormous difference between the sort of boys Auden and Isherwood picked up and those to whom Britten found himself drawn – the predominantly young, middle-class, prep-school types, such as Dunkerley and Barton – and this is where both Pears and Berkeley fell short. Auden and Isherwood sought like-minded young men – sexually sorted, up for an adventure. There was at the time plenty of currency to the Forsterian notion of finding love or sexual experience in the arms of a working-class young man who was homosexual by nature or grateful for the extra income and the entrée into a social or artistic milieu that came with the territory. Those so inclined could view such liaisons as political; cross-class relationships were a sign of a progressive society, were they not? The young men in such relationships were thought to be able to look after themselves, hence the lax attitude, by today's standards, toward their age. But this attitude was also a direct offshoot of the law. Whereas the 1885 Criminal Law Amendment Act prescribed the heterosexual age of consent at sixteen, no such minimum existed for homosexual sex. The same Act extended the so-called buggery laws to cover *any* sexual activity between men; homosexual relations with an adult were as illegal as they were with a fourteen-year-old boy.*

It was predominantly a mix of paternalism and political commitment that prompted Britten to open the Old Mill to a Basque refugee boy in late April 1938, a matter of weeks after moving in himself. A comedy of manners ensured that this poor fish out of water stayed only two weeks, but it was a further reiteration of Britten's attachment to boys of twelve or thirteen. It was therefore somewhat out of character for Britten, in June, to write to Wulff Scherchen, now a good-looking, willowy eighteen-year-old schoolboy, living with his mother in Cambridge. 'I do not know whether you will remember me or not – but in 1934 – during the Festival of Modern Music in Florence – we spent a long time together – especially one day in Siena.'

There was no particular reason for Britten to think Scherchen gay; they had met when the boy was only thirteen, and Britten had a bad

---

* Hence Isherwood, aged thirty-three or thirty-four, sleeping with 'a genuine teenage stud' at a New York brothel in 1938. 'Looking back, I get the impression that [this boy] jumped from adolescence to middle age without ever pausing to be a young man.'

nose for such things, anyway. But Scherchen was a refreshing departure from Britten's type. He was older and came from an artistic family; he was brought up in Germany, a country without the peculiarly English brand of moralizing and sexual hypocrisy, and had his own artistic side, a love of literature. And though he would go on to marry and have children, he was then relaxed enough in himself to embark on a close friendship, then relationship, with another man. He responded immediately and effusively to Britten's letter, including a sub-Byronic description of his happy memories of Siena ('pleasant reminiscences of a glorious past!'). Arrangements were made for Wulff to visit Snape in July.

23

If it took a while for the relationship to catch fire, Britten's hectic schedule and Scherchen's summer travels with his father were at fault. In June Britten was busy finishing his Piano Concerto, commissioned by the BBC, its premiere to be in an August Promenade Concert under Henry Wood. The previous December Hawkes had mentioned a possible concerto to Kenneth Wright, the BBC's assistant director of music, who jumped at the idea. Britten would be both composer and soloist, and his previously vague thoughts on a concerto now had a deadline. Here, finally, was the opportunity for him to seal his reputation as an eminent composer-pianist in the Romantic tradition.

The BBC held certain expectations of these concerts, as it did of the concerto it was commissioning. With its cheap tickets and programmes of popular warhorses leavened by 'novelties', the Promenade Concerts attracted a sizeable, passionate audience whose diet was enlarged by Wood's catholic tastes and the BBC's broad cultural remit. In 1938 all the Beethoven and Brahms symphonies were programmed, as were two or three each by Haydn, Mozart, Schubert, Dvořák, Tchaikovsky and Sibelius. There were ten concertos for violin, twenty-nine for one or two pianos, and fifty chunks bitten from Wagner's corpulent oeuvre. The commission was a tricky undertaking for a composer whose music was admired in specialist circles, derided in others, and unknown to the great majority of concertgoers. Hawkes knew this: his 1937 Christmas present to Britten was a handful of piano concerto scores, to be consulted where necessary.

Britten wrote the work at speed in Peasenhall, Earls Court and Snape, zipping between the three as he organized his new residences and tossed off *The World of the Spirit* in time for its June broadcast. There were ballet galas and informal concerts to attend (through which to woo prospective patrons), and much discussion with friends and colleagues about potential projects large and small, feasible and ridiculous. It was a busy time, and in the wide range of commitments and collaborations it was unlike any previous period in his life. He was at Snape in early May to receive Hawkes's splendid housewarming present – a high-quality radiogram, which picked up 'any station from Omsk to Tomsk', as Britten phrased it in his letter of thanks. In June he was at the ISCM Festival in London for performances of *Variations on a Theme of Frank Bridge* and his violin Suite, where he met and befriended Aaron Copland, whose *El salón México* caught his ear. Britten recommended him to Hawkes, who signed him up. The gift and this recommendation were symptomatic of the easygoing, mutually respectful relationship composer and publisher had developed by the late 1930s. Britten was fond of Hawkes, enjoyed his company and old-money ways, while for his part Hawkes was attentive to his artist, alert for opportunities, one eye on the fast-developing music industry in London, another on the stately, almost European scene in New York.

Britten finished the concerto in July and was elated with the result. The feeling lasted all the way through the first and second informal play-throughs, orchestrating, constructing the full score and rehearsals with Wood. After the first of these he told Hawkes that it 'certainly sounds "*popular*" enough', which is what both men had intended. The performance on 18 August 1938 – a wash of shirt studs and tailcoats – gave him his first popular success. When it was over, a crowd awaited him outside the artists' entrance to Queen's Hall, mobbing him as though he were a movie star.

He received a critical larruping for the piece, however, which says a little about the concerto and a lot about the make-up of the English music establishment at the decade's end. 'This is not a stylish work. Mr Britten's cleverness, of which he has frequently been told, has got the better of him and led him into all sorts of errors, the worst of which are errors of taste,' wrote William McNaught in the *Musical Times*. The *Christian Science Monitor*'s critic thought the 'concerto is, in the best sense of the word, youthful; its weaknesses are mostly those of youth'.

And the Elgar devotee and one-time composer Ferruccio Bonavia reported in the *Daily Telegraph* that 'Mr Britten will do better things and more substantial things when his thoughts turn, as they must, to matter rather than manner'.

It is easy to write off these observations as throwbacks to an earlier time in English music. Too many are simply variations on the critical shorthand that dogged Britten in the second half of the 1930s: facility over substance. The *Musical Times* said much the same thing about his Frank Bridge tribute after its June ISCM outing. 'Britten's Variations for string orchestra, brilliantly written though they are, do not wear well, and fail to achieve coherence as a whole.' The anonymous *Observer* critic who reviewed the work's first London performance the year before was terser. 'Mr Britten's Variations were worse than we have been told, but better than we had feared.' He was described in turn as clever, ineffective, undeveloped, promising, a bright young star fading, an exploiter of a brilliant faculty, a sower of wild oats and a fritterer of natural gifts.

The Bridge circle, however, came to much the same conclusion about the Piano Concerto. The day after the premiere Fass wrote to her friend Daphne Oliver:

> I expect you'll have been as disappointed in Benjy's work as we were & loving him so much made it difficult for us, as we cldn't hurt his feelings before the event, as the knowledge of our opinion would easily have done. In one way, because he has so many young friends who adore & flatter him for his brilliant talent & who only live on the superficial side of life, it won't hurt him at all, but pull him up, if the criticisms in the papers are harsh. The orchestra & Wood liked the work very much – as it's amusing to play – & every orchestral device is employed with brilliance. – but of *music or [originality]* there is no trace – And if Benjy develops some day later on, he will see the insignificance of this work as it must be to all real musicians.

There is much to unpack in this pen-sketch – the devotion, the suspicion of the Bright Young Things with whom Britten now associated, the question mark over his achievement and potential, and the tense play-acting by his mentor and friends that must have followed the concert.

The concerto is by no means as bad as Fass made out. Britten's melodic gifts let him down in the final movement, though, given the ironic and political associations of much of his music at the time, it is impossible to believe that the rather gawky march has no deliberately bland martial connotations. Britten was clearly unhappy with the original third movement, with its Rachmaninovesque big tune: he replaced it in his 1945 revision with a downcast Impromptu, a long-limbed piano melody from which he conjured a series of set-piece variations, the grand theme in the final movement of Prokofiev's Piano Concerto No. 3 evidently on his mind. Yet the Toccata does just what it sets out to do – channel the spirit of Liszt – while the Waltz, which starts as a whimsical dialogue between piano and individual instruments before whipping up a Viennese ballroom frenzy, is at once sardonic and serious. The new piece was a perfectly credible vehicle for Britten the performer; once the few subsequent performances were completed, Britten would never again be heard in such virtuosic concerto repertory.

Yet even its weaknesses (and those of other Britten works in the late 1930s) do not fully explain the critical antagonism. Some of it stemmed from the instability of the industry in London in this decade. Everything was new: electrical recording, broadcasting, orchestras, full-time orchestral contracts, a PRS with teeth and income, disproportionate unemployment fuelled by the near-overnight disbandment of cinema orchestras. Comparison between the London orchestras and those in Vienna or Berlin might still have been invidious, but the standards of the LPO and the BBC Symphony Orchestra were far ahead of the cash-strapped ensembles of the century's first three decades. There were new journals to report the activities of the BBC and new journalists to write in them. Jewish immigration after 1933 caused much unrest among London musicians: the posturing Incorporated Society of Musicians worked hard to prevent the country from being 'overrun with every class of foreign musician' (its actual target only slightly veiled), while its new president, Beecham, complained in 1939 how unfair it was that a small section of the community was expected to absorb a disproportionate share of émigrés. This protectionist line had been pushed by the Musicians' Union for different reasons at the beginning of the decade when it argued for a general ban on 'foreign artists of no reputation and of mediocre attainments'. No blanket ban ensued, though the union was happy enough to flex its muscles to prevent certain foreign soloists from performing in England when the occasion or interested party demanded.

1. Britten's substantial childhood home at 21 Kirkley Cliff Road, Lowestoft, Suffolk.

2. The view from the Britten house towards the mercurial North Sea, which exerted a strong influence on Britten's music from childhood onwards.

3. The cast of *The Water Babies*, Sparrow's Nest Theatre, Lowestoft, June 1919. Britten as Tom sits on his mother's lap.

4. Prosperous middle-class English life after the First World War: Robert and Edith Britten host a tea party at 21 Kirkley Cliff Road. Britten and Beth (*right*) sit on the ground with a friend.

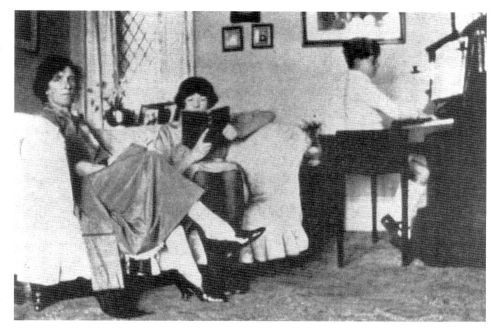

5. Life at home: a fierce-looking Edith Britten listening to her son, aged eight or nine, playing the family piano, as her daughter Beth reads.

6. Britten on the Lowestoft seafront, around 1929.

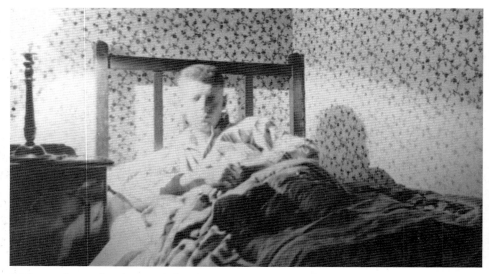

7. The student in his digs on the Cromwell Road, London, *c.* 1932.

8. Britten and his great teacher and mentor Frank Bridge, 1930. 'I heard conversations which centred round the arts; I heard the latest poems discussed, and the latest trends in painting and sculpture.'

9. Britten in the Old Mill, Snape, which he bought in 1937 and moved into the following year after renovations were complete. Ralph Hawkes's housewarming present, a high-quality radiogram able to pick up 'any station from Omsk to Tomsk', is in the foreground.

10. The Old Mill, *c.* 1940.

11. 'Oh my darling, I love you. Yours ever, Wulff.' Wulff Scherchen in the late 1930s. Britten carried one of Scherchen's poems in his wallet for years.

12. Britten with his lifelong love, Peter Pears, at the Old Mill, *c.* 1943.

13. Two Englishmen abroad: Britten and Pears at Jones Beach, Long Island, *c.* 1940.

14. 'I always feel very young & stupid when with these brains – I mostly sit silent when they hold forth about subjects in general.' The composer and librettist of *Paul Bunyan* in New York, April 1941. Despite (or because of) Britten's sense of intellectual inadequacy, W. H. Auden had a significant influence on him for more than a decade.

15. 'The trees they grow so high . . .'
Britten with Bobby Rothman,
to whom he formed a doting
attachment, Amityville,
Long Island,
c. 1940–41.

16. Britten rehearsing a new
style in America, c. 1939–40.

17. American liberation, c. 1939–40.

If musicians struggled to keep up with the quicksand culture, critics could hardly be expected to do better. Some were protected by anonymous bylines and wrote accordingly. Others were new to the job, grabbing opportunities where they saw them (Burra); still others had cut their teeth in a time before the seismic changes of infrastructure (Bonavia). This was a climate of fear, ignorance, novelty, opportunity and opportunism, and into it came a modern English composer more talented than any other the critics had seen or written about. Some were perceptive: there were weak pieces, though Britten was temperamentally unable to see or accept this from them. Others were decidedly not, but critics had no ears or point of reference, and found themselves parroting the damaging critical line about Britten's easy facility and empty heart. Either way, their intemperate language, their connection to a part of the industry Britten held in low esteem at the best of times, and their jejune analyses drip-fed the disillusionment Britten came to feel for his country and profession in the last years of the 1930s. They made his decision to leave that much simpler.

24

'And what about its effect on a certain person of importance?' Auden asked a few days after the concerto's premiere. Scherchen had tuned in to the broadcast and written an appreciative note, boldly venturing that he found the last movement 'pompous', earning a touchy reprimand. In the weeks that followed there were many letters, much making of plans, and growing intimacy. Auden sent Britten a guide to seduction: stay at home with him rather than go out; play the piano; appear comparatively indifferent emotionally; be friendly, but cold; take no notice if rebuffed. 'Permanando vincimus', he signed off humorously ('we conquer by penetrating', a pun on 'permanendo vincimus' – 'we conquer by persevering'), though Britten's poor Latin at South Lodge almost certainly left him with insufficient facility to translate the questionable advice.

Encouraged by Britten, Scherchen started writing poetry – a creative outlet certainly, but it was also a vehicle for expression of the unspoken and ambiguous, a map for uncharted waters. A poem written in October,

soon after Britten had visited the Scherchens in Cambridge for the third
time, suggests things were not quite as ambiguous as all that:

> I love you, oh, beyond all comprehension.
> but should I not restrain and guide that love?
> for can I give you aught that you already not possess?
> your music calls and I become your slave
> yet linger I and dare not go, nor dare I stay.

Both of them were new to relationships, but were doing just fine. In letters between them in the lead-up to Christmas, which Scherchen was to
spend at the Old Mill, the cloak of poetry was unnecessary. 'Oh my darling, I love you. Yours ever, Wulff . . . I'm feeling absolutely desolate.
Don't ever leave me darling. xxxx'.

Britten's first Christmas in his new home was a week of meals, visits,
tobogganing and, probably around New Year, consummation of his
relationship with Wulff. Scherchen conceived a poem in the last two
days of 1938, which he completed on 10 January 1939 and 'dedicated
to B. as part-payment of an unpayable gift: his friendship.'

> lost to the worlds,
> beyond all stars,
> alone, yet one,
> two beings lie.
>
> oblivion rules
> their minds, their hearts,
> while tranquil there,
> voluptuous, they love.
>
> away from hate,
> above all scorn,
> but in their love,
> they know existence.
>
> time has no sense,
> music no charms,
> beauty is lost,
> in lover's frenzy.

Britten folded the poem wallet-size and carried it with him for years.

Scherchen was later embarrassed about the sexual aspects of his time with Britten, if justly proud of the emotional connection between them, and he dissembled when describing their relationship. Yet this was a true love affair, and, perhaps unexpectedly, Britten took to it speedily and naturally. He was attentive, affectionate, quasi-paternal and clearly enjoyed the physical dimension. ('Good-night, my darling – wish "lost to the world" were going to be appropriate to-night & all other nights too,' he wrote to Scherchen on 22 January.) There were meals together and visits to Cambridge, and Scherchen was introduced to Britten's circle of friends and collaborators. Coldstream wrote of a party at the new flat in Hallam Street, W1, into which Pears and Britten moved in January 1939, which was a gay old affair. Guests included Auden and a boy he had picked up, Isherwood and his new boyfriend, Spender and his girlfriend, Pears, 'a German boy friend of Benjamin's', and Hedli Anderson, who sat on the piano and sang her way through some of the *Cabaret Songs*. It was an entrancing milieu for Scherchen. There were jealous outbursts from Berkeley, who could not quite understand why Scherchen had succeeded where he had failed. But mostly the Auden crowd was delighted that Britten had finally dived in and found the water to his liking. 'To my friend Benjamin Britten, composer, I beg / That fortune send him soon a passionate affair', Auden had written two years earlier in his collaboration with Louis MacNeice, *Letters from Iceland*. Here it was.

But things quickly went wrong. Perhaps Pears was playing a long game, doing what he could to prise Britten away from his young lover. It is true Britten and Pears had become close, and there was no one else in the singer's life. And the idea to go to America originated not with Britten but with Pears, who had planned to spend a few months there rekindling friendships and contacts before returning to England after the summer. (Britten reneged on an earlier plan to go there with Berkeley.) But this does not explain why Britten lost his nerve or his interest in Scherchen. It would be tempting to say the relationship just fizzled out, were it not for the contradictory letters sent by Britten in the following months. 'I got heavily tied up in a certain direction, which is partly why I'm crossing the ocean!' he told Copland in May 1939. Yet simultaneously he was sending Scherchen letters overloaded with sentiment. 'Much love, my darling, it's still horrible being away from you – & I'm looking forward terribly to seeing you again – it won't be long – luckily time goes very fast.'

Britten stopped keeping his diary around the time he first wrote to Scherchen, but the correspondence in these months paints him as confused and conflicted. For all the excitement and sensuality of his first sustained relationship, he seems not to have been convinced a few months in that the two of them formed a good match. Perhaps Britten's paternalistic approach prevented them from meeting as equals and the relationship from developing. There were other factors. Asked to meet Britten one night, Scherchen was shocked to discover their rendezvous point was a gay bar. The environment repelled him – as it probably did Britten, or would do soon. It put an uncomfortable label on his relationship with Britten, and made him wary about their future.

Meanwhile, Berkeley was once more trying his hand, which revolted Britten and reinforced the desire to escape. Whatever physical relationship had come into being between the two, and whatever hopes Berkeley held for their future together when he became the lodger at the Old Mill, Britten was having none of it. 'Hedli, what a bloody fool I was about all that,' he wrote harshly to Anderson in late 1939. 'One sees so much more clearly when one's away. He's just NO GOOD.'

Complicated relationships were not the only spur. There was talk of a Hollywood film, which if it were to happen would make a trip to America necessary. And he just could not shake the feeling that he was unappreciated in England, which the cool critical response to the Piano Concerto reinforced. 'One had a struggle to get things performed,' he said in 1959. 'It was frustration that sent me to America. I felt there was a wall of laziness and apathy against new things.'

This was a disingenuous characterization of the last months of 1938 and early 1939, when Britten's works were performed almost as soon as he finished them. It is more that after the Piano Concerto he was preoccupied with music for various films and theatre works (including another Auden–Isherwood play, *On the Frontier*, in November, and J. B. Priestley's *Johnson over Jordan* in February), which he did not consider real music. He was frustrated with himself for needing the work when he would much have preferred to be writing his own music. Yet in composing for a major new Priestley play, he was working with theatrical royalty – an eminent left-wing author and playwright (he would end up on Orwell's notorious post-war list of card-carrying Communists and fellow travellers) who was successful and passionate about music. There was potential for future collaborations, which would keep Britten in bread and ale while his reputation as a serious composer developed. The BBC also provided him with plenty of opportunities: on 21 April 1939 it broadcast a programme devoted to Britten's art music, which included two Rimbaud settings, completed only a month earlier, of what would become *Les Illuminations*. Britten recognized the broadcast as an important event. 'You see – the first *complete* concert of one's music is a pretty good trial – & the fact that it was a great success makes one rather bucked,' he wrote proudly and admonishingly to Scherchen, who had missed the broadcast.

There was one final element in his indecision and confusion, the most poignant by far. As Hitler marched his troops into Bohemia and Moravia in mid-March, contravening the Munich Agreement Chamberlain had brandished with such hollow confidence the previous September, Britten became desperate at the disintegrating situation in Europe, which tied together a number of the political, social and artistic threads then preoccupying him.

> After Munich the morale of Europe seemed about as low as it could get. Things were becoming steadily more rotten ... Not that I was running away from war when I went to America. At that time – the spring of 1939 – there was no certainty that war was coming. But I wanted to have nothing to do with a military system that, to me, was part of Europe's decay. Mistakenly, as it turned out, I felt that Europe was finished. And it seemed to me that the New World was so much *newer*, so much readier to welcome new things.

This idea had currency late in the decade. Thomas Mann, an emblem of Old World culture, announced in 1938 that America was to be his new home. 'For the duration of the present European dark age the centre of Western culture will shift to America,' he grimly predicted. Likewise, Walter Benjamin, attempting to extract himself from Denmark in late 1938, two years before his suicide, was unsure 'how long it will continue to be physically possible to breathe European air'.

Britten's eloquent memories of the reasons he left England were those of a mature, successful man many years after the events he describes, yet his diary in the late 1930s plainly charts his disquiet over Hitler and the rise of National Socialism. 'Think of Wien, under Nazi control,' he wrote on 13 March 1938, one day after German troops marched into Austria to considerable public jubilation from political sympathizers,

'– no more Mahler, no lightness, no culture, nothing but their filthy, lewd, heartiness, their despicable conceit, & unutterable stupidity.' When in September 1938 Basil Wright suggested they put forward the Piano Concerto for the following year's Baden-Baden Festival, Britten firmly quashed the idea. There was no Semitic blood in his family, he responded to Wright's enquiry. 'But I shouldn't bother about anything in Germany for me or the Concerto – because, even if you succeeded in getting a date for me there, I don't feel I could accept it. Admittedly music has nothing to do with politics – but when politics pokes its slimy finger into music that's a different matter.'

The spiralling political situation preoccupied Auden and Isherwood. Their melodrama *On the Frontier*, which they dedicated to Britten, is a thinly veiled account of life under Hitler, a fictional war being waged against a neighbouring country. It was their English swansong, for on a bitterly cold day in early 1939 the two sailed for America. In doing so they were in one way replicating a pattern of 1920s and 1930s literary England: Norman Douglas, Aldous Huxley, Bertrand Russell, Somerset Maugham, Stephen Spender, Osbert and Edith Sitwell, Julian Bell, Katherine Mansfield, Evelyn and Alec Waugh, Graham Greene, Robert Graves and Lawrence Durrell were just some of the English writers who left their homeland in these decades, however temporarily, seeking a more conducive and creative environment. 'I have plumped against England,' wrote Cyril Connolly in 1929. 'I am tired of the country . . . I do feel it is a dying civilization – decadent, but in such a damned dull way – going stuffy and comatose instead of collapsing beautifully like France.' Nor was the motivation always political: travel in the 1920s and 1930s provided an opportunity for illicit delights – an encounter with an obliging young lighthouse-keeper (Tom Driberg), say, or a seemingly endless supply of thirteen-year-old 'cooks' and companions (Norman Douglas). Travel was a disguise, and Britten well knew his friends' tales of easy love and experiences abroad.

So amid all the confusion, all the conflicting thoughts and emotions and the 'spiritual fogs' in which Britten found himself (his words a year later), he jumped at Pears's invitation to follow Auden and Isherwood to America. It would provide a cooling-off period, an opportunity to decide what he thought his prospects were with Scherchen and with England. Not least, he was relatively prosperous at the time, partly because of the seventy guineas he had just collected for his jazz-inflected score for Priestley.

He broke the news to Scherchen callously. In mid-April Wulff came from Cambridge to London expecting the usual intimacy, only to find himself at a farewell party for Britten and Pears. In the month since Britten made up his mind to go, he had said nothing to Scherchen, wary then and thereafter of conflict. While guests laughed and drank, Wulff sat in the corner by himself, alternately knocking back gin and sobbing. Britten took him to the station in a taxi and the boy disappeared into the night. Either in the taxi or some time in the following days they resolved to break up.

Two weeks later Britten and Pears hosted a more sober affair. Friends and family dropped in, availed themselves of the bottle of sherry on the floor and said their goodbyes. The next day at Southampton they met the Bridges, who had driven there to bid their adieus. As they prepared to board the *Ausonia*, bound for North America, Bridge handed Britten his Giussani viola, a handsome, mellow instrument, a gesture that more than any other symbolized the end of Britten's long apprenticeship. There was an accompanying note:

> So that a bit of us accompanies you on your adventure.
> We are all 'revelations' as you know. Just go on expanding.
> Ever your affectionate
> & devoted
> Ethel & Frank
> Bon voyage et bon retour.

Teacher and pupil never saw each other again.

3

Exile

America, England, 1939–1945

I

When Coleridge fled England in 1804 it was on a brig bound for Nelson's fleet in the Mediterranean, a hostage to morphine and mephitis. Britten did considerably better. The *Ausonia* was part of the Cunard fleet, a Royal Mail ship that for sixteen years had criss-crossed the Atlantic between England and Canada. The lower decks were crowded with refugees and émigrés making good their escape, who kept much to themselves. The English bourgeoisie occupied the upper deck, taking cocktails with the captain and enjoying lavish meals. Britten dismissed the upper-deck passengers as 'dull colonials', though many attended his recital with Pears, which assured some on-board celebrity. The trip was dreary. Icebergs slowed their progress at one point, bobbing against the hull all night. A day later fog slowed them first to a crawl, then to a halt; at night the horn sounded its warning into the darkness, preventing both catastrophe and sleep. Otherwise they fell into a routine of ping-pong, walks on the deck and reading – Pushkin's *Boris Godunov* for Britten, which later made its influence felt, in the Mussorgsky operatic version, in *Peter Grimes*.

He did no work; the circumstances were hardly conducive and he was too tired, his emotions too mixed. He wrote a long letter to Scherchen, full of endearments, intimacies and regret. 'What a fool one is to come away – the more I think of Snape & the visits to Cambridge & yours to Snape – the more I feel a fool to have left it all.' In this his voyage resembles Coleridge's – the archetypal Romantic flight from the heart, the emotional uncertainty helping to explain why his plans were so ill formed. He and Pears talked vaguely of a month or so around Montreal or Ottawa; a road trip to Vancouver; a journey down to New

York. There remained the whispery potential of a film, *The Knights of the Round Table*, another of Hollywood's promiscuous trawls through English history which captivated American studios and audiences in the 1930s. This alone would keep Britten in America through autumn. 'I've come with the guy I share a flat with in London,' he told Copland. 'Nice person, & I know you'd approve.'

Never a spontaneous being, Britten relaxed once they reached Montreal, trying new things and slowing down after a gruelling winter. He took a cabin with Pears in the Laurentians, a spectacular part of the country north of Montreal, packed with lakes, mountains, forests and resorts. They played tennis, went walking and canoeing, and heard some French Canadian folk songs – 'La Perdriole' and 'Alouette' among them – which later that year were woven into *Canadian Carnival*, Britten's open-plains orchestral work, its debt to Copland evident. Settled in the log cabin, he pulled out the incidental music he had been sketching for a different Arthurian fantasy, a BBC drama *The Sword in the Stone*, and finished it smartly, before returning to the violin concerto he had been writing for some months. The Vancouver trip fell by the wayside as Pears became fidgety about money and prospects. Other plans emerged, but there was something delightfully improvised about these early weeks and months, so different from the routine of Britten's life for most of the 1930s.

Far from home, Britten grew even more reliant on Hawkes. Whether chasing visas, commissions, payments or performances, the publisher proved a real force. He dispensed advice ('I beg of you not to "flirt" with the film people too much, until they really want you'), and was an excellent sounding board. For such a playboy businessman, Hawkes sensed Britten's potential and had an unfailing touch in promoting his young client; he would need such belief and commitment once the war had begun in earnest. In May, Hawkes sent Britten word that the savvy contemporary-music conductor and patron Paul Sacher was interested in the Rimbaud cycle, if only Britten could get on and finish it. (This may well have been Hawkes's own initiative, not Sacher's.) Britten immediately mapped out how the completed work might look, though he told Hawkes that 'management reserve the right to alter the programme', which management eventually did.

The alterations illuminate one aspect of the maturing Britten at work. The idea for the cycle had been brewing since Auden first introduced him to the poems. Sophie Wyss described a train journey in 1938 during which Britten came over to her, eyes blazing, full of the wonder of Rimbaud, thinking about what to do with the poems he had just read. He told her then that he was going to set them for her, yet which songs, their order and the architecture of the cycle would not be settled until late in the composition process.

A similar method marked a number of his mature song cycles. 'The work is planned, and then when the plan of the work is fixed – is finished – the actual notes are decided on,' he told the Earl of Harewood in 1960. But it was not a case of notes being shoehorned into a prescriptive scheme, regardless of their merit. It changed from genre to genre, piece to piece, and however much each work was carefully planned (and each was), an element of Britten's subconscious remained in the mix. 'I think E. M. Forster describes that very well in *Aspects of the Novel*, when he says that one must always be prepared as a creative artist to let the characters take charge,' he told the critic and friend Donald Mitchell in 1969. 'And I can quite often go to the paper perfectly clear that what I'm going to do, and to find that it doesn't work out quite like that. And I think one has got to have faith in one's subconscious, that it's going to direct one rightly.' It is important not to overplay this influence – Britten's mental maps were always finely detailed – but there were frequent surprises.

Each work was also hostage to more prosaic influences – the relationship between keys, for instance. 'Interlude' in *Les Illuminations* is little more than a rickety bridge between two disparate tonalities that had been thrown together, a touch gratingly, in the late ordering of songs. Britten was fond of saying he did most of his work away from his desk and this was true. 'The composer is really only writing down the result of many hours' thinking, many years of experience.' Often this experience showed its hand in problem solving, not strategic planning – an extension to an Interlude in *Peter Grimes*, say, when the staging required it – which nudged the piece in a new, unexpected direction.

Intimate letters to Scherchen continued, distance providing Britten no resolution, only further heartache. If the trip was a long game by an amorous Pears, he played it remarkably well. On the *Ausonia* and in their cabin in the Laurentians, their friendship asserted itself as a meeting of minds and equals, something quite distinct from the type of bond Britten had hitherto sought. Then in Grand Rapids, Michigan, visiting friends of Pears's, they became lovers.

2

Pears and biographers have described the time in Grand Rapids as a light-bulb moment – the instant in which each man realized his feelings for the other. Pears, for example, wrote to Britten in January the following year, 'I shall never forget a certain night in Grand Rapids', a theme he revisited in 1959 and again in 1974 ('it is *you* who have given *me* everything, right from the beginning, from yourself in Grand Rapids!') And this was undoubtedly the first physical manifestation of a friendship that had gently unfolded over the previous years. Yet Britten remained emotionally entangled with Scherchen. Only a few days before travelling to Toronto and then on to Grand Rapids, he wrote to Scherchen that, despite the resolutions they made when he left England, he could not help thinking about him. 'I love you more everyday – & seeing all these people (& some very nice & attractive) can't put you out of my head. So there! There's a declaration.' (This was his mature writing style – a mixture of businesslike assessments and confidence, as if there was simply no time for anything further.) On 27 June, a week or more after Pears and Britten first slept together, his tone towards Scherchen had not changed. 'No more news, my darling. No need to reiterate that notwithstanding all the many & various people I'm meeting I still feel very much the same about you. Peter is being very nice & we're getting on well. He sends his love.'

There was an element of Britten having his cake and eating it. Yet it's more likely that Grand Rapids was not quite the light-bulb moment Pears and others later suggested, that it was less a consummation of love than two close friends falling into bed together. Of course their relationship had moved onto a new level, but it was not necessarily a signal of potential or permanence in Britten's mind. With their American plans still unformed and with every intention that they would later in 1939 return to England, where Scherchen remained keen ('I have lost something very important to me with your departure . . . You see, for all my resolutions I have not given you up'), Britten was determined to keep his options open. And of course Pears was physically and intellectually distinct from the boys Britten habitually liked.

In the following months, as their professional plans fell into place, as Europe slid into war and as Britten's relationship with Pears further intensified, his ardour for Scherchen quietly slipped away. Even so, in November 1939 Britten was writing to Enid Slater, 'I'm afraid alot of resolutions have gone up in thin air – especially, funnily enough since the war' – a direct reference to Scherchen, whom Britten had often discussed with Slater. And as late as 8 December Britten was telling Scherchen, 'O – if all this bloody business would clear up – or *if* you could come over here. *That's* what I want most of all.' Yet when Pears wrote to Britten a mere month later, he signed off with, 'I'm terribly in love with you.' And by then, it seems, his feelings were at last fully reciprocated. Britten and Pears were able to acknowledge the substance of their bond.

Before then, Scherchen played the role of absent muse. The thin, gaudy *Young Apollo* for piano and strings, which Britten dashed off in July for the solicitous Canadian Broadcasting Corporation, was inspired by the final lines of Keats's *Hyperion*: 'and lo! from all his limbs / Celestial Glory dawn'd: he was a god!' Britten's rapt contemplation of Apollo's/Scherchen's golden tresses did not inspire great things. It was probably a jealous Pears who ensured its withdrawal after only two performances; it was all a little too close to the bone. 'I ought to have the courage to destroy all of the above,' Britten wrote in his fiftieth year when *Young Apollo* and a few other lost works from the era were brought to his attention, 'but they have a kind of gruesome fascination for me like old photographs.' Instead it lay undisturbed, entombed in one cupboard or another, published only posthumously.

He had considerable success with *Les Illuminations*, however. Britten was no doubt as thrilled by the poet's biography as he was with the poems themselves. Arthur Rimbaud (1854–91) was a modern-day troubadour, a (prodigiously talented) Bosie to Paul Verlaine's Oscar Wilde. Together they drank and fought their way around Paris, London and Brussels – the teenage Rimbaud handsome and headstrong, Verlaine an often bewildered, jealous consort. Still, the words flowed as they egged each other on, in dirty beds and taverns. Eleven years earlier, in his *Quatre chansons françaises*, Britten had responded inventively to Verlaine's poems; now it was the turn of the impetuous young lover.

It is not so fanciful to suggest that Britten saw Scherchen as a tame version of Rimbaud, the untrained lover-poet of an older artist. The Rimbaud setting 'Antique', dedicated to Scherchen, is, like *Young Apollo*, a sketch of mythological beauty. 'Oh, gracious son of Pan! Thine eye – those precious globes – glance slowly; thy brow is crowned with little flowers and berries.' Britten's setting is exceptionally sensuous: the strings sound like an Italian street band of guitars and mandolins. There is a solo violinist in the troupe who toys with the singer before inviting his comrades to join him in doubling the voice, a gesture of approval or complicity. It is a depiction of uncomplicated, *reciprocated* love.

The movement dedicated to Pears, 'Being Beauteous', is even more impressive. A beautiful creature lies dying, blood spreading quickly from her wounds, colouring the snow around her as though a shadow or halo. In defiance of her condition and the distant, indifferent city noises, she stands up – tall, straight-limbed, composed. This is no recovery, though; she is leaving the world and her body behind in a Mahlerian transformation. 'Being Beauteous' shares the same slow pulse as Scherchen's movement, the same slow-moving harmonies gradually crowded out by invading chromaticism, but there are many more layers. It was completed before leaving England; Scherchen's movement is undated, but was probably written in America. Two of the songs, 'Marine' and 'Being Beauteous', had outings of their own before the first complete performance in London's Aeolian Hall on 30 January 1940.

Though written for soprano (which suits it best), the cycle was harvested by Pears for his own use and in May 1941 he recorded the complete work with the CBS Symphony Orchestra conducted by Britten. The recording provides a fascinating indication of the singer Pears was becoming and the conductor Britten already was. Photographs of the session show Britten much as Fass described him conducting in 1938: 'If he goes on for ever he'll *never* be a conductor – you never saw anything so stiff & held in.' Yet Fass was mistaking physicality for musicality. The recording is so organic, with such careful rubato and ensemble, it is difficult to believe Britten had previously conducted only a handful of performances. Pears's voice is lyrical and resonant, stuffed full of overtones, without the slight curdling vibrato he developed after the war. It has a lazy coloratura (the fast runs are skated over at times), few colours and an unstable top. But everything else is there: the mixture of head and chest voices, the well-judged *portamenti*, the word painting ('*clocher à clocher*' (bell-tower to bell-tower) chimes with impeccable onomatopoeia). He had found a new teacher six months or so before the recording, a tough New York-based Australian singer, Clytie Mundy, who helped turn him into Britten's worthy muse and interpreter.

3

Their first impressions of America were positive. They were fêted in Grand Rapids and invited to a dizzying round of parties, press interviews and meetings. Pears planned his first complete recital of Britten songs for broadcast, while Britten contemplated the various offers waved under his nose. 'I might as well confess it now,' he told his sister Beth in June 1939, 'that I am seriously considering staying over here permanently.' Nothing was certain, and if war came it would, he thought, bring him home. Yet artistically he felt the comparison between England and North America invidious. 'I am *certain* that N. America is the place of the future.' He may have only been rehearsing his argument, but in these early months away the idea of turning his back on England caused him no grief. Music meant something in America, so he thought. He spoke of consistently brilliant reviews for the New York premiere of *Variations on a Theme of Frank Bridge* on 12 July (Frieder Weissmann conducting the New York Philharmonic at Lewisohn Stadium) and even if this was not true (as it was not), it seems the bad or indifferent ones affected him less.

There were drawbacks, of course: New York made the same sort of impression on him as London; loud, brash, dirty, fast-paced, staggeringly beautiful, alive and bewildering, and with an intellectual sophistication that made him uneasy. In 1939 it was more of a melting pot than London, African-Americans aside. Immigrants were everywhere, pursuing the great American Dream – working on building sites, selling possessions in junk-filled street markets or scavenging for them elsewhere, opening delicatessens. Vendors hung full kosher chickens in the shop windows on Hester Street. Pan Am's new long-range Clippers flew passengers and mail from New York to Southampton in twenty-nine hours, via Shediac, Botwood and Foynes. Shares changed hands at the Stock Exchange according to the fluctuating prospects for peace in Europe and the swift trade of the American iron and steel industry, the magnificent glass and steel groined vaults of the old Penn Station testimony to this industry. Albert Einstein entered the lion's den of Princeton Theological Seminary and gave the faculty either a fig-leaf or fresh meat when he argued that scientific knowledge provided no guidelines for ethical behaviour.

At Café Society ('The Wrong Place for the Right People'), a former speakeasy on West Fourth Street, a young Billie Holiday ended her gigs with a new protest song: 'Southern trees bear strange fruit, / Blood on the leaves and blood at the root, / Black bodies swinging in the southern breeze, / Strange fruit hanging from the poplar trees.' The civil rights movement was emerging. John Steinbeck's *The Grapes of Wrath* had just been published and the following year would win a Pulitzer Prize. Glenn Miller and his big band returned to Carnegie Hall, drooping their way through *Moonlight Serenade*. Raymond Hood's art deco complex in Midtown Manhattan, the Rockefeller Center, was completed, Rockefeller himself driving in 'The Last Rivet'. It was a city of staggering verve, vision and achievement. 'Wystan compares it to a great Hotel,' Britten later told his brother-in-law Kit Welford, '& it's a damn good comparison.' Isherwood was less generous, describing it as a 'nervous breakdown expressed in terms of architecture', a mad performance staged solely for their benefit, the locals delighted at their presence.

Thirty miles or so east of Manhattan, over the 59th Street Bridge to Long Island and through Queens and Nassau County, lies the picturesque village of Amityville, close to where F. Scott Fitzgerald placed his bootlegger Jay Gatsby. It was home to Dr and Mrs Mayer, two German émigrés who spent much of the 1930s playing a careful, defensive chess game with their family, moving individual pieces out of harm's way, before reuniting in Amityville in 1937. Dr William Mayer was an intelligent, cultured Jew, dominated by his straight-speaking wife, who worked at the Long Island Home, a 'Private Sanatorium for Nervous and Mental Diseases'. Elizabeth Mayer, a pianist by training who had dark, penetrating eyes and spoke six languages, met Pears when, in 1936 at Southampton, he joined the ship on which she was making her escape from Germany. The two travelled on to America and afterwards remained in occasional contact. In June 1939 Pears wrote to her proposing they meet for lunch or tea; it was a propitious suggestion.

The Mayers represented Old World cultural values in a New World setting and became enormously important figures in the lives of both Britten and Pears. Britten described Elizabeth in a letter to Enid Slater as 'one of those grand people who have been essential through the ages for the production of art; really sympathetic & enthusiastic, with instinctive good taste (in all the arts) & a great friend of thousands of those poor fish – artists.' She offered Britten the unwavering love and support he had experienced with his mother, and what began as a weekend visit in August turned into an extended stay. They were soon addressing each other as 'darling' and 'dearest' – endearments that had characterized young Benji's correspondence with his mother – and Elizabeth's letters to Britten on his trips away from Amityville read like those of a supportive and perceptive parent. The Mayers and their house were the ideal antidote to frenetic New York, a recreation of everything Britten loved in his childhood.

There was a touch of Friston to the place as well, the sort of genteel salon milieu he was used to with the Bridges. Elizabeth's son Michael remembered soirées ('Miss Otis Regrets', a Britten–Pears staple at the time, was frequently trotted out), luncheons and parties, and much laughter among artistic guests and family friends. They dipped into Sigmund Spaeth's worthy 1936 study, *Great Symphonies: How to Recognize and Remember Them*, reciting the mnemonic aids its author created to the tunes of various symphonies – the third movement of Beethoven's 'Pastoral' Symphony, for example: 'The peasants are dancing and prancing together, / The weather means nothing to them, ha, ha, ha!' They went to see every movie featuring Deanna Durbin, the 'sensational Canadian songbird' as she styled herself, whom they dismissively referred to as 'Deanna Dustbin'; they were glued to the radio for every episode of *The New Adventures of Sherlock Holmes*, with Basil Rathbone as the detective, Nigel Bruce his sidekick; they swam and sunbathed at Jones Beach, a popular stretch of ocean front, parkland and bay water; and they enjoyed the attentions of Mrs Mayer, who found them more stimulating than her own children, their middlebrow humour notwithstanding. Neither Mayer twigged that Britten and Pears were lovers – not in the slow-burning months of 1939, but not later either, when their commitment to each other was unshakeable. 'My mother was never aware of such things,' Michael said, however unlikely this seems. 'My mother thought that [my sister] Beata ought to marry Ben, you see; but she lived in another world.'

By the beginning of September they were all living in another world. 'War is on us this morning,' wrote Virginia Woolf blandly on 1 September, as though commenting on a cloudy day. Auden, back from New Mexico, sat in 'a dive on Fifty-Second Street' on the same day that more than a million German soldiers marched into Poland. Here he contemplated the expiration of a 'low dishonest decade', writing what became perhaps the most famous poem of the 1930s, 'September 1, 1939', which would haunt him for the remainder of his life.

> Waves of anger and fear
> Circulate over the bright
> And darkened lands of the earth,
> Obsessing our private lives;
> The unmentionable odour of death
> Offends the September night.

Two days later, Britain and France declared war on Germany; within a week most of Britain's dominions had fallen into line.

War did not provide Britten with any clarity; there was too much confusion, too many conflicting notions of what the hostilities would mean. 'London and the country are buzzing with rumours,' wrote the *New Yorker* journalist Mollie Panter-Downes on 3 September,

> a favorite one being that Hitler carries a gun in his pocket and means to shoot himself if things don't go too well; another school of thought favors the version that he is now insane and Göring has taken over. It is felt that Mussolini was up to no good with his scheme for holding a peace conference and spoiling what has become everybody's war. The English were a peace-loving nation up to two days ago, but now it is pretty widely felt that the sooner we really get down to the job, the better.

It was an impossibly difficult time. Friends and family advised them variously to come home, to remain where they were, to take out American citizenship. Britten talked, improbably, of working as a secretary in Washington's Library of Congress and, more obviously, of writing music for military bands. Hawkes thought he could pull strings and place him in charge of just such an ensemble should he come home, this being the mildest form of military service he could conjure. And throughout, Britten wrote of his homesickness, frustration at not knowing what was happening and uncertainty over his future. But he was hardly consistent. Later in October he told Hawkes that he would remain in America for as long as it was possible, yet it seems by then his homesickness had been assuaged temporarily by Elizabeth Mayer's ministrations, the increasing intimacy of his relationship with Pears, and the re-emergence of the pixie Auden in his life.

It was assuaged also by the prospect of two big projects: a commission from the Japanese government for an orchestral work to celebrate the 2,600th anniversary of the Japanese Empire, and an operetta on the subject of the mythical lumberjack Paul Bunyan, which he had begun discussing with Auden. The commissioned short symphony was to net him almost £600 – his entire income in the year leading up to his departure. Money was once again tight and nowhere near as portable as it had been, so he viewed the commission as a boon. Both works he saw as a vehicle for his pacifism, which events had helped focus. 'I'm making it just as anti-war as possible,' he told the *New York Sun* of the symphony in April 1940, a comment he repeated to various friends. Lennox Berkeley duly responded, his wounds slowly healing. 'I'm glad to hear that the Jap. Government commission is really happening, though that they should commission an anti-war work seems a piece of disconcerting irony.' It was a prescient but unheeded observation.

4

In the early months of 1940, as he worked on the two projects, Britten was felled as surely as one of Bunyan's trees. He had uticaria on his face and body: 'I've got all new skin over my face, hands & feet – so for once I'm quite clean! (don't even whisper it about – but it's possible that I've had a strange kind of scarlet fever!!)', he wrote to Beth on 15 March 1940. His throat was sore and tonsils infected: 'His tonsils are quite rotten apparently and must come out at the first suitable moment,' Pears told Beth on 20 February. His teeth hurt – one was later removed – and 'he had a long and horrible nose-bleed which left him pretty weakish'. His temperature remained high: 'Dr Mayer who was in charge was confident about it, but when his temperature suddenly went up to 107° for a bit last Sunday night, he got a specialist to come down on Sunday and look him over. Well, apparently, he's all right and taking it very well (heart, lungs, chest, etc. in perfect condition),' Pears told Beth.

Much of his care was overseen by the kindly Mrs Mayer, her doctor husband and their daughter Beata, and once a final diagnosis was made – streptococcus – there was a new class of drug, sulphonamide, to combat it all. As his treatment dragged on, as doctors put fingers in dykes and plastered over the damage, as lesions disappeared and skin grew back,

Britten slowly recovered and by the end of the year thought he could put it all behind him. 'But everyone agrees that as long as he is careful and looks after himself, there's not the least likelihood of anything untoward happening,' Pears told Beth.

'Outwardly the ailment was infected tonsils,' Britten recalled in 1960. 'But the real cause was my mental perplexities. It was a frantically difficult position.' If his later recollection sounds simultaneously understated and melodramatic, there is no doubt he found these months draining and, on occasion, life threatening: he really was very ill. But there were also 'mental perplexities'. Britten and Pears remained unsure whether to stay in America on its own merits, and uncertain whether they would be required back at home for national service. They had no idea how they would get there if called back, since passenger liners were requisitioned by the navy and transatlantic travel halted, and they did not know how their pacifism would be viewed now their home country was at war. 'I find, as you do too,' he wrote to Beth and her husband at the end of June 1940, 'that if one's mind's upset, that one's body usual[ly] gets that way too.' Berkeley didn't help. His letters stressed duty and patriotism, nationhood and enemies, which sent Britten into transatlantic rages. He directed these at his friends and family, not Berkeley himself, which became standard behaviour from here on. And he found Ethel Bridge's letters uncharacteristically and depressingly full of flag-waving.

Such arguments became more prevalent in Britain as the phoney war transformed into something more tangible – a mixture of conscription and munitions, of Churchill now in charge of a coalition government, of German troops marching through France before occupying Paris. A spiteful poem did the rounds:

> The literary erstwhile Left-wellwisher would
> Seek vainly now for Auden or for Isherwood:
> The dog beneath the skin has had the brains
> To save it, Norris-like, by changing trains.

To his surprise and annoyance, Isherwood found himself stung, grasping to explain his feelings. 'If I fear anything, I fear the atmosphere of the war, the power which it gives to all the things I hate – the newspapers, the politicians, the puritans, the scoutmasters, the middle-aged merciless spinsters.'

Even literary allies of the two pilloried writers kept the debate alive – whether wittingly or unwittingly is not always clear. Cyril Connolly described them as 'ambitious young men with a strong instinct of self-preservation, and an eye on the main chance', though he was equally disappointed in England for losing them. Harold Nicolson, MP husband of Vita Sackville-West and an old friend of Auden's, chastised the poet in a *Spectator* column, adding barbs for Isherwood, Aldous Huxley and academic philosopher Gerald Heard. To Nicolson they were diminishing the intellectual rationale in America for war, at exactly the time when American participation was a highly sought prize: 'four of our most liberated intelligences refuse to identify themselves . . . with those who fight.' Evelyn Waugh weighed in, predictably, transforming Auden and Isherwood into the fictional poets Parsnip and Pimpernell in his comic novel *Put Out More Flags,* a romp through London society at the beginning of what he called the Great Bore War.

> 'What I don't see,' she said (and what this girl did not see was usually a very conspicuous embarrassment to Poppet's friends) – 'What I don't see is how these two can claim to be *Contemporary* if they run away from the biggest event in contemporary history. They were contemporary enough about Spain when no one threatened to come and bomb *them* . . . It's just sheer escapism,' she said.

Britten was not named in the House of Commons or the pages of the *Spectator,* nor was he yet the subject of spiteful doggerel. But he was certainly one of the targets. In December 1940, a year almost to the day before the attack on Pearl Harbor that would draw America into the war, he was careful to spell out to a journalist from the *New York Sun* that he was not master of his own destiny. 'He's been told he will be sent for when and if he is needed,' the article ran, reiterating advice Auden also received. 'Apparently England has taken to heart the lesson of the last war, in which so many of her musicians were lost, and it is encouraging to know that even nations fighting for their existence are thinking of their cultural and artistic futures.' (If this came from Britten he was sadly wide of the mark, although perhaps he intended it as a smokescreen.)

In early 1940 Britten was already aware of the brewing hostility at home towards the young Britons living in America. In September 1940 Hawkes warned him of the climate. 'There is no doubt at all that we are going to have difficulty in getting performances of your works and caustic comment has been passed on your being away.'

This was still to play itself out when, in early 1940, émigré artist Josef Scharl, an old friend of the Mayers from their Munich days, sketched Britten. He remained ill and the finished piece captures an anxious young man: the crispy hair and the slightly lopsided lips are brilliantly done, but it is the worried eyes that reveal the tension he was already experiencing. (It is far from the sketch used on the cover of Christopher Headington's short biography of 1982, where he looks like a pirate.)

For all the loose talk and consequent indecision, America provided some balm. There were musical opportunities Britten thought non-existent in England. 'Whatever struggle American music may have had in the past for its fair share of public recognition,' he said in early 1940, 'today the composer here, compared with his English brother even in normal times, has a very rosy prospect.' Americans drew no distinction between old and contemporary scores, thought Britten, as was the numbing case in England. Moreover, American composers benefited from private and public patronage, a gung-ho approach to recording, Hollywood commissions, school bands, concert societies, passionate audiences and extraordinary orchestras grown from refined German seeds. Even when Britten came to leave he was gracious about his adopted land. 'I am sure there never was so much music-making even in Imperial Vienna as there is here now.'

Much of it was undertaken by émigré composers and performers, making America more connected with Continental modernism than England was before the war. Stravinsky, Schoenberg, Bartók, Martinů, Milhaud, Eisler, Krenek and Weill were transforming American opera, orchestral programmes and university faculties, while conductors such as Arturo Toscanini, Otto Klemperer, Fritz Reiner, George Szell, Fritz Busch, Bruno Walter and Dimitri Mitropoulos were influencing the standard and role of performance in American culture. It is an astonishing list. What lured them to America over England was much the same things that had attracted Britten: the number of quality orchestras and opportunities and the culture of private patronage fuelling them. These Britain lacked, as eminent foreign musicians well knew from their visits during the 1920s and 1930s. Aspects of the British music industry were transformed by immigration, but it was America that bagged the truly great émigré composers and performers.*

The country influenced Britten outside the concert hall too, allowing him a break from the preoccupation with political ideology that characterized his work in the second half of the 1930s – *Sinfonia da Requiem* aside. Whereas in England he was often left struggling to keep up with Auden's jackdaw ideas, America required no political commitment. Perhaps it was just as well: on their voyage to America in January 1939, Auden and Isherwood relayed to each other their disenchantment with politics and their conviction that art was unable to effect any lasting change in society. Auden took this further a few weeks later in his literary autopsy of W. B. Yeats: 'the honest truth, gentlemen, is that, if not a poem had been written, not a picture painted, not a bar of music composed, the history of man would be materially unchanged.' He was being cute, playing roulette with rhetoric: nonetheless, here was the decade's great architect of art-as-protest washing his hands of the whole idea. Though the seeds of his defection were sown as far back as 1936 in Spain, it was a remarkable volte-face, one he worked at further in 'The Prolific and the Devourer' (1939). In a time of war, he asked, is it the artist's duty to enlist, to serve the military machine in other ways, or is it his duty to stand back from the fray, creating beautiful works capable of inspiring better behaviour?

Britten was not ready to abandon entirely the habits of the previous years. And though it was tempered with time, he retained a conviction that music could influence public thought and action, however indirectly. But in America he had no cause to further, no protest march to join and no substantive contact with the American left. The brave new world of American politics Britten now encountered was what he and his circle had been arguing for during the previous five years. Taking office in 1933, with the after-shocks of the Wall Street Crash and the collapse of the American

---

* There was conservatism as well, to which the home-grown composer Charles Ives reacted with such ferocity and imagination, not content to serve up tepid imitations of nineteenth-century European scores to a New World twitchy about its cultural relationship with the Old, paradoxically determined to punch considerably below its weight in the matter of indigenous composition. Isolated from these traditions and from emerging American ones, Conlon Nancarrow and Ives in the first half of the last century produced some of their country's most startling and original musical works. Unsurprisingly, their voices were not much heard at the time, which offers a corrective to Britten's rose-tinted view of contemporary music in America.

economy still the dominant fact of political life, Roosevelt drove through a raft of progressive legislation, part of his New Deal. Social security, banking, agriculture, labour, the environment, the stock exchange and home ownership were all subject to reform and bailouts in Roosevelt's first term.

The largest of the schemes, the Works Progress Administration, employed millions of Americans during the late 1930s building roads and bridges, landscaping parks and erecting public offices and auditoriums. Improbably, the WPA also created artistic works to put inside the auditoriums – literary, musical, dramatic and cinematic, some cringingly worthy, some good, and all of it, for want of a better term, socialist art. Thousands of performances were funded and, in this, Roosevelt's grand scheme directly touched Britten and Pears. Moreover, it undercut traditional forms of patronage in America, those of big business and old industrial money. The contrast with the culture Britten had left behind in England could not have been more profound. The old political aspirations were superfluous; utopia was all around him.

In other ways America disenchanted him. His letters in 1940 contain many attempts to define the continent; influenced no doubt by homesickness, they suggest both seduction and conflict. He thought Roosevelt a great man of ideals, good at the brokering as well as the vision. Yet he deplored the foul back-street politics of New York and was suspicious of the thuggish Irish Catholic dominance of the police force and the Democratic Party. ('The Irish Catholics are the great curse of this State – that's why the police in New York are so unscrupulous, hard & rude.') He was disgusted by the lynchings Billie Holiday sang about and was mindful of the treatment dished out to pacifists in the previous war. ('The things that were done to pacifists or pro-Germans in the last war were unbelievable – & since then there have been plenty of examples of crowd-hysteria – the Klu-Klux-Klan – negro-lynchings & burnings.') He was sour about the superficiality of popular culture with its fickle crazes and feeble trends, disliking the gullibility and hysteria of the masses, best exemplified by the panicked public reaction to Orson Welles's broadcast of H. G. Wells's *The War of the Worlds* in October 1938 ('the Martian visit', in Britten's understated description), which listeners took to be live reportage. He found many customs alien. 'Ten cents, Albert?' he asked of conductor Albert Goldberg when discovering he must pay to use a lavatory. 'Ten cents for shitting?' He was unsympathetic towards American isolationists – a contorted position for a pacifist to take – and at the same time commending a country that refused to engage in war-fare. ('They're fed up with Europe – they didn't like its peace – and they're suspicious of its war. They're full of advice as how to run the rest of the world – & refuse to take any of the consequences.')

America was a land of enterprise and opportunity, but there was also something necrotic about it, surprising him in such a young continent. 'In some ways this country seems to have the corruption of the Old World & little of its tradition or charm,' he told Kit Welford in April 1940. It was a common enough response among émigrés and refugees. The Austrian journalist and critic Alfred Polgar, who sailed to America in October 1940 with Heinrich Mann, his nephew Golo and the sophis-ticated beauty Alma Mahler-Werfel (who escaped France with a suitcase packed with her first husband's scores and the original manuscript of Bruckner's Symphony No. 3), never really settled in California, deter-mining instead to live just long enough to 'enjoy the end of the awful mess made by that monstrous arsehole'.

Britten was aware he could not reconcile the conflicting views of his adopted land. This was impossible even for an American, he thought. 'What one state thinks will be laughed at by 45 of the others – what is possible for the West is impossible for the East – the New Yorker is as much like the Southerner as a Norwegian is like a Turk – and says so too.' But the problem was less with America, more with how he was coming to view himself. Fevered, finding it difficult to work and missing his fam-ily desperately, Britten articulated the theme that would come to define him as an artist. 'You see – I'm gradually realising that I'm English – & as a composer I suppose I feel I want more definite roots than other people.' This was written as early as April 1940, when he was not yet through his illness, and the idea would ferment over the coming months, increasing in potency. Its impact on Britten and on English music in the second half of the twentieth century would eventually be profound.

5

His illness hijacked his work, making the composition process more intense, the deadlines tighter. As chance would have it, this phase of his sickness was bookended by two major performances: the American premiere of the Piano Concerto on 15 January 1940 with the Illinois

Symphony Orchestra under Goldberg, Britten as soloist (on no fee, as it was a WPA performance), and on 28 March the Violin Concerto with the New York Philharmonic Orchestra and Antonio Brosa, conducted by John Barbirolli. 'I had a *terrific* success in Chicago,' he told Beth, 'like one dreams of! 14 calls – & cheers & shouts of speech!' Britten was immediately invited back for a concert in May, to include the first American performance of *Les Illuminations* with Pears. ('By-the-way are you going to let me conduct the old work?' he asked Goldberg in his polo club way. 'No aspersions being cast of course, but I do like to wield the old baton!')*

The Violin Concerto is structurally more adventurous, less reliant on set pieces for effect than its stablemate – a restless, hypnotic work from the start. The violin meanders through its opening melody, refusing to put down roots. Later, it thrums away like a street busker: the orchestra has stolen the original melody, playing it half-speed, insisting that time stand still, and the soloist is left with little option but to play along. The oriental chromatic musings in the middle movement are a little workmanlike, despite the sure-of-foot Britten scherzo encasing them. But Britten compensates for the flaws with great theatrical gestures. One is at the beginning of the third movement, following a cadenza in which the violin picks over the bones of the first movement. Here the trombones glide into the texture like a great ship at sea sounding its foghorn in warning. From this one growling utterance, an austere passacaglia emerges. The phrase is repeated by different instruments, sometimes rhythmically altered, the soloist all the while performing miraculous acrobatics high above. It is an unusual sound-world, one quite unlike anything Britten had hitherto created. And it is mesmerizing.

His use of a passacaglia here, the first instance in his music, was a happy consequence of life in Amityville, where Britten and Pears were slowly working their way through the piles of piano duets in the Mayer home: Schubert, of course; Mozart, naturally; but also scores by

---

* Britten and Pears pulled out two weeks before the concert, citing financial worries – it was no longer possible to transfer money from England overseas and the men panicked – but Britten's suggestion for the rest of the programme illustrates his progressive taste. 'The Overture *must* be classical and lightly scored,' Elizabeth Mayer wrote on his behalf, listing as possibilities Gluck's *Iphigenie in Aulis*, Beethoven's *Prometheus*, Rossini's *La Scala di seta*, Mozart's *Cosi fan tutte* or a concerto grosso by Handel. After the interval he suggested symphonies by Mozart (Jupiter), Schumann (1, 2 or 3), Beethoven (6), Mahler (4), or Schubert (5 or 7).

Buxtehude. What an incongruous spectre this last composer must have been on Long Island at the end of the 1930s, long before musicians regularly mined the seventeenth century for repertory or curiosities. Britten was thrilled to have stumbled upon him, telling Berkeley in September 1939, 'Since my discovery of Mahler I haven't been so excited over anything. I think he's so much better than Bach!!!' It was quite a call, but he was responding to Buxtehude's rule-breaking – much as he once did with Stravinsky – and the unsettling, dangerous quality this introduced to each score.

Auden captured these domestic performances in his 'New Year Letter (January 1, 1940)', dedicated to Elizabeth Mayer, in which a Buxtehude passacaglia, played in the sun-drenched Mayer cottage, is invoked as a counter-weight to the barbarity of war: it represents order, intellect and the European culture then threatened. It was a vital chance discovery; perhaps only Britten's 1956 trip to the Far East, midway through the composition of his vast ballet *The Prince of the Pagodas*, had a comparable impact on a half-finished work. Buxtehude's harmonic language and love of the passacaglia form was the bounty here. (Schoenberg in *Pierrot lunaire* (1912) and Berg in *Wozzeck* (1922) both used passacaglias, though unusually these appear not to have registered with Britten.) These ideas and techniques would make themselves felt in later works, not least *Peter Grimes*. Yet the encounter was important for quite another reason: it encouraged Britten to look at other early music, hopeful of similar revelations. In such pioneering fashion he came to champion the work of Henry Purcell, a discovery that also revolutionized his own music.

The Violin Concerto's premiere aroused great interest and applause. Britten shuffled onto the stage afterwards, a gangling lad of twenty-six, dressed in his father's tailcoat, and bowed awkwardly to the enthusiastic Carnegie Hall audience, his shyness almost overwhelming him. ('Frankly, he didn't look like the composer of his D minor concerto,' thought the critic of the *New York World-Telegram*, Louis Biancolli. 'But, then you never can tell in music,' he added sagely.) Backstage the voracious pianist Harriet Cohen cornered him and said in earshot of everybody, 'Let me be your mistress,' a generous if terrifying offer. But he was privately thrilled with the performance, delighted with Brosa's deft dispatch of the virtuosic writing and his ability to locate the work's heart – somewhere near the beginning of the downcast passacaglia.

Britten never enjoyed his premieres – and they became no easier with age. If he was performing the work himself, he could be physically sick beforehand, at which point he downed a restorative finger or two of brandy and crept on stage. Every composer reacts differently to a first performance, yet certain things are common. The composer must evaluate whether the performance is a true likeness of what is in the score and whether the score is a true likeness of what was in his head. If it is, he must determine whether the piece actually works. To do this he must separate his experience of the performance from the audience's. All this occurs before the applause has sounded, the final bows have been taken. Thereafter are the receptions, the patrons, the casual comments and arid pontificating, and of course the critics. None of Britten's touchiness surrounding a premiere was a pose or an impersonation of how a composer ought to behave. These were terrifying occasions, and no amount of brilliance or success shielded his vulnerability.

6

With the fever temporarily lifted and the concerto premiere behind him, Britten set to work on the Japanese government commission, which had finally been confirmed. The spirit of the concerto's passacaglia hung over him as he worked, his first major piece to be conceived and completed in America. In ambition and scale it suggests the perspective Britten was then acquiring concerned not just where he wanted to live, but how he wanted to write. He wanted big forms, bold gestures. And in this hybrid symphony and symphonic poem, he painted from a much larger palette than before. The startling, clumping opening is part Mahler, part Britten's own 'Funeral Blues': the timpano is struck with both sticks, the sound decaying almost immediately. However heartfelt the dedication to Britten's parents, we are left in no doubt that those in this cortège are mourning European democracy. It is a march of unremitting bleakness. Not even the whirligig scherzo that follows manages to lighten the mood: it is another of Britten's fast-sketched dances of death, punctuated by trumpet fanfares, dislocated and clashing, as though sounding from opposing sides of some monstrous battlefield. There is hope, of sorts, towards the end, where the shrieking cluster chords give way and the movement unwinds slowly towards a Mahlerian climax. There is a touch of *Das Lied von der Erde* to it – the quietly ecstatic transformation from one world to the next – which is the only part of the work that could feasibly be considered a parental tribute. It is a work of astonishing power and achievement, and represents a real advance in both ambition and structure on the pieces that preceded it.

In these details and martial effects, *Sinfonia da Requiem* can be considered a rehearsal for the much later *War Requiem*. Yet the latter was a peacetime work, a protest voiced far from enemy lines. *Sinfonia da Requiem* had no such protection or perspective. It was composed in the fever of battle and illness, commissioned by an imperialist government that for some years had been waging war on China. It was as uncompromising an offering as could be imagined.

Something does not add up. Britten surely knew about the Sino-Japanese War as he wrote the work; Auden and Isherwood had travelled to China in 1938, publishing *Journey to War* the following year, and Auden was wont to lecture almost anyone on the subject. ('I get very depressed running all over the place chatting about China,' he said on his return to England. 'Does it do any good?') Yet the war did not seem to fire Britten's imagination or indignation, certainly not in the way that Spain had done a few years earlier. Numerous times in 1940 he informed friends, a little smugly, that he was to visit 'Tokio' for the first performance, which caused him no further comment or condemnation. Surely he was aware of the propaganda value for the Japanese of such a visit?

So Britten was either ignorant of the extent of Japanese aggression in the East, or he intended his symphony to be a Trojan horse, launching an attack on Japanese imperialism and warmongering from within the city walls. If the latter is the case, he could not have been so surprised that the Japanese stopped its entry through the gates. 'Mr Benjamin Britten's composition is so very different from the anticipation of the Committee,' wrote Prince Konoye to the Japanese Foreign Office in late 1940, subsequently forwarded to Boosey & Hawkes in America, 'which had hoped to receive from a friendly nation felicitations expressed in musical form on the 2,600th anniversary of the founding of the Japanese Empire.' There followed a petulant response from Britten and more diplomatic hand-wringing, before the great celebrations came and went, *Sinfonia* quietly dropped from the programme.

It was as if, invited to a Japanese tea ceremony, Britten began to lecture his hosts about their patriarchal customs and ridiculous, restrictive gowns. Yet from the beginning Britten was clear in his mind about the nature of the piece – its Christian framework, its anti-war message and its public memorial to his parents – and early in the commissioning process communicated his ideas to Leslie Boosey, who ought to have taken him aside and countered his naivety. His indignation was partly because he was short of cash and badly needed the commission fee. He had already spent $95 of it on a 1931 Ford, and had treated the Mayers to an expensive dinner in the French Pavilion at the 1939–40 New York World's Fair, taking large-denomination notes from his wallet one at a time, saying as he did: 'First movement, second movement, third movement'. Would he now have to pay back the advance? But Britten was also prickly at the perceived snub; he was proud of a work in which his technique and vision were united with complete assurance, without any of the telltale tics and flaws that can be identified in some of the hastily composed works of the 1930s.

7

At the end of 1940, while all this diplomacy was under way, Britten and Pears moved from their Amityville sanctuary into an old Georgian terrace at 7 Middagh Street, Brooklyn. They were mindful that contacts and opportunities would be found in the heart of New York, not in suburban comfort and isolation on Long Island. It was a sort of doll's house, made of brick and brownstone, spread over five storeys, with Tudor trim on the façade and an equally incongruous wooden portico. The terrace no longer exists; the row was demolished in the 1950s to make way for the Brooklyn–Queens Expressway. But it occupied a thriving corner of town, only minutes from Brooklyn Bridge and the Columbia Street Waterfront District, with uninterrupted views over the harbour to the Lower Manhattan skyline.

It was less a house than a salon, less a salon than a 'year-long party', in the words of historian Sherill Tippins. Britten and Pears shared it with Auden, a young Carson McCullers, whose bestselling *The Heart is a Lonely Hunter* appeared that year, the fiction editor of *Harper's Bazaar* George Davis and the writers Paul and Jane Bowles. The designer Oliver Smith was there for a while, as was the stripper Gypsy Rose Lee, who was then writing her first book, *The G-String Murders*, a detective novel set in the dingy world of an old burlesque theatre on

42nd Street, which was soon thereafter turned into a successful film. Others came and went with the seasons.

The house had its own touch of burlesque. Auden, a mixture of martinettish landlord and dorm mother, collected rent ($25 a month for Britten and Pears), shopped for food, arranged laundry and dispensed advice, overseeing proceedings with complete authority. Mealtimes were scheduled, conversations marshalled, chaos kept (just) at bay. Leonard Bernstein thought it a madhouse; the Swiss writer Denis de Rougemont, who visited in 1941, thought that 'all that was new in America in music, painting, or choreography emanated from that house, the only center of thought and art that I found in any large city of the country'. It is a hyperbolic description, yet there can be no denying he had observed an A-list artistic crowd.

It was not all carnival. Auden's dogmatic personality ensured tenants were brought face to face with the questions he had posed in 'The Prolific and the Devourer' and 'New Year Letter': to what extent is the artist a part of the state machine and how does this change in wartime? Auden had written these ideas almost abstractly, yet the summer and autumn of 1940 ensured abstraction was no longer possible, even in distant America. Paris fell, Dunkirk hosted its own lethal theatre, and great swathes of London were destroyed in the Blitz. 'Everytime we have a thunderstorm (& they're pretty bad & frequent here),' Britten told his sister at the end of June 1940, 'I imagine what it must be like in your bombardments.' The war was now more serious.

Those in 'February House' (Anaïs Nin's nickname for it, in recognition of the large number of residents with February birthdays) had further cause to think on Auden's proclamations: at Middagh Street they rubbed shoulders with many European émigrés, guests at the year-long party, who talked with urgency of the countries and politics they had left behind. Kurt Weill and his wife Lotte Lenya (who would marry the homosexual Davis after Weill's death), various members of the Mann family, and Salvador Dalí were just some. (Dalí and his wife would later move in.) A visitor might encounter McCullers crouched in a corner, a flagon of sherry under her arm or a teacup of plonk at her fingers, her mind on her next book; or Davis naked at the piano, cigarette in mouth, his matinee-idol looks on full display; or Britten and Pears rehearsing songs in the front parlour. Louis MacNeice came for a meal and described its occupants as 'the way the populace once liked to think of artists – ever so bohemian, raiding the icebox at midnight and eating the catfood by mistake. But it was very enjoyable and at least they were producing.'

Britten celebrated his twenty-seventh birthday in February House soon after moving in. It was a day after Thanksgiving and the household decided on a large dinner in honour of both occasions, adding names to the guest list with abandon. The Mann and Mayer siblings, Copland, arts patron and impresario Lincoln Kirstein (and anyone he saw fit to bring), McCullers's ex- and future husband Reeves McCullers, Auden's lover Chester Kallman, and Swiss writer Annemarie Schwarzenbach all came. McCullers bought a crate of champagne and a turkey that would have fed only six people had Davis not replaced it with a sturdier bird. A feast was duly prepared.

Auden was in his element – shouting directions, practising his German with Golo Mann, holding forth on any subject (a transcript of which would make a great book, thought Mann). This was not Britten's natural milieu; it was too noisy, too intellectual, and few sitting round the table bothered to take prisoners in an argument. (Paul Bowles recalled later that, though he and Britten had meals together every day for four months, 'he and I had nothing memorable to say to one another'.) Yet he did what he could on this party night, which included an impromptu performance with Pears. And he joined in the charades and the game of Murder, for which the creaky old house – haunted, thought Davis – was ideally suited. The night finished with an improvised ballet: Pears and Davis danced wildly to *Petrushka*, swinging from curtains and hot-water pipes, whether accompanied by a gramophone recording or by Britten on piano is tantalizingly unclear.

For their duo performance the two musicians no doubt took the temperature of the room and then presented the *Cabaret Songs* or the like. But it is possible they also gave a preview of Britten's most recent work, *Seven Sonnets of Michelangelo*, completed only a month earlier. These songs overlapped with the two major orchestral pieces of the time, *Sinfonia da Requiem* and *Diversions*, and illustrate Britten's ability to juggle several large-scale works at once, a practice the mature composer did his best to avoid.

The Michelangelo settings form an impassioned love letter to Pears, ripe with unrestrained feelings and emotions. They are by no means cloud-free; the tribulations between lovers are there as well, and Britten catches them with an occasional thread of menacing restlessness. And it is likely they were not written solely with Pears in mind. Long after Britten's death Scherchen recalled him 'complaining of a "mental block" over a Michael Angelo Sonnet & "putting it away"'. If the initial inspiration for the songs was probably Scherchen rather than Pears, when the time came Britten was happy to adapt the idea and give the old ring to a new lover.

It is certainly possible that two of the seven songs, undated in their composition drafts, were written in 1938 or 1939, as Scherchen remembered. When Britten wrote to Enid Slater in April 1940 he told her he had a 'sudden craze for the Michael Angelo Sonnetts' and had set half a dozen of them. Only three drafts have dates before that of this letter, which leaves open the possibility he had pulled the two undated songs from his case. Regardless of when these two songs were conceived or composed, *Seven Sonnets of Michelangelo* is the first complete work written specifically for Pears to sing, inspired by (or partly adapted to) the timbre of his voice and the nature of his feelings for the dedicatee. In this last element, the songs reflect the origins of the sonnets, written for the handsome young Italian Tommaso dei Cavalieri, Ganymede to Michelangelo's Zeus. 'My will is in your will alone, my thoughts are born in your heart, my words are on your breath. Alone, I am like the moon in the sky which our eyes cannot see save that part which the sun illumines.' This was their relationship, Pears later said.

Seven Sonnets is not strictly a cycle. Or more accurately, it was not conceived as a cycle in the manner of Schubert's *Winterreise*, one song leading logically into the next. It is more in the mould of *On This Island* – a collection of songs composed over a relatively long stretch by Britten's standards, in moments snatched from other commissions and commitments and then reordered for performance and publication. By 1940 Britten had of course already completed a few orchestral song cycles, not least *Les Illuminations* – a work also squeezed between other commitments, individual songs composed out of sequence. Later cycles tended to be composed in more concentrated periods, though the order of the songs' composition and that when finally published did not necessarily coincide. And occasionally Britten would write a surfeit of songs for a particular cycle, as with the two Hardy poems originally written for *Winter Words* in 1953 which did not find a place in the completed work; three extra Rimbaud settings in the case of *Les Illuminations*; an unused epilogue to his Donne cycle; three surplus songs for *Who are these Children?*; and the extra song composed for his Indian-summer collection, *A Birthday Hansel.*

There is a recording of *Seven Sonnets*, probably made in early 1941, in which Pears sounds occasionally stilted, at other times wary of the demands made of him. There are no more colours in the voice than are in his April 1941 recording of *Les Illuminations*, but there is power and warmth. He has a top B in his armoury, which he dispatches with relish in the lines quoted above from Sonnet XXX. Britten plays with great stillness, pacing the songs with care and precision, particularly the concluding sonnet, which unwinds ecstatically over a mutating ground bass.

All the accompaniments are stripped back, in contrast to the substantial thickets he created at the same time in *Sinfonia da Requiem*. There is also an attractive feeling of antiquity to some of the songs, as if Michelangelo's poems were to be matched with contemporaneous musical techniques. Quite apart from ground bass, in Sonnet XXXI the left hand plays a simple cello part, a figured bass-line in effect, which is fleshed out in the right hand with increasingly dissonant harmony, unmoored from the material beneath. (These roles are reversed in the following sonnet.) Yet for all such nods towards Baroque music, it was Italian bel canto repertory that influenced Britten here, inspiring in him melodies of simple beauty, a showcase for his lover's emerging voice.

Britten and Pears gave the first public performance of the cycle only when they returned to England, at London's Wigmore Hall, in September 1942. The Italian text (and lack of translation in the programme) may have cloaked the representation of Britten's and Pears's feelings for each other, but there was no ambiguity in one key area: the performance marked the debut of what would become arguably the most important musical partnership in post-war Britain – more significant even than Walter Legge and Elisabeth Schwarzkopf. It was a bravura gesture, a gauntlet thrown down on behalf of English song and music-making, and would subsequently be recognized as an event of great significance.

8

For $10 per rehearsal, in late 1940 Britten was appointed director of the Suffolk Friends of Music Orchestra, a semi-professional band, 'a post which requires a great deal of energy, a certain amount of skill and an infinite amount of tact', he confided to Albert Goldberg. Scrappy as it was, the orchestra provided Britten with his only apprenticeship as a conductor. He never lost the physical stiffness Fass identified. 'In the beginning,' Imogen Holst said after his death, 'he didn't even know – he told me, Ben himself – how to raise his arm for an upbeat; and we've seen him year after year get better and better, and it's taken him twenty years.' Yet this suburban scratch orchestra helped him develop the courteous, no-nonsense approach to rehearsing and performing that would become his post-war trademark.

Money was the motivation here, however, not a quest for podium hours. Performances of his works had dried up almost completely in England, partly through circumstance, partly through hostility. His scores continued to sell, yet the sums generated were trifling and from early 1940 all money earned in Britain was required by law to remain there. (The full score of *Variations on a Theme of Frank Bridge* sold forty-one copies in 1941, *A Hymn to the Virgin* a little under three times as much.) There were performances in America – the piano and violin concertos, *Sinfonia da Requiem* with the New York Philharmonic and the Frank Bridge variations among them – but they did not make a huge material difference. Nor did American sales of scores. Britten found himself in a similar position to another exile, Béla Bartók, whom he once encountered at the New York office of Boosey & Hawkes, sitting in a corner counting out his stipend, reliant on the patronage of his publisher. Nor was Pears earning anything significant from performing; he took on his own directorship, that of the Southold Town Choral Society at $15 a rehearsal, to help make ends meet.

Amid this financial hardship, Britten was approached over the directorship of the music department at the University of New Mexico, Albuquerque, which came with an astonishing salary of $32,000 (£8,000). 'Later on I may find it necessary to hold such a position,' he told composer and academic Douglas Moore in declining, 'but for the time being I think I'll risk just being a freelance composer, doing hack-work maybe, but in the composing line.' Perhaps Hollywood would come to the rescue, Britten told himself, not for the first time, but his decision only emphasized how precarious his position was.

Commissions were the answer: a percentage lump sum on signature, the rest on completion or performance, which generally came about quickly because of the speed at which he worked. Sometimes the commissions were hackwork – music for a CBS adaptation of Hardy's *The Dynasts*, for example – other times more elevated in design and execution. One of the latter had come his way in 1940, when the overbearing but rich one-armed pianist Paul Wittgenstein, brother of the philosopher Ludwig, commissioned a work for piano and orchestra, and paid Britten $700 for the privilege. It is a contemplative piece, a series of short but rather beautiful variations on a dramatic theme, which opens the work with the same sort of rhetorical power of a Strauss tone poem. Britten went from one hand to four in a subsequent work, the slight *Introduction and Rondo alla Burlesca*, written for the husband-and-wife team of Rae Robertson and Ethel Bartlett. Yet these were friends, not so much commissioners as grateful exponents.

Elizabeth Sprague Coolidge, the generous and insightful music patron, commissioned a string quartet from Britten in late 1940, a task that gained in poignancy when, on 10 January 1941, Bridge died at his home in Sussex, aged only sixty-one. Britten wrote to Coolidge offering his assistance (and that of Brosa and Pears) if she had 'any concert or ceremony in mind in memory of our dear friend Frank'. It was not much, but given how helpless Britten felt just then, and how far he was from the Friston circle that had so shaped his boyhood, it was the best he could manage. After the war he made good his debt to Bridge by programming and performing his music whenever he could.

Lincoln Kirstein paid him $300 for a chamber orchestration of Chopin's *Les Sylphides* in 1941, and came good with another project only months later – a suite based on Rossini tunes, *Matinées musicales*, a companion piece for Britten's first such suite, *Soirées musicales* of 1936. Together the two Rossini tributes formed a new ballet, with choreography by Balanchine, no less. Britten also worked with Auden on his radio adaptation of a D. H. Lawrence short story, 'The Rocking-Horse Winner', which CBS aired in April 1941 as a follow-up to *The Dark Valley* of the previous year. This earned Britten $75. Between these commissions and various advances from his publisher, Britten's income for the year was a little over $1,640 – then around £400. It was less than he had been earning in England and a little toothless in the face of New York's higher cost of living, which was now documented for Britten and Pears in the carefully annotated household bills Auden prepared for the tenants of Middagh Street. Living on Long Island with the Mayers had insulated them from such expenses.

It was nonetheless enough to make him think America was a land of opportunity. The performances were high-profile: Carnegie Hall; the New York Philharmonic and the Boston and Illinois orchestras; conductors John Barbirolli, Albert Goldberg, Serge Koussevitzky and Izler Solomon, with Eugene Goossens buzzing around in the background, programming Britten's works in Cincinnati for the following season. He had ready access to many of the most prestigious American companies, and doors opened at the slightest of touches. He forged an uneasy friendship with Leonard Bernstein, who would become such an important architect of post-war American culture, though Britten found his flamboyant personality nauseating, on one occasion thumping him in the chest to stem his conversation and extravagant behaviour.* And Britten's compositions were now better: more even, more adventurous and often enough on a larger canvas, which he handled with verve.

Yet the city was intent on souring his outlook. 'New York is the worst,' he told Enid Slater in June 1941, 'a struggling mass of scheming, shallow sophisticates & the lowest kind of every race under the Sun.' And life at Middagh Street, though never dull, became more and more draining. It was dirty, diseased (bedbugs chomped away) and too unpredictable for such an ordered man. The parties became longer and stranger, the itinerant visitors more random, more improbable. Pears coped a little better, but even he found it uncomfortable after the warmth and happiness of Long Island. This discontent brewed during the first half of 1941, and prompted their escape to California in July. But before they could once more take refuge in flight, the work that should have been the pinnacle of Britten's partnership with Auden was to have its premiere.

9

Quite how *Paul Bunyan* ended up as it did says a lot about the state of Britten's mind in the early 1940s. His aspirations for the piece, as recorded in the *New York Sun* a year before the operetta's premiere, were sound. 'Bunyan in a way symbolizes the pioneers of the whole world, the men

---

* It was probably Bernstein who dismissed English music as 'too much organ voluntary in Lincoln Cathedral, too much Coronation in Westminster Abbey, too much lark ascending, too much clod-hopping on the fucking village green'.

who opened up new country, who conquered without killing, who were the noblest kind of adventurers.' These are lovely sentiments (though they were more probably a poetic enhancement of a journalist's sketchy notes than Britten's exact words; his rhetoric was rarely so elevated), linking the work with a more general 1930s literary preoccupation: the exploration of new frontiers, metaphorical and literal. *Annie Get Your Gun*, Irving Berlin's smash-hit Broadway musical of 1946, emerged from these ideas and was no doubt the type of show, and success, to which Auden and Britten aspired. Their operetta was originally intended for school halls, but from early on both men had Broadway in their sights.

The mythical giant Paul Bunyan, so large at birth that it took three storks to deliver him, and who dug the Grand Canyon by allowing his axe to drag behind him as he walked with his friend Babe the blue ox, remains a popular figure in American folklore. Perhaps aware that many Americans would view these Englishmen's colonization of their myth as presumptuous or arrogant, Britten suggested in his interview that sometimes 'strangers see such things more clearly'.

The piece they created shows otherwise. Unlike Berlin's musical, or for that matter Weill's *Aufstieg und Fall der Stadt Mahagonny*, which is a dark and cynical portrait of a Wild West dystopia, its economy run on prostitution, whisky, horses, poker and theft, *Paul Bunyan* is not really sure what it wants to be. Is it an American backwoodsman version of a Norse legend? A medieval morality play? American history according to Vico's cycle of ages: the divine, the heroic and the human? Whatever Auden's motivation, it would seem both men had only the slightest hold on American culture and sensibility when setting to work on the piece, as confident as Dickens in the previous century that American audiences would lap up any old nonsense. There is a barb in this messy creation story, as there is in Dickens's *Martin Chuzzlewit*: Bunyan takes his leave of his fellow lumberjacks on the eve of the Machine Age (an obsession of Auden's at the time): we are left thinking that the apple has been picked from the tree and that American history – the bad more than the good – is just beginning. (Dickens has Chuzzlewit travel to America to make his fortune, where he rudely dismisses the New World and those who populate it.) American audiences and critics resented what they considered a patronizing lecture, an imperial report card, just as they had Dickens a century earlier. 'In the plot, as in the score, is a little of everything, a little of symbolism and uplift, a bit of socialism and of modern satire, and gags and jokes of a Hollywood sort, or of rather cheap musical comedy ... It seems a rather poor sort of a bid for success, and possibly the beguilement of Americans' was one of the milder dismissals.

As the criticism suggests, Britten responded in kind to Auden's jumbled libretto, careering between ballad and folk song, blues and bel canto, hymn tune and show tune. Only in the aria sung by the philosopher-bookkeeper Johnny Inkslinger, with its gentle chromaticism, its incrementally thickening orchestral texture and its tweaking of simple vocal phrases, do we hear Britten's true voice rather than his expert ventriloquism. It is an aria in reverse, another example of gradual revelation. The vocal fragments act as incoherent stutterings and give the impression of thoughts being processed there and then. It is only at the end of the aria that the fragments are knitted together and we hear a full phrase of touching melismatic beauty.

Auden later owned up to his ignorance. 'The result, I'm sorry to say, was a failure, for which I was entirely to blame, since, at the time, I knew nothing whatsoever about opera or what is required of a librettist. In consequence, some very lovely music of Britten's went down the drain.' The problem, in part, was that he did not have Isherwood to rely on – the 'cool-headed play-doctor', in John Fuller's words, 'making viable constructions out of the fertile mess that Auden provided'. And the libretto was written much earlier than the music, when Auden had been in the country for less than a year. Yet the problems are knottier than this. A modernist poet had no need of something as old-fashioned as plot: Auden's lyric poetry before *Bunyan* is full of episodic, fleeting images, political commentary and wild jigs of fantasy, and even the larger poetic works do not have the taut, narrative quality of a long Tennyson poem. In Auden's hands, *Bunyan* was a magic-lantern show, a selection of striking contemporary images kitted out in old costumes and threaded together with an improvised narrative.

Britten did his best to keep up, as he did in previous collaborations with Auden, but there is a huge difference between assembling an anthology and writing an opera, and it shows in *Paul Bunyan*. Perhaps there is a comparison to be made with *Mahagonny* after all, not simply in its bleak portrait of the American frontier with its own cast of lumberjacks, but in that it also suffers from the tensions that existed between *Mahagonny*'s creators, Weill and Brecht.

Auden would improve with age: his libretto for Stravinsky's *The Rake's Progress*, written with Chester Kallman, is a masterful narrative embellishment of a series of Hogarth etchings – material as scant as he had to hand for *Paul Bunyan*. And his reordering of certain scenes in his poetic translation of *The Magic Flute* shows his determination to make a plot sensible, as Fuller has suggested. But these operas were still some years away. As it is, we are left like Stephen Spender, regretting the lost opportunity. 'I mean the sort of unwritten masterpiece of the [twentieth] century – the early part of this century – is the collaboration between Auden and Benjamin Britten. That ought to have been written and I think they both knew it ought to have been written.' This knowledge would increase in poignancy in the 1960s and 1970s.

If Auden learned from his mistakes, so did Britten. *Peter Grimes* and *The Little Sweep* aside, which like *The Rake's Progress* are built on suggestive but by no means complete narratives, in all his other operas Britten worked from pre-existing stories. The contemplated but unwritten operas were also to be adaptations of famous works, with the exception of the original space-age fantasy 'Tyco the Vegan'. The Church Parables required some fleshing out, though less than one might imagine. All his remaining stage works use existing plays or novels as templates.

Of course, changes to the sources were made. The first of his Church Parables, *Curlew River*, was moved from Japan to the marshy bleakness of East Anglia – as were *The Little Sweep* and *Albert Herring* before it (the latter transplanted from France). Captain Vere in *Billy Budd* survives into an old age of self-recrimination and potential redemption, whereas Melville killed him off in battle. *A Midsummer Night's Dream* had huge chunks of the original removed, at the expense of the human characters, but demonstrating touching empathy with the forest world and its inhabitants. Yet these were relatively minor alterations – positioning Britten far from Alfred Hitchcock, who once mischievously said, 'Today I would be unable to tell you the story of Daphne du Maurier's *The Birds*. I read it only once, and very quickly at that.'

Not for nothing was Britten an admirer of Dickens, a master of plot, suspense and episode. ('Jo?' Dickens wrote of a crossing-sweeper in his working notes for *Bleak House*. 'Yes. Kill him.' It is no stretch to imagine him writing an identical note for Little Nell. Britten was often almost this clinical with his characters.) 'I am a great reader and lover of

Dickens,' Britten said in 1963, 'but although many of the scenes I could think of operatically, I would find the overall shape almost impossible to cope with. One, however, I have thought about seriously.'* He needed these buttresses in his stage works, regardless of the tinkering and larger structural alterations he effected in the source material. Six years after commenting on Dickens, with a swag of operas to his name, Britten made an observation of E. M. Forster which is as illuminating of his own process as it is of the writer's: 'Here one may perhaps observe that the construction of Forster's novels often resembles that of the "classical" opera (Mozart – Weber – Verdi) where recitatives (the deliberately un-lyrical passages by which the action is advanced) separate arias or ensembles (big, self-contained set pieces of high comedy or great emotional tension).' For Britten fiction shaped opera, and opera shaped fiction. But in both, to him, plot was paramount. This was the ultimate lesson of *Paul Bunyan*.

10

California was part menagerie, part Garden of Eden. Britten and Pears drove across the continent in an old Ford borrowed from friends, taking nine days to cover the 3,000-odd miles, and in California encountered a world of humming birds, coyotes, fireflies and citrus trees, fed from dams and irrigation pipes that spread across the land like great arteries. They worked each morning and for much of the afternoon, often motoring down to a beach to bathe before dinner, a Pacific rehearsal of Britten's post-war Suffolk habits. Bed was early and sleep sound. Their hosts were the pianists Ethel Bartlett and Rae Robertson, who were attentive and generous – almost to a fault: during these months Ethel fell in love with Britten, a situation Rae attempted to resolve by withdrawing his claim to his wife, a spectacularly misplaced act of gallantry. Pears acted as peacemaker, a role he later perfected, yet the incident suggests that in the two years or so of their friendship with the couple, the men had not disclosed the true nature of their relationship.

* This was probably *David Copperfield*, a book he read and reread as a teenager. It is a good example of Dickens's episodic narratives, and also features a romantic friendship between the schoolboy David and the slightly older James Steerforth, both of them boarding-school pupils, which no doubt resonated.

Despite the awkwardness, which grew exponentially, Britten worked and worked in a small shed in the Robertsons' garden, desperate to commit to paper all his thoughts while he was still able to do so. Not for the last time in his life, he worried that circumstances would rob him of his ability to compose. 'At the moment my greatest wish is to write as much as I possibly can,' he told Scherchen, 'while I am still able & allowed to – because one never knows how long it will last, & I have such a hell of a lot to want to say.' He completed his second piece for the duo, the still-night *Mazurka Elegiaca*; wrote the bulk of his *Scottish Ballad* for two pianos and orchestra (which he thought a poor piece, too beholden to the Scottish folk songs at its heart, which is an accurate assessment); and finished and dispatched his first numbered string quartet, which was scheduled for its premiere in Los Angeles in late September 1941.

Britten described himself at this time in a letter to his sister Barbara. A new hairstyle, brushed back from the forehead, a sourer temper, weighing in at nine stone six (up ten pounds from that to which *Paul Bunyan* had reduced him a month earlier), his face smooth from now-daily shaves. Photographs show him relaxed and smiling, belying the strained circumstances. In one he is dressed in dungarees, heavily tanned, looking to the world like an itinerant fruit picker, a welcome contrast to his usual jacket and tie.

Finally they visited Hollywood – for an occasional concert at the Bowl (conducted by Barbirolli) and for some informal business meetings from which nothing eventuated.* The place repulsed him: its pagodas and Spanish villas, road congestion and awful driving, fat and pampered children, the thoughtless Californians with their bogus medicines and body culture, and no doubt the food as well – crunchy salads of iceberg lettuce and the gloopy orange sauce that so startled other émigrés. All this sent him into a fug of depression. 'Money, time, distance – nothing has the old meaning,' he complained to Scherchen. 'It explains why so many of the films that come from Hollywood, although

---

* Britten admired Barbirolli more than he did the conductor's British peers, though three years later, having experienced his unsatisfactory conducting of the *Sinfonia da Requiem* premiere with the New York Philharmonic on 29 March 1941 – the speeds in the outer movements too slow, the inner poorly shaped – said 'the party isn't *really* first rate'. The critic of the *New York Herald Tribune* on 31 March 1941 was more generous, though he took back with one hand what he offered with the other: 'Except for his fine work in the *Sinfonia da Requiem*, this was not Mr Barbirolli's afternoon.'

technically so good, are artistically so rotten. All the weaknesses of the civilised world, all the lack of direction, find their epitome in California.' It was much as Isherwood later described it: 'California is a tragic country – like Palestine, like every promised land.'

There were compensations, for 'it was in California, in the unhappy summer of 1941, that, coming across a copy of the Poetical Works of George Crabbe in a Los Angeles bookshop, I first read his poem, *Peter Grimes*'. An article by E. M. Forster in the *Listener* of 29 May had alerted him to Crabbe's poetry, about which he was wholly ignorant. Forster wrote beautifully of this strange man and his work. 'Even when he is writing of other things, there steals again and again into his verse the sea, the estuary, the flat Suffolk coast, and local meannesses, and an odour of brine and dirt – tempered occasionally with the scent of flowers. So remember Aldeburgh when you read this rather odd poet, for he belongs to the grim little place, and through it to England.' For a man already homesick, hostile to his environs, Britten was struck with nostalgia for England, Suffolk in particular. With the same sense of wide-eyed wonderment with which he accosted Wyss on the train three years earlier, volume of Rimbaud in hand, he wrote to Elizabeth Mayer, 'We've just re-discovered the poetry of George Crabbe (all about Suffolk!) & are very excited – maybe an opera one day . . . !!'

Quite who recognized the operatic potential of these bleak, damp poems is not clear. It says something about Britten's confidence and certainty in himself – despite hardships and homesickness – that the recent debacle with Auden had not poisoned the genre for him. And it says something about Britten's inexperience that he was happy enough to march on in this new venture with such incomplete source material – a collection of character sketches and gloomy, unrelated episodes, but no overarching narrative. (Grimes is the subject of only one poem out of twenty-four.) Yet once they were back in Amityville, Britten outlined ideas for the Act 1 Scene 1 scenario and staging – full of storm clouds and rising tides, with word of a foreign boat in trouble off Southwold and whispered stories about the thuggish, drunken Grimes and his previous apprentice, dead by suicide. Pears also thrashed out a scenario, which includes a church scene, a monologue from Peter to the boy that ends with his 'accidental murder', and a manhunt. Thereafter, Grimes enters the stage, fevered and hallucinating: 'the Sea calls him. Just as he is about to leap in, enter Ellen, ahead of crowd. She calls to him.

Too late, he says, & jumps in.' It is a rough sketch, unsubtle and melo-dramatic, yet anyone familiar with the opera would recognize it immediately.

After Auden, Britten was learning a new, gentler form of collabor-ation and liked it. His sure dramatic instincts, shaped to a degree by Pears's literary taste and input, were to dominate the opera's compos-ition. As Pears commented in a later broadcast, 'by the time we came back to London, the whole story of *Peter Grimes* as set in the opera was already shaped and it simply remained to call in a librettist to write the words'. He was not entirely accurate – a number of people helped form the piece in England and turn it into something subtler than the Ameri-can sketches suggested – but the balance of power implicit in Pears's observation would characterize most of Britten's post-war operas.

When in early 1942 he came to choose a librettist for *Grimes*, he first turned to Isherwood, not Auden. Isherwood read Crabbe and looked at their ideas for the rough shape of the work, but finally and resoundingly cried off any involvement. 'I'm sorry, but I don't see any possibility of collaborating with you and Peter on the *Peter Grimes* libretto.' His problem was time, but 'frankly, the subject doesn't excite me so much that I want to *make* time for it'. He was convinced it would never work as an opera.

All this was some months off. And there was one more important event before they could leave California: the first performance of Brit-ten's String Quartet No. 1. The genre belonged to his youth: he had used it to help crystallize his technique and harness his somewhat wild har-monic ideas, initially under Bridge, subsequently Ireland. But then came the whirl of contemporary poetry, of political works and larger forms; a string quartet could hardly expect to keep up with this smart crowd. In accepting the commission, however, Britten was joining a remarkable club: many eminent composers enjoyed Coolidge's patronage, and her links with the European avant-garde had helped shape America's music industry in the first decades of the twentieth century. Like Schoenberg's Quartet No. 4 and Bartók's Quartet No. 5 before it, Britten's Quartet No. 1 is dedicated to this most cultured patron.

What a difference there is between this work and Britten's earlier essays in the genre. It is not that Britten ignores the formal considera-tions that reined in the adventurousness of his earlier works – the headstrong *Quartettino* aside. The work has a classical skin (the

separate movements, sonata form and imitative writing would not surprise Haydn), yet it readily discards it when inspiration demands. It is
full of song-like melodies, of the ready virtuosity of the Violin Concerto,
where detailed, idiomatic string writing and phrases pass effortlessly
from instrument to instrument, movement to movement, transformed
along the way. It is a strong riposte to the accusations of facileness that
had plagued him in the late 1930s; it is almost as though the piece was
composed from inside out, rather than Britten taking a form and fitting
it with music. 'The Britten has an extraordinary explosive force,' Edith
Sitwell wrote of the quartet in 1943. 'In spite of the fact that I've just
had a most debilitating cold, it is still exploding in my head with a
blinding light followed by new ideas, points of view, even new vision.'

Britten was delighted with the performance by the Coolidge Quartet,
technically and musically. (The ensemble was far better than the quartets that played his early string works.) The *Los Angeles Times* ran a
mostly perceptive critique on 22 September, a day after the premiere, in
which the ideas were admired if not always the sounds. Whether Britten
saw this review on the day is unclear. He was busy with Pears, making
good their escape from their 'selfish, self-indulgent, conceited' hosts,
setting off back across the continent in the Robertsons' car, an irony
evidently lost on the self-obsessed composer.

II

On the East Coast, Britten dashed off an 'occasional overture' for
the conductor Artur Rodzinski and the Cleveland Orchestra, a deal
Hawkes brokered. 'I'm afraid (again, between you & me!) I didn't do an
awfully good job,' he told Beth. Here Britten's assessment is harsh. Even
if it does not know how and when to end, it is a work of its time and
place – full of prairie sounds, barn-dance extemporizing on solo fiddles
(prefiguring the band music in *Peter Grimes*) and a still, solemn chorale,
which gives way to brilliant chromatic fanfares and a blazing climax. It
seems that Rodzinski did not perform it, then or later; the manuscript
remained behind in America after Britten returned to England, forgotten for thirty years. When it resurfaced in 1972, Britten had no memory
of it whatsoever and no especial desire for reacquaintance; it was pub-

lished only posthumously, under the title *An American Overture*. His reaction captures well how he looked back on the final months of 1941. 'My recollection of that time was of complete incapacity to work; my only achievements being a few Folksong arrangements and some real-isations of Henry Purcell. I was in quite a psychological state then . . .' Biographers and film makers have jumped on this remark, proffering it, alongside a corroborating statement by an American friend, as evidence of a breakdown.

The friend concerned was David Rothman, who ran a hardware store in Southold, Long Island, and who sat on the committee of the orchestra Britten conducted. Rothman's wife, who was seeking treat-ment for a nervous breakdown, was a patient of Dr Mayer's. Britten went to stay with the family one weekend in early November 1941 and to David he unburdened his anxieties. Much later Rothman recalled this and an earlier occasion when Britten shed tears on seeing that there were more people in the orchestra than in the audience for their concert. 'He wanted to stop writing music, and wanted to work in my store.' It was not a serious proposition: it was a sulky, frustrated, foot-stamping reaction to things not going his way, nothing more. Nor is any trauma evident in home-movie footage of Britten on his weekend away – at a family picnic, smiling as he eats a hamburger and blows on a toasted marshmallow – or in the upbeat thank-you letters sent to his hosts. 'Ben to Southold,' Elizabeth Mayer wrote in her diary, making no mention of an altered mental state, 'had a good time with the Rothmans, played at salesman in store, brought presents for us all.'

He was, evidently, plagued by indecision. En route to the East Coast, high on Crabbe and homesickness, Britten and Pears met Isherwood and 'discussed the whole business of going home . . . in particular, the idea of going back and being a Conscientious Objector. I came to the conclusion that for me personally, it was a little bit like insisting on being a vegetar-ian in a group of people who aren't.' They argued the toss: if they were going to live in England for the rest of their lives, which they told Isher-wood seemed likely, they should go back as soon as feasible and declare themselves pacifists. A few weeks before his Southold trip Britten said much the same thing to Coolidge, adding that 'I am not telling people because it sounds a little heroic, which it is far from being – it is really that I cannot be separated any longer from all my friends and family'.

A little over two weeks later, he told sister Beth the opposite, mentioning future commissions and a life for them all in America after the war.

News from England was scarcely positive. 'It is not encouraging to see others thriving on a culture which they have not the courage to defend,' a music-loving RAF officer had written to the *Musical Times* in June 1941, sparking fierce debate. The editor eventually came down on the side of the RAF officer, suggesting that 'there are even worse fates than being unable to go on living and "composing in America", and one of them may be the consciousness of having saved one's art and skin at the cost of failure to do one's duty'. At the same time the baritone George Baker, an honorary official of the Royal Philharmonic Society, wrote angrily to the *Sunday Times* about the composer's absence while other young musicians were directing their energies towards winning 'the Battle of Britain; a programme in which Mr Britten has no part'.*

Britten's 'psychological state' was only partly to do with this indecision and the temper back home: mostly the problem was that he had come back to Long Island with no firm compositional plans and no commissions in place. He was banking on nebulous prospects, drawing advances from Boosey & Hawkes ($200 on 17 November, the same again a month later) and found himself in a more tenuous position than at any time in the previous two and a half years. Was America going to fail him? The thought made all the medium-term prospects, all the introductions and game planning, of little comfort. 'Yer pays yer money (or yer doesn't!!) & yer mikes yer chice,' as he wrote to Goldberg on another matter, his best Bronx gangster voice on show. He was a gun for hire, happy to do anything for a bag of cash, but found no takers. It was in this frustrating climate that the homesickness, the lack of immediate opportunities and his sense of duty coalesced, hardening his thoughts towards his adopted country. Auden threw in his twopenn'orth: 'You'll never be a well man while you stay in America.' Within two weeks of his visit to the Rothmans, Britten was telling Koussevitzky that he expected to leave for England early in the New Year. He and Pears sought passage home and the cloud passed.

---

* Much later, as chairman of the society, Baker would sound out Britten on his willingness to accept its prestigious Gold Medal. In graciously accepting, Britten had either put behind him Baker's unfortunate intervention or, more likely, had forgotten.

I 2

As Britten mulled over the matter of turning Crabbe's poems into a full-length opera, he was slowly, almost unknowingly, drifting apart from Auden, his literary mentor. The folk songs and Purcell realizations Britten dismissed so lightly in 1972 were evidence of his new approach to the setting of English poetry outside Auden's influence. Britten's discovery of Purcell's songs and his exposure to this remarkable prosody (the inherent rhyme and metre of verse, which Purcell identified and elevated to an extraordinary degree) came at a fortuitous time: Purcell could take Auden's place.

In an essay Britten wrote for the first performance of *Grimes*, he addressed this question.

> One of my chief aims is to try and restore to the musical setting of the English language a brilliance, freedom, and vitality that have been curiously rare since the death of Purcell. In the past hundred years, English writing for the voice has been dominated by strict subservience to logical speech-rhythms, despite the fact that accentuation according to sense often contradicts the accentuation demanded by emotional content. Good recitative should transform the natural intonations and rhythms of everyday speech into memorable musical phrases (as with Purcell), but in more stylized music, the composer should not deliberately avoid unnatural stresses if the prosody of the poem and the emotional situation demand them, nor be afraid of a high-handed treatment of words, which may need prolongation far beyond their common speech-length, or a speed of delivery that would be impossible in conversation.

It was a high-wire act. The composer who spent much of the early 1930s a hostage to musical form was talking now about the freedom that came from following the methods of prosody instead. Other composers had attempted to do the same – Janáček, for example, who created musical syntax out of Czech speech rhythms in the first decades of the century – yet Britten was arguing on behalf of the English language, with its own patterns and declamatory style. With Purcell as a guide, Britten proposed to remove the shackles of nineteenth-century Austro-Germanic form from musical settings of the English language, while at the same time saving it from nineteenth-century British literalists. It was quite a manifesto.

His first Purcell settings were undertaken some time in the initial American months – 'The Knotting Song', and 'Hark the ech'ing air!' from *The Fairy Queen*. Britten and Pears included them in a recital in Riverhead, New York, in November 1939. The latter is an ecstatic colloquy between voice and piano, the small amount of text spread over a large number of bars, each filled with ornamentation, onomatopoeia, repetition of words or phrases and the sort of free-wheeling coloratura Pears was yet to master. The musical phrases are of wildly varying lengths, while the joyful piano realization embroiders the text with great skill and cheek.

Britten's vocal works before his discovery of Purcell were not all one note per syllable – *On This Island* proves this – but thereafter his vocal writing contained the brilliance, freedom and vitality he identified in Purcell's songs. From *Peter Grimes* to *Canticle I 'My Beloved is Mine'* and the unmoored vocal writing of the Church Parables and *Death in Venice*, the impact was profound.

The challenges in setting English texts had concerned him for several years before his immersion in Purcell. He avoided the issue in *Les Illuminations* and the *Seven Sonnets of Michelangelo*, saying later of *Les Illuminations* that 'it was something in the setting of the foreign language which enabled me to have a freedom which set in my own language wouldn't have existed'. It was Purcell who helped him recognize that such freedom was also possible in English.

His other experiment at the time, arrangements of English folk songs, was not of the same significance. The songs, published as *Folk Song Arrangements*, volume 1: *British Isles*, in 1943, nonetheless performed three functions: they were a modest vehicle for Pears; they allowed Britten to pay tribute to various new American friends through individual dedications; and, courtesy of some innovative harmony and piano writing, Britten was able to cock a snook at those fusty English folk-song collectors and their hymn-like arrangements. 'Parry's national ideal was, in fact, the English Gentleman (who generally thinks it rather vulgar to take too much trouble),' he wrote in 1941 in an essay pointedly called 'England and the Folk-Art Problem'. 'From Parry and his associates there arose a school of composers directly influenced by folksong, to which belonged virtually every composer known here until recently, except of course, Elgar and Frank Bridge.' Britten mined the same vein, setting 'The Salley Gardens', 'The Ash Grove' and 'Oliver Cromwell' among others, but what he created from the raw material was worlds apart from the arrangements of Parry, Cecil Sharp and the like, who tiptoed reverentially and unimaginatively around the original songs.

There is an urban–rural tension to each Britten arrangement; the countryside is dragged, sometimes kicking, into the modern city, which is full of strange noises and foreign customs. Yet the behaviour and values in each song are determinedly rural. The whole volume is a revelation: there are harmonic colours, narrative themes and a hint of patriotism that would have been unlikely, if not inconceivable, only three years earlier. The arrangements demonstrate a composer alert to every dramatic nuance and musical opportunity inherent in the original songs.*

Britten dedicated one of these early folk songs to Bobby Rothman, David Rothman's adolescent son, who forgot about it until the 1970s when a neighbour brought it to his attention. He then rifled through the family piano stool and found a copy of the first edition. Bobby's song, 'The trees they grow so high', is a troubling piece. It narrates the short life of a teenage boy, told through the eyes of the older girl to whom he is betrothed, much against her initial wishes. They marry at sixteen, have a child at seventeen, and a year later she is mourning him. Britten perhaps identified a loose connection between the boy protagonist and Bobby, but if so it was nothing more profound than that they were both teenagers.

Commentators have identified autobiographical motifs in the song, particularly lines such as, 'I called for my true love, but they would not let him come, / All because he was a young boy and growing.' This would be quite a stretch were it not for the fact that Britten apparently confessed to the Mayers' daughter Beata, after one of his trips to Southold, that he had fallen in love with Bobby.

There were certainly acute feelings on Britten's part, which Bobby

---

* There was one mishap. In the sad and sinister child–adult world of 'Little Sir William', a 'Jew's wife' slays the poor boy with a penknife. (In one popular version of the folk song the boy is called Sir Hugh, while the murderer is a 'Jew's daughter'.) In a subsequent printing of the Britten setting she was silently transformed into a 'school's wife' (an unusual new class of villain), though not before the first print-run had further perpetuated the folk song's medieval anti-Semitism.

himself recognized, at least in retrospect. 'I was a little overwhelmed that someone should be so fond of me.' Yet their time together was more Huckleberry Finn and Jim than anything more threatening. They would go out on Bobby's rowing boat, casting for blowfish or rigging up a sail. Or they might go for long walks, talking all the while. There were occasional sleepovers when Britten would share a bedroom with Bobby, both of them chatting until they fell asleep. And later, once Britten returned to England, they corresponded. It was a more innocent time, of course, but neither parent saw anything predatory in Britten's behaviour. On one occasion, at bedtime, Britten asked, 'Bobby, would you mind terribly if before we fell asleep I came over and gave you a hug and a kiss?' which Bobby thought perfectly natural.

Once Humphrey Carpenter's biography appeared in 1992, with Beata Mayer's recollection of Britten's feelings for the boy given some space, Bobby became more guarded, careful to stress that Britten had been far fonder of him than he had been of the older man. Yet he was also careful to exonerate Britten of any wrongdoing. 'He *was* very fond of me,' he told Donald Mitchell in 1992, 'but there was never any words, any activity, any suggestion on his part – and this is all very clear to me – that this extended any further than plain fondness for another individual in a very social way.' In the early 1940s Bobby was uninterested in music and unaware of Britten's stature; nor for that matter did he know exactly what another Long Island resident, a Mr Albert Einstein, did for a living. Each was just part of the milieu, flowing in and out of the house for dinners or chamber-music evenings, the composer at the piano and Einstein playing the violin (with what Britten thought poor intonation*). To Bobby, Britten was a friend of his parents' who nonetheless had an uncommon ability to make him feel the centre of attention. No doubt there was more going on beneath Britten's carefully controlled exterior, as there was beneath the surface of the avuncular relationships he had forged with various boys in the late 1920s and 1930s. Yet Britten's friendship with Bobby played out platonically, much

---

* This was perhaps a little uncharitable. On 3 February 1941 *Time* reviewed a concert given by Einstein at Princeton as a benefit for the American Friends Service Committee. 'Einstein proved that he could play a slow melody with feeling, turn a trill with elegance, jigsaw on occasion. The audience applauded warmly. Fiddler Einstein smiled his broad and gentle smile, glanced at his watch in fourth-dimensional worriment, played his encore, peered at the watch again, retired.'

as similar friendships would with other teenage boys over the remainder of his life.

Britten's friendship with Bobby Rothman tells us a little about his relationship with Pears. Though this was the first of Britten's infatuations in the two years since he and Pears had become lovers, both men instinctively realized that such passions operated somehow outside their relationship. It was as unthreatening to their bond as it was to the boy himself. (It would not always be thus.) Little correspondence exists between Britten and Pears while they lived cheek by jowl, so it is difficult to get a clear picture of their relationship in its early years. From mid-1942 onwards, back in England and often apart, they wrote each other free-falling love letters which suggest a strong and intimate rapport. There is, however, one revealing pen-sketch of Britten and Pears in America, made in late 1941 by Charlie Miller, a student Auden hired as a cook and housemate in Ann Arbor, where he was then teaching. Miller tells of their visit to the house:

> Benjy smiled as soon as anyone looked at him, but I don't remember hearing a note of laughter from that pale, patient face. As he sat in Wystan's blue upholstered chair, I was impressed with his melancholy, his generally passive attitude, even while Peter and Elizabeth [Mayer] rocked with laughter ... Peter, handsome and irresponsible, loomed large over his Benjy, and I didn't need Wystan to tell me, as he did in a murmured aside, 'Now there's a happily married couple.'

It is a picture of the 1930s Britten – passive, serious, dependent – and a long step from the ruthless man he was becoming. Yet Miller's description of their dynamic rings true. Moreover, his sketch confirms that in the company of their intimates, Britten and Pears were happy to demonstrate the true nature of their relationship.

13

The last months in America passed in a whirl of concerts and hastily convened farewell dinners. There were the first performances of *Scottish Ballad* in Cincinnati with Goossens, and *Diversions* in Philadelphia with Eugene Ormandy, the work's truculent commissioner and dedicatee on piano. Wittgenstein had lobbied Britten for all sorts of changes in the piece and had even penned his own cadenza – all of which Britten ignored. 'To Benjamin Britten's concert,' Isherwood wrote of the premiere. 'Benjy and his friend Peter Pears met me afterwards. They are leaving soon for England, where Benjy has decided to register as a C.O. We all got sadder and sadder and drunker and drunker.' There were concerts featuring *Les Illuminations*, one earning a blistering rebuke from cranky critic and composer Virgil Thomson. 'I found the work pretentious, banal and utterly disappointing, coming from so gifted a composer. Mr Pears, who sang it [had] neither correct French diction, nor a properly trained voice.' It was a reminder that American critics were not necessarily any less hostile than those back home, and that Pears's technical development as a singer was incomplete. There were barnstorming performances of *Sinfonia da Requiem* by Koussevitzky and the Boston Symphony Orchestra ('I really think the orchestra is the best I have ever heard,' Britten told Coolidge, no small accolade given his experiences in Vienna). And as a farewell gesture to his friends on Long Island, Britten and Pears gave a recital in the Southold High School auditorium, which included an early public airing of a handful of folk-song arrangements completed only a few weeks earlier.

Britten also performed Beethoven's Sonata, Op. 10 No. 2, and Chopin's Scherzo No. 2 in B flat minor at the recital. Nothing would prompt public performances of such repertory after the war; they belonged to a younger Britten, the one who on Auden's advice played through Beethoven sonatas in the Old Mill as part of his seduction of Scherchen, the boy sitting on the floor, heart in his hands, transfixed by the beautiful music surrounding him. Or Britten six months or so earlier, improbably playing Tchaikovsky's Piano Concerto No. 1 from memory in an informal domestic performance, the later critic John Waterhouse busking his way through the orchestra part on a second piano, Auden looking on with glee. 'I knew pretty well for sure that he was going to be a great composer,' Waterhouse later said, 'but I had had no idea that he was already a great pianist.'

It is a shame he dropped all this repertory, that audiences never had the chance to hear him play these sonatas that he came to deride so publicly, or this concerto, or this difficult spinning-top Chopin Scherzo; all of it suited him down to his sinews. Clifford Curzon remembered him playing the Chopin Scherzo in joint recitals during the second half of the war, Britten grumbling about his limited technique but enjoying the virtuosic outing all the same. And pianist John Lindsay remembered Britten in a lesson on Chopin's fourth Ballade in the late 1940s discussing the angels he thought occupied the sparse, still passage a minute or so before the end, swift rapids on either side. 'He just made you feel music wasn't to do with dots on paper; it was to do with an experience in time, and [how] it would sound.' This is what was so special about Britten's playing, what he would articulate in Aspen after the war: the magic comes only with the sounding of the music.

Had they stayed in America, it would have been difficult to sustain the Long Island idyll much past this point; six days before the Southold school recital America entered the war. At first it was exciting: America was now an official ally, yoked to Britain through common aims. But soon the excitement and unity gave way to political squabbling and bureaucratic restrictions. Britten acquiesced to the fingerprints, registration, permit photographs and the like, and wryly observed that it took sugar rationing and the consequent shortage of Coca-Cola to make the war's impact properly felt.

Either America's involvement in hostilities or his impending departure prompted a flurry of political observations. He characterized Churchill as a sort of fiery revivalist tent preacher dispensing flowery phrases and hollow promises of redemption. 'What an impossible old gas-bag he is, just like a Baptist minister! I wish he, and all that crowd would go. If they *are* going to have a war, I wish they'd do it properly.' To Kit Welford he wrote of the unsuccessful attempts to ban German and Italian music, of the uniforms everywhere (echoing Virginia Woolf) and the jingoism. 'It makes me sick, especially as I loathe the Star-Spangled-Banner, and its awkward harmonies,' he said, rather undermining his broader political point.

After his deliberate silence on political issues during the previous two and a half years, these letters jar. It is likely he was girding up for re-entry into war-torn England. He was no clearer about what he and Pears might do on their return, but at least the options had narrowed. They would seek official music positions, either with the military or with the new Council for the Encouragement of Music and the Arts, or they would register as conscientious objectors and see where that took them.

Britten was composing a little. He toyed with a proposed concerto for Benny Goodman, but his heart was not in it and it came to nothing. And at Ann Arbor he and Auden tried to give shape to an idea for an oratorio, which Auden eventually published as *For the Time Being*. The oratorio would eventually play its own part in their estrangement, but before that Britten would complete another Auden work, *Hymn to St Cecilia*, a lovely closing to an extraordinary collaborative friendship. He worked on this while he and Pears waited in vain for a ship, their bags packed, exit permits finally issued.*

Two things of significance occurred while they awaited passage. Following the January performances of *Sinfonia da Requiem* in Boston, Koussevitzky asked Britten how it was possible that such a dramatic composer had yet to write an opera. Britten pointed out that planning such a piece, collaborating with a librettist, making the composition sketch and writing nearly a thousand pages of orchestral score demanded freedom from all other work, which was a financial impossibility at the time. But he went on to entice the conductor with the scenario he and Pears had created from Crabbe's poems, and, soon after, Koussevitzky commissioned the opera in memory of his recently deceased wife. He stumped up $1,000 for the project (£250), not enough to give Britten the freedom he craved, in America or England. ('If he had asked more we would have paid it,' Koussevitzky told *Time* in 1948.) The opera would still have to jostle with other works – the quickly dispatched, well-remunerated commissions from the BBC, for example. Yet it was a big-hearted gesture and it allowed Britten to clear some much-needed space in his head in which to conceive and compose a grand opera.

The second significant event was a letter Auden sent Britten at the end of January 1942, as he contemplated his friend's departure. Commentators have long suggested that this sermonizing letter caused a rift between composer and poet, yet, prickly as Britten was, he was by then well used to such lectures from Auden, even if increasingly less sympathetic to them. Pears was sure no single event effected their post-war estrangement, observing in 1980 that 'Ben was on a different track

* Not without a hitch: J. Edgar Hoover's signature appears on a February 1942 document concerning Pears's nominal association with a politically undesirable organization. It is addressed to the Visa Division of the Department of State, redacted and declassified in 1995: 'It was reported in July of 1940, that one —— of New York City was either a Communist or had radical tendencies.' The document came back to haunt him on a much later trip to the United States.

now, and he was no longer prepared to be dominated – bullied – by Wystan, whose musical feeling he was very well aware of'.

Auden's letter is simultaneously loving, stern, workmanlike, prescient, intimate. He sets out his latest thinking on the artist and society. 'Goodness and Beauty are the results of a perfect balance between Order and Chaos, Bohemianism and Bourgeois Convention. Bohemian chaos alone ends in a mad jumble of beautiful scraps; Bourgeois convention alone ends in large unfeeling corpses.' It is the Auden of the 1940 'New Year Letter': 'To set in order – that's the task / Both Eros and Apollo ask; / For Art and Life agree in this / That each intends a synthesis.' It is not at all certain that Auden believed such a synthesis was possible, even if the process was necessary. The danger, he wrote, was that in seeking this balance, Britten would end up tied to bourgeois convention.

> Your attraction to thin-as-a-board-juveniles, i.e. to the sexless and innocent, is a symptom of this. And I am certain too that it is your denial and evasion of the ~~attractions~~ demands of disorder that is responsible for your attacks of ill-health, ie sickness is your substitute for the Bohemian.
>
> Wherever you go you are and probably always will be surrounded by people who adore you, nurse you, and praise everything you do, e.g. Elisabeth, Peter (Please show this to P to whom all this is also addressed). Up to a certain point this is fine for you, but beware. You see, Bengy dear, you are always tempted to make things too easy for yourself in this way, i.e. to build yourself a warm nest of love (of course when you get it, you find it a little stifling) by playing the lovable talented little boy.
>
> If you are really to develop to your full stature, you will have, I think, to suffer, and make others suffer, in ways which are totally strange to you at present, and against every conscious value that you have; i.e. you will have to be able to say what you never yet have had the right to say – God, I'm a shit.

It is a thoughtful, heartfelt assessment, part of it directed at its author as much as its recipient. Britten responded in kind, quibbling only over his misapprehension that Auden was describing his relationship with Pears as juvenile.

The remarkable thing about Auden's observations is the degree to which they are a template of Britten's post-war life and art; it is almost as though he had neither the desire nor the imagination to step beyond them. The environments he built for himself *were* warm nests of love; he replaced Elizabeth Mayer with Imogen Holst and other such figures, and recreated in Aldeburgh the sort of buzzing artistic milieu and comfortable domesticity he had experienced on Long Island. The creative relationships he had with others sometimes *were* laced with suffering. In his work, Auden's correlation between goodness and beauty turns up time and again. When Captain Vere summons his officers immediately after Billy Budd has killed the villainous John Claggart, he sings urgently, painfully, 'Beauty, handsomeness, goodness coming to trial.' In *Death in Venice*, Aschenbach ponders the first of Auden's binaries, the balance between Order and Chaos, not long before his death, paraphrasing Plato's retelling of Socrates's conversation with Phaedrus.

> Does beauty lead to wisdom, Phaedrus?
> Yes, but through the senses.
> Can poets take this way then
> For senses lead to passion, Phaedrus.
> Passion leads to knowledge
> Knowledge to forgiveness
> To compassion with the abyss.

Britten never showed much sympathy for the abyss; discipline, order, self-control were his allies, as they were Aschenbach's. Plato's vision of chaste, loving concord between man and boy resonated with him, of course; yet to depart from this compact was to court the abyss, to muddy the waters of childhood, a time in his life the adult Britten did his best to protect. Auden had his own arguments with such sophistry, as his letter makes clear: the mind cannot lie to the body, any more than the body can lie to the mind, he would have countered Plato. In his ordinary play *The Habit of Art*, Alan Bennett has Auden remonstrate with the composer about his opera-in-progress. 'No amount of dressing Tadzio up as a vision of Apollo can alter the fact that Dionysus for you comes in a grey flannel suit or cricket whites. This is an old man lusting after a boy, and Apollo has got fuck all to do with it.' It was not quite like this, or at least not solely: Britten's attraction to boys was strong and would last his lifetime, though propriety always won out.

'I think the effect of America was to broaden one, encourage one and to shake one. I was in danger of becoming parochial, and this worried me,' Britten said many years after his return. A month after receiving Auden's letter he wrote to Kit Welford of the importance of discipline in his work, observing that 'in art, as you know, the bias is to the other direction, that of anarchy and romantic "freedom". A carefully chosen discipline is the only possible course' – essentially paraphrasing Auden's words. Auden got one fundamental thing wrong, however. The bourgeois conventionality of Britten's post-war life helped drive his work. It was his disguise as he set to work on his devastating explorations of contemporary society.

On 16 March 1942 Britten scribbled his farewell in the Mayers' guest book. 'The end of the week-end,' he wrote, a reference to his first visit to the house one Saturday in August 1939, a young idealist unaware of how far the Mayers' hospitality would extend and how much America would change him. Mayer took Britten and Pears to the pier and they boarded the *Axel Johnson*, an old Swedish freighter, in marked contrast to the relative comfort of their 1939 crossing. 'The Ides of March,' Mayer later wrote in her diary, distressed that these remarkable men were slipping through her fingers. From Boston nine days later, Britten wrote to her, 'We are really only now fully realising what a civilised life we have been living with your dear selves.' Yet during Britten's turbulent, often unsettling American years, it had been evident how much this loving relationship, this stable environment, meant to him and his work.

14

They disembarked in Liverpool a month later. Crossing the Atlantic itself took only twelve days, which they spent in the company of foul-mouthed recruits who whistled loudly as they passed the men's cabin, almost as if they were setting out to disturb Britten as he worked. The long gap between departure and arrival on 17 April was due to the slow initial crawl from New York to Boston and then on to Halifax, and repeated repairs to the ageing freighter. Concerned that they contained some intricate enemy code, New York customs officers confiscated Britten's manuscripts – much like the official in Waugh's *Vile Bodies* who retains a draft of the poor booby Adam's memoir when he disembarks at Dover ('Particularly against books the Home Secretary is').

Unperturbed, Britten recreated the sketches for *Hymn to St Cecilia* from memory, finishing the piece en route to England.

Auden's St Cecilia is a sort of organ-playing superhero who can summon pagan goddesses with her beauty and angels with her song; she can harness the trumpets of the apocalypse and has dominion over the fires of hell. 'Blessed Cecilia, appear in visions / To all musicians, appear and inspire / Translated Daughter, come down and startle / Composing mortals with immortal fire.'

It is a leaner work than *A Boy was Born* – as is its companion, *A Ceremony of Carols*, also composed (primarily) on board the *Axel Johnson*. In many ways both pieces belong to the earlier period of Britten's fascination with derring-do figures from early Christianity and liturgical prayers in their honour. The project had long been on his mind: as far back as January 1935 he noted, 'I'm having great difficulty in finding Latin words for a proposed Hymn to St Cecilia.' Auden eventually trumped whatever Latin words Britten may have found. Taking his lead from John Dryden's 'A Song for St Cecilia's Day, 1687', Auden in late 1940 completed an ornate appreciation of the saint whose religion, or a version thereof, had recently reclaimed him. He dedicated the poem to Britten. It was at this point that the shape of the work began to emerge in Britten's mind, though it took the enforced solitude of the *Axel Johnson* to bring it to fruition.

In the unaccompanied piece, Britten toys with the simplest of ideas: he juxtaposes elongated spellings of musical phrases with fast-moving versions of themselves – an early example of the heterophony that would preoccupy him from the 1960s onwards. In the opening pages, the male voices act as clackety organ pedals, over which the treble voices whip through the text, moving three times faster than their lumbering colleagues, hushed and reverential as they describe Cecilia and her powers. Then follows a homespun imitative section, a scalic tune sung over yet more organ pedals, Britten matching Auden's sudden change of metre.* It is a marriage of musical and linguistic forms. He introduces an *organum* effect in the subsequent solos, the medieval polyphonic technique whereby an ornamental solo line sits atop a single note (in Britten's case a chord), creating ever-changing harmonies as it ducks

---

* Remo Lauricella spoke of Britten's 'fascination with Beethoven's scalic melodies and his use of scales compositionally' in the early 1930s.

and weaves. Doffing his cap to blessed Cecilia herself, Britten has these soloists impersonate musical instruments: the alto sings *quasi Violino*, an open-stringed barn-dance call; the tenor *quasi Tromba*, a militaristic bugle fanfare; the soprano is a flute, the bass a timpano. It is an imaginitive tribute to the patron saint of music, on whose feast day Britten was born. It was also a tribute to his friend Auden, as Pears later recognized: 'Perhaps he may be said to have said goodbye to working with Wystan with his marvellous setting of the Hymn (Anthem) to St Cecilia.' That is too dramatic a retelling – at the time, Britten and Auden fully expected to continue working together – but it gives some indication of how the friendship was later viewed and compartmentalized.

From London, two days after disembarking in Liverpool, Pears wrote to Mayer, 'This cannot be called life here. It is just an intermission.' They found the capital drab and shabby, in fact a little sordid. Britten decried England's provincialism yet loved its lush countryside, finding no contradiction between the two views. He thought the music still terrible – bad orchestras and conductors performing a handful of popular symphonies in the unhelpful acoustic of the Royal Albert Hall, a sorry substitute for the much lamented Queen's Hall, which the previous year was destroyed by an incendiary bomb. Yet he recognized the demand for music in such circumstances, an almost spiritual thirst. There was no evidence of the previous year's sniping at his absence or achievements; in its place Britten experienced an exaggerated kindness, which left him suspicious of the unspoken thoughts. Significantly, the funds that had accrued in England during his absence allowed him breathing space.

He had missed the thrills and privations of London during the Blitz: civilians sleeping on the Underground's rickety wooden escalators and gloomy platforms; domestic pets put down in their thousands by harried owners and complicit vets; the bombing raids on St Thomas's Hospital, the Houses of Parliament and chunks of the East End, where the earth swallowed double-decker buses whole and where, from street level, the landscape looked like a grimace in which teeth had been pulled from the gum; the gas masks and drills; the harvesting of tin and wrought iron for weaponry, the gates of Battersea Park included.

Yet Britten identified many smaller changes. Food restrictions were severe, fluctuating with the country's changing military fortunes: anyone over five was allocated a ration book, which carefully limited supplies of bacon, sugar, tea, meat, cheese, butter, lard, eggs, sweets and preserves. Powdered egg and milk filled the gaps, as (according to rumours) did unattributed horseflesh. There were no mere rumours where whale meat was concerned. Beer was diluted and cocktails were little more than coloured water. ('For a good cocktail, or a nice bit of Rum one would sell one's soul,' Britten told Beata.) Petrol dried up and clothing was purchased with coupons – two for a pinafore, nine for an unlined mackintosh. Houses were cold: central heating barely existed (except in the Old Mill, a neat, forward-looking touch) and fires were usually lit only in the late afternoon.

United Press journalist Joseph Grigg, based in Berlin until America's entry into the war, when he was interned and subsequently exchanged for a displaced German, identified certain similarities between the German and English capitals. 'People stumble around in the same black-out. There is no great difference in the basic rations. There are queues, propaganda posters, thin newspapers and uniforms everywhere. You meet some of the same war-time shortages and hear people grumbling about much the same sort of annoyances.' Churchill celebrated the stoicism of the British people, though Britten and Pears noticed intense weariness not far beneath the mask. 'All the excitement of the "blitz" (except for isolated spots) has died down,' Britten told Mayer, '& people seem very, very tired.'

They camped out in the houses of different friends and family – Beth and Barbara, naturally, but also the Slaters, and Pears's parents in Barnes – as they searched for a place of their own. This would continue until September, when they moved into a house in Cheyne Walk, Chelsea, right by Battersea Bridge. They shared it with Ursula Nettleship, a friend from before the war, who worked as an administrator for the Council for the Encouragement of Music and the Arts (CEMA), a connection Britten and Pears would exploit to everyone's advantage.

The biggest shock in London was the uniformed soldiers everywhere, GIs included, some with visible wounds or missing limbs, which made Britten and Pears in their civvies conspicuous and self-conscious. Yet something pertinent to both had arrived with the soldiers. Many of these young men, away from home and their families for the first time in their lives and fatalistic about their chances of survival, threw themselves into the homosexual subculture that had sprung up around Piccadilly Circus and Leicester Square. Bars were packed with American, French, Polish, Canadian, Australian and British soldiers, freed from the moral constrictions of peacetime or their religious upbringing. Piccadilly Circus Underground station was a notorious pick-up point, and late at night uniformed soldiers milled about, with anonymous sex or solicitation on their minds. (Before the war it had been Marble Arch and Hyde Park Corner, where, according to radio producer J. R. Ackerley, 'a pound was the recognised tariff for the Foot Guards then; the Horse Guards cost rather more'.) Military records and copious memoirs suggest that many such negotiations occurred in seedier situations, in the public lavatories around Piccadilly Circus and beyond.

These liberated men were abetted in their sexual adventures by the nightly blackouts, which transformed London into a city of opportunism, danger and risk-taking. The capital was 'a paved double bed', observed Quentin Crisp. Basil Reeve suggested that Pears had been a 'great haunter' of these clubs at the time Britten and Pears became a couple. Perhaps he had fallen back into old habits, but it is once more difficult to separate Reeve's antagonism towards the singer from what actually happened. Pears was frequently on his own in London or on tour, where opportunities would have presented themselves. Britten was less interested in such things, but then he was often at Snape, writing furiously, blind to London's supposed allure.

They were both immediately in demand. Pears, his voice transformed from the spindly instrument it had been pre-war thanks to his lessons with Mundy and work with Britten, jumped at the title role in Albion Opera's production of Offenbach's *The Tales of Hoffmann*, which he shared with another English tenor, Henry Wendon. Albion Opera was a fly-by-night company and the standard was probably not high, but Pears had no professional stage experience and knew little about what such a large undertaking entailed. His first performance was 6 May, less than three weeks after their return to England, which speaks to his quick musicianship and new resolve. 'Peter sang so well,' Britten told Mayer, 'acted so delightfully, and was such a ravishing personality on the stage, in Hoffmann, that everyone was delighted & more than surprised.' Britten was not surprised: there must always be tenors and heroes, he went on, and Pears to him was both.

This engagement was one consequence of the informal performance they gave to Ralph Hawkes immediately on their return, at which the publisher heard for the first time a number of Britten's recent works. Repertory included *Seven Sonnets of Michelangelo*, which had not yet been performed in England, and which made a strong impression. Curiously, given his later practice, Britten sketched a number of other works in these early weeks back in England, which he discussed with Hawkes but which he never completed, including a sonata or partita for chamber orchestra, which later morphed into an improbable 'Overture and Fugue' for piano, strings and timpani, before falling victim to a deficit of time or inspiration. His important composition just now was *Peter Grimes*. Without delay he commenced work on it with his old friend Montagu Slater, an Oxford graduate from a working-class family with fantastically broad literary interests and achievements, probably having flagged the potential collaboration from America. 'He has splendid ideas,' Britten wrote to Mayer in early May. 'It is getting more and more an opera about the community, whose life is "illuminated" for this moment by the tragedy of the murders.' This is itself an illuminating comment, suggesting a brutality in Grimes's behaviour (note murder, not accidental death) quite removed from the more nuanced character we know today.

Their most pressing task was not the new opera or Pears's unexpected role debut: both men were eligible for conscription according to the National Service (Armed Forces) Act 1939, and to avoid this fate it was necessary to register as conscientious objectors, citing either religious or political reasons. There were four possible outcomes from registration: unconditional exemption; conditional exemption; a directive to register for non-combatant service; complete rejection. It was possible to initiate an appeal, though this could and often did result in appellants being moved from one of the two middle categories to the fourth. The decision of the Appellate Tribunal was final and if a 'conchie' refused to accept the decision or contravened a particular wartime directive he could be jailed, as Michael Tippett discovered. Conscription for women was introduced in 1941 – mostly for factory or munitions work – yet they had an easier time with exemptions, which were issued freely to mothers.

In a pre-emptive statement to his local tribunal, written on the same day he updated Mayer on *Grimes*, Britten formulated his thoughts on war and pacifism. 'Since I believe that there is in every man the spirit of God, I cannot destroy, and feel it my duty to avoid helping to destroy as far as I am able, human life, however strongly I may disapprove of the individual's actions or thoughts.' It was an unconscious paraphrase of Edna St Vincent Millay's poem 'Conscientious Objector', published in

1934, which begins, 'I shall die, but that is all I shall do for Death'. In Britten's statement there followed a nice line about how he viewed his work. 'The whole of my life has been devoted to acts of creation (being by profession a composer) and I cannot take part in acts of destruction.' And then he made the less plausible suggestion that Hitler, were he to conquer England, could be overcome by passive resistance, his fascism somehow undermined. These views were consistent with his beliefs in the previous decade, now made more urgent. He had applauded Chamberlain's attempts at appeasing Hitler, to the extent of welcoming the September 1938 Munich Agreement and expressing no reservations about the consequent carve-up of Czechoslovakia.

In his hearing on 28 May, the composer represented by Canon Stuart Morris, general secretary of the Peace Pledge Union, Britten stuck pretty much to this script, offering to work for CEMA and the Ministry of Information in lieu of military service. There were some telling diversions and concessions, however, which were recorded in the tribunal's report and hint at his leaving a flaky impression. 'I do not believe in the Divinity of Christ,' it records him saying, 'but I think his teaching is sound and his example should be followed.' He acceded to joining the Royal Army Medical Corps if so ordered, and generally underplayed his long-held pacifist beliefs ('I think with the Quakers I might find a spiritual home'). He was ordered to serve as a non-combatant, the third category of registration.

Britten's appeal on 18 August was more hard-hitting – not least because he was convinced he would soon be working on a farm, or digging trenches and roads, or even going to prison. He garnered letters of support from Hawkes, the BBC and from Bridge's widow, the latter recalling an occasion when she pointed out to the teenage Britten the smartly uniformed soldiers at Hyde Park Barracks. 'I hate all of it & what it stands for,' was his response as he turned his back, unimpressed by their finery or beauty. Britten himself also showed more grit. 'I could not conscientiously join the RAMC or the non-combatant corps because by so doing I should be no less actively participating in the war than if I were a combatant against which service the Tribunal recognised the validity of my objection.' Here, flanked by Slater and William Walton, Britten experienced 'one of those (for me) rare rays of light, when everything seemed so clear & simple ... and I wasn't caught by any of the childish inanities, which usually defeat the most intelligent

"Objectors"!!' This time round he was successful. The tribunal informed him that he would 'without conditions be registered in the Register of Conscientious Objectors' – an unconditional exemption, a status enjoyed by only 3,000 Britons (one of them Pears), six per cent of the total number of conscientious objectors (compared with under 0.003 per cent of COs in the First World War). He was free to get on with his work.

15

The theological muddle Britten found himself in with the local tribunal is illustrative of his evolving religious beliefs. His childhood faith had by now disappeared. Defining himself as a potential Quaker did not pin him down to a particular Christian narrative, for Quakers form a remarkably broad church: agnostics rub shoulders with evangelicals. In fact, Britten rejected the idea that his pacifism required any sort of Christianity as a crutch. In his appeal he argued that the 'Local Tribunal failed to appreciate the religious background of my conscience trying to tie me down too narrowly to a belief in the divinity of Christ'.

Various churchmen, musicians and scholars have done their best to tie him down to this very thing. 'His religious beliefs are central to his life and his work,' asserted his first biographer, Eric Walter White. 'As a devout and practising Christian, he has been keen, whenever possible, to work within the framework of the Church of England, and many of his compositions have been planned accordingly.' Pears was not as forthcoming, yet he still granted Britten the tenets of faith: 'He was religious in the general sense of acknowledging a power above greater than ourselves, but he wasn't a regular churchgoer.' So too did the great pianist Murray Perahia, who found himself discussing religion with Britten over their first lunch together. 'I'm not terribly religious in my ordinary life,' Britten told him, 'but when it comes to music I'm a very Christian composer.' And the author of one recent study of the composer has performed all sorts of contortions to assert that Britten's sense of morality was evidence of his Christian faith, the one apparently impossible without the other.

It is to be expected that Britten's thoughts on religion would change over time, yet it seems that the ideas he communicated to Lennox

Berkeley about God and faith at the time of Peter Burra's death in 1937 that prompted the older composer's admonishment were unchanged in the early 1940s. Donald Mitchell's friendship with Britten postdated the war, but he was nonetheless sure that Britten was not in any fundamental way a religious person, a view shared by the Earl of Harewood. Perhaps wary of adding agnosticism or atheism to a charge sheet that already included pacifism and homosexuality, Britten gave the impression of going with the flow of holy water that ran strongly through the military, Parliament, schools, universities and other important institutions. 'What he respected and admired was faith or religious tradition,' Mitchell thought, 'which in the past celebrated aspects of humanity and human life, without which we all know the world would be much poorer. But that didn't mean that he thought that it was religion or faith that actually was responsible for those remarkable aspects of human nature, which he so greatly valued.'

Certainly in his adult life he maintained friendships with a number of religious figures, from the cultured Revd Walter Hussey – who commissioned Britten's asylum reverie *Rejoice in the Lamb* – to Leslie Brown, Bishop of St Edmundsbury and Ipswich, whom Britten befriended in the last months of his life. And he was happy on occasion to take the Church's coin, if not its communion, much as countless artists have done for centuries. But the commissions and the religious themes in his music were simply a reflection of the society in which he lived. This is what he meant when he told Perahia that he was a Christian in his music, or what Tippett meant when he asserted, 'We are both of us religious composers, i.e. bound, *religati*, to a sense of the numinous, but Britten is more properly Christian.' He was at most a mild-mannered deist who believed in a historical Jesus and admired his teachings, but on other related matters remained agnostic. 'I am not sure that he would really have called himself a Christian,' Pears told Tony Palmer in his 1979 documentary *A Time There Was*. 'He may have called himself a Christian, but only as a follower of Christ – not as a member of the church, I don't think. And certainly not as a communicant.' He was a deist in a theists' world, a bar-room brawl he would never win. He decided to cause no further offence and used what he could from religious stories and parables to demonstrate aspects of human behaviour, beautiful and ugly alike.

The appeal of Quakerism was not solely the pacifism at its core. The

Quakers' historical refusal to swear oaths of office meant there was a long tradition of opting out of the club-land institutions Britten found distasteful – not just the military, but law and medicine as well. Quakers campaigned against slavery throughout the second half of the 1700s and were the first body to ban it, which put wind in the sails of Benjamin Franklin. Quakers existed in a culture of equal rights and espoused what amounted to a form of non-political socialism: the duty of society to look after its weakest. Slaves in the eighteenth century, women in the nineteenth, Jewish children escaping Hitler in the twentieth: the precise cause mattered not, for the principle in each was the same. In their campaigns the Quakers found themselves frequently swimming against the tide. There was a flavour of anti-authoritarianism to their core beliefs, which was perhaps related to the distrust many Quakers felt for the Christian notion of an all-powerful deity, watching over his creations with pride or disgust, ready to intervene (or not) when required.

It would take some time and practice for Britten to sort out his relationship with the English post-war Establishment – the great juggling act that characterized his mature life and works – yet this element of Quakerism appealed to him hugely; it had already been rehearsed at school and at the Royal College of Music. Meanwhile he was happy to explore in his works the varying influence of institutional religion on human behaviour, from the wholly good to the unambiguously wicked.

16

The sudden burst of correspondence between Britten and Pears as the singer took his show on the road demonstrates the depth of their relationship on their return to England. 'I don't think you really know how much I need you and want you always,' Pears wrote in late May 1942. Britten reveals a more insecure side, at one point berating Pears for missing an arranged telephone call. 'Why the hell can't you organise your times abit,' he thundered. It is impossible to tell if there is a greater subtext to this outburst, one that would mitigate the sense of spitefulness and self-obsession the complete letter portrays. Britten himself thought he had gone too far, furiously back-pedalling with a telephone call before Pears received the tirade.

Britten's letters often included admonitions of one transgression or another, usually involving punctuality or a broken promise. There were references to tiffs and spats, which Pears batted away and over which Britten obsessed. Yet the endearments were equally strong. 'I love you very much, & I wish to God (reverently, this time), you were here in bed with me,' Britten added to the above serving. And on another occasion, 'I am still a little disturbed by our saturday night tiff – Worrying as to whether I am not good for you – not caring enough for your health & work. But, in all humbleness I say it, give me a chance to reform, my dear. I swear in the future I will look after you.'

For all their endearments in the correspondence, for all the temperament and intensity, Britten and Pears were discreet about their relationship in public, bemused rather than distressed when they discovered that the Robertsons ('the two old gizzards', as they had evolved in Britten's mind) had spread gossip about them to Barbirolli ('I wonder if they told him the truth'). They confided in trusted friends, though they were occasionally known to divulge details to unsuspecting acquaintances, as if the secret were sometimes too big to keep. 'I don't care who knows,' Britten told Pears in June 1942, not quite accurately.

Awaiting his appeal, Britten worked hard with Slater on the opera about 'a fishing village, full of storms, & sailing boats, & murders', as he described it melodramatically to Bobby Rothman. Though he would come to decry the notion of the ivory tower, of artists working away in isolation from the world around them, Britten's converted windmill in Snape served this purpose during the war. Not for him the rough and tumble of literary Soho or Fitzrovia, the brawls and the heavy drinking, the loud talk and scant production in what Cyril Connolly called a 'five-year sentence in gregarious confinement'. He escaped to Snape as often as possible, sometimes bringing Slater with him, other times luxuriating in the solitariness and isolation. The travel was wildly impractical: trains to Saxmundham from London were infrequent and a car or taxi was required from the station to the Old Mill, which became more difficult and expensive as petrol was further rationed and the use of private cars restricted.

There were a number of important performances over the summer, which no doubt added weight to Britten's appeal to the Appellate Tribunal. On 8 June Sophie Wyss and Boyd Neel performed *Les Illuminations* at the Wigmore Hall, and on 22 July, as part of the Promenade Concerts, there was the first British outing of *Sinfonia da Requiem*. The performance prompted some of the usual carping in the London papers and journals. J. A. Westrup continued his pre-war campaign against Britten, as if nothing had changed, previewing the orchestral work in the *Listener*. 'Britten has published work after work displaying a complete technical assurance; and if nothing but technical assurance were looked for, there would be nothing but praise for his music. What disturbed this critic was the feeling that the technique had become an end in itself.' The smart pianist, critic and musicologist William Glock, still some years from founding Dartington's summer school and being appointed BBC controller of music, ran with the same line. 'Up till now most of us have been saying that Britten fritters away his talent; and we inspect each work in the hope of finding an extra inch of depth.' What a dispiriting re-entry into the English music scene; could critics not notice Britten's greater musical assuredness in such a brilliantly sculpted piece?

Yet there were hints there and elsewhere that the critical tide might be turning. The writer and musician Edward Sackville-West, cousin of Vita, later Baron Sackville and partner of critic Desmond Shawe-Taylor, and soon to be a close friend of Britten's, wrote a perceptive critique in the *New Statesman*. He placed *Sinfonia da Requiem* very much in its times, further identifying the role Britten's music might play in England – during the war, but thereafter as well:

> Our reactions to the idea of death become simpler in times when that event tends to be a sudden matter rather than gradual. Feelings become less mixed, love and admiration remain whole, self-pity shows for the self-indulgence it is. This astringency makes for the kind of single-pointed attitude which results in considerable works of art. At the Albert Hall, on July 22 many among the audience must have felt that the fact underlying the experiences of the last three years had at last been given a satisfying form.

Auden might have rejected the idea of the poet as seer, and three years later Spender would envisage 'the possibility of a society organized in such a way that it is completely independent of the values which are maintained by art' – a consequence of brutal warfare and a determination to avoid its repetition. Yet here was Sackville-West with a prescient rejoinder, and he was no partisan. In the July 1944 edition of *Horizon* he would write an important article on Britten's music, including the observation that the 'surface brilliance, the versatility, the passion for applause that were the bane of Britten's early music, will continue to lie in wait for unguarded moments'. This was a scattergun assessment, though more shot hit the target than Donald Mitchell and Philip Reed would later concede in their magisterial edition of Britten's letters.

The other great performance at this time was the premiere of *Seven Sonnets of Michelangelo* at the Wigmore Hall on 23 September 1942. The hall is a discreet presence on Wigmore Street, tucked away behind a wrought-iron frame and canopy, looking to the world like any other bit of neo-Georgian Marylebone. Designed by Thomas Collcutt, it is a keyhole laid flat, an ancient burial chamber, if you like – a treasure hall approached by a narrow corridor – originally built as a small concert venue attached to the London shopfront of the German piano maker Bechstein. It was an ideal venue for the premiere of Britten's songs. Because of its design, the blackout was easily enforceable; patrons entered the hall and were cocooned from warfare and world-weariness. And because of its brilliant acoustic, artists sounded as good as they ever could. This was Pears's first major showcase since returning from America, with none of the props – literal and metaphorical – of *Hoffmann*; it was bound to be a defining occasion.

The audience listened attentively to the mixed bag offered: Ireland's Elgarian Violin Sonata No. 2, the first British performance of Bartók's *Contrasts*, and Bliss's Quintet for Clarinet and String Quartet. Britten's songs, which came immediately after the interval, brought them to their feet. Where had Pears been hiding all this time? Gramophone company His Master's Voice signed them up on the spot and they entered the studio in November to create a recording that even today is full of revelation. Ireland, who shared the Wigmore green room with Britten, was afterwards frustratingly silent on meeting his former pupil. But he liked the songs – or at least defended them from their detractors.

Critics responded as generously as the audience. Pears's development as an artist was noted, while Sackville-West was moved to describe *Seven Sonnets of Michelangelo* as 'the finest chamber songs England has had to show since the seventeenth century, and the best any country has produced since the death of Wolf'. It was a gratingly hyperbolic account – Mahler quite obviously wore this mantle – but the emotional thrust of his argument remained.

Here were the early, unexpected shoots of Britten and Pears's public rehabilitation. They were still only in the initial months of their return and their exemptions from military service were yet to be granted. Animosity towards them remained in parts of the BBC, with various conductors and impresarios muttering grave imprecations into their beards and telephones, and among patriotic members of the public. Yet they had experienced a far softer landing than they could ever have dared hope. All they needed to complete their homecoming were a few more high-profile appearances – or perhaps the imprimatur of a trusted figure or organization.

17

The English pianist Myra Hess, who was created a Dame of the British Empire a year before Britten's return from America, had enjoyed a good career in Europe and across the Atlantic since her 1907 debut. She was a regular at the Promenade Concerts, unfazed by celebrity recital partnerships with the likes of Nellie Melba and Fritz Kreisler, and had become an iconic figure in England's musical scene. She was a no-nonsense performer with an impassive face and hair coiled like Princess Leia's. In the early stages of the Second World War she initiated a series of daily lunchtime recitals at the National Gallery, by then stripped of its permanent collection, most of which had been moved to safety underground in Wales. The concerts were a gift to a country now in disarray, its future uncertain and its vein of distinguished (Aryan) German soloists blocked.

The recitals were remarkably effective propaganda and soon became a metaphor for the pluck and fortitude Londoners exhibited in the wreckage of the Blitz. Metaphor became reality on one occasion, when a delayed-action bomb went off in Trafalgar Square. According to Spender, who was attending the recital that day, 'the musicians did not lift the bows from their strings. A few of the audience, who had been listening with heads bowed, straightened themselves for an instant and then resumed their posture.' (How different from the reaction of the drama critic Philip Hope-Wallace, caught in a theatre during an air raid, who said to himself, 'How squalid to be killed at this disgusting little farce.')

There was a similar experience four years later when Edith Sitwell stood in the Churchill Club to recite her poem 'Still Falls the Rain', her celebrated response to the air raids Spender wrote about. A doodle-bug bomb was heard buzzing overhead, yet Sitwell merely raised her eyes to the ceiling before continuing her strangely workaday recitation (if a contemporaneous studio recording is any indication), with her imperious sing-song voice and delayed cadences, so at odds with Britten's later solemn and angry setting of the poem. The audience was entranced by her defiance and authority, according to literary editor John Lehmann, and by 'her unspoken asseveration that poetry was more important than all the terrors that Hitler could launch against us. Not a soul moved, and at the end, when the doodle-bug had exploded far away, the applause was deafening.' Sitwell downplayed the incident in a letter, leaving open the possibility that the exaggerated narrative of British stoicism was pervasive by 1944, even to someone of Lehmann's sophistication. But both incidents illustrate an unexpected development in British culture: the artist as wartime hero.

Other countries had stitched together their own versions of this mythology. *Time* on 20 July 1942 famously put Fireman Shostakovich on its cover, his face framed by a gold helmet and round, thick spectacles, his beloved Leningrad burning in the background. (The magazine's catalyst was the American premiere of his 'Leningrad' Symphony, a microfilm of the score having been carefully dispatched to the West only a few months previously.) Yet even under Stalin's corrupt and anti-intellectual dictatorship, great musicians had a higher profile in the Soviet Union than they did in England, where the concept of the artist as hero was uncharted territory. It was not in Britten's personality to exploit this new notion cynically, however; music to him was no mere means to an end, nor was it a form of political leverage. In a shift from his pre-war views and a prefiguring of his post-war stance, Britten had returned to England wanting to be useful as a musician and to be of public service. His desire to give something back to the demoralized and culturally ravenous British public, his hope of avoiding military service, and the potential for full rehabilitation all overlapped in the concerts organized by CEMA and Hess.

Hess had not mightily impressed Britten at a BBC concert ten years earlier when she and Henry Wood performed Beethoven's Piano Concerto No. 4. It was technically proficient, but to Britten's mind the cadenzas were ridiculous and 'she & Wood have no idea of the 2nd movement – it's Andante *not* adagiossississimo' (a rare written display of Britten's humour). There are enough recordings of her in the years of her National Gallery concerts to suggest that she would never have captured Britten's imagination, at eighteen or twenty-eight. These recordings of Brahms, Mozart, Bach and Beethoven show her to be a genuine and generous performer, with a nice touch and without tricks or affectation. Yet she was not a particularly profound musician; nor was she a great rhetorician, often insensitive to harmony and gesture, frequently stumbling in her live performances at the gallery (the 'Appassionata', in one recorded instance), as if to underline her proud assertion that she had never played so much and practised so little in her life. There are few of the breathtaking moments that punctuate a Schnabel recording. Queen of a narrow island, Britten would probably have said of her.

None of this was particularly important then, except for the fact that Hess was an early player in the culture wars that would dominate Britain's music industry after 1945. What type of artist would define the country's music-making when a national infrastructure was finally hammered into place? Would sentiment prevail over dispassionate assessment? Would the infrastructure resemble the German model – musicians in long apprenticeships with master teachers or in opera houses, and a public raised on live performances from childhood – or would it be the ad hoc system of training, concerts and appreciation that Britain had embraced in the first three decades of the century? Gerald Moore was not the only British musician to decry the *status quo ante*, however gentlemanly his style while doing so. In his 1962 memoir he wrote of eminent foreign artists being at the mercy of a suspicious, mercurial public and press, often taking years to establish themselves in London. Paradoxically, Moore noticed that at the same time British singers were routinely passed over for Continental artists, because of 'the besotted idea held by our public that no British artist could possibly be an authoritative singer of Lieder'. It was a mad playground, a reminder that the whole culture of serious music was relatively new in England and built on shaky foundations. 'All that the English permitted themselves to see of Europe was characterized by the Salzburg Music Festival, French Impressionism, the Lake of Geneva, and of course the museums and art galleries,' Spender wrote of late-1930s Britain. As the country set about shifting from this position there were bound to be inconsistencies, slips, failures and embarrassments amid the triumphs (sometimes accidental). There were bound to be as many mountebanks as visionaries – probably far more.

For their recital at the gallery on 22 October, Britten and Pears preceded *Seven Sonnets of Michelangelo* with Schumann's *Dichterliebe*. This was an inspired yet risky choice: here were two English musicians, one better known than the other, setting up their market stall inside the fortified gates of Austro-Germanic culture, determined to counter the sort of prejudice Moore described. If the gallery concerts were in some way forerunners of post-war British culture, this particular recital was remarkably close to the final product, a manifesto as much as a performance. No recording exists, and their commercial disc of Schumann's cycle was not made until 1963, when Pears's voice was at its zenith. Yet it is possible to imagine from this late-ish recording the exceptional musicianship and the limpid, musical piano playing that must have filled the gallery space that day. How much the audience must have hoped for its own 'wondrously beautiful month of May' (the cycle's opening words) some year soon.

Britten and Pears's work for CEMA was not as elevated, but they were equally committed to it. There were recitals in factory canteens and village halls, with poor facilities and pianos – notes sticking on the way down or the way up and small children noisily rolling pennies along wooden floors – where they performed to audiences that had never heard of Schubert, much less Britten. At each concert they were starting from scratch, unable to make assumptions on their audience's behalf.

Spender identified an unprecedented enthusiasm for the arts in these war years, 'because people felt that music, the ballet, poetry and painting were concerned with a seriousness of living and dying with which they themselves had suddenly been confronted'. He watched audiences at the gallery sitting in rapt attention as though listening for a message from artist or composer, thinking that if they concentrated hard enough they would come close to decoding the mysterious dialogue between performer and the eternal truths inherent in great art, affirming faith and joy in the process. 'There was something deeply touching about this interest in the arts; it was one of the few things which can still make me regret the [end of the] war.' Purcell, Handel, Schubert, Schumann and Britten: the spiritually and culturally deprived audiences for Britten and

Pears's recitals supped on a rich and splendid diet. After a concert, if no accommodation in town was available, they returned to London on packed, blacked-out trains, stopping at every station, standing most of the way. There was an improvised air to each recital, which did not concern them in the least; the two used the experience to formulate ideas about audiences and programming, which would shape their thoughts in Aldeburgh and beyond after the war.

18

Britten's constellation of friends was smaller now and had lost some of its sparkle. Spender was in London, an improbably handsome and literary member of the Fire Service, now married to pianist Natasha Litvin (though managing thereafter to keep one toe in gay waters, as his unexpurgated diaries show), and he and Britten saw a little of each other. Curiously, Britten does not rate a mention – not even a footnote – in Spender's frank and touching *Abschied* to the era, *World within World*, which is thickly populated with brilliant artists and intellectuals of the 1930s and 1940s. Britten saw a lot of Louis MacNeice, now married to his old friend, cabaret singer Hedli Anderson, and kicked around with him some potential collaborations, a few of which eventuated: three programmes as part of a BBC–CBS series, *Britain to America*, broadcast between September 1942 and January 1943; *The Dark Tower*, a radio play broadcast by the BBC in December 1945; and a beautiful song composed in late 1942, a setting of 'Cradle Song for Eleanor'. 'Sleep, my darling, sleep; / The pity of it all / Is all we compass if / We watch disaster fall.' It is heavily infused with the sounds and affections of Britten's mid-1930s world, rocking gently in time with the cradle, yet was not performed until fifty years later. (The proposed song cycle was never composed, alas.) He also saw a lot of the Slaters as the two collaborators worked at the opera libretto – Montagu snaggletoothed and taciturn, Enid warm and sympathetic. And he was back in touch with Ronald Duncan, rekindling a relationship that would bear fruit (not all of it ripe) in 1945 and 1946. But the many others who had swum in Auden's stream were either away or otherwise occupied. Britten did not miss them; he was busy enough with CEMA and his opera libretto, sustained by his correspondence with Elizabeth Mayer, who sent food parcels and stale copies of the *New Yorker* in addition to protestations of unstinting love and support. Britten found the tight circle to his liking, a stabilizing force after the carnivals of the 1930s and February House.

There were new friends in the first year or so back: the pacifist pianist Clifford Curzon, an ex-pupil of Artur Schnabel and Nadia Boulanger, and his wife the harpsichordist Lucille Wallace, who entertained Britten in their Highgate home or their cottage in Cumbria, filling him with good food and a sense of domestic calm; John and Mary Behrend, arts patrons every bit as enlightened as Coolidge, if with less capital behind them; and Joan Cross, the tough wartime director of Sadler's Wells Opera Company, with her bright, even soprano voice, who would most sympathetically create the role of Ellen Orford in *Peter Grimes*, but who was somehow more at home as the later monsters Lady Billows and Queen Elizabeth.

Some old friends no longer satisfied him. Wulff Scherchen, back in England and hardened by experience as an incarcerated enemy alien, was 'impossible' and 'vindictive' now in Britten's eyes. And Sophie Wyss, of whom he was still fond, earned his disapproval for her performance of *Les Illuminations* at the Wigmore Hall. He thought it coy, subjective and whimsical, but mostly he wanted to wrest the cycle back for Pears's exclusive use. The situation was fanned by Wyss's husband, who was furious with Britten and protective of his wife. Diplomatically, Wyss talked to Britten of other repertory, other potential collaborations, but his heart was not in it. 'I'm too fond of her to be rude, & not interested enough to be critical. In other words, just weak, weak, weak,' he wrote to Pears, revealingly. (By late 1944 the fondness barely survived. 'Sophie's at it again – another long letter – including a nice lot of copies of press cuttings, showing how good she & I are together – the woman's a moron. How can a person be so daft?') He hated confrontation, but was nonetheless determined to have his way. His solution here was to push Wyss away with indifference, like a young, disappointed lover.

The two did record five French folk songs a year later, and these suggest Britten's behaviour towards her was not solely the consequence of his proprietorial feelings towards Pears. The disc reveals an attractive if old-fashioned sound. But it is also a little sluggish, which would have been intolerable to Britten by this stage – notwithstanding Pears's continuing vulnerability in this same respect. Wyss was a genuine force in

Britten's life and music in the 1930s, but she did not survive Pears's emergence as a soloist; nor did she measure up to Britten's vastly increased knowledge of voice and vocal technique in the 1940s. He met her when he was green in the art of collaborating, and she fell victim to a whole new set of requirements in his artistic colleagues – loyalty, an easygoing nature, exemplary musicianship – which would characterize his work for the remainder of his life.

Britten and Pears's constant separation in the last six months of 1942 helped them further define what they wanted from each other and from the alliance itself. The squalls and reconciliations were an inevitable part of the process. Sitting in an unprepossessing hotel in Birmingham in December, Pears attempted to describe their bond in a letter to Britten that is at once wise and touching.

> You know, I've been thinking an awful lot about you and me. I love you with my whole being, solemnly and seriously. These last times have made me realise how serious love is, what a great responsibility and what a sharing of personalities – It's not just a pleasure & a self indulgence. Our love must be complete and a creation in itself, a gift which we must be fully conscious of & responsible for.
>
> O my precious darling, parting from you is such agony – Just hearing your voice is joy.

No direct response has survived, though other correspondence contains variations on this theme, as Britten and Pears address the tensions born of distance, proximity and love.

19

On 30 September 1942 Britten told Elizabeth Mayer that 'the opera libretto is *finished* (& excellent too)'. The major disagreements were yet to come – Slater silent and intransigent, puffing on his pipe in defiance of Britten's entreaties for yet more alterations – but this first draft was an impressive achievement. In less than six months Britten and Slater had turned some quickly sketched characters and plot-lines into a working libretto. Slater had identified opportunity where his contemporary, Isherwood, had seen only melodrama. No other work pushed *Grimes* from Britten's thoughts. CEMA and the like filled his diary as the year progressed, and he grabbed idle moments to finish off *A Ceremony of Carols*, a piece that in other circumstances would not have taken seven months to complete. Yet his mind was otherwise totally focused on how best to tell the story of the Borough and its inhabitants.

Enid Slater remembered this period as one of great happiness, of Britten and her husband reunited after the enforced break in their friendship, traipsing through the countryside at Snape or Risborough, fleshing out their ideas. Their young daughter Bridget was also charmed by him. 'I was impressed by his unpredictability and his irritability. I was never sure when he would turn into a fractious fury or gently join us in a game,' she later said. 'It is going so well & I'm very keen on his whole attitude to the subject – Very simple, full of respect for Crabbe, and with real stage experience,' Britten told Mayer in June. Slater wrote with a thoughtful mixture of prose, four-stress lines and rough rhymes and in discussion with Britten introduced in these early months two key episodes: the villagers' procession to Grimes's hut, hell-bent on confronting him over his behaviour, and the ecstatic, orgiastic manhunt in the third act.

Slater's later intransigence was part practical, part political. He had been a committed member of the Communist Party of Great Britain since the late 1920s and, like the 1930s Auden, saw no distinction between art and ideology. The party's causes included trade unions (particularly miners'), anti-fascism and the unemployed workers' movement. Hitler and Stalin's pact of August 1939 robbed it of some momentum, though Hitler's betrayal of the pact and the subsequent routing of German forces at Stalingrad brought the party new popularity, however temporarily.

The libretto of *Peter Grimes* has had to bear a lot of weight over the years. It is a parable of the outsider – this much Britten and Pears made clear – but it is also a metaphor for the savagery of war: the viciousness of the villagers, with their gang mentality, high-street morality and lynching tendency, is both extreme and credible. Slater was sympathetic to the two ideas, but his background ensured the opera was to some extent also a commentary on capitalism. Class, poverty and oppression fired his imagination. (It is possible he or Britten knew *Ein ernstes Leben* (1932) by Heinrich Mann, Golo's uncle and Thomas's brother, with its stark depiction of German fishermen and their families trapped in brutal penury.) In a 1935 article in *Left Review* he flagged his commitment to 'knowledge of the ordinary world of people and of things, the world of work, the world of everyday economic struggle'. It was the documentary film world of John Grierson, though Slater had a much bigger axe to grind.

The Borough is a pre-industrial community (the opera is set in 'about 1830'), its economy governed by the sea and those living in the big houses above the High Street. The villagers are trapped in a cycle of desperate poverty, a cycle Grimes hopes to escape by fishing the sea dry and then acquiring wealth, a house and a respectable marriage. It is a classic bourgeois narrative. Grimes fails in his attempt to escape proletarian life and his suicide is the outcome. But his aspirant trajectory is set in play the moment he acquires his first workhouse apprentice before the opera begins; the second apprentice merely confirms his ambition and vision and splashes a Dickensian backdrop to the opera, one of exploitation and greed.

Slater gently pushed his Marxist reading of Crabbe's Borough, of the struggle of the working classes to live an honest, decent life. Britten initially seemed happy enough with the reading: it was to this notion that he was responding when he told Mayer *Peter Grimes* was becoming an opera about the community, and partly these ideas informed his essay in the Sadler's Wells handbook accompanying the opera's first production. 'In writing *Peter Grimes*, I wanted to express my awareness of the perpetual struggle of men and women whose livelihood depends on the sea – difficult though it is to treat such a universal subject in theatrical form.'

Despite the throat-clearing prior to his return, Britten was not overtly political in these years, preferring to keep his head down while he worked. There was the occasional exception. On 12 June he commented wryly to Pears on MI5 obstructing Slater's attempts to join the Ministry of Information owing to his Communist Party membership – 'a nice paradox with the new "alliance"!!', a reference to the Anglo-Soviet alliance against Hitler concluded on 26 May. On the same day as his letter, *The Times* led with the new compact, reproducing George VI's glad-handing message to the Soviet President, Mikhail Kalinin. 'This treaty consecrates the efforts of our two countries in the hard and bitter struggle they are waging, and pledges them to wholehearted cooperation and mutual support in the years that will follow our victory.' All sins were forgiven – including Stalin and Hitler's awkward alliance in the early war years – not least as the Red Army gradually turned the tables on the Germans.

The king's message was emblematic of the good feeling towards the Soviet Union in the second half of the war.* Slater therefore had no incentive to steer clear of explicit or implicit positive depictions of socialist experiments in his work. Even those suspicious of Stalin had to recognize that Britain's wartime economy was run on the principles of central government control and expenditure, which were the primary buttresses of the Soviet system. It was a long way from laissez-faire capitalism, which had not run untethered in Britain since the beginning of the nineteenth century, but which had nonetheless long been a dominating philosophy in British economic policy.

Comradeship between composer and poet lasted only until March 1943, when Britten confessed to Pears that Slater might not be the 'ideal librettist'. He went on to list potential alternatives, each of whom was quickly discounted: Auden ('there are the old objections, & besides, he's not to hand'); MacNeice ('more or less the same objections'); Sackville-West ('I doubt whether he again is a good enough poet'). The problem was not the overall shape of the work as Slater envisioned it (though already by 1943 Britten was certain the opera had different angles); it was more the writer's working habits, which Britten found too slow, too methodical, and with doubts about the quality of his poetry. No music had yet been composed, but Britten was nonetheless shaping the opera in his head and wanted from Slater a flexible and mercurial response to his ideas. 'I see so clearly what kind of music I want to write for it,' he told Pears, '& I *am* interested in the people & the situations, & interested in a musical way.' But perhaps there was a problem with the opera as political allegory: Grimes remained too much of a pathological case – 'no reasons & not many symptoms', as Britten told Erwin Stein – and this needed fixing, a process Slater seems to have resisted, or found difficult to respond to in time.

---

* There is a photograph of Britten smiling beneath the hammer and sickle, part of a delegation of British composers, taken at either the first British performance of Shostakovich's 'Leningrad' Symphony in June 1942 or at a barnstorming 'Salute the Red Army' event in February 1944. Britten looks incongruous next to Granville Bantock, Sir Arnold Bax and his former teacher, Ireland.

In 1946 Slater published the libretto as he thought it should have been set. The differences are, for the most part, minor: a word changed here, a stanza reordered there. But in Grimes's final scene, Slater has him present an almost Socratic monologue about the death of his apprentice. 'You're not to blame that he went down. / It was his weakness that let go. / He was too weak. Were you to know?' This compares poorly to the wide-eyed mad scene in the opera, full of melodic and textual references to earlier events, with the crowd baying offstage somewhere and Grimes barely comprehending what has happened, let alone what must now happen: 'The first one died, just died ... / The other slipped, and died ... / And the third will ...' As late as 24 February 1945 Britten wrote to Ronald Duncan, 'We are having a terrific time with Grimes – & Peter & I are pretty well re-writing his part. Montagu agreed to the new mad-scene, & I kept your part in it fairly quiet, altho' I murmured that you helped us abit!' Duncan clearly served him well in this instance, though the individual interventions – most of them necessary, most pointing to the composer's deep dramatic instincts – do not diminish the extent of Slater's responsiblity for this bold and progressive libretto.

20

Britten became ill again. Accurately or not, he usually linked each of his adult illnesses with his infant pneumonia, the principal source of the slow-burning paranoia concerning his health in childhood and beyond. In the last months of 1942 the illness was influenza, and then in March 1943, measles. Finally, in November 1943, the flu returned, scuttling his thirtieth-birthday plans and leaving Pears to nurse a truculent patient unable to eat or get excited over his lover's thoughtful gifts, which included a book of Michelangelo lyrics. Doctors blamed his easy susceptibility to flu on the sulphonamide he had taken in 1940, which had spoiled his immune system. He must give up coffee, they warned sternly. On this occasion, Britten thought he was just run down, not least from his appellate hearing.

The measles in March 1943 had a greater immediate impact on his work than the November influenza: Britten was admitted to the Grove Hospital in Tooting, South London, a motley collection of wards, isolation wings, staff quarters, kitchen and mortuary. Built to cater to victims of scarlet fever and diphtheria, as the century progressed and vaccines appeared the hospital welcomed patients suffering from other, often milder diseases. Britten stayed for two weeks in complete isolation, describing it as a 'gloomy hole' with comic food and an uncanny, magnetic attraction to German aeroplanes, which droned overhead, upsetting the children in the wards. The doctors treated him like a film star, hinting at an intimate knowledge of his music. The Grove allowed the convalescing Britten to conduct a much slower-paced version of his life. He wrote letters, read old copies of *Horizon* and thought about his opera and other works. From Hawkes he requested a score of Strauss's *Der Rosenkavalier* so as 'to pick the old man's brains for my opera!' After the Grove he was prescribed complete bed rest, which he used as an excuse to pull out of projects to which he had committed himself out of either duty or opportunity. These included a score for the film version of George Bernard Shaw's *Caesar and Cleopatra*, which he had been toying with – none too enthusiastically – for some months.

Unlike six months earlier, there now seemed no limit to his prospects. The directorate of the Promenade Concerts sniffed around for novelties, earning a rebuke from Britten that applies to today's culture as much as to his own: why not older works? Why not the Violin Concerto, *Variations on a Theme of Frank Bridge*, *Les Illuminations*, *Sinfonietta*, or even the new orchestral versions of four of his British folk-song arrangements? Why this constant demand for premieres, especially given how busy he was, how overstretched he found himself?

Later, once he had recovered, Hawkes attempted to rein in his profligate composer, determined to avoid future collisions or extractions. At the end of June 1943 he listed the works to which Britten was committed: an anthem, 'Rejoice in the Lamb'; 'Serenade for Strings, Voice and Horn (Consisting of six items)'; 'Ceremony of Carols' ('One more Carol is to be added, together with a Harp interlude'); 'Sonata for Orchestra'; cadenzas for Mozart and Haydn concertos, the former for flute, the latter for harpsichord. 'Beyond these you should start no other new composition but devote yourself – upon the completion of the above works – to the Opera for Koussevitzky, the Ballet for Sadler's Wells and the Cantata [*The Rescue*] for the BBC.' Hawkes had a point: it was a huge workload. The 'Sonata' was never written, nor was the ballet or flute cadenza. The list makes no mention of the Prelude and Fugue for eighteen-part string orchestra which had received its premiere five days earlier by its dedicatees, Boyd Neel and his orchestra, and now needed prepping for publication. Nor does it include the various Purcell realizations he completed, almost for relaxation, during these months and in the year to come. Or *The Ballad of Little Musgrave and Lady Barnard*, composed 'For Richard Wood and the musicians of Oflag VIIb – Germany, 1943'. Moreover, he was yet to write a note of *Peter Grimes*, and his diary remained full with performances. There was desperately little room to undertake new works, willingly or otherwise.

One work on Hawkes's list was already completed by the time the publisher collared his charge, while another was almost done. The completed work was the cantata *Rejoice in the Lamb*, commissioned by Walter Hussey for the fiftieth anniversary of the consecration of St Matthew's church, Northampton. It is a setting for choir and organ of poems by Christopher Smart, a sort of Holy Fool who produced a series of prophetic, reverential madhouse ravings. Smart was yet another gift from Auden, who no doubt enjoyed the comic-book biblical characters who skip their way through the poet's disjointed zoological narrative: Balaam and his ass; Ishmael and his tyger; Daniel and his lion. There is a section full of musical instruments, each of which Britten impersonates with the same knowing clarity he brought to the 'instrumental' section of *Hymn to St Cecilia*. The cantata lasts only fifteen minutes or so, but it is a captivating piece – a stroll through an over-curated nineteenth-century natural history museum as much as through a church. 'That is still your best yet you know,' Pears would write about the work to Britten in October 1944.

The work nearing completion was Britten's *Serenade*, for tenor, horn and strings, most of which he composed in the Grove during his sickness and convalescence. These 'horn songs', as he termed them, were written in a mad rush and near fever, Britten having rifled two books for material: *Poems from the Works of Charles Cotton* and the 1927 edition of Arthur Quiller-Couch's *The Oxford Book of English Verse*, one of the school prizes he was awarded on leaving Gresham's. On the back flyleaf of his Quiller-Couch edition, under his scribbled banner 'Night', are the titles of sixteen poems that caught his eye. This list is itself an anthology of English verse: Shelley, Thomas Campion, Robert Herrick, William Habington, William Collins, Blake, Wordsworth, Byron, Thomas Lovell Beddoes and Sir Philip Sidney – in addition to most of the poems he finally set. Sackville-West helped him whittle it down and perhaps suggested the Charles Cotton and Blake texts, which earned Britten's appreciation (as well as the work's dedication) and probably prompted Sackville-West's declaration of love in December 1942, deftly batted away by Britten.

There is something intriguing about the works Britten composed at the peak of one illness or another: fever heightened his imagination. They include his *Rhapsody* for string quartet, written in Gresham's sanatorium in early 1929; *A Hymn to the Virgin*, composed on 9 July the following year, its creator pulled from classes with a high temperature and ushered back to the sanatorium; preliminary work on *Sinfonia da Requiem* during the early months of 1940; *Serenade* in the Grove; the skittish, combative sixth of the *Seven Sonnets of Michelangelo*, which is dated 12 June 1940, the end of two weeks of fierce pain from a tooth extraction; *The Holy Sonnets of John Donne*, composed in August 1945 when Britten was in bed with a high fever, an adverse reaction to a typhoid vaccination; *The Prodigal Son*, which was interrupted in 1968 by Britten's hospitalization for endocarditis; *Death in Venice*, created in the shadow of major heart disease and impending surgery; and *Phaedra*, during his hopeless convalescence from this literally heart-breaking operation.

There were other times when he was too weak to compose or forbidden to do so by doctors. Or when he suffered from depression, such as April 1943, or between December 1948 and March 1949 when anxiety and exhaustion halted work on *Spring Symphony*, a traipse through the sunny Suffolk countryside that belies the circumstances of its composition. Yet even these circumstances or directives were often brushed aside; Britten would sneak manuscript paper to his bed, sketching the ideas that gave him no peace – a fevered Romantic, his senses altered, imagination untrammelled. And in such circumstances music flowed from his head and hand.

Serenade was Britten's way of keeping Pears foremost in his thoughts. The tenor was now away more often than not: 'he is permanently with Sadlers Wells Opera,' Britten told David Rothman in May 1943, '& a very glamorous & popular heroe he makes!' His Hoffmann had given rise to a host of roles: Rodolfo in *La bohème*; Tamino in *The Magic Flute*; the Duke in *Rigoletto*; Alfredo in *La traviata*; Almaviva in *The*

Barber of Seville. Later there would be Ferrando (*Così fan tutte*) and Vašek in *The Bartered Bride*.* Some of the roles he learned in a couple of weeks, an indication of the company's frantic, last-minute programming, but also testimony to Pears's maturing voice and fast-accumulating stage experience. Britten drank in this experience vicariously, but attended performances as often as he could, analysing every move, breathing every phrase. He was a shadowy figure in the wings, or crammed into the small stage box in London's New Theatre, or waiting for Pears at the stage door, impatient to whisk him off to a meal or their lodgings. Britten later wrote that he attended twelve performances of *La traviata* in such circumstances, at which point he felt he was only just beginning to know the piece and 'appreciate its depths of emotion, and musical strength'.

There were oratorios as well, and recitals with substitute pianists when Britten was ill or busy elsewhere. Pears was enjoying an impressive and somewhat unexpected career as a soloist, sowing the seeds of his post-war professional life. In photographs he looks handsome and commanding: his Alfredo is in a stiff collar with tousled hair, his Vašek a mix of village idiot and earnest morris dancer. It gave Britten much pleasure to think of his absent lover, to imagine him in these roles, to regret their missed performances together and to write him new music: 'what a curse it is that I haven't been able to do these concerts with you – but at least I've been able to write things for you, – better than nothing.'

When he wrote this to Pears, Britten was immersed in the world of Keats, the poet venerated by Wilde and Tennyson and Shelley. Home from the Grove, licking his wounds, impatient for the recovery of his health and routine, Britten had the same day set Keats's sonnet 'To Sleep', which would end up as the seventh movement of *Serenade*. The poem depicts a still night in which the protagonist begs for release from the many woes of daylight and the burdensome responsibilities of conscience and consciousness. 'Then save me, save me, or the passèd day will shine / Upon my pillow, breeding many woes.' Britten was attracted to the Romantic potential of night, aware also of the nightmarish possibilities of sleep, as the anonymous 'Dirge' in *Serenade* and the Wordsworth setting in the later *Nocturne* demonstrate. He enjoyed it

---

* A *danseur*, released from the army by the exiled Czech government, was in charge of training the English ballet in the native dances, in which girls dressed as boys to make up the depleted numbers.

for other reasons, too, for the 'chance for your subconscious to work when your conscious mind is happily asleep'.

Britten treated Keats reverentially. The peaceful night is depicted with primary chords that slip down chromatically, as though eyelids drooping, a stillness soon interrupted by a series of sharp jolts, loud and foreign in the nocturnal landscape. His is a sensitive reading of the words, alert to the short-breathed panic that can accompany sleeplessness. He had lived with the poem for some time before setting to work, his illness still afflicting him.

Pears was not the sole muse here. The virtuoso horn player Dennis Brain was only twenty-one when Britten first met him in early summer 1942. Principal horn in the RAF Orchestra, Brain played 'as flexibly and accurately as most clarinettists, & is a sweet & intelligent person as well', Britten told Mayer. Brain dispatched solo horn repertory pitch-perfect, as though playing scales at a piano. Both musicians were thrown together on Britten's score for *An American in England*, Brain impressing the composer with his extraordinary poise and talent. He was a gentle soul too, which appealed to Britten. At one of these early rehearsals he asked Britten to write him a concerto, which did not turn out quite as Brain intended, the composer deciding instead on an orchestral work for horn and voice.

Serenade is more layered than a horn concerto, however, and the selection of poems reflected the possibilities of the horn as much as those of Pears's voice. There are the bugle calls Tennyson evokes in 'Nocturne', while Jonson's 'Hymn', with its opening line, 'Queen and huntress, chaste and fair', simply begs for the horn calls of a forest hunt. The Jonson setting is a thrilling dialogue between voice and horn: at times the singer interjects with short, punctuating phrases, at other moments he performs in reckless imitation of the horn's brazen fanfares. Jonson's huntress is the goddess Diana, bold, luminescent, in charge, which Britten matched effortlessly.

The conductor Norman Del Mar, then a fellow horn player in the RAF Orchestra, recalled Britten at the 1942 rehearsal with Brain, plying him with questions about the instrument. Can you pull a top C from your hat? How does pitch change according to the way you stop the horn with your fist? How do harmonics on the natural horn work? Brain's answers made their way into *Serenade*'s Prologue and identical Epilogue, a horn call made up of natural harmonics and strange, other-worldly sounds. Listeners are immediately transported deep into the forest, as surely as they are at the beginning of Britten's *A Midsummer Night's Dream*, where string glissandi portray creaky branches and dry summer air. Both Britten works inhabit the world of Richard Dadd, the Victorian murderer, Bedlam inmate and fantastic artist whose evocative paintings depict the dangerous and alluring world of fairies and the supernatural. And both works politely drop the safety curtain once the performance is finished, cutting us off from the magical forest world and the suggestive, erotic power of night.

Serenade's premiere, once more in Wigmore Street's own magical if tatty night kingdom, was on 15 October 1943. The conductor Walter Goehr assembled a scratch band equal to the occasionally difficult string writing, and Pears and Brain stood on the wooden platform, eyeing the assembled friends and general public, and the London critics there for either feast or famine, and literally played off each other. The critics found it a feast, saluting Pears's beautiful tone and phrasing and Brain's understated virtuosity. But their greatest praise was for Britten's sensitive selection and treatment of the nocturnal poetry. 'Five years ago I used to listen rather sadly to my predecessor, Fox Strangways, while he told me of his good fortune as a young man in being able to hear Brahms's mature works as they came out,' wrote William Glock in the *Observer*. 'Now I feel differently for in Benjamin Britten we have at last a composer who offers us visions as great as those. His new Serenade, op. 31, a set of six songs for tenor, horn, and strings, surpasses everything else of his in strength and feeling.'

They made a recording in 1944 under Britten's direction, which gives a good indication of how the premiere must have sounded. Pears has a more even instrument than three years earlier – a little wild on his top B flat, but otherwise secure in the long phrases and masterful as he had been earlier in his word painting. So too is his coloratura much better than before, a consequence of all those Alfredos and Almavivas he had trotted out in provincial British theatres. Brain dispatches his part with ease, plucking his top Cs from the air like fruit from a low branch. There are a couple of surprising missteps, quickly corrected – a reminder that this was new and challenging terrain for a horn player and that musicians then thought differently about the need for second, third and fourth takes. (There was no editing the pale wax discs.)

For all the virtuosity, for all the explication of poetic image as sound,

Serenade is an unexpectedly safe work, especially after the freewheeling *Michelangelo Sonnets*. ('I still think I prefer *Les Illuminations*,' commented Boosey, never much fun, after the premiere, 'and in any case I am distrustful of a work of this character which causes too much enthusiasm at the start.') It is harmonically straightforward, and when Britten is not using the voice in word painting, he is luxuriating in the sound and registers of Pears's instrument, which he had come to know so well. 'It is not important stuff,' Britten said of the cycle to Mayer in early April, six months before the premiere, 'but quite pleasant, I think.' This was Britten's usual self-deprecation, yet it is a fairer assessment of the work than its reception and later canonical privileges would allow. Britten, tucked up in an isolation ward in the Grove, devouring with pleasure a book on Constable, harnessed the great artist's bucolic spirit and composed his own pastoral landscape. There is the occasional patch of briars and there are spectres in the background, but the work is an unambiguous and slightly nostalgic paean to the country he had gratefully reclaimed as his own.

2 1

In February 1943, with Pears averaging five performances a week and Britten yet to compose his nocturnal idyll, the couple moved out of the house they shared with Ursula Nettleship in Cheyne Walk (£1 each per week plus telephone and bills) and into a maisonette occupying the top three floors of a Georgian terrace at 45A St John's Wood High Street. This remained their London base until 1946. They engaged a cook who performed magical feats with their rations (no doubt relying on the complicity of the grocer whose shop was on the ground floor) until she became ill, which disrupted the lifestyle into which they had fallen. The London base was necessary, of course, given Pears's whimsical touring schedule and Britten's various projects and collaborators, yet the composer spent as much time as possible away from the capital. It was partly to do with the civvies that branded him almost as surely as uniforms branded the soldiers everywhere about town, but mostly he found it difficult to write in London, too noisy, too frantic – the same complaints he had with New York. After his unproductive 1942, he was determined to compose more.

The bombing and destruction of London did not so much soften his views on war and Germany as reinforce them. Snape was not immune to attack: Allied and enemy bombers flew overhead and klaxon sounds at night summoned him from bed, away from the surrounding glass windows. But London bore the brunt of the attacks. Writing to Pears from the Grove, his sympathies were with the 'enemy': 'think of what the Germans are going through now – poor devils. How I wish to God it would all stop. I feel every day that it goes on longer makes things worse – takes us all further into the mire of hate & hopelessness.'

There was no doubting what the Germans were going through. During 1943, as Britain stepped up air attacks (a consequence of an exponential increase in munitions and trained airmen), the *Daily Telegraph* reported raids with breathless *Boy's Own Paper* enthusiasm. 'Hamburg has had the equivalent of at least 60 "Coventrys", Cologne 17, Dusseldorf 12, and Essen 10' – a reference to the catastrophic bombing of the cathedral city of Coventry in November 1940. Spender recalled the BBC's news bulletins being little better. '"We gave" *(long pause)* "Jerry" *(long pause, followed by the next three words spoken very quickly)* "a jolly good" *(long pause)* "Pranging."' Even without the *Telegraph* for corroboration there was anecdotal evidence within earshot, since many of the Allied bombing raids began from airfields in East Anglia. 'Knowing how I feel when they come here, I can't feel pleased for people on the other side, when [the bombers] go out,' Britten told Bobby Rothman.

Retribution left him cold; his views on the war did not change according to one side's progress, the other's regress. Britten was strangely uninterested in the implications of pacifism, of how it would make England vulnerable to attack and brutal occupation if more of his countrymen had subscribed to it. Instead he occupied the Arcadian territory of first principles: war was wrong and any arguments about implications were irrelevant. This was the stance taken by the Peace Pledge Union, with which Britten continued his association. He had been consistent in this belief since adolescence and remained so after the war. In 1967, at a dinner hosted by (Jewish) musicologist Hans Keller, Britten declared that Israeli soldiers should have lain down in front of Arab tanks rather than fight. It was a somewhat eccentric reading of the geopolitics, but heartfelt nonetheless. Keller argued with him, which initiated Britten and Pears's precipitate departure – a display of what the musicologist labelled the composer's 'aggressive pacifism'.

It was indeed aggressive. By 1967 Britten brooked no dissent on almost any topic, even from a pro-Israeli Jewish intellectual whose views and friendship he valued. Yet there was no substantive difference between the Britten of 1967 and that of twenty-five years earlier. In the early 1940s Hawkes argued with Britten over his pacifism before offering his respectful disagreement and full support, much as Isherwood had. It was not the reaction of every friend or colleague. American composer Marc Blitzstein had not let him off so lightly, warning him at a party in New York in the early 1940s that the next time they met he would ask Britten 'how he squared his conscientious objection to the war with doing propaganda work for the BBC'. Based in London with the US Army Eighth Air Force, Blitzstein was in the audience for the premiere of *Serenade*; Britten avoided him.

For all his relative isolation from the daily grind of war and his new-found status in the public eye, disputes such as that with Blitzstein or with military-minded patriots occasionally brimmed over. Critical letters to the *Musical Times* were small beer, but a more serious dispute occurred in October 1943, when Arthur Bliss, the BBC's director of music from 1942 to 1944 and onetime *enfant terrible* of English music (improbable as that seemed by the early 1940s), made it widely known he thought it unfortunate to appoint Britten to conduct his score to Edward Sackville-West's radio play *The Rescue*. Britten eventually withdrew from the engagement with some dignity, but he was left in no doubt that his pacifism was the primary cause of Bliss's hostility. 'I have my great friends for my work,' he wrote elliptically to Mayer in December 1943, 'and at the moment they seem easily to outweigh my enemies – but for how long, one can't say, nor does it matter.'

One of these friends was the free-spirited composer Michael Tippett, almost nine years Britten's senior, but with none of the younger man's success and profile. Perhaps as a partial consequence, Tippett had fared poorly in his local tribunal hearing in 1940 and subsequent appeal. He refused the Appellate Tribunal's directive to serve as a non-combatant and was duly sentenced to three months' imprisonment in Wormwood Scrubs. It was here that Britten and Pears gave a celebrated recital on 11 July 1943, assisted by the gangly Tippett turning pages. ('Incidentally,' wrote John Amis, who was with Britten and Pears that day, 'Michael was tickled pink to take over the prison orchestra from Ivor Novello, who was in for petrol-coupon diddling.')

Britten and Tippett maintained a lifelong bond despite their differences in temperament: the one garrulous, carefree, openly curious about everything and everyone; the other guarded, suspicious, private and proper. In *The Habit of Art*, Alan Bennett has the middle-aged Britten spit out Tippett's name as 'the one the students listen to, model themselves on. The money is on Michael.' Whatever truth there is in the composers' changing fortunes in the 1960s, their friendship survived in remarkably good shape. It was Britten who insisted that Tippett exhume his oratorio *A Child of our Time* from the drawer to which Walter Goehr advised him to consign it, and Britten who agitated for its 1944 premiere. And it was Tippett who really got Britten's mettle, writing thirty years or so later in the touching obituary of his friend, 'I want to say here, personally, that Britten has been for me the most purely musical person I have ever met and I have ever known.'

Enchanted by an early performance of *Seven Sonnets of Michelangelo*, Tippett composed *Boyhood's End* for Britten and Pears, an apposite work in so recent a friendship. It is a setting of prose by William Henry Hudson, writer, naturalist and ornithologist, which evokes a world of tree climbing, cream-coloured eggs, grassy banks and bulrushes, mirages and mysterious sounds. Tippett does not consistently catch the poem's mixture of boyhood insouciance and nostalgia; there is a central section of reverent contemplation, which fulfils a possible structural need in the music but is at odds with the rough-and-tumble vignette it depicts. But the cycle is an impressive achievement – the piano part slightly clumsy on paper (crafted at the instrument through a process of trial and error by the non-pianist composer), yet effective to the ear.

Britten and Pears performed the work at Dartington on 10 October 1943 and at the Wigmore Hall the following year, the first recital prompting fan mail from Imogen Holst. Holst, the spindly, brilliant, eccentric daughter of composer Gustav, was director of music in the arts department at Dartington, a position she retained until 1952 when she moved to Aldeburgh to assist Britten on *Gloriana*, thereafter remaining a key figure in his life and in that of the Aldeburgh Festival.

Holst's letter initiated a revealing response.

It is also encouraging that you too sense that 'something' in the air which heralds a renaissance. I feel terrifically conscious of it, so do Peter, & Clifford, & Michael Tippett & so many that I love & admire – it is good to add you to that list! Whether we are the voices crying in the wilderness or the thing itself, it isn't for us to know, but anyhow it is so very exciting. It is of course in all the arts, but in music, particularly, it's this acceptance of 'freedom' without any arbitrary restrictions, this simplicity, this contact with the audiences of our own time, & of people like ourselves, this seriousness & above all this professionalism. One mustn't and can't deny the many heavenly genius[es] of the last century, but it is also a greater sympathy with the earlier centuries that marks this thing perhaps the most clearly.

'Renaissance' was not a word to be thrown about lightly just then. There was already supposed to have been one at the beginning of the century, when Elgar, Vaughan Williams, Bax, Rutland Boughton and numerous others emerged as supposed giants of British musical culture. Britten was largely dismissive of this renaissance and its authors; there seemed to be so little to show for it. The letter is polite and respectful of the nineteenth- and twentieth-century geniuses he would be hard-pressed to identify, yet Britten probably thought these 'renaissance composers' and their teachers were the voices crying in the wilderness, heralding a bright time ahead.

22

In late 1943 Mary Behrend commissioned a double portrait of Britten and Pears. The artist was Kenneth Green, eight years Britten's senior, whom the composer had met soon after his return to England and who would soon design the Sadler's Wells productions of *Così* and *Peter Grimes*. In December they squeezed in sittings between Pears's performances and Britten's composing. Green's portrait is a formal, almost stilted work, which could almost be a parody of Hans Holbein the Younger's *Double Portrait of Sir Thomas Godsalve and his Son John* (1528), both men staring to their left in sombre compliance. Holbein's subjects at least have a strong familial resemblance through which the connection is made explicit: bulbous noses, cleft chins and apple cheeks.

In Green's portrait the men fix on slightly different points, Pears a patrician aristocrat, made thinner from his stage exertions, Britten softer than in photographs, his sharply delineated lines smoothed over. There is nothing to connect them as the genre requires. It is possible their arms are touching, yet even this is not explicit. Green purposefully keeps their relationship ambiguous, perhaps relying on their recent, public musical partnership as a fig-leaf.

There was much malicious gossip about them at the time. Edward Downes, then a student at the RCM and later a distinguished conductor and Britten interpreter, remembered a toxic 'corporate antagonism' at the college towards Britten due to his whispered homosexuality and evident pacifism; other students at the time remember the same, John Lindsay recalling a caretaker saying: 'Oh, couple o' nancy-boys. They ought to be in the bloody army.' And there's a fair chance that Bliss's reaction to the pacifist Britten was exacerbated by homophobia; Basil Douglas, a perceptive music administrator who shared a flat with Pears in the late 1930s and was later manager of the English Opera Group, remembered Britten being considered 'very off-colour' by the music department's grey-suits. Quite whether Behrend's enlightenment ran to knowledge of the exact nature of their relationship is unclear; perhaps this explains the cool, rather classical composition of the double portrait. Yet the painting was not intended as a public statement, for all Green's caution; it remained in Behrend's private collection until 1973, when she donated it to London's National Portrait Gallery. And whatever the artist's intentions, whatever the work's degrees of disclosure and disguise, it is a fittingly serious portrait of two of the key players in England's wartime cultural renaissance.

Green also completed a solo portrait of Britten, probably at the same time (the clothes are identical). It is a more rough-hewn work, no doubt a hurried preparatory study for the double sitting, left to one side once the artist was sure he could capture Britten in oils. For all its haste, there is more humour in the smile, more lift to the brow, more life in the eyes than in the double portrait. Pears described it to Mayer in August 1944: 'Kenneth Green is a *real* painter – his portrait of Ben (my first picture as collector) is lovely – always different, every day – like Ben!' In the same letter he attempted to describe Britten two years or so after their return. 'He is a lovely mature person, no less vital but stronger and broader.'

A few weeks after Green finished the paintings Britten finally started to give music to the ideas that had fired him since 1941. The libretto was at last done, Britten told Mayer in December, unaware of the further surgery to come. Slater had given flesh to a host of minor characters: Auntie, the fast-talking landlady of the Boar, the Borough's disreputable drinking hole; her ever-changing 'nieces' who tease the village men with exaggerated coyness before moving on, as itinerant as Lowestoft's herring-girls; Ned Keene, the apothecary, who peddles authentic drugs (laudanum, a cheap opium derivative), not miracle cures, like that other great operatic quack, Dulcamara, in Donizetti's *L'elisir d'amore*; Bob Boles, a shrill, unhinged Pecksniffian Methodist evangelist and fisherman, who seeks salvation in unlikely sources; and Mrs Sedley, the town's Miss Marple, who prowls the streets in her worn black satin bonnet, piecing together the puzzle of Grimes's behaviour. Grimes is rendered sympathetically, as is his sole friend, Captain Balstrode, and the schoolmistress Ellen Orford, who *almost* rings true as a character. But most of the villagers come out of it badly.*

Regardless of such progress in the opera's structure, meaning and characterization, the timetable they were then working to was impossibly tight: the premiere was planned for Koussevitzky's Berkshire Music Festival in Tanglewood in summer 1944. Britten was sanguine about the schedule – unrealistically, given that he only began work on the Prologue in the second week of January – yet it was a tall order for everyone else involved. Fortunately for Britten, Koussevitzky cancelled his festival for the remainder of the war, and amid slow and sometimes hostile negotiations with Sadler's Wells, which Britten settled on as a replacement, the opera's premiere slipped back to April and then June 1945.

At the end of February 1944 Britten played through to Pears what he had composed of *Peter Grimes*, singing all the parts in his low, droning voice – no quality, but much character. Pears found the occasion 'tremendously thrilling', dispensing a little advice about pace and the delivery of text. It was this occasion that prompted Pears's comments

---

* Britten's former publisher, Hubert Foss, wrote a critical but remarkably thoughtful appraisal in the *Listener*, unconvinced by anyone but Grimes. 'But turn aside from the dominating character, cast a living glance at Ellen Orford (who is too good to be true or explainable), and you find pasteboard characters, each bearing a dramatic and musical label, but unreal . . . Bob Boles and Mrs Sedley merely state identities in an operatic plot.' Perhaps this was Foss having his revenge, though the issue of characterization in Britten's operas would haunt the composer all his life.

about Grimes's queerness being unimportant; he was certain that what-ever its weight, it should not obtrude into the music or words. 'P.G. is an introspective, an artist, a neurotic, his real problem is expression, self-expression. Nicht wahr? What a part! Wow!'

There were other informal performances as the opera progressed: a play-through at Curzon's home in Cumbria this same winter, Britten breathing life into an old upright with yellow keys, rain thrashing the cottage windows; an 'awful gabble-through' in March or April 1944 for Sackville-West, who was to write a major article on it and who responded with a number of specific criticisms, which Britten took with thin-lipped good grace. And there was an important play-through at Sadler's Wells in August, a matter of weeks after he had completed the second act, when 'Ben came and smashed it out on the piano', according to Joan Cross, a performance that earned the executive's imprimatur.

By his own reckoning Britten was now spending half his time in Snape ('the view as heavenly, as Constable, as ever'), the rest in London or on the rickety concert circuit. Beth remembered the hard graft of Britten's time at Snape: her brother at his studio desk by 9 a.m. at the latest, remaining until 1 p.m.; a walk after lunch, during which more of the music was mapped in his head and sometimes sung, to the amuse-ment of passing villagers; three more hours at his desk. There was the odd tantrum – 'My bloody opera stinks, & that's all there is to it,' he complained to Pears in June – but it was a mostly productive and congenial time. Moreover, it established the working pattern of the remainder of his life.

Beth also remembered less cerebral events during the year: doodle-bugs flying in over Thorpeness, the village five miles east of Snape, made visible by their tail lights. If they turned down the coast, south towards Ipswich and then London, villagers in Snape were safe; if they turned inland, those at the Old Mill would take refuge under the stairs. One doodle-bug hit the village in late October 1944, missing the Old Mill's roof by only a matter of feet, exploding at a farm in nearby Priory Lane. Britten welcomed in a local family whose home was left uninhabitable by the blast, yet still stuck to his timetable, leaving others to dispense hospitality.

By now he was onto the scoring, which he whipped through at speed. Ronald Duncan once observed Britten holding a conversation while at the same time scribbling away at the full score; by this stage in the composition process all the thinking had been done. Britten's manuscript sketch, with its scratchy references to particular instruments – 'strings only', 'horns', 'ww', 'Tuba Db Fg. Gong etc' – underline how automatic a process orchestrating was for him.

23

Occasionally a concert took him from Snape. On 2 November 1944 he performed with Pears what was by then a typical mix of composers and centuries: Dowland, Purcell, Schubert and Britten (*Seven Sonnets of Michelangelo* and some folk-song arrangements). Though such programming today is textbook, it was unusual then. So too were single-composer concerts in which different genres were juxtaposed: songs, a string quartet, solo piano works. Britten and some friends planned a number of such concerts, and though only the first occurred, at the end of April 1944, their vision was no poorer for it. On this occasion an enthusiastic crowd piled into the Wigmore Hall to hear Curzon play Schubert's improvisatory Piano Sonata in D, D. 850, and Britten and Pears perform *Die schöne Müllerin*, their first outing with this cycle.

Later in the year Pears wrote about their rehearsals. 'Work with you is totally different in kind from any other sort. It becomes related to life immediately, which is more than any of the other stuff I do, does (including "Così").' There are evocative photos of Britten and Pears in this time rehearsing in the circular studio at the Old Mill, heavy drapes in the background ready to be drawn at nightfall against the Luftwaffe. Their faces are united in absolute concentration. It did not seem to matter how long Britten had lived with a particular score (and by 1944 this young man of thirty had already been playing, composing and absorbing music for over twenty years), he thrived on instinct. His repertory expanded with the years, and there would remain surprises and joyful discoveries, which filtered into his own music or shaped the way he thought about other people's.

A much later filmed performance of *Die schöne Müllerin*, with comical Viennese candelabra dotting the stage, shows Britten with his thin, flat fingers articulating each song distinctly, approaching modulations with care. He is alternately the rushing brook, the clattering mill, the impatient youth and the polite lover – at first bashful and then heartbroken. In the sixth song, 'Der Neugierige' (Curiosity), the miller lad asks the brook whether the miller maid loves him: yes or no, he tentatively demands, as though the stream is a magic mirror. Britten's playing in this one moment perfectly captures the hesitancy and trepidation of the youth.

The film establishes that Pears was a similar beast. Though Imogen Holst came to distrust Pears as a musician, describing him late in life as a philistine, and though the couple's correspondence is full of slights and apologies and their lives punctuated by misunderstandings and disagreements, the shared instinctive response to music was their pact. In footage of them working on *Winterreise* in the late 1960s they are relaxed and of equal authority. Pears revels in the barking dogs in the piano part, matching his words to the narrative of the accompaniment.

Britten could be intransigent in rehearsal. He was adamant about tempo. 'I can't help feeling you know,' he wrote to Erwin Stein in 1943, 'that there *is* only one tempo for every piece of music – at least, maybe one tempo for one person! Maybe it's something to do with heartbeats or slow or fast metabolism!! I know I suffer agonies when I feel the tempo wrong. But why, I can't say.' Was it association, he wondered, perhaps familiarity with particular speeds from gramophone recordings (which, in this era of short-sided 78s, were often bizarre). He had always been critical of 'wrong' tempo, whether it involved an unfamiliar or unrecorded work or was something well known. This was the core of much of his frustration with the London performances he derided in his teens and twenties, and it would cause tension between Britten and conductors of his own works after the war.

Record producer John Culshaw later admired Britten's remarkable memory for tempi – no means a given with professional conductors, for whom tempo is often an inexact science. Britten could pick up where he left off in a recording session days earlier at exactly the same speed. Or he could record an opera out of sequence, which would then be put together in the editing suite, each piece of the puzzle fitting neatly with the others. He was complimentary when others managed this 'one tempo', as with the 'damn good conductor' Charles Münch performing *Variations on a Theme of Frank Bridge* in November 1944. ('The L.P.O. isn't so hot an orch., but he made them play wonderfully, & had a very good idea of the piece.')

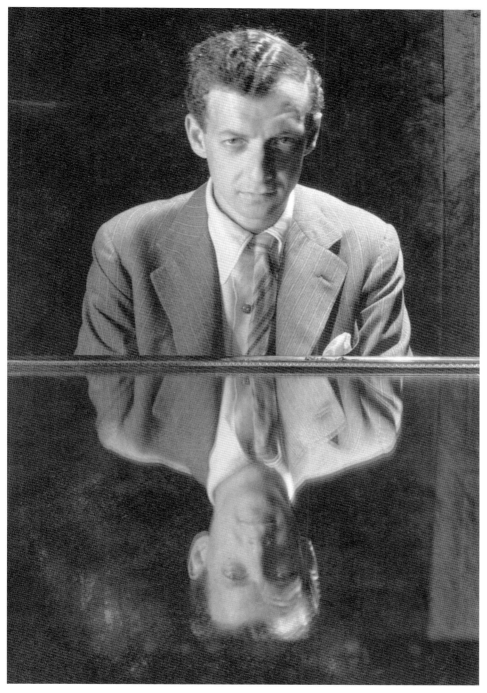
18. The celebrated composer of *Peter Grimes*, photographed by Cecil Beaton, August 1945.

19. The *Peter Grimes* team at Sadler's Wells: Britten, designer Kenneth Green, director Eric Crozier and conductor Reginald Goodall.

20. 'This is whatever day I say it is!' Grimes ignores Ellen's protests and takes his apprentice fishing on a Sunday. Joan Cross as Ellen Orford, Pears as Grimes and Leonard Thompson as John, Grimes's apprentice, in the first production at Sadler's Wells, June 1945.

21. Christmas meeting of the new English Opera Group, 3 Oxford Square, London, December 1946. From left to right, John Piper, Eric Crozier, Joan Cross, Pears, Britten, Anne Wood and Erwin Stein.

22. Bump-in for the English Opera Group at the Jubilee Hall, Aldeburgh, June 1949.

23. Some of the original cast of *Let's Make an Opera* (1949) off on an outing in Britten's 1929 Rolls-Royce.

24. Austerity England: Britten and Pears buying vegetables from greengrocer Jonah Baggott in Aldeburgh High Street, 1948.

25. Britten and Pears with George and Marion Harewood, being rowed by George Behrend on Thorpeness Meare during the second Aldeburgh Festival, 17 June 1949.

26. Pears, E. M. Forster, local schoolboy Robin Long, Britten and fisherman Billy Burrell off Aldeburgh beach, August 1949.

27. Britten working with Forster and Crozier in August 1949 on the libretto of *Billy Budd* in Crag House – its proximity to the sea quite clear.

28. In Venice for the premiere of *The Turn of the Screw*, September 1954: Erwin Stein, Britten, Sophie Stein, Basil Coleman, Pears.

29. Rehearsals for *The Turn of the Screw* were fraught. Designer John Piper and librettist Myfanwy Piper, with their children Clarissa and Edward, join Britten, Pears and director Basil Coleman for an apparently tense street picnic in Venice.

30. 'Peter Quint, you devil!' Pears as Quint, David Hemmings as Miles, and Jennifer Vyvyan as the Governess in the original production of *The Turn of the Screw*.

Münch's concert and the Schubert recital with Pears afforded a rare escape from the sheer slog of completing the opera. There was still no house for it: negotiations with Sadler's Wells were foundering amid uncertainty about the theatre reopening in time, which left the production team scouting around for an alternative. Covent Garden, as yet without the permanent company that would help define post-war British music, expressed interest, perhaps using an ad hoc ensemble, a consequence of Boosey & Hawkes's recent financial stake in the theatre. Britten was left alone as much as his curiosity and personality would allow, bequeathing the practicalities of staging the opera to the careful and efficient Eric Crozier, who had been passed the job by Tyrone Guthrie, then a producer at Sadler's Wells. ('I suppose it's a sort of love-murder really, isn't it?' Guthrie asked Crozier, somewhat unpromisingly, on hearing its synopsis.) Crozier, a warm, private man, with an aquiline nose and smiling eyes, who had cut his teeth at the Old Vic theatre before joining Sadler's Wells, threw himself into it.

Despite his isolation and solitary work, Britten was now earning good money. In 1942–3 his gross income was £945, which was made up of a little over £87 from CEMA; around £70 from other concert clubs (his and Pears's standard joint recital fee was £26. 5s., of which their agent took ten per cent, the remainder split equally); private income from rent of the Old Mill and the like; OUP, which generated a few funds; and bankable income from Boosey & Hawkes to the sum of a tremendous £1,142 – almost double Britten's gross income in the last financial year before the war – though it was whittled down once advances and loans were taken into account. His 1943–4 income was even greater: total professional earnings amounted to £1,169.* In both years there were the sort of offsets that feature in a musician's tax return to this day: agents' commissions, hotels and travel, scores and recordings, concert tickets, piano tunings, telephone and telegram expenses and upkeep of evening dress. This had left him in his first year back in England with a surplus a few shillings above £420; the following year it was £100 higher.

With financial security, certain character traits emerged or were consolidated – greater generosity, for instance. Britten had been supportive of his two sisters in the early war years when there was little money to go round; now there were fewer financial restrictions, he enjoyed his

---

* £43,000 today.

benevolence. The house in St John's Wood was big enough to accommodate not only Britten and Pears, but also the Stein family, made homeless from a fire that could easily have destroyed the manuscript score of *Peter Grimes*, then in Erwin's possession.* He remained thrifty in his tastes and spent little on himself – the art collecting was ahead of him and was anyway driven by Pears – though in November 1944 he viewed a large, deserted rectory in Iken; the Old Mill was now too small, he had decided, and too full of the ghosts from his twenties. He was on the lookout for something more suitable.

There is a well-travelled anecdote concerning Britten and his publisher. Early in Britten's career, Hawkes would be asked at annual board meetings where were the returns on the company's continued and generous investment in Britten. At the first meeting following *Peter Grimes* Hawkes awaited the question and when it did not arise, he asked it himself. 'Aren't you going to ask me about Mr Britten?' It is a nice story, and Hawkes deserved every bit of vindication the opera brought his way. Yet it is clear from royalty accounts in the last years of the war that the company's investment was already proving canny.

24

'I have actually just this moment written "End" to the opera score,' Britten told Mary Behrend on 10 February 1945. Rehearsals began soon after and they were fraught and thrilling in equal measure. Sadler's Wells, now full of life once more after the dark war years (the homeless families that occupied it following the Blitz rehoused elsewhere), had agreed to undertake the new work. Various principals received chunks of the vocal score just as soon as Erwin Stein reduced it from Britten's manuscript and Boosey & Hawkes produced it. Pears was impossibly busy: he sang seven performances of four different operas between 12 February and 1 March. Britten travelled to Manchester to be with him, coaching him on his newest role, Grimes, between performances and rehearsing their programmes for a trip to France: three orchestral concerts (which Britten shared with Münch and Manuel Rosenthal) and a recital in early March,

* The manuscript was either jinxed or blessed: it had almost been destroyed once before, when a frozen water pipe burst in the Devon cottage in which Britten was working.

all under the auspices of the British Council. The war was slowly winding down: Stalin's troops liberated Auschwitz on 27 January and on 21 April they marched into Berlin, precipitating Hitler's suicide nine days later. Those both pro-war and anti-war would use the startling, sickening revelations from Auschwitz and other concentration camps in support of their stance; in Britten they would breed a quiet but increased resolve.

There is little correspondence in these months while they rehearsed; that which exists crackles with energy and excitement. To Ronald Duncan he wrote encouragingly about a possible opera based on Chaucer's *Canterbury Tales*, which he remembered from his final English exams at Gresham's, the idea of which they had discussed in previous months. To Behrend he wrote optimistically of the string quartet she wanted to commission from him. He joined CEMA's music panel, committing himself to the quarterly meetings, however improbably. With Kenneth Green he took long walks, describing in detail what he needed from the designs for *Peter Grimes*. They had to be realistic; symbolism and abstract ideas, such as those that would in Britten's mind blight the 1947 Covent Garden production, were to have no place here. And when Slater dragged his feet over various requests or changes, the silences in their collaboration growing heavy, Britten did his best to remain patient, not always with success. 'Our collaboration, in retrospect, was built around his silences,' said Crozier, whose role, increasingly, was to calm the turbulent waters flowing between composer and librettist. 'He could be noncommunicative to an astonishing degree – he was not necessarily antagonistic, but had a genuine block (something I encountered later in other authors) about the threat of having to alter anything he had once thought out and written down.'

Green took Britten's ideas for the opera's design to heart – perhaps a little too much so, Crozier later thought. 'I hope that other producers and designers, blessed with more adequate stages, will explore the value of a more poetic realism in its staging.' Green's costume sketch of Grimes is a conscious inversion of Pears in the double portrait, the face of each closely resembling the other, a straggling mop and a patched, filthy coat replacing the portrait's neat hair and tidy jacket. Green drew inspiration for the design from a series of old black-and-white postcards depicting hearty fishermen in pullovers and shapeless oilskins, sucking on pipes. There is more than a touch of Dickens to the other designs: a baker with a tray of buns on his head; a retired army officer with pointed shoes, monocle and handsome thigh-length frock coat; Auntie looking more like Dickens's Miss Flite than tavern mistress and pimp. They are well executed and fulfilled Britten and Crozier's desire to 'convince our audience of the truth of place and people'. Yet they also represent the literalness with which Britten viewed theatre design and would continue to do so for the next fifteen years, not always to a work's benefit. And they needed a bigger stage and less cloistered set to let them breathe.

Sadler's Wells was riven during the rehearsal period. Disaffection poisoned the atmosphere and obscured, to many involved, the historical nature of their undertaking. Edmund Donlevy, creating the role of apothecary Ned Keene, identified the 'quarrelsomeness, overweening ambition, envy, fear of unemployment, hysteria . . . which have appeared in so many guises during the last six months or so and which have done more to damage the artistic standard of the company's work than anything else could possibly have done'. Joan Cross resigned as director of Sadler's Wells in order to stem the malicious comments flowing her way; at Britten's insistence she had cast herself as the leading female role when there were others capable of playing it, so the story ran. And the outsider status Britten later identified in connection with the opera, which to a large extent he had avoided while composing it, now characterized his relationship with Sadler's Wells. The chorus music was too difficult to sing and the highly rhetorical score was beyond the competency of an orchestra full of wartime deputies grown fat and complacent on their diet of *Così*, *La traviata* and *The Barber of Seville*. Cross found her part difficult to memorize and perform, having long supped at the same table as the orchestra.

Some of this was known by the critics and interested opera-goers introduced to the piece a week before opening night. The principals assembled at the Wigmore Hall, a venue that had brought nothing but good fortune to Britten and Pears since their return from America, and an attentive, excited crowd turned up to find out what all the fuss was about. Britten sat at the piano, mercifully dumb, while Crozier provided narrative links between various arias and ensembles. In such unprepossessing circumstances did the sounds of *Peter Grimes* first entrance an audience.

Around this time Tippett walked into Sadler's Wells and spied Britten in the pit. Perhaps Britten needed to demonstrate a point to the orchestra or its conductor, Reginald Goodall, an uncompromising and imaginative musician, twelve years Britten's senior and a staff conductor at Sadler's Wells. Or perhaps Goodall wanted to check for balance from the auditorium and Britten obliged by stepping onto the podium. A press photographer at just this time (29 May) captured in detail what Tippett could only surmise inside the gloomy theatre, observing his friend's slight frame as a shadowy silhouette in the pit, illuminated by orchestral sconces. Britten leans against the entrance to Sadler's Wells on Rosebery Avenue, his jacket, waistcoat and tie all very Oxbridge, his bony hands clutching the enormous manuscript score of *Peter Grimes*. His eyes are more like his father's than ever before, his expression old and serious. The same features are evident in Pathé newsreel footage taken around this time, where a surprisingly relaxed Britten sits at what sounds like an old saloon-bar piano playing the opera's first 'Sea Interlude'. Tippett's impression is far more revealing than any picture, however, for he wrote about what he heard. And what he heard blew him away: the sounds coming from the orchestra; Britten's authority as a performer and composer; the sheer scale and audacity of the undertaking. 'It is difficult for us now, after so many years, to realize what this event, in every sense, meant, not only to us in England but to, I think, the musical world in general.'

A week later, on 7 June 1945, Guthrie wrote to Cross, 'Affectionate best wishes for tonight. I want here & now to put on record that, win or lose with the press & public, I absolutely support the policy of doing this opera; & congratulate you on the grit with which it has been carried thro' in face of difficulties.' It was exactly one month since Germany's unconditional surrender. An excited, expectant audience was about to hear the same sounds Tippett encountered in rehearsal, and see the stage heaving with Kenneth Green's version of soberly dressed Suffolk villagers. Among these villagers was Hobson, the Borough carter, constable and silentiary. Underpinned by nothing more than a couple of bassoons and clarinets, Hobson drew himself to his full height and summoned the principal witness in a coronial inquiry: 'Peter Grimes! Peter Grimes! Peter Grimes!'

Middle

4

Rehabilitation

England, 1945–1951

I

Bouverie Street is a little over a mile from Sadler's Wells, a small inlet off Fleet Street which until 1960 housed the *News Chronicle*. All newspapers in this part of London had long abandoned the letterpress printing that had brought Dickens his wide readership, the teams of nimble-fingered compositors made obsolete by the clanking of Linotype. A single operator now did the work of ten, and did it faster. Important events of an evening could be written up and typeset in time for the print deadline, concerts and plays included. Critics had to move smartly from theatre or concert hall to booth, where their scribbled notes were hurriedly transformed into 400-odd words for the next day's paper. It was not an ideal system: many of the most important premieres of the first half of the twentieth century – often demanding, difficult works – were reviewed in the dailies with rushed or clumsy incomprehension. Modern composers and playwrights were left fighting not just the reactionary nature of performers and audiences, but also a system in which critics scarcely had time to breathe, let alone think, before committing their opinions to print.

If, after the premiere of *Peter Grimes*, *News Chronicle* music critic Scott Goddard filed his copy in person, he would have travelled from Sadler's Wells down Farringdon Road to Fleet Street, crossing Charterhouse Street on his way. On his left at Charterhouse he would have passed Smithfield Market, now a forest of rubble and twisted metal; it was destroyed on 8 March 1945 in one of the last and most devastating V2 attacks on London. Such scenes were commonplace in the city, yet Goddard – like most critics and commentators at the opera's first performance – drew no comparison between his surroundings and what he had just seen on stage.

It is curious that no British critic at the time came close to the sharp analysis of the American writer Edmund Wilson. 'This opera could have been written in no other age, and it is one of the very few works of art that have seemed to me, so far, to have spoken for the blind anguish, the hateful rancors and the will to destruction of these horrible years.' Or that no one publicly identified in the piece the wider social and political critiques evident in contemporaneous works by Orwell, say, or those that would soon be picked over in Arthur Miller's *All My Sons* (1947) and *Death of a Salesman* (1949) – both of which, like *Grimes*, end with the suicide of the protagonist – or would be found in the plays of that angry young man John Osborne in the coming decades, his sharply sketched characters Jimmy Porter, Archie Rice and Alfred Redl each at odds with society, each nonetheless drawing our sympathy and interest.

It is not that Goddard was an unperceptive critic. He had identified Britten's originality eleven years earlier with the performance of *A Boy was Born* and had thereafter kept a watchful eye on his development. And it is not as though he went into the theatre cold: the opera was the talk of the town, and he had probably attended the Wigmore Hall introduction the previous week. He was right about much of the piece, identifying the mean social instincts of the villagers who hound the fisherman into lunacy. He appreciated the skill in the choral and orchestral writing (though he found balance in the pit wanting), and thought Pears and Cross profoundly moving. 'It is an astonishing work to meet for the first time.' Yet in conclusion Goddard inadvertently touched on something that explains why his profession, on the whole, saw only trees where there was a dense wood before them. 'Will this new opera succeed? The public is fickle, and on its unstable temperament all depends no matter how good the work or how fine the performance.' What would (or could) a country without a sustained history of opera creation make of this startling, multi-layered work?

If any theatre in England was to succeed with a modern opera it was Sadler's Wells, which in the 1930s had attempted to kick-start an operatic tradition. Yet even one of the theatre's governors, scholar and critic Edward Dent, whom Britten had met in Florence in 1934, found it a difficult space to love. He derided its drab colouring, peculiar angles, obstructing staircase, and stage, which was too close to the audience for Wagner, too far for Mozart. Dent was equally, if more artfully, critical of the company's manager, the fabled Lilian Baylis, for whom the terror of debt was never far away. 'I'm an ignorant woman,' Baylis at one time told Dent, deflecting his long campaign on behalf of Beethoven's only opera. 'I don't know anything about *Fidelio*; I've never seen it; I only know it's always been a failure at Covent Garden.' The threepenny operas that resulted at Sadler's Wells – the artists underpaid, the productions under-rehearsed, the sets and costumes improvised from anything close to hand – she yanked from the schedule without ceremony if the house was not filled to capacity for the second and third performances.

The sad reality was that the sums simply did not add up. Britain in the first decades of the twentieth century had no sustained opera culture; it had no sustainable one either, many muttered darkly. There was no government funding for the arts and no state-run theatres as in Germany. Nor was there the private patronage of the sort that was then keeping New York's Metropolitan Opera afloat, where cultured émigrés and wealthy industrialists dug deep to assure themselves that theirs was no mere saloon town, far from the world's musical epicentre. Thomas Beecham had for three decades channelled his family's pharmaceuticals money into operatic ventures, which sometimes burned with rare intensity for Britain in these decades, but they were not ongoing propositions – sometimes little more than an event in the London society calendar – and did little to allay the impression that in Britain there seemed to be only an occasional appetite for this suspiciously Teutonic art form.

Britten was clear-sighted about what was needed. 'I am passionately interested in seeing a successful, permanent, national opera in existence – successful both artistically and materially,' he said at the beginning of 1944, when scarcely a note of *Grimes* was committed to manuscript. 'And it must be vital and contemporary, too, and depend less on imported "stars" than on a first-rate, young and fresh, permanent company – Sadler's Wells have made a good beginning.' By this stage, having frequently visited Pears on tour with the company, he had begun to see enthusiasm for the art form, as he had noticed considerable interest in the contemporary music he and Pears included in their recital programmes. The only question was whether this enthusiasm would survive the peace.

There was public acclaim for *Grimes* on its opening night – though not immediately. The young boy playing Grimes's fated apprentice thought something was wrong when complete silence followed the orchestra's final notes, lasting minutes, he asserted. Joan Cross said the same. 'There was silence at the end and then shouting broke out. The stage crew were stunned: they thought it was a demonstration. Well, it was but fortunately it was of the right kind.' There was curtain call after curtain call, bouquet upon bouquet, with Britten, a matinée idol in white tie and tails, stiffly accepting applause. Later he would get better at this, to the point where his sisters would chide him for taking too many bows. But just then it was a welcome if confronting experience. The premiere sold well enough; it was the post-war reopening of Sadler's Wells, after all. But for the rest of the season, as word got out, it was packed to the gods, easily rivalling the productions of *La bohème* and *Madama Butterfly* then in repertory. Had she lived to witness it Baylis would have been astonished.

Part of the enthusiasm was because June in the capital was one big party. Austerity prevailed, but it was to be ignored for the moment. Bunting hung from St Pancras's Gothic redbrick façade. Inside the station, families evacuated to the country for the duration of the war returned to their homes. The remaining few Underground bunkers were dismantled. Churchill could be seen out among the electorate, stumping for votes, breezily confident of the outcome. Spivs peddled dodgy ration books and bottles of whisky made from weak tea. Troops poured back into the capital – at first on leave and then clutching their demob papers – romping in the fountains in Trafalgar Square and spilling out of pubs around Piccadilly Circus in full agreement with the billboard above stating 'GUINNESS IS GOOD FOR YOU: GIVES YOU STRENGTH'. There were parties, shows, clubs and revues – one of the latter overseen by Black Venus, the leggy and legendary Josephine Baker – and the Odeon, Leicester Square, screened David Lean's new Technicolor film adaptation of Noel Coward's *Blithe Spirit*.

The audience at the *Grimes* premiere was a snapshot of this dazed, exuberant London in the month following VE Day. There were young women in bright civvies – some style and colour, at last – and young men in uniform. There were pre-war patrons of the theatre, some unaware what they were attending, and 'gallery oldtimers' who had set up camp stools in the ticket queue twenty-four hours earlier. Society women dusted down their tiaras and brushed their furs before stepping out for a real event. Britten's old foes, those Grand Old Men of English music, were in attendance – the RCM's Sir George Dyson and Ralph Vaughan Williams (or Mr Williams, as Britten mischievously referred to him) – as were their presumptive heirs, William Walton and Yehudi Menuhin.

Old musicians staffed the pit, having played their way through the war on the same endless regional tours on which Pears honed his craft, rubbing shoulders with young students. Horn player Edward Downes was among them, punch-drunk on the experience of playing extraordinary music and pocketing £1. 5s. a show. Goodall thought the orchestra not up to the score's demands and Crozier later described the standard as 'little more than competent'. Others took a more indulgent view, given the circumstances. Tea ladies served patrons in the two intervals, dropping crockery at the beginning of the subsequent acts, either a clanking parody of the brash new score or an act of solidarity with the company singers who found themselves excluded from the undertaking.

A year later Goddard wrote of the lead-up to the premiere. 'It became impossible to mention the work without discussion degenerating into argument. Nothing could be discovered of its artistic quality, so heavy was the cloud of sociological, political, even ethical bickering surrounding *Peter Grimes*.' Much of the bickering was small-minded stuff – about casting, or the role of contemporary opera in a repertory house – yet some was more important – the role of opera in contemporary British society, or what post-war British culture should look like and, perhaps more to the point, how it should be funded. The response to *Grimes* put paid to any suggestions that it was wrong for Sadler's Wells to devote so much time and money to a new work by a young man, despite the hostility with which many in the company continued to view the piece: Britten had delivered a breathtakingly confident and beautifully paced opera from unpromising source material, the vocal writing lyrical yet powerful, the orchestration full of the virtuosity and gritty darkness of *Sinfonia da Requiem*, the cumulative effect overwhelming. The opera's success, however, ensured that the other points of argument rumbled on, as Britain set about building its post-war cultural infrastructure. Britten sensed his role in the renaissance, even if he could not yet quite envisage the details. As he presciently wrote to Imogen Holst in late

June, 'I think the occasion is actually a greater one than either Sadler's Wells or me, I feel. Perhaps it is an omen for English Opera in the future.' A month later he was discussing with Cross and Crozier the formation of a new company based at Dartington, which would produce his next opera.

The squabble had its benefits, however, as did the applause: it acted as a smokescreen for the work's leftist, pacifist creators who had cut their teeth in a more outspoken decade and were determined that their new work should be far more than a collage of pretty sounds and pictures. It was another of Britten's Trojan horses, a point missed by Goddard and his colleagues who were all too busy ascertaining the opera's significance to work out its meaning. This was a technique to which Britten would return time and time again.

2

Buoyed by the opera's success and his overnight celebrity, Britten did two unexpected things. First, on 20 July, he called a press conference. (This makes it sound a little grander than it probably was.) The Potsdam Conference, at which Truman, Stalin and Churchill were thrashing out the future of Germany, was then under way and Britten had things to say about it. 'Mr Churchill's high living at Potsdam is an offence that stinks to high heaven. It is a political indecency – a moral crime.' Britten went on to list details of Churchill's high living, faithfully recorded in *Peace News*: feasts of turkey, ham, eggs, steaks, melons, strawberries, all accompanied by fine wines and whiskies. 'All around is the stricken enemy people, hungry and facing greater hunger; not far away are the people of France, Belgium, Holland, Norway. They have been hungry for years and are still hungry.' It was not solely the stricken enemy. Britain would suffer under rationing until the early 1950s, as MPs grimly surveying the whale and seal steaks on the menu of the House of Commons dining room knew only too well.

Britten did not vote Conservative in the 5 July general election. It was not so much the antipathy he felt towards Churchill specifically, though this played its part; it was more that he was sympathetic to the broad thrust of Labour's manifesto in what became the great reformist government of 1945. Labour was promising a lot: a speedy end to the war in the Far East and the successful demobilization of servicemen and women; jobs for all; world peace; education and welfare reform; a tax-funded national health system; town planning; nuclear defence; the nationalization of major industries; the creation of a wide-reaching agricultural policy. It was radical stuff, beyond even the greatest aspirations of Britten and his fellow travellers in the 1930s. Yet no one, from the king to the prime minister's deputy, Labour leader Clement Attlee, to Stalin himself, seriously expected the warrior Churchill to lose the election. And when Britten called his press conference, a little under a week before the 26 July vote count, he was anticipating a return to the bad old days of Torydom. He was no doubt as surprised as Attlee when the leader of the Labour Party found himself on his way to Potsdam to take Churchill's place at the table.

There were few other such outbursts in Britten's life: his public manners and reticence grew with his celebrity. Unlike those of his friends who rarely saw a soapbox without mounting it, Britten shied away from potential public controversy in the post-war years, preferring to channel his social criticism into his works. There were relatively few signatures on petitions or Letters to the Editor, and nary a political aside in the many radio interviews he undertook post-*Grimes*.* A rare and revealing exception was a 1963 interview: 'Politicians are so ghastly, aren't they? After all, the job of politics is to organize the world and resolve its tensions ... My social feelings are the same as they have always been. I disbelieve profoundly in power and violence.' There would be recitals in aid of a particular cause – the Quakers, or the War Resisters League, or UNESCO ('Not only is modern war completely irrational and suicidal; it is also completely immoral,' Britten and Pears would write in a 1949 programme note) – and his name lent to a number of social-justice organizations, but mostly he kept his opinions to himself. If this sounds like a wasted opportunity, it is worth contemplating Britten's second unexpected move in the month or so following *Grimes*.

He met the celebrated violinist Yehudi Menuhin in July at a party hosted by Boosey & Hawkes. Menuhin had volunteered his services to a Jewish organization working in conjunction with the United Nations

---

* In 1952, however, he was a signatory to a letter to *The Times* suggesting there should be a pacifist element to the coronation service, in counterpoint to the militaristic pomp and circumstance in planning.

and was soon to travel to Germany to perform for survivors of the concentration camp at Bergen-Belsen in Lower Saxony and for German civilians in surrounding towns and villages, now destroyed. With only a week or so to go before the trip, Britten asked if he could replace the scheduled pianist, Gerald Moore. Over four days in the last week of July the two musicians gave nine concerts amid what Menuhin labelled 'the saddest ruins of the Third Reich', performing works by the Jew Mendelssohn and the Germans Beethoven and Bach, as if to prove that music was to emerge unscathed from the barbarism.

It had been only three months since British and Canadian soldiers first entered the camp, accompanied by the BBC journalist Richard Dimbleby, and discovered corpses heaped throughout the compound like piles of leaves, yellow skin stretched like canvas on a hull. Most of the dead were women, the teenage Anne Frank somewhere among them. By cruel irony, their bodies, ravaged by sickness and malnutrition in life, were in the uncommonly cold spring almost impervious to decay in death. Some of the bodies had had their livers, kidneys and hearts crudely cut from them by starving prisoners, whether when alive or dead British medical teams did not determine. Those who had survived the neglect and cruelty of their captors contended with the ill-prepared and under-resourced British Second Army, impotent in the face of the wasting diseases tuberculosis, dysentery, typhus and typhoid. The stench was apparent up to five miles from the camp. Doctors distributed antibiotics and amoebicides liberally, and food was scavenged on behalf of the prisoners; yet death was never far away. 'This day at Belsen was the most horrible of my life,' Dimbleby broadcast, describing in shocking detail the 'awful, ghostly process of emaciated, aimless people, with nothing to do and no hope of life'.

Circumstances improved in the following months, but it was a fitful affair, with treatment improvised by teams of English medical students and dragooned German doctors and nurses. The smell, the harrowing experiences of the prisoners, and the death of many thousands of survivors even after liberation meant Britten and Menuhin encountered a horrific scene. 'Men and women alike, our audience was dressed in army blankets fashioned by clever tailors among them into skirts and suits,' Menuhin later wrote. 'No doubt a few weeks since their rescue they had put a little flesh on their bones, but to our unaccustomed eyes they seemed desperately haggard, and many were still in hospital.'

For the remainder of his life Menuhin talked of his experiences at Belsen. He would describe the recitals themselves or chat with people who cornered him after concerts in Britain or Israel or Australia to tell him they had been there too.* And of course Menuhin would perform the same pieces from the Belsen programme many times again. Other visitors to the camps talked of near identical experiences and reactions. The American photographer Lee Miller, *Vogue*'s war correspondent from 1944, also travelled in Germany immediately after the war and recorded her experiences in explicit words and images. 'I IMPLORE YOU TO BELIEVE THIS IS TRUE,' she cabled her editor, aware that what she was forwarding scarcely seemed credible. A year after the war she would describe herself as still inarticulate from shock, and later, much later, she would assert that she had never managed to lose the 'stench of Dachau' in her nostrils.

For decades Britten barely spoke of the camps, except in the most superficial way. Menuhin said they did not talk about their experience during their visit or afterwards, on the occasions that friendship and artistic collaboration brought them together. Once in the early 1960s Britten mentioned his time in Germany simply and evasively, almost defying the skilled interviewer, Murray Schafer, to probe more deeply. 'We gave two or three short recitals a day – they couldn't take more. It was in many ways a terrifying experience.'

It was only at the end of his life that he could speak of Belsen with anything like the weight it deserved, and even then it was only to Pears and a few other confidants. It was almost as though he thought some things just could not be articulated. After the composer's death Pears relayed the core of these conversations to film director Tony Palmer, noting that Britten had admitted to him 'that the experience had coloured everything he had written subsequently'. For Britten, Belsen was an almost *inevitable* consequence of war; his experience there verified his conviction that war was always wrong.

The first of his post-Belsen works to pulse with the hatred of warfare is *The Holy Sonnets of John Donne*, composed immediately on his

---

* One inmate, cellist Anita Lasker (later Wallfisch), thought Menuhin played soullessly, which he could do, but 'concerning the accompanist, I can only say that I just can not imagine anything more beautiful [or] wonderful. Somehow one never noticed that there was any accompanying going on at all, and yet I had to stare at this man like one transfixed as he sat seemingly suspended between chair and keyboard, playing so beautifully.'

return. It occupies a desolate landscape which in style and content was a complete departure for the composer, its vision every bit as nightmarish as Berlioz's 'March to the Scaffold' or Rimbaud's *Une saison en enfer* (A Season in Hell). As with these two works, it was forged in high fever, though sickness in Britten's case, not addiction: he was laid up in bed as he sketched the songs, delirious from a post-trip typhoid vaccination.

The potential for Britten's Donne settings had existed before Belsen; they were ordained from the moment, in Britten's words, that 'Auden got us to take Donne seriously', some time in the final part of the American years. Yet the cycle's composition in the wake of the Belsen experience ensured it was a different work from what it would have been earlier. Belsen unlocked Britten's righteous fury. He worked, feverishly, at the layers of meaning in Donne's memento mori, at their universal truths and contemporary resonances, at the aching loss underpinning many of the poems and the poet's attempt to reconcile this with belief in God. He identified and honed Donne's patterns and symmetry, his individual colours, his beauty of imagery, and matched the exalted Jacobean texts with a musical language distilled from later Purcell. And in each setting Britten sublimated every word he would never speak about Belsen.

> Oh my blacke Soule! now thou art summoned
> By sicknesse, death's herald, and champion;
> Thou art like a pilgrim, which abroad hath done
> Treason, and durst not turne to whence hee is fled,
> Or like a thiefe, which till death's doome be read,
> Wisheth himself deliver'd from prison;
> But damn'd and hal'd to execution,
> Wisheth that still he might be imprisoned.

As the Red Army advanced through Poland in 1944 and news of the camps and the slaughter surfaced, other artists reacted with dumb horror to what they saw and heard. Picasso filled a canvas with the brutal, gruesome image of bodies messily piled one on top of the other, dead eyes staring out, the hands of one corpse bound. And though Britten never specified the connection between the new cycle and his experiences in Germany, the link is as obvious as it is in Picasso's *The Charnel House*. 'The theme of the *Donne Sonnets* is death, as you know,' he later allowed. 'I think the connexion between personal experience and my feelings about the poetry was a strong one. It certainly characterized the music.' Yet the work is also a coda to *Peter Grimes*: even though it is much darker, its bleakness more concentrated, *The Holy Sonnets of John Donne* covers similar ground, the ground that Edmund Wilson identified. It was completed, with exceptional speed and certainty, in a little over two weeks. Britten dedicated it to Pears, who gave the first performance at the Wigmore Hall on 22 November, the composer's thirty-second birthday.

<h1 style="text-align:center">3</h1>

In certain practical ways their lives did not change after *Grimes*, at least not in the short term. Pears went back on the road with Sadler's Wells, singing in *The Bartered Bride*, *Così fan tutte* and *La bohème*. He was an unlikely Rodolfo, perhaps – too patrician, his voice too small for the great Act 1 aria – and other members of the company, still smarting from the troubled *Grimes* rehearsal period, pounced on the weakness. Yet he emerged from the final war years as an operatic soloist of distinction, which also lent him a certain steeliness. His stature as a performer gave Britten enormous pride, though tinged with trepidation: opera singers lead itinerant lives, and Britten was no better at separation after the war than he had been during it. While apart, they wrote constantly, and the correspondence gives the temperature of their relationship: loving, infatuated, admiring.

Britten's post-vaccination illness dragged on for a month, much of which was spent in bed. He tried to placate Slater, who was upset at not being sent proofs of the vocal score of *Grimes*, but ended up wearily batting away his objection. ('If you insist on seeing the proofs, of course ring [Ernst] Roth – but do remember the urgency.') The friendship was more or less over; any remaining embers were extinguished the following year when Slater published his own version of the libretto.

Slater's position in Britten's life was effortlessly assumed by another pacifist, the charming, puckish, somewhat roguish playwright and poet Ronald Duncan. Britten had consulted Duncan throughout the composition of *Grimes* whenever Slater's intransigence became too much, and Duncan had demonstrated key qualities: flexibility, discretion, loyalty and speed. They were working together on their own project at the same time, a 'masque and anti-masque' called *This Way to the Tomb*, a satire on religion and human gullibility. In addition to some mood music and a setting of words from Psalm 70, Britten contributed idiomatic miniatures for voice and piano, which did not delay him long. (The songs were posthumously published and nowadays appear occasionally on concert programmes.)

John Lindsay, then a student at the RCM, played in this production, and his description of life in the house on St John's Wood High Street evokes a complete inversion of the brownstone community in Middagh Street, Brooklyn. There was a live-in housekeeper, who cost the household £182 a year in wages and keep, taking instructions from Britten and Pears, and from Sophie Stein, who ran the place with style. Stein's school-age daughter Marion was a serious pianist (with Fanny Waterman she would later found the Leeds International Piano Competition), practising long hours, while Stein's husband Erwin, when not overseeing Boosey & Hawkes's growing catalogue, gave lessons and consultations at home, often enough helping decode works by his teacher Schoenberg. Meals were ordered affairs, sometimes waited on by Marion, punctuated by Britten's childish humour and an understood amount of veneration towards the insecure composer, who wanted nothing more than to be liked and loved. In Lindsay's assessment, 'he'd go quite boyish, you know, as though he knew that he deserved the praise but he wanted to be a little bit coy about it'. Duncan later recalled a similar vignette. Meeting with Britten soon after he completed Act 1 of *The Rape of Lucretia* in 1946, he found the composer close to tears, complaining of Beth, 'I've been three days waiting for her to ask me to play it.' Lindsay occasionally encountered Britten practising the piano – some Bridge works just then, his powerful fingers able to conjure any colour or effect – or with Erwin playing through Mahler's symphonies on the piano, Stein distilling every detail of Mahler's tempi and phrasing into the performances.

There were fights behind this ordered façade. The composer Arthur Oldham, a friend and sometime tenant, witnessed faces being slapped. And Lindsay captured the temperamental differences between Britten and Pears:

> Well you couldn't get so friendly with Peter as with Ben. Peter was always like the schoolmaster. He was ready to correct you and censor you from

a lofty point of view. Ben was a friend who was genuinely wanting to bring out whatever there was in you, not push it down and say it wasn't right or anything . . . You felt a freedom with Ben, that music was a great adventure, it wasn't something that you did right or wrong, but within limitless opportunities, you know, of expression.

This contradicts a piece of biographical shorthand – that Britten was forever touchy on the subject of music. Perhaps Lindsay's interest in Britten's scores made him immune to such prickliness, though Oldham also found him generous with his thoughts and enthusiasms. Or perhaps the age difference worked in both men's favour.

While Duncan was the librettist of Britten's new opera, Crozier was the architect. As an eighteen-year-old schoolboy he saw La Compagnie des Quinze perform André Obey's play *Le Viol de Lucrèce*, and was overwhelmed by the story's impact and the physicality of the twelve actors on stage. He promptly ordered a copy of the play from Paris and translated it. A few weeks before the premiere of *Grimes*, when the guerrilla warfare at Sadler's Wells was at its peak, Crozier remembered these experiences of twelve years earlier and put forward *Lucretia* as a possible subject for Britten's next opera. Crozier did not stop there: he 'suggested that we should form a small company of gifted singers on the French model, with ourselves as artistic directors, no chorus, and the smallest group of instrumentalists that Ben would find acceptable for chamber opera'.

The idea was more out of left field than might appear. Crozier had spent two years managing Sadler's Wells productions on tour – eight shows a week of three or four different operas. The stagings grew in size and sophistication as the war progressed, but Crozier knew of Guthrie's touring production of *The Marriage of Figaro*, which had begun life in October 1940 with an entire company – creative team, soloists, chorus, orchestra and technicians – numbering twenty-six. (This was quite a step up from productions earlier in the century that went on the road with an orchestra comprising a harmonium, piano, trombone and fiddle.) If this number could be made to work for *Figaro* (a moot point), imagine what could be achieved if an opera were conceived with a small number of musicians on stage and in the pit.

This was the radical part of Crozier's suggestion. Wartime English audiences had responded to grand operas snipped here and watered down there. But there was no precedent for so-called chamber opera, not since the Baroque era anyway. Moreover, the idea came at the same time that England was trying to prove that it could sow and grow its own grand opera company. Britten, the most conspicuous indigenous contributor to the art form since Beecham (and with much greater significance), was now proposing an unexpected detour.

Perhaps in quickly agreeing to Crozier's proposal Britten was remembering one of the few crumbs of comfort in the *Bunyan* fiasco, a prescient sentence in an otherwise damning *New York Times* review: 'What is done by Mr Britten shows more clearly than ever that opera written for a small stage, with relatively modest forces for the presentation, in the English language, and in ways pleasantly free from the stiff tradition of either grand or light opera of the past, is not only a possibility but a development nearly upon us.' Crozier and Britten discussed the idea with their friends at Dartington Hall, Dorothy and Leonard Elmhirst; Duncan found a 'man with money', as Britten reported to Pears, who stayed in the picture for almost exactly the amount of time one would expect in a film financier; and Crozier's suggestion slowly gained form and momentum through the second half of 1945 while Duncan prepared the libretto of *The Rape of Lucretia*.

4

Other performances intervened, however, and other premieres. In October Britten and Pears made a fleeting visit to Paris and Bordeaux where they performed a now typical programme: Purcell, Schubert and Britten (*Michelangelo Sonnets* and French folk-song arrangements – the latter a nice morale-boosting gesture). His correspondence records no impressions of post-war Paris, disarmingly frozen in 1939 as it was, but he must have been touched by the programming of *Les Illuminations* (with piano) and his violin Suite in the following month's Concerts de la Pléiade, a series founded in 1943 as 'a kind of clandestine revenge against the occupation', as Olivier Messiaen put it.

To commemorate the 250th anniversary of Purcell's death on 21 November, Britten programmed and performed two concerts at the Wigmore Hall on consecutive nights. On the surface it appeared to be an almost defiantly antiquarian gesture from contemporary music's new hero; most of Purcell's works were scarcely known in this era, even less performed. But his reasoning was simple. 'Henry Purcell was the last important international figure of English music,' he wrote in the recit- als' programme booklet. 'Ironically the continent of Europe has been more aware of his greatness than the island which produced him. But that he should be to the English public little more than a name in history books is not altogether strange, for he is the antithesis of the music which has been popular for so long in this country.' It was a jab to the jaw of the knighted and otherwise honoured composers of his youth, a reminder, if one were needed, of the low regard in which he held the great majority of his predecessors. It was also an explanation for why Britten had such a success with *Grimes*: his music was so different from the nineteenth-century English symphonies, the folk-ridden tone poems and the pale imitations of Brahms he had grown up hearing – and, early on, replicating. ('This is going to be almost as bad as the Brahms influ- ence on English music I fear,' Britten said of Sibelius in 1936.) Britten, like Purcell, was composing English music of international appeal.

Tippett shared Britten's admiration for Purcell and joined him in the tribute. They chose anthems, fantasias and a trio sonata, secular songs and duets, and even a performance of *Ode for St Cecilia's Day* (1692), a feast that fell on the same day as the second of these concerts, performed by the Morley College Choir under Tippett's direction. The continuo realizations were all by Britten, a task he relished since it allowed him to get inside the composer's head, to imagine how he ticked, to admire 'those very Purcellian qualities of clarity, strangeness, tenderness and attack'. He was working from scant material. There were no modern editions, and much of the music was simply not avail- able. That which was came in archaic scores, such as the 1714 edition of *Harmonia Sacra* Imogen Holst presented to Britten and Pears in 1945. These editions contain little more than a vocal line over a figured bass – a series of numbers printed under a bass-line, indicating what the harmony should be to those who knew the code, but nothing else besides: 'cold, unfilled-in lines', as Britten later put it. His task was to turn this shorthand into a convincing musical and dramatic narrative, for Purcell's songs are nothing if not dramatic. This he did with com- plete ease, keeping one foot in Purcell's world, another in his own, to produce accompaniments that sound simultaneously 'authentic' and freshly minted.

Britten's tribute did not stop with these concerts and realizations.

With Pears he returned to the National Gallery on 23 November for more Purcell, the building's walls marked by large, unfaded rectangles of still-missing paintings, as Isherwood would observe a little over a year later. The symbolism of the concert here was strong.

There were other, more subtle tributes. The two Britten premieres in the Wigmore concerts were his String Quartet No. 2 and *The Holy Sonnets of John Donne*, both 'composed in homage to Henry Purcell', the programme stated. Britten had been toying with the idea of a second numbered quartet for some time, encouraged by Mary Behrend and her philanthropic urges, and once he had completed the Donne settings and recovered from his fever and illness he set to work. Behrend received the formal dedication, though it was really Purcell on his mind: the work is infused with the clarity, tenderness and strangeness Britten identified in his great forebear's melodic lines. Britten's Donne settings also look back to the free-falling vocal lines of Purcell's songs. The strongest connection between the two works is the passacaglia that ends them (a Chacony in the case of the quartet). Purcell used this form to represent the passing of time, to make his listeners experience such passing temporally, rather than merely have it described to them in words. The same occurs in the Britten works. The quartet's final movement occupies a strange, austere world: harmonies shimmer and slip from one berth to the next; a cello cadenza provides an enticing hint of the solo cello suites Britten would write twenty years later; and slowly, slyly, a series of twenty-one variations on the opening unison melody unfolds, some of them wandering far from home.

'I'm so glad you got pleasure from it,' Britten told the dedicatee after the concert, 'because to my mind it is the greatest advance that I have yet made, & altho' it is far from perfect, it has given me encouragement to continue on new lines.' This was the first occasion Britten spoke of a new direction post-*Grimes*, and it is true that the quartet (and Donne sonnets) was a contrast to the more opulent works he had been composing since 1940. It was the perfect genre too: his musical argument needed to be precise and concise. Proceeds from the concerts were intended for survivors of the 1943 Bengal famine, a humanitarian disaster resulting in the deaths of several million Bengalis, a total pushed higher by British military tactics in the area and a high-handed colonial response. Britten sent a cheque for over £350, which included either his commissioning fee or a further donation from Behrend.

Britten's other great tribute to Purcell dates from this time. Basil

Wright, now producer-in-charge at the GPO's wartime successor, the Crown Film Unit, had commissioned a score from his former confrère for a film with the working title 'The Orchestra and its Instruments' (it would be released as *Instruments of the Orchestra*). One of Britten's old *bêtes noires*, Malcolm Sargent, was involved as host and conductor, working to the composer's script (though Slater is credited for it). In the finished film Sargent walks to a podium in Denham Studios, his hair and teeth glistening, the orchestra spread high and wide on rises, and announces to an imagined audience, 'Many of you may have heard and seen a full symphony orchestra playing in the concert hall. Many more of you must have heard one over the radio. But today I want to take this great musical box to pieces . . .' Britten had already done all the work for him, breaking the orchestra down into its constituent elements, showing off each tiny cog, before reassembling it in a breathtaking fugue. The climax comes courtesy of a grand restatement of the work's opening melody, a simple tune by Purcell, which is grafted onto the fugue with spectacular results. 'That's the champagne moment! Fucking great!' is how the actor David Hemmings later described it, no musicologist he. Britten himself was delighted with his handiwork, jumping about and laughing in the sound-recording session. Plotted almost a year earlier in his pocket diary, he completed the work on the last day of 1945, in the same month in which he composed twenty minutes of incidental music for Louis MacNeice's radio play, *The Dark Tower*. To Hawkes he wrote of his 'Purcell variations', 'I'm hoping that the latter may be useful for the ordinary orchestra repertoire, but I'm not sure yet.' History has proved him right: *The Young Person's Guide to the Orchestra* is one of his most popular and performed works.

It capped off an extraordinary year for the young composer. In iconic if technically poor photographs taken by Cecil Beaton in August, Britten appears dour and spectral, his reflection in the Steinway smudged, the pose stiff and artificial. He was now the composer of *Peter Grimes*, a serious mantle, and was framed accordingly by the gadfly Beaton, renowned for his society portraits, fashion shoots and recent war photographs. (What did these two gay artists, whose names would be linked in less fortunate circumstances in the early 1950s, talk about as the lights were positioned, the camera put in place?) Yet he was still young at the time of the session (thirty-one) and though he was serious and focused, he was not yet the dour figure in these photographs.

Hawkes had pushed him for repertory for the many fine American orchestras, but was having little success promoting his talented charge. Britten was sanguine about the difficulties: 'don't be too depressed if things aren't too good about me in the U.S.A. Let matters take their course there. I'm afraid that I am conceited enough to feel that eventually they'll come round, as this country & the continent have – but at the moment my music is neither ordinary enough or shocking enough to hit them.' It was a fair assessment (and prediction), not too far from Virgil Thomson's acerbic dismissal of Britten's music after hearing *Paul Bunyan* on the grounds that it 'is easily recognizable as that considered by the British Broadcasting Corporation to be at once modernistic and safe'.

Regardless of the vicissitudes of the American market, he was doing well financially: his gross income in the 1945–6 tax year was £2,155.* Some of this came from recitals with Pears, but most was from Britten's compositions. He spent the tax year finishing off and mounting one opera, before moving on to the next. If not quite matching Verdi's punishing schedule of one hundred years earlier – *Alzira* in August 1845, *Attila* in March 1846 and *Macbeth* a year later – it was an impressive undertaking by British and twentieth-century standards. In his December 1945 letter to Hawkes, Britten addressed both his earnings and the new contract being drafted. 'I wonder if you would mind if I went back to the original method of only receiving what I earn, & when I earn it,' he suggested, nervous at the advance against earnings of £600 per annum (up from £400) Hawkes was proposing. Britten ended his letter with another revealing comment: 'Don't be away too long, nor become too infatuated with the New World. The Old World's got quite abit of life in her yet.'

5

Britten composed the first notes of *The Rape of Lucretia* on 23 January 1946. 'It is loathsome starting pieces,' he wrote the following day to Pears, who was away rehearsing the Sadler's Wells revival of *Peter Grimes*. 'I always regret that I'm not a coal heaver or bus-driver and not have to depend on things you can't control.' He was exaggerating, for of course he was in control – at least up to the moment, usually fairly

* £75,000 today.

late, when his subconscious kicked in and the broad shapes conceived in his head were filled in with wondrous detail.

Something had shifted, however, in his approach to composition. He was now free to choose both his projects and his collaborators. Though he was still sketching the occasional incidental score, these were favours to old friends, not necessary sources of revenue. Yet if his experience with Slater on *Grimes* had taught him anything, it was to trust his dramatic instincts. In his mind, the pipe-puffing ideologue Slater was the stumbling block in their collaboration, never the clear-sighted composer. It is not hard to trace the perceived flaws in this partnership back to those of an earlier collaboration, on another eponymous opera, *Paul Bunyan*. It was an issue he was determined to solve: he had to work with sympathetic, amenable librettists.

This determination came with its own set of problems. It was Slater, after all, in a whip-smart letter to Britten in December 1944, who fought to keep the women's quartet in Act 2 of *Grimes*, which at the time Britten was attempting to jettison; whatever Slater's limitations as a collaborator, he was a good, old-fashioned dramatist. And no amount of Britten's theatrical flair – evident from the moment he identified operatic potential in Crabbe's poetry – would compensate for the fact that *Lucretia* was put together in under a year and experienced none of the careful word-by-word paring and slow-boil preparation of *Grimes*. Any number of problems in the opera would never have made it to the stage had Britten been dealing with the intransigent Slater, rather than the more biddable Duncan.

When Britten began putting notes down on paper, the opera's intended home had barely been settled. The governors of Sadler's Wells made a stab at wooing Britten and his like-minded colleagues, suddenly conscious of what they were losing, but it was too little, too late. Glyndebourne's visionary entrepreneur Rudolf Bing had stepped forward, only a year before he would help found the Edinburgh Festival. Bing recognized Britten's aspirations for what they were and went to work on John Christie, Glyndebourne's ambitious squire.

Christie and Britten never warmed to each other. They were both cultural fellow travellers, in possession of similar revolutionary tendencies. Both had sharpened their ears and tongues in response to the crude performances in 1930s England and the infinitely better ones they experienced on the Continent. Their feelings about English music-making outlasted the war, Christie unleashing an impressive tirade on the nascent Arts Council in July 1946, observing that 'the whole of the orchestral work in London is lamentable from the London Philharmonic Orchestra downwards'. He was not very wide of the mark.

But for all their similarities in outlook, their personalities almost guaranteed conflict. Christie was a bullish visionary, an Old Etonian and decorated ex-army officer; Britten was a single-minded pacifist who detested confrontation, who had accumulated what he thought was almost limitless artistic capital through the success of *Peter Grimes*, and who was choosy about how and where to spend it. But in 1946 any reservations were put to one side, since at that moment their agendas exactly aligned: the canny impresario was determined that Glyndebourne, dark during the war years, would reopen the year after and had already entered into negotiations with Beecham to conduct (and probably help bankroll) one or more productions. With the speedy and predictable breakdown of these talks, Christie settled on the operatic talk of the town, whose magic he was keen to obtain for his theatrical relaunch.

For a time there was concord. Scarred by the vitriolic and sometimes chaotic rehearsals for *Grimes*, Britten was uninterested in large, sceptical choruses and other such unknown quantities; he wanted to collaborate with a smaller, hand-picked team, free from distractions and the gossip and innuendo to which he was suddenly more sensitive. This suited the set-up and philosophy of Glyndebourne admirably, where long rehearsal periods had been established as the norm. To give Christie his due (especially given the unfortunate opinions about Britten and his operas that emerged from these initial post-war seasons), he was determined to give the composer space and artistic freedom, regardless of how much he came to regret doing so.

One area where Christie relinquished control was touring; though he shared none of Britten's enthusiasm for the practice (despite Bing's prescient conviction that Glyndebourne was a portable and powerful brand), Britten insisted in their discussions that they must take the new opera on the road: Manchester, Liverpool, Edinburgh, Glasgow, Oxford and London would all see *Lucretia* in its opening season. Britten liked the unfettered enthusiasm with which regional crowds had responded to canonical operas on tour during the war, in contrast to what he saw as the cynicism and pretentiousness of metropolitan patrons and press. Britten viewed touring as a way of circumventing the existing cultural elites and infrastructure. He could be directly in charge of disseminating his work, without its being diluted by others and without its being the sole preserve of the upper middle classes. It was his way of democratizing culture – in the same spirit as the 1944 Education Act, which made fundamental changes to the provision of secondary schooling in England and Wales. This direction in his thinking was reinforced in the following years, and the habit, once gained, was not easily shaken. He was pleased when his music was taken up by other exponents, other organizations, but he often did not try over hard to conceal the impression that the authentic experience of these scores was to be found in his own performances.

Not only regional Britain caught his eye. In the crippling winter of 1945–6 when, in a cruel postlude to the war, cold, desperate Berliners felled the centuries-old trees in the Tiergarten for firewood, Britten and Pears travelled to Amsterdam. It seemed abandoned. There was no food or heating of any substance. They travelled by horse and carriage from their spartan hotel to the Concertgebouw for the first Dutch performance of *Les Illuminations*, snow flurrying around them, thoughts of Tchaikovsky's Russia uppermost in their minds. The charming, eccentric Charles Münch conducted, and the audiences responded warmly, gratefully even, to the two English musicians and their fanciful excursion into Rimbaud's France. Britten told Hawkes of these concerts and of wider Continental interest: Holland, Belgium, Italy, Greece, Sweden and Czechoslovakia all wanted to know what the composer of *Grimes* and the celebrated English tenor were planning next. Stockholm was gearing up for a new production of the opera in March, while Basle, Antwerp and Zurich would mount it a few months later. Pears and Cross starred in Zurich, singing in German, not without incident.* There would be recitals in St Gallen, a Zurich Radio broadcast and concerts in the capital featuring *Les Illuminations* and *Sinfonia da Requiem*, with Britten rehearsing in German, again not without incident as he thought on his feet, making specific instructions in his second language. It was too soon for invitations from Germany itself, though Italy's inclusion on the list was a sign of thawing relations. (In 1950 the English Opera Group would be invited to Germany, and, in pressuring Britten to accept, the Foreign Office appealed directly to his sense of patriotic duty.)

* 'This Peter Grimes will be long remembered,' one critic wrote of Pears, 'even though the singer was somewhat inhibited by the unfamiliar language – the British had no qualms about singing in German in front of a German audience!'

In such circumstances it is no surprise that Britten again rebuffed Hawkes's croaky siren calls from America. It was not only the time and distance involved, with arduous transatlantic flights and miles separating the two coasts; nor was it his memory of the various slights and ongoing sense of vulnerability he felt while in the country. It was more that the positive reception of his music on the Continent was a reminder of its Austro-Germanic roots, which he was delighted to acknowledge. From the scores he played as a child, through the example of (late) Bridge, to his own dabbling with expressionism in the 1930s and 1940s, the influences on his mind and music were closer to hand than across the Atlantic. 'Peter & I have found, without any doubt, that our work is exportable eastwards; and my music is going so well in that direction, that my sympathies rather naturally lie there too. Besides, once having tried the American Way of Life, I feel, inspite of its silly muddles, really a part of Europe.'

Hawkes pushed on without Britten's direct involvement. He commandeered Clytie Mundy's New York apartment to host three private salon performances in which excerpts from *Grimes* were featured. Koussevitzky and his protégé Bernstein attended the last of these – as did Auden, who reported to Elizabeth Mayer that it was much better than the first of the showcases, except that 'he was not so satisfied about the tempi'. (Auden had surprisingly little to say about Britten's spectacular success in the genre.) Britten left Hawkes to it. He would go on only two concert tours of North America – in 1949 and then, twenty years later, cap in hand, seeking funds to rebuild the Snape Maltings concert hall – and would not live to see American audiences take his operas fully to their hearts, as they eventually did.

6

In a stairwell, or perhaps backstage, at Sadler's Wells, Britten encountered Edward Dent at a performance of *Peter Grimes* in February 1946, the opera's first revival season. Although the cast was almost identical to that of the first run, Britten found little to love this time round. In the few seconds they were together, Dent gave Britten his hurried, somewhat mealy-mouthed impressions of the work: how he enjoyed the opera a little more every time he saw it; how some of it was profoundly moving; how it reminded him here of Massenet and there of Liszt. It was a ghastly meeting, with the composer bristling at the suggestion of overt musical reminiscences in the score and Dent trying to dig himself out of the hole. His letter the next day only made matters worse, for he managed to imply that Britten was an ingrate to boot: 'Don't be ungrateful; no English composer has ever had such chances before.'

Britten sat on the letter for two weeks, fuming as he pushed on with *Lucretia*, before finally snapping back.

> Thank you for writing to tell me you'd changed your mind about Peter Grimes – although it would be difficult to measure the harm that was caused to some fine people & some important ideas by your first opinion.
>
> Why you & your young critics bother yourself about 'reminiscences' I cannot understand. That is the easiest & most provincial form of criticism. As Brahms said 'any fool can see that'.
>
> But anyhow, thank you for your good wishes for the opera and for Peter Pears abroad.

His anger at Dent's criticisms was genuine (he would be disheartened to discover that this approach to the criticism of contemporary music remains to this day), but the letter captures far more. Here was Britten saying to an eminent representative of the English music establishment what he had long thought: that the country's music industry – from its composers to its performers, from programmers to critics, from the academy to those who had sabotaged the proposed British Council-funded recording of *Grimes* (Walton *et al.*) – was second-rate. Some months later, when Britten's old piano teacher Arthur Benjamin declared 'that in you this country has found the "universal British composer"', he was pushing against an unlatched gate.

Other pedantries could not be dealt with so easily. The Theatres Act of 1843 stipulated that every new work intended for the British stage be sent to the Lord Chamberlain, 'at least seven days before the first acting or presentation thereof'. (A similar requirement had been in place since 1737.) The Lord Chamberlain's officers would read the submitted play or libretto, write a report, and a licence would be granted subject to any specified alterations. Theatre managers were happy enough with the procedure, since it cost them little and a licence ensured they were immune from prosecution for offence. Authors were understandably less sanguine. A few years before Britten was born the writer J. M. Barrie mounted an unsuccessful campaign against the lofty censorship; the system limped on until 1968, by which time, thanks to John Osborne and those like him, the intellectual climate had changed.

Peter Grimes had earned its licence in May 1945 with the following bland summary from the Lord Chamberlain's reader:

> Peter Grimes was a fisherman who lived a villainous life, murdered more than one apprentice and died in a madhouse. The libretto of this Opera seems to follow the plot of the poem, though here he goes down with his boat and commits suicide.
>
> It is all very wafty and nebulous and I don't pretend I can make sense of the plot from the verses, but there is no offence in them or in the production. Perhaps Benjamin Britten's music will carry it through.
>
> Recommended for Licence

It was not so straightforward for *Lucretia* – the story of a virtuous Roman noblewoman who is raped by an Etruscan prince and kills herself in front of her loving husband as a consequence – and the Lord Chamberlain's intervention in February 1946 had significant repercussions for both the submitted opera and Britten's subsequent dramaturgical style.

Nancy Evans, who shared the title role with Kathleen Ferrier in the opera's opening season, wrote of *Lucretia* many years later that 'moral perceptions have changed during the past 40 years, and some young singers and directors occasionally state the belief that Lucretia secretly longed to be raped by Tarquinius. The notion destroys the essence of both the heroine and her tragedy.' In recent decades such readings have been relatively commonplace, but for the opera to work must Lucretia's resistance to the swaggering Prince Tarquinius be absolute?

The Lord Chamberlain's report suggests that Duncan and Britten thought no such thing. 'Physically Lucretia is starved of passion, so when Tarquinius succeeds in arousing her desire, he quickly accomplishes his purpose.' In support of this interpretation of the rape scene, the reader of plays, H. C. Game, cited one passage from the submitted libretto.

Male Chorus: He takes her hand

And places it upon his unsheathed sword.
Female Chorus: Thus wounding her with an equal lust
A wound only his sword can heal.

'I most certainly think we should draw the line at the somewhat transparent effort by the Chorus on page 5 of Act II to wrap up an ugly fact in pretty language. It is little better than the obscenities in "Lady Chatterley's Lover".' The licence was granted subject to the removal of the offending quatrain.

It was tame stuff compared to the language of D. H. Lawrence's novel.* Nonetheless, Duncan's libretto offended moral decency: Lucretia was a willing participant in Tarquinius's actions. It was a departure from Shakespeare's narrative poem on the same subject, as it was from Duncan's sources, Obey, Ovid and Livy. But it was there nonetheless, contradicting Evans's later assertions about the fundamental nature of Lucretia's tragedy.

Britten and Duncan replaced the offending lines as directed:

Tarquinius:	Poised like a dart
Lucretia:	At the heart of woman
Male Chorus:	Man climbs towards his God,
Female Chorus:	Then falls to his lonely hell.

Yet one quatrain does not a new opera make. Librettist and composer had smudged but not erased Lucretia's complicity. When Collatinus lovingly tells his wife, 'If spirit's not given, there is no need of shame', Lucretia replies, 'Even great love's too frail / To bear the weight of shadows', before killing herself. Why such a tragic action if she is the innocent victim of a crime? Collatinus was closer to the truth than he knew.

Lucretia thereafter wandered off in a strange direction. It was late in the writing process and Britten was desperate to send the score to the copyist, desperate as well to set off on his month-long visit to Switzerland, and so, when he asked for two new sections, Duncan quickly wrote 'a hymn to the Virgin Mary as the obvious symbol of chastity',

---

* A 1960 dramatization of the book by John Harte could still rile the Lord Chamberlain. 'The following is disallowed: The word "cunt" (twice) . . . The word "maidenhair" . . . The word "fucking" (twice) . . . Mellors must be reasonably clothed, at least in pants.' It was tame too compared to Shelagh Delaney's 1958 play *A Taste of Honey*, which made the Lord Chamberlain similarly twitchy: 'The following line on page 37 will be omitted: "Worn out but still a few good pumps left in her".'

which he thought would be a fitting counterpoint to the rape, and for the epilogue gave the Male and Female choruses 'some universal comment on the entire tragedy ... Perhaps reverting to the position of Christians'.

It was an odd lurch, saddling the opera with metaphors that were never part of the original narrative, wrenching it from its original time-frame, c. 509 BCE. The historical moral of the fable is that Tarquinius's deed led to the end of the Roman Kingdom and the founding of the Roman Republic, a bone on which there was already quite enough meat. 'It is an axiom among kings, to use / A foreign threat to hide a local evil,' the Female Chorus announces in the opening pages of the opera, whetting our appetite for an ageless commentary on power and politics. Yet instead Duncan cobbled together the anachronistic Christian interlude and epilogue as they stand today, heavily influenced it seems by T. S. Eliot's trick of balancing Christianity and modernism in his *Four Quartets*, or W. B. Yeats in 'The Second Coming', or Edith Sitwell in her 1940 poem 'Still Falls the Rain'.

In Sitwell's highly impressionistic response to the blitzkrieg, war imagery is melded with the story of Christ's crucifixion and redemption. Yet what succeeds brilliantly in her poem, not least a pacifist streak, is simply clumsy in Britten's opera. He may have sought musical ballast, but the epilogue throws the work out of kilter, providing opera directors with a huge challenge. David McVicar's solution in his fine Aldeburgh/English National Opera production of 2001 was to have the Female Chorus look at the Male Chorus with a mixture of incomprehension and disdain while he fulminated from the pulpit, 'In His Passion / Is our hope / Jesus Christ, Saviour. He is all! He is all!' How ridiculous seemed this glassy-eyed preacher-man, bleating God and mercy when a woman has either been raped or unfaithful and has taken her own life in consequence.

'The composer and poet should at all stages be working in the closest contact, from the most preliminary stages right up to the first night,' Britten wrote later, a little pleased with himself at such a calm collaboration following the bruising of *Grimes*. 'It was thus in the case of "The Rape of Lucretia".' His sheer facility ensured there was no opportunity for sober contemplation during the writing process and some lame dramatic ideas slipped through as a result, unchecked by Crozier or

Pears or a more sceptical librettist. A year on from *Grimes*, it casts doubt on Britten's dramatic instincts.

There was one positive aspect to the Lord Chamberlain's intervention: that which was explicit was now made ambiguous. Evans may have been certain of her character's innocence, yet an equally distinguished Lucretia from the 1960s, Janet Baker, thought otherwise. 'If she weren't in danger from his sexuality she wouldn't be frightened. If she had been emotionally uninvolved, she wouldn't have felt guilty after the rape.' It is telling that two such eminent Lucretias, each with a close connection to the work's composer, could position themselves on different sides of the fence. Regardless of the opera's flaws, the dramatic ambiguity that emerged as a consequence of the Lord Chamberlain's directive was thereafter a vital feature of Britten's works for the stage. But the ambiguity in each of these subsequent pieces was intentional and conceptual, not the by-product of more censorial times.

7

Britten's fumblings in *Lucretia* also illustrate his somewhat narrow understanding of women. He had plenty of female friends, though the relationships were often more maternal than coequal. Or they were complicated by professional dealings, by the deference that crept in as he grew older and more famous, or by amorous feelings on their part, which quickly brought the curtains down. Canny friends – from Enid Slater and Elizabeth Mayer onwards – sensed what he wanted from them. Elizabeth Sweeting, an early manager of the English Opera Group, thought he 'looked for a surrogate mother in every relationship [with a woman]'. There were exceptions: the painter Mary Potter maintained a long, close friendship, partly through her unfussy manner, partly because she and Britten were both hard-working artists. So too did Princess Margaret of Hesse and the Rhine (whom he called Peg). He found Donald Mitchell's wife Kathleen great company in the late 1960s and 1970s, as he did the formidable Cynthia Nolan, wife of the painter Sidney Nolan. ('If Britten could have an amiable relationship with Cynthia he should be acknowledged as a man of great social gifts,' Nolan's biographer Tom Rosenthal observed. 'She was a total monster.') And Marion

Stein remained a lifelong friend, Britten's loyalty towards this remarkable woman unshakeable.

Yet in his operas he gives the strong impression of incomprehension. Of course he was not solely responsible for his characters, notwithstanding how hands-on he was as a collaborator, and one of his favourite librettists was a woman. But for every Queen Elizabeth – a gloriously evocative portrait, hard-nosed and vulnerable in equal doses – there is a Kate Julian, Owen Wingrave's cardboard-flat fiancée. For every Governess, an Ellen Orford or a Mrs Herring or a monstrous Mrs Noye, swilling gin and gossiping to her ghastly friends – not much more than rough sketches or clichés. Britten totally avoided the issue in four of his operas, in which the casts are wholly male. (One of these, *Curlew River*, has a woman as the protagonist, though a man performs the role.) As for the men in his operas, they are a mad, flawed bunch, but each is brilliantly drawn – Collatinus and Essex aside.

The problem is less about Britten's sexuality – still less about misogyny – and more about empathy. The doggedly heterosexual Richard Strauss was sympathetic to his male characters, even when they play second fiddle to a slew of smart, complex women. Even Baron Ochs in *Der Rosenkavalier* is fundamentally attractive, regardless of how boorishly he is often played. But Britten was often not interested in the fate of his female characters, beyond their being someone for the men to love, abuse, or react against – a Nancy to Bill Sikes.* Myfanwy Piper, his librettist for the much later *Owen Wingrave* (1970), tried to rescue Kate from Britten's indifference towards her. 'Britten took [the character] Mrs Coyle's view of her that she was an impossible and arrogant girl, not worthy of the thoughtful Owen.' Kate is no gentle dove in the Henry James novella, though fidelity to an author's original characterizations had never bothered Britten before. But in *Wingrave* Kate is simultaneously unformed and repellent, which is no mean trick, and the drama would have been much stronger had she been more sympathetic. Another of his librettists, Eric Crozier, took a broader shot at this subject in his unpublished notes on Britten. 'Homosexuality was the predominant influence in the choice of subjects for his operas,' he asserted, not quite accurately. 'He had all the capacity for a great opera-composer . . .

---

* Dickens's slight female characters have ignited academic argument since the 1970s, his own daughter having written that her father did not understand women at all.

but he lacked the essential humanity, the broad range of compassion and understanding necessary for the purpose.'

This question of female empathy was on Slater's mind when in 1944 he wrote so passionately to Britten about Ellen Orford. He first implored Britten not to build up Balstrode any more than they already had, since his role was explicatory, nothing more. 'The old stock companies used to have a name for it. They called him Charles's friend ... In Hamlet he's Horatio. His job is that he is the receiver of confidences, the giver of good advice, and the bloke who stands by at the climax.' Then Slater rode to Ellen's defence. 'I said I regretted losing Ellen's quatrain ... But the more I think about it the more I'm convinced that it is simply the clue to Ellen's whole outlook and character and it should at all costs be the curtain line of that scene.' His argument prevailed – surprisingly, given the men's short tempers at the time – and Ellen is left to sing of her complicated feelings for Peter, and men generally. 'They are children when they weep / We are mothers when they strive / Schooling our own hearts to love / The bitter treasure of their love.' It was a small victory for her character – and it was Slater's, not Britten's.

Britten's approach to the noblewoman Lucretia was similarly tin-eared, starting with his casting. He first heard Kathleen Ferrier in the final days of the war at a performance of Handel's *Messiah* in Westminster Abbey, and was struck by her nobility, beauty and stillness, by the warmth and range of her voice. She had no stage experience, however, and agreed only reluctantly to take the role. ('I can't act, what am I to do?' she asked Cross early on. 'I don't know anything about acting.') Britten was unconcerned: 'I knew that for Lucretia you couldn't have a sexy dame, which Kathleen certainly wasn't!' She was required to emit just those traits Britten identified and admired in her, wandering around the stage as though in a Handel oratorio; he could join the remaining dots, he thought.

Such a tactic undermined the character Lucretia, a portrait of power, honour and female sexuality. Ferrier got away with it, just, though long after her untimely death Pears said he preferred Evans in the role. But by then a fairly unsophisticated characterization of Lucretia had become entrenched.

Janet Baker's thoughts on the role of Lucretia conflicted with how she played her. It was partly an offshoot of voice type – all those Caesars and Octavians and Composers she performed throughout her distinguished career. And even when not singing male characters she was often cast as one queen or other, which she acted with regal hauteur. Britten was captivated by her voice and musicality, and did not seem to worry that she was no more a 'sexy dame' than Ferrier. But it is telling that these women – together with Cross and Evans and Jennifer Vyvyan – were all cut from similar cloth, so distinct from the voluptuous Hedli Anderson, Britten's cabaret singer of choice in the 1930s. It is almost as though a more complex or overt version of female sexuality was too confrontational for him – on stage as in his life. So into his operatic world came a series of chastely comforting women, performing often unformed characters, unable to do very much to improve them.

8

The new company at Glyndebourne started well. Britten had brought with him a few evacuees from the Sadler's Wells implosion: Pears, Crozier, Cross, Edmund Donlevy and Owen Brannigan, the first two immeasurably enhanced in the public eye by *Grimes*. To the list was added designer John Piper and conductor Ernest Ansermet – a compromise brokered by Bing, who did not rate the 'little man' Reginald Goodall; the latter had to be content assisting Ansermet and conducting the second cast. The rest of the singers were assembled from acquaintances or by recommendation (Ferrier suggested Evans). It was a harmonious group of thirty – only four of them foreigners, Britten proudly told Hawkes – which began rehearsals immediately on Britten and Pears's return from the Continent, flushed with the success of their various concerts and the Zurich *Grimes*.

Yet as time went on fault lines were exposed. Crozier and Britten took against Bing, and Christie's bullying manner started to irritate. Christie remained supportive, though to his mind contemporary chamber opera strayed too far from Glyndebourne's *métier* – Mozart and the like. There was no significant Arts Council recompense for this and the tour later in the year lost him a bundle, as the company played to tiny houses throughout the country.

It is true that Christie wanted to play entrepreneur-squire on his own patch and resented funding a tour. In key ways he was right to do so: at the end of 1947 the council would conclude that the regional activities it funded 'do not ... touch the mass of the working-class, even to the extent they did during the war' (Spender's regret), and it would wind back its support. It was not just Christie: even Hawkes gave the impression that the new company was a distraction from Britten's main task. He sold the idea of a Swiss premiere of *Lucretia* to Switzerland's three opera houses, leaving no room for a tour there of the Glyndebourne production and contradicting the year-long exclusivity deal on which they had agreed. Hawkes also rightly encouraged Britten over a proposed commission from the new Covent Garden company for the 1947–8 season. Britten was keen but wary: 'it must be clear that I have the veto on performers & producer & conductor. I have no faith in an organisation which has [Constant] Lambert as assistant conductor, & on the Committee behind it – Walton & Dent.'

And then of course there was the fact that critics generally hated *Lucretia* at its premiere on 12 July 1946. Ernest Newman asked 'what had become of Mr Britten's sense of the theatre and his feeling for his tragic subject', which led him to include some of the more absurd passages in the libretto. Another critic described the audience around him tittering at these moments. Britten's friend Grace Williams had strong things to say about the text, as did Michael Tippett. 'If you're now going to write a comic opera for Christ's sake don't use this librettist,' he told him backstage after the dress rehearsal. Britten took it badly, even from such a close friend, while Tippett, like Dent before him, followed up his comments with a letter. Apology dispatched, he went on to say that 'the dramatic qualities never really put *all* the characters or all the *character* of the characters into play': it was not just the women here who did not ring true. Even Queen Mary put her oar in. 'Tell me, Mr Britten, what made you choose such a subject?' she asked following a Glyndebourne performance. 'Well, I am rather interested in that sort of thing,' he found himself replying, to his long-lasting embarrassment.* Britten took some of the criticism to heart, effecting slight revisions the following year. But he dug in his heels over the fundamental shape of the work, epilogue included. It had a huge success in Holland in October that year (it sounds fine on the surviving broadcast recording) and Britten no doubt told himself that philistine British audiences and critics were the problem, not the piece itself.

* The response continued to be critical for decades. After a 1972 performance of *Lucretia* in Belgrade, Sviatoslav Richter wrote: 'The actual subject matter I find unappealing and even see a certain banality in it, a quality I'd rather not associate with Britten.'

Tensions of a different sort surrounded the first American production of *Peter Grimes* in the chaotic atmosphere of the summer school at Tanglewood, Massachusetts: musicians were painting backdrops or operating the lighting plot when they should have been in rehearsals; singers spent time in madrigal groups instead of learning the opera's difficult choruses; Bernstein conducted a giant orchestra, half the musicians allocated the outer acts, the rest the inner, cohesion nowhere to be found; two different casts of young singers in the principal roles, most of whom went on to only modest careers (though Britten used the Balstrode, James Pease, in his later recording). Crozier was drafted in to clean up the mess and left England immediately after the subdued premiere of *Lucretia*. He swiftly brought some order to proceedings, telling Koussevitzky he would leave immediately if the musicians were not allowed to focus solely on *Grimes*. And focus they did, rehearsing up to twelve hours a day where necessary, far outside the protective clutches of a musicians' union. Yet Crozier still despaired at the results, cabling Britten after one rehearsal and telling him to stay put. Bernstein was relieved: 'I wouldn't want Bengy coming all this way out here and upsetting my tempi!'

Yet Britten read Crozier's cable as a call to arms and flew across the Atlantic, where he shared a hotel room with Auden, who smoked in bed, to the composer's fury. No doubt they discussed *The Duchess of Malfi*, Brecht and Auden's adaptation of Webster's play, for which Britten was writing music. (The score is lost.) And Auden almost certainly tried his hand once more on the matter of his 'Christmas Oratorio', the sprawling poem Britten thought he would set at the end of his American years. Auden had good reason to try: for a Christmas 1944 BBC feature Britten had filleted some short lyrics from the whole to create two beautiful carols – a taste of the work's potential, which he recognized: 'One day, in a matter of years, I am going to get down to the Christmas Oratorio,' he wrote to Mayer in December 1946. 'That has got to be set, even if no one performs it. It'll probably last three evenings!' The day never came.

There was little Britten could do to save the Tanglewood *Grimes*, and the performance upset him greatly: this shy, diffident, slightly mistrustful man, as Bernstein found him on this trip, watched his great opera lurch from one misfortune to the next. Sitting next to Koussevitzky (who referred to the opera as 'Peter und Grimes' in a short speech to the audience before the performance), he did his best to hide his feelings. Photographs of the event show him smiling, cutting an elegant figure in white dinner jacket and black dicky bow. But backstage, waiting to take his curtain call, frustration took hold. He cadged a cigarette from Crozier, disguised himself with a cap lest this uncharacteristic behaviour appear disrespectful to the artists, and puffed away ineffectually. Auden and Copland were in the audience and at the party afterwards no doubt attempted to talk him down. Auden was impressed by the piece, though acknowledged the performance was poor. Critics were perceptive and appreciative, though this did little to assuage Britten's mood. 'There's no use pretending it was professional – this was a very lively student performance,' he ungraciously told *Time*. The 'bad nightmare', as he described it to Mayer – compounded by a much-delayed flight home, which no number of Marx Brothers films or luxury food items could counter – set him further against America.

9

'It was a decaying district of huge early Victorian houses, built when servants were plentiful and cheap and almost impossible to manage without them.' Thus Crozier's description of the patch of Paddington into which Britten and Pears moved in late August 1946, two weeks after Britten returned from the America debacle. Pears had bought the house at 3 Oxford Square two months earlier and now oversaw arrangements. The Steins came with the furniture, and Pears's elderly parents moved in as well, soon thereafter objecting to the food, to Sophie's running of the house and to Marion's piano playing. It was not an easy environment, yet the younger inhabitants put up with the complaints and the graceless behaviour for a little over two years, by which time both parents had died.

Britten was already thinking about a new opera. Christie had rashly requested a new piece while *Lucretia* was still being rehearsed, unaware how much he would lose on the tour. Britten and Duncan had tossed around a few ideas long before Christie's invitation, including the tragic love story of Abelard and Héloïse and *The Canterbury Tales*. But Britten wanted to write a comedy after the harrowing *Lucretia*, as he had told Tippett. Cross suggested *Mansfield Park*, Austen's stroll through the Georgian landed gentry. Christie was predictably excited by the idea (he no doubt admired the capitalist Sir Thomas Bertram), but so too was Britten, and Duncan set to work on a libretto. It is an intriguing idea – not least whether Britten would have been more successful with the tough, cynical Mary Crawford than he later was with the black-hearted Kate Julian. Yet on a visit to London, a draft of Act 1 in his satchel, Duncan discovered from Marion Stein that Britten was at work on quite another opera, *Albert Herring*, with Crozier as librettist. He was flabbergasted: the two had spoken often on the phone without mention of the other work. 'I now confronted Ben. He admitted the position, looked sheepish but gave no explanation.'

Britten and Duncan had other projects on the boil – 'half a dozen other pieces in our heads', including a cantata for Ferrier on the subject of Hylas, the beautiful mythological warrior prince. Duncan also adapted Jean Cocteau's *L'Aigle à deux têtes* in 1946, to which Britten contributed a national anthem for brass and percussion. (The play earned a short Broadway run the following year in a production starring Tallulah Bankhead.) There would be another Duncan play, *Stratton*, in 1949, for which Britten composed incidental music, and they collabor-ated over a small anthem on the occasion of Marion Stein's wedding. Britten also still intended to undertake the large-scale oratorio 'Mea Culpa', a response to the bombing of Hiroshima, which they had planned, shell-shocked, in the paralysing aftermath of the explosion. But the critical thrashing *Lucretia* received made him wary of working with his old friend on a new opera: it was *Paul Bunyan* all over again.

Like Auden before him, Duncan was hurt by Britten's sudden change of heart. He loved their work together, which was straightforward and amusing, and foresaw a long and bountiful partnership. 'Ben and I knew that, left to ourselves and undivided by the spite of the uncreative, we could write an opera a year for the next twenty years, taking no more time than three to four months on each.' In one sentence Duncan unknowingly put his finger on exactly what had gone wrong in the com-position of *Lucretia*. Slater arguing every toss was what Britten needed, not an opera pushed out in a matter of months. They would continue to kick around the occasional idea, whether through sentiment or continu-ing admiration is unclear, but Britten now had other goals.

There were a few incidents at this time that suggested Britten's behav-iour towards Dent and even Duncan was here to stay. At a dinner in July with Erwin Stein and Etienne Amyot, a programme-planner with the nascent BBC Third Programme, Britten launched what Amyot described as a hysterical attack on the corporation's policies and commitment to high art. Why would the new programme stream be any different? 'It was a very sticky dinner until drink made both of them a little more amiable,' Amyot dryly reported to his boss. Amyot sidelined Stein as best he could ('obviously his Svengali') and talked Britten round, getting him to agree to compose a fanfare for the Third Programme's opening concert on 29 September 1946. This was the slight *Occasional Overture* – limited raw material, heavily mined – which Boult conducted and which Britten withdrew soon afterwards.

It was not only business associates who earned such tongue-lashings. When Sackville-West wrote an appreciative but unvarnished review of *Lucretia*, Britten argued back, point for point. 'My own feeling about works of artists whom I love & trust, is that when there are passages I don't like or understand, that it's my fault, & that if I work hard enough or love enough then one day I shall see the light!'* Critics ought to be John the Baptist types, not the Herod kind, he added. By contrast, Britten leaped on Imogen Holst's appreciative letter ('It is a 1946 B minor mass,' she wrote of *Lucretia*) to thank her for her perceptive comments of the work's spirituality. 'I have never felt so strongly that what we've done is in the right direction, & that the faded "intellectuals" are dangerously wrong!'

Crozier found him straightforward enough just now. He set up camp in the attic room of the Paddington house and spent much time in Britten's company. The new opera was their main preoccupation, though extracting themselves from Glyndebourne was a delicate and time-consuming operation. They met or talked on the telephone daily. Crozier helped draft Britten's articles and arranged photographic sessions with a studio. They went on holidays together and talked music and theatre the whole time. 'Our friendship was so close and so enduring that some people took it for granted that I must be a homosexual, but I was not,' Crozier later said.

It was Crozier who had suggested Maupassant's short story 'Le Rosier de Madame Husson' (Madame Husson's May King) as a potential comic opera – inspired by the Sadler's Wells production of Mozart's *Così fan tutte* and by Pears's performance as the simple country boy

---

* 'I am an arrogant and impatient listener,' Britten wrote in 1951, 'but in the case of a few composers, a very few, when I hear a work I do not like I am convinced it is my own fault. Verdi is one of these composers.'

Vašek in *The Bartered Bride*. And it was Crozier who had earned himself the role of librettist as a result. He was the ideal colleague and companion: smart, theatre-wise, stimulating and sympathetic, with none of Duncan's highfalutin language, and none of Auden's didacticism. On the *Lucretia* tour to Amsterdam in October he displayed all these qualities, and they returned from the trip enthusiastic about transplanting Maupassant's May King from a small French town to an even smaller Suffolk village, the imaginary Loxford. Britten presented him with a copy of the libretto of Verdi's *Falstaff*, to his mind the most perfect of its kind ('Eric, a present from Amsterdam, very confidently, Ben'), and both men set to work.

The split from Glyndebourne was almost inevitable from the moment Christie discovered how much he had lost on the *Lucretia* tour. Christie's feud with the Arts Council showed no sign of abating, which meant that touring funds would once more need to come from his own pocket. By mid-October Britten and Crozier had a plan: they would form their own opera company, which would tour Britain and the Continent, including a season at Glyndebourne if Christie were agreeable. It was a hubristic undertaking. Working capital of £12,000 was sought – far shy of the £31,000 they would spend in 1947 – only £3,000 of which would come from the Arts Council. 'Britten's music is an important thing,' the Council's music director Steuart Wilson wrote in a memo, but 'should *he* have to make a company to exploit it?' The short answer, of course, was no. Britten was then in conversation with David Webster, general administrator of Covent Garden, about a new work and a new production of *Peter Grimes* planned for 1947. Webster exhibited nothing but goodwill towards this brilliant if touchy talent. Yet the talent had now seen his first three operas suffer from unsympathetic administrations, real or imagined, and was not inclined to make it four. 'If there were a superb orchestra and superb opera company available,' Crozier said in a 1947 radio interview, Britten and Piper at his side, 'then I suppose your tendency would be to write works for them, but in the present circumstances, if you want high standards of performance, you have to create an ensemble yourself and that has to be a small one.'

The thinking behind Britten's new company was spelled out in an early 1947 manifesto. 'We believe the time has come when England, which has never had a tradition of native opera, but has always depended on a repertory of foreign works, can create its own operas. Opera is as much a vital means of artistic expression as orchestral music, drama, and painting. The lack of it has meant a certain impoverishment of English artistic life.' The manifesto listed names: the artistic triumvirate was to consist of Britten, Crozier and Piper. Singers were to include Pears, Cross, Evans and various other soloists from *Lucretia*, accompanied by pit musicians such as oboist Joy Boughton and flautist John Francis. The company's name was to be the English Opera Group.

The fledgling EOG boasted some impressive supporters. The founding board included the Rt Hon. Oliver Lyttelton (later Viscount Chandos) as chairman, Sir Kenneth Clark, Tyrone Guthrie, Ralph Hawkes and Erwin Stein. Dorothy Elmhirst chipped in £2,000, finally able to realize a version of her Dartington dreams. The snag was that the Arts Council was busy creating its new company at Covent Garden, which the council's founding chairman, John Maynard Keynes, had made a priority. Keynes was determined England would have a national opera company every bit the equal of those pre-war monoliths in Berlin and Vienna. And he was almost equal to the task: in the year to 31 March 1948, the Arts Council would distribute £193,440 in grants, £98,000 of which went to Covent Garden. (Sadler's Wells scooped £23,000 of this pool.) Despite Keynes's best paternalistic endeavours before his untimely death in 1946, however, the Covent Garden grant was hopelessly inadequate for the new company's needs. This soon became apparent and a begging-bowl culture emerged and remained in place for some decades. On top of its other operatic pursuits, the Arts Council did not have enough funds for the EOG, nor was there anyone within the organization with the enthusiasm required to launch Britten's vessel or help it significantly when it started taking water. Of course this just made Britten more sure: how could everyone be so blind? In the following years, as the administration of the EOG kept Britten away from his desk more and more, he would have cause to revisit the decisions of late 1946.

10

Before the year was out, Britten returned to the Netherlands for concerts with Pears, slipping into the programme three of his new folk-song arrangements. There was also an outing of *The Young Person's Guide to the Orchestra*, with Britten as narrator, his Noel Coward voice (his own description) filling the Concertgebouw, locals lapping it up. His profile remained high in Britain too. There was a UK tour with Pears – sixteen recitals in twenty-one days. And there was the Leicester Square premiere of the film *Instruments of the Orchestra*, a low-key affair compared to the first ever Royal Command Film Performance in the same cinema earlier in the month. (Then the teenage Princess Elizabeth and her parents came to see *A Matter of Life and Death*, with David Niven as the handsome squadron leader complete with pencil moustache.) There was no overall strategy, however, no homeland promotional campaign: Britten performed when and where it suited him.

Curiously, it did not suit him to conduct the BBC Symphony Orchestra, or the London Symphony Orchestra or other such ensembles in the capital. No doubt there were conversations and invitations, but it now seems extraordinary that London was not on his radar. In July 1946, as part of the Cheltenham Festival, he conducted Noel Mewton-Wood and the London Philharmonic Orchestra in the first performance of the revised Piano Concerto, but he surrendered the podium to Basil Cameron in the August Proms performance with the LSO. The BBC continued to issue invitations for new works, but most of these Britten declined.

He was busy, of course: in the last months of 1946, while he waited for the *Albert Herring* libretto, he knocked out a short organ work, *Prelude and Fugue on a Theme of Vittoria*, and a handful of folk-song arrangements and Purcell realizations. Yet there was more to his low profile in London than his crammed schedule. Despite renewed public enthusiasm for music in the capital after the war, despite the many talented orchestral musicians reclaiming their positions after demobilization, and despite Beecham's formation in 1946 of yet another orchestra, the Royal Philharmonic, Britten was still suspicious of the scene. His estimation of Beecham had not moderated – if anything it had hardened: when Beecham lashed out at Covent Garden over its appointment of a German music director, Karl Rankl ('It must be . . . because ignoramuses and nitwits who brought this about – this disaster – were under the impression that the functions of a musical director in an opera house were of such exotic, intricate and profound a nature that only a person of the sublime intelligence of a Teuton could grasp and manipulate them'), Britten threatened to send him a muzzle. Britten's dealings with Boult and Sargent over *Occasional Overture* and *The Young Person's*

Guide to the Orchestra, respectively, initiated no change of heart either; he thought Sargent's prim preference for the subtitle of the latter, 'Variations and Fugue on a Theme of Henry Purcell', over the more colloquial title the worst sort of English snobbery. It was easier, and safer, to stay out of their orbit. When Grace Williams chided him in 1949 for writing so little for large orchestra, he responded, 'I like to write for what is handy & don't call one performance every five years under Boult or Sargent "handy" – do you?'

The brave new world of opera seemed no safer. Britten's negotiations with Covent Garden over the proposed commission made it patently clear that the opinion he had expressed privately to Hawkes had been picked up by the organization – at least in its broadest brushstrokes. 'I can confirm that all the details of the casting, designing and production would be in the hands of Karl and myself in consultation with you,' Webster told him in November 1946. Some of the men Britten happily derided reciprocated his hostility; wartime prejudices lingered and new ones emerged. But these grumbling administrators were in a difficult position: what were they to do about these historical grudges and slights now that the other party had become, overnight, so famous?

Britten held no such blanket reservations about the European conductors with whom he associated – quite the opposite. Ansermet, friend and imaginative interpreter of Stravinsky, impressed him, as he had done as long ago as 1932. Eduard van Beinum and Rafael Kubelik were invited to Oxford Square in November 1946 for a dinner rustled up by Britten's housekeeper, twelve years after van Beinum caught Britten's ear in a radio broadcast of Strauss's *Don Quixote*. He was also the conductor of the Concertgebouw performance of *The Young Person's Guide to the Orchestra*, and would give the premiere of Koussevitzky's new commission – 'a symphony with voice, the voice to be an integral part of the orchestration', as Koussevitzky stipulated – there in July 1949 as part of the Holland Festival. Walter Susskind, who had escaped Prague just in time in 1938 and whom Britten encountered in 1942 conducting Pears in *The Tales of Hoffmann*, was invited to lead *Albert Herring*. Münch he liked and had thought gifted ever since his performance in 1944 of *Variations on a Theme of Frank Bridge*. He saw a little of Hermann Scherchen, who conducted Pears in Britten's *Serenade* in February 1947, and was distraught four years later when Josef Krips's famously poor eyesight resulted in (or was the excuse for) the conductor's withdrawal from the premiere of *Billy Budd*. He was delighted with Rankl's critical success conducting *Carmen* at Covent Garden in January 1947, his first production as music director – enthusiasm tempered somewhat during the 1947 *Grimes* by the conductor's difficulty in finding Pears's tempi. Britten was furious at what he thought of as deprecatory obituaries for his hero Artur Schnabel in 1951. He adored every aspect of Victor de Sabata's 1950 London performance of *Falstaff*, writing to this most musical of conductors in rage and embarrassment when he read the condescending notices in the London papers.* And Britten was at home in the company of Peter Diamand, the cultured Dutch-naturalized administrator of Austrian descent, who acted as his and Pears's European agent at the time, booking them their many Continental tours and engagements.

This enthusiasm was no mere cultural cringe, the sort of automatic prejudice against home-grown artists that had characterized much of the English music industry in the nineteenth and early twentieth centuries. Britten did not rate Hans Oppenheim, Christie's head of music staff. He thought Bruno Walter prone to serving up 'slop' in his performances, notwithstanding their cordial relations and Britten's youthful enthusiasm for his Mahler evangelizing. And Duncan observed how, late in life, Britten held Carlo Maria Giulini in low regard (though this contradicts his enthusiasm for him in the 1960s). But the sort of connection he felt with Erwin Stein that linked Britten with old European traditions and lineages – Schoenberg and Mahler – trumped what England then had to offer.

It was in this mood that at an Arts Council advisory panel meeting at the end of October 1947, 'Mr Benjamin Britten called attention to the desirability of hearing not only new or unfamiliar music, but the advantage of hearing foreign performers in familiar repertoire.' The panel, on which Britten sat for two years, noted that it 'does not oppose the entry of foreign musicians into Great Britain, provided that the principle of reciprocity be observed as far as possible.' This was also the time in which William Glock could be sacked as the *Observer*'s music critic for his zealous support of modern composers like Bartók, and a V&A

---

* This affection vanished two years later in a meeting between Britten, his new publisher at Boosey & Hawkes Ernst Roth, and de Sabata concerning his proposal to mount a truncated version of *Billy Budd* at La Scala. When de Sabata picked up a vocal score and pointed to an aria he thought came too late in the opera, Roth responded, 'You mean that it should come earlier on?' 'No, no, it must be left out.'

exhibition of Picasso and Matisse could achieve public notoriety. At the same panel's first meeting since incorporation, in late October 1946, Webster could say of the new company at Covent Garden, 'There were no foreigners in the chorus or orchestra and the five foreigners among the Principals were all Americans. The Music staff was English, with two exceptions. All the operas would be given in English.' Britten was proud of his predominantly British EOG team, but this was something altogether more troubling, a numbing parochialism. When Ansermet spoke at an international conference in Geneva in September 1946 under the banner 'European Spirit', arguing that music was fundamentally a European phenomenon, it could just as easily have been Britten talking. Britten's response to the 1948 film *This Modern Age: The British – are they Artistic?*, which contains footage from the original Glyndebourne production of *Albert Herring* and cameos from Myra Hess and Robert Helpmann, is unknown but easy to imagine.

To hear Britten's accent or to observe his sober jackets and knitted ties no doubt reassured some of the more conservative members of the Arts Council panel. To all appearances he was an English gentleman – the very figure he had derided only a few years earlier in relation to Hubert Parry. He was anything but, of course, though the balance between insider and outsider was still being settled. When Diamond later described Britten and Pears's post-war recitals as a revelation, he was identifying their context and their quality. But to the two musicians, their recital tours were a way of stepping outside the cultural insularity of Britain; the jackdaw Dutch, with their wide range of languages and trade, were the ideal audience for their performances of Purcell and Schubert, Mahler and Britten.

I I

In December 1946 Crozier decamped to Snape to work on *Herring*. Pears was away: it was *Messiah* season, much as Easter was Passion season, which kept him on the road. Beth had moved out of the Old Mill that September and a newly installed live-in housekeeper, Barbara Parker, kept Britten and Crozier well fed. Much of the libretto had been knocked into shape by mid-October, but was then carefully picked apart by Britten and Crozier before being reassembled.

As in the Maupassant original, a village committee meets to select a virtuous young woman as the year's May Queen. Once each potential candidate is ruled out for varying shades of immorality, the hapless Albert is proposed as a May King, a startling if progressive departure from convention. At the coronation feast in his honour the white-suited Albert drinks lemonade that has been spiked with rum by the cocky butcher's boy Sid, who sees the festivity and the villagers for what they are. Albert discovers a taste for rum, which he indulges that evening, spending £3 of his £25 booty in a series of pubs in a neighbouring village. When Albert's May King wreath is found the following day on the road, crushed by a cart, all Loxford assumes he is dead. He returns midway through their mourning, however, dishevelled and dehydrated, and when most of the villagers turn on him for his behaviour and heartlessness towards his distraught mother, he shrugs them off: it was her fault for coddling him so, for giving him no space to breathe.

There were already slight differences between the Maupassant and Crozier stories. Maupassant's Isidore is no mummy's boy, while Albert, whatever his new sense of freedom and determination to continue to taste life's pleasures, does not end up the village drunk, Isidore's fate. (Isidore eventually dies from alcoholism.) But now that Britten had begun putting notes down on paper, all sorts of snags presented themselves. Should the recitatives be in verse? What should the Mayor say in his speech? What did Albert get up to as he kicked over the traces? Words were snipped and characters honed – not least the young lover Nancy, one of Britten's successful female creations (though much of the credit can be given to Crozier, who was then falling in love with her namesake, Nancy Evans, the first performer of the role). A month or so earlier Crozier had complained that there was no time for him to read and look up all that he wanted before beginning writing. Pressed, he trawled his memory, dredging up poetry, biblical quotations, poetic metaphors and much else besides.

There were two fundamental differences between Albert's and Isidore's worlds: class and sexuality. Gisors, Isidore's home town, is as petty and as provincial as Loxford, yet in relocating the opera from Normandy to Suffolk Britten and Crozier suddenly had to deal with the suffocating awfulness of the British class system, with a character quite distinct from anything France could throw up. Orwell's 1941 shiny-eyed prediction of how post-war Britain might look may not have turned out quite so ('The Stock Exchange will be pulled down, the horse plough will give way to the tractor, the country houses will be turned into children's holiday camps, the Eton and Harrow match will be forgotten'), yet there was still more than a whiff of working-class emancipation in the air. On New Year's Day 1947, a matter of weeks after Britten and Crozier had kneaded out yet more lumps from the libretto, Britain's mines were nationalized. 'The great majority of miners are not politically minded,' noted sociologist Ferdynand Zweig soon after, 'but all of them have an enormous – I would say overwhelming – class consciousness.' It was one of the ticking bombs of the 1920s and 1930s, and one of the reasons for Churchill's surprise defeat in 1945; there was a strong public perception that this well-fed Tory and his colleagues would leave things much as they were.

Crozier did not intend the opera to be political. Early on he told Evans he needed to rebut the proposed director Carl Ebert's insistence that the production should express both the 'social criticism' of the comedy, and the 'mendacious prudery' of the characters – a perceptive observation from this cultured émigré. 'Now I must write a long letter back in words of one syllable, explaining that this isn't an Expressionist or Trotskyist attack on the upper classes of a decadent England, but a simple lyrical comedy.' Crozier's unworthy reaction aside, composer and librettist expended all their sympathies on the opera's working-class characters, in the best tradition of much literature and documentary works from the 1930s and 1940s. It was on Sid, Nancy and Albert that they lavished attention and thoughtful characterization. Britten was no class warrior: in other operas he was happy to depict the brutality and destructiveness of the working classes, as *Peter Grimes* makes clear. But in *Herring* it is the bumptious dowager, Lady Billows – the 'Lady Bracknell of opera', as her creator, Joan Cross, described her – and those who pander to her, who attract the writers' affectionate ridicule.

'His setting of words is remarkable: he transforms them in a curious way, and it's very fascinating when the words are one's own, like seeing them suddenly in colour after black-and-white,' Crozier told Evans in December. He was spot on: Britten could inflect a word or sentence in ways his librettists never even considered. Britten's gift to Crozier of the libretto to *Falstaff* was not wasted, either: Sid and Nancy are versions of the young lovers Fenton and Nannetta and they too are given music of shimmering eroticism. As in *Lucretia* there are instrumental doublings, and the dusky stillness Britten evokes between scenes in Act 2, joining bass clarinet and alto flute in a quiet, slow dance, the embrace ever tight, is a great example of his orchestral imagination, particularly with so few instruments on hand. At times the libretto sounds a touch clunky, the rhymes forced and wearisome, but Britten loved setting Crozier's everyday language (so unlike that of his previous operas) and was excited about having to find a musical equivalent. The end result is perfectly clear in its symbolism: working-class British people – around seventy-five per cent of the population at the time – are good, simple folk with natural appetites; the aristocracy is a deeply flawed institution, worthy of ridicule; and middle-class aspiration and respectability are overrated.

A large portion of these working-class appetites was sexual. A prevailing view of working-class Britain was that it was untroubled by the hypocrisy and stifling sexual etiquette of the middle classes (the aristocracy had its own separate rule book), especially before the 1967 legalization of homosexual acts. There was much truth in this – never more so than after the war, when social boundaries were left far more amorphous following the home-front events of 1939–45. Before the war, shy on their own ground, Auden and Isherwood had sought satisfaction further afield, finding complete sexual freedom among working-class youths in late 1920s and 1930s Berlin, which they communicated gleefully to Britten. So did many of their peers (and an occasional peer of the realm), finding release among the guardsmen and sailors who, in pre-Wolfenden Britain, were happy to supplement their wages any way they could – as Forster and the art historian-cum-spy Anthony Blunt could verify. It is no coincidence that so many gay writers before the war escaped their stifling conservative upbringing in the arms of working-class boys, only to eulogize their class and politics in their work. Britten was obviously not made this way; he had been prudish about Auden's pre-war sexual excesses, uncertain how he should apply the lessons to his own life when his taste remained so public school. But he was intrigued by Auden's utopian depictions of sexual freedom and socialist ideals all wrapped up in one parcel.

The question of whether Albert is gay and the opera a coming-out parable was never put to Crozier, though he died as recently as 1994. There is only the slightest hint in Maupassant that there were deeper reasons for Isidore's shyness with girls: 'Was it a mere conjecture concerning mysteries shameful and unknown, or repugnance for the degrading embraces ordained by love?' After this single sentence Maupassant left the topic well alone. Yet however much Albert is modelled on the shy, stammering Vašek in *The Bartered Bride*, it seems likely that the two characters do not share the same sexuality. There are enough nods and winks to this end: 'Girls don't care for chaps like me,' Albert bemoans in Act 1. At the end of Act 2, when Albert returns from the coronation feast – 'decently squiffy' as the Lord Chamberlain's reader put it – the opera slips from comedy into far murkier waters. In a poignant near-mad scene, echoing the full-blooded version at the end of *Peter Grimes*, Albert despairs at his fate. 'How shall I screw / My courage up to do / What must be done by everyone?' And later, home from his escapades, he tells 'Of a night that was a nightmare example / Of drunkenness, dirt, and worse . . .'

These could, of course, point to a more traditional story of liberation. (Peter Hall's celebrated 1985 Glyndebourne production had him pull from his coat a pair of women's bloomers at this point, subtle as a hammer.) Albert's near-final words in the opera underline his newfound freedom as he offers the village children peaches, the generosity of the gesture not lost on post-war audiences still smarting over what they paid for the fruit imported from France. Although it is all tantalizingly ambiguous, it is impossible to believe that Britten did not acknowledge the seed he was planting. *Herring* is the ideal comic counterpoint to *Grimes*, and social oppression threads its way through both Loxford and the Borough, neighbouring Suffolk villages. Once *Herring* reached the stage there was none of the conflation of composer and character that *Peter Grimes* generated, though Charles Stuart in the *Observer* noted in Albert 'a shyness so tormenting that opera goers of a certain sort are sure to start grubbing frantically for bits of Freud between the lines'. Freud was invoked and misunderstood in equal parts in these years, never more so than when a domineering mother was near by. Yet Stuart came closest of all contemporary commentators to identifying one of the opera's subtexts, the sexuality of its title character.

12

'We've fallen (literally) for ski-ing which we do passionately & erratically. But we work of early mornings & late nights to keep the conscience clear.' Drained by the year's labours, in January 1947 Britten escaped with Pears to the Swiss village of Zermatt, sharing the top half of a chalet with the British Council's assistant representative in Switzerland, Lionel Billows, and his future wife. Britten brought a draft libretto and composition sketch of *Herring*, which he chipped away at, with the Matterhorn as his backdrop. Several times he asked Stein for manuscript paper to be sent so he could begin scoring, filling the dark winter evenings with this untaxing, near-reflex labour. At the beginning of February they left the village for a month-long concert tour: Zurich, Winterthur, The Hague, Stockholm and Copenhagen. Crozier joined them, working on the rewrites demanded by Britten, kicking around ideas for the proposed Covent Garden commission. They eventually settled on an opera about the English Civil War, which came to nothing.

They had escaped what was, by the end of January, a freakishly cold British winter. Throughout the country pipes froze, huge snowdrifts brought cars and trains to a standstill, coal was scarce and electricity cut out without warning, and gas pressure in the cities fell to around a quarter of its normal level, reducing Hyde Park on one occasion to eerie blackness. Isherwood visited the capital for the first time since before the war and was struck by the squalor of London, the drabness of once fine restaurants, 'wallpaper hanging in tatters from the walls of the Reform Club', the miserable cold and constant reminders of mortality, and the poor occupants, with their wartime faces, lined and tired, and their covetous glances at his new overcoat. 'This is a dying city,' his friend William Plomer told him. Tennessee Williams was also in town, writing to his agent, 'I guess England is about the most unpleasant, uncomfortable and expensive place in the world you could be right now.' The poet and editor John Lehmann identified something more than physical discomfort, a 'kind of mean puritanism that the newly triumphant Labour MPs and their officials appeared to have decided was the proper wear of the day'. Were there to be no fruits of victory?

It was a time of great social shifts: besides the cold weather and ongoing food rationing there were frequent strikes; there was the piecemeal implementation of the Beveridge Report, whose architect was determined to rid Britain of its five 'Giant Evils' – Want, Disease, Ignorance, Squalor and Idleness. All of this gave the simmering class narrative more zip; was this what working-class soldiers had fought and died for?

Against this backdrop, Crozier's denials of *Herring*'s political subtext are not credible. Britten was sensitive to the grinding deprivation, despite his relative privilege. From Zermatt he wrote to his sister Barbara, imploring her to enjoy the metaphorical fruits of his ration book if things remained too bleak for her. He also sketched the boorish fellow countrymen he encountered in Alpine trains and restaurants, able to travel freely for only the second winter season since the end of the war: they were rich, snobbish and blasé to a man.

Though he wore it lightly, the concerts helped make Britten a relatively wealthy man. His gross income for 1946–7 was an astonishing £4,185,* nearly double his earnings in the previous financial year. (Rank-and-file players in the BBC Symphony Orchestra were on £15 a week – £780 per annum.) When in 1946 *Horizon* surveyed established writers on the income needed for a comfortable existence, no one came close to this figure. Orwell suggested £10 a week after tax for a married man, £6 if single. Herbert Read thought £1,000 per annum. Spender suggested that an unmarried writer living in London needed £500 or £600 per annum after tax. 'A married writer, if he makes his wife his cook, needs £700. However, if he has children, if he does not wish his wife to be a domestic slave and if he has any social life, he needs £1,000 a year or more ... Try to earn £1,000 a year or more from writing today and see what happens.'

Britten's tax deductions for the year included £30 worth of gramophone records; £25 each on publicity and on first-night expenses for *Lucretia*, £47 on concert tickets. He also listed £321 on motor-car expenses: in summer 1946 he had bought a 1929 open-top Rolls-Royce Shooting Brake (its left-hand running-board missing in a famous 1949 photograph, lending it an air of shabby gentility), which he would keep for eighteen years and which prompted Vaughan Williams's copycat acquisition. ('Well, why shouldn't I? Ben Britten's got one!')

Social unrest made him even more aware of his privileged position; he threw further support behind causes dear to him. On 18 April, the travels and crippling winter behind them, Britten and Pears performed Schubert's *Die schöne Müllerin* at Friends House, the handsome, historic Quaker headquarters in Euston, in aid of the pacifist organization War Resisters' International. They put their names to a written appeal (which reads more like Pears's work than Britten's) that is a heartfelt summary of their pacifist views. Invoking the contempt heaped on pacifists when the WRI was founded twenty-five years earlier, and incorporating a line

---

* £135,000 today.

from Roosevelt's 1941 State of the Union address (his so-called Four Freedoms speech), it identified happier, more confident times.

> Since Napoleon first cursed the world by introducing military conscription, growing numbers of young men, and lately, young women too, have refused to become the tools by which war has brought the world to its present sorry plight ... Pacifism is not a new doctrine, but it is still the most revolutionary of them all. It calls for a new social order and a world-wide patriotism. In the atomic age it has become, not an alternative to war, but the only possible way leading to a world order where there shall be no more war, but 'Freedom of Speech, Freedom of Worship, Freedom from Want, and Freedom from Fear.'

As little as two years earlier it would have been impossible to say such things out loud; two years later, however, in 1949, such thinking would be given its own sturdy platform, the First International Peace Conference in Paris, which adopted Picasso's *Dove of Peace* as its emblem. ('I have never understood how one could make it a symbol of peace,' Picasso naughtily dissembled. 'It is an extremely cruel bird.')

In the same month Ebert heard *Herring* in a play-through and declined Britten's invitation to direct it. Whether Crozier had come round to Ebert's way of thinking about the opera's social underpinning by then is unknown, but he and Britten were relieved not to be working with Christie's man, despite his distinguished pedigree (which included time as a pupil of the great modernist Max Reinhardt). Britten was still busy with the scoring and was only cursorily involved in finding Ebert's replacement – curiously, for it was a key appointment: *Herring* was the EOG's first production and comic opera is so often a director's graveyard. They brought on board Frederick Ashton, born in Guayaquil and raised in Lima but who now spoke and dressed as though from Eton, who had gained a reputation before the war as a talented choreographer (mostly at Sadler's Wells) and who had recently directed Massenet's opera *Manon* at Covent Garden, with only mixed success.

It was a remarkably progressive appointment, given Britten and Crozier's conservative taste in staging. And though it started well, with a young team collaborating on a large, unusual project (only five minutes or so shorter than *Grimes*), tensions soon developed along predictable lines. Principally, Crozier and Britten objected to the way Ashton directed it as a farce. In playing comedy, Britten later told Janet

Baker, one must not think the situation amusing oneself, since 'the characters were not in the least amusing or eccentric to themselves, which is precisely why an audience thinks them to be so'. It was a fair point, though Britten and Crozier seemed unable to communicate their reservations directly. Instead, they formed a united front with Pears against poor Ashton, whose lack of self-confidence left him ill-equipped to fend off the attack. 'Ben and his friends behaved impossibly during *Albert Herring*,' he later told Keith Grant, a successor to Elizabeth Sweeting as manager of the EOG. He could not bear their cliquishness, and distrusted the reverence and intensity that Britten expected in the rehearsal room. 'I can't stand much more of this,' he would mutter, before going out for a cigarette.

Yet Ashton pulled it off. At the dress rehearsal the audience at Glyndebourne laughed loudly in all the right places, much to the disgust of Christie, who thought them vulgar. The first performance on 20 June 1947 was a more sober affair, though the public responded warmly, demanding Britten's return to the stage for more and more curtain calls. The 'mischievous old mad-man J.C.' (Britten's label for Christie) greeted his bejewelled guests with an unhappy expression and the words, 'This isn't *our* kind of thing, you know.' It is difficult to imagine a more wonderful irony.

The critics mostly found it not much their thing either. It was a charade, a miscalculation, a trifle, second-rate. Ernest Newman returned to his theme of a year earlier: 'In Mr Britten I see a first-rate opera talent going partly to waste because of a failure to find the right libretto, a failure due in the first place, I suspect, to an insufficient perception on his part of where his real strength lies, and in the second place to a certain confusion as to what is and what is not worth doing in opera today.' Newman got himself into a hopeless tangle over the vernacular libretto, the supposed impossibility of recreating speech rhythms in music and the foolishness of trying (Janáček, then barely known in England, had most emphatically disproved this canard). Yet he was spot on about Britten's problem with his libretti. William Glock was positive, but even he suggested that perhaps the opera was too hastily written. Circumstance and Slater had put the brakes on Britten's speed when *Grimes* was being stitched together; no such mechanism was in place for either *Lucretia* or *Herring*, the librettist of each falling into line and offering no resistance to Britten's ideas. The source material for each was suggested, jumped on and turned into a full-scale opera production inside a year. This had no bearing on the quality of the music, but it did mean decisions about shape and structure were made in haste, not always to the work's advantage.

This was less of a problem in *Herring* than in *Lucretia*. Yet with some notable exceptions, critics did not understand the piece, did not find its heart and were unaware of its targets. Perhaps this is why Britten could dismiss them with a weary sweep of his hand, and why Crozier survived the mauling where Duncan had not. Diamand, spooked by the English reviews, attempted to renege on his agreement to host *Herring* in Holland, but was talked round. And when following the Glyndebourne season the company headed off to Amsterdam for performances of *Lucretia* and *Herring*, and later on to Lucerne (Britten, Pears, Crozier and Evans piling into the composer's Rolls), they encountered a different critical climate. 'Incidentally,' Britten wrote to Erwin Stein after Amsterdam, 'it's nice to have Albert taken seriously by critics!' *Herring* was even reviewed in *Le Figaro* by Frederick Goldbeck, in remarkably warm terms. 'Far from despising them, Britten adores his characters. He treats his world – old trouts and scarlet women, flirts and thoroughly bad lots, mayor, vicar and constable – like an enchanting tribe of savages who are performing an initiation rite for a young chap who is no more innocent than you or me.' Britten had created a world of tradition, innocence and parody, thought the paper – 'a game of allusions and knowing winks'. Such Continental sympathy only hardened Britten's attitude to British critics and the traditions they represented.

13

The tour was thrilling (it included a concert in the Tonhalle, Zurich, the EOG soloists singing music by Thomas Morley, Orlando Gibbons, Purcell and other early English masters) and the operas hugely successful. Moreover, the travelling party was completely relaxed. At one hotel Crozier overheard a short exchange between a chambermaid and a porter, the latter eyeing with disbelief the decrepit luggage and boxes fastened with string to the back of the Rolls. '"Eh bien? qu'est-ce qu'ils sont?" [Well, what are they?] " 'Sais pas. Peut-être des romanichels?" [Don't know. Perhaps some gypsies?]'

Crozier observed on this trip that 'there was something absurd about travelling so far to win success with British operas that Manchester, Edinburgh and London would not support'. Freight and travel costs for forty people were absurdly high; notwithstanding British Council support, the EOG estimated a loss of £3,000. Moreover, the company did not really have enough quality singers to present rotating casts in two different operas, which the tour, as structured, required. Though invitations to foreign festivals brought prestige, such touring was simply not economically viable. Thrashing such thoughts about – in the Rolls or in a café somewhere – Pears suddenly piped up, 'Why not make our own Festival? A modest Festival with a few concerts given by friends? Why not have an Aldeburgh Festival?'

It was an absurd idea. Wartime petrol rationing remained in place, as it would until 1950, the government too broke to import American oil. Old cars were left in garages; new ones could take two and a half years to be delivered. Suffolk laboured under an eccentric rail network, with a small locomotive puffing the eight and a half miles from Saxmundham into Aldeburgh only infrequently, and there were no motorways binding the county. Aldeburgh had not benefited from nineteenth-century growth as Lowestoft had. The town's theatre could not rival even Lowestoft's Sparrow's Nest: Jubilee Hall, a former roller-skating rink, was a doll's house with a tiny stage and only 300 seats. The beautiful local church was a possibility for concerts, though both chancel and sanctuary were small, and it came with a bishop who demanded there be no Sunday performances and 200 free seats for parishioners. A festival in Aldeburgh, then, would probably be an elitist affair: tickets would be in short supply; the scale of performances would be limited by budgets and venues; audiences would need to be local or own cars; and men with low regard for the folksy tastes and assumptions of other British artistic directors – and some post-war audiences – would be in charge of programming. The last point aside, an Aldeburgh Festival would be an inverse of the new Edinburgh Festival, Bing's creation, the idea for which was being talked about at Glyndebourne in its first post-war seasons. What on earth was Pears thinking?

In fact he was remarkably close in spirit to the visionary Keynes, who in July 1945 had argued Britain needed more theatres. 'And let such buildings be widely spread throughout the country. We of the Arts Council are greatly concerned to decentralise and disperse the dramatic

297

and musical and artistic life of the country, to build up provincial centres and to promote corporate life in these matters in every town and county.'

The Arts Council's £500 grant in 1948 would turn out to be the best money it ever spent, for the new Aldeburgh Festival fulfilled all the council's aspirations and then some. It also helped deflect criticism that the council was shovelling most of its funds into the new opera company at Covent Garden, strangling other ventures and possibilities. The grant appears stingy from today's perspective, but it accounted for over a fifth of the inaugural Aldeburgh Festival's income. With favours called in and artists performing for little or nothing, a black economy was fast constructed, which allowed the festival to achieve more than should have been possible from the moment the words escaped Pears's mouth.

It would also allow Britten and Pears to spend time together. As in the early months following their return from America, Pears was often away on tour, and a febrile correspondence resumed. More mundane topics crept into the letters. Courtesy of some generous, creative accounting on Hawkes's part, Britten bought a handsome new house at 4 Crabbe Street, Crag House, on the seafront in Aldeburgh, into which they moved in late August. The house now needed furnishing, which occupied Britten in his letters to Pears, underlining the couple's increased prosperity and cosy domesticity. (Britten's gross income in 1947–8 was £5,022,* up more than £800 on the previous year.) 'The walls will be white with an offness of pink,' Britten in September 1947 wrote to Pears, who was singing in a rare British performance of Mahler's *Das Lied von der Erde* at the inaugural Edinburgh Festival. 'The greatest need otherwise is lampshades ...' Pears responded in kind: he began collecting art to hang on these pinkish-white walls. A small Constable to begin with, then another; a few Sickerts over time, one a radiant red-dressed *chanteuse*; a Blake, a Cotman, a Boudin, a Spencer Gore and a Turner of dubious provenance; a couple of Pipers; two Duncan Grant male nudes, which were hung, slightly incongruously, next to a queenly photograph of Edith Britten overlooking Britten's large wooden bed; and a rather wonderful Diana Cummings canvas of thuggish boys playing football, brutal, cubist heads on their shoulders.

By the time of Britten's death the collection was impressive. Although Pears was the driving force, Britten did enjoy art, often finding himself

* £150,000 today.

spellbound by a painting or sculpture. Some of his public comments about art were simplistic or glib; in his mind art, like music, was to be experienced, not talked about. But in a March 1948 letter in response to a broadcast of Bach's *St Matthew Passion* from Amsterdam, in which Pears sang the Evangelist, there are hints of the depths of his appreciation and of the way he experienced and processed visual art. Discussing the three narrative and spiritual levels of the scourging of Christ in the *Passion*, he said that 'it reminded me strongly of the agonised marked body in the Colmar altar, & then the serene head above it'. There is nothing remotely serene in the Christ of Grünewald's Isenheim Altarpiece, yet the twisted body – with its graphic scourging marks and the bloody claw-like hands, fastened upwards with thumping great iron spikes – had left a strong impression.* This was partly because Britten looked for narrative in paintings, as he did in literature; abstract art was a murkier world to him.

Other mundane daily matters are relayed in their correspondence: progress on any particular composition (rarely illuminating), the walks, the weather, the sea, the invitations to tea where Mr Britten could meet Mrs so-&-so who's *very* musical. (The new house may have brought Britten immediate contact with his beloved, cranky North Sea, but with the proximity came the dowagers, retired colonels and admirals – their outlook anathema to the man who had boycotted the OTC at school – all serviced by an underclass of domestic workers.) The letters also show their deep musical connection and regard for each other in their separate projects, and evidence their protective love. Aware that Pears was hopelessly miscast in the gruelling Mahler, Britten dispatched encouraging messages from Aldeburgh to Edinburgh, determined to help him through the demoralizing experience. There is sympathy on behalf of the bad conductors Pears reported working with; apologies for a temper tantrum following an unsatisfying recital of *Die schöne Müllerin* together, Britten's performance anxiety increasing with the passing years ('Don't be depressed about the Schöne Müllerin. It *wasn't* bad, & I'm sorry I was so stinking to you ... But please, just because I'm a nervy, & upsetting bedfellow, don't give me up'); and special pleadings on behalf of John Ireland, with whom Pears was performing.

---

* Historically, it made a similar impression on the lepers and syphilitics cared for by the monks who commissioned it, equating their pain with Christ's.

Treat him well, Britten begged, no doubt assuaging some guilty feelings about his old teacher.

The fact remained that they were even more often apart than in initial post-war seasons, which Britten hated. While the festival was intended, in part, to balance these frequent periods of separation, it is evident that Pears simultaneously enjoyed his liberty. In the last month of Britten's life, Pears went from his lover's bedside for a concert tour of America and Canada and a week of master-classes in California, which later left him burdened with guilt and a sense of futility; by then, however, it was ingrained behaviour. But there were also concessions on his part. Pears's connection with Suffolk was negligible and his partner's new house on Crabbe Street and the nascent festival anchored him to the county in a way that caught him by a not entirely welcome surprise. Pears remained, in essence and temperament, a Londoner.

Britten's London meant concerts and visits to the dentist, auditions and endless meetings – an exterior world of 'telegrams and anger', in Margaret Schlegel's words. For Pears the capital meant galleries and exhibitions, young artists to patronize and flirt with, restaurants and friends to enjoy. So he fought against the country life Britten so loved – the quiet walks, simple food, swims several times a day during summer – and threw himself into his work. This took him far from Crag House, with its grand piano, numerous fireplaces, windows crusted with sea salt, and a study overlooking the gunmetal sea with its ferries and fishing boats, catches of sprat and herring unloaded on the hard shingles. In 1948 Britten and Pears were photographed in Aldeburgh High Street buying vegetables. Pears looks happy, relaxed and more handsome than usual. Yet in 1951 he visited Aldeburgh only six times, sometimes for a mere matter of days. At Crag House he joined in the meals and games, and played piano duets with Britten, but he returned to London with some relief.

Crozier plugged the gap as best he could and their friendship and creative partnership intensified in the late 1940s. While Pears was in Edinburgh, Crozier was in Aldeburgh, working fitfully on the libretto of *Saint Nicolas* during the day (a commission from Lancing College, Pears's old school), relaxing with Britten at night over meals and wine and informal performances of Schubert, Buxtehude and Bach preludes and fugues – a layman's crossword puzzle in essence. Britten was busy composing *Canticle I 'My Beloved is Mine'*, intended for a memorial

concert on 1 November 1947 honouring Dick Sheppard, founder of the
Peace Pledge Union. Sheppard picked up the dedication, but the new
work was essentially a love song to Purcell and Pears.

The latticework piano opening, a barcarolle in which the right hand
is nudged out of vertical alignment with the left, immediately establishes the distinctive landscape; it is the territory of Purcell's *Divine
Hymns*, five of which Britten realized in the three years before composing *Canticle I*. Then follows a coruscating vocal line: ecstatic displays of
coloratura over a thrumming harp-like accompaniment ('Ev'n so we
joined / We both became entire / No need for either to renew a suit / For
I was flax, and he was flames of fire'). Then there is a plinky child's duet
between voice and piano, and finally a reverential hymn, interrupted by
a simple line that sounds as though it is played on a viola da gamba,
before *Canticle I* culminates with Francis Quarles's words: 'That I my
best beloved's am, that he is mine.' It is simple stuff, but so perfectly
executed that those present in Central Hall, Westminster, for the premiere could hardly have missed the crackling electricity between tenor and
pianist. What polite and peculiar times were these when such a display
could go unremarked? And what a mean-spirited man Frank Howes of
The Times must have been, finding the piece's word painting a little too
obvious, before grudgingly conceding the work's cumulative power.
Britten would later have his revenge.

14

'I'm up to my eyes in work & worry,' Britten told Duncan a little after
the premiere, now busy with the new production of *Peter Grimes* at
Covent Garden. 'Really grand opera is too much of a strain – the organisation of the Garden is nil – our opera group is a rest cure compared.
Tony Guthrie has some fine ideas of production, but on the whole, I'd
rather have Eric.' Part of him was determined to identify problems at
Covent Garden similar to those he had encountered at Sadler's Wells, to
prove that such obstacles were systemic to the art form outside the
EOG. But Covent Garden was in the aftermath of a difficult birth.
Bricks without straw, thought conductor Eugene Goossens, as he
declined the offer of the music directorship. Where were the British singers
the company was so confident of finding? And if not home-grown

singers, where were the foreign performers who would undertake roles in English? There were conductors on hand – lucky émigrés mostly, who had jumped ship in time – though Karl Rankl was territorial in this area, as conductors tend to be. A string of scrappy productions defined the company's early years – including *Carmen* ('This British Carmen is all wrong' was the headline in the *Evening News*) and *Der Rosenkavalier*. This was partly a matter of taste and judgement, partly a consequence of Webster's dilatoriness and Rankl's limitations as a musician.* Britten's prejudice ('we have no English tradition of opera acting at all'), fuelled no doubt by Stein's negative reaction to the production standards in *Carmen*, was not without basis.

He pretended that he did not mind Guthrie's conception of *Peter Grimes* or Tanya Moiseiwitsch's moody designs. 'I think a piece like Grimes *can* stand a different – non-realistic production,' he told Mary Behrend unconvincingly in response to her post-first-night consolation. Yet he thought the show lame, lost his temper over and again throughout rehearsals, unable to divorce himself from his great opera, and was a miserable wreck on the November opening night. Even the weather conspired against it: a pea-souper infiltrated the theatre through the props door, enveloping the stalls in a thick, eerie fog. Critics liked what they could see, however. After a year of missteps at the new company, here was a modernist production of an English opera on the stage at Covent Garden; observers fell on it with palpable relief. 'The dear old critics follow along three or four years behind as usual – what bores they are!' Britten told Berkeley scornfully if inaccurately.

Guthrie's particular production highlights a number of aspects of post-war British theatre. In design, its shift from the cramped realism of the original to quick-sketch abstractness prefigured trends on the British stage in the 1950s and 1960s. (Production costs were slightly over £5,000 compared to £7,000 for *Carmen* and almost £12,000 for *Turandot* in the same year.) This in turn placed emphasis on the psychological strata of the opera – the aspect of this production Britten unfairly thought lacking. It was an almost inevitable conflict, as Britten ceded control of his work to others, especially in an artistic climate he continued to find

* 'Rankl, the surprise appointment as Music Director, wrought no miracles with the orchestra and many of the early performances were pedestrian,' Harewood later wrote, though in fairness he was fighting a culture of orchestral substitutes, whereby players sent along a colleague in their place if a more lucrative engagement came up.

mediocre. He would soften over time, but he always expected literal readings of a score and its stage directions. In the early 1970s he could still find fault with the Covent Garden production of *Grimes* commissioned to replace the Guthrie–Moiseiwitsch conception, complaining to John Tooley that a curtain should have been lowered between scenes as stipulated in the score.

Colin Graham, nineteen years Britten's junior and a product of Stowe and the Royal Academy of Dramatic Art, who directed his first new Britten opera in 1958 (*Noye's Fludde*) and his last in 1973 (*Death in Venice*), thought this was nothing personal – or perhaps nothing analytical. 'Ben often said to me he knew it was a fault on his side but ... if he'd liked people or the production in the first production, he could never stand variations on that subsequently.' It was a wholly emotional response. He liked some of Guthrie's ideas for *Grimes* and nodded assent when both director and designer came to talk to him later about the production scheduled for the Metropolitan Opera in February 1948, but he never got Guthrie's measure. They worked together on *The Beggar's Opera* the following year, during which Guthrie antagonized Pears, who played the role of the highwayman Macheath in a full-bottomed Louis XIV wig. 'You look as if you're doing Stainer's *Crucifixion* on skates at Scunthorpe,' Guthrie at one point bellowed, later telling Britten that only a 'real man' could play the role. Britten took umbrage on Pears's behalf – and that was it for Guthrie. How strange that Britten, with his strong dramatic instincts, had no feeling that he was working with a great innovator of twentieth-century British theatre.

It was partly because he felt so comfortable working with John Piper, whose watery, often beautiful backdrops came to define the EOG's aesthetic; director was far less important than designer, Britten thought. Piper had designed and painted the sets for Spender's *Trial of a Judge* in March 1938, which Britten saw twice. Post-*Grimes*, with Kenneth Green dropped from Britten's life and imagination, Piper was enlisted to design *Lucretia*. He was thereafter responsible for all Britten's major stage works, the composer enjoying his easy friendship and collaboration. Little got between Britten and this former war artist – with his long face, sunken cheeks and sad eyes – probably because each admired the other's work. There was an occasional point of friction: Britten needed to have clear in his head how a production would look before he could compose the music, while Piper thought it impossible for him to design an opera before he heard how it sounded. It was a conflict they never resolved – Piper usually gave in, and worked from a draft libretto – yet it left their friendship intact.

'We don't want realism or naturalism,' Britten told Piper unconvincingly when he took on *Lucretia*, without offering any suggestion for what might be put in its place. Piper's wife Myfanwy was later asked whether Britten had a strong sense of how each opera should look. 'Well yes, in a way, but he trusted the person he chose to do it.' He was fussy about where singers would be and how long it would take to get from one position to the next, and whether the set included a porch or a door; otherwise, he had his hands full completing each new work. He liked Piper's modern aesthetic ('Whatever he touches has magic'), thinking it a better match for his own than Green's naturalistic designs for *Grimes*, but otherwise did not have much to say.*

Thus it was Piper who in 1946 at Glyndebourne put the adolescent, boastful soldiers at the beginning of *Lucretia* in front of a moody green-blue sky, dotted with rich crimson tents, a daub of yellow in one to indicate a roaring fire. And it was Piper who spent days thinking about the opera's last-minute Christian additions, before remembering the windows of the thirteenth- and fourteenth-century English churches he so loved, and borrowing their colours for his backdrop. He had to approve any props: a vegetable basket or a sack of grain had to be designed and painted, not just bought in a junk shop and thrown on the stage. Yet because the productions all happened at such speed, the operas sometimes ended up occupying a no man's land between the high stylization of La Compagnie des Quinze and 1920s West End stagings of English drawing-room comedy.

Piper saw the stage as his own huge canvas, which literally it was. There were downsides to this approach: the backdrops may have hinted at depth and perspective, may have suggested a whispery, watercolour atmosphere, but against them the singers could look as though they were pasted in, beautiful stickers in a children's picture book.† Guthrie

---

* Britten occasionally reacted to specific aspects of a design. He insisted that the Governess in *The Turn of the Screw* arrive at Bly by coach, for instance, to which Piper argued that a 'coach would be realistic in manner, foreign to everything else, foreign to the evocative and atmospheric sense of the scenery'. Britten fought back, before finally conceding that the coach was evident in the lurching music he composed for the scene, and let the matter drop.
† Piper conceded this when he wrote of a scene in *Lucretia*, describing the set as 'in essence pictorial or architectural rather than theatrical, and it throws a heavy burden on the

aside, the *Regietheater* revolution was still many years away; just now the job of an opera director was to move singers on and off the stage as though playing chess, working around the set provided by designers, painting the characterization with a broad brush. For these reasons, Piper's 1951 set for *Billy Budd* was much more successful. The ghostly, unpainted wood of the Main Deck formed a brilliant contrast to the pitch-black backdrop, while Between Decks looked like the bleached skeleton of a whale, a spinal column linking a mass of ribs. This was director Basil Coleman's idea: he wanted to emphasize the link between Melville and the opera he had inspired.

Britten's approach to design evolved over time, particularly as production standards improved in Britain, at Covent Garden in particular. When *Budd* was revised and revived in the 1960s, Britten was adamant that the set should somehow be made less realistic, a reflection perhaps of Crozier's canny line about the ship being an image of the world, not a mere vessel. Such thinking finds its resonance in the great productions of the opera today, in which the rigging and the masts, the sails and cannon, are often done away with and the psychology and psychoses of the piece made more prominent as a result. Piper also evolved. His 1954 designs for *The Turn of the Screw* were far more abstract than anything he had done before, and thereby more theatrical. For *A Midsummer Night's Dream* (1960) he junked the green leaves and tree trunks he had grown up with, steered clear of Max Reinhardt's dewy 1936 visions (with 'birds and beasts, waterfalls and rivulets' and 'little piccaninnies', as a Warner Bros. featurette put it at the time), and plumped instead for 'shades of diluted Chinese ink, with sometimes additions of Chinese white, making tones of silver grey'. And *Death in Venice* (1973) was far more of a visual montage than Britten's early operas, one scene melting into the next, as though put together in a film studio editing suite.

In 1947 Britten's objection to Moiseiwitsch's designs for Covent Garden were that they were at odds with the piece and period: 'of all my operas it's the most realistic', he later told Coleman. Moiseiwitsch thought Britten clung uncommonly tightly to this idea of naturalism in *Grimes*, despite what he said to Behrend at the time, and she was right.

---

producer if he is to make the scenes played in front of these arcades "work" in an interesting and lively way'.

She thought Britten viewed the Borough as a 'cosy' environment – 'friendly until it became savage, and somehow we'd got to get the whole of the village on to the set; and Guthrie took a much bigger, bolder, broader – I think monumental – view of the opera which has since proved over the years to be the right one'. This was not wholly the case, since Britten was attuned to the work's wider metaphors. But Moiseiwitsch's characterization of the composer's personality and theatrical sense is accurate. Only a year after this *Grimes* he would object to all the sheets and laundry hanging everywhere on her set for *The Beggar's Opera*, blind to the marvellous, claustrophobic effect it produced.

In these early years Britten seemed knitted to staging that was at once adventurous *and* conservative. This was Piper's approach too. Piper was what cultural and literary historian Alexandra Harris has termed an English Romantic Modern, an artist able to combine his interest in modernist ideas with his fascination for rural settings and (ecclesiastical) architecture. Perhaps Rural Modern is a better term, since it contradicts modernism's claim to being a solely metropolitan phenomenon. More, it would allow Piper his post-abstract works as well as his flint cottage in the countryside, with neither water nor electricity.

There were plenty in this particular country club – Waugh, Woolf, Forster, the Sitwells, Betjeman and Britten among them; even the London-based Eliot was an honorary member. What they managed to do in their work was translate modern, urban ideas into rural settings, exploiting the tension between the two for narrative gain. In Britten's output, such tension fuels the oppression in *Grimes* and the hypocrisy in *Albert Herring*. Modernist gestures are there in the countryside folk-song arrangements, *Spring Symphony*, the eerie, downcast world of *Winter Words* and in the guttural climax of *Billy Budd*. Even *War Requiem* manages to bog down pastoral poetic traditions in the muddy trenches of the Western Front, knocking the stuffing out of every one of these traditions with each rifle shot and glassy-eyed soldier's corpse.

Britten may have been sensitive to the poor training in stagecraft of young opera singers in the conservatoriums, and he pledged the EOG's support to Cross in 1948 as she founded the National Opera School. But for all such progressive inclinations, he still wanted his works to *look* simple: he despaired that his operas' musical economy was rarely matched by visual economy. His works had to speak for themselves. Piper was all for this, as were Crozier and the directors who succeeded him; yet this philosophy, instead of heightening the theatrical experience, often deadened it – whether the static *Lucretia* (Piper), the scrappy *Dido and Aeneas* (Sophie Fedorovitch) or the picture-book *Let's Make an Opera* (John Lewis).* There could be something almost wilfully untheatrical about the productions. 'When I hear the words "good theatre" I feel for my revolver,' commented Piper in 1948, suspicious of those cunning sorcerers who held their audiences' attention with what he thought were nothing more than cheap theatrical tricks.

'They were innovatory things, those operas of his,' Piper later said of the Britten premieres, 'and I hope that my scenery was innovatory along with that.' While this is true, Moiseiwitsch was more prescient of the changes that would take place on the British stage in the coming decades. Britten's crippling 'fear of people he didn't know' (Myfanwy's description) meant he collaborated with those who made him feel safe and did not challenge him socially or intellectually. As a musician he rarely put a foot wrong. But as a man of the theatre, he was governed by his fear of the unknown, fear of anything outside his imagination or comprehension. His collaborators were either similarly minded or tiptoed around this fear gingerly.

What Britten would make of today's productions is easy to imagine. 'I saw the ugliest opera ever in Frankfurt the other night,' he wrote to Myfanwy in January 1954, 'with a revolving stage, which wouldn't or couldn't keep still! Don't let's have any of that – –!!' It was much like Dent's warning in 1946 of what Britten would encounter on the Continent in new productions of *Peter Grimes*. 'The first idea of a German producer is to upset the entire scheme of production and do something entirely different. Things may have changed in the last ten years, but I doubt it, and you will probably find Zurich and Basel obsessed by the German styles of ten or fifteen years ago.' If pushed, Britten would have generalized the distinction between the production styles as Crozier and Graham versus Guthrie and Moiseiwitsch. In many ways, however, the great productions today – with their revolving stages and so-called ugly

---

* Piper himself was critical of the last two. 'Sophie F. is the answer to the producer's prayer,' he told Britten when the birth of his son meant he could not undertake the design, 'but it is no use pretending that she is a feast for the eye, as a rule … The children's opera didn't look good enough, and I think could have looked better *at the same cost* … I think it of real importance that future works you have a hand in should look fine, and out-of-the-way, if you know what I mean. Sophie is *in*-the-way, if anyone ever was.'

theatrical ideas – are more in tune with the ambiguity, complexity and modernist magic of his operas than were most of the original shows. Too often the first productions were hostage to their times, the haste with which they were assembled, the scant money at hand, the internal squabbling in the companies, a culture unused to the art form, the monolingual stage language of those involved, and the subtle yet simultaneously unadventurous visual aesthetics of their creators.

15

'The Covent Garden Grimes was a grave disappointment,' Britten wrote to Henry Boys in November 1947. 'Only the great art of Joan & Peter, some moving conducting by Reggie, & some fine conceptions of movement from Guthrie saved it from complete mediocrity.' The public embraced it, however. Covent Garden scheduled a remarkable fourteen performances in the 1947–8 season, which played to houses averaging two-thirds full. In all it was seen by a paying audience of 18,606 – close to the total audience figures for the ten performances each of *Tristan und Isolde* (with Kirsten Flagstad) and *La traviata* (with Elisabeth Schwarzkopf). The EOG's short season at Covent Garden in October (three performances of *Lucretia*, seven of *Herring* in its first London outing) was less successful, with houses averaging a touch over half full. When Britten wrote to Behrend about the lamentable set-up at Covent Garden, he asked rhetorically if it must be this way in any big house. 'But anyhow it more than confirms my feelings that the small opera is the thing – in spite of the nice noises one can make with an orchestra of 85 & chorus of 60!' He would many times be left wondering if British audiences on the whole preferred the nice noises of a large ensemble.

Britten was much in the air in the late 1940s – literally so in the case of a quick-fire series of BBC broadcasts with Pears. And a marvellous, eclectic repertory the concerts and broadcasts presented: Bridge, Purcell, Schubert, Berkeley, Schütz, Buxtehude, Monteverdi, Handel and songs and realizations by Britten himself. There was Mahler as well, including 'Der Tamboursg'sell', the splendid, sorry tale of a wretched drummer-boy, sentenced for desertion, trudging his way to the gallows to the beat of a solitary field drum. (Britten would emulate this miniature four years later, on a grand scale, in the final scene of *Billy Budd*.)

Grumblings within the BBC that Britten was over-represented in the schedule had no effect; the complaints would arise again from time to time, yet in the space of only a few years Britten had been transformed from a pacifist outsider to a central figure in contemporary British culture. The BBC was hardly likely to ignore this, regardless of the petty jealousies governing areas of the bureaucracy and Britten's own suspicions about the corporation; they were ideal bedfellows.

The same would eventually be said of Britten and the commercial recording industry, though only after a series of fits and starts. Much later he would observe, 'Anyone, anywhere, at any time, can listen to the B minor Mass upon one condition only – that they possess a machine. No qualification is required of any sort – faith, virtue, education, experience, age. Music is now free for all.' The gramophone had shaped his adolescence, had broadened his education and outlook, and fuelled his certainty that there was a world of music far removed from the mediocre performances he experienced in England in the 1920s and 1930s. It had served its purpose at a time when opportunities to hear really fine concerts were thin on the ground, and his characterization of recording was therefore unfair.

Recording companies came and went, every bit as transitory as Waugh's great comic creation, The Wonderfilm Company of Great Britain. The young pup Decca, criticized for its 'rackety, harsh, and overamplified' recordings in the mid-1930s, invested in new technology and adopted a more innovative approach to artists and repertory than its bigger, more established rivals (though early Britten recordings on the label infuriated the composer). The technology leaped ahead during wartime; wax discs gave way to magnetic tape and the era of the long-playing record was just around the corner, soon followed by stereo reproduction, which is when Britten would come into his own as a recording artist. HMV and Decca squabbled over their 'exclusive artist' in the late 1940s, each pressing its credentials. (Decca would eventually win.) 'Benjamin Britten has only to blow his nose and they record it!' a 'disgruntled elderly composer' (Vaughan Williams?) complained to critic Stephen Williams, who published the remark in September 1947. More accurate was the assessment of another (anonymous) critic. 'Britten is also a cult. He is indisputably the Golden Boy of contemporary music, immensely successful and immensely fashionable. His success is due to two causes: exceptional gifts and exceptional opportunities for putting them over.'

Yet he was creating many of the opportunities himself: rural tours; the performance and compositional style that slipped effortlessly into European concert halls and opera houses; programming ideas brimming with originality and vitality. It was churlish to suggest opportunity just landed in his lap, though of course it often did. Radio and gramophone were welcome additional ways of familiarizing new audiences with the strange, intoxicating sounds of *Lucretia*, *The Holy Sonnets of John Donne*, *Michelangelo Sonnets*, *Serenade*, his folk-song arrangements and other works besides. This was the medium through which many people came to know Britten's music well – including Pears's uncle, who reprimanded the two for the morally questionable content of 'The Foggy, Foggy Dew', with its tale of the weaver lad who beds a fine maiden out of wedlock. It was mild compared to the reality of his nephew's relationship, but his intervention indicates how far from Britten's coterie his music had now reached.

16

With *Messiah* season upon them once more, Britten loped off with Crozier for a break in Dublin, loving the easy supply of goods and food still rationed or expensive in England, but distressed by the poverty – urchins hawking bunches of violets on the streets, dirty workers dressed in rags, the huge disparity between rich and poor. He retreated into happier territory – the nocturnal songs he was then conceiving for Nancy Evans, rootling through second-hand bookshops as he had in California with such conspicuous success, this time on the prowl for the poems that would make up *A Charm of Lullabies*. The cycle, with its easygoing allure, crafted for Evans's chocolatey voice, was almost a deliberate riposte to the modernist or metaphysical poets that had occupied his imagination since first meeting Auden more than ten years earlier. He composed it quickly and dispatched it to Evans on 17 December 1947, a mere two weeks before its premiere in The Hague.

Christmas was a happy affair in Aldeburgh, with the Steins decamping from London. Britten played host, making Crag House warm and welcoming. He produced a whole tub of butter as a seasonal treat, which the guests giddily devoured; it was a present from Duncan, a reminder of past friendship and an implicit plea for future collaboration.

(This was probably the same Christmas Slater sent Britten an antique map of Suffolk.) Britten remained friendly with Duncan, which was not true of Slater; there was no friendship left there. Both writers belonged to his past – a past in which, Britten later admitted, his own lack of stage experience had led to some bad mistakes in his early dramatic works. He had revised his way out of a few of these in *Lucretia* earlier in the year, but nothing would entice him to return to the plodding, frustrating Slater, despite how well the collaboration had served him.

Duncan's present was a reminder of the dispiriting experience cooking and eating remained in Britain after the war. Apricots, olives and butter, rice and lemons, oil and almonds: 'I came to realize that in the England of 1947, those were dirty words that I was putting down,' Elizabeth David later said. Britten, David's senior by one month, was unaffected by the food writer's clarion call in the 1950s and the slow-burn revolution in British cuisine. He remained trapped in the world of rationing and inter-war food, a world of mutton and braised oxtail, jugged peas and Floating Island. When asked in 1971 to contribute their favourite recipes to a cookbook celebrating famous musicians, Britten and Pears submitted Miss Hudson's Soup as a starter – the bone of a good English sirloin, simmered for three hours with plenty of onions, celery and carrots, the dish named after their Mrs Tiggy-Winkle housekeeper from 1948 to 1973 – followed by Soles Red House ('go down to the beach first thing in the morning and buy your soles. The fishermen will clean them for you on the beach'). The main was to be served with new potatoes and small peas – accompanied by Wine Society Chablis – and followed by Dark Treacle Jelly and biscuits with blue Cheshire cheese. The spread looks a little plain next to pianist Claudio Arrau's ornate Lobster Bisque.

Post-Christmas, Britten began work in earnest on the Lancing commission – the college's imposing Gothic Revival chapel, dedicated to St Mary and St Nicolas, informing both the archaic spelling of the protagonist's name and some of the acoustic effects weaved into the score. Though a cantata, not an opera, and lasting fifty minutes, not two-and-a-half hours, *Saint Nicolas* is as dramatic as *Herring* and taxed Crozier accordingly. He struggled to find a shape for it, yet ended up constructing a taut cradle-to-grave narrative, with gentler, subtler language than he used in *Herring*. Britten responded with delight. At first he found it difficult to conceptualize: the piece was to be sung mostly by students, and the mixture of subtlety and simplicity foxed him. 'Yes, writing's all most exciting & interesting,' he told Pears as he composed the first notes, 'but it doesn't get any easier.'

Nicolas was another of Britten's superhero saints. He appears first as an adult, looking back on his life – much as Captain Vere would do three years later in *Billy Budd* (another Crozier collaboration). And then suddenly he is a boy, his passage from boyhood to adult marked by the tenor soloist taking over a single treble phrase, 'GOD BE GLORI- FIED' ('To be sung by the youngest boy in the choir', the score stipulates), that has six times punctuated the story of his birth and which is now bellowed out, an octave lower, with great effect. When Nicolas is chosen as Bishop of Myra, the choir and congregation sing a rousing arrange- ment of the hymn 'All People that on Earth do Dwell', a few years before Vaughan Williams's showy arrangement of the hymn for the coronation of Queen Elizabeth. This, too, is a thrilling moment, inspired by the Netherlands performances of *St Matthew Passion* where the congrega- tion performed the chorales. Nicolas calms the sea; he brings back to life the three boys pickled by the barbaric if entrepreneurial village butcher; he feeds starving multitudes from a single sack of corn, no fish to hand; he does good deeds and takes on Constantine the Great, who does not; and finally he goes to his death with great dignity and a Nunc Dimittis. There are some historical jolts: the 'Old 100th' hymn tune dates from the mid-sixteenth century and the Nunc Dimittis is the version from the 1662 Book of Common Prayer – quite some centuries after Nicolas lived. And there is the odd musical jolt: the words 'Serve the Faith and spurn His enemies!' sung at Nicolas's enthronement are set as a cum- brous fugue. For all these niggles, Britten was captivated by the story, writing the piece in about three weeks, forswearing further commissions 'for 20 years (or thereabouts)'. Lancing graciously allowed the cantata an out-of-town try-out in the June 1948 inaugural Aldeburgh Festival, but a month later the work's joyous sounds filled the school's splendid sandstone chapel, Pears awash with schoolboy memories.

17

In late January 1948 Britten and Pears embarked on one of their light- ning Continental tours: five weeks in Switzerland, northern Italy and the Netherlands. Germany still did not feature on their itinerary, though this was more to do with contacts than anything more sinister. Pears could write to Britten at this time of 'that old Nazi Mengelberg', but only because he was in Amsterdam working with Dutchman Eduard van Beinum, who survived German occupation with far less of a taint than his co-principal conductor Willem Mengelberg; this was Pears's oblique, very English comment on the situation. Britten was distressed and moved to find Europe so sad and worried, so slow in its recovery, even some distance from the Reich's ruined epicentre.

The trip caught him in a curious mood. He was overworked and snippy, finding himself apologizing to Pears and other friends. 'Deep down in my much scarred conscience I'm aware of having behaved like a beast,' he told Walter Hussey in March, 'firstly for having been stupidly touchy, & then out of sheer slackness not doing anything to prevent that impression from growing.' The touchiness was no worse than usual, but his refusal to conciliate with anyone other than Pears was new. He was also resentful of composing pieces to strict deadlines ('e.g. every piece I've written in the last four years!'), craving time and space to think quietly about the works he would like to pour from his pen (not least a Requiem for Gandhi, whose assassination on 30 January upset him hugely) and about music in general. 'If *only* I had time to go back over the past work and correct or alter as I want to do,' he later told Beth, 'but always people are waiting to rehearse, and it is not fair to keep them waiting.'

Amid such anxiety Britten pulled out of a planned tour of America in late 1948. It was not solely that he was overworked: he had heard bad things about the Metropolitan Opera production of *Peter Grimes* in February, conducted by Emil Cooper, and disliked how he was characterized in the *Time* article celebrating it (not least the assertion that he never answered letters, an affront to this most assiduous correspondent). Olin Downes's dismissive, condescending notice in the *New York Times* topped it off. ('So the opera, for us, is only the façade of an opera. The choruses are oratorio choruses, not operatic.') He once more identified the vital distinction between the openness of Continental thought and the narrowness and lack of generosity in England and America. 'It is fantastic how much separated general American & European artistic (if not otherwise as well) ideas are today,' he told Hawkes from Amsterdam. 'The enormous sympathy one feels for one's ideas on the continent, even compared with England, is most moving.' Almost as an afterthought, echoing a similar assertion to Hawkes some years earlier, Britten added, 'I am conceited enough to believe that it will come round in the end!'

There were contradictions in Britten's desire for space and time to think: simultaneously he relished the onerous responsibilities of the EOG and the nascent Aldeburgh Festival. He did budgets in his head, calculating income and expenditure with impressive speed; he suggested repertory in an imaginative and utilitarian manner, determined that festival musicians should perform in numerous guises; he negotiated exclusivity deals and calculated insurance premiums mid-letter; he thought up commissions and talked up the festival in the foreign press; and on the overheated trains between Milan and Zurich he worked some more on *The Beggar's Opera*, which would need to be completed quickly on his return.

Like Hawkes, Boosey was aghast at Britten's responsibilities, telling Anne Wood, Pears's old friend and now general manager of the EOG, that he would not be at all upset if the group collapsed since it would allow Britten more time to compose. Crozier passed on the treacherous message to Britten with some embarrassment and anger; surprisingly, he took it in his stride. He liked the busy schedule, and Boosey would have to accept whatever volume of work he produced.

It was not sustainable, however, and in cancelling the American tour Britten was almost foreshadowing the collapse he would suffer at the end of 1948 – or at least scheduling time in which to have it. Perhaps even he knew early in the year that the pace at which he worked could not ultimately be maintained, even if the year continued with the same frenzy of composing, performing and producing.

The Beggar's Opera is infected with this frenzy. As usual he left himself little time to work: ten weeks separated his return from the Continent and the premiere. Much of the groundwork, however, had already been done some centuries earlier. English poet and dramatist John Gay had pilfered widely for his bawdy 1728 opera, choosing popular songs and ballads from England, Ireland, Scotland and France for the bulk of the piece, lifting other tunes from major and minor composers of the seventeenth and eighteenth centuries. Yet they still needed arranging. Britten worked from a 1923 edition of Gay's opera, as sparse as an old hymnal, scribbling in the margins his ideas for adapting the tunes, some of which were no longer than half a minute in duration. Attracted to their wide leaps, peculiar modes and severe mood, Britten treated each as if it were a stand-alone folk song, not worrying about trying to recreate an eighteenth-century sound in the chamber orchestra. He conjured canons from these simple melodies; or a martial chorus, punctuated by brilliant hunting-horn calls; or a folk-fiddle accompaniment, full of scratching bows and open strings; or an ensemble magicked from one of Gay's solos. 'I feel that most recent arrangements have avoided their toughness and strangeness, and have concentrated only on their lyrical prettiness,' he wrote, and acted on his convictions. He egged himself on to more daring and provocative accompaniments, giggling as he went.

A 1951 BBC internal memo from the composer Herbert Murrill, head of music, says much about Britten's realization of the opera, and even more about the BBC and audience tastes at the time. 'I believe it would be right to suggest that the Beggar's Opera would be more acceptable to Light and Home listeners in Austin's or Dent's edition and that the vastly more debatable Britten realisation be given on Third.' This was the BBC at its pernickety worst, acting like a Victorian museum curator deciding where to put the exhibits without causing offence to those lining up to view them. Britten had to put up with this sniping, particularly from the generation of composers that had gone through the London colleges with little to show for their efforts and had gravitated towards the BBC in the 1920s and 1930s. (It was Murrill who, in 1949, would complain that Britten's music was over-represented in the Third Programme's schedule.) Britten and Dent exchanged polite letters at the time – their respective realizations of Gay's opera being produced simultaneously – though there is no doubt that the younger composer lumped the older one in with those frustrated administrators, organists and academics, however unfairly.

Guthrie was an ideal collaborator if only Britten would realize it, this brilliant man who looked like a retired squadron leader but who possessed a great mind and finely tuned social conscience; he was determined to emphasize the beggarly existence 'of people made reckless, even desperate by poverty, but in whose despair there is none the less a vitality and gaiety that the art of elegant and fashionable people too often misses'. There is a touch of *Peter Grimes* in this description, though both composer and director saw more inherent nobility in the villainous underclass peopling this new opera than Britten had ever found among the villagers of the Borough.

Perhaps this aspect of the performance alienated those audiences for whom the famous and successful 1920s Frederic Austin production – full of diatonic chords and wigs and wide-cuffed sleeves – was a happy memory. To others, Britten's score was at fault. 'It would be an ingenious literary experiment no doubt to rewrite "Baa Baa Black Sheep" in the style of T. S. Eliot,' wrote the critic of the *Evening News*, 'but one suspects that some of the simple charm of the original would be lost.' Other critics were more admiring (including Edward Sackville-West, who, like Guthrie, made a mischievous swipe at Pears's sexuality by commenting on his 'natural unsuitability to the part of Macheath'), but it held little sway with the opera-going public. '*Where* are those lovely *tunes*?' Moiseiwitsch recalled audiences moaning as they emerged from the theatre. 'The tunes were there, but Ben had done magical things with them and it was so savage and cruel and marvellous. Guthrie and I had a field day.' Moiseiwitsch was spot on; there *is* something savage and cruel and marvellous about Britten's realization, which is hardly played today. Even Pears felt ambivalent about the piece, and two years later a new version was mounted, rescored for a virile baritone Macheath, sung by Bruce Boyce.

The EOG had hoped for some of Austin's stardust and commercial success to visit its own enterprise (it remained in a parlous financial position), but was sorely disappointed. Crozier and Britten had strong-armed Boosey into donating the firm's share of royalties, and had earlier negotiated the sale of rights for a film that never made it beyond development. Even so, the EOG finished the first week of *The Beggar's Opera* with an overdraft of £8,000. Notwithstanding the company's tiny administration, the opera's small casts and production budgets (a total of £5,400 in 1948), they had not yet made a success of their model of chamber opera. The continuing financial pressure would have immediate and far-reaching repercussions for the EOG's leading figure.

18

They were on much surer ground with the other bold experiment of 1948: the inaugural Aldeburgh Festival, held from 5 to 13 June, advertised in a smart, red and black brochure that cost 1d. and was distributed throughout local towns. A description of Aldeburgh in an 1844 gazetteer held good a hundred years later: it was a 'sea-port, fishing town, and delightful bathing place, pleasantly situated on the site of a picturesque acclivity, rising boldly from the German Ocean'. Forster was less polite about it in the *Listener* article on the poet Crabbe that set in train such wondrous events. 'It is a bleak little place: not beautiful. It huddles round a flint-towered church and sprawls down to the North Sea – and what a wallop the sea makes as it pounds at the shingle! Near by is a quay, at the side of an estuary, and here the scenery becomes melancholy and flat; expanses of mud, saltish commons, the marsh-birds crying.' These sounds, this melancholy, infused Crabbe's poetry, and more than 130 years later they had a similar impact on Britten's music.

The sea exerted a hypnotic influence on Britten – far more so than on any other twentieth-century composer – and had done since childhood. It was partly a consequence of growing up directly overlooking the North Sea, hostage to its moods and temper which he depicted so deftly in the *Four Sea Interludes* from *Peter Grimes*. And partly he was transfixed by its rhythm, its percussive beat punctuating his walks on the shingle beach as he set about solving that day's problem. Though it returned time and again as a setting in his music, from *Peter Grimes* to *The Golden Vanity*, he was interested equally in its metaphors – a consequence of all the nineteenth-century poetry he had read as a boy and of Auden's thoughts in the 1930s and 1940s on the imagery and meaning of the sea. Slowly, also, as the religious certainty of his childhood slipped away, he clung to it as proof of a numinous force of nature, as inexplicable but as powerful as God.

The festival founders were hoping that this same sea and the austere characteristics described by Forster somehow worked in the town's favour. Then, as now, it swelled in summer, filling up with golfers and sailors, but no one knew whether it could cater for a new, arty-not-hearty crowd, one enjoying urban pursuits in a rural area. 'There were several difficulties at first,' recalled the festival's first chairman, Lady Cranbrook, an Aldeburgh resident, with classic aristocratic understatement. 'There was pacifism, *God Save the King*, and applause in church.' They dealt with each as best they could, but still the air dripped with antagonism towards the 'long-haired types' pushing the new venture, threatening the town's summer character – a comic and not very convincing counterpoint to Britten's conservative, dapper appearance and the Rolls occasionally parked by the church. The parish vicar was unpredictable, not beneath preaching fire-and-brimstone sermons against homosexuality, to the obvious shock of Britten's friends and supporters. In an effort to further hostilities, he relied on those whom Cranbrook, with a Mitfordian flourish, referred to as Aldeburgh's 'antibodies' to spread gossip and malice in equal measure.

Facilities were primitive. Eminent artists changed costumes in cottages close to Jubilee Hall, legging it to the wings just in time. The hall's tight fit left the harp with nowhere to go but the edge of the stage, disguised as best it could be, while the timpani were muted with colourful eiderdowns. Later, when an orchestra pit was excavated, water seeped into the hall during floods or high tide. And if maroons sounded during a performance – as they did in this first festival – 'floaters' abandoned their posts backstage as scenery shifters to launch the town's lifeboat. Despite all this, from humble origins there grew what Cross later called Bayreuth in England.

In this first year there were lectures by Sir Kenneth Clark on Constable and Gainsborough; Tyrone Guthrie on contemporary theatre; the Arts Council's Steuart Wilson on the future of music in England; William Plomer on Suffolk writer Edward Fitzgerald (an exotic bird with clipped wings); and Forster on Crabbe and *Peter Grimes* – and what a different work it would have been had he written the libretto. 'I should certainly have starred the murdered apprentices. I should have introduced their ghosts in the last scene, rising out of the estuary, on either side of the vengeful greybeard, blood and fire would have been thrown in the tenor's face, hell would have opened, and on a mixture of *Don Juan* and the *Freischütz* I should have lowered my final curtain.' There was an exhibition of works by Constable, lent from the collection of Dr H. A. C. Gregory, the fruits of considerable passion and cattle money. Three showings of *Herring* were shoehorned into Jubilee Hall, while the purloined performance of *Saint Nicolas* took place in Aldeburgh Church and was repeated a week later. ('The church seemed alive,' Forster said of the performance he attended.) There was a concert by the Zorian Quartet, which included Tippett's restless Quartet No. 2 and Bridge's *Phantasie* quartet, with Britten at the piano, paying his dues. And there was a recital by that most musical of pianists Noel Mewton-Wood, stepping in for an indisposed Clifford Curzon, elevating Britten's ropey old piano stool to the required height by putting hard-bound music scores to good use. There was also an appearance by Britten and Pears, declaring love and comradeship in a performance of *Canticle I*. When they stepped out into the chancel of the parish church, their suits and demeanours sombre, they established a precedent that would characterize (and subsidize) the festival for the next twenty-five years.* As Cross put it, 'the great quality, the great core of the whole of the Aldeburgh Festival was Ben himself.'

National critics were not invited, which caused some resentment and a change in policy in the festival's second year. Britten kept an open house throughout the nine-day event, which, as time went on, was overseen by Barbara, who had to absorb or deflect her brother's impatience and tantrums. Britten extended his hospitality to music critics once they began attending, though he had one rule: 'You must never, but never, let Frank Howes come in,' he told Sweeting, having kept score for some years.

The festival's first president was George Lascelles, 7th Earl of Harewood and cousin of princesses Elizabeth and Margaret, who lent his blue-blood name to the letterhead. Britten and Harewood had first met during the interval of a Sadler's Wells performance in 1943 and the earl subsequently attended the premiere of *Grimes*. He sat in Christie's box at an early performance of *Lucretia*, no doubt heeding J.C.'s warning not to be shocked at some of the strong language. ('Of course, that *is* how soldiers talk,' Christie explained to this ex-POW.) He was cultured and knowledgeable, as was to be expected of a future director of Covent Garden, the Edinburgh and Leeds festivals and English National Opera, and was amassing what would become an important collection of commercial and private recordings. He founded *Opera* magazine in 1950 and would prepare four editions of *Kobbé*, the opera bible. He married Marion Stein in September 1949, after she had sought Britten's advice on whether a commoner could hope to sustain such a relationship in English society. Harewood remained a close friend of Britten's for slightly longer than the marriage survived.

In the programme book – itself a work of simple elegance and artistry, edited by Crozier, which patrons picked up for 5s. – Harewood wrote of creating a festival that belonged to the local community 'in the sense that Mozart did to Salzburg'. Bayreuth, Salzburg . . . It was a very English disease, this determination to rationalize an artistic venture in terms of Continental precedents. (Harewood was sufficiently aware of it to warn against 'the emptiness of the imitative', however.) Though this was never Britten's conception of things in the post-war expansionist, acquisitive culture, new British festivals looked to old models for ideas, inspiration

* In 1948 the recital's surplus was £172.

and acts. Not Britten. 'It is not a festival for propagating one's own works,' he told Harewood in 1960; 'this is not a festival like Bayreuth, which is obviously designed for Wagner's own works.' No one quite knew it in 1948, but the Aldeburgh Festival would make a virtue out of generating sublime, unrepeatable performances from within its small family of artists, programming repertory from four centuries, much of it unfamiliar to concert-goers. Salzburg and Bayreuth had long ceased to be able to make such boasts, while Edinburgh, determined to show it was truly international, could not have been less interested in the Aldeburgh model – a modest festival, with its few concerts given by friends.

The irony, of course, is that the Aldeburgh Festival was parochial by definition, the description Britten disparagingly threw at just about every other British musical venture. But the festival defied the conventional meaning of the word since its founders and their friends were such extraordinary talents. Despite Britten's protestations to Harewood about not propagating his own music, he increasingly wrote for the small community of performers and patrons whom Harewood in 1948 hoped 'may feel that the hosts have at least not hired the entertainment for their guests, but have provided it themselves'.

It was no hollow boast – more domestic Schubert in style than empire-building Wagner – and from the late 1950s onward, Britten left the peace and security of Aldeburgh with reluctance. The entertainment Harewood spoke of would over the years include significant Britten premieres – from the three Church Parables (EOG) and three cello suites (Rostropovich), to *Songs and Proverbs of William Blake* (Fischer-Dieskau), *Death in Venice* (Pears) and *Phaedra* (Baker). Aldeburgh Festival audiences were full of people who must have wondered what it would have been like to be present at the first informal performance of Schumann's *Dichterliebe*, when the magical postlude dispels the anger and despair of the final song, or the day Schubert sat at his piano and ground his way through the sparse, chilling texture of 'Der Leiermann' (The Hurdy-gurdy Man), the conclusion of *Die Winterreise*. Those passionate, enlightened audience members would realize that in Aldeburgh they were witnessing something like the twentieth century's equivalent. 'People were hearing history,' pianist Graham Johnson said of Britten's musical partnership with Pears. 'To hear a great composer play the piano is half what he actually does and half the awareness that you are taking part in a historical moment.'

19

It is no coincidence that the two times Britten hit a block compositionally were while he was working on a large orchestral piece. Opera has its own momentum – a collaborative process in the first instance and then teeming with adrenalin once it hits the rehearsal studio. But there is no escaping the loneliness of large-scale orchestral composition, the sheer slog of it all, the process driven by one person with no team in the wings. In late 1948, and again in late 1955, Britten threw his hands up and pencil down. Each time he was hit by exhaustion masquerading as something else. Touring Holland in early December 1948 with Pears, Britten fell ill with what was suspected to be a stomach ulcer, forcing him to pull out of one concert and limp through the rest. On their return a correct diagnosis was made: he was suffering from exhaustion and depression and was ordered to spend three months resting.

It had been an impossibly busy year, its tone set in February 1948 with his appearance on the cover of *Time* magazine. Arthur Oldham later asserted that this changed everything for Britten, and certainly this year his behaviour towards friends shifted, his schedule fomenting conflict but allowing little time or inclination for resolution. 'I'm crotchety, & take it out on my friends!' he told Piers Dunkerley in December. The festival was followed by another EOG tour – to the Holland Festival once more, this time with *The Beggar's Opera* – and the official premiere of *Saint Nicolas* at Lancing. Britten and Pears left August free and spent it in Aldeburgh, swimming, eating, entertaining and reading poetry. But once September arrived and the new season commenced, the EOG was back on the road, including a twelve-day run at Sadler's Wells, *The Beggar's Opera* alternating with *Albert Herring*. Pears, unable or unwilling to sit still in Aldeburgh during the dates originally allocated to the American tour, headed off across the Atlantic anyway. He booked lessons with his old teacher, Clytie Mundy, and planned time with friends, including the Mayers – all of which had a predictable effect on Britten's mood. Throughout 1948 there were slow-burn and more urgent compositions, and constant approaches for new works – the correspondence would pile up on Britten's desk until he dictated negative or holding-pattern responses to his housekeeper, Miss Parker. By the time he and Pears headed to Amsterdam in early December for performances of *Saint Nicolas* and a recital in the Concertgebouw, Britten was well primed for some form of physical or emotional collapse.

A significant factor in his exhaustion and depression was the suffocating financial situation of the EOG. The first Aldeburgh Festival had generated only a small deficit, a little over £300, which buoyed all those concerned and ensured the experiment would be repeated in 1949. But the same could never be said of the opera company. It made a modest surplus for its appearance at the festival (£15), a consequence of a greatly reduced fee, a fair serving of goodwill and the surprisingly minimal carpentry expenses involved in turning Aldeburgh's former skating rink into an opera house. Such ameliorating budgeting was impossible outside Aldeburgh, and the group finished the year with an overdraft of £5,400.

Crozier, barely making ends meet himself, would in February 1949 write a damning, passionate letter to the Arts Council, accusing it of supporting 'only those enterprises that are spectacular in intention, certain of wide publicity and likely to be immediately popular'. He took aim at an organization that 'doubles the large Covent Garden subsidy of £60,000 in the current year and threatens to halve the small English Opera Group subsidy of £5,000, which pampers the successful at the expense of the struggling venture'. His figures were not quite right – Covent Garden's subsidy in 1947–8 was actually £98,000 once a vital supplementary grant was taken into account, a figure that grew to £120,000 the following financial year – but it seemed shocking to him, and to Britten, that such an important venture as the EOG, run on string and air and headed by the country's most significant musician, should attract so little state support. In these early days of the EOG and the festival, Britten was involved in every detail. Later, those around him established a balance between discretion and disclosure, protecting him from himself, but just now there was no escaping the EOG's financial problems even had he wanted to.

Boosey may have been right to pray for the EOG's collapse. The constant money problems were offset by the stimulation the group engendered in this composer-impresario, but total control meant total responsibility, a trade-off Britten had come to realize and desire in the aftermath of the first production of *Grimes*. In these early days of the Arts Council, with off-the-record conversations taking place in theatre foyers and bars, it was difficult to dispute Crozier's criticisms. The council's heart did not seem to be in Britten's venture.

Part of the problem was encapsulated in a throwaway remark Britten made in 1963. 'Some people seem to want another *Grimes*, and still another! But they are mistaken if they expect me to give it to them. I have different challenges before me and I respond to them.' He was thinking this way long before the 1960s: in the second half of the 1940s he seemed to take pleasure in sabotaging the notion of another *Grimes*. In May 1948 he wrote to Webster of his concerns about Covent Garden's production of *Peter Grimes*: it was chronically under-rehearsed, badly miscast, demonstrated a disregard for the printed score and suffered from the lack of involvement of the original creative team. It was a damning list, one that Webster clearly took on board, for later in the year he revisited the proposal put forward two years earlier: a new grand opera by Britten for Covent Garden.

Britten had not ruled out the genre; he had toyed with the Civil War idea, after all. But he responded badly to Webster's dilatoriness, which was a poor substitute for the immediate reaction he demanded and was used to from his inner circle. Webster's substitute for the stalled Britten commission can hardly have been reassuring: *The Olympians* by Arthur Bliss to a libretto by J. B. Priestley, a puzzling mixture of Shakespeare's *A Midsummer Night's Dream* and Strauss's *Ariadne auf Naxos*, which would suffer a stillbirth at its September 1949 premiere. Still Webster persisted, and this time circumstances were more in his favour: Britten, Forster and Crozier had spent some of summer 1948 discussing a new grand opera, something way beyond the scope of the EOG. Yet still Britten dragged his feet. 'I am afraid I can in no way commit myself about a first performance until it has at least begun to materialise. Then I shall have to see if your Company includes the kind of people I should want for the opera, and above all whether you and Karl [Rankl] could agree to my demands.'

Publicly Britten argued that he was wedded to chamber opera on aesthetic grounds, but much of the problem was that neither Covent Garden nor Sadler's Wells offered a viable alternative. If one had existed, perhaps Britten's professed commitment to chamber opera would have given way to a string of grand operas, as Boosey wished. But the absence of an alternative company in Britten's mind encouraged him to continue to stage his own operas, staggering between exhilaration and exhaustion.

While depression was by no means an inevitable consequence of exhaustion, in December it came. 'It is one thing thinking gaily about a possible free time,' he told Pears, '& another being ordered to rest for 3 months, & to have to forgo all the things with you, my darling, to have to be separated too, for so long from you at times when I thought we'd be travelling & working together.' There were more fights and misunderstandings throughout his recuperation, usually initiated on the telephone and then cleared up in print. ('Perhaps after all we'd better NOT telephone, because we always get cross,' he told Pears in February 1949.)

If there was an advantage to their separate lives just now it was that Britten found Pears to be 'so very severe a critic' – to the extent that he was reluctant to try out new ideas on him lest he damn them. Strolling through Central Park with Donald Mitchell in the 1960s discussing a new piece, Britten suddenly volunteered: 'You know, sometimes I'm nervous of talking about these new ideas I have, because Peter has such a strong personality and such strong reactions that if he says, "That's a silly idea" or something, I'm put down straight away, I can't go on with it.' John Tooley, Webster's assistant then successor at Covent Garden, frequently experienced Pears's deflating influence on his partner. Decisions made by Britten and Tooley would be overturned once the composer had discussed them with Pears, Britten sheepishly ringing Tooley soon after: 'Well, John, I've been thinking about what we talked about last night and I'm not quite really sure that we ought to do it this way.' Sometimes these were practical interventions – a rehearsal schedule, or a touring plan; at other times it was a throwaway remark or a petty dismissal of another singer. Though at his doctor's insistence Britten had put his manuscript paper aside, his mind still whirred with ideas, not least the new grand opera. In poor health and temper, who knows how he might have reacted to a negative word about the project from Pears?

20

Contained within Forster's flights of fancy about a *Grimes* composed to his libretto was a broad hint: the ageing writer would like to collaborate with Britten on a new opera. So, in mid-January 1949, Forster came and stayed at Crag House for a few days to kick around one of Britten's ideas. The men were not yet close, though Britten felt a sense of gratitude towards Forster for introducing him to Crabbe's poetry, repaying him by dedicating *Albert Herring* 'to E. M. Forster, in admiration'. Their correspondence then intensified. Despite the nearly thirty-five-year age gap, they shared a similar background and outlook. Forster was more an Edwardian, of course, raised on the era's casual misogyny, which was not far beneath the surface of the homosocial culture of King's College, Cambridge, where he now lived. They had friends in common; Forster alone had waved Auden and Isherwood on their way from Waterloo Station in January 1939 (later ordering them to stay away and 'see us sink from a distance') and he was close to William Plomer, who soon became a favourite Britten librettist. Both men explored social and political themes in their works, with Forster displaying none of Britten's unsureness with female characters (he had resolved early in the century to 'get a less superficial idea of women'). Britten balanced the slate with the greater courage he showed in dealing with homosexual themes. (Forster's novel *Maurice*, written in 1913 and passed like prized contraband around a smallish circle of mostly homosexual men, Britten and Pears included, remained unpublished in his lifetime, partly from the author's conviction that the public had no stomach for a happy ending to a gay love story.) He was a respected, elderly writer who had published no new novel since *A Passage to India* in 1924, but whose correspondence crackled with acute social and literary ideas and observations which Britten could never equal.

They were well matched in their values; it was Forster, after all, who famously stated in 1938 that 'if I had to choose between betraying my country and betraying my friend, I hope I should have the guts to betray my country'. Spender caught the older writer's qualities brilliantly in a thumbnail sketch: self-effacement combined with positive assertion of his views; whimsicality combined with precision; pagan amorality combined with complete preoccupation with moral issues; love of freedom combined with absolute self-discipline. Some of these describe Britten as well, as does Spender's conclusion: 'He is one of the most comforting of modern writers, and at the same time one of the most uncomfortable.'

Forster had been slow with ideas following Britten's initial invitation; he was in any case lacking confidence. 'Unluckily I have not got my mind on to a subject yet, which is the real feebleness of this letter,' he wrote in October 1948 to Crozier, who was acting as midwife. 'My feeling is that you ought to start and do the thing – calling on me to look over your shoulder when you will.' He felt he was not the appropriate person to write a comic opera, on which Britten was then keen, asserting that 'comedy must be either satirical or nostalgic'. But apart from being instinctively drawn to large-scale opera ('I want grand opera mounted clearly and grandly,' he told Britten in December), he had no plan. For a while they toyed with the story of Margaret Catchpole, the Suffolk servant girl, buccaneer, lover and convict, but it never took flight. Then Britten remembered the small reprint of Herman Melville's *Billy Budd* he had picked up on tour in England after the war.

Billy Budd is the story of an honest, patriotic, handsome young sailor, press-ganged into the British navy at the time of the French Revolutionary Wars, who wins the hearts of all those he serves alongside. He is wrongfully and maliciously accused of mutinous deeds by John Claggart, the villainous master-at-arms, whom he strikes and kills with a blow when his severe stammer blocks his words of defence. The man-of-war's respected, bookish Captain Vere, who fully comprehends that Claggart's vindictive attraction to Billy is the real crime, nonetheless directs the drumhead court to follow to the letter the Mutiny Act; propriety *and* desire are Vere's 'mind-forg'd manacles', in Blake's phrase, for he too has noticed the wholesome recruit. Billy is found guilty and hanged from the yardarm; Claggart is committed to sea with full naval honours.

It is a poised, unsettling parable of good and evil, right and wrong, of Christ or Adam, and morality and conscience in wartime – an ideal story for Britten. He proposed it to Forster, who needed little convincing: he had written on Melville and this particular story in *Aspects of the Novel* in 1927, which may be where Britten first learned of it. A rather beautiful sentence in Forster's book would have caught Britten's eye: 'Melville – after the initial roughness of his realism – reaches straight back into the universal, to a blackness and sadness so transcending our own that they are undistinguishable from glory.'

That was the hook, the notion of extracting broad philosophical observations from such particular, local circumstances. Much later, when Crozier and Forster reunited to effect the opera's revisions – restructuring the original four acts into two, rehabilitating the piece – Crozier would talk of this quality in the novella.

> Now, it would be true to say, wouldn't it, that in this particular case of Melville's story of *Billy Budd*, he's not concerned only with one ship at one moment in time; he's concerned with what I called earlier the quality of extension that in a sense that ship is an image of the world. It is a world, which reflects the stresses and problems and concerns of our own world, and floats on the sea of time and of infinity.

Britten was grateful for the cogent explanation. 'It certainly seems like that when I read that story. Whether Melville was as aware of that as we are, I don't know.' (He was.)

Yet Crozier was sceptical at first. He was summoned to Aldeburgh for Forster's visit (or one in late November), aware of some great scheme in the wind, but unaware of the correspondence and conversations that had already occurred between Britten and Forster. He was fed breakfast and given the book to read, devouring it at a sitting. Crozier immediately felt it was his role to stress the enormous difficulties of the undertaking. How could the staging work? Who had ever heard of an opera with an all-male cast? How could an operatic hero have a paralysing stutter? Britten and Forster calmly dealt with each misgiving, biting their tongues all the while; they had been living with the subject for longer. Britten did a child's drawing of a ship in profile – all beams and stick figures – to help orient themselves through the narrative, which Forster labelled in his scratchy hand and to which John Piper stuck in his subsequent stage design. Then Britten scribbled down the main events of the story, which is much how the opera plays out: 'Press-gang & boarding'; 'Scourging of slack after-guardsman'; 'Natural depravity of Claggart'; 'Attempt to bribe Billy'; 'Frigate chase'; 'Interview with Claggart & Billy in cabin'; 'Murder'; 'Trial scene'; 'Vere's speech & discussion'; 'Verdict'; 'Vere tells Billy'; 'Execution'.

A few days after the visit, Forster sent Crozier a 'rough-out for Vere's opening speech', a prologue to the events described by Melville. The odd word is scribbled over, but it is almost identical to what we know today. 'I am an old man who has experienced much. I have been a man of action and fought for my King and Country at sea . . .' Forster added a canny postscript: 'N.B. in the story Vere dies soon after. But had better live on.' He was hooked, impatient to get on with it after six months of foot-dragging. Britten asked Crozier to collaborate on the libretto to counter Forster's lack of theatrical experience.

Britten was also keen to develop the work, yet remained ill and depressed, and before devoting his energies to it would need to clear his desk of his *Spring Symphony* for Koussevitzky and a new children's opera intended for the second Aldeburgh Festival. Pears stepped in with a plan for Britten's recuperation. 'Peter's taking me away to Italy on Sunday for three weeks,' Britten told Duncan, '& if that doesn't cure me I feel nothing else will!' So in late January 1949 they set off for two weeks in Venice and one in Portofino, eating like farmhands, which calmed Britten's stomach and nerves. They walked for miles each day, in the churches, galleries and alleys of a winter-bound Venice largely free of tourists, happy in their own company. They marvelled at the silent rhythm of the city, at the gondolas they caught on the lagoon, at the church bells that punctuated the day almost too diligently. They basked in the winter sun on visits to surrounding towns and villages, and hiked in the mountains. With Forster's prologue now in his hands, Britten's mind was alive to the great potential of *Billy Budd*. 'I am feeling a new person,' he told Mayer from Portofino, 'impatient to get back to work for the first time for months!'

Venice would be called on once more to work its magic when, in infinitely sadder circumstances, Britten returned there for a final visit a year before his death. Here he completed his String Quartet No. 3, a work that clangs with the bells of Santa Maria della Salute and bobs with the rhythm of the canals. In 1949 the magic was not the city's alone, for, back in Aldeburgh in early March, Britten wrote to Pears: 'Lovely as Venice, Bellini, the little Carpaccio boys, Mimosa and the wine-dark sea off Portofino were, my happiest & most treasured memory is of the wonderful peace & contentment of your love & friendship. Love, such as I felt we had in those 3 weeks, is a rare thing – as beautiful and luminous as this sea outside, & with endless depths too. Thank you, my dearest.'

2 I

They returned to another EOG financial crisis, as common as the wind in the company's early years: the Arts Council had cut its subsidy from £5,000 to £3,000. A solution was close at hand, though Britten did not yet know it: the children's opera would become a commercial hit, leavening the EOG's inky ledger and partially ameliorating an ongoing source of anxiety. They could all be forgiven for not predicting this success; there was no especial reason post-war British children would be interested in opera, even one dressed up as an 'Entertainment for Young People'. The clue was in this subtitle, however, for Britten saw the project as akin to *The Young Person's Guide to the Orchestra*, a didactic show for children. The new piece was originally conceived as a film, the first part demonstrating how an opera is put together, the second the short opera itself. The film was eventually dropped, but the structure survived; all that was required was a story. Britten was fond of Arthur Ransome's *Swallows and Amazons*, a popular Lake District children's adventure full of pemmican, pirates and grog, yet he opted instead for a dramatic expansion of Blake's poem 'The Chimney Sweeper'.

Britten juggled his three projects, doggedly determined not to learn the lessons of the previous year. In early March Forster and Crozier spent two weeks at Crag House working on *Budd*. 'Morgan is the careful, wise mind who will write most of the text and dialogue,' Crozier told Evans. 'I am the technician and will write what is needed in the way of songs and shanties.' His role was greater than that, however, which Forster recognized by sharing the librettist's royalty. Each day, immediately after breakfast, they huddled around the fire in Crozier's room. They talked endlessly, Britten's skeleton sketch to hand, suggesting ideas, rejecting most, scribbling lines, discussing technical points concerning life on a warship. One or both would then write up each episode and the drafts were pored over, scribbled on, sometimes amalgamated, sometimes scrapped and begun again. A beautiful libretto began to emerge. 'A prose libretto is rather unusual and it had to be in prose because I can't write poetry,' observed Forster bluntly. He would later decry the 'small but ceaseless drag towards recitative' he thought a prose libretto initiated, acknowledging, however, that emotionally he was what Britten and the story both needed. ('I found his terse, vivid sentences, with their strong rhythms, melodically inspiring.')

Britten, at the other end of the corridor orchestrating his *Spring Symphony*, would meet them for elevenses, read what they had written, give his thoughts and then head back to his study. Despite the Italian break, he was not yet better, his depression not yet beaten. The weather did not help: it was an unseasonably cold spring, culminating in storms and frightening swells, flooded basements and further erosion of the seafront – all a dress rehearsal for the savage flooding of early 1953. Crozier thought Britten wretched. 'Something is worrying him, spoiling his temper, jamming his work, and throwing his tummy out of gear.' He guessed the problem was a sort of revulsion against *Budd*, an inability to see clearly its shape and meaning. Both librettists talked him down from this particular precipice; he remembered what he had first identified in the novella and his dark mood lifted somewhat. But it would take the completion of the symphony to effect more lasting change.

'I like the Spring Symphony,' he told Pears later in the month, 'apart from one still beastly bit that I <u>can't</u>, <u>can't</u>, <u>can't</u> get right, but I suppose I shall one day.' The piece is a stomp through the pastoral Suffolk of Constable and Gainsborough – schoolboys swimming in the stream at Flatford, and even spring light replacing weak winter sunshine. A chill wind blows through the first movement (another of Britten's prologues) but soon gives way to the accoutrements of spring: the merry cuckoo, nightingales and larks, spring lamb, rye reaching chin height, the whistling boy driving his team of oxen, country maidens and fair shepherds – all of which Britten latched on to with his keen sense of mimicry.

It is easy to miss the symphony's deeper themes amid so much bucolic revelry. Britten wrote that the work is 'a symphony not only dealing with the Spring itself, but with the progress of Winter to Spring and the re-awakening of the earth and life which that means'. Donald Mitchell has identified the similarity between this cycle of life, death and renewal, and Mahler's great *Das Lied von der Erde*; it is a neat comparison. Mahler's influence is found not just in the philosophical subtexts; or the use of choir, soloists and boys' voices within a somewhat disguised symphonic form ('It is in the traditional four movement shape of a symphony,' Britten said, 'but with the movements divided into shorter sections bound together by a similar mood or point of view'); or the venue for the premiere, the Concertgebouw in Amsterdam, Mahler's ghost ever present; or Britten's use of a cow horn, which hints at the Alpine cattle that wander the stage in Mahler's Symphony No. 6, bells around their necks clanking with abandon. It is more that Britten handles the large orchestra much as Mahler does, at times treating it as a small chamber ensemble, intimate colloquies demanding our concentrated attention, at other moments giving it free rein.

There is another ghost hovering over the work. Britten plucked Auden's 1933 poem 'A Summer Night' from his well-thumbed copy of *Look, Stranger!* and gave it whispery prominence in the symphony's second part. The words jump from the score with a jolt, a reminder of how long ago emotionally their collaborations and lives together were, yet simultaneously how recent it actually was. It was an odd poem to include, dealing with broken love, memory and reconciliation, the paragraphs dealing with reunification left unset. Was Britten's motive here renewal, or was it valediction?

The symphony, intended for a previous Boston season, had been postponed amid Britten's illness and overwork. Once more Koussevitzky gallantly ceded the premiere to another organization, and so on 14 July Britten and Pears were in Amsterdam for the first performance (repeated a day later in Scheveningen), a full month before Koussevitzky was to conduct the work at Tanglewood. Pears was singing, of course, joined by Ferrier and Dutch soprano Jo Vincent, the Dutch Radio Chorus and the Boys' Choir of St Willibrorduskerk ('70 little Dutch toughs', as Britten described them, a little improbably, to a gay friend), conducted by van Beinum. And in good voice they were too, if a private, crackly, off-air recording of the performance is anything to go by. Tempi were close to Britten's later recording, and the audience, Field Marshal Montgomery among its ranks (much to the composer's annoyance), responded rapturously. Not even the critics – Dutch, American or English – found much to quibble with, which marked a shift in Britten's critical fortunes. Desmond Shawe-Taylor thought the piece represented a considerable advance in Britten's writing. 'It is as though the springtime of his genius – raw, brilliant and tender – were itself also about to ripen into high summer.' For all the acclaim at the time, performances today are nowhere near as frequent as the work merits; it is thought, unfairly, to have aged badly.

The Britten of the late 1940s would have given Shawe-Taylor short shrift. 'I have no respect for criticisms anywhere,' he told Mayer in January after reading the poor notices for *Lucretia* in the American press sent by Hawkes, 'but these (even the friendly ones) touched a bottom that even England cannot surpass!' (Kurt Weill, whom Britten met in Maine in the summer of 1940, revelled in the roasting Virgil Thomson gave *Lucretia*, having seen a preview of the opera himself, which he thought contained no music, just orchestral effects. It was much like Truman Capote's dismissal of Jack Kerouac: 'That's not writing, that's typing.') A month later there appeared in the *Times Literary Supplement* an anonymous review of Eric Walter White's thoughtful 1948 monograph on Britten, which concluded by lamenting that 'the author's image of the composer springs from a mood too uncritically admiring to satisfy any readers except those belonging to the small but powerful sect which threatens to kill with kindness one of the most naturally gifted of contemporary British composers'.

Britten remained temperamentally unable to distinguish between astute and wayward criticism; to him, any problems perceived by critics were in the eye of the beholder. It was not that he thought his work flawless, but, he complained in 1952, not once were any offending passages identified and solutions proffered. It is an unfair characterization. For every glib adjective or analysis pegged to one of his works there was a considered, insightful critique. Libretti were picked apart, their flaws skilfully analysed and the architecture of the operas dissected. Numerous critics would rightly pounce on the flabby muster scene closing the original first act of *Billy Budd*, a full nine years before Britten did the same thing.* There were clearly observations worth making, observations those close to Britten seemed unable to make (as Forster would soon discover), and quite distinct from the clubby pontificating and gossip that passed for much music criticism in the 1940s. There were good critics and bad, and sometimes they were both. Britten's hatred of Frank Howes is unfair when his whole body of criticism is considered, for instance. It is true that many critics struggled to keep up with the massive changes in post-war British culture and were perhaps ill-equipped for this new world. Nor was it only Britten who bridled: in 1950 Stravinsky wrote dismissively of 'the old London press idiots and the new British chauvinists [the arts establishment]'. Britten could only ever see the bad critics, however, and found nothing to learn from the good.

A photographer caught the thirty-five-year-old composer leaving the Concertgebouw after the *Spring Symphony* premiere, his Bogart-in-*Casablanca* trench coat buckled high and tight, a large bunch of lilies in his hands, with beaming, well-dressed Dutchmen applauding him. Britten returns their smiles, uncharacteristically insouciant, strangely youthful. Scarcely any other photograph of him matches it.

22

With the symphony off his desk, but its premiere still three months away, Britten's mood finally lifted. 'I have seldom seen Ben so cheerful as he is these days,' Crozier told Evans in April 1949. 'He is loving writing the children's opera and goes about with a beaming smile.' He

---

* In an otherwise unperceptive review, Ernest Newman in the *Sunday Times* wrote: 'The action would have gone better in two acts than in four; by that means we would have been spared a good deal of repetition and padding and one or two scenes that are too "operatic" in the unflattering sense of the term, the worst example being the ensemble of the ship's company in praise of Captain Vere at the end of the first act. I could imagine something of this sort happening on the deck of H.M.S. *Pinafore* but hardly on that of H.M.S. *Indomitable*.'

composed *The Little Sweep* in three weeks – Crozier having expanded Blake's poem into a serviceable libretto – without stopping to think about what he was doing or how it was sounding, as he told Pears. He also confessed how little he liked writing an opera without a part in it for Pears, something he rectified when it came to recording *The Little Sweep* in 1955: Pears puts in an unlikely cameo as Clem, the working-class son of the evil sweep-master Black Bob, in which he sounds like a 1930s Oxford undergraduate at a sherry party, as indeed he had once been. Britten auditioned children in Ipswich and was startled at the high standard of the urchins and aristocrats rustled up by the local Co-op choir. He threw himself into the production, dropping in on rehearsals whenever time permitted, joking with the children and enjoying their easy companionship. It was a work in which Britten was able to skip through his own childhood. He went birdwatching near Orford, incorporating into the opera the songs of the herons and chaffinches. And he put the Britten children's own rocking-horse back into harness, decades-old sugar lumps rattling around inside it.

The Little Sweep is only the second half of *Let's Make an Opera*. As in the original film plan, in the first half various characters decide to put on an opera and go about explaining to the audience the art form's intricacies – a children's *Ariadne auf Naxos*. The wordy, clichéd dialogue of the original remains a problem, despite various attempts over the years to fix it, and it was left to the EOG's music director, the young English conductor Norman Del Mar, to plug as many gaps as he could, using his charm and powers of coercion to teach the audience the choruses they were to help sing in *The Little Sweep*. The opera's libretto reads much like a *Famous Five* adventure, full to the brim with exclamation marks, everyone proclaiming his or her slightest thought in quick-fire dialogue. 'Of course it's all very slight, an occasional piece, so occasional that it may not survive the dispersal of the present company,' Shawe-Taylor wrote about a performance at the Cheltenham Festival in July. Yet all were delighted to discover he was wrong. Its June premiere in the Jubilee Hall contributed to the success of the second Aldeburgh Festival and *Let's Make an Opera* was a mainstay of the EOG for years to come. It beguiled British audiences, young and old, on radio, television, gramophone or in the theatre, and gave many their first operatic experience. It also underlined an evolving appreciation of opera in Britain as the art form slowly became part of the cultural vernacular.

Almost without warning, Britten and Crozier's relationship fell apart. 'I have known since early this year that Ben was done with me,' he told Evans in July 1949, 'and that we could not work together again – for some years, anyway.' There is nothing in their correspondence to suggest a split. On the contrary, it is astonishing how many plates Britten and Crozier kept spinning: programming, writing, planning, fundraising, directing, casting and performing. Only the ongoing precariousness of the EOG caused the occasional crashing down. Crozier kept up with it all, describing his activities to Evans with barely contained exuberance.

He would not have been oblivious to any change in temperature. Perhaps Britten started getting that nervous little look in his eyes in Crozier's presence, the one he got when trapped in a bad performance. Or perhaps Crozier's long-standing debt of £200 or his workaday play for *Let's Make an Opera* came between them. Or perhaps Crozier suspected that Basil Coleman, the young (gay) director who had come into the Aldeburgh orbit as assistant producer on *The Beggar's Opera*, who made a success of *Let's Make an Opera* and whom Britten much liked, would usurp him. It was possibly none of these things or a combination of all. Regardless, Crozier seemed almost determined to sabotage the friendship. Stressed by the crippling alimony he was paying his ex-wife, he wrote to Hawkes requesting an advance on future royalties. Hawkes sought Britten's reaction, which was one of fury: Crozier had not first consulted him and Britten felt trapped by the implications. He was *satisfied* with Crozier's work within certain limits, he replied, the praise faint. The libretti were neat and Crozier's stagecraft was invaluable in *Billy Budd*. 'But if you decide to give him this guarantee against future royalties, I *cannot* feel myself bound always to use him as my librettist.' Britten's letter remained on his desk unsent for some weeks and Crozier's request was declined before Hawkes received it. But the damage was done. In June 1949 Crozier resigned from the EOG in search of better paid employment.

Britten was perplexed by his behaviour and remained so for many years. 'Eric really is a pretty puzzling man,' he later told Donald Mitchell. 'He just walked in here one day and said, "I think the Aldeburgh Festival has gone on long enough. It ought to stop. And in any case, whether it stops or not, I'm stopping. Goodbye."' But at the time Britten was determined to keep relations good and their various projects on track, so he responded positively to a direct plea from Crozier for financial help. 'We can't afford, personally or professionally, to let these "iron curtains" interfere!' The *Budd* collaborators gathered in Aldeburgh in August, feigning normality, though Crozier took a cottage nearby rather than stay at Crag House. Crozier found Britten more relaxed with him than he had been for some time, so he told Evans, though he also thought him *generally* tense, 'as though he were going through a prolonged internal crisis'.

Picture Post caught them at work, Forster and Crozier in ties, Britten in shorts and beach shoes, sitting in the window frame of Crag House, a string of beach huts visible in the background. Another photograph shows Forster and Britten on a boat, their hands posed ineffectually on the tiller, in the company of Pears, a local fisherman, Billy Burrell, and a young lad, Robin Long.* They look at ease with each other in the photograph, and Crozier described the partnership to Evans in these terms. 'I do not think there ever was a happier collaboration than this one between Ben, Morgan and me. We are thrilled by the work, we like each other, we respect each other's viewpoints, and yet we are all so entirely different in our experience and gifts.'

For now, it was relatively plain sailing. Britten, blissfully free of other compositional commitments, took control of the tiller, requesting a new scene here, a new character there. They chipped away at the draft libretto, tightening it, making every word count. It was *Peter Grimes* all over again and the opera was to benefit similarly from the attention. Forster, unused to any form of collaboration but determined the libretto be a literary work in its own right, thought himself a little stale and dazed in the discussions, before going to his desk and turning each new idea or revision into blank verse.† The working pattern continued throughout 1949 and much of the following year until Britten retreated into his study in Aldeburgh with his huge manuscript, printed with more staves than he had had to think about in some years (*Spring Symphony* aside), and both his collaborators found themselves kept at bay.

---

* Late in his life Burrell enjoyed pulling out this photograph and talking about his easy friendship with Britten (his broad, Suffolk accent not always easy to comprehend) and of his then physical similarity to the handsome Billy Budd. Britten tacitly acknowledged this by taking Burrell to a performance of the opera and inscribing a vocal score for him.

† The Lord Chamberlain's unperceptive reader thought little of his efforts. 'Opera libretti seldom reveal literary merits. This one reads as badly as most; but it has been set with astonishing virtuosity by the composer, and the result is a deeply moving narrative.'

23

Work on the new opera was disrupted by Britten and Pears's recital tour of the USA and Canada, held over from the previous year, which they began on 23 October 1949 in New York City. Hawkes had finally won the day. There were appropriate Barnum touches: twenty concerts in all, with New York as a bustling base camp, and the flyer was modern American PR – distinguished faces smiling into the middle distance; press quotes ('a brilliantly talented musician, with unlimited imagination and impeccable technique' – an Italian newspaper's verdict on Britten); the imprimatur of no fewer than five gramophone companies; and a typically wide menu from which to build each programme. It was slick, modern and desperately un-British. The strange twists of fate, industry and migration had left mid-century America far better equipped than Britain for a headline tour by two such men performing such music.

Their reaction to New York had not improved. Britten hated the tropical heat, as he termed it, the noise and the overwhelming claustrophobia of it all. 'This town is hell,' he told Sweeting, Dorothy Parker at his side, a view he expanded for the benefit of another friend: 'beastly, hateful, sinister, stupid, snobbish, unimportant New York'. But what different men they were from the last time they were in town together.

It was the era of Rubinstein and Toscanini, Heifetz and Klemperer; the most eminent soloists and conductors were treated in America as movie stars, not mere musicians. Rubinstein could command as much as $85,000 for a creaky Hollywood film – this in addition to the $3,500 he demanded for each of the hundred-odd concerts he gave every year. Even Myra Hess was safe box-office, having done the hard graft to establish a North American career before the war; her concerto appearances with the New York Philharmonic in its 1949–50 season earned her $7,000. Britten and Pears, softly spoken, somewhat diffident English gentlemen, sat uncomfortably with the new breed of celebrity performer. The difference in style would assume greater significance in Britain in the coming decade, when the domestic industry became increasingly attuned to this American cult of celebrity, fused with a brittle sense of masculinity.

Despite the positive reception to their concerts, Britten's American and Canadian net remittances for the tour amounted to little more than £600. It was apples versus (imported, rationed) oranges: the beleaguered pound was devalued from $4.03 to $2.80 a month before they set sail, putting a scythe to their American earnings. It did not matter greatly: Britten's gross income in 1949–50 was £7,512,* almost eight times what he earned five years earlier, the bulk of it Boosey & Hawkes royalties. His immediate predecessor as *enfant terrible* of English music, William Walton, a year from his knighthood, was earning around £3,000 a year at the time, John Piper £4,000.

There were some pleasures to be had on tour and near misses to be regretted. Percy Grainger, the eminent free-spirited Australian composer and pianist, whom Britten much admired and whose footprints can be identified in his earlier folk-song arrangements, hoped they might meet. It did not happen on this trip, though subsequent encounters left Britten struck by the sprightly old man's warmth, originality and charm, which he recreated in an exuberant, freewheeling gramophone recording of Grainger's music some years later, and which he honoured by 'lovingly and reverently' dedicating his late *Suite on English Folk Tunes* to the Australian. When Hawkes introduced Britten to the great Scottish viola player William Primrose, Britten wasted no time telling him that he was 'needed' in Aldeburgh, aware he had to enlarge his festival family and conscious he had little money with which to do so. Primrose consented and Britten sweetened the invitation by snatching time away from *Budd* in May to compose for the violist his *Lachrymae*; he had forgotten his promise and composed it overnight following a telephone call from Primrose asking where it was. 'It's in the post,' Britten found himself dissembling. It is a poised work that nods and dances away gracefully to a slow, melancholic pavane by John Dowland. (Britten's reworking of the piece for viola and small string orchestra, crafted in the last year of his life, comes much closer than the original version to recreating Dowland's striking melancholia and in evoking the distant, haunting sounds of Elizabethan court life.)

On the West Coast for three weeks, Britten met the émigrés Stravinsky and Schoenberg, whom he had so long admired. Schoenberg attempted to see Britten in the interval of one concert, only to be turned away by an attendant with the news that Britten was in the bathroom

---

* Over £210,000 today.

throwing up; the waspish old composer put this down to drink rather than nerves. Britten was similarly cool: 'not what you'd call a *magic* composer', he later told Imogen Holst, and indeed Schoenberg was a dour old stick.

His meeting with Stravinsky began more propitiously, which, given their personalities, is perhaps surprising. The Russian attended two of the Englishmen's concerts and entertained them at his home. Stravinsky talked about the little of Britten's music he professed to know: *Grimes* in score, *Lucretia* from a poor local amateur performance, and even *Night Mail*, which he had seen two years earlier and liked, fortuitously stumbling across Auden's lyrics at exactly the time he was searching for an opera librettist. The 'little boy who likes Stravinsky' no doubt talked admiringly of the scores that had liberated his adolescent imagination – *The Firebird* or *Le Sacre du printemps*. And they must have discussed the proposed Stravinsky chamber opera for the EOG, which Hawkes had attempted to broker in 1947 but which morphed into the grander (and far more lucrative) *Rake's Progress* for another company.

Perhaps it is a mistake to meet our childhood idols. Stravinsky gave the distinct impression that he had not listened to *Lucretia* closely, claiming that his new opera would include *secco* recitatives accompanied by piano, a real innovation. Britten spluttered over this boast, for *Lucretia* is full of such passages. (In fairness, it is possible the amateur performance Stravinsky heard was with piano alone, in which case the textural distinction between recitative and aria would have been unclear.)

All the subsequent animosity between the pair can be dated to this meeting. Stravinsky wrote to his friend the composer Nicolas Nabokov (a first cousin of Vladimir) about 'Aunt Britten and Uncle Pears', the homophobia more explicit in the original Russian. 'Britten himself makes a very nice impression and has a huge success with an audience. He has an unquestionable talent as a performer (especially at the piano).' Nabokov picked up Stravinsky's barb and told it to Isaiah Berlin, who was thereafter fond of 'quoting' Stravinsky: 'Britten is a vonnnderrful ... accompanist', the pause theatrical and damning. Britten returned the compliment as soon as he could. In rehearsals for *The Rake's Progress* under two years later, Auden could be heard telling anyone who would care to listen that Britten, who had seen the score, liked the opera very much – 'everything but the music'. Auden probably learned this from

Mayer, not from Britten himself. And Mayer no doubt delighted telling Britten Auden's assessment of Stravinsky in rehearsals: 'he cant conduct . . . doesnt know the score . . . is deaf.'

Thereafter the gloves were off. Snide asides were made by both, in person and in print, culminating in Stravinsky's brutal assessment of *War Requiem* and its reception. 'Kleenex at the ready, then, one goes from the critics to the music, knowing that if one should dare to disagree with "practically everyone", one will be made to feel as if one had failed to stand up for "God Save the Queen".' Stravinsky even visited Britten in a dream, holding up one of his scores and pointing out its faults. It would remain an odd, slightly obsessive relationship on both sides. Yet Britten, the vastly more insecure of the two, suffered the most, viewing his elder as a great vulture at his shoulder, ever ready to pick at the bones.

More successful was the reunion with Isherwood, jittery from nicotine withdrawal, who immediately put Britten and Pears at their ease. He threw a party to celebrate Britten's thirty-sixth birthday, cramming the house with attractive young Californian men who leaped at the opportunity to meet the eminent visitors but who quickly thereafter lost interest. 'In this gay setting, where celebrity snobbery was replaced by sex snobbery,' Isherwood wrote, 'Ben and Peter were just a pair of slightly faded limey queens, who were, furthermore, too shy and too solidly mated to join in the general kissing and cuddling.' It was the beginning of the Beat Generation, which would pass Britten by.

They escaped Los Angeles. With Isherwood and his young man they undertook a short road trip: Palm Springs, Mount Palomar and Laguna Beach, the tallish musicians bobbing away uncomfortably and uncomplainingly in the back seat. Somewhere along the way, the two old friends alone, Isherwood asked Britten if he ever slept with other men. No, Britten replied, 'I still feel the old charm.' Isherwood responded in mid-December by writing to Britten, expressing how profoundly moved he was by their strong, seemingly inviolable bond. 'It is so right, and so simple and obvious, and so astronomically rare in this world of lies and vanity and half-promises and emotional cowardice.'

Britten was never free of his other responsibilities while on tour. His correspondence is peppered with references to the Italian translation and UK premiere of *Spring Symphony*; or his need for the latest version of the *Budd* libretto, his mind brimming with ideas; or programming and casting directions for the EOG and the Aldeburgh Festival. Cables arrived on either side of the Atlantic demanding attention, and in this way, perhaps, he was more the American-style impresario than he would ever care to admit.

24

Immediately on their return, Forster came to Crag House ready to plug the libretto's various holes. The opera had still not been officially commissioned, despite various high-level conversations about how it might fit into the planned 1951 Festival of Britain, conversations that started in late 1948 and ran on until the end of 1950. The festival – the brainchild of *News Chronicle* editor Gerald Barry, who found a sympathetic ear in Attlee's deputy, Herbert Morrison – had two functions: it was to look back to the might and glory of mid-nineteenth-century industrial Britain as captured in the 1851 Great Exhibition, and at the same time anticipate (assisted by some smoke and mirrors) such future glories in a country still in many respects on its knees. The Arts Council seemed more wedded to the festival's first goal, commissioning a number of backward-looking works for churches, women's institutes, military band, brass band and massed choirs from a series of worthy if dull British composers. One of the few hints of modernism in the council's vision was in the design for a new arts complex to be built south of the Thames on the site of the disused Lion Brewery, the neighbourhood in which much of *Oliver Twist* takes place (and in 1948 still looking every bit as sinister).*

In its favour, the Arts Council was determined Covent Garden would mount a new opera 'on the grand scale'. The commissioning process, however, was a circus, replete with comic interludes, poorly worded scripts, and Britten taming lions and walking ropes. Many of the composer's *bêtes noires* were involved at one time or another: Sadler's Wells, Glyndebourne, Covent Garden and the Arts Council. Yet it was Eric Walter White's careful stewardship of this last body that prevailed.

---

* When Churchill returned to power at the end of 1951 he crankily refused to follow through Labour's plans to erect permanent buildings in place of the temporary pavilions buttressing the new concert hall, thinking the scheme too socialist. EOG's sage chairman, James Lawrie, thought the prime minister's attitude had wider artistic implications: 'I am extremely disturbed about the probable attitude of the new Government to expenditure on such awful unnecessary things as Art . . . I don't want to be too gloomy, but I don't care much about the temperature in Whitehall insofar as I can gauge it.'

Amid runaway budgets and a fair amount of mutual recrimination between Britten, the Arts Council, Sadler's Wells and the Edinburgh Festival – not least the accusation that Britten's aspirations for the work had grown extravagantly since he first embarked on it and that he was evidently against the whole Festival of Britain in the first place – Covent Garden would eventually announce plans for the premiere of *Billy Budd* in October 1951, which later slipped back to December. There would be little money in it: the Arts Council had earmarked £500 for Britten's fee – small beer compared to the extraordinary $20,000 (£7,000) Stravinsky would soon extract from La Fenice and La Scala for *The Rake's Progress* – but there would be a shiny new production of the opera which would not trouble the EOG's precarious accounts.

Harewood thought the objections of Sadler's Wells were less to do with budgeting, more to do with the opera's disquieting subject matter and a niggling doubt over whether Britten could pull it off. It seems extraordinary now that this could have been so. Here was Britten's first foray into grand opera since *Peter Grimes*, a work that had reshaped Britain's operatic landscape; surely *Budd* would have the same impact. Yet none of Britten's operas since *Grimes* had created so big a splash, cynics countered; why should this one? Arthur Benjamin was hardly alone in thinking that his former student's work had deteriorated following *Grimes*.

There were layers to this criticism. Britten's retreat to Aldeburgh and his refusal to have much to do with London, while he simultaneously went about developing a strong Continental profile, meant that much of what he had done since 1945 had occurred off camera. The musicians and administrators then madly refashioning Cockaigne from the ruins of London – building new concert spaces, funding new orchestras, creating a new BBC programming stream dedicated to art music and serious culture – could be forgiven for reading this as a snub. Yet when performances occurred in the spotlight, such as the UK premiere of *Spring Symphony* in the Royal Albert Hall in March 1950, Britten was left nursing his usual frustrations. On this occasion van Beinum spent all his time teaching an under-rehearsed choir its notes and entries rather than structuring and polishing the overall performance. At the final rehearsal Britten found van Beinum despairing at the nonchalant attitude he encountered in the musicians and administrators of the London Philharmonic Orchestra.

341

This was Britten's great dilemma at the start of the new decade. He personally oversaw an arts festival and an opera company, both of which ran on goodwill and farthings but still spent most of their time in the red, yet he had no confidence in the artistic integrity of the metropolitan organizations that could rid him of his onerous responsibilities and provide a home for his works. So in February 1950, at the end of a Scottish recital tour with Pears, he directed Boosey to pay direct into the Aldeburgh Festival's funds an unexpected honorarium from Koussevitzky for *Spring Symphony*, while a month later he donned a sailor's costume to attend a fancy-dress ball in aid of the EOG, *Tatler* snapping the distinguished musical figures and minor royalty in their rented finery.

Yet there were signs Britten was softening his stance. The fact that either Covent Garden or Sadler's Wells was even being considered for the new opera was progress. Moreover, in March Britten accepted an invitation from the London County Council to join its Festival Hall sub-committee, deliberating in print and person about acoustics and other musical matters, not least Ralph Downes's controversial design of the hall's organ, which exercised him considerably. 'What I am sure we shall get is something miles away from [the] Wurlitzer organs one is so tired of hearing in our major Cathedrals and Concert Halls,' he had told Downes on his appointment, later promising him a concerto to help launch it. (Downes's design prompted Vaughan Williams's resignation from the committee; he was happy with his cathedrals as they stood.) And in July Britten gave evidence to an Arts Council panel on the future of opera and ballet in Britain.

It was a revealing interview. He condemned the 'shockingly low' standard of singers emerging from the London colleges, whose poor training made it impossible to distinguish between the 'acting-deaf, or whatever you call it' and those who had not been taught the first notion of stagecraft. He talked unconvincingly about the attraction of the English to the small rather than to the very big, which he thought would see the string quartet ultimately prevail over the symphony orchestra. (On another occasion that same year he asserted that the British public could distinguish between 'Great music and Big music', a neat distinction.) He emphasized the need for British composers to hear their operas in performance so they too could learn stagecraft. 'What makes Puccini a greater composer of operas than, in my humble opinion, a great composer, is that he knows how long it takes a person to cross the room.' He batted down a Beecham witticism without even trying and rejected a suggestion that English was an ugly language to sing.* He also delicately trod on the grave of a revered artist in Britain: 'Surely we agree that if Melba had been able to act, it would not have been worse; it would have been better.'

His association with the London County Council's sub-committee was less fortunate. For all its noble, progressive aspirations in building the replacement for the much-mourned Queen's Hall, the council demonstrated a mindset every bit as regressive as that of the Arts Council's advisory panel when it came to planning what to put inside it. In January 1951 Britten saw a brochure for the Royal Festival Hall's inaugural concert season, which featured his unholy trinity of conductors, Beecham, Boult and Sargent, with the London Philharmonic, chillingly signifying the *status quo ante*. (Arturo Toscanini had originally been enlisted for the opening concerts.) Having heard nothing of the planning of the concerts and possibly believing it was here his contribution might have been most valuable (as the Arts Council had hoped), Britten resigned immediately. 'I regret to say that I do not approve of them [the concerts] and I cannot allow the public to connect my name with them.' In such fashion – two steps forward, two straight back – his dance with the capital continued.

25

There were other, quite different hurdles as the *Billy Budd* commissioning process rumbled on. Forster was seventy-one and slowing down. He needed to be met at train stations or deposited back in Cambridge. ('Oh my darling, darling Ben, please don't drive so fast my dear, dear darling.') He could not comprehend Britten's fast pace and full diary, nor his tendency to abandon *Budd* mid-sentence for other commitments.

* Viscount Esher: 'Sir Thomas Beecham told us that the dampness of our climate must always make it impossible for English people to sing, and that it does something to the throat. Do you believe in all that?' Britten: 'I think it is extremely witty and I think it is absolutely untrue. For one thing, I think that the gentleman himself would admit that the most resonant voices come from Wales, and Wales, I should have thought, was one of the dampest parts of the country.'

Forster's health was fragile and he was worried, not entirely melodramatically, that he might die before completing the libretto. In March and April 1950 he bedded down at Crag House, recuperating from a (second) prostate operation, recording in his diary his many ailments with almost ghoulish fascination, from aching feet and bleeding toe, to leaky bladder and tender left testicle. It was in Aldeburgh during the weekend of 22–3 April that he heard for the first time his Act 1 words set to music.

What remarkable occasions the informal first performances must have been throughout Britten's life, from the early days of Bridge looking over his shoulder, pencil in hand, to the final years of his life when, unable to play, he ceded the piano stool to other musicians who could give sound to his shaky musical hand. Basil Coleman, who was to direct the first production of *Budd*, was transfixed by a later complete play-through.

> As well as playing from the piano score, Britten half-sang all the vocal parts, giving a vivid idea of the characterizations he had in mind ... and as the daylight faded in the room round him and the terrible events of the story developed, Britten became more and more immersed in them himself. At the finish he was exhausted, physically and emotionally. It was very apparent how much the work meant to him and I did my utmost to hold onto those first images and impressions as they came flooding over us, for use in the production.

They were certainly enervating events for Britten – intimate and revealing in equal measure. In such circumstances, admiring and appreciative noises were required of those present. There was so much to be taken in. Later, perhaps, a question could be asked or a comment made, but was not always well received. David Matthews, who worked for Britten at Aldeburgh during the late 1960s, observed that he 'would sort of screw up his face when you were on the verge of saying anything dangerous – you knew when to stop'. Of all Britten's friends and colleagues possibly only Erwin Stein, with his quick ear and impeccable pedigree, was allowed anything more, and he always couched his comments with care.

The beginner Forster was unaware of the protocol, so while the Harewoods and Ralph and Clare Hawkes looked on, he outlined his reservations concerning the lament Britten had composed for the minutes following the flogging of the poor young Novice in Act 1. 'He has done dry contrapuntal stuff,' he wrote afterwards to his lover Bob

Buckingham, 'no doubt original and excellent from the musician's point of view, but not at all appropriate from mine.'

It is an inaccurate description. Forster could have gleaned none of the orchestral colours from Britten's performance at the piano, but even so it was no arid fugue he was playing. The contrapuntal writing – a languorous duet between saxophone and bass clarinet – is almost incidental to the chorale it encircles, in which the crushing brutality of life on board a man-of-war is touched on by a small chorus of onlookers, the Novice's fellow sailors. The two wind instruments duck and weave through the texture, through the wretched Novice's cries of pain and shame, through his friend's hollow assertions that both will pass. It is cumulatively a giant punctuation point, like the chorales in Bach's Passions, the participants almost standing outside time. It is slow, certainly: perhaps Forster imagined the words he had written for the Novice travelling much faster; perhaps he conceived them being spat out by the young sailor, not wrung from him tortuously and picked up and underlined by the onlookers. Nonetheless, it was a tin-eared response from this moderately musical author, to which Britten reacted predictably badly. Forster soon after took his recuperation elsewhere.

He was not aware of his faux pas, however, only of a certain inexplicable *froideur*, and so there were more such confrontations as the score slowly emerged. Crozier found himself in the unusual if welcome position of keeping the peace, never more so than after the play-through of the original Act 2 in late November, the day after the composer's thirty-seventh birthday. Here there was a new complaint: Britten's treatment of Claggart's big monologue.

Monologues are ungainly devices in the wrong hands. There is narrative to be advanced or psychology to be plumbed, and few audiences forget the monologue is simply a vehicle to these ends. Yet in the right hands – Janáček at the end of *The Cunning Little Vixen*, the Forester singing of death and renewal; or Verdi in *Otello*, Iago declaiming, 'I believe in a cruel God / who has created me in His image / and whom, in hate, I name' – puppeteer and strings are nowhere to be seen.

It was Iago's 'Credo' that Forster had in mind when writing the aria. Forster had Claggart contemplate Billy's beauty and goodness, before recognizing that the comparison with his own black soul was too invidious to be allowed. Forster even had Claggart predict Billy's fate – at the yardarm and then in a watery grave – before the sailor growls his demonic pledge, 'I, John Claggart, Master-at-Arms upon the *Indomitable*, have you in my power, and I will destroy you.' Britten probably had the lesser-known Grand Inquisitor's aria from Verdi's *Don Carlos* on his mind when he set to work on the monologue – the gravelly first half of which is more amorphous than Verdi's 'Credo' – and Forster was left unmoved by his efforts. It was nothing to do with Britten's limitations as a singer; whatever these were, his orchestral piano playing and his characterization of the work always came across in these informal performances. Forster simply found nothing in this dark aria to match the heights of his prose – or, more likely, found nothing that matched the showy bravura of Verdi's 'Credo'.

A week or so later Forster expanded his criticism in a much-quoted letter to Britten. 'I want *passion* – love constricted, perverted, poisoned, but nevertheless *flowing* down its agonising channel; a sexual discharge gone evil. Not soggy depression or growling remorse. I seemed [to be] turning from one musical discomfort to another, and was dissatisfied.' The reaction crippled Britten, who sought solace and advice from Pears, Stein and Crozier, the latter sagely telling him not to tinker with the aria until he had completed the next act. Crozier then told Forster of the composer's extreme sensitivity to the slightest criticism, information the writer greeted with surprise and gratitude. Britten left the monologue well alone and continued with Act 3. With distance, however, he decided that Forster was perhaps onto something, for in July the following year, a matter of weeks before he completed the composition draft, he refashioned the monologue into something resembling the aria or 'more recognisable form' his collaborator had sought.

The problem was that Forster was used to greater deference than he thought the collaboration afforded. To the many writers and scholars and young gay men in his address book, he was a venerated elder statesman of English letters. Nothing in his previous friendship with Britten prepared him for the composer's single-mindedness. Forster could himself be prickly, as demonstrated by his letters to Buckingham, full of slights and grudges, real or imagined. When this same November Britten and Crozier called on Forster in Cambridge to discuss a troubling scene, eminent writer bawled out eminent composer, addressing him 'like some low-class servant who deserved to be whipped. Then he stalked off into the night.' A coda to this episode appears in Forster's final diary entry for 1950. 'I am rather a fierce old man at moments . . .

and he is rather a spoilt boy, and certainly a busy one who rushes whither he sees most immediately to do, with whomsoever, and leaving no matter whom or what behind him.'

This was somehow more than the expected tensions born of a close, exacting collaboration. *Billy Budd* was the product of a different collaborative experience for Britten: for the first time since *Paul Bunyan* he was working with a librettist whose talent matched his own. More significantly, the work has legitimate claim to being Britten's greatest opera. Before a word was written, before Britten sketched his toy ship and batted away Crozier's objections, Forster told the composer about the novella's 'lovable (and hateable) human beings connected with immensities through the tricks of art'. It was not a bad lodestar, and Britten responded with his own great tricks of art. He braided Melville's silver whistles into the score, each as shrill as a sea hawk. He created a battle scene of visceral impact, cut through with thrilling martial fanfares and booming great guns of war, the latter haunting Vere into his old age. He played with the dull, insistent rhythm of the sea and gave the sailors lyrical lullabies and jocular shanties to sing. He accompanied Billy in his exuberant meeting with Captain Vere with the sounds of a navy bugle, and gave him a dry tin whistle for the resigned aria he sings on the gun-deck near the end of the opera, chained between two cannons, which tootles away in an amateur, improvised manner. He took Melville at his word in the scene in which Vere informs Billy of his fate ('Beyond the communication of the sentence, what took place at this interview was never known'), depicting it only in a series of thirty-four primary chords of different colour, volume and suggestiveness, the fierce grating spasms of the brass chords giving way to muted but definite resolution. The sequence's meaning was left deliberately ambiguous, as was the composer's wont, yet forgiveness, understanding, love and wisdom can all be read into it – and certainly have been.*

And in this manner Britten created 'the horrible texture of a fabric that should be woven of ships' cables & hawsers', as Melville described his other great story, *Moby-Dick*. Britten's last sure touch was saved for

---

* Australian artist Sidney Nolan met Britten for the first time when he was composing the section, and was told by the composer what 'an intense experience it was to envisage the scene and to write it'. Nolan was enthralled by Britten's description of his creative process, how 'it kind of steals into you in some way and then reaches a peak and you can do things then, under the influence of that situation, that you can't otherwise do'.

the moment following Billy's hanging, where he composed music of overwhelming, expressionistic power, a violent gesture unequalled in his output – the shrieking great climax of the 'Libera Me' (Deliver Me) in *War Requiem* aside. Taking his cue from Melville, who describes a muffled murmur of 'capricious revulsion' emanating from Billy's crewmates as they witness the dangling corpse, Britten gave his chorus grunting, violent cries, which explode in rage, teeter on the edge of revolt, and which only then are put down forcibly by the ship's lieutenants. It is a shivery, unforgettable moment in the theatre.

Forster's tricks included incorporating a lot of Melville's words and phrases, which so effectively evoke the particular style of the late work, so different from his masterly *Bartleby* in mood and language: 'Struck dead by an angel of God! Yet the angel must hang!'; 'Do you come to me, Master-at-arms, with so foggy a tale?'; 'ruddy-tipped daisies'; 'the sweet and pleasant young fellow'; and much of Billy's monologue in the darbies (handcuffs), including the slow, long-vowelled sentence, 'I'm sleepy, and the oozy weeds about me twist', the last word almost whispered in Britten's setting, to devastating effect. Forster reused some of his own words, too. When the Novice sings 'It's fate, it's fate. I've no choice. Everything's fate', he is borrowing George Emerson's words to Mr Beebe in *A Room with a View*, which show up the shallow determinism of both the young press-ganged sailor and the young lover George.

Forster's greatest trick was in rehabilitating Vere, 'rescuing' him from his creator, as he put it in early 1949. 'We felt that Melville was disgracing Vere,' Forster later said of the trial scene, and certainly, amid the prim remonstrations and lawyerly recitation of statutes in the novella, it is difficult to feel any sympathy for his behaviour. Britten thought the same: 'for my own particular point of view of the way that Melville made Vere behave in the trial would not have been sympathetic or encouraging to me to write music.' So Forster and Crozier leavened Vere's behaviour in the trial, much as Slater had chipped away at Crabbe's Peter Grimes, urged on by Britten and Pears. They made his lieutenants more authoritative, less overwhelmed by the circumstances and their responsibility for Billy's fate. We are made aware of Vere's dilemma, and we feel sorry for this poor man, caught between universal moral truths and earthly laws. It is a revisiting of Coleridge's fascination with men placed 'in an absolute Dependence on Powers & Events, over which they have no Control'.

Yet there is more to it even than this, for we also recognize in the opera what Vere identified in Claggart – repression and desire – and his faint realization that were he to show Billy mercy or discretion he would be acknowledging these feelings in himself, an impossibility then and ever.* So he talks instead of God and judgement and forgiveness and other woolly metaphysics. It appears we *are* meant to think of Billy as Christ, despite Forster's early dismissal of this approach, but we end up instead thinking of him as Isaac, docilely consenting to God's and Abraham's brutal sentence. And we see at the core of Melville's parable – the work of one unbeliever, Melville, magnified by the convictions of another, Forster – a bolt of utterly cruel and heartless behaviour. Britten could not have joined Forster in mocking religion to this extent (or to the extent Melville does in *Moby-Dick*), yet his views on its fallibility would have ensured he went along with the basic narrative. At the end of his life Britten thought they should have gone one step further in their refashioning of Vere and had him step in to save Billy (as he argued with Rosamund Strode). Yet the power of the opera lies in the realization that, though such discretion was available to him, Vere chose not to exercise it. Earthly laws prevail and Vere is haunted into his old age by how useless were these man-made laws, clutching on to Billy's last-minute benediction of him with ever-increasing discomfort.

There is a final point to consider. American cultural historian Howard Franklin has identified in Melville's *Billy Budd* an exposé of the moral culpability of capital punishment, fraught arguments about which were prominent in late-1880s America. The dates fit, yet whether anything else does is impossible to say. But Franklin's thesis offers a way of thinking about *Billy Budd* as a work of philosophical weight and protest, its lessons as relevant today as when it was written – for the first time by Melville in the late 1880s and then once more, in the mid-twentieth century, by three Englishmen holed up in a small town on the edge of the North Sea.

---

* On encountering Britten's *Billy Budd* for the first time, writer Jennifer Higgie perceptively described it as 'an exploration of men's inability to love each other openly, either physically or spiritually'. 'Oh, that is ridiculous!' Carmela Soprano would counter, as she did to her children and their friends at dinner one night when they suggested something similar. 'I'm sorry, but *Billy Budd* is not a homosexual book . . . *Billy Budd* is the story of an innocent sailor being picked on by an evil boss.' The only mention of the homosexual subtext of the opera in its first season was in a French newspaper.

26

With the 1950 Aldeburgh Festival behind him (which included the UK's first complete German-language performance of Bach's *St Matthew Passion*) and after a recital with Pears in Holland at the end of June (*Dichterliebe* and Copland's *Old American Songs*) and then a short holiday in Italy in the first half of September, Britten succumbed to more illness and depression. He pulled out of a recital with Pears and a performance of *Spring Symphony*, staying in bed to nurse a throat infection and high temperature. Marion Harewood, as she now was (Britten and Duncan had hastily assembled the meandering *A Wedding Anthem* for the previous year's nuptials, a poor-man's *Rejoice in the Lamb*) and soon to give birth to Britten's godson David, provided him with a bottle of 1943 Saint Emilion, no doubt fetched from the cellar of one of her houses. Good wine and cars were among Britten's few indulgences, and the bottle cheered him enormously.

Billy Budd pushed his life into a particular rhythm, much as *Grimes* did six years earlier. Not even the repeal of petrol rationing in mid-1950, which freed up the Rolls, distracted him from the task. He was obsessed by the piece, far more so than by any previous opera, and he remained in Aldeburgh as much as possible, depression and anxiety his companions, in a house made cold by fuel economies and bitter east winds. 'It is a strange business this, creating a world which finally ends by dominating oneself,' he wrote to Marion Harewood.

But the death of Ralph Hawkes on 8 September shook him. It was the end of fifteen years of friendship and canny advocacy, and it started the slow unravelling of Britten's relationship with the publishing house Hawkes had co-founded. Towards the end composer and publisher were no longer as thick as they had once been (Erwin Stein and Anthony Gishford were Britten's day-to-day contacts), yet Boosey's philistinism and Ernst Roth's antagonism were constant reminders of Hawkes's warm urbanity and his scouting eye.

He tinkered with an old work, something old age and illness would make more common. At the prospect of a Heifetz performance he slightly revised his Violin Concerto, as he would again in 1954 and once more in 1965. 'I hope what I have done is to leave the work as it would have been had I been able to write it in 1939 with my present experience,' he told his old friend Albert Goldberg. 'I think I bit off then a bit more than I could chew!'

And of course he had the EOG to worry about; its new manager, Henry Foy, who was either corrupt, incompetent or just a bit mad, had plunged the group into further financial chaos after making off with the little money that was on the books. In mid-November Britten went to the Arts Council, cap in hand, and managed to secure a special Festival of Britain grant of £5,000 and an advance of an identical amount on the following year's subsidy, staving off the EOG's immediate liquidation. No one thought the increased state subsidy was here to stay.

To concentrate on *Budd*, Britten resolved not to give any performances during 1951. He stuck to this resolution as best he could, leaving Pears free to moonlight with other partners, among them the glum, inspiring wizard Erich Kleiber, who in January was in the Covent Garden pit for *The Magic Flute*. Britten broke his resolution a few times: in February he returned to Friends House in Euston Road for a performance of *Die schöne Müllerin*, and at Easter, with all but the opera's Epilogue complete, he darted to Vienna for a recital with Pears. On his return he found himself devoting some hours learning Tippett's exuberant song cycle *The Heart's Assurance* for its May premiere at Wigmore Hall, a Pears commission for the couple that ended up being a loose fit. It was Noel Mewton-Wood who braved Decca's studio in 1953 to record it with Pears, while twelve years later, on the occasion of Tippett's sixtieth birthday, Britten added a spiky postscript to his tribute, 'I wish your piano parts weren't so difficult!'

Despite his best efforts, May was impossibly busy. Britten conducted both his *Spring Symphony* at the newly opened Royal Festival Hall and, from the harpsichord, his sober realization of Purcell's *Dido and Aeneas* with the EOG at the Lyric, Hammersmith. Saddled to Monteverdi's *Combattimento di Tancredi e Clorinda*, the new *Dido* helped make up a three-week Britten Festival in Hammersmith, part of the much grander Festival of Britain then under way. A complex rotation of artists and operas – *Lucretia*, *Herring* and *Let's Make an Opera*, in addition to the double bill – ensured a seven-shows-a-week diet of Britten's works for the stage, which, despite every precedent, generated a profit of £1,140. At the same time he put his mind to two prospective works for the EOG. The first was a children's opera, an adaptation of Beatrix Potter's *The Tale of Mr Tod*, which never found its way clear of Potter's publisher and its punitive copyright. The second was an adaptation of Henry James's *The Turn of the Screw*, which he confessed was almost more than he could face just then, spent as he was by *Budd*. And finally, at the end of the month, he travelled to Wiesbaden with the EOG (*Lucretia*), after which they all set up camp once more in Aldeburgh for the festival.

Dido, to which the Elmhirsts had generously pledged support in December when it looked as though the EOG would go under, was relatively little labour for quite a lot of love. Britten solved the troublesome end of Act 2 – six lines of text for which no music exists – by borrowing snippets from three other Purcell works. Mostly he was applauded for his solution, though there was predictable sniffiness in some quarters. He responded with a letter to *The Times*. 'Until such a happy event as the discovery of the missing numbers occurs, I believe it is better to restore the original symmetry of the work with Purcellian material than to leave this wonderful musical building with a large hole in it.'

There were other distractions, of course. He somehow found time to compose *Six Metamorphoses after Ovid*, beguiling pen sketches for solo oboe – inspired by the Roman poet's long narrative poem – which dart around the monophonic instrument, creating a brilliant, luminescent tapestry from a single thread. It was premiered during the 1951 festival on Thorpeness Meare, two miles up the road from Aldeburgh. Yet all other activities were secondary to his real task. The sea shanty sung by Billy and his mates gave him grief, yet he refused to allow it to delay him: he wrote music without words, sketching the rhythms for Crozier and Forster, telling them to find something suitable, which neither did. (Forster enlisted the help of his Cambridge friend and colleague, Kenneth Harrison, who came up with the solution – a boisterous tongue-twister with improbable Audenesque rhymes.) And progress was marked by the steady production of vocal score fascicles, from which the cast, chorus and conductor were to learn the opera.

Illness slowed him down once more during July and August – this time cystitis, for which he took sulphonamide, as he had ten years earlier. Yet in the fog of this illness and subsequent depression he managed to scribble 'August 10th 1951' on the last page of the composition draft. The pure mechanics of orchestration then took over, though even Britten conceded that there were an awful lot of notes. He paused long enough to become irritated by Auden's pronouncements on opera, reproduced in *Tempo* magazine, a definite hardening in attitude towards the poet.* 'Really the old serpent excelled himself in the current Tempo – some quite memorably inane remarks!' He was more frank to the Harewoods about *The Rake's Progress*. 'I feel miserably disappointed (I have done since I first saw the libretto & first few pages of the score) that easily the greatest composer alive should have such an irresponsible & perverse view of opera (of the voice & of the setting of words & of characterisation in particular).' This was a brief excursion from his routine. Mostly he kept his head down.

Forster came to stay at Crag House early in September, demanding attention and consideration, infuriating Britten by asking him to play bits from the opera he had already heard, offering scant comment in return. 'He doesn't seem able to grasp it at all – or [be] really interested in the musical side of the opera!' Britten complained to Stein. At a play-through for the production team, Forster infuriated Britten by saying, 'I was very, very moved. Why didn't you bring those chords back?' Britten, white with rage and exhaustion, pointed to either the end of the great aria Billy sings in the darbies or Vere's Epilogue, where the interview chords are revisited, somewhat embroidered. 'Look! There they all are!'

27

He left all this and the bad autumn weather behind, escaping in mid-September with Pears, Coleman, Oldham and the twelve-year-old local schoolboy Robin Long for a pointedly slow two-week Rhine cruise. They hired a motor launch from a boatman in Lowestoft, skippered by Burrell's brother John, an old navy hand too fond of drink. They sought their sea legs by spending the first night stationary on the River Alde, sailing out the next day. They crossed the North Sea, a child's boat in a bath knocked this way and that, sometimes terrifyingly so. At each stop they walked and explored new towns or villages. They ate the occasional meal in a restaurant or *Kneipe*, though Pears and Coleman were

---

* 'In opera the orchestra is addressed to the singers, not to the audience,' Auden wrote. 'An opera-lover will put up with and even enjoy an orchestral interlude on condition that he knows the singers cannot sing just now because they are tired or the scene-shifters are at work, but any use of the orchestra by itself which is not filling-in time is, for him, wasting it.'

happy enough to cook food for the whole party, shuffling about in the small galley. Leaving Cologne they found themselves with ships on either side, tugs pulling seven or eight barges at once. When things looked bad, when it looked as though either the barges would sink them or the long ropes ensnare them, Pears announced, 'I think I'll go below and shave now.' Before heading home they got as far as Bingen, a small town tucked under the Rhine knee in south-west Germany.

Back in Aldeburgh Britten rewarded the Harewoods for their friendship (and for George's unwavering encouragement when Forster blackened his mood) by dedicating the new opera to them. Harewood had heard the work in progress, comparing its emotional impact to that of *Otello*. Britten would have thought the praise too fulsome, yet was no doubt relieved to hear it.

The rehearsals were frantic. Covent Garden did not yet have adequate permanent studios on site and time in the theatre was limited; the cast became an itinerant troupe of medieval players, making their way to somewhere in Hammersmith, or the Welsh Workman's Club, or some such hall in Gray's Inn Road. Rehearsals were not helped at all by the slapstick array of ailments among the creative team: Britten's bad ear, Coleman's septic foot, Forster's slow-healing broken ankle and Crozier's ulcerated stomach. The conductor, the Austrian Josef Krips, had seemed happy with each instalment of the vocal score as it arrived, which from the first suggested the shape and scale of the whole. Yet as he got closer to the premiere on 1 December, aware of its importance and with one eye on the London critics, he grew less and less sanguine. When the orchestral score arrived in manuscript, with its tiny staves covered in Britten's scratchy, hurried notation, Krips panicked, saying it would be impossible to learn the work in time. Harewood convened a crisis lunch at his London home in Orme Square, where he and Stein attempted to keep Krips on board the listing ship. Regardless of the smiles and reassurances with which the conductor left the Harewoods', he went home and immediately resigned from the production. Britten reluctantly stepped into his shoes, which was the last thing he felt like doing.

From senior management down to the cast's smallest powder monkey, Covent Garden did him proud. Acknowledging there was no baritone in Britain who matched Melville's description of Billy, Webster happily searched further afield for a more handsome specimen. In

America he discovered the barrel-chested Theodor Uppman, who maintained his good looks and pleasing, naive personality to the end of his life and was here an ideal counter to Pears's Vere and Frederick Dalberg's Claggart. Since it was an all-male cast, the chorus had to be augmented, which Webster acceded to willingly, though yet more men should probably have been found. The lighting operators who had survived the war or the allure of the far more lucrative film industry worked at an antiquated console of dials and slides and flicking meters, and did their best to give the team the atmosphere on stage they sought – the moody shadows beneath deck and the stark contrast of the great whale bones. In all aspects Britten was thrilled with the courtesy and co-operation, with the willingness of everyone to get behind the difficult new work, to soak up its language, to respect its dark, unsettling themes. How different it all was from 1945.

'WISHING YOU A TRIUMPH TONIGHT LOVE WYSTAN AUDEN IGOR STRAVINSKY.' Given his recent grandstanding, it is impossible to say whether Auden intended this cable as an inflammatory or as a heartfelt gesture. Kenneth Clark caught Forster after the opening performance on 1 December and told him, rather wonderfully, that it was 'one of the great masterpieces that change human conduct'. Audiences and critics were less sure. 'One always resents having it dinned into one's ears that a new work is a masterpiece before it has been performed,' wrote Stephen Williams in the *Evening News*, 'and Benjamin Britten's *Billy Budd* was trumpeted into the arena by such a deafening roar of advance publicity that many of us entered Covent Garden on Saturday (when the composer conducted the first performance) with a mean, sneaking hope that we might be able to flesh our fangs in it.' Williams did not, though many of his colleagues did – some of them far from the mark, others penning insightful critiques. With distance, Britten was able to write to Forster on his eightieth birthday in 1958, remembering with pleasure the collaboration, observing that 'the result is certainly one of my best operas – although the world is going to take sometime to find that out'. He was completely right.

5

Establishment

England, 1952–1955

I

Late one morning in February 1952 the sonorous voice of BBC announcer John Snagge interrupted the scheduled programme. 'This. Is. London. It is with the greatest sorrow that we make the following announcement. It was announced from Sandringham at 10.45 today, February the sixth 1952, that the King, who retired to rest last night in his usual health, passed peacefully away in his sleep earlier this morning.' He was only fifty-six, and although his lungs had been slowly shutting down, the King's death was unexpected. There were no doctors at his bedside or nurses monitoring his sleep; instead it was left to a royal valet, on discovering that he could not wake His Majesty, to sound the alarm. Princess Elizabeth was in Kiganjo, Kenya, with her husband, and it was as Queen that she made her sad journey home. The ripples from the King's death reached Britten and initiated a gradual but marked change in him.

An immediate consequence was that the Third Programme's schedules were thrown over to sombre programmes and coverage, postponing the first broadcast of Britten's *Canticle II*. The new work was a curious if revealing undertaking. With *Budd* much on his mind and under his skin, Britten had in January turned to the biblical story of Abraham and Isaac as the source for another canticle. Melville may even have given Britten the idea, for at one point in the novella he suggests that Vere 'may in end have caught Billy to his heart, even as Abraham may have caught young Isaac on the brink of resolutely offering him up in obedience to the exacting behest'. In the early 1950s Britten still managed to walk the fine line between appreciating religious parables and undermining them. He liked the stories – for artistic, cultural and certain

356

spiritual reasons, and of course their popular resonance in a country of churchgoers – sometimes steering them towards a secular destination. Not often enough for Forster, who thought Britten a little too forgiving of Christian ideology, a little too blinded by the shimmering beauty of its imagery. Forster conceded the attraction of the tenderness, pity and love at the core of Christianity, but hated how they were conditional on certain beliefs and behaviour. 'What with this and what with the historical difficulties,' he wrote to Britten in late 1948 with touching understatement, 'I have to find my emotional explanation of the Universe, for of course I must find one, elsewhere.'

So this Quakerish, low-church, sometime deist continued to be drawn to the myths and monsters of early Christianity. In certain instances he is the young penitent of his Suffolk childhood and early London years; in others the religious sceptic, repulsed by the cruelty at the heart of the tales and the ready transference of their moral to contemporary society. *Canticle II 'Abraham and Isaac'* is from the former category, as are the majority of such works at the time: there is a white-bearded, controlling, mostly benevolent God at their core.

Britten took a pencil to his copy of Alfred Pollard's *English Miracle Plays, Moralities and Interludes*, whittling down the long story of Abraham and his son into a tight dramatic arc. He cut Isaac's more extreme protests and mundane comments, leaving him in docile acceptance of his fate. (At one point in Pollard's version the considerate son worries aloud that so much spilled blood will ruin his clothing.) He brilliantly fashioned the Trinitarian voice of God in a simple homophonic duet for Pears and Ferrier, accompanied by piano, the contralto's near-angelic status in Britain helping the imagery no end. It was far from the bellowing Old Testament treatment he would later give God in *Noye's Fludde*, as it was from the voice he had given the invisible, eponymous hero of *Paul Bunyan*, a God proxy. Amid ecstatic leaps, sparse piano harmonies, and improbable benedictions given the circumstances, Isaac asks for his father's blessing, which is duly offered, along with that of Isaac's unwitting mother and, for good measure, the Holy Trinity.

Rembrandt had captured more of the story's barbaric, hollow-souled cruelty in his *Sacrifice of Abraham* (1635). He placed a fairly mature Isaac in the centre foreground, lying on a pyre of sticks and twigs, his father's splayed hand covering the boy's face, an angel wrenching Abraham's other hand from a silver knife frozen mid-air. If there is a hint of such cruelty in Britten's treatment it is only in the section where Abraham 'doth kiss his son Isaac, and binds a kerchief about his head', any time during which a divine intervention could call matters to a close; the intervention is a long time coming.

For all its unquestioning recitation of the story, *Canticle II* is a work of great poise and simple beauty. The narrative arc conforms to what pioneering psychiatrist Elisabeth Kübler-Ross would seventeen years later identify as the five stages of grief: denial, anger, bargaining, depression and acceptance, though Britten manages redemption as well and gives each stage a different musical and metaphysical character. The piece leaped quickly onto and off the page: it was composed in the early weeks of 1952 and premiered on 21 January in Nottingham. Tippett greatly admired the work's opening, in which the piano spells out a simple, warm arpeggio and where God is made to sound as though he was composed by Pérotin in the twelfth century (Pears having recently excavated the composer on one of his archaeological digs), the two voices bound *in organum*. Tippett told Britten what he thought of it, to which Britten is reported to have replied, 'Yes, that's worth a million dollars.' It doesn't sound like Britten – too brash, too boastful for such a simple idea – though he was proud of the *Canticle*'s first page. Two years later he would return to the idea of disembodied voices issuing demands and devising brutal tests of loyalty, this time in a non-religious context – by no means the only connecting rod between *The Turn of the Screw* and the humble yet well-constructed *Canticle II*.

At the first performance on 21 January 1952 Ferrier tripped as she left the stage, wrenching her back, which Britten and Pears put down to a simple misstep. Only in the following months, when it became apparent her recent treatment for breast cancer had been unsuccessful, did they remember her stumbling on stage and realize its significance.

Despite Ferrier's sickness, Britten was determined to record the piece with her (she shared its dedication with Pears) and scheduled some possible studio dates in that year and the next. But her body was slowly breaking down and each date passed without the recording being made. Her unusual, marvellous voice was almost the last thing to go, however, and Britten pounced on the idea of recording *Canticle II* and a handful of other works at her house, Ferrier propped up in her sickbed. Another operation intervened, however, and a few months later she was dead. Britten nursed his own 'special selfish grief' that neither this nor any other of his works composed for Ferrier had been commercially recorded.*

The real impact of George VI's demise on Britten was not felt until March 1952, when he and Pears repaired to a ski resort in Gargellen, Austria, following recitals in Vienna and Salzburg and a long strenuous year. They walked in brilliant late-winter sunshine and worked at their eccentric skiing, their faces tanning as they went. The Harewoods joined them and one night before dinner, over glasses of schnapps or fruit brandy, the conversation turned to the idea of national opera. Why did such pieces exist, and what were they in each country? *The Bartered Bride* in Czechoslovakia, suggested Britten; *Manon* in France; *Meistersinger* in Germany (though it was a bitter pill for Britten); *Aida* in Italy ('It's the perfect expression of every kind of Italian nationalist feeling, national pride,' notwithstanding its setting, Memphis and Thebes during the reign of the Pharaohs). Yet where was the English equivalent? 'You'd better write one,' Harewood told his friend.

It is a slightly odd idea for a composer to set out to write a national opera. Or at least it was a slightly anachronistic idea for mid-twentieth-century Britain, a country without any of the nineteenth-century operatic traditions and historical reformations that gave rise to the genre on the Continent. In his operatic quest Britten echoed Vaughan Williams, of all people, for twenty years earlier V.W. described *Meistersinger* in the language of nationhood. 'Here is no playing with local colour, but the raising to its highest power all that is best in the national consciousness of his own country. This is universal art in truth, universal because it is so intensely national.' Britten was captivated by the idea and the challenge of capturing the nation's essence in a single work, alive too just then to the pioneering spirit of opera in his homeland, alert to its culture of opportunity and invention. There was no reason *not* write a national work, he reasoned, one that Britons would cling to as loyally as the villagers of Oberammergau do their passion play and the Salzburg Festival their annual showing of Hofmannsthal's *Jedermann*.

The discussion lingered through dinner and beyond. They talked about whether it should be about Tudor or Elizabethan times and whether Henry VIII was too obvious, too villainous, a subject. Finally

---

* Both the studio recording made a day after the London premiere, two days before the King's death, and a BBC tape of the second live performance were later destroyed, in sinister circumstances, Britten thought, before he had the chance to purloin either.

Elizabeth I was suggested. Harewood had recently read Lytton Strachey's unconstrained biography *Elizabeth and Essex* (1928) and talked it up enthusiastically. It was fitting: the 1953 coronation of a new Queen Elizabeth would be marked by an opera about the old. Britten had only one condition: he would undertake it only if it were made an official part of the coronation celebrations – a revealing proviso.

At the end of the skiing holiday they said farewell to Pears, who returned to England for concerts, and travelled on to Zurich. There they saw *Eugene Onegin* for the first time, which seems scarcely credible today. From Zurich they went to stay with Harewood's cousins, the Prince and Princess of Hesse and the Rhine, who soon became fast friends of Britten and Pears. And from there they travelled to Wiesbaden for the disastrous first German production of *Billy Budd*, the piece cut significantly and lumbered with a poor translation and cast, and bad conducting to boot. Britten sought solace in drink, at one point after the performance sitting at the Hesses' piano, all thumbs, to impersonate an inebriated concert pianist attempting the opening of Tchaikovsky's Piano Concerto No. 1. It was an unexpected return to 1940 Brooklyn and the easy, slapstick humour of February House. As soon as they were all back in Britain Harewood got in touch with another cousin, Sir Alan Lascelles, then the Queen's private secretary, to seek royal assent for the new opera. By early May it was granted, only thirteen months before the coronation. The possible children's opera was shelved, its librettist William Plomer press-ganged aboard the new vessel, and Britten set about battling an impossibly tight timetable and Pears's sullen, myriad objections to the project.

2

Britten cleared his diary for the year – or at least his version of clearing his diary. There were performances of *Budd* to conduct in Britain and abroad, and recitals with Pears to honour. (Others were farmed out to Mewton-Wood and lutenist and guitarist Julian Bream.) And there was another Aldeburgh Festival to oversee, the most austere yet following the high expenditure and working deficit of 1951. The basic structure of the 1952 festival stayed in place for the remainder of the decade: one opera; two orchestral concerts with chorus; an opera concert; a chamber music recital; a Mozart and Haydn programme; a choral concert; a 'big name'; a programme of music and poetry; 'Music on the Meare', an outdoor performance in nearby Thorpeness; lectures by distinguished artists and thinkers; and the Britten–Pears recital, which still helped subsidize the whole affair.

It was also the year in which France once more held Britten to its bosom, even if the grip this time was not as tight. In Paris in late May for two performances of *Billy Budd* (presented by Covent Garden), Britten and Pears looked with wonder at the treasures in shop windows, yet were generally unimpressed by Parisian society, by the cold sophisticates and sniffy critics. Nancy Mitford described the *Budd* performances as an outstanding failure – too long and too dull for French taste – which is certainly how *Le Figaro* reviewed the work ('long and annoying'). It was also how Auden saw it, if Walton can be trusted as a source. ('Auden's just returned from Paris,' he wrote to Christopher Hassall, 'where he'd seen both B.B's; & said he thought the opera absolutely the end & hadn't gone down too well.') *L'Aurore* reported the French composer Henri Sauguet expressing relief that he did not have to pay for his ticket and noted the eminent writer Florent Fels's dismissal of the opera's homosexual subtext. Perhaps the performance was bad or the surfeit of intervals infuriating; these were otherwise strangely off-key reactions.

The Englishmen were more taken with Aix-en-Provence in July and here the affection was returned. It was another road trip with the Harewoods, who matched Britten's Rolls with a stately Austin Princess, the cars transported over the Channel on a night ferry. The trip was not purely recreation: Britten and Pears gave a recital in the grand old Cour de l'Hôtel de Ville – full of tapestries and fine woodwork – which bewitched the locals. The rest of the time in Provence was spent exploring, eating and bathing, before the party moved on to Menton and then Salzburg for further recitals. They were comfortable in each other's company – Marion a beautiful, gentle, conciliatory figure, passionate about music; George a serious, cultured man, interested in everything; Pears a gadfly, skipping from topic to topic; Britten focused but relaxed, chatting away easily one minute, silent with his thoughts the next. Britten and Pears made a show of resenting the concerts, though they were planned from the beginning to cover the expense of their opulent hotels and hearty meals.

During these travels and other trips Britten's mind never strayed far from *Gloriana*, the title they had settled on. He wanted a simple, clear narrative from Plomer, the thoughtful South African writer and friend of E. M. Forster, one punctuated by scenes of royal pageantry, which were never to descend to 'just folk dances and village green stuff', as he told Harewood. (Britten originally thought Duncan, aided by Harewood, might undertake the libretto if Plomer declined, though the prospect left him understandably unenthusiastic.) The pageantry would come to compromise the opera's narrative, as the various parties involved in the premiere sought different things from the same occasion, flexing their muscles to that end. At this early stage, however, Britten saw the pageantry as a vital illustration of Elizabethan life, not mere trimming for a royal gala.

Britten and Plomer worked from the scribbled notes the composer made reading both Strachey's book and J. E. Neale's 1934 biography of Elizabeth. It was much as Forster and Britten had done with *Budd* and Melville, and Britten with other collaborators before. By early July the scribbles had become a road map. There were to be three acts of two scenes each, the latter two acts containing a 'diversion'. Key events were listed: an early quarrel between Essex and Mountjoy; an intimate meeting between Queen Elizabeth and Essex; a grand ball at Richmond Palace, which included the episode of Lady Essex's dress and the announcement of her husband's commission to Ireland; Essex's arrival back in England, unsuccessful in his campaign against the rebel Tyrone; his sentence to death for conspiring against Queen Elizabeth; finally her own death.

Britten was prescriptive about how these sketched incidents might be knitted into an operatic narrative, supplemented by the Elizabethan atmosphere in which he was then immersing himself. Britten and Plomer visited the National Portrait Gallery in mid-July to look at paintings of the opera's protagonists. Britten bought monochrome postcards of pictures by unknown artists of Elizabeth, Essex, Cecil and Raleigh for stimulation. The Queen on the postcard is heavily disguised, for she was toothless and bald at this stage of her life. She wears a richly textured gown flecked with jewels and a high ruff to hide her neck and jowls. Her face is fierce and overly painted, eyes dark and haunted ('the traces of beauty were replaced by hard lines, borrowed colours, and a certain grotesque intensity', writes Strachey). Essex is handsome and looks surprisingly humble, his beard soft, his chest adorned with honours. Cecil is a ghostly figure, his thin face emerging from dark clothes and background. Later in the year Britten and Plomer visited Hatfield House, built by Cecil in the early 1600s and occupied by his direct descendant, Lord Salisbury. There they entered a world of Elizabethan wonder: a grand staircase carved from oak, adorned with small figures; the Long Gallery with its gold-leaf ceiling; the Marble Hall with its fine carvings and seventeenth-century tapestries; huge fireplaces at every turn, large enough to roast a whole pig; exquisite crystal goblets; armaments and paintings throughout, including the stunning Rainbow Portrait of Queen Elizabeth, painted near the end of her reign, deceptive and alluring in equal measure; a library lined with books from the sixteenth century onwards; and a letter in Elizabeth's hand, which thrilled Britten.

From Provence he reacted to Plomer's draft of Act 1 and to his outline of the remaining two acts, his scrappy annotations all over Plomer's neat, cursive longhand. The metre and rhymes of the recitatives were too square; could a word be taken out here and there? Could the crowd respond more at this point and, at another, could Essex have a more personal reaction to what was being said? Didn't the Queen call Essex 'Robin'? Couldn't Lady Essex change into her fine gown immediately prior to the ball scene and not be wearing it beforehand in the garden, which seems quite wrong? Finally he suggested a stunning, cinematic ending to the opera, 'a quite unrealistic slow fade out of the Queen', which he detailed as though it were a camera script for the GPO Film Unit.

> Signing of warrant. Take lights down except for a spot on Elizabeth. Then, so as to suggest her mind is on Essex, play an orchestral version of the 'Brambleberry' song, while people come & hand her documents to sign, consult her on matters – to which she replies automatically or not at all. Then finally, perhaps one might suggest she's dying; some doctor tells her to go to bed – she won't, but continues to stand there gauntly, like some majestic fowl, & slow fade of all lights to show the end. Could you think about this?

Plomer did think about it, but not for long: 'I like *very much* your suggestions about the final scene of the opera.' Queen Elizabeth is indeed left standing at the end like some majestic fowl – the phrase likely inspired by Strachey ('The fierce old hen sat still, brooding over the English nation'), since Britten was never a great one for analogies. The various revisions, with Britten's snips and cuts, made the scene conform even more to his original prescription.

There was no time for prevarication; Slater would have been no use to him at all. Britten was respectful of Plomer's work and his warm, easygoing nature. He consulted him on changes or requirements, often sketching alternative lines, leaving Plomer to 'tidy up the whiskers', in Rosamund Strode's neat phrase. Requests and queries were often made, literally, on the back of a postcard. Britten asked for postcard confirmation of his suggestion that the tumbler they had planned be replaced by a small boy dancing a morris jig, his face painted black, typical aristocratic entertainment of the day. On another occasion Plomer sent Britten a postcard with an idea for the opera's penultimate act: 'I wonder whether the ballad-singer in Act 3 Sc 2 might not be *blind*.' (The ballad singer, a narrative device perhaps inspired by Hardy's poem of the same name, was needed to bridge the seventeen months between Essex's return to London and his beheading.) There were requests for little scraps of dialogue, to which Plomer responded immediately. Plomer's recuperation in November from a minor operation slowed them down, but only momentarily. When Britten requested a speech for Essex at the end of Act 2 in response to his commission to Ireland, a recuperating Plomer sketched something immediately and duly dispatched it from his nursing home. Britten straight away slotted it into the score. ('Armed with the favour of our gracious Empress, I am armed like a god.') Through such polite, efficient correspondence and the occasional visit to Aldeburgh, the opera took shape. There was none of Slater's foot-dragging, Duncan's poetic excesses, Crozier's prickliness, or Forster's occasional tantrums. It was a remarkably harmonious experience and would be repeated three more times in the following decade.

3

Relations were less harmonious between Britten and Covent Garden. The ballet corps, slighted at being left out of the prestigious royal gala, attempted to stake some sort of claim on the evening. Webster tried to placate Britten, but the strategizing and tact he had displayed with *Budd* deserted him, partly because he thought it a huge mistake to premiere the opera as part of a gala: the wrong people would attend, he said, not least because a reigning monarch had not attended a first night at Covent Garden in more than 200 years, as Pathé footage proudly claimed.* Britten was unwilling to heed Webster's advice, to the detriment of the work and his reputation. The friction was once more not helped by Webster's plodding style, which engendered great loyalty among his staff but made Britten explode with impatience. Webster was unaffected by the moody outbursts. He greatly enjoyed the authority and gravitas Britten brought to the house, noting in an internal memo how highly regarded he was at Covent Garden. 'The orchestra adores him as much as it dislikes others' – a litmus test not many conductors pass. In November Webster offered him the music directorship of the company, an idea Britten entertained for a short time before deciding that the parties and people, desk work and layers of bureaucracy, and sheer slog of conducting operas were beyond him.†

Having made his forecast about *Gloriana*, Webster seemed almost duty-bound to see it fulfilled. Britten thought the obvious solution to the ballet corps' objections was to include 'two little ballets in the opera where they can hop around & make their little bows' (no dancer he) and urged Webster to resolve the matter of the choreographer, since he was unable to write the scenes without discussing them first with the person who would stage them. The ballet corps thought Britten's suggestion insulting and continued to agitate for greater involvement. When in November Britten heard there were plans for a separate ballet on the evening of the gala, before *Gloriana*, he wrote another of his letters to Webster. 'Anyhow you know that only over my dead body, & dead opera too, will there be a ballet before Gloriana that night. Let them prance on their points as much as anyone wants *after* but *not* before.'

The doughty, fierce Ninette de Valois had no intention of giving up without a fight. (In 1946 Covent Garden had appointed Sadler's Wells Ballet as its resident dance company.) The idea of a separate ballet was dropped and she reluctantly agreed to release one of her ballerinas for

* This view was shared by the Queen Mother, who after a royal performance of Constant Lambert's ballet *Tiresias* in July 1951 assured Webster that 'this Ballet will have a much greater success at subsequent performances. It is most interesting but we do not bring the kind of audience that responds well to a first performance of this kind.'
† Covent Garden thought much the same once he declined: 'The general view of the Board was that it would be a serious misuse of Mr Britten's great talents, if he were to undertake the job.'

the opera. Yet Madam, as she was known, issued a list of demands if her company was to take part, among them an expansion of the Masque Scene and John Cranko's replacement by Ashton as choreographer. Britten was simply no fan of the art form: 'if it were a serious art it would have a notation by now,' he grumbled. He held his ground on both points and de Valois and the company fell into resentful compliance.

Pears was away through much of this time, giving concerts and recitals in Britain and abroad, to which Britten listened on the radio whenever possible, cursing the poor reception or bad conducting, often both. Pears was caught in London during the great pea-souper of December 1952, smog enveloping the capital, bringing it to a halt, after which he returned, weary and grateful, to Aldeburgh. His returns from abroad were happier occasions: he would wend his way to Suffolk, armed with one treat or another – a whole Stilton, which trumped any of Miss Hudson's plans and would promptly be served, port at its side, to anyone in Crag House.* Most often he was not there long enough to get itchy feet.

With Pears away, some of the ongoing traumas of the year were relayed in their correspondence, though it was almost as though Britten did not even have time for letters, except for those flying back and forth to Plomer. He pounced on those from Pears, which were as affectionate as ever and which prompted effusive protestations of love. Yet his schedule, and Pears's ambivalence towards the new opera and his role in it – Essex – meant they wrote of other things: plans for a new London flat, settling in 1953 on an apartment in a forbidding block in Regent's Park, dismantling their Melbury Road ménage (where they had been renting two rooms from the Steins since 1949, having given up their place in Paddington); or the occasional idea for the coming festival; or the fierce storms in January 1953 that lashed the crumbling Aldeburgh foreshore and flooded Crag House's sitting room, filling the cellar with muddy water and causing extensive damage to fittings and wiring. Britten told Duncan the flooding was the reason he seldom listened to gramophone recordings any more, because 'the labels on most records floated off and then, out of sheer perversity, sank down and dried upon another record', as though in a scene from Disney's *Fantasia*. More perilous were Britten's manuscripts, fortunately stored above the water-line,

---

* Miss Hudson's namesake, the landlady of 221B Baker Street in Arthur Conan Doyle's Sherlock Holmes stories, encountered similarly unpredictable behaviour in the two bachelors she looked after.

which Miss Hudson carried up further into the attic and buried beneath pillows.

There is a detailed account of the eight months leading up to *Gloriana* made by an eccentric and wonderful woman who blew into Aldeburgh at the end of September 1952, like Mary Poppins, and never left. Imogen Holst had maintained a cordial friendship with Britten for some years. They corresponded over performances or new works or old music and each had great respect for the other's gifts. She was slim, high-spirited, gauche and a spinster, literally and in character.

Mary Potter painted Imo in 1954 in a shapeless smock, her hair pulled tight behind her head, expression blank, round blue eyes staring out to her right, just above Potter's easel. (Rosamund Strode, Holst's successor, was certain she was memorizing a score while she posed, probably one of the Bach Passions.) Other images of her in these years capture her poised at Britten's side, ready to turn pages in recital, or conducting on Thorpeness Meare, her face as animated as a jester's. She was all these things and more. It was easy to mock the clothes, the exaggerated effusiveness and the blind adoration she felt for Britten, which teetered on the brink of love, and many did. But she was a fabulous musician: a knowledgeable, musical, thorough all-rounder, who arrived in Aldeburgh at Britten's invitation to help him score his new opera and plan future festivals. Here she created a vital role for herself, which Britten thereafter could never do without. He paid her terribly, somehow not putting his mind to her penurious situation, naively assuming that her father's compositions – *The Planets* in particular – generated enough for her to live on, whereas she had signed over her share of royalties to her mother. She furnished her bed-sittingroom in a house behind the parish church as though she were eighteen or a member of a religious order: there was a bed, a chair, a table and the Bach *Gesellschaft* edition. It could have been one of Britten's student lodgings; here it served a woman of forty-five.

For her first eighteen months in Aldeburgh she kept a diary, the flavour of which she established on her first day in the job, following evening drinks with Britten. 'We were talking about old age and he said that nothing could be done about it, and that he had a very strong feeling that people died at the right moment, and that the greatness of a person included the time when he was born and the time he endured, but that this was difficult to understand.' It was an extraordinary statement, the idea that achievement must be measured against the opportunities and restrictions of an era. Britten would be sadly tested against the notion that people die at the right moment in his final year.

It was Holst, not Pears, who saw first-hand the creative evolution of *Gloriana* and associated events. She recorded Britten's highs and lows, his ongoing feud with Covent Garden over the gala, his attempts to write a will (his lawyer gloomily advising that his most likely fate was to die in an air disaster with Pears), and his relaxed approach to money ('Good old Peter Grimes,' he would chime, much as he had ten years earlier pulled American notes from his wallet at the New York World's Fair, giving thanks for *Sinfonia da Requiem**). She detailed his plans to adopt two displaced children from the UN camps in the Hessen region of Germany, 'because he realised that it was unlikely that he'd ever marry and have children of his own, and he'd got such an immense instinct of love for them that it spilled over and was wasted'. She wrote of the play-throughs of the opera and the huge mood swings they engendered in Britten, and of her own response, a heady mix of ecstasy and admiration. She described the minutiae of the intransigent festival committee, an *Albert Herring* ensemble comprising the mayor, the vicar, the manager of Barclay's Bank and a few other worthies, who dragged Britten's mood down without even trying. (Of the Friends of Aldeburgh Festival he said, 'if only they hadn't got the English habit of having to hate what they love.') She noted Britten's mischievous attempt to write a telegram congratulating Vaughan Williams, who had just turned eighty and looked much older. 'What do I say? Many happy returns?'

She listed the meals and the calendar of drinks consumed in Crag House: fine red wine most often, but champagne and spirits for Britten's thirty-ninth birthday party in November 1952, delicious Pouilly at times, cider if sunny, the odd glass of sherry during the day or before the cinema, a Guinness after physical exertion, and Drambuie or rum or cognac as a nightcap after taxing rehearsals or frustrating meetings. It was life devised by P. G. Wodehouse. She wrote of her scolding reaction to Britten playing through both of the Brahms sonatas for clarinet/viola, with Erwin Stein at the piano, much as she despaired of his reading

* By the end of 1948 *Grimes* had been performed in Antwerp, Basle, Berlin, Boston, Brno, Brussels, Budapest, Copenhagen, Graz, Hamburg, London, Los Angeles, Mannheim, Milan, New York, Paris, Philadelphia, Rome, Stanford University, Stockholm, Sydney, Tanglewood and Zurich.

Sibelius symphonies in bed at night, solely to check whether his prejudice against both composers still held. ('Sibelius, he decided, probably wrote when he was drunk.') She noted with glee his occasional flights of fancy and skittish behaviour – the games and jokes after dinner, or his stepping forward from the December darkness to insist the local carol singers target the home of the grand Aldeburgh woman who had previously objected to the noise they made, as though he was in a Dickens novel or on a Victorian Christmas card. And she detailed the activities of the Aldeburgh Music Club, which Britten and Pears formed in April 1952, for which she conducted Purcell's music to *Timon of Athens*. The club had the faintest flavour of *The Ladykillers*, the black comedy starring Alec Guinness still three years away, in which an improbable collection of crooks gathers in a large house overseen by an eccentric landlady, supposedly to rehearse chamber music when in fact they are plotting an audacious heist. But the Aldeburgh amateurs, with Britten and Pears in ties and on at least their third instruments, could really play.

She wrote down his thoughts about other musicians – 'how wretched it is that composers took the trouble to write *just* what they wanted and then they so seldom got it' (this in a response to a broadcast of Berlioz's *The Childhood of Christ* featuring Pears and conducted by Malcolm Sargent) – and his thoughts about her – 'well I must say I find *you* go to the head rather' (in response to Holst declining wine with lunch because, as she told him, his presence was intoxicating enough).

Mostly, though, her diary records the fog of depression enveloping Britten in these months. 'Then at dinner he said he'd been depressed *all* the time,' she wrote at the beginning of December, not even a long walk on the marshes and the sight of a flock of curlews lifting his mood. 'The Opera goes on ahead,' he told Peg Hesse on 11 December, 'in a way I'm so rushed & exhausted that I don't know whether it's wonderful or dreadful. Probably it's neither, just, as usual, somewhere in between.' It was not solely his battles with Covent Garden that made him this way. He was unsure how to write the Elizabethan dances, much as he had been stuck, at a similar stage, over the shanties in *Billy Budd*. Nor did he feel confident about composing the last, cranky argument between Elizabeth and Essex, where so much prose had to be wrestled into a reasonable form. Holst helped with the first of these: she darted to Oxford to learn the steps of various Elizabethan court dances, which she taught to Britten immediately on her return, the rhythms and metrical relations of which he incorporated into the score. And he solved the final argument between queen and soldier, their duet unwinding as slowly as a clock, and with it their relationship. She helped Britten with his scoring too, ruling and barring staves on the large manuscript paper in preparation for his quick work. He whipped through the orchestration at speed, determined to complete his task by mid-March 1953, when he was to leave for a two-week holiday in Ireland with Pears and the Harewoods. He filled his fountain pen with black ink so the score could be easily photographed, apologizing to various correspondents for contravening the etiquette that restricted this colour to condolence letters.

Britten was enormously grateful to Holst for her support and said so often: 'it belongs to you as much as to anyone,' he told her on the day of the gala. But she could help only intermittently with his depression during the months leading up to this night; it clung to him resiliently throughout Pears's long absences, through the small wins and larger setbacks with the festival, through the manifold crises with the EOG (starved of his attention while he composed his grand opera) and its manager, Elizabeth Sweeting, who found herself usurped by Holst's easy intimacy with Britten and resentful of the intrusion.

4

Although bare-boned and light on psychology, the reader's report prepared for the Lord Chamberlain at the end of May 1953 contains a serviceable synopsis of *Gloriana*.

> Historical operas always read like a kind of stuttering primer for infants, and this is no exception. In Act I, Essex and Mountjoy, rivals for the Queen's notice, are united in loyalty to her service by her own intervention. In Act II, Essex' ambition leads him to disaster. He desires to lead the campaign in Ireland and is allowed to through the machinations of Cecil, who realizes that the favourite will come to grief. In the third act, Essex, having failed to destroy Tyrone is arraigned and executed for treason. The Queen, who has toyed with the idea of loving Essex is left, an old dying woman, meditating on greatness against a background of shadowy symbols of her past. This simple plot is bulked out with a masque and various scenes of Elizabethan high and low life.

> Page 52 In this scene a housewife empties a chamberpot from a window over one of the characters. This is not, in any sense, germane to the plot; and I do not see why Her Majesty (who will be attending the premiere) should be confronted with an incident that we would not permit even the Crazy Gang to get away with. The pot can easily be changed for a basin or other less intimate vessel. And I would suggest that a special note be added that the alteration must also be made in the printed script.

How quaint to read of such strictures as late as 1953, for though it was not yet the Lord Chamberlain's last hurrah, it was getting close.

In the culture of fear and censorship, Britten and his librettists opted for a mixture of compliance and evasion, burying controversial themes so deep in the drama that the Lord Chamberlain's readers found themselves singling out nothing more than unsheathed swords and chamber pots. Audience members with an ear for it picked up the bat squeaks of sexuality, repression, politics and dissent at the core of each opera – much as certain motifs were evident to those inclined to look for them in Noel Coward's plays in the 1930s. Those without the ears stamped 'RECOMMENDED FOR LICENCE' on the scripts and libretti submitted for approval. As theatre freed itself from these binds in the 1960s, often spectacularly so, Britten would go in a different direction from both the mainstream and his works in the previous two decades.

The last weeks of May were full of tweaks. Naturally there were errors in the parts, which Holst corrected quickly and guiltily; they were her responsibility. The young English conductor John Pritchard, whom Britten had found so impressive in Bellini at Covent Garden, was here a disappointment; he clearly did not know the score well enough, which left the cast deflated and nervous. Britten's occasional appearances on the podium during rehearsals only underlined Pritchard's limitations. Britten paced the auditorium, *willing* Pritchard to be better, observing at one point, 'You know, the more simple I try to make my music, the more difficult it becomes to perform.'

'Queen Salote of Tonga is among the many distinguished guests who attended the first night of a new British opera,' Pathé footage announced. 'Many who journeyed far to attend the coronation add further colour and sparkle to this royal evening,' the camera panning over two very black dignitaries. Thousands of people lined Bow Street to watch such noblemen and women arrive. Locals stood on their balconies, Covent

Garden porters on long benches outside pubs, while children on the pavement waved flags, enjoying both the occasion and the privilege of staying up so late for it. It certainly felt like a celebration, though none of the easygoing atmosphere followed the Queen inside the building.

The sad fact is that not even Britten in the pit could have saved the evening. The Grand Tier at Covent Garden on 8 June 1953, six days after the coronation, contained thirty-one members of the royal family, including members of various royal houses of Europe and a certain Group Captain Townsend, whose relationship with the Queen's sister was about to remind people uncannily of the events of 1936. Around 15,000 commoners had applied for expensive gala tickets, though only 1,400 were available since Covent Garden needed 600 for its own guests. Apart from the royal party, tickets were allocated to members of the royal household, diplomats from every country imaginable, Cabinet and Shadow Cabinet ministers, delegates of the Commonwealth Prime Ministers' Conference, foreign royalty, Commonwealth parliamentary delegates, members of the Colonial Office, and lords, dowagers and scions of the great noble families, including Lord Montagu of Beaulieu, whose life would soon be linked to Britten's in quite another way. Covent Garden and the Arts Council did their best to lighten the mix, inviting principals of the music colleges; a sprinkling of the era's eminent artists, musicians, writers and actors, including Elisabeth Schwarzkopf, Henry Moore, John Betjeman and Douglas Fairbanks Junior; and the knighted composers and conductors with whom Britten maintained defiantly sour relations: Barbirolli, Beecham and Boult had declined their invitations, yet Bliss, Bax, Sargent, Walton and Vaughan Williams were seated in a clump in the orchestra stalls – every one a knight, bar V.W., who had the vastly more prestigious Order of Merit instead.

5

Harewood described the premiere as 'one of the great disasters of operatic history', and even in a crowded field, this is difficult to dispute. The audience greeted the work in near silence, their polite applause dampened by dress gloves and a general fug of bewilderment, Britten leaning forward in his box hissing 'Clap, damn you! *Clap!*'; there was just enough of an ovation for three curtain calls. Nor was the royal family any more receptive, if Noel Coward is any guide: 'Dickie and Edwina [Mountbatten] brought Princess Margaret to the Café last night; very amiable. Benjamin Britten's opera *Gloriana*, for the Royal Gala Performance, apparently a bugger. Dull, without melody as usual with Mr B., and not happily chosen.' It was not solely that this grand gathering did not know how to behave at the opera; it was also that the audience – and evidently the royal family – felt this subtle, psychological portrait of a monarch at the end of her life and powers was unsuitable fare for such a formal and optimistic occasion. Britten and Plomer had stuck too closely to Strachey's reimagining of this great, majestic fowl, one who swore and spat, who struck tables with her fist when she was angry, and laughed raucously when amused. What a vulgar portrait on such an occasion, and what a rebuff to all that beef-witted talk about a new Elizabethan age. Webster's prophecy was fulfilled, though he was the last to find comfort in his prescience.

Critics also greeted the work with puzzlement. The consensus was that there was too much pageantry, too little drama, and that the episodes and years celebrated in Strachey were poor foundations for an opera. There is merit in some of these observations, for *Gloriana* is an episodic work, coming across more as a series of folio etchings than chapters of a tautly written book. There is also a surfeit of narrative devices in the piece (often Britten's Achilles heel), clogging the opera's arteries. The Masque scene is long and is soon followed by a grand ball at the palace of Whitehall, which takes place to the beat of a very Elizabethan drum: six brilliant courtly dances are played and pirouetted to. And then there is the third act, with its extended scene involving the blind ballad singer, his boy, and his cast of many – a narrative device Britten had used once before in *Paul Bunyan* and would return to in *Owen Wingrave*; here it does not quite come off. Coleman's production, abetted by John Piper's static, opulent design, only served to reinforce the episodic, picture-book nature of the piece.

Yet critics were wrong to suggest there was nothing dramatic in the sometimes touching, but mostly manipulative, delusional and rebarbative relationship between Queen Elizabeth and her soldier. The way the relationship unfolds and implodes is compelling. ('But make him into the traditional hero,' Britten later answered Behrend's criticism of Essex, 'or his relations with the Queen more simple and direct, we cannot. This part of the story must always remain elusive, but to me always fascinating.') And the contrast between the public world of the ageing warrior queen and her private hopes and desires is extremely well drawn – never more so than when Essex bursts into Queen Elizabeth's boudoir before she has dressed, her make-up not yet applied.* Moreover, Essex's incompetent, foolhardy warmongering in Ireland and his impotent truce with Tyrone are given a good run, Britten and Plomer both taking their cue from Strachey. 'Under the combined influences of casualties, desertions, disease, and the garrisoning of distant outposts, his army was melting away.' What was England doing in this strange, savage land, attempting to acquire what was not hers? Shakespeare hints at similar thoughts in *Henry V*, written in the same year as Essex's campaign in Ireland; in *Gloriana* it is more blatant. Cecil counsels the Queen: 'Tyrone is still a rebel / And Ireland not yet ours. / Not ours, but might be Spain's, / Might easily be France's: / For want of forthright action / He forfeited his chances.' In these few lines Britten and Plomer captured the expansionist policies of the British Empire, which lasted not so many more years, when along with the British Raj they faded away.

The score itself is brilliant. Queen Elizabeth jumps from steely histrionics to tender lyricism in a beat; the orchestra skips with ease from Elizabethan sounds to Britten's middle-period language – tonal set pieces, dissonant harmony ratcheting up the tension, snatches of leitmotif – never more so than at the end of Act 2: the reedy sounds of the court orchestra playing a Coranto are gradually and ominously underpinned by the full orchestra, which pushes towards its own great climax, threatening but never quite managing to swallow the small Elizabethan band whole. 'The work seems to me the best I have yet done,' he wrote to Mayer at the end of August. This is not the case, as Britten must have known, but, in the context of the opera's venomous reception, it was a forgivable claim.

---

* Perhaps Plomer or Britten saw the 1946 revival of Somerset Maugham's play *Lady Frederick* at the Savoy, starring Coral Browne as the honourable heroine of a certain age who pushes away her young aristocratic lover by letting him see her at her morning toilet. 'The great difficulty, you know, is to make both your cheeks the same colour,' she tells the horrified young man as she daubs over her yellow, lined face.

6

In a country that had only been in the opera business for ten years or so, suddenly everyone had an opinion of the coronation work. 'Even the porters in the Covent Garden vegetable market will put down their baskets and argue about it,' wrote Beverly Baxter MP. The subject matter, music, hint of *lèse-majesté* to the premiere, and of course the expense: each provoked debate. (*Gloriana* cost £24,000 to get to the stage, almost three-quarters of which went on costumes; *Grimes* in 1947 had cost slightly more than £5,000). Critics and supporters – the latter including Vaughan Williams – slugged it out in *The Times* and elsewhere. 'Public resentment, intense and widespread,' wrote family-planning pioneer, eugenicist and amateur opera critic Marie Stopes, 'is not at the cost but that the opera was unworthy of the great occasion, uninspired, missing the main glories of the times, its music inharmonious and wearisome, and with at least two scenes profoundly affronting the glorious memory of Queen Elizabeth I, hence unsuitable for public performance before Queen Elizabeth II.'

The critic Martin Cooper thought the animosity was fuelled by a widespread jealousy of Britten's privileged position in English society (he was created Companion of Honour in the Coronation Honours List) and that commentators displayed 'an almost sadistic relish or glee that has little to do with the musical merit or demerit'. The jealousy and resentment had been brewing for a while – and not solely among critics. The previous year William Walton had written to Christopher Hassall, the librettist for *Troilus and Cressida*, the opera he was then writing, mocking Britten's royal connections and consequent privilege. 'B.B. has to give up all his engagements and Covent Garden which is already broke, has to compensate him. But there it is, we've no friends at Court so we must put on a smiling face and pretend we like it.'

There was more to the vitriol than digs at Britten's friends at court. It was as if the jokes and whispers, the raised eyebrows and winks, and the more virulent displays of homophobia that had followed Britten and Pears since their return to Britain eleven years earlier were no longer kept in check by English good manners and social restraint. Tippett identified the origins of the shift in a cabal of composers in the late

1940s, including Elisabeth Lutyens, Constant Lambert, Alan Raws-
thorne and Walton, who would go boozing with Dylan Thomas,
Louis MacNeice, critic Cecil Gray and artist Michael Ayrton, where
they nursed their resentment with their Guinness and 'entertained
absurd fantasies about a homosexual conspiracy in music, led by Britten and Pears'. It seems ludicrous now, yet when Britten was offered
the music directorship of Covent Garden, Walton's curt response
was, 'There are enough buggers in the place already, it's time it is
stopped.' (Walton remained mired in jealousy of Britten all his life, notwithstanding their nominal friendship and mutual protestations of
admiration.)

The cabal's paranoid homophobia was a thin disguise for professional jealousy. Ireland described it well in a 1954 letter to his former
pupil, writing of the 'maze of jealousy your well-deserved success has
aroused in the world of pygmies'. Yet by the mid-1950s there were
others, without a dog in this particular fight, chanting the same slogans.
In July 1955 an embittered Sir Steuart Wilson, formerly of the Arts
Council and, until April, Webster's unhappy deputy at Covent Garden,
announced to *People* his campaign to rid the industry of homosexuals.
'The influence of perverts in the world of music has grown beyond all
measure. If it is not curbed soon, Covent Garden and other precious
musical heritages could suffer irreparable harm.' Wilson's dealings with
Britten at both the Arts Council and Covent Garden had been extensive.
Moreover, he had accepted Britten's invitation to lecture at the first
Aldeburgh Festival and was distantly related to Pears. But there was no
mistaking his targets. The minor composer Walford Haydn was asked
to comment. 'Homosexuals are damaging music and all the other arts. I
am sorry for those born that way, but many acquire it – and for them I
have nothing but contempt. Singers who are perverted often get work
simply because of this. And new works by composers are given preference by some people if the writer is perverted.'

Wilson was boarding an already crowded bandwagon, for his complaints reflected a wider concern in the 1950s with the impact of
homosexuality on British society. In May 1951 two of what would
become known as the Cambridge Five disappeared from England, to
resurface in Moscow four years later. Guy Burgess was a flamboyant,
louche homosexual, while Donald Maclean – Britten's exact contemporary and fellow Old Greshamian – was a handsome bisexual. Both

were double agents and their defection precipitated a lazy public conflation of homosexuality and treason. Cold War paranoia fuelled such
thinking, helped no end by Churchill's puritanical home secretary, Sir
David Maxwell Fyfe, who in late 1953 initiated a McCarthyite witch-
hunt against gay men. (Maxwell Fyfe attended the *Gloriana* gala,
captured on Pathé footage looking uncannily but appropriately like a
beady-eyed bald eagle.) Churchill was caught in a bind: he wanted to
prove to the Americans the trustworthiness and security of his government, yet was unexercised by the defections. 'I think he merely wrote
them off as being decadent young men, corrupted by drink and homosexuality, and the whole story lowered his not very high opinion of the
Foreign Office,' his joint principal private secretary, Jock Colville, later
said. The prime minister's characterization of these decadent young gay
men, however, with their loose grip on patriotism and propriety, did
nothing to stem the paranoia of many others.

At Maxwell Fyfe's behest, ever greater numbers of good-looking
young constables – so-called 'pretty police' – found themselves assigned
to quite different beats, entrapment on their minds. In October 1953 the
newly knighted John Gielgud was arrested in a public lavatory, giving
his name as Arthur Gielgud and his profession as clerk, hoping to avoid
public humiliation. (This trick had worked seven years earlier for Alec
Guinness.) A month or so before Gielgud's arrest the Labour MP William Field was detained in similar circumstances and resigned his seat,
while six years later the South African choreographer John Cranko
would be arrested in Britten Street, Chelsea (of all street names), escaping with a fine. Cranko's arrest was reported on the front page of the
Daily Express, and in a commentary which drips scorn at the 'chi-chi
world' of eminent gay artists, the choreographer was described as 'the
latest on the list of famous stage names who have been found guilty of
this squalid behaviour . . . these are evil men. They have spun their web
through the West End today until it is a simmering scandal. I say they
should be driven from their positions of theatrical power.' (This was
what the *Sunday Express* wrote about Gielgud, further arguing that
such criminals should be stripped of any honours bestowed on them.)
Eminent mathematician and cryptographer Alan Turing, who during
the war helped crack Nazi codes and after it was a computer pioneer,
was convicted in early 1952 of indecency under the same law that
put Oscar Wilde in jail. Offered a choice between imprisonment and

chemical castration, Turing chose the latter. His death two years later was possibly suicide.*

The police did not restrict their interest merely to those caught in the act. 'Scotland Yard are definitely stepping up their activities against the homosexuals,' the editor of the *Evening Standard* told the newspaper tycoon Lord Beaverbrook in January 1954. 'Some weeks ago they interviewed Benjamin Britten. This week I am told they have interviewed Cecil Beaton. No action is to be taken against either.' By interviewing such distinguished Britons, yet not arresting them, Maxwell Fyfe and Scotland Yard were both conforming to and running contrary to the rules. Eminent American sociologist Edward Shils put it well in his 1956 book *The Torment of Secrecy*. 'The secrets of the governing classes of Britain are kept within the class and even within more restricted circles ... No ruling class discloses as little of its confidential proceedings as does the British.' Whether such interviews were intended to shame the men or to warn them is unclear, as is Britten's response, though it was probably like the occasion in 1949 when Sir John Redcliffe-Maud, permanent secretary of the Ministry of Education, invited Britten to call on him at his Curzon Street office, and there told him that his friendship with his son was to cease. Britten reacted furiously, indignant at the distortion of his relationship with the boy (one of the dedicatees of *The Young Person's Guide to the Orchestra*). Perhaps it was even worse in 1953, being hauled before a police officer with sinister Orwellian precision, his eminence the lightest suit of armour.

Arrests increased dramatically, police scouring the address books of those they caught, looking for clues about other offenders or evidence of homosexual rings.† When Lord Montagu was arrested in 1954, accused of sexually assaulting two boy scouts, police went as far as altering a date in his passport to strengthen the prosecution. The case was dismissed, but Montagu was immediately rearrested on different charges, which the police and director of public prosecutions made sure

---

* Although a coronial inquest returned a verdict of suicide, recent scholarship suggests the verdict was unsafe and the thesis put forward originally by Turing's mother – that her son poisoned himself accidently by ingesting cyanide fumes in the small laboratory he installed next to his bedroom – more likely.

† Raiding a discreet gay club, an officer commented on the large number of men's names in the membership book. 'You might say the same of the Athenaeum,' the proprietor responded, 'or, for that matter, of the Police Force.'

were carried, employing disgraceful (and illegal) tactics. Ironically, it was Maxwell Fyfe who initiated a committee, led by the headmaster then University of Reading vice-chancellor John Wolfenden, to examine the laws under which these men were charged. The public nature of certain prosecutions put wind in the committee's sails but its 1957 recommendation that homosexual behaviour between consenting adults should be decriminalized no doubt caught Maxwell Fyfe, now Lord High Chancellor of Great Britain, by surprise.

There was the occasional voice of dissent. In late October 1953, a week after Gielgud's arrest, E. M. Forster protested in the pages of the *New Statesman* about the inhumane treatment of homosexuals. 'If homosexuality between men ceased to be *per se* criminal – it is not criminal between women – and if homosexual crimes were equated with heterosexual crimes and punished with equal but not with additional severity, much confusion and misery would be averted; there would be less public importuning and less blackmail.' (Jailed in 1953 for indecency, writer Rupert Croft-Cooke said of those he encountered in Wormwood Scrubs: 'There were several blackmailers who had found in homosexuality a rich and ready harvest.') It was difficult for such voices to be heard above a reactionary press with the law on its side. In May 1952 the *Sunday Pictorial* included a helpful full-page guide to identifying homosexuals – a dress rehearsal for its 1961 article, 'How to Spot a Homo'. (Tweed jacket, suede shoes and pipe. Or if this netted more than Kinsey's 1948 estimate of one man in ten being gay, as seems likely, look instead for his mincing step.) Those who could best articulate the need for change often felt unable to do so, lest they incriminated themselves; Plomer, who was almost arrested in 1943 for soliciting a sailor, is only one such example.

The Lord Chamberlain did his bit, writing to Laurence Olivier as early as 1951 to canvass his opinion on the depiction of homosexuality on stage. On the one hand, thought the Lord Chamberlain, society was far more broadminded now. On the other, 'The subject will be very distasteful and embarrassing in mixed company of all ages and also that the introduction in plays of new vices might start an unfortunate train of thought in the previously innocent.' The response of the scarcely disinterested Olivier is unknown (numerous biographies have suggested he had homosexual affairs). By the end of the decade certain rules were in place: the word 'pansy' was allowed but not 'bugger'; there were to be no embraces between men; and so forth. The list was long and narrow. Measured change was the outcome, unlike the fierce, combative stance on other subjects taken by John Osborne and others in the mid-1950s. Noel Coward, who had learned the codes of sublimation in the 1920s and 1930s, much as Terence Rattigan did in the 1940s, disapproved of Osborne's explicitness, writing in his diary that he could not 'understand why the younger generation, instead of knocking at the door, should bash the fuck out of it'. All the same, they must have looked on in wonder at the sheer brazenness of Osborne's *Look Back in Anger*, as all the while they tiptoed around the themes buried deep in their hearts. Such a revolution was impossible amid the puerile talk of Walton and his like. Their homophobia was a strong currency which they spent indiscriminately.

7

In this context, those so inclined viewed *Gloriana* as a deliberate provocation to genteel British society. It had a gay composer, librettist, director, conductor, choreographer and producer (David Webster). It was based on a book by a gay writer and starred a gay tenor as Essex. A gay interior designer spent £1,660 on temporary renovations of the royal box and the auditorium. Had de Valois prevailed in her desire to use Ashton, the choreographer would still have been gay. And it was all served up to the Queen at a gala celebrating her coronation. Not for a moment did it occur to the very proper Britten that either the commission or his artistic team was inappropriate or provocative. Nor was he on a crusade, challenging the pharisaic arguments swirling around just then and those who mounted them. The cards had simply fallen this way and this was his team.

Then there was the problem of a scholarly book on Britten, published the previous year, which most critics thought far too admiring of its subject. Edited by Hans Keller and Donald Mitchell, and containing essays by colleagues and musicologists, the volume is often perceptive. Britten was initially pleased, but later, depressed by his inability to give the ballad-singer scene in *Gloriana* a decent shape, he told Holst it made him feel like a rabbit being dissected by grubby schoolboys. Keller's essay, with its assertion that heavily repressed sadism was at the heart of his music, particularly disheartened him: he hated such psychological interpretation and generalizations.

Those who thought the book reinforced the 'cult of Benjamin Britten' laid about his new opera with a big stick. Many of the critics of *Budd* now vented a broader sense of frustration and disappointment: Britten was not conforming to their expectations in his return to grand opera. By the time of the royal gala, the simmering resentment and barely veiled homophobia were all that much greater.

'The fact that the press failed to be in any way happy or receptive confused us all,' Britten told Mayer at the end of August, 'but the public as usual, dear things, kept its head & at the end of the run was coming in large numbers & taking the work to its heart.' It was a brave front: the opera did miserable business in its final showings, and its return early the following year for three performances was even worse. 'But – there is no point in glossing this fact over – we all feel so kicked around, so bewildered by the venom, that it is difficult to maintain one's balance.' Pears delivered his own broadside after the first performance: what did Britten think he was doing, making himself vulnerable before such an unsympathetic, metropolitan crowd? Didn't it confirm they were better making music in their own festival or with their own opera company, controlling the circumstances of production and, on occasion, the critics who were permitted to see it?

Plomer was more sanguine. 'On the whole I think we have seen a healthy reaction to a new work of art. All the ferocities, the knowingnesses, the superficialities, the stampeding sheep-in-wolves'-clothing, the second thoughts, the timidities, the jealousies, and so on, amount, it seems to me, to a real tribute to your powers.' Plomer was right: the opera and its reception revealed much about contemporary British society. But Britten could not see it this way. Pears's debilitating intervention – fuelled partly by his dislike of his role (another roistering, straight anti-hero, only a few years after Macheath), the critical response to his performance as Essex and the reinforcement that his voice was just not big enough for Covent Garden when up against a big orchestra – helped nudge Britten once more in the direction of smaller forms and more intimate settings. Harewood was convinced the opera's reception injured Britten personally as well as musically. 'It shut him in on himself and he became even more private. He had made a great public gesture and the public had, so to speak, rejected him.' Moreover, the whole affair undermined the 'influence of those of us who had hoped he would gradually assume a metropolitan as opposed to a micropolitan stance'.

This last point is of huge significance in understanding Britten's career in the late 1950s and 1960s.

Some colleagues and observers also accused Britten of being in thrall to royalty and the echelons of society it represented. It is true his milieu had shifted as a result of his friendship with Harewood. Two weeks before the coronation he attended a small dinner at Orme Square for the Queen and the Duke of Edinburgh, hosted by the Harewoods, during which excerpts of the new opera were performed for its dedicatee, Queen Elizabeth. The Queen would later open the Aldeburgh Festival's new concert hall at Snape – not once, but twice – and there would be handwritten letters and other dinners, one of which found composer and monarch sympathizing with each other over how far in advance their respective diaries were filled. There would be a further royal commission (*A Birthday Hansel* in 1975 for the Queen Mother) and an invitation from the Duke of Edinburgh to write something for the choir of St George's Chapel, Windsor (Britten's 1961 *Jubilate Deo in* C). Britten and Pears would occasionally stay with the Queen Mother at Sandringham, and Britten greatly enjoyed his friendship with Harewood's cousin and his wife, the Prince and Princess of Hesse, who soon distinguished themselves in Britten's eyes as ideal travelling companions. 'I would have been a Court composer,' he once told Tippett, 'but for my pacifism and homosexuality.' (Montagu Slater thought Britten *did* become a court composer and wholly disapproved.)

Yet Britten also told stories against himself in this society. He described a breakfast at Harewood House in Yorkshire at which he found himself sitting next to Harewood's mother, Princess Mary, daughter of George V. It was soon after Christmas Day 1950, when the Stone of Scone was stolen from Westminster Abbey, and HRH asserted that Communists were surely behind the theft, likely escaping with the precious artefact by boat down the Thames. The theory tickled Britten. 'What a *wonderful* idea, ma'am; wouldn't it be funny if they had!' He had mistaken her diagnosis of dire conspiracies for black humour, and Princess Mary, a tough old bird, sat in frosty silence, most displeased.

Britten seemed to take their company in his stride, feeling neither unworthy nor privileged. It was this quality that so annoyed Auden, what he thought of as 'Ben's lack of daring, his desire to be The Establishment . . . playing it safe, settling for amiability as guard against his queerity, but insisting on the innocence of adolescence as if this was a courageous attitude'. Yet the same quality was much a feature of 1950s Britain. In his scorching article of 1955 on the state of British intellectualism, Edward Shils drew invidious comparisons between the mid-century breed and that in the 1930s. Where was the bite, the fire in their bellies? Where was the trenchant social criticism? What had produced the extraordinary degree of self-satisfaction, the ease with sovereign authority? 'Outside the China of the Mandarins, no great society has ever had a body of intellectuals so integrated with, and so congenial to, its ruling class, and so combining civility and refinement.' Auden would have said this applied to Britten, an artist who had created out of his life and work a compelling narrative of the outsider, but who nonetheless enjoyed his opportunities and his friends at court. He thought such refinement ridiculous in a musician from Lowestoft, one moreover who had earned his spurs in the scrappy fights and artistic protests of the 1930s. Auden was proud of his scars from that decade and his escape from the Establishment. Britten was proud of his own scars, and his royal friendships and relations were never allowed to affect his mature work adversely. In fact, these friendships sometimes afforded him a further layer of disguise.

8

In the back of his copy of Thomas Hardy's *Collected Poems*, a present from Isherwood when they met on America's West Coast in 1949, Britten scribbled the titles of twenty-one verses that caught his eye. He was entranced by Hardy's landscape – the dark, brooding Dorset countryside, punctuated by Iron Age hill forts and barrows, its heaths and vales swirling with Celtic spirits. He loved the pictorial quality of the poems and their low supernatural hum. Like Dickens, Hardy was inspired by the impoverishment and inequalities of Victorian society; his prognosis, though, was far gloomier. He was an ideal match for Britten.

There was no particular scheme in his selection of poems, no plodding journey through a cold, dead winter landscape, as Wilhelm Müller and then Schubert had imagined in *Winterreise*. But the lyrics and ballads Britten plumped for offer a bleak picture of Dorset – an icy wind blasting the weathervane – as they do of England in the decades at the turn of the century, Victoria's shadow ever present. Britten's use of Hardy's title,

Winter Words, along with various other overlaps of tonality and texture, suggest Schubert was on his mind as he composed this new cycle for Pears. The mood lifts on occasion, however, which cannot be said of *Winterreise*. 'Wagtail and Baby' flicks and darts along nicely, as do the fluting, fluttering birds in the piano accompaniment of 'Proud Songsters (Thrushes, Finches and Nightingales)'. 'The Children and Sir Nameless', ultimately excluded from the published collection, is a quick sketch of grumpy aristocratic self-aggrandizement, full of hunting calls and noisy children in hobnail boots putting paid to Sir Nameless's carefully laid plans for posterity: the statue he commissioned when alive, now set into the floor of his parish church, is scuffed and rebuffed by local children.

The journeying boy in 'Midnight on the Great Western', with a third-class ticket stuck in his hatband and a key on a string around his neck, is in Britten's hands every bit a refugee child or evacuee from one war or another. He is dispatched to a new life somewhere, but we never know where, for the narrator is too English to ask. (In Hardy's *Jude the Obscure*, the disturbed boy nicknamed 'Little Father Time' is travelling alone to live with his father, Jude, in Aldbrickham. The atmosphere in both is identical.) The accompaniment lurches and chugs, and the train whistle changes pitch as the locomotive moves, a Doppler effect that Britten pulls off with some fancy pedal work.

Religious cynicism is pricked in 'The Choirmaster's Burial', a tale of a pompous, modern vicar (as self-important as Swallow in *Peter Grimes*), who decides that a read service will be quite enough for the interment. Once the choirmaster is in his grave, the hymn-tune accompaniment of the song's first half gives way to an ecstatic reverie, the chalky spirits of old village musicians at his graveside honouring his work and their traditions, no doubt welcoming him to their ghostly fraternity.

Then there is the small, poor boy busking at Upway station, his violin thrumming away without much purpose, line, or beauty (Britten characterizing the instrument as surely as Schubert depicts a hurdy-gurdy at the end of *Winterreise*), who probably leaves the station without a coin in his hand or food in his stomach. In the magnificent final song, 'Before Life and After', we are asked to ponder a time of nescience, Eden before the fall, when 'None suffered sickness, love, or loss, / None knew regret, starved hope, or heart-burnings'. It slowly builds and builds, copper twisting onto a coil, until the great climax, after which we are let down gently, alone with our prelapsarian thoughts.

Britten began writing the songs in March 1953 – in the downtime between completing the coronation opera and rehearsing it – finishing them six months later. They were a fine-featured contrast to the plump *Gloriana*, as well as a contrast to his most recent cycle for Pears, *The Holy Sonnets of John Donne* from as long ago as 1945. (*Winter Words* is technically a collection of songs, much like *On This Island*, though it is almost always performed as a cycle.) Britten's piano writing had been pared down even further in the eight years since the sonnets, Schubert the model, where so much is said with so little. It is no coincidence that in those eight years Britten had become a great Schubert accompanist, so alive to the ebb and flow of Schubert's harmony, so sensitive to the way he coloured words. His proficiency in another's music did not necessarily translate into his own, of course, but Britten was learning to trust himself with sparse textures, with thinner harmonies and fragmented melody – a foretaste of great things to come.

Bursitis in his right arm and shoulder did its best to derail him, though the correct diagnosis would not be made until October. The pain had been with him on and off since *Billy Budd*, providing him with another excuse to dislike conducting, if any were needed. 'I suppose it's because I'm too tense nearly all the time,' he told Holst by way of explanation of the illness, but perhaps also the dislike. Britten eventually cancelled a number of autumn performances – including his first full recital tour of Germany with Pears and his appearance on the podium for the revival of *Grimes* at Covent Garden – yet for now, with another festival in June behind him – including a barnstorming lecture by Auden on 'The Hero in Modern Poetry', Britten keeping his distance throughout the short visit – he fell in with the alluring rhythm of a Suffolk summer, tending his *Gloriana* wounds all the while.*

There were cricket matches, brass-rubbings, sketching expeditions and games of tennis; there was sailing and bathing – some of it at night, phosphorescence transforming the bathers into eerie sea creatures – and much domestic music-making, Britten snickering his way through recorder ensembles ('he gets such giggles that his eyes swell, his ears

---

* It was around this time that Auden wrote his reaction to *Gloriana*, only to have his letter returned to him, torn into tiny pieces. Auden's comments to Elizabeth Mayer probably give some flavour of his letter to Britten: 'It has some of the best operatic music in it, I think, Ben has done yet, and the Piper sets were superb. Didn't care for the libretto and neither Joan Cross nor Peter should sing anymore on the stage.'

grow scarlet and his whole face is suffused with tears'). There were picnics, conversations about poems and books (Hardy's grim *Jude the Obscure*, Britten describing it as only just bearable), and motoring trips into the flat, yellow countryside. He managed to put off prospective guests whenever he could, but was still host to a procession of friends: Tippett; the Harewoods; baritone Otakar Kraus and his family; James Bernard, a young composer Britten had met in the lead-up to *Grimes*, who helped prepare the full score of *Billy Budd* and went on to his own successful career as a composer of scores for Hammer Horror films; and Paul Rogerson, a young man Britten met on the first night of *Billy Budd* and who soon became a Jesuit novice, saddening the composer.

There was still much to think about: the festival and the proposed new theatre, which Britten had discussed more seriously of late; a new opera, *The Turn of the Screw*, put to one side while *Gloriana* was composed; plans for a new residential music school, possibly in Aldeburgh but definitely away from London ('I don't see the advantage of sending the students to hear Sir Malcolm conducting'). Otherwise he did his best to empty his head, and by 8 October seemed well enough to give the first performance of the Hardy songs with Pears at Harewood House. It did not go particularly well. Soon afterwards a new osteopath made the correct diagnosis of his condition and told Britten to stop playing for three months. He was reduced to writing music left-handed and letters on a typewriter, errors galore, travelling to London for weekly treatment.

Depression returned. He was no good when not composing, and Pears took Britten's withdrawal from their joint performances badly. But for his fortieth birthday in November 1953 Britten relaxed over a long, boozy lunch in the company of friends and family, drinking first schnapps, then beer in silver mugs, and finally champagne alongside a meal of chicken and puddings and rich sauces. The spell did not last: he spent a week in London receiving daily treatment for his arm, which tired him and did not seem to help. And in early December, griefstricken by the recent death of Bill Federick (his 'very dear friend' as the *Evening News* would coyly term him), Noel Mewton-Wood dashed a tumbler of gin and cyanide against his apartment wall and ingested the fumes. Britten learned of his death two days later, and to Holst expressed his despair. Why did the people he liked and admired find life so difficult? Why was the gap between madness and sanity so small? It was like the death of Peter Burra, which had brought Britten and Pears together in

1937, only sadder, somehow more ordinary, more squalid. Pears took it personally, grieving for his friend but also despairing over who would now play for him when Ben did not.

With his arm only half responding to treatment and his work on hold, Britten decided to spend Christmas with the Hesses in their home, Schloss Wolfsgarten. He liked the quiet seriousness of the season in Germany, the lack of commercialism. As for their circle, 'It is a curious, circumscribed, little world,' he told Erwin Stein, 'this international Royal clan – there were, for instance, seven princes to the family Xmas dinner! Some are fascinating, Barbara of Prussia, and Francis of Bavaria, some dull or just effete.'

There had been no unified response from the German royal families to Nazism. Queen Victoria's great-grandsons, the Princes of Hesse, were enthusiastic cheer-leaders of Hitler's regime, and the dictator played them, much as he did the Catholic Church, for the constituency they represented. Many German princes were members of the Wehrmacht before their sudden expulsion in 1943, triggered by Hitler's gathering paranoia. Yet Prince Ludwig of Hesse had joined the reserves of the Wehrmacht only reluctantly, and in 1943 was placed under house arrest along with his Scottish wife, formerly the Hon. Margaret Campbell Geddes, whom he married just before the war. And Franz of Bavaria, Britten's fellow guest at Christmas dinner, who turned six a little before the outbreak of hostilities, belonged to a family of even grittier stock. His father opposed Nazism, taking his wife and children to Hungary, some of whom (including Franz) were swept up in the 1944 occupation and sent to a series of concentration camps, Dachau among them.

Britten did not relay to Stein any of the political conversations from around the table at Christmas dinner, but he was clearly attracted to the Continental high culture of the Hesses and their relations. The strange mixture of tension and normality, of Britten instinctively making no moral distinction between the German war and the British war, would have its most poignant resonance only a few years later, when at the end of *War Requiem* the ghosts of two opposing soldiers meet somewhere in the bloody glob between their trenches and try to make sense of their predicament.

His immersion in this world is telling for another reason: the British government, first under Attlee and Bevin, then Churchill and Eden, was either not interested in playing any role in the reconstruction of Europe or was incapable economically of doing so. Britain rebuffed France's Schuman Plan, whereby the production of coal and steel in Europe would be under a central autonomous body, and watched from the sidelines as one card was placed on top of another: the European Coal and Steel Community, the European Economic Community and the European Atomic Energy Community – all formed in the space of five years. There was something wilfully isolationist and inward-looking about Britain in the 1950s, as if determined not to capitalize on its wartime victory, instead proudly showing off its never-quite-healing scars. Germany, on the other hand, was simultaneously the guardian of the musical culture to which Britten belonged and a progressive force in a Europe that was slowly being rehabilitated. The contrast between the two countries cannot have been lost on the composer.

At Wolfsgarten he reflected once more on the *Gloriana* debacle and tried desperately to figure out what had gone wrong. He decided ultimately that audiences felt confused or betrayed by the opera's 'simplicity and directness, the fewness of the notes. This has been confused with thinness of invention.' Time would show if they were right, he mused, though he thought they were not.

9

Throughout the depression and debilitation that took over as 1953 wore on, his mind was occupied with ghosts other than Hardy's. Britten was eighteen when he first heard a broadcast of Henry James's 'wonderful, impressive but terribly eerie & scarey play "The Turning of the Screw"', which he followed up immediately by reading the novella. Now he found himself, more than twenty years later, adapting James's story for the operatic stage. He had thought about a new opera for the EOG for some time, aware he had neglected the company during the long gestation of *Billy Budd* and composition of *Gloriana*. And though he would end up writing the piece in only four months – hampered by the bursitis and an operation in March 1954 – this opera also had a relatively long gestation. While scouting around for a subject he reread the novella at Pears's suggestion, and as early as May 1951 mentioned it as a possibility. It had to make way for *Gloriana*, however, and the 1953 Venice Biennale, which was to host the first performance, passed without a note having been written; it was eventually programmed in the twenty-seventh International Festival of Contemporary Music in Venice in September the following year.

The book tells the story of two young orphans in an English country house, their uninterested guardian away in London. 'The servants, wicked and depraved, corrupt and deprave the children,' James wrote in his notebook in January 1895 after hearing the story, however improbably, from the Archbishop of Canterbury. 'The children are bad, full of evil, to a sinister degree. The servants *die* (the story vague about the way) and their apparitions, figures, return to haunt the house *and* children, to whom they seem to beckon, whom they invite and solicit, from across dangerous places.' Following the deaths, the guardian dispatches a young and inexperienced governess to look after his wards. She is enchanted by life at Bly and the man who sent her there. Soon, however, she sees the ghosts of the servants, Peter Quint and Miss Jessel, and becomes convinced they have not relinquished their corrupting hold on the two children. From this point, the story plays out its chilling denouement.

It was Myfanwy Piper, who with husband John was the dedicatee of *Winter Words*, who had mentioned the book's operatic potential to Pears some years earlier. Myfanwy was now asked to prepare a synopsis. Britten originally thought Plomer would write the libretto, but Plomer, raised in South Africa in a culture thick with supernatural notions, was unsympathetic to James's 'gingerly northern hauntings'. And Piper's filleting of the novella so impressed Britten he saw no need to try to change Plomer's mind.

Myfanwy, two years older than Britten, was a bright, elfin creature, straight out of a portrait by Memling or Modigliani, with a degree in English from Oxford and a largish, demanding brood to care for. She was not a professional writer or librettist; she had two children's books to her name and the odd unfulfilled contract in her desk drawer, but it was more as editor of the highbrow journal *Axis* in the mid-1930s – a quixotic, foredoomed attempt to inspire in the English an interest in abstract art – that she earned her literary stripes. She knew everyone, so it seemed: Kandinsky, Brancusi, Mondrian and Giacometti from a trip to Paris in 1934; Graham Sutherland, Henry Moore and their generation of English artists through her stewardship of *Axis* or through John; Kenneth Clark, John Betjeman, the Sitwells and their literary fellow travellers. Even activist and heiress Nancy Cunard had drifted into her milieu: she turned up in August 1937 at the Pipers' ramshackle farmhouse near Henley-on-Thames in Oxfordshire, her black boyfriend in tow, on the weekend Britten, Auden and others repaired there to thrash out the Group Theatre's most recent crisis. ('Hello, Maud,' Margot Asquith famously greeted Cunard's mother ten years earlier, news of Nancy's *outré* friends and behaviour having pinged around town, 'what is it now – drink, drugs or niggers?')

Like Britten, Myfanwy was a product of the 1930s. More, she possessed a good editor's eye and conversationalist's ear. Both of these qualities informed the libretto she wrote for Britten. She distilled James's ambiguous novella into a series of vignettes, threaded loosely with a string of unsettling hints and images. Don't worry about having the characters act in a haunted way or say spooky things, Britten told her; leave all that to the music.

Unlike her predecessors, Piper was too busy with her family to decamp to Aldeburgh for long stretches. 'She is so good, but is so occupied with being a wife & mother,' Britten complained to Coleman at the end of May 1954, two months after the surgery that for the moment corrected his arm, aware that the premiere was a matter of months away. But the distance worked to the advantage of both, allowing careful contemplation of each stitch in the fabric. Piper was not railroaded into the instantaneous fixes that had scarred previous operas, *Lucretia* most notably. Instead, Britten telephoned through each change or request, or wrote to her if the ideas were complex. Some requests were tiny: he replaced 'It is all a mistake' with 'It is all a wicked lie', having composed a startling, elongated phrase for the Governess and Mrs Grose to sing and liking the whip-crack sound of the substitute word. And he decided on 'was free' instead of 'made free' to describe Quint's relationship with young Miles, the former sounding more ambiguous, somehow less sexual.

He scribbled such corrections throughout his draft libretto – changes in metre, new rhymes, even lighting directions when they occurred to him – and asked Piper for her thoughts. He plucked sentences from the original novella and sent them her way if he thought them better than what she had come up with, as he had done with Plomer and Forster before. And in meetings with Coleman, who was once more to direct, he honed the opera's structure, deciding on one occasion that what was needed was a prologue: Act 1 was looking a little short, he explained to Piper, though only a Britten made of sterner stuff could have passed up the narrative potential and pitfalls of the existing James prologue.

James was not so easy to pin down. 'Only make the reader's general vision of evil intense enough,' he said of his story, 'and his own experience, his own imagination, his own sympathy (with the children) and horror (of their false friends) will supply him quite sufficiently with all the particulars. Make him *think* the evil, make him think it for himself, and you are released from weak specifications.' Harewood recalled a surprising disagreement with Britten over this. In a lively conversation it soon became evident that Britten thought the ghosts in the story real, overturning decades of Freudian literary criticism. Harewood, on the other hand, thought the whole point of the novella was that the reader is never quite sure whether the ghosts exist or are a figment of the governess's fevered imagination. In this, Harewood was replicating James's line, but also that taken by Edmund Wilson – his world and Britten's unexpectedly overlapping once more – who decided the young governess was insane.*

Piper thought it did not come down to one version or the other. 'I don't think Ben really took sides: but James's story certainly underlines his [Britten's] own emotional attitude to the corruptibility of innocence. That evil exists whether in life or in the mind . . . and is capable of corrupting – or perhaps not necessarily corrupting but causing the loss of innocence – he was, I think, quite certain.' The question is who is corrupting whom.

Britten wrote at great speed. Holst recalled copying the vocal score in batches, six or so pages at a time, and immediately posting them to Boosey & Hawkes to be prepared for the cast; 'it seemed incredible that a composer could be so sure of what he wanted that he would risk parting with the beginning of a scene before he had written the end of it.' Only two sections caused him trouble, the Prologue and the denouement,

---

* And if not insane, there were certainly malign governesses. In her book *Governess Life: Its Trials, Duties, and Encouragements* of 1849, Mary Maurice wrote that 'frightful instances have been discovered in which she, to whom the care of the young has been entrusted, instead of guarding their minds in innocence and purity, has become their corrupter – she has been the first to lead and to initiate into sin, to suggest and carry on intrigues, and finally to be the instrument of destroying the peace of families'.

the drafts of which cast some light on how Britten viewed the power struggles and relationships in the work.

His first draft of the Prologue was badly stilted. It has none of the suggestive harmony and Victorian atmosphere of either the novella or his final draft, in which the audience feels as though it is gathered beneath gently hissing gas lamps, steeling itself to hear a terrifying ghost story, a sense of foreboding overtaking before the Prologue has ended.

The final scene, in which Quint and the Governess slog it out for young Miles's soul (or body?), caused Britten much more trouble. He wrote four drafts, which was unusual; generally he erased errors rather than reach for a new sheet of manuscript. This time the changes were too great, and the drafts depict different degrees of collusion between the adults in the lead-up to Miles's denunciation ('Peter Quint, you devil!'), ultimately suggesting different degrees of culpability in the child's death.

First Britten tried making Quint solely responsible. Then he made the Governess join Quint in singing his beguiling melody from earlier in the opera, in Quint's key. In his third draft Britten played with the idea a little further, reinforcing their joint responsibility for the boy's death. In the final draft he stepped back from such an explicit reading. The Governess and Quint both urge Miles on, but once he shrieks out the manservant's name, Quint sings his sinuous melody alone – this time in the Governess's key. While Quint bids him farewell, she embraces poor Miles, comforting him in his distress, and only once the ghost is gone does she realize the boy is dead. It is a devastating moment and she cries out in anguish, revisiting Miles's haunting 'Malo' song from Act 1, as Piper always planned she should.

What exactly has she won? She has pushed Quint away from Miles and has seen off Miss Jessel, but she is left with the boy dead in her arms. It is unclear whether she literally suffocated him with her love and comfort, or whether the spectral showdown, and Miles's enforced denunciation, robbed him of his lifeblood. The Governess's morality has not trumped Quint's. And we cannot be certain that the 'you devil' is not directed at the Governess, rather than Quint, since she, after all, has goaded Miles into betraying his mate. Likewise, when she sings 'What have we done between us?' it is not clear that she is not addressing Quint rather than the dead boy in her arms. It is the most ghastly pyrrhic victory.

I O

Henry James's own interest in dramatic ambiguity ('Make him *think* the evil, make him think of it for himself'), his delight in making his readers join the dots, and his repressed sexuality (which often influenced the choice and shape of his stories) were a good fit for Britten. It is curious that the novella did not occur to him sooner: one of his great talents, after all, was his eye for stories that would work as operas, especially those involving only a handful of characters. The speed with which decisions were taken occasionally affected his judgement, but his strike rate in finding stories for his operas was high. When Crozier later sniffed about how many of them contained a homosexual sub-narrative, he was technically accurate; yet he was remarkably grudging about what was clearly a primary creative force for the composer. In James, in Melville and Crabbe, and even in Maupassant, Britten recognized a certain kinship, felt happy in the author's company and was inspired to write great things.

In her libretto, Piper did Britten one disservice. In the colloquy between Quint and Jessel at the beginning of Act 2, where she found herself having to put words into the mouths of ghosts that are silent in the original James story, she turned to Yeats's great 1919 poem 'The Second Coming' and eyed one section.

> Turning and turning in the widening gyre
> The falcon cannot hear the falconer;
> Things fall apart; the centre cannot hold;
> Mere anarchy is loosed upon the world,
> The blood-dimmed tide is loosed, and everywhere
> The ceremony of innocence is drowned;
> The best lack all conviction, while the worst
> Are full of passionate intensity.

Piper plucked one line – 'The ceremony of innocence is drowned' – and gave it to the ghosts, first Quint, then both in a duet. It is a clunky appropriation. In Yeats it points to a time before the First World War, before the Easter Rising and the Russian Revolution, those chilling blueprints of disastrous twentieth-century imperial conflict. In *The Turn of the Screw* it is used to suggest that all bets about childhood innocence are off.

Piper thought she was on safe ground. 'What is absorbing and fascinating about *The Turn of the Screw* is not the sin that lies beneath the fine mist of evil, nor yet the Governess's unfulfilled love, which it was at one time the Freudian fashion to make responsible for the whole affair, but the vulnerability of innocence at all ages.' Of course this is a significant part of the work, bringing it close in spirit to 'Before Life and After', the final song of *Winter Words*. Yet incorporating Yeats's line formalized the idea of corrupted innocence – particularly that of children – as a major motif in Britten criticism. It became the shorthand with which his work thereafter was viewed and discussed – not solely by critics and biographers, for whom it became a modern-day Rosetta Stone, but by those close to him as well.

It is not as though the notion has no substance. 'I think if one looks back over the operas that I have written up to date,' Britten told Crozier in 1960, 'one does find a kind of pattern running through them, but I must admit that I haven't been very conscious of that pattern. But I think you are quite right: there are certain conflicts which do worry me a great deal, and I want to say things about them in musical terms.' There had certainly been early hints in this direction. There is the tiny vignette in *Quatre chansons françaises*, where the little child sings his nursery rhyme out on the street while his mother lies dying inside the house. As soon as she is interred under the cold stone floor of the cloister, he takes up his song once more: 'Sorrow is a fruit: God does not permit it to grow on a branch too weak to bear it.' Or there are the narrative underpinnings of *Hymn to St Cecilia*, in which the children are thrust into the adult world and instructed to stay there, seeking forgiveness for the crimes of others: 'O weep, child, weep, O weep away the stain, / Lost innocence who wished your lover dead, / Weep for the lives your wishes never led.'

In 1980 Pears explained why he thought the theme was so attractive to Britten. 'The point is, everything seemed so simple when he was a boy ... simple and delightful for the most part. But as he grew up, he began to be increasingly disillusioned – in MAN – I suppose. So this idea of a lost child, lost childhood, lost innocence, and the search for that innocence, became of fundamental importance to him.' This is fine as far as it goes – and it goes a good distance. But it can also limit the scope of Britten's works, narrowing their true targets. It is now impossible to hear the end of *Winter Words* without somehow *knowing* this is Britten hankering after the innocence of his boyhood. Or watch *Peter Grimes* without thinking about the poor apprentice boys, their childhoods roughly taken from them, when, in Suffolk in the 1820s, with the Elizabethan Poor Law on their side, every one of those fishermen would have had his own apprentice (chimneysweeps were still allowed six each), and no doubt they died like flies in the rough and tumble. Or view Miles as anything but an unwitting victim. Or see Billy solely as a symbol, not a man. These ideas are part of each story, but should take their place in a much wider scheme.

Britten was infuriated when critics tried to depict him as a Johnny One Note. He told a *Guardian* journalist in 1971 that he was 'never aware of himself thinking, "Here's a nice story about innocence destroyed again"', before conceding 'he supposes he does have an instinctive tug towards it'. Colin Matthews remembers having tea with him in the early 1970s when Britten read out loud a critical review of *Owen Wingrave* in *Opera* magazine, which included the observation that all Britten's operas were concerned with the theme of innocence, at which point Britten exploded, throwing the magazine across the room. 'That is absolute rubbish!' He was so angry that Matthews did not feel he could ask him the question: if they're not about innocence, what are they about?

Betrayal, Britten would have replied. People of all ages can be betrayed, as can values, societies, loyalties, trust, confidences, friends, countries, words and aspirations. Grimes betrays Ellen, and he in turn is betrayed by his own community (not without cause: he is the dreamer Britten and Pears desired him to be, but a fairly ham-fisted one). Albert Herring betrays his society's values, but they are values worth trampling into the dust on the road to Campsey Ash. Lucretia betrays either her husband or herself, her lust or her mistaken sense of social propriety bringing about her death. Captain Vere betrays Billy against his own wishes, but had he not done so he would have betrayed his feelings towards the young sailor and to the repressive laws of monarch, empire and navy. Queen Elizabeth is betrayed by Essex and, like Vere with Billy, by her own desire for the coltish nobleman. Owen Wingrave is betrayed by his family and fiancée, who equate his pacifism with cowardice. And Miles is betrayed by almost everyone he meets: his childhood might literally be full of ghosts, his death a form of spectral collateral damage, but the opera's story is infinitely more complex and troubling than the loss of innocence theme of the Yeats line.

And these are only the operas Britten completed. The works he contemplated are full of such betrayals: the Civil War opera (social and political); *King Lear* (political and filial); *Mansfield Park* (class and romantic); *Anna Karenina* (ditto). 'Happy families are all alike; every unhappy family is unhappy in its own way' is the opening line of *Anna Karenina*, but it applies as well to the others. Conflict is occasionally resolved happily, but the moral is more often found in the betrayal than the resolution. In his 1960 conversation with Crozier, Britten said he always began the process of writing an opera by observing the characters and their conflicts in the source material. It is not that he thought plot would look after itself: *Paul Bunyan* had put paid to this notion. It is more that it was character and conflict that immediately caught his eye. Crozier pressed him on this, observing that Britten was 'not really interested in human conflict simply in finite terms', but in its broader meaning and metaphors, with which Britten concurred.

If audiences think Britten's operas are concerned solely with the theme of innocence, they go looking for it, remaining blind to everything else. Coleman was adamant that Miles's yelping denunciation at the end of *The Turn of the Screw* is intended for Quint alone; he directed it that way in the original production and even as an old man could not comprehend how it could be otherwise, despite Britten's assertion to a friend in 1955 that they had 'left the same ambiguities as Henry James did, and in the particular case you mention the boy's final cry is addressed to no one on the stage at all'. Stein thought it was not quite as ambiguous as this in Britten's mind, telling the young opera director Anthony Besch that the composer unequivocally intended Miles's denunciation to be of the Governess, not Quint. Suddenly the opera is less about Miles's corruption, more about his collusion with the adult world, furious at what the Governess has taken from him. Here is Britten exploring the tension between the innocence of childhood and the shimmering potential of (sexual) experience – a more apposite Yeatsian ideal. Britten was drawn to the story in the same way that the young poet Wilfred Owen was drawn to Keats's *Endymion*, the preface to which he quoted in a letter to his mother, hinting at his own sexual turmoil. 'The imagination of a boy is healthy, and the mature imagination of a man is healthy;

but there is a space of life between in which the soul is in a ferment, the character undecided, the way of life uncertain, (yes!), and the ambition thick-sighted (yes indeed!).' It could easily be Britten describing Miles.

The political backdrop to the operas further muddies these boyhood Arcadian waters. Post-war Britain was a bold socialist experiment, Clement Attlee, William Beveridge and John Maynard Keynes its architects. The concept of state responsibility and intervention was played out in the second half of the 1940s through new institutions such as the National Health Service, the National Insurance Act and the Arts Council, and through the nationalization of coal mining, gas, electricity, the railways and much else besides. If ever there was a time to explore notions of personal and corporate responsibility, to examine the relationship between the individual and the state, it was in England in the late 1940s and early 1950s. These were the years in which Graham Greene repeatedly spun powerful tales about personal betrayal in morally ambivalent times. The post-war Britten was no ideologue, and though he was sympathetic to the basic humanitarian ideals of the new institutions, he was also attuned to the potential for their corruption or failure. And with much of Europe charred and ruined, he remained wary of those whose behaviour was indebted to ideology, faith or repression.

Britten wrote what he felt, intrigued by the frictions and conflicts between characters in the stories and poetry he read both recreationally and when on the prowl for source material. He was of the class and the generation-but-one so tragically betrayed by its elders in the bogs of the First World War; like Wilfred Owen, he felt the betrayal keenly. It is not certain he always identified the moral weight of his works or their likely impact. He made a lovely observation about Mozart to Crozier, which applies equally well to his own operas. 'I feel that with Mozart, for instance, that he is writing about Figaro and his relationship with Susanna and the Countess, and is not always quite clear of the tremendous moral significance that these pieces are going to have for us.'

II

Soon after the 1938 partition of Czechoslovakia the photographer Erich Auerbach set off on foot from his homeland for London. There he set about creating an extensive photographic portfolio, charting Britain's unsteady emergence from hostilities with skill and empathy. An amateur musician, Auerbach was at home photographing the great visiting and resident soloists and conductors of the post-war era. They relaxed in his presence, forgot he was there, and his collection today, perhaps more than that of any other photographer of the time, charts the emergence of a confident British music industry. It contains pictures of Schwarzkopf, Dietrich Fischer-Dieskau and Wolfgang Sawallisch in the EMI studio listening to playbacks of *Capriccio*; Pierre Fournier, looking more like a circus clown than a brilliant cellist, his accompanist Gerald Moore a butcher; Bernstein on the podium, looking like nothing his musicians had ever seen before; Klemperer recording Beethoven's Symphony No. 9, his soloists including Hans Hotter and Christa Ludwig; Rubinstein playing at the Royal Festival Hall; Boult in the audience of the same venue for a Schwarzkopf concert, every bit the Edwardian gentleman; a vulpine Glenn Gould, backstage there, his gloved hand holding a glass of something cloudy; Stravinsky in dark glasses at the Savoy, looking like a gangster.

Auerbach was in Venice in September 1954 for *The Turn of the Screw*. He captured a street picnic near Teatro la Fenice in a rehearsal break: the Pipers and two of their children, Britten and Pears and the EOG's manager Basil Douglas sit in a tight circle on some steps, eating sandwiches, looking stressed and glum. It was another fraught production period, though there were mitigating circumstances this time. John Piper had matched Britten's cinematic conception of the opera with a minimalist set, which through clever lighting, gauzes and panels was able to suggest the tower at Bly, or the house's beautiful grounds, or the church, or Miles's bedroom, shifting between them all as seamlessly as did Britten's score. His designs had depth and perspective, evoking a brooding, unsettling atmosphere. But it was all too complicated for the Italian stage hands – who had to move it on and off in between rehearsals to accommodate other productions – and for the lighting operators, who sat at antediluvian consoles, wondering how on earth they could create the subtle shifts and fades required to match Britten's music and Piper's design. Colin Graham, in Venice as the EOG's young stage manager, had taught himself Italian the previous winter and now found himself negotiating with the head of the union, doing his best to ward off a strike.

Graham prevailed and the opera opened on 15 September 1954.

It was swelteringly hot, and the performance began a little late because of an overrun on one of the broadcasting networks taking the premiere live. David Hemmings, the boy playing Miles, later recalled the final scene and the shattering moment when Jennifer Vyvyan, the Governess, reprised his 'Malo' song. He was in tears in her arms, she was giving the aria all it was worth, and the audience sat there in a sort of appalled, mesmerized silence as the curtain came down, remaining that way for a while. 'It started slowly,' Hemmings later said, 'and soon there was this rush of enormous enthusiasm from the audience – which absolutely took you by the bowels and broke your heart. We didn't quite know what had happened. There was something like forty-three curtain calls. It was one of those special nights.'

Afterwards, the cast and creative team attended a ball thrown by the mayor of Venice – Myfanwy Piper in a floor-length gown, Britten dressed much as he was for the Tanglewood performance of *Grimes* all those years ago, his white single-breasted dinner jacket now upgraded to the double-breasted Bold Look then in fashion – and at four in the morning found themselves walking home through an empty St Mark's Square. Arda Mandikian, who sang Miss Jessel, launched into a Greek folk song. Pears and Vyvyan joined in, the sound echoing around the square. Then Vyvyan gave an encore of the 'Malo' aria. People emerged from the shadows to watch, or opened their windows or came out of doorways. Britten stood smiling, relieved, thrilled with how the evening had gone.

The critics were also pleased. One or two thought Britten had opted for Version A of James's story, in which the ghosts are invented by the Governess; most others went with Version B, in which they are real – a little too real, thought Shawe-Taylor, who disliked their dialogue and proximity. But words such as genius, gripping, intense, miraculous, masterpiece and tour de force turned up with frequency in the reviews. Once again, it took a French newspaper to use the word 'homosexual' (which more than any extensive sociological study encapsulates the critical and cultural differences between France and Britain in these years) when Antoine Golea in *L'Express* wrote of 'the composer's customary intense preoccupation with homosexual love and the futility of struggling against it'.

Despite protestations that he neither read nor cared about the opinions of critics, the positive reception comforted Britten, memories of *Gloriana* still fresh. John Ireland listened to the first broadcast and a later one from Sadler's Wells in October, describing the score as 'the most remarkable and original music I have ever heard from the pen of a British composer . . . I now am (perhaps *reluctantly*) compelled to regard Britten as possessing ten times the musical talent, intuition and ability of all other living British composers put together'. It was a handsome tribute from one of these living composers, and Ireland later repeated it, watered down, to Britten himself. Yet none of this – the good reviews, appreciative letters, public success – effected a rapprochement with the wider industry. To Britten it just reinforced how wrong everyone was about *Gloriana*.

12

Of all the adolescent boys in Britten's life, David Hemmings came closest to upsetting the balance at Crag House and its successor, the Red House. Whenever he was asked, which was quite often, the adult Hemmings took great pains to exonerate Britten from any inappropriate behaviour. Without doubt there was love and infatuation on both sides of the relationship, which had intensified in the two months leading up to the premiere, the twelve-year-old Hemmings living with Britten in Aldeburgh. There was schooling of sorts laid on for the boy, but mostly his time was spent rehearsing or taking singing lessons, swimming or playing tennis, or walking on the beach where fishermen taught him to mend nets and invited him to join them for a snifter at The Mill, a dingy pub on the seafront. Britten would tousle his hair and kiss him on his head or cuddle him, and Hemmings would come and sleep in his bed when scared by the unrelenting crashing of the North Sea against the shingle, or when he was lonely, or just for the hell of it. Hemmings *père* had dispatched his son to Aldeburgh with the fatherly observation, 'You know he's a homo, don't you,' which turned out to be a redundant warning.

Britten did find Hemmings physically attractive. The boy was old for his age, good-looking, knowing too, aware of the effect he had on Britten. The young conductor Charles Mackerras, a bright-eyed, larrikin Australian who was then working with the EOG, thought Hemmings played up mercilessly to Britten's adoration. 'Ben's behaviour was so much that of the besotted lover that one thought that maybe he might have behaved improperly with him eventually.' Some of those involved in the EOG had previously thought this about other attractive boys singing parts in the operas. Soprano Margaret Ritchie, who created the role of Miss Wordsworth in *Albert Herring*, started looking out for young David Spenser, the first Harry, when the company was on tour. And when it was over she visited Crozier and asked him to use his influence to stop Britten writing parts for pre-adolescent boys. Anne Wood, the company's manager, also picked up on Britten's attachment to Spenser: fearing the worst, she made it her business to barge into rooms without knocking, hoping not to find anything untoward, wrongly confident she would.

In Venice it was Joan Cross's turn to be chaperone. She made obvious her concerns about the closeness and what she thought the inappropriateness of Britten's relationship with Hemmings. Coleman later thought her general unhappiness during the opera was less to do with this relationship and more with the fact that she was at the end of her singing career (she would retire the following year); she was now singing a *comprimario* role, that of a housekeeper, whereas a year earlier she was queen. But others were also concerned. Pears, who normally took such infatuations in his stride, was one of them, telling the harpsichordist and conductor Raymond Leppard after Britten's death that the Hemmings episode was 'nearly catastrophic' and would not have needed much for it to escalate into a scandal.

Hemmings did not see it this way. 'Was he infatuated with me? Yes, he was. He was a gentleman; there was no sort of overt sexuality about it whatsoever. It was a very kind and loving and very gentle relationship.' Moreover, had Britten tried anything on him, 'I think it would have embarrassed him a damn sight more than it would have embarrassed me at the time.' He was more than able to look after himself.

This is not to say that over the years there were no boys without Hemmings's street-smartness, made vulnerable as a result. Thin-lipped Aldeburghians would observe each new boy and say to themselves, 'Here's the latest', before bruiting it about town. Mitchell thought Britten had a touch of Quint to him – possessive, mesmerizing, magicking somebody's heart away. Yet Hemmings thought part of his attraction for Britten was his knowingness, not his sexless innocence. David Spenser thought it had been the same with him in 1947. Of all the middle-aged men Carpenter interviewed for his biography in the late 1980s and early 1990s who had known Britten when they were young, only Jonathan Gathorne-Hardy could relate an occasion when Britten overstepped the mark. He was in a towel following a bath at Crag House, when 'Ben came up with an extremely soppy, sentimental look on his face, and put his arms round me, and kissed me on the top of the head. And I made the speech which I'd long prepared. I said, "No, Ben, it is not to be!"' And nor was it. They went downstairs, drank Martinis together, and no doubt tucked into one of Miss Hudson's hearty meals. Gathorne-Hardy was eighteen at the time.

Most contemporaneous and subsequent commentators have concluded that such infatuations had no bearing on Britten's relationship with Pears. It is true that each wrote openly to the other of the cute blond boys in Switzerland; or the young toughs in Amsterdam; or the sweet English poppets on a train; or the bellboys in one hotel or another – much as they might correspond over bad conductors or spicy food. Yet the Hemmings episode was more intense than those before, different from young Bobby Rothman in the early 1940s when Britten and Pears had been together only a few years. Anne Wood thought the early infatuation with Spenser, not the later clumsy advance to Gathorne-Hardy, was an accurate measure of the men's relationship. 'One could just see cracks in the relationship, and [because] that seemed so important it was a pity.' Hemmings noted that Pears was 'furiously jealous' of their friendship, though he did not find out about this until almost forty years later.

Pears shared some of Britten's penchant for young men, and he went along a certain distance with his lover's attraction to adolescent boys. They were both distraught about Paul Rogerson's departure for the priesthood, for example, though it was Britten who described the novitiate in terms of love.* Britten and Pears both talked about adopting a child, though it was Britten alone who enacted a version of this, asking Ronald Duncan whether he could be a second father to his son Roger. 'And as you see, we've always got Briony,' Duncan said casually of his daughter in agreeing to Britten's suggestion, and an already strong bond between Britten and Roger grew stronger still.

Anne Wood was right: there seemed to be more distance between

---

* 'Do you know, Paul & I fell in love with each other, if that is how you can describe it, a whole year before we met,' Britten told Holst, adding that it was Rogerson who, at the premiere of *Budd*, came and asked him whether he remembered the concert a year earlier when the two of them had stared at each other for some time.

Britten and Pears than ever before. The infrastructure of their relationship remained, but they lived such different lives. Colin Graham was
sure Britten was celibate by then and Robert Tear maintained that *Canticle I* was written as a peace offering following the mutual recriminations
that erupted when Pears strayed while on a foreign tour. Their love and
admiration were evident in their letters and reunions. But there were
also jarring notes, Hemmings aside. Pears could now be terribly offhand
to his partner, especially if Britten was working on a piece that did not
involve him, or did not appeal to him. Holst was at Covent Garden at
the end of December 1956 for the final rehearsal of *The Prince of the
Pagodas*, his large-scale work for the Royal Ballet. It was a distressing
rehearsal – not least because Britten was in the pit, his arm causing considerable pain once more, and he had never before conducted a ballet,
which requires such different skills from conducting opera. Dancers
jump to the beat of someone else's drum, and Britten was wholly unused
to this style of working, to the way they breathed and gave away everything but simultaneously nothing with their bodies compared to singers.
Ninette de Valois would come out front periodically, sit behind him in
the pit, and ask for one thing or another: a clearer upbeat for her dancers, perhaps, or a query about tempo. Pears, having wandered in for a
little of the rehearsal and taken stock of the moody, desperate situation,
saw Britten in the break. 'What am I to do?' Britten wailed. 'I don't
know what you're going to do,' Pears responded, 'but I'm going to have
a haircut.' And off he went, leaving Britten bewildered, without anyone
other than Holst to help later with taxis and bags and his depression
over the new work. She fumed on his behalf.

There were many other such instances, in both art and life – the *Gloriana* broadside, or Pears not offering to take the wheel and turn the great
Rolls around when they had parked in a tiny area, Britten making a hash
of it because of his arm. Or Pears responding to an enthusiastic query
from a BBC producer after the final rehearsal for the British premiere of
the Cello Symphony: 'I don't know. I've never heard it.' Or his reacting
ambivalently to Britten's appointment to the House of Lords, and
clearing up the mess a month later: 'In the middle of all those worries
which you can't get rid off, don't – please don't – include one that in any
possible way makes you think that I "mind" about the Lordship. I am
proud and touched but in *no* way resentful or jealous – I repeat over &
over again – in no way!' Or the day of Britten's funeral, only hours after

the country's greatest composer since Purcell, and a superb conductor, was interred in the cemetery behind Aldeburgh parish church, when Pears announced to the remaining mourners at the Red House, 'Slava [Rostropovich] says I must conduct.' There was something wilful and distasteful about it all – almost as though Pears needed to demonstrate his power, or flex his muscles, or attempt to step out of Britten's long shadow.

There was more to it than this. 'Peter is always right,' Holst told Mitchell less than a year after Britten's death, 'about everything.' So Britten found it difficult to tell Pears he was singing flat in a recording session, or that he was unhappy with his performance in *Gloriana* one night, expressing his glum wrath to Holst instead – how he ought not to 'have dragged Peter away from the Matthew Passions and things that he loved doing, since he was obviously unhappy in opera'.

Yet Pears was not solely to blame; neither man could be told anything. So they hinted, or fumed, or picked at scabs, or got others to do their dirty work. It would all blow up and be followed by tender reconciliations, but then Pears would go away once more – on tour or just to London – and the silly slights and differences would accumulate once again. Perhaps it was no worse than it had ever been, though the time they now spent apart was much greater, and recent years had left Britten with little space for anything but composing. It was in this context, in April 1953, that Britten told Holst that if Pears 'found the right girl to marry he supposed he'd have to "lump it" and that nothing would ever interfere with their relationship'.* Perhaps it was a Forster–Buckingham ménage he here envisaged, the patient May in the background tending both husband and writer, or a beaten-down reaction to Pears's tantrums over *Gloriana*. Or it was acknowledgement of the cracks that Wood identified.

There was none of this friction and tension with the middle-class adolescents who caught Britten's eye and heart. They looked up to him with uncomplicated adoration, sometimes enjoying the frisson of sublimated sexuality, often not. In their company he could step outside the adult world for a time and revel in the company of those who for once

---

* John Lindsay remembered a similar conversation concerning Britten in the mid- to late 1940s. 'In fact there was one time Ben actually wanted to get married, and we were all talking about who would be suitable for him, because he did want to have a family; but you know, it never came to it actually. I shouldn't think Peter would allow anything like that for one moment.'

found him straightforward, and he them. 'It's often a problem that these youngsters seem to think I want to go to bed with them,' he complained to Mitchell, improbably and a little disingenuously, when one boy had become too clingy. Yet it would seem that, having worked out what he wanted from these friendships and what he was willing or permitted to give, everyone else was meant to glean and follow the unstated rules.

13

In late September 1954, two weeks after the premiere of *The Turn of the Screw*, Britten wrote to Edith Sitwell seeking permission to set perhaps her most famous poem, 'Still Falls the Rain', as a memorial to Noel Mewton-Wood. He did not have a huge amount of time: it was intended for a concert at the beginning of December to mark the first anniversary of Mewton-Wood's death, and Britten had a two-week Continental recital tour and the London premiere of *The Turn of the Screw* to navigate. Yet he had done all his thinking about the new work, without knowing it, over the previous year. The musical language is straight from his most recent opera: sparse textures and pared-down piano writing in an episodic framework, with short motifs repeated, their impact cumulative.

By the 1950s Dame Edith cut an eccentric figure. 'Her features seemed carved as though out of alabaster, in which were cut narrowly watchful eyes, amused, kind, cold, sad, or even at moments incisively shrewd,' Spender described her late in the war. With her angular face, raven-black clothing, clunky jewellery and large collection of turbans, she looked more prophet than poet. 'The trouble with most Englishwomen,' she once said, 'is that they will dress as if they had been a mouse in a previous incarnation ... they do not want to attract attention.' She did. Her friendship with Britten was recent yet warm and, having long admired his music, she was thrilled he wanted to set her words.

There is no obvious connection between the poem and Mewton-Wood, except that the piece Britten composed occupies a barren landscape. He told Sitwell that in the poem's 'courage & light seen through horror & darkness I find something very right for the poor boy'. Written for tenor, horn and piano, this third *Canticle* growls and clumps along, a series of sullen instrumental variations divided by clear, still, lyrical stanzas. The mood Britten created for Sitwell's words is almost apocalyptic – the stillness following an air raid, a sole survivor looking out at the wreckage. Where Sitwell quotes from Marlowe's *Doctor Faustus* – 'O Ile leape up to my God: who pulles me doune' – Britten has the tenor declaim the words in a demented *Sprechstimme*. There is resolution of sorts in the Bachian chorale that follows: 'Then sounds the voice of One who like the heart of man / Was once a child who among beasts has lain – / "Still do I love, still shed my innocent light, my Blood, for thee."' But it is not a convincing resolution. There is anger that such bloody destruction could be allowed by a benevolent God, anger at the slaughter of Christ and the senselessness of war. It is far more barbed than its predecessor.

The concert was postponed, as it happened, until the end of January 1955. Pears was ill, doing his best not to pull out of the run of Walton's *Troilus and Cressida*, which premiered at Covent Garden on 3 December. He croaked and half-spoke his way through the opening night, buoyed by pills and champagne, and then cancelled subsequent performances without much regret: he thought the whole thing badly shaped, too long and looking shoddy on stage. Britten distractedly continued the hunt for the subject of a new children's opera – Arion, perhaps, the ancient Greek poet thrown off a ship and rescued by dolphins. Or Phaeton, the boy who drives his father's chariot across the sky, dragging the sun behind him, and is killed by Zeus before he can crash it into the earth. Icarus or even Medea, who murders her brother Absyrtus. ('What a girl she was,' Britten commented dryly to Plomer.) But nothing stuck.

Britten sensed it was the end of one era and the beginning of the next. In late April 1955 he wrote of this feeling to Sitwell, who had finally felt able to describe the devastating impact Britten's setting of her poem made on her. ('I am so haunted and so alone with that wonderful music and its wonderful performance that I was incapable of writing before now ... It was certainly one of the greatest experiences in all my life as an artist'). Normally Britten responded to such letters in one of two ways: I think this is my best piece yet, he would say to his intimate friends. Or to those outside the circle, he might say: one is always fondest of one's youngest child. But Sitwell and the new piece prompted a different response.

I must confess I was nervous about writing it; it is such a great poem, & I was well aware of the responsibility. Where I think I *have* succeeded is to have the wit to put nothing in the way of the wonderful words, & that of course is largely why the effect on the listeners is so intense. I can only be grateful to you, my dear Edith, for having written them. But in another way too I am grateful to you; writing this work has helped me so much in my development as a composer. I feel that with this work & the Turn of the Screw (which I am impatient for you to hear) I am on the threshold of a new musical world (for me, I am not pretentious about it!). I am worried by the problems which arise, & that is one reason that I am taking off next winter to do some deep thinking. But your great poem has dragged something from me that was latent there, & shown me what lies before me.

It was an honest and accurate reflection on his work and future, all the more remarkable because it stemmed from a well-crafted yet modest piece.

It was not solely his change in style, however – this shift away from the luscious orchestral textures of the works from *Grimes* to *Gloriana* to more intimate soundscapes, putting nothing in the way of wonderful words – that marked the end of the era. Since returning to England in 1942 Britten had been continuously involved with one opera or the next. He had scarcely had any time to think, and the operas slid between great and flawed creations as a consequence. Every flaw can be traced to the speed with which he was working and his truculent impatience with those collaborators who slowed him down or questioned his judgement – regardless of the degree to which such resistance benefited the finished work. Britten was not now proposing a period of self-reflection and analysis; he really did believe the public and critics were to blame when an opera of his did badly. But he was determined to reflect on the type of composer he wanted to be and the type of music he wanted to write.

Britten was a far brittler character now than in 1942. When Stein chose not to attend the recording sessions for *The Turn of the Screw* in January 1955, he found himself bawled out by the composer, who threw his old friend's words back at him with derision, something the younger Britten would never have done. 'I don't see how one can, as you ask me from time to time, make strong representations to Leslie Boosey to allow you to come abroad to important performances, if the first complete operatic recording of mine happening on your own doorstep isn't important enough for you to attend.'

He was also far wealthier. His income for the year ending 5 April 1955 (the day on which Churchill resigned as prime minister, health and power waning) was £12,800* – almost six times what he earned in 1945–6, the breakthrough year of *Grimes*. Wealth made him more generous, but pricklier too; it somehow testified that he was right. A touchy self-righteousness entered his correspondence around now, with phrases of his friends and colleagues singled out in examination, the possibility that he had misunderstood the content or context never entertained. Occasionally the friends and colleagues would bite back. In the aftermath of *Gloriana*, as Britten lashed out at those close to him, Roth wrote admonishing him for listening to his friends and their distortions, rather than the facts of any situation. 'I do not seem to have an adequate weapon against persistent vilifications and your readiness to listen to them.' Mostly though, they absorbed the blows. It's just Ben, they'd tell each other. But this new Ben – or perhaps this old Ben, with the patina of restraint and good manners stripped away – appeared more often now.

* Over £275,000 today.

6

Prosperity

The Far East, England, 1955–1963

I

At the end of October 1955 Britten and Pears packed Aertex dress shirts, white tie, casual clothes (summer and winter), sleeping pills, scores and books – though very little manuscript paper. New visas in their passports and exotic inoculations in their veins, they said goodbye to their miniature dachshund Clytie (named in honour of Pears's singing teacher), and took the night boat to Holland. They would be away for almost five months, time enough for the deep thinking Britten craved. The first leg of their travels was well-charted territory for them both: Holland, Germany, Switzerland, Austria. They ate too much, drank too much, and gave recitals and concerts at every stop, showcasing Britten works from the early 1940s onwards. They revelled in concert halls grand and modest, pianos good and bad (one in Geneva, a sixty-year-old Steinway, now as knackered as an old carthorse), and were fêted by audiences and consuls alike, the latter overseeing official dinners crammed with yet more rich food and wine. They were driven too fast along narrow streets in Amsterdam and kept awake at night by the chimes of clocks adjacent to the various grand hotels in which they stayed. In Vienna they attended a poor performance of *Die Meistersinger* at the newly reopened Staatsoper – destroyed by Allied bombs in the last months of the war and meticulously rebuilt – marvelling at the care with which the house had been brought back to life, drawing an invidious comparison between its splendour and the shabby gentility of Covent Garden.

Yugoslavia was new for them both. They enjoyed the countryside, populated by bony horses and smiling peasants, so different from Suffolk, and saw a production of *Grimes* in Zagreb sung in Serbo-Croat,

409

which was what Flanders and Swann had in mind in their gentle 1953 sketch, 'A Guide to Britten'.

> Sung all over the civilized world. And in America.
> Pierre Grimes!
> Pedro Grimo!
> Pyotr Grimsky!
> Peter J. Grimes!

In Belgrade they met Yugoslavia's twinkly-eyed President Tito, with his high cheekbones and easy smile, which belied his extreme toughness. Britten was struck by his 'curiously attractive personality' and by the cultured, sympathetic members of his government, though he remained silent on Tito's authoritarian ways. Despite the poverty and shabby hotels, despite the dirty trains and many receptions they attended (displaying them as trophies as much as welcoming them), they were touched by the country's efforts to define itself outside Moscow's suffocating grip. They were struck, too, by a love of music in the cities, which generated rapt, full, young audiences at each of their recitals. In Maribor, a picture-postcard city on the Drava, Britten celebrated his forty-second birthday, performing on a piano that 'jangled like an old barrel organ'.

Thereafter they travelled east, to Istanbul, where they decamped to the new Hilton, a luxurious counterpoint to their gloomy digs in Belgrade. Their room overlooked the Bosporus and the start of Asia, which served to emphasize how far they were from home. They found the city strange and wonderful, if bewildering: the smells, food, music and squalid conditions in which most Turks lived were all disquieting, and Britten never dispelled the feeling that the country was a powder keg awaiting flint. (The Istanbul Pogrom, directed at the city's Greek minority, had occurred a little over three months earlier.) They were overwhelmed by Hagia Sophia, the great Byzantine cathedral-cum-mosque-cum-museum, with its extraordinary dome covered in golden mosaics and high galleries supported by massive stone trunks. And they could not quite get over the smaller Byzantine churches, converted into mosques during the Ottoman Caliphate, their ornate walls plastered over. After the abolition of the Caliphate in 1924, many of the small churches were restored, the plaster removed and the brilliant mosaics that so offended Islamic belief revealed, looking as if they were made only yesterday. Britten was thrilled that suppression had led to preservation.

He thought the indigenous music dull, and was buoyed by the great interest in Western scores (not least his own) among young people. He and Pears gave a few recitals and in Ankara attended a bad performance of Verdi's *Un ballo in maschera*. But their concert schedule was lighter than in Europe, for which they were both grateful. From Turkey they flew to Pakistan via Beirut and on to Bombay the next day.

India made an immediate, lasting impact: the climate, the vultures and monkeys and jackals, the warmth of the people, the elegant saris and beauty of the landscape. They grappled with whom to tip: shoe cleaners, bedmakers, liftboys, porters and waiters – each had a claim, yet bumbling Anglo-Saxon embarrassment usually prevailed and the impoverished workers left unacknowledged. They were pushed between one dry reception and the next. 'Although I'm not any more alcoholic than most other people, a little gin *does* help to get through such functions,' Britten wisely wrote to Roger Duncan. They had an informal lunch with the reformist prime minister Nehru and his daughter Indira Gandhi, and were entertained by the great sitarist Ravi Shankar. This was no Cook's tour.

'Like everything they do,' Britten wrote in response to the Shankar performance, 'it seemed much more relaxed & spontaneous than what we do, & the reactions of the other musicians sitting around was really orgiastic. Wonderful sounds, intellectually complicated & controlled.' There were to be two more such responses to indigenous music – in Bali and Japan – and each would influence Britten's own work. Most striking was the more relaxed approach to living and performing. Was it transferable back home? On Christmas Day they visited the Taj Mahal and on Boxing Day lazed in the sun, full of the previous day's mince pies, plum pudding and other such colonial relics. Britten wondered whether they couldn't just stay there for three weeks, not moving anywhere, not seeing anything. Instead they flew in toy aeroplanes and visited temples and tea factories, empire men to their toes. On New Year's Eve they were at a literary dinner in Calcutta, followed by a noisy party, the eminent American choreographer Martha Graham cornering Britten at one point to demand a ballet from him. And the next day they were at lunch in a gentlemen's club, uncomfortable with the number of coloured servants in these post-independence days. ('One is embarrassed by the excess of servants in even quite simple households,' Pears wrote in his diary.)

In Singapore early in the new year they performed *Dichterliebe* and *Die schöne Müllerin*, Pears despairing at the great barn in which the concerts were held, singing like a pig, he thought. They ate Chinese food for the first time in their lives, impossible as this now seems, Britten settling for the safest thing he could see on the menu; the chopsticks defeated him and, too polite to sip soup from the bowl, he went to bed hungry. The Hesses joined them for the travels in Indonesia.

On the island in and around Denpasar there were gamelan rehearsals, trance dances, shadow plays, processional and purification dances, and vast, theatrical cremations to attend. Britten had known of Balinese music since meeting the composer and ethnomusicologist Colin McPhee early in his time in America (he also performed McPhee's two-piano *Balinese Ceremonial Music* in the States and then back in Britain). He owned a few gramophone recordings featuring gamelan orchestras, which supplied him with some of the alluring sounds with which Quint goes about his business in *The Turn of the Screw*. Yet he was still unprepared for the intoxicating impact these orchestras had in the flesh: 'they are fantastic, most complicated & beautiful, & they are *everywhere*! . . . the air is always full of the sound of gongs, drums, & metallophones!' He amused local musicians by singing back to them the short scale on which they had improvised at length, distilling their elaborate soundscape into just five notes – a bit like the bird charmer they watched in Agra who whistled commands to his canaries to thread beads onto cotton, hop through rings and catch small coins thrown in the air.

At each new destination there was correspondence to deal with. The EOG was haemorrhaging funds once more, its tour of *Let's Make an Opera* at the end of 1955 doing dire business. And the festival demanded a few decisions, though Holst's recent appointment as third artistic director (effectively replacing Crozier) ensured much happened without Britten's participation. Any problems or requests that came his way he dealt with as automatically as ordering pre-dinner cocktails.* From Denpasar in late January, buoyed by the long gamelan session he heard that morning, Britten cabled de Valois: 'CONFIDENT BALLET READY FOR

---

* 'I think Venus & Savitri the best alternative,' he wrote to Basil Douglas at the end of December regarding EOG plans, 'but I strongly advise rearranging the week so that we *don't* start the first Friday, but have the performances on the Monday & 2nd Saturday – expensive in fares, I know, but dangerous to have a *non*-1st perf. outside the usual span of the Festival.'

MIDSEPTEMBER LOVE BRITTEN.' His confidence was misplaced and the ballet, first discussed with John Cranko in late 1953, announced by Sadler's Wells in January 1954, and begun in early 1955, would vex him at almost every stage. But the shot in the arm from the morning performance was genuine, and heady gamelan sounds would ultimately transform the stalled work.

In fact, the experiences in Bali could not have come at a more opportune time. As Britten emphasized to Edith Sitwell, months before boarding the boat in Harwich, he knew he was on the threshold of a new, indefinable musical world. In Bali he heard colourful, ecstatic, contemplative works built from the smallest of melodic cells, something he had just achieved, writ large, in *The Turn of the Screw* and *Canticle III*. Was this the musical clarity, order and discipline he sought? So he listened to the live music with extra care. He wrote down on manuscript paper the Balinese names of the dances and sketched a number of the simple scales he had distilled from the source. He fleshed out some of the harmonic elaborations of these scales ('repeat indefinitely,' he noted without irony), which would show up seventeen years later in *Death in Venice*, much as he notated them now.

This was not the only Balinese influence on *Death in Venice*. On 19 January 1956 the party joined Dutch artist Rudolf Bonnet for dinner at his home in Ubud, the small town he had made his home since the late 1920s (a period of internment during the war notwithstanding). Along with German painter Walter Spies, Bonnet was part of a gay expat community in an area that became renowned for its art and sex tourism. Some who came here were real artists, interested in local culture and in spearheading indigenous painting and sculpture; others were drop-outs or criminals or rogues – characters from a Somerset Maugham story – attracted to the amenable post-colonial lifestyle and the accommodating nature of the Balinese. Bonnet belonged in the former camp, as did Spies; though their work includes a fair number of nude adolescent boys, both were interested in creating something fantastical from the fusion of European and Asian artistic ideas, Spies managing to transplant an almost Chagallian aesthetic to a Balinese setting. McPhee attempted much the same in his musical work there in the 1930s. He knew Spies and carried on affairs with compliant young Balinese men, his wife pretending not to notice. But McPhee was genuine in his attempt to preserve Balinese music as all the while he created something new from it. The culture was perhaps not as free in the 1950s as it had been two decades earlier, though Australian artist Donald Friend would find it obliging when he moved there in the late 1960s and acquired an array of young Balinese houseboys.

Britten was circumspect about this aspect of the island, of the beautiful young men at every turn, ready to provide all sorts of hospitality for a coin. The presence of the Hesses probably inhibited him, and any opportune behaviour would have transgressed the understanding he had with Pears (infatuation, but not action, at least on Britten's part). Whatever the reason, Britten disguised any longings behind a pronounced interest in the music he heard and dancing he saw. Paradoxically, Prince Ludwig felt far more relaxed about admiring the physical beauty of the boys, describing them in his diary. At the dinner with Bonnet, shirtless youths in sarongs and white headcloths, flowers stuck behind ears, provided the musical entertainment. 'The slim young people with their brown lithe bodies, looked quite glorious by the light of a few lamps,' Prince Ludwig wrote. 'It is understandable that people can fall uninhibitedly in love with these savage beauties with their somewhat sad faces.' How natural it all seemed, the loving of young men without the censure of society. These distinct versions of morality or custom – of the easygoing Balinese versus a buttoned-up Westerner – find their reflection in *Death in Venice*.

They made their way back to Java and then to Solo in Central Java, travelling in rickshaws to primitive lodgings. In an era before quick international bank transfers, they found themselves cadging money from a taxi driver when funds dried up, a comical inversion of process. Broke, they spent a twelve-hour train journey back to Jakarta through bandit country, consuming nothing but bananas and warm beer. The stress of all this put Britten to bed with an upset stomach and he cancelled a planned recital in Medan. They returned to Singapore and flew to Hong Kong for a recital there, and on to Macau for another. Then to Japan, which provided Britten with his final surprise of the trip.

This leg of the journey started badly. They had had trouble obtaining visas. And Britten held on to a wartime cartoon version of the Japanese – 'the Yellow races look very strange & suspicious – whereas the Brown, the Indians, or Indonesians, look touching & sympathetic, & can be very beautiful' – and after the tranquillity of Bali, the visit was impossibly frantic, packed with meals of raw fish and sake, official

31. On sabbatical: Britten in Tenganan, Bali, January 1956. The sounds he encountered there revived his stalled ballet, *The Prince of the Pagodas*, and thereafter influenced his orchestral writing.

32. Desmond Doyle as the King of the North, attempting to win the affections of the heiress to the Middle Kingdom, in *The Prince of the Pagodas*, Covent Garden, January 1957.

33. *Noye's Fludde*, 1958. Britten instructing sceptical boys in the art of producing the sound of raindrops from mugs slung on string.

34. Britten obliging Mrs Panda, Mrs Wolf and Mrs Monkey with autographs.

35. Britten in the mid-1950s playing tennis with polymath Laurens van der Post at the Red House, Aldeburgh, then owned by the artist Mary Potter. A few years later Britten would leave the busy seafront in Aldeburgh by swapping Crag House for the Red House.

36. Britten and director Colin Graham leaving the Red House in the composer's Alvis, June 1964. Graham directed many Britten premieres.

37. Britten and Mstislav Rostropovich rehearsing for the first performance of the Cello Sonata in the Red House studio, June–July 1961, with members of the English Chamber Orchestra looking on. In the 1960s Rostropovich assumed the role of alternative muse, sometimes at Pears's expense.

38. Britten turning pages for Sviatoslav Richter in recital with Dietrich Fischer-Dieskau, Aldeburgh church, 20 June 1965.

39. 'My subject is War, and the pity of War.' Rehearsal for the premiere of *War Requiem*, Coventry Cathedral, May 1962. Britten talks to co-conductor Meredith Davies, Pears and Dietrich Fischer-Dieskau elevated above the chamber orchestra on the right. Graham Sutherland's tapestry *Christ in Majesty* is the backdrop.

40. Part of Britten's royal circle: Prince Ludwig and Princess Margaret (*right*) of Hesse and the Rhine with the Countess of Harewood on Thorpeness Meare during the 1957 Aldeburgh Festival.

41. 'It is a curious, circumscribed, little world, this international Royal clan – there were, for instance, seven princes to the family Xmas dinner!' Schloss Wolfsgarten, home of the Prince and Princess of Hesse and the Rhine.

42. Imogen Holst,
mid-1950s.

43. Rosamund Strode, *c.* 1980s.

44. Donald Mitchell, June 1976.

45. Britten on the gritty shingles of Aldeburgh beach,
June 1964, at the time of the premiere of *Curlew River*.

dinners with the British ambassador and the like, press conferences, their very first televised recital, geisha entertainments and tea ceremonies, kabuki dramas, perplexing etiquette, temples and gardens, meetings with local musicians and concerts performed by Japanese ensembles. Japan never quite won them over ('It is far the *strangest* country we have yet been to; like, in a way, going to a country which is inhabited by a very intelligent kind of insect'), and possibly Britten's memory of the *Sinfonia da Requiem* fiasco still rankled, but while there he had an artistic epiphany. Twice they attended a performance of *Sumidagawa*, a traditional Nō play, which Britten counted as 'among the greatest theatrical experiences of my life'.

> Of course it was strange to start with, the language and the especially curious kind of chanting used; but we were fortunate in having excellent literal translations to follow from, and we soon became accustomed to the haunting sounds. The deep solemnity and *self*lessness of the acting, the perfect shaping of the drama (like a great Greek tragedy) coupled with the strength and universality of the stories are something which every Western artist can learn from.

The story itself is affecting: a madwoman searches for her lost child, who has been kidnapped by thieves, and stumbles upon his grave. But of greater influence on Britten was the heavy symbolism and stylization of the theatrical tradition: the simplicity of the story and economy of means, the slowness of pace, beautiful costumes and the mixture of chant, singing and speech. 'It all offered a totally new "operatic" experience.' Moreover, he encountered the performance style at exactly the right juncture. The sounds and complex rhythms of the gamelan orchestras would be felt sooner in Britten's music, yet the impact of Nō theatre, starting with *Curlew River* in 1964, was easily as great.

The remainder of the mammoth journey – the flights, receptions, short breaks in Ceylon and Bombay and the overnight stay on the way home in Wolfsgarten – played out fairly predictably, but the experiences in Bali and Japan stayed with him. 'We've flown (not counting boats & trains) about 25,000 miles,' he wrote to Roger Duncan on 11 March, six days before returning to Aldeburgh, 'visited 16 countries, packed & unpacked just on 100 times, given nearly 40 concerts, heard nine quite different kinds of musical traditions, seen countless different arts, talked to Turks, Indians of all sorts, Chinese, Indonesians, Malayans, Siamese,

Japanese – not counting the many kinds of Europeans. And feel much richer for it.'

2

Britten was changed by the experience, but outward circumstances remained much the same. It was the EOG's tenth season, yet the company's footing was as precarious as ever. The ballet needed completing and a conductor to be secured. Festival programmes needed finalizing and Decca recordings had to be scheduled. And plans for a new theatre in Aldeburgh remained on the table, a fundraising campaign for which was to be launched at a grand garden party in September, Britten asking Sitwell to invite her new friend Marilyn Monroe as guest of honour. There were other works to think about, not least a big cantata about St Peter, a stablemate for *Saint Nicolas*, for which Duncan had written a libretto, and performances in May of *The Turn of the Screw* at the Théâtre des Champs-Elysées to fit in. And there was the singular problem of Britten's 'devoted wife', a mentally unstable woman who had begun sending him letters c/o Boosey & Hawkes declaring love and more besides, one day trying to ambush him backstage after a performance of *The Turn of the Screw*. 'Let me in – I *am* his wife! I deserve to be there. Where's his dressing room?' Her family intervened soon after this scene and committed her to an institution, but it was a troubling episode.

To David Webster he hinted at how little he would mind if the ballet were postponed, and he steeled himself for a showdown if Covent Garden could not come up with a decent conductor for the premiere. By the beginning of August he knew the ballet had slipped back in the schedule until at least Christmas, which gave him just enough breathing space. He took Holst with him to the Hesses' summer castle in Switzerland for three weeks, where they worked for four to five hours a day solely on orchestrating. Yet it was another two months after his return from Schloss Tarasp in early September before he could finally write to Prince Ludwig, 'That b. Ballet is <u>FINISHED</u>, & I feel as if I've been just let out of prison after 18 months hard labour.' A week later he was on a recital tour in West Germany with Pears, surfing the general unrest caused by the Soviet invasion of Hungary – a savage Kremlin riposte to the country's hopeless aspirations to some measure of autonomy – and Eden's skulduggery in Suez.

West Germany was the great success story of post-war reconstruction: its annual growth in the 1950s was almost eight per cent of GDP. Yet the big cities they visited – Düsseldorf, Cologne, Munich – remained shell-shocked. Churches were built on bombsites, rubble left all around; families still lived in houses with great chunks missing from roofs or façades; skeletons of once-fine buildings awaited buyers with the imagination, sentiment and funds to restore them. Britten and Pears noted the vast concert halls and the *Bierkeller*, the bomb-gutted cities and the docile, distressed Germans, who sat gratefully while the music of their countrymen was performed by two Englishmen, while Europe wondered what brinkmanship would come next.

Notwithstanding Britten's hard labour, *The Prince of the Pagodas* is a curious work. Cranko's scenario was something between *King Lear* and *Beauty and the Beast*, as might be expected of this most puckish character, with his hypnotic wolf's eyes and love of fantasy. An ageing emperor has two daughters, one evil, the other virtuous, sadly without her father's favour. Kings from the four compass points come to court the haughty, vain, eldest daughter, after which her sister is borne up to Pagoda Land by flying frogs, where she cavorts with a giant salamander – a prince in disguise. They return to her land and ultimately claim the throne, the prince in human form. Cranko listed all this in an early scenario, which Britten kept at his side as he composed the ballet, the timings of each dance written out in Cranko's neat hand. Britten complained that the choreographer was nowhere to be found when he had queries and ended up making decisions in the dark or turning to Holst, whose knowledge of dance was greater than his. He kept a score of Tchaikovsky's *Swan Lake* close at hand and took inspiration from the ballet's fantastical plot and Grimm-like characters.

For all its metamorphoses and twists of fancy, *Swan Lake* is the work of an opera composer *and* symphonist; the plot is advanced by a taut symphonic argument that etches a gripping narrative arc. By contrast, Cranko wanted a work in which only the milestones were provided; it was otherwise all about imaginative, magical divertissements, the audience pinning it together as best it could. It was a bad match for Britten for two reasons. Because he knew nothing about dance, he abdicated all narrative responsibility to Cranko, which would never have happened had the piece been an opera. In fact, not since his film and radio days and the unfortunate *Paul Bunyan* had Britten sat in his study with a stopwatch and someone else's synopsis, creating a score to order. Cranko later asserted that Britten talked through the scenario and made suggestions that were incorporated. If so, there is little to show for it. It seems more likely that Britten's strong, instinctive ideas about narrative (not always infallible) gave way to Cranko's expertise. As a consequence Britten found himself reverting to a manner of collaboration he had long left behind.

The second area of vulnerability was that Cranko's scenario, his plan for colourful episodes at the expense of a tightly argued plot, appealed to the more facile side of Britten's brain. He took Cranko exactly at his word, composing episodes himself: a march here, a waltz there, a pas de deux in between. Arguably this is the function of a ballet composer, though Tchaikovsky demonstrated what could happen with a much larger canvas. There is much brilliant music in Britten's score – not least in the second act, where gamelan takes hold of the texture, almost throttling it with clanking percussion writing and mesmeric little cells that whirr along like spinning tops – but there is also the workaday stuff Britten could toss off when a deadline loomed.

It was almost inevitable he would end up conducting the premiere. Ansermet, who earned his stripes as conductor of Diaghilev's Ballets Russes in the 1910s and 1920s, graciously declined. Webster was slow in working down Britten's list of alternatives – first Rafael Kubelik, second Rudolf Schwarz – and eventually appealed to Britten that the ballet needed him, which by then it did. 'I never wished to conduct,' he told Plomer afterwards, 'was already seedy when the rehearsals started, & the performances were really agonising. After three of them, my doctor put his foot down, & here I am, for a month, doing absolutely nothing, on a dreary diet, & thoroughly low.' (Robert Irving and Kenneth Alwyn took over the run.)

The production boasted a gorgeous design by Piper, especially for the second act, which featured exquisite pagodas looking like giant triffids or frill-necked lizards, and a striking luminescent crescent moon. And there was spectacle and acrobatics at every turn. The public warmed to it, thought Britten, and Covent Garden found itself in the enviable position of having to schedule extra performances. But the ballet critics disliked the choreography and conception, while music critics disliked the score, which seemed to be neither one thing nor the other. Cranko's divertissements seemed pigheadedly old-fashioned in one so young (he was not yet thirty), especially in comparison to what had happened in dance since the 1920s. (Mayer, who saw a later performance in New York, told Britten, 'I thought Cranko's ideas could have been better knitted.') They all missed the point of how successfully the gamelan sounds evoked an exotic, scented other world, scratching their heads at this so-called clumsy pastiche. Even as perceptive a critic as Donald Mitchell tore into Britten's second-act incorporation of an 'Indonesian (?) percussion band': 'once the ensemble's tinkling has been savoured, its motivic stagnation becomes painfully tedious.' It seemed British ears were not ready for such borrowings of a music so little known. As ever, amid the carping and befuddlement, there were razor-sharp observations, not least from Felix Aprahamian in the *Sunday Times*. 'Once again, Britten is seen responding best to definite dramatic or descriptive concepts; in their absence the music suffers.'

3

In Aldeburgh nursing his bad arm, Britten wrote Elizabeth Mayer a touching letter of consolation on the death of her husband, William, in December. It was more thoughtful and reflective than his usual hurried correspondence – to Mayer and to other friends – and uncharacteristic in its poetic language. He recalled his time in America and pointed out that though three out of his forty-three years did not constitute a large proportion, this time and these friends had shaped him. 'In every way they were formative years; we were children before, men after. You both gave us strength, & courage to see ourselves & to face what we saw. You were both rocks who knew & loved the past, & yet were not daunted by the future.'

Free of the ballet, he was able to clean out yet more stables. He wrote to the EOG's chairman, James Lawrie, about the recent tenth-anniversary London season, which almost scuttled them. The concept of the EOG only worked in particular circumstances, he told Lawrie: festivals, with their specialized audiences, and in countries where opera is a part of the daily diet. Look at the success of *Lucretia* or *Herring* or *The Beggar's Opera* in Germany and Holland. 'However, in England the general public is operatically much more conservative, and our financial backing has not been adequate for us to do enough performances to win it round.'

He was being polite, for it is not so much that Britain was operatically conservative, more that it was still for the most part operatically illiterate. Yet the EOG was an uneven teacher, programming new or obscure small-scale works and favouring simple design and direction; how did this relate in the public's mind to the grand works of yore? There were hits: *Let's Make an Opera* helped train young audiences in the delights of opera, while *The Turn of the Screw* was a critical success and was popular with audiences in its initial seasons. And there were commissions and rehabilitations: Berkeley's *A Dinner Engagement* (1954) an example of the former, Gustav Holst's *Sāvitri* (1908) and Thomas Arne's *Love in a Village* (1762), arranged by Arthur Oldham, of the latter. Yet even Norman Del Mar thought they went on performing *Let's Make an Opera* too long, while in late 1956 *The Turn of the Screw* averaged audiences of only thirty-nine per cent for its six performances at London's Scala Theatre. The disarray in which many European companies found themselves post-war fuelled the EOG's success on the Continent; what would happen to the group's touring schedule when, like the Vienna Staatsoper, these companies managed to put their houses in order?

Maureen Garnham, the EOG's secretary, thought Britten had simply lost interest in his company. Yet it was more that Britten, pulled in every which way, found himself exhausted by the EOG. 'We are, I fear, still very dependent on you,' Basil Douglas wrote to him in December 1955, 'and I'm so sorry that we do not seem to be able to do without you ...' This dependence, which originally stimulated Britten, now ground him down. The Aldeburgh Festival, while similarly cash-strapped, cost far less to run and managed to absorb blows with greater equanimity. It was also separate from London, unlike the EOG, which was an even greater attraction. Britten proposed that the EOG should narrow its focus, close down its London office, and be run as a subsidiary of the festival. The group, he argued, should be more a creator than an impresario. There would be regular showings in Aldeburgh, such as the planned gala performance of *Albert Herring* to mark the tenth festival in 1957, much of the original cast assembled for the occasion (including Cross, who came out of retirement to sing Lady Billows, and Pears, a newly created Commander of the British Empire). There could be tours and visits to other festivals, such as the planned performances of *The Turn of the Screw* in Stratford, Ontario and Berlin later in the year, but they must be funded from someone else's purse. Stephen Reiss, in charge of the festival since 1955, calculated the restructuring would save more than £3,000 a year in administration costs alone.

There is one sorry observation to make of Britten's letter to Lawrie: it was such a long time coming. From the EOG's first year it was somehow inevitable. Christie was far nearer the mark than Britten and Crozier and their back-of-the-envelope calculations: there were not the funds to run and tour an opera company, regardless of how small and innovative. The EOG was perennially on the brink of insolvency, its creative team devising ever more ingenious ways of surviving. All the new-dawn hopes in 1947 of overcoming the country's artistic impoverishment were genuine, as was Britten's negative assessment of the existing or nascent British opera companies. Yet the landscape had changed markedly in ten years, without Britten working out where to position himself in it. He himself admitted this in 1966. 'What one wasn't prepared for was the emergence of Covent Garden so soon: I was probably wrong not to realise that that would probably have given one a stage to work for, but it didn't seem at all likely or even possible at that time.'

It is impossible not to wonder about the mainstream opportunities he missed through his loyal, quixotic stewardship of the EOG and foot-stamping dismissal of other companies – lucrative commissions from abroad, like Stravinsky's for *The Rake's Progress*, or an understanding with Covent Garden that it would be the principal home of his operas, much like Verdi's relationship with La Scala or Richard Strauss's with Dresden. It is not that Britten could have feasibly been more productive in the years between his return to England and this late recognition of the EOG's unviability; six full-length operas, a children's stage work and one realization is a remarkable achievement. (He could not have composed so many operas had they all been the size of *Grimes*.) Moreover, his small-scale opera *The Turn of the Screw* remains one of his most popular and performed works. Yet it is still possible to feel a sense of loss for what he did not compose in these decades. Britten thought that those who asked him in the early post-war years when he was going to write another *Grimes* were looking for a carbon copy of his first major stage work. But some simply regretted the works he was not composing while his focus was on his small company.

Garnham and Douglas thought Britten's change of heart treacherous, especially since he had written so kindly and positively to Douglas a year earlier when the young director was in a funk over his future and that of the company. Ironically, Douglas's letter to Britten on his world tour, bleakly analysing the current and potential finances of the EOG and making for depressing reading, lit the fuse. Moreover, Britten thought Douglas a fine-weather sailor, ill-equipped to steer the poor EOG through the choppy waters in which it too often found itself. Angry telephone calls ensued, bitter letters exchanged. Douglas was hurt that Britten seemed incapable of ever breaking bad news to colleagues, thereby exacerbating the pain, while the composer argued back every point in his stubborn, pedantic manner. Regardless, it was a good decision – a cutting of losses, as Britten put it – and provided proof of the new path on which he now travelled.

4

The Aldeburgh Festival benefited most from the change in his composition and performance priorities, from his desire to write more and administrate less. In its first ten years the festival presented what was to hand: Britten, Pears and their friends, much as the tenor had originally envisaged. But with Britten's time so taken up with opera, Aldeburgh was host to relatively few Britten premieres. Only four of the seventeen pieces he composed in the 1950s and allocated an opus number were given their first outing in Aldeburgh; in the 1960s fully two-thirds of his numbered compositions, and a handful of others besides, received a festival premiere. 'I like at the moment to write pieces which suit the buildings and the occasions down in Suffolk,' he said in 1966, though the shift can be dated to the late 1950s, to the change in his thinking and to Reiss's certain stewardship of the organization. Reiss modestly put his visionary success down to the fact his predecessor, Elizabeth Sweeting, rode everywhere on a bicycle and thus never explored the far-reaching churches into which he took the festival. But this is to downplay the amazing chemistry in the organization late in the decade. Even those Britten works commissioned by outside bodies were composed with one eye on the festival's programme. Though Britten

disparaged comparisons with Bayreuth, in the 1960s Aldeburgh increasingly became associated with his music and major premieres.

Britten's attachment to the county had never wavered. The fast pace
and squalor of New York had pushed him towards defining himself in
terms of place – England, in the first instance, but increasingly Suffolk. He
began to resemble Constable in his determination not just to live in the
county but to depict it in his work. East Anglia was the setting for whole
operas – from *Grimes* to *Herring* to *Let's Make an Opera* – and the
source for some of his folk-song arrangements. Its flat landscape dominates the opening of his *Spring Symphony* and its birds twitter away in
numerous works. As the 1950s progressed and he did everything he could
to avoid a metropolitan life, Suffolk began to mean even more to him.
There was a danger that such a retreat would leave him shielded from the
chance encounters and conversations that give writers their ideas, but
Britten had never been particularly interested in such sources. As he aged
he looked around him for inspiration, writing works that now colour the
way we view the county, much as Constable had done before him.

The shift in Britten's priorities was evident in a letter he sent Ronald
Duncan in February 1957, telling his old friend he had decided to put
St Peter to one side. 'I get terribly worked up about a thing, then cool
off, & then, if the idea was originally a good one, come back with
renewed vigour to it.' He cited *Grimes*, *Spring Symphony* and *The Turn
of the Screw* as examples, yet for the remainder of his life Britten would
compose almost no piece without a specific performer or performance
in mind. Nebulous projects such as St Peter no longer had a place. There
would be the occasional idea for an opera, which he would churn
around for some time before rejecting, and there were numerous orchestral works contemplated, not least a concerto for string quartet and
orchestra, which he had discussed with Del Mar as far back as 1948 and
still thought he might write. Yet such ideas came to nothing. He was
more tired than before, more prone to depression, and was anyhow
determined to avoid the logjams of the previous fifteen years.

In this spirit he pocketed fifty guineas from the government of the
newly independent Malaysia for a national anthem, to contain a 'slight
oriental strain'. Britten did not think much of what he came up with – a
modest song, which jumps between several related keys with surprising
agility and which jingles with *Turandot*-like orientalisms – and was not
unduly surprised when it was rejected as unsuitable for the sober-minded

Malaysians. He nonetheless asked Boosey to recover the manuscript since 'it might come in handy for some other Eastern nation' and was glad enough of the further fifty guineas the Malaysians sent him as a sop.

He was on surer ground with the remarkable quartet of works that occupied him for the twelve months from autumn 1957, two of which were premiered at Aldeburgh. The first was another present to Pears, though the Hesses picked up the official dedication. *Songs from the Chinese* is a collection of six songs for tenor and guitar, settings of Chinese poems in translations by sinologist Arthur Waley. Guitar was a recent enthusiasm for Britten, notwithstanding the strumming balladeer in *Paul Bunyan*. The subtle, thoughtful guitarist and lutenist Julian Bream, twenty years Britten's junior, sparked his interest. He played at the 1952 Aldeburgh Festival and never really left, forging a close recital partnership with Pears that helped paper over Britten's illnesses and composition schedule. Pears and Bream both loved Elizabethan lute songs, Pears in particular since they allowed him to float his voice and colour the often striking words with élan. Britten liked it that Pears had a different recital partner – on a different instrument and with a distinct repertory – which took the pressure off him to be available always for Pears's concerts and whims. (After Bream arrived, he stopped playing Dowland songs with Pears.) He arranged six English folk songs for them between 1956 and 1958, including 'I will give my love an apple' and the forlorn 'Bonny at Morn', which they added to their repertory.

There is something courtly, almost formal to these folk-song arrangements, but they also point to a composer comfortable with the instrument and its associations. It is no surprise, then, that *Songs from the Chinese* is a set of finely sculpted miniatures. The poems themselves are full of well-sketched images rather than great profundities, though there is a haunting sense of nostalgia to three of the middle songs, which can easily be lost in the dust and rambunctiousness of the outer settings. 'The Herd-Boy', with its depiction of a young lad standing shoeless on his ox's back, driving it home, is a snapshot from Bali, while 'Depression' is a chilly evocation of old age.

> Turned to jade are the boy's rosy cheeks;
> To his sick temples the frost of winter clings.
> Do not wonder that my body sinks to decay;
> Though my limbs are old, my heart is older yet.

The second of Britten's significant works from these twelve months is *Noye's Fludde*, based on another miracle play. He started plotting the piece in mid-August 1957, before composing the Chinese songs, working in a third-class cabin on board Canadian Pacific's *Empress of Britain*. (Britten and Pears had forgone first-class luxury in solidarity with other EOG members travelling to Stratford, Ontario, for performances of *The Turn of the Screw*.) But the cramped quarters and crowded public spaces depressed him and his mood did not improve for the three weeks they were there. Ghosts from the 1939 visit haunted them at every step. They swam in lakes (Britten finding the still, saltless water effete) and went to countless official receptions and informal dinners, filling themselves with local fare: stuffed chickens, sweet corn, relishes, meatloaf, peach pie, squash and wine jelly. They gave press conferences (asked the difference between *The Rape of Lucretia* and *The Turn of the Screw* by a keen reporter he mischievously replied, 'The notes are the same, but they are in a different order'), and despaired at various aspects of Coleman's staging of the opera. They were glum over a performance of *Sinfonia da Requiem* ('As Erwin Stein would say, it was bad of course, but it could have been worse,' Pears wrote), and were heartbroken to hear of Dennis Brain's death in a car accident. 'One is left aghast when one thinks of the loss sustained by English music in these two deaths [Brain's and Mewton-Wood's] and that of Kathleen Ferrier, all young artists at the beginning of dazzling careers, in the space of only four years,' Britten wrote a few months later. Finally, they were worn down by the almost excessive politeness of Canadians, escaping whenever they could to drink whisky in toothmugs as though in a Fitzgerald short story. 'Neither of us can wait to get back to England, away from this very kind, hospitable, beautiful, rich, boring country,' Pears told the Hesses.

Britten managed to think through the new work while there, and was able to begin his composition draft at the end of October. *Noye's Fludde* behaves like an opera: it contains a handful of principals and an abundant chorus of bilingual (English and Greek) animals and birds; it has a large orchestra (150 in the original production), and tells a dramatic story, if not necessarily one blessed with the element of surprise. Yet it is a hybrid work, as much cantata as opera. Britten conceived it along the lines of the original Chester miracle plays, which were performed by ordinary people, not actors: local craftsmen and their families, supplemented by choristers from the town's church playing children's roles, would take their show on the road, visiting different parts of town, the sets and props transported on a single cart. So in *Noye's Fludde* the audience participates, much as it does in *Saint Nicolas*, singing three well-known hymns at crucial junctures, while hymn fragments and snippets of plainsong turn up elsewhere. There are children galore, drilled in the elementary roles over the preceding months. Nor is the orchestra conventional: a professional ensemble of only ten players is supplemented by amateurs playing recorders, bugles, handbells, strings (some on open strings, others pushed no further than third position), and a battery of percussion instruments, including mugs slung from a string. (There is a famous photograph in which Britten demonstrates his new instrument to attentive, sceptical schoolboys who do not give the impression they are witnessing tin being transformed into gold.) It is a mad circus when it gets going, but it embodies Britten's thoughts on the vital role of serious music in the community and in children's education.

The characters are roughly sketched. God is a cranky, bellowing old tyrant; Noye is henpecked at home and from heaven; Mrs Noye is a burlesque figure, bumping and grinding along with her fellow drink-soaked gossips. With its disparate elements, it is not particularly cohesive musically, but it has some special moments. The hymn 'Eternal Father, strong to save' is given startling treatment – a whirling, breathy accompaniment, a creeping bass and a high, teetering descant. And the final hymn, sung to Tallis's Canon, provides the piece with its powerful climax, the professional singers rising above the congregation and the bugles and the chinking percussion. Britten finished the composition draft on 18 December 1957, fleshing it out into the unusual full score over the following few months.

5

There was one interruption. As his fame and fortune increased, Britten came to find Aldeburgh too public, the house on Crabbe Street too exposed. With Mary Potter's collusion he came up with a solution: they would swap houses. Potter was now divorced from her husband, and her children were adults: her house, tucked away behind the golf course, half a mile inland from town, was too big and too expensive for one person to maintain. Potter and Britten had their properties valued, talked to bank managers, and soon agreed on a price for his privacy and her security.

A former farmhouse, with outbuildings and generous grounds, the Red House dates from the early seventeenth century. It is substantial but not excessively so. Both floors are divided by narrow, dark corridors, which connect the many rooms and never quite dispel the impression of a warren. It is, 'alas, away from the sea, but thankfully away from the gaping faces, & irritating publicity of that sea-front', as Britten told Edith Sitwell. There was a tennis court, a croquet lawn and a studio in which he could 'bang away to my heart's content'. There was space for the art collection, and potential for all sorts of redecorating, refurbishing and, ultimately, rebuilding. Best of all, it captured Pears's imagination in a way Crag House never quite managed. London would still exercise its hold on him, and in the Red House they maintained separate bedrooms. Even so, the new place gave a much better impression than Crag House of being home to both.

The move at the end of 1957 was further evidence of Britten's shift in thinking, of his attempt to wrench back some privacy, to concentrate on more intimate genres and types of performance. Despite every effort to live his life out of the metropolitan spotlight, he had maintained a very public career for twenty years. Some months before moving he listed the recent honours this career had brought him: recognition from the Catholic Stage Guild of Dublin (1950) – 'A perfectly hideous statuette of a deformed St Cecilia'; Honorary Freeman of the Borough of Lowestoft (1951); an award from the Music Critics Circle in New York for *Spring Symphony* (1952); Membership, Swedish Academy of Music (1953); Honorary D.Mus., Queen's University, Belfast (1954); Honorary Membership, Accademia Nazionale Cherubini di Musica, Florence (1955); Honorary Membership, Académie Royale des Sciences, des Lettres et des Beaux-Arts, Brussels (1955); Honorary Membership, American Academy and of the National Institute of Arts and Letters, New York (1957); Honorary Membership, Accademia Nazionale di Santa Cecilia, Rome (1958). He overlooked the Companion of Honour.

Britten's *Nocturne*, for tenor, seven obbligato instruments and string orchestra, the third of the four glorious, more intimate compositions composed in late 1957 to 1958, was the first work to be composed entirely in the Red House. *Nocturne* straddles Britten's old and new worlds, revelling in the sparse textures that shaped his most recent works, but retaining a black glossiness that looks back to pieces from the early 1940s. It is one of his greatest works – subtler and more integrated than *Serenade*, and far more ambitious. 'It won't be madly popular because it is the strangest & remotest thing – but then dreams are strange & remote,' he told Marion Harewood, wrongly as it turned out.

He achieved cohesion in three ways. First, he selected poems that complement each other, evoking a world of dreams, of Puck's night and silence. Having scoured among other things Carol Stewart's *Poems of Sleep and Dream* and Cecil Day Lewis's recent edition of *Palgrave's Golden Treasury*, he scribbled a possible sequence of texts in an old Gresham's notebook.* He included poems by Shelley, Tennyson, Words-worth, Owen, Keats and Shakespeare. Sitwell's 'The Youth with the Red-gold Hair' was crossed out and replaced by Middleton's 'Mid-night's bell goes ting, ting, ting' – not the last time he would be attracted to the onomatopoeia of night. The poems were a nod to his schooldays, but they were also the compilation of a real poetry lover, someone who had read anthologies since boyhood. It was also the work of someone capable of locating a poem's essence in a single couplet or stanza and unsentimental about culling the rest.

Second, Britten wrote 'link' between each poem on his scratchy list and duly composed a rocking string ritornello that returns throughout the piece, separating the poems yet simultaneously binding them together.

Third, he allocated a different obbligato instrument to each poem as glue, matching the subject matter with the instrument's associations. There is a barking bassoon for Tennyson's kraken, the monster deep below the sea ('Then once by men and angels to be seen, / In roaring he shall rise and on the surface die'). There are timpani in Wordworth's terrifying depiction of the French Revolution's September Massacres, which thump away underneath the description of the brutal mob upris-ing, prisoners murdered in their cells and priests killed in the streets. A cor anglais accompanies the ghosts in Owen's bleak poem 'The Kind Ghosts', which has all the languorous weight of Lucretia's death scene. It was an idea lifted straight from Mahler's *Des Knaben Wunderhorn*,

---

* The notebook, which contains thumbnail sketches of numerous works, was not the only throwback to his public-school days just then: he used a schoolboy pocket diary for appoint-ments, replete with information about the American birdman Clem Sohn and other such phenomena.

in which the condemned drummer-boy ('Der Tamboursg'sell') sings his sad farewells to his comrades accompanied by this doleful instrument.

Britten also played against type. The horn obbligato has none of the post or hunting associations that fired the Romantic imagination. Instead, it is one moment a clock chiming midnight, the next mired in a howling impersonation of dogs, or the caw of a raven, or the low, guttural mewls of a cat. Almost certainly he was thinking of Dennis Brain's effortless virtuosity while composing it.

Britten was thrilled by the poetic images. There is a beauteous boy of Coleridge's invention who for Britten was another of Mahler's *Knaben* – all jaunty, whistling insouciance, bathed in moonlight, watched by a curious or aroused onlooker. The Wordsworth presents yet another Mahler connection, a mirror image of the ghostly drummer in 'Revelge', say, or the marching sentinel in 'Der Schildwache Nachtlied', the sleepless narrator replaying his awful memories, his past fears compounded by present uncertainty, until finally he acknowledges that there will be no sleep that night.

The best he saved till last. The setting of Shakespeare's 'Fair Youth' Sonnet 43 – possibly written for the handsome Henry Wriothesley, 3rd Earl of Southampton – is another of Britten's slow reveals, as though the whole cycle was composed with this one poem in mind.

> When most I wink, then do mine eyes best see,
> For all the day they view things unrespected;
> But when I sleep, in dreams they look on thee,
> And darkly bright are bright in dark directed.

It builds as incrementally as does the final song of *Winter Words*, all the obbligato instruments now part of the texture, the cumulative impact overwhelming. And then, suddenly, it winds down, the tenor almost whispering, 'All days are nights to see till I see thee, / And nights bright days when dreams do show thee me.'

He wrote it quickly once he got down to the task, composing direct into full score, though to Peg Hesse he described it as 'a tremendous effort to write – each note being squeezed out like that last dollop of toothpaste out of an empty tube. This tube rather wants a holiday.' He also told her it was a 'very odd' piece, a curious assessment he would later modify: the whole thing is a compelling mixture of classic understatement and theatrical flair.

Nocturne – its last song in particular – was a stunning dress rehearsal for the language setting in *A Midsummer Night's Dream*, a work soon to fill his imagination. In its exploration of the power and possibility of night, and the compelling marriage between danger and beauty, it prefigures not just *A Midsummer Night's Dream* but a host of 'night works' in the early 1960s: the superb 'Um Mitternacht'; the Elegia movement of the Sonata for cello; *Night Piece (Notturno)*, the lean, moon-flecked compulsory work for competitors in the 1963 inaugural Leeds International Pianoforte Competition; and his piece for Julian Bream, *Nocturnal after John Dowland* (1963), a series of reflections on Dowland's drowsy 'Come, Heavy Sleep', which dashes and dives along the fingerboard, evoking a strange and alluring netherworld somewhere between Elizabethan England and the moon-drunk poet in Schoenberg's *Pierrot lunaire*. 'But night and dreams – I have had a strange fascination by that world since a very early age,' Britten told Donald Mitchell in 1969. '[Night] can release many things which one thinks had better not be released; and one can have dreams which one cannot remember even, I find, in the morning, which do colour your next day very darkly.' It was Milton's world in *Comus*: 'What hath night to do with sleep?'

Fittingly, Britten dedicated the cycle to Alma Mahler-Werfel, the great composer's widow. He met her first in New York at the beginning of 1942 and though they were not often to see each other, they corresponded warmly if occasionally and held each other in high regard. It was perhaps an unexpected friendship, this sensitive, puritanical man and the spirited *fin de siècle* beauty, with her sparkling humour, strong opinions on music and art, and impressive array of eminent ex-lovers. Britten's veneration of her first husband and Alma's cultural heritage ensured any potential points of conflict were avoided. (On one occasion she asked Britten to complete her former husband's unfinished Symphony No. 10, as she did Shostakovich, which flattered him hugely but which he declined.) And Alma did admire his music, possibly hearing it for the first time at the Mayers in February 1942 – perhaps a domestic performance of *Michelangelo Sonnets*. Seventeen years later, in response to Britten's request to dedicate *Nocturne* to her, she telegraphed the composer: 'MY HAPPINESS IS ENORMOUS I CANNOT FEEL OR THINK OF ANYTHING ELSE MY DEEPEST THANKS.'

6

With no time to think between works, Britten set six poems by the German lyric poet Friedrich Hölderlin, the last of his quartet of stunning pieces, as a present for Prince Ludwig on his fiftieth birthday in November. They occupied sparser territory than ever before, but they contain certain musical and philosophical ideas that he would refine in the coming decades. The sinuous melody of 'Hälfte des Lebens' (The Middle of Life) is underpinned by a gentle, rippling accompaniment, which is much the sound he would give Aschenbach at a key moment in *Death in Venice*. The almost medieval hymn tune of 'Die Linien des Lebens' (Lines of Life) is accompanied by long chromatic threads played by both hands in canon, independent, overlapping and culminating in a coda reminiscent of the powerful conclusions to *Winter Words* and *Nocturne*. And the beautiful youth Alcibiades asking Socrates why he looked at one so young with love in his eyes is accompanied by a single line of melody on the piano, as though the boy is accompanying his own question on a lyre. Socrates's answer also prefigures a scene in *Death in Venice*: 'Who most deeply enquires, loves what is liveliest, / And true Virtue perceives, who has observed the world, / And at moments the sages / Must be yielding to Beauty itself.' It is sung to chords of shimmering simplicity, as though the words uttered form an inviolable truth.

Britten was inspired by poor, mad Hölderlin and guided by Schubert and his bare accompaniments. 'How few notes there are in Britten's compositions, yet how much thought and feeling!' Rostropovich would say of the works from the following decade, and the description applies here. *Sechs Hölderlin-Fragmente* eschews the more obvious pictorial accompaniments of previous Britten cycles. Instead, Britten almost replicates the *sound* of the German words, marrying accompaniment with language. The little gem 'Um Mitternacht', the composition draft of *Children's Crusade* and an unpublished part-song aside, these were his only settings of German, a homage to his cultured friend Prince Ludwig and to the lied genre itself.

The first performance of *Nocturne*, which replaced a Mass he had thought he might write for the Leeds Festival, was in mid-October 1958. Pears sang the glorious poems, of course, but Britten was not on the platform with him. The Austrian-born, British-naturalized Rudolf Schwarz conducted instead, directing the BBC Symphony Orchestra, which a year earlier had Malcolm Sargent as its chief conductor, and before him Boult. In such circumstances it is no surprise Britten never managed to establish a relationship with the orchestra, a situation exacerbated by the personal and musical antipathy he felt towards its concert master Paul Beard. ('I have had many years of experience of him, and my last was the worst – only respect and affection for Rudi Schwarz prevented me walking out of the whole affair.') He was unsympathetic to the orchestra's track record and performances.

Britten greatly admired its new chief, Schwarz, however. Quite apart from including him on the list of potential conductors of *The Prince of the Pagodas*, a year before the *Nocturne* premiere he congratulated him on his performance of *Variations on a Theme of Frank Bridge*. 'It had great understanding, and great warmth. I realize that once or twice perhaps the orchestra did not do exactly what you wanted; but it was all such wonderful music making, and that is what I enjoy the most . . . I am sure it is a great thing for English music that you have undertaken this very important position.'

It is easy to see why Britten was enamoured of Schwarz's conducting. In recordings from the 1950s he demonstrates exquisite care and grace, phrasing Schumann's Piano Concerto with such delicacy that his soloist, Myra Hess, sounds clumpy in comparison. His sense of structure is unerring, one section logically melting into the next. Schwarz was self-effacing with it all too, taking great care over new works; this placed him at odds with London critics and audiences who would have preferred a little more showiness, a little more 'Flash Harry' Sargent. His performances were far from the messy, insouciant outings of his predecessor, who was deftly criticized in an internal BBC memo in the early 1950s: 'Neither wind nor strings were able to phrase because of his heavy-handed 4-square beat.'

It is also easy to create a profile of Britten's ideal musician based on the conductors and soloists with whom he collaborated in this decade and the next. Virtuosity in and of itself was of no interest to him. He required a distinctive sound, good technique and an authentic curiosity about each composer. He naturally liked musicians who were at home in his own music, but almost more importantly, at home in that of his heroes: Mozart, Schubert, Mahler. What he prized most was musicality. Individual phrases needed to breathe ('Pears has always possessed the all-important gift of being able to *phrase* music,' he would say, 'of singing a series of notes in such a way that they make *sense*, musical sense').

There had to be space around a chord, and harmony had to be allowed to speak with its own rhetoric. He appreciated an almost feminine sensibility in performance, in which even the smallest detail was attended to, the architecture of any piece underlined cumulatively, not through grand and empty gestures. This is what Britten and Pears achieved in their lieder performances, which Graham Johnson thought fresh and daring, and so outside the prevailing traditions – in Britain and on the Continent.

At one time or another, therefore, Britten found himself admiring Mewton-Wood, not Myra Hess; Clifford Curzon, not Harriet Cohen; Dinu Lipatti, not Maud Randle; Schnabel, not Vladimir Horowitz; Schwarz, not Bruno Walter; Menuhin, not Adolf Busch; Mackerras, not Del Mar; Meredith Davies, not Colin Davis; George Malcolm, not Douglas Guest; de Sabata, not Tullio Serafin; Kubelik, not Hans Knappertsbusch; Ansermet, not Eugen Jochum. (He was not swayed by the Toscanini–Furtwängler binary; he liked them both.) His preference had nothing to do with an artist being gay or straight, male or female; it came down to a performer's musical instincts and sensibility. 'The notes I handle no better than many pianists,' said Schnabel in 1958. 'But the pauses between the notes – ah, that is where the art resides.' He could have been describing Britten.

Schwarz's relative failure with the British public and critics was a harbinger of the stylistic changes in performance in the 1960s that would once more leave Britten isolated from the mainstream. Georg Solti made his Covent Garden debut in 1959 with *Der Rosenkavalier*, a year after he embarked on the first ever complete studio recording of Wagner's *Ring* cycle, and was two years later appointed music director, a position he retained for ten years. Solti represented a new, aggressive style of conducting in Britain: hardbitten, tempi pushed to the limits, the conductor's persona a throwback to the autocratic types who stalked the concert halls in the first decades of the century and Continental imagination thereafter. It was the antithesis of everything Britten stood for. But it was also antithetical to Beecham and Boult, with their quick wit or earnest gentlemanliness. It was a new bellicose style of performance, but also of behaving. Solti was nicknamed the 'screaming skull' by the musicians, which was soon known beyond Covent Garden. Opera audiences took a while to take him to their hearts: he was frequently booed in curtain calls and attacked by critics. But during the 1960s he came to be accepted and admired by audiences and musicians (Britten included, on occasion, surprisingly), who equated his autocratic ways with authority and professionalism. Most insiders no doubt approved of his publicly stated aim to transform Covent Garden into the greatest of opera houses, but many had their toes stepped on along the way.

A similar transformation was under way at the London Symphony Orchestra, which had struggled to find its feet in England after the war, often assembling a motley crew of players. The orchestra survived on fees from Decca and film studios and by playing for choral societies and festivals. Josef Krips began to turn it round in the early 1950s, but resigned in 1954 following a dispute with management. By the end of the decade his place had been taken by Pierre Monteux, a grand old man in his mid-eighties with an impressive walrus moustache, quiet authority and links back to the young Stravinsky and middle-aged Diaghilev. Under Ernest Fleischmann's pugnacious, no-nonsense management, the LSO was on its way to becoming a professional, driven ensemble.

If it is a coincidence that the new, masculine style of performance emerged just as the witch-hunts and the increasingly public grumblings about gay cabals running the arts were taking place, it is a remarkable one. This is surely what William Glock was hinting at in his 1955 review of Walton's *Troilus and Cressida*: 'whatever we may decide about the imaginative quality of the music, he has set us an example of spacious-ness and competence and of sheer masculine vigour that is very welcome in English opera just now.' Glock remained a (measured) fan of Britten, but he was frustrated with the musical climate in England, which showed no awareness of trends on the Continent – of Luciano Berio and Pierre Boulez, of Karlheinz Stockhausen and Luigi Nono, and of music emerging from the Darmstadt hothouse, where every year an inter-national summer school played host to young avant-garde composers. Ironically, Britten was more aware of the contemporary European scene than most Englishmen, though his knowledge and experience showed their hand in ways often too diffuse for Glock. Glock's appointment as the BBC's controller of music in 1959 was a turning point, and his interest in muscular Continental trends in performance and compos-ition was to have huge bearing on British taste and music-making.

So Schwarz's reign was almost a last hurrah for the type of conduct-ing Britten appreciated and represented, though he did not know it at the time. A leaner, hungrier crowd would follow – Antal Doráti at the BBC SO, Sergiu Celibidache as guest with the LSO, and the young Daniel Barenboim with the English Chamber Orchestra, in a much gentler incarnation of his later self. The decade's music-making was monumental, hawkish, superhuman, Strauss's *Ein Heldenleben* (A Hero's Life) as a road map and Karajan a role model. They had stereophonic sound on their side, too, which invited such grandeur. One such proponent was young Colin Davis, chief conductor of Sadler's Wells Opera from 1959, who played a big role in the LSO's rejuvenation in the 1960s. He would succeed Solti at Covent Garden and was, meantime, happy enough to emulate some of his habits. Davis, in turn, passed the baton to a string of British conductors who have pursued a breathless approach to Britten's scores, far from the composer's own nuanced music-making in which each bar flowed effortlessly into the next and each performance added up to much more than the sum of its parts. The exceptions – like Simon Rattle, who has long demonstrated great empathy with Britten's music and style of music-making – have been few and far between.

Most of the young conductors Britten employed to work with the EOG fell by the wayside for musical reasons, or they were a bit pedantic (Del Mar), or unreliable (Pritchard). Occasionally they fell short of Pears's exacting if fallible requirements and met the same fate. Charles Mackerras was made of sterner stuff – a fine musician with a scholar's mind. Like Walton and his crowd he found homosexuality amusing, and in rehearsals for *Noye's Fludde* made a wisecrack about its being conveniently full of young boys. John Cranko heard of the remark and passed it on to Britten, who flew into a rage. Mackerras was summoned to the Red House, where he encountered an icily calm composer. 'Because I like to be with boys, and because I appreciate young people, am I therefore a lecher?' Mackerras was upset by the encounter and lashed out at Cranko for his part in it, only to be told, 'When suddenly you hear something like that, however long you may have worked together, suddenly you hate that person.' That was it for Mackerras and Aldeburgh, at least for a while. He had only himself to blame, and recognized his foolishness, especially concerning a musician he adored. It is no coincidence that by the late 1950s, given the cultural shifts in British music and society, Mackerras felt comfortable with such lazy homophobia all the while he was the guest and colleague of a gay man; in pre-Wolfenden times such an attitude was common, even prevalent. He was hardly the only offender in Britten's circle. Bream, bizarrely asked what dangers existed for a single young man in Aldeburgh, responded that it was best to 'keep your back to the sea at all times, though not forgetting to watch out for the early morning bavers' – Britten among them, was the implication. It was an old disease, and not even close friends of Britten and Pears were immune.

7

BENJAMIN BRITTEN and PETER PEARS
RECORD EXCLUSIVELY FOR DECCA

A full-page advertisement in the 1958 festival programme book had listed the various Britten works now available on disc: *Les Illumina-tions* and *Serenade*, performed by the New Symphony Orchestra, Decca's ad hoc house band in the 1950s, conducted by Eugene Goos-sens; *A Boy was Born*, *Saint Nicolas* and *Rejoice in the Lamb*, conducted by Britten; *The Turn of the Screw* with the English Opera Group. Also listed were a number of 'Aldeburgh Festival Records', including per-formances of Haydn symphonies and Britten at the piano for Mozart's Concerto in A, K. 414. Britten had been making commercial recordings of his works for almost twenty years, though it took the unveiling of LP discs in the late 1940s for the relationship between Britten and Decca to blossom. There was no money in it; the explosion of interest in record-ings belonged to the 1960s, a world of stereo sound and the Beatles. Sales in the 1950s were relatively modest; overarching austerity left British music lovers with little spare money to build record collections. The greatest sales of new Britten releases were in America, of all places.

Britten was caught unaware by the invention of stereo recordings. When in 1956 HMV proposed a stereo recording of the Piano Concerto, Britten had to request information about the new technology. This is a curious omission, since Decca had started experimenting with stereo two years earlier. (The first commercial releases were not until 1957, however. *The Turn of the Screw*, the first complete recording of a Britten opera and released by Decca in 1955, was in mono.) Decca quickly established itself as market leader, and Britten, who made his first studio tape when electric recording was only ten years old, entered into an exclusive agreement with the company. Britten releases came thick and fast, the time between a work's premiere and it first recording contracting rapidly. It is almost as though he had been waiting for the new technology.

There was a backlog of works to deal with, so at the end of 1958

Britten and his team entered Walthamstow Town Hall – a glorious 1930s pile looking every inch a politburo headquarters – to record *Peter Grimes*. A complete recording had long been mooted – by EMI, the British Council, the BBC, Covent Garden and Decca, the latter urging patience and careful planning, which ultimately prevailed. John Culshaw, Decca's brilliant young producer, drew up complicated treasure maps dotted with microphone placement, singer entrances and stereo sound effects. The recording was a child of the stereo age, one of the first, with 'all the life and realism of a stage performance', as Decca boasted in advertisements the following year. Britten assembled a great cast, reluctantly conducting the orchestra and chorus of Covent Garden himself, throwing out his back on the final day of taping. It was a huge undertaking, yet he revelled in the planning and scheduling and the way it all seemed to fit together. Thereafter he spent days with Culshaw or his Decca colleagues before entering the studio, mapping the best possible stereo imaging for each scene, an architect at his drawing board.

The recording did well enough: 2,706 complete sets were sold in 1959, while a separate disc of the *Sea Interludes* sold a little over half this number. The discs reminded critics of what they had so admired in the young composer almost fifteen years earlier. No doubt the recording underlined what they identified as a lack of quality in his subsequent operas, but they kept such views to themselves. In the new age of stereo, which would turn schoolboys into collectors and *Gramophone* into the industry bible, critics lavished praise on the *Grimes* discs. The writer Peter Shaffer even incorporated the recording into his 1966 screenplay *The Pad (and How to Use It)*, in which the awkward Bob attempts to seduce Doreen: 'I know what I'll play you! (*Grabbing an album*) PETER GRIMES! Decca's done the most marvellous recording of it.'

Britten was in and out of Decca studios in the following years, recording a whole bag of his own works and those of others: *Nocturne* in September 1959; Schubert's *Die schöne Müllerin* in October; *Noye's Fludde* in November 1960 and July 1961; *Sechs Hölderlin-Fragmente* in November 1961. He had suddenly discovered the means by which to circumvent critics, to control every aspect of performance and, as much as possible, public reception. 'As you know,' he would write to Ernst Roth, his publisher at Boosey & Hawkes, four years after recording *Grimes*, 'I value very highly the authentic recordings of my works, and wish to keep my contact with the Decca Company (who is most sympathetic to the idea) very close indeed ... It does not seem to be understood in the firm that these major recordings are to be encouraged in every way rather than to be regarded as a nuisance.' Britten's involvement in these 'authentic' recordings helped them acquire canonical status – much as Stravinsky's participation in his recordings did for his (though the Britten releases are far superior). More, it was a solution to the grinding relentlessness of touring and to the penury that had clipped the EOG's wings: there were other ways for audiences to hear his music. And it reinforced the distinction between this phase of his life and work – the Red House phase, with its privacy and intimate compositions – and that which came before.

Recording would also contribute to his rapidly increasing wealth. Mechanical royalties in 1958 amounted to a little over £1,200; in 1961 they were more than £1,800, which rose to £2,700 in 1962 and £1,000 more the following year. Where his income in the 1954–5 tax year was a little under £13,000 (considerably short of playwright Terence Rattigan's taxable income of £32,000 the following year) and in 1960–61 was a little over £20,300, in 1964–5, buoyed by the release in 1963 of the *War Requiem* recording (which sold an astonishing 300,000 sets in its first year), it was a gargantuan £48,000.* Britten's wealth was the product of a whole portfolio of activities, but recording increasingly played its part. It served as town crier, pronouncing Britten's new achievements to a willing public, generating interest in his performances and published scores. The discs helped establish Britten as an international star, acting as a public catalyst, transforming his fate and fortune. Those who had never heard Britten and Pears perform *Die schöne Müllerin* in the tiny Jubilee Hall, or at Friends House in Euston, could now experience their great artistry at one remove.

8

In July 1958 Erwin Stein died unexpectedly from two quick strokes. Britten was devastated by the loss of such a great mentor and friend. 'I feel absolutely dazed, as if an anchor in these stormy days were taken

---

* Britten's income in these years equates, respectively, to £280,000, £370,000 and £765,000 today.

away from me,' he told Sophie in a tender, touching letter of condolence. Stein was such an important figure in Britten's life. He was not the Svengali that Etienne Amyot had identified in 1946: instead he represented a tangible connection with the music and culture Britten so admired and, to varying degrees at different times in his life, emulated. Harewood put it well in a later tribute to his father-in-law, quoting a young musician who told him Stein's death 'deprived this country of the sort of musical influence we most lacked and we could least do without – someone with the whole of European culture behind him who yet lived and thought in the present and was able and prepared to impart this wisdom without preaching'. It was an illuminating comment in the context of British music stretching its wings in the 1960s, attempting to fly out from the shadow of Continental cultural imperialism and define an indigenous version. Britten's tribute to his great friend and colleague was apt: at a memorial concert at Friends House on 30 January 1959 he conducted the first London performance of *Nocturne*, a ghostly thread running through Stein back to Mahler himself. 'It is heart-felt, communicative and supremely elegant: the music of a lyrical poet who is not dismayed, or even embittered, by the world he sees around him,' wrote Desmond Shawe-Taylor in response, not quite capturing Britten's prevailing outlook.

A few weeks before the memorial service, George Malcolm conducted a performance of *A Ceremony of Carols* at Westminster Cathedral, with Osian Ellis on harp. Britten attended, young priests bringing salvers of cocktails into the cathedral afterwards for the adult musicians, perhaps taking their cue too literally from Graham Greene's *The Power and the Glory*. Britten was blown away by the performance and by the Continental sound the boys made, so distinct from the hooting Anglican tradition prevalent from Victorian times onwards, full of 'aw-merns' or 'oo-moons'. The 'whole choir sang with a brilliance & authority which was staggering – owing to you, my dear, I know, & I do sincerely send my congratulations', Britten told Malcolm afterwards and resolved to write them a work. He scribbled an idea for a Sanctus in the back of his pocket diary (on a page intended for sports fixtures and results), an ecstatic, leaping, full-throated cry: 'Sanctus!' It made its way largely unaltered into the composition draft of the Missa Brevis (or 'Mass in short trousers', as he later wrote on his copy of the published score, borrowing Donald Mitchell's phrase), which he completed in late May 1959. The whole piece, with its crunchy, dissonant organ writing and cleverly constructed vocal lines – much of it derived from a simple plainchant intonation – was premiered on 22 July 1959 at a celebration of the Mass.

There were numerous other requests in these years for liturgical music – companion pieces for his youthful *Te Deum* in C, and another from the patient and persistent Walter Hussey – a few of which he accepted and were completed in the early 1960s. One was his scrappy Psalm 150, composed for the centenary celebrations of what was formerly South Lodge School, which Britten scored for two-part children's voices and whatever instruments lay to hand. Yet from 1963 onwards, following hints of a dramatic departure the year before in *War Requiem*, his thoughts on religion took him down a different path.

The big works occupying him as one decade clicked over to the next were a commission from the University of Basle for its quincentenary, *Cantata academica, carmen basiliense*, and his ongoing plan to spin some sort of dramatic work from his experiences in Japan. The Basle commission bogged him down as he grappled with the difficulties of setting medieval secular Latin – an unappetizing chunk of the university's charter, adapted and dressed up a little by philologist Bernhard Wyss. ('O citizens of Basle, may you always be praised for having fostered so noble an academy.') Britten referred to it as his 'Swiss homework', though this undersells what he came up with. The gentle serialism he played with in *The Turn of the Screw* – a twelve-note theme providing melodic material for the fifteen scenes and variations that follow – is given another outing, here poking fun at academe, a rich target. Significantly, *Cantata academica* was another rehearsal for *War Requiem* (though there is no sting in its tale), and it does the public stuff well: courtly fanfares; a fugue that builds and builds until hijacked by wind sonorities lifted straight from Stravinsky's *Symphony of Psalms*, Britten a teenager once more; the scrumptious writing for the four vocal soloists. For such a dry text, everything is well characterized. Strauss could have written the pompous bass arioso for his own Baron Ochs, while a later intimate soprano arioso, with snatches from a *canto popolare*, is ravishing. It is a pity the work is not much performed today.

Britten had contemplated an adaptation of *Sumidagawa* ever since his encounter with it in Japan. Plomer had prepared a draft libretto, which Britten admired, yet he kept furnishing reasons for the project's postponement: another piece needed attention; or he and Pears were just heading off on tour; or the festival was upon them once more. The behaviour used to drive Forster mad. It was not until April 1959 that Britten told Plomer he simply could not find a way to reconcile the oriental story with its likely setting, a medieval Suffolk church. Nor could he see a way to write music for the original story that did not sound like clumsy pastiche. This had caused the block. But what if the whole thing could be Anglicized and Christianized? What if Nō theatrical customs could find their equivalent in English monastic dramas of the tenth and eleventh centuries? And what if the strange, austere sounds of the Japanese masked players and the small, unlikely band of instrumentalists could find their equal in Western music? Plomer expressed relief and set to work. He dumped the Japanese names and Buddhist themes, rephrasing them in Christian language and imagery. The 'millions of Buddhas' became numberless 'Saints and martyrs'. He scribbled directions to himself on the draft – 'expand with fenny details' and 'de-jap a bit' – and came up with a title, 'Curlew River', named after the long-billed fen bird. It was an impressive start, though there were to be a few more interruptions, one almost immediately.

9

Two months before Britten's medieval epiphany, Pears left Britain for a month-long tour of Canada with Julian Bream. His career was thriving independently of Britten, and though he enjoyed the success and acclamation, he was left guilty and ostensibly frustrated by his long and frequent absences. It was sometimes as though he was not quite sure he wanted the prize he had claimed. 'Why shouldn't I recognise that you are such a large part of my life that without you my life is dry and stupid and dull,' he wrote from Canada.

Homesickness inspired such protestations. But so too did the feeling that they had made a lucky escape in 1942 – from America, but also from the old crowd. Pears caught up with Auden at Lincoln Kirstein's house in New York a few days after arriving, and though cross with himself for his sulkiness, apportioned all blame to his fellow guests. 'Wystan looking like Oscar Wilde painted by Picasso or somebody was just the same as always, dogmatic laying down the law about opera translations & librettos, Chester puffy & gossipy & Lincoln nervous & sensitive & dotty, with a nice wife.' Britten was sympathetic in response:

'what *is* one to do about him? Nothing, I suppose – just keep away.' They just could not abide Auden's grandstanding, certainly not on the subject of opera, and they fumed and boiled away whenever one of his lofty pronouncements about their art form was brought to their attention.

It is probably no more than a coincidence that not long after Pears's encounter with Auden, Britten again put 'Curlew River' aside and set to work on an operatic adaptation of Shakespeare's *A Midsummer Night's Dream*, intended for the 1960 Aldeburgh Festival. Coincidence or not, here was a text Auden could neither equal nor criticize. But language was only half the battle. He still had to structure the opera, stepping gingerly through the minefield of characterization and meaning in Shakespeare, all the while cutting the play to shreds. Where would Britten's dramatic instincts lead him this time?

Working from a Penguin edition (later pretending they used only the First Folio, which they somehow thought gave their venture a seal of authenticity), Britten and Pears set about truncating Shakespeare's great play. Their main problem was the expository scene with which it opens, four days before the marriage of Theseus and Hippolyta, in which the various mortal relationships are established. It was too long and static for opera, and they culled it, saving important passages for later. But Britten still had to relay the vital information contained in the scene. Like Bottom, who begs of Peter Quince to 'write me a prologue', Britten asked Myfanwy Piper for a short summation of the act. She came up with an intelligible textual contraction, in which two Heralds discuss the impending royal wedding and Hermia's cranky defiance of her father's choice of Demetrius as her husband when her heart is with Lysander. 'Lord Theseus gives her till his Nuptial day to make her choice: death, or the cloister, or Demetrius.' Yet Britten thought Piper's effort creaky and decided against placing someone else's words next to Shakespeare's. So with Pears he came up with the one line of invented dialogue in the whole opera: to Hermia Lysander decries the sharp Athenian law 'Compelling thee to marry with Demetrius', which more or less covers Shakespeare's Act 1.

Britten was anyway not much taken with the play's mortal couples, with their dreary problems and incessant whining; it was the woodland world that captured his imagination, inspired not least by 150-year-old oaks in the nearby Suffolk woods, planted not for timber but for the pheasants they would harbour. In the back of his Penguin copy, Pears sketched a synopsis beginning with Shakespeare's Act 2, Scene 1 – the Fairies and Puck – and this plan prevailed: 'The wood – dark night', Britten would write at the head of his composition draft. Emboldened, they contracted Shakespeare's timeframe into a single night and day and set about reordering the play.

Britten's Penguin copy is a treat to examine. Long used to keeping any number of plates spinning in the air, Britten now turned his organized mind to the plight of his characters. Did any single line require knowledge of another, one now excised or placed later in the sequence? Was a character's reaction at any point predicated on a previous slight, now removed? It was an extraordinarily complicated operation ('a fascinating problem, only heart-breaking to have to leave out so much wonderful stuff', he told Plomer), yet the paperback is marked up and scribbled in with great certainty. Whole lines are dispatched with apparent ease, arrows joining previously separated stanzas, the words of one character now given to another. The musicologist Mervyn Cooke, more than thirty years after the premiere, noticed Britten and Pears, amid all their excisions and reordering, made only one mistake: they neglected to marry off the two mortal couples before Theseus sends them to bed at the close, carnal delights awaiting. It was a slip-up, though the opera is none the worse for it.

It is the worse for the two-dimensional characterization of the young lovers. Stripped of the bulk of their back-stories and left with little more than combative dialogue before they slip into docile concord in the third act, they are difficult parts to pull off. Yet Britten's sympathetic treatment of the Mechanicals ('I can say the rustics, perhaps, resemble some of my very good friends in this part of the world'), the waspish characterization of Oberon as a counter-tenor, and the terrific handling of Puck and the Fairies even the balance. Having pounced on the word 'mounseer' in the Shakespeare (an Anglicized version of 'monsieur'), Britten cast the Fairies as boys. He was determined, however, not to turn them into the cute, toothless creatures of Victorian imagination, which lingered well into the twentieth century. He looked instead for something 'very different from the innocent nothings that often appear in productions of Shakespeare. I have always been struck by a kind of sharpness in Shakespeare's fairies . . . Like the actual world, incidentally, the spirit world contains bad as well as good.'

Britten's approach to Puck was equally innovative: he conceived him as a tumbler, an adolescent circus acrobat who romps through the opera dispensing clumsy mischief, invisible to the mortals around him as he speaks Shakespeare's words. This characterization would have earned Auden's ungrudging approval: in the 1940s he lectured American students on the play. 'You use Puck for a day when you get up and it's raining, you cut yourself shaving, you hurry over breakfast, you miss your train, your boss is sarcastic, your favorite lunch seat is taken, a bar drunk bores you with his life story, the potatoes are undercooked at dinner, and you quarrel with your wife.' Puck is our mythological explanation for events or circumstances that conspire against us – a grenade lobbed or a spell cast by unseen forces.

Many people at the time identified Britten's setting of Thisbe's mad scene in the Mechanicals' play as a parody of that in Donizetti's *Lucia di Lammermoor*. There are certain musical connections, namely the dialogue between voice and flute, yet Britten was also mocking the public response to *Lucia* in its February 1959 outing at Covent Garden, which overnight made a star of Joan Sutherland. Britten attended probably the third performance, but found it a desperate evening, as he related to Pears.

> Lucia has been the *wildest* success, & dear Joan S. has become a prima donna (very good for George [Harewood], of course) – but it was the most horrid experience. It is the most awful work; common & vulgar, very boring, no subtleties, poor tunes (the old Sextet is the best – Donald Duck & Clara Cluck), just as if Mozart, Gluck & all (written in 1835) hadn't existed. Apart from Joan (who sang it well, it suits her perfectly, but to my taste with no real musicality or warmth – she'd been taught the Italian style like a dog is taught tricks) & Geraint [Evans], the singing was poor, the orchestral playing feeble (Serafin isn't interested in the pit), & it looked like an Italian copy of a Landseer, even to the gauzes imitating old dirty varnish. Hideous!

The audience screamed and roared, and regardless of whom Britten turned to in each interval, seeking allies in the bars and boxes of Covent Garden, he found his sour view rebuffed. It was such an important event, a milestone for the opera house and a personal success for Sutherland, Webster and Harewood (now working there), and Britten found himself at odds with popular and critical opinion.

So he had his petulant revenge, mocking their response with a hammy mad scene of his own – a ruthless, unfair parody. 'Thy mantle good; what stain'd with blood!' sings Pyramus on discovering his lover's cloak, his panic rising, and it does not take much imagination to picture Britten conjuring up Sutherland's bloody gown and face (the sheer amount of blood having earned the disapproval of old-school Serafin). And when Thisbe, who has survived the lion's attentions, her mantle bloodied, discovers the body of Pyramus, she wails her distress. Here Pears, in Jubilee Hall and a bad wig, replicated Sutherland's long, dark hair, her wide-eyed expression, and the dramatic movements and direction Franco Zeffirelli had carefully given her (earning the disdain of the more histrionic Callas).

The Jubilee Hall was expanded for the 1960 festival (hence Britten's decision to write a new work to stage in it), as was the programme. Stephen Reiss saw it as his job to achieve Britten's wishful thinking, and a much bolder vision for the festival emerged in the 1960s. Before then the programming and scale of performance were limited by circumstances. 'I think the shape of the Festival – that is, the works you want to perform in the Festival – is very much dictated by the town itself, the buildings, the size of those buildings, and the quality of those buildings,' Britten told Harewood in 1960.

It is odd that Britten was not more ambitious for the festival in the 1950s. He had backed a scheme in 1954 for a new theatre (of desperately plain design), but he was strangely sanguine when the project was shelved due to local antagonism and lack of funds. He was no Wagner, who bullied and fought and harangued until Bayreuth was built. 'Ben was the more down to earth,' wrote Reiss much later, 'and Peter the more creative, not as one might imagine.' Even when wealthy, it was hard for Britten to step out from his impecunious mentality; instead, he wrote within the limits dictated by the buildings at hand, and did so without any sense of greater ambition or regret. 'Ultimately, it is to me the local things that matter most.'

It was not that he was unable to forecast the long-term success of his works. 'If it is any good,' he said of *Dream* a week before the premiere, 'it will get many different interpretations in many different places and all with translations.' Covent Garden would lead off, picking it up for a new production in 1961 directed by John Gielgud, designed by Piper and conducted by Solti.* This quick turnaround of a new Britten opera

---

* Gielgud did not really appreciate the opera, asking his stage manager John Copley, 'Oh John, why did Benjamin write such hideous music to these beautiful words?' Solti, however, remembered the great Shakespearean Gielgud sitting in a tiny room coaching the boy

by a British company other than the EOG represented a shift in attitude towards him. It was fortunate, since the opera had been squeezed into the marginally expanded Jubilee Hall, to its detriment, and John Cranko made rather a hash of it. At Covent Garden it had more space, and a larger string body with which to flesh out the sound (it works better with a bigger string section than Jubilee Hall allowed).

Within its first year *Dream* was seen in Berlin, Edinburgh, Göteborg, Hamburg, Milan, Pforzheim, Schwetzingen, Tokyo, Vancouver and Zurich. It was an international hit – Britten's biggest since *Peter Grimes*. Pears picked up the librettist's royalty, Britten the grand rights that flowed from main-stage performances (and which he often denied himself in EOG productions, funnelling them to the EOG through deals done with his reluctant publisher), and the opera helped contribute to the age of prosperity he was soon to experience.

'It *was* a joy to set those heavenly words,' Britten wrote to Marjorie Fass in July, and they certainly inspired great sounds. From the opening pages, in which the wood creaks and groans and slowly comes to life (and which in his manuscript looks just as it sounds, a beautiful, feathery sketch surrounded by air and space), to the transformation from the woods into Theseus's palace, Britten did not put a foot wrong. He was able to separate life from music, much of which was composed while he was suffering once more from severe depression. 'I was so saddened by your poor old voice this morning,' Pears told him in December 1959, 'and everything gloomy and dismal that I have been thinking of you all the time and wondering what I can do.' None of this shows. Nor is there much fat in it: the orchestra comprises as few as twenty-seven players, and Britten luxuriated in its chamber sonorities as much as its potential as a full ensemble. The royals, the lovers, the rustics and the fairies have very different styles of music, from Tytania's and Oberon's haughty fight in the opening scene – full of huge leaps and jealous disdain – to the plodding grandeur of Bottom, a yokel Falstaff, to the martial music of the Fairies, to Hippolyta's sarcastic asides and Theseus's warm, wise utterances at the end of the piece. Britten was thrilled by the personality of the characters as much as by their language. He dismissed the suggestion by a reporter that there was something almost

---

playing Puck in his line, 'Lord, what fools these mortals be!' junking that great, resonant voice for something more boy-like.

hubristic about setting Shakespeare's words. 'Shakespeare can look after himself and however well or badly or much I cut the work, the text – thank goodness – remains.' Critics thought it a strong marriage, this brilliant contemporary composer setting a great English play, and were generous to a man. 'That Britten would make a success of the venture was almost a foregone conclusion; and so he has.' Or, 'The local event has a national significance and an international future.' This too was a shift.

<h1 style="text-align:center">10</h1>

The contest between Lysander and Demetrius for Hermia's affections had its offstage parallel. Harewood had fallen in love with a violinist, Patricia Tuckwell, and his marriage imploded. Britten responded sympathetically to Harewood in autumn 1959 when the news first broke, but his view hardened over time. Following a lunch with George and Marion in March 1960, Britten described the couple: 'the latter radiant, in excellent form, she is a splendid girl, the former ghastly, filthy behaviour, & looking awful.' Marion begged Britten to be nicer to Harewood, but he was furious with his friend, writing him a highly charged letter decrying his betrayal. Although the friendship limped on for five more years, Britten's loyalty to Marion ultimately prevailed.

The break caused both men great sadness: Harewood was a cultured, smart colleague as well as friend, at both Covent Garden and the Aldeburgh Festival, as different as possible from the gentlemanly amateurs who historically had run much of Britain's music industry. It was a friendship they would both miss hugely, an eventual rapprochement coming too late. Britten's was a curiously unforgiving response, especially given how wretched Harewood felt about it all and how often Marion tried to calm Britten down. But he would not budge. To Roger Duncan he wrote, 'I wish people just occasionally would think of the result of their actions. I am also rather worried about you, old boy, worried lest you think that this kind of sexual laxity is the way most of the world behaves, or *should* behave.' It was the morality of his upbringing, his own homosexuality aside.

Back in the dark days of depression – in late 1959, as he worked on *Dream* – Britten's physician ordered rest and recuperation, and immediately following the 1960 festival Britten did his best to comply. But there were four performances of *Dream* in the Holland Festival in mid-July – the EOG's fifteenth consecutive annual visit – where a dizzying round of press conferences, interviews and dinners consumed him. In Holland they solved a few of Cranko's more erratic staging decisions, though it would take the new Covent Garden production to iron out the superficial characterizations, knockabout farce and incoherent arguments of the original production. Britten dealt with Cranko openly and honestly, sympathizing with him over Covent Garden's decision not to use him for its production. 'I must confess that when they (D. Webster, Solti & the others) put their criticisms of the Aldeburgh production the other day I was in the difficult position of agreeing with many of the things they said, & so unable to defend you.' Both men professed continuing affection, though neither their friendship nor working relationship survived. Counter-tenor Alfred Deller, who like Ferrier before him had come to the opera with no stage experience, was also dropped by Covent Garden after critical reviews in the original run. Britten remained loyal to Deller, however, using him in the 1966 recording.

In key ways Harewood was replaced in Britten's life by the excitable Mstislav Rostropovich, four years Harewood's junior, whose performance of Shostakovich's Cello Concerto No. 1 in London in September 1960 brought them together. Thirty-three years old, a graduate of the Moscow Conservatory where his teachers included Semyon Kozolupov and Shostakovich, egg-bald, with a curiosity about everything and a love of contemporary music, Rostropovich was a formidable musician and ebullient personality, with a very Soviet career: the permits and concerts and tours carefully vetted by the glamorous if sinister Madame Yekaterina Furtseva, Soviet minister of culture. Cello playing of this stature simply did not exist in England. They became close quite quickly.

As they had once done so happily with the Harewoods, Britten and Pears would take holidays with Rostropovich and his wife. 'From the beginning I felt at ease with him,' Galina Vishnevskaya later said of Britten. 'I'm sure that everyone who was lucky enough to know that charming man must have felt the same sense of simplicity and naturalness in his company.' Although the memoirs of this tough prima donna are full of such hammy observations, her recollection is not without merit. Rostropovich spoke virtually no English and Britten no Russian, so they conversed in what they called 'Aldeburgh Deutsch', which for primitiveness had few lexical equals, ensuring their relationship, at least to begin with, was primarily musical.

When Britten met with Rostropovich the day after the Shostakovich concert he agreed to write him a sonata if he would come and play it at the following year's Aldeburgh Festival. Rostropovich warned of Soviet restrictions, but Britten drafted a letter and secured the requisite permissions. On holiday in Greece with Pears and the Hesses soon afterwards, where he attempted to put the whole matter of the EOG's governance behind him (the group was now to be administered by Covent Garden), he mapped out the new piece.

His doctor's warning to rest hung heavy in the air, but there remained a recital tour of Germany and Switzerland and recordings of *Spring Symphony* (Decca) and the revised version of *Billy Budd* (BBC) to navigate. In December, finally, he set to work on the sonata. The Shostakovich performance showed Britten he was writing for a musician with no weaknesses, no areas that he needed to bolster or disguise, as was the case with Pears – not that either of them would say so out loud. It was an emancipating experience. He turned the instrument into a guitar one moment, an organ the next, a gypsy violin at another. There is a restlessness to the first movement, a sustained breathlessness to the second. The piano writing is more opulent than in any work since the mid-1940s, while the genre itself is a reminder of Britten's teenage years when he accompanied his chums in Romantic string sonatas. The whole piece is episodic yet cohesive. It was mostly finished by mid-January 1961.

The work exhilarated him, and for much of the decade and beginning of the next it was Rostropovich, not Pears, who acted as Britten's muse. There would be no further song cycle for Pears – Britten's traditional gesture of intimacy and commitment – until the dour *Who are these Children?* in 1969. Meantime there was a string of works for Rostropovich: a sonata, a concerto (of sorts), a set of cadenzas for a Haydn concerto and two extraordinary solo cello suites – a homage to Bach as much as to Rostropovich – with a third in 1971. There was also a song cycle for Vishnevskaya, and one for German baritone Dietrich Fischer-Dieskau. Pears was not entirely neglected. Britten composed for him principal roles in the three Church Parables of 1964, 1966 and 1968, among other things. But for most of the decade Britten looked elsewhere for musical inspiration.

Rostropovich arrived for a rehearsal at the flat in St John's Wood, which Britten and Pears had taken in 1958, not long after moving to the Red House. Both he and Britten were nervous and took refuge in drink. (Rostropovich later averred that he needed four or five large whiskies to get ready.) But thereafter they played and played, stopping only for a quick meal nearby, before returning to the apartment and the piece. 'He had understood the work perfectly,' Britten wrote to Vishnevskaya afterwards, 'and of course played it like no one else in the world could.'

Three months later they gathered at the Red House for a more sober rehearsal, captivating the members of the English Chamber Orchestra looking on, Erich Auerbach snapping away with his camera. At one point the ebullient Russian, thrilled by the experience, jumped up to hug the reserved Briton. The first public performance was in the Jubilee Hall on 7 July 1961 and they soon after recorded it for Decca. The recording sparkles, each man playing off the other with a sense of danger and occasion, rubato at every turn. The same qualities are evident in their recording of Schubert's Arpeggione Sonata, which they included in their Aldeburgh recital. Rostropovich had never before played this extraordinary work and presumed it was easier than it is, arriving at Aldeburgh without properly knowing it. He tripped up at various points in rehearsal, which Britten did his best to accommodate. 'I was able to play all the notes that were there without panicking,' he later said, though the performance still teeters more than once.*

The recital exemplified what the festival was now becoming: a showcase for major premieres and performers. The *Times* critic William Mann, who had succeeded Britten's sometime adversary Frank Howes, wrote of the concert: 'Often he seems to be playing for the delight of musician friends; this time he was met with a cellist who plays with him as though he had to satisfy the rigorous judgement of the composers themselves.' This was music-making of the highest quality – an intense, brilliant dialogue between equals. Nor was it confined to the Rostropovich recital. Pears and Britten performed Schubert's *Winterreise* at the same festival, Pears having waited until he turned fifty to take it on. Mann admired Britten's 'astonishingly full and vivid understanding of what Schubert's musical vocabulary says in *Winterreise*', by no means

* Almost fifty years later, Olga Rostropovich played the recording to her father as he lay unconscious in bed, close to death, and noticed him shed a tear.

an isolated critical response. Their 1963 recording hints at what the festival audience encountered: a more burnished sound from Pears, with his careful, sometimes exaggerated German, and Britten's peerless playing, with the structure of each lied unfolding with absolute certainty. Reiss helped change the festival culture in the 1960s so that such events became frequent and treasured.

I I

Wilfred Owen's reputation was slight when Britten set 'The Kind Ghosts' as part of his *Nocturne*. A woman sleeps untroubled while the bodies of the men she loved, or some quite like them, line the trenches, their ghosts leaving her to sleep peacefully. 'They move not from her tapestries, their pall, / Nor pace her terraces, their hecatombs, / Lest aught she be disturbed, or grieved at all.' It fitted the song cycle thematically – an unsettling coda to Wordsworth's slaughter. Cheered on by Siegfried Sassoon, Owen's poems were passed around a certain crowd of sophisticates in the 1930s, 1940s and 1950s, like Rimbaud's slightly earlier in the century. But it was only in the 1960s, a decade in which authority was pushed against and when anti-war Britons once more had a high-profile conflict on which to peg their protest, that Owen's poetry achieved lasting popularity.

Owen's poems are steeped in mud, blood and homoeroticism, the words given a grim context of gargling blood and froth-corrupted lungs. Owen adored and idealized the lads he served alongside or above, describing their eyes or smiles, their fingers or hair, their white teeth. The Roman poet Horace lent him the title and ending couplet of perhaps his most famous gas poem – 'Dulce et decorum est pro patria mori' (It is sweet and proper to die for one's country) – but it was Owen who labelled it 'the old lie'. The poet's readership extended beyond gay men and pacifists (Edith Sitwell was an early champion), yet there was a gay sensibility and fierce political undercurrent to his writing that made him a good fit for Britten.

Britten now felt freer to set such texts. He was an Establishment figure, not a young 'conchie' expected to suffer in silence the slings and arrows of wartime Britain. Society had shifted as well, amid CND protests, busy American airbases, the burgeoning 1960s counter-culture, and the broad conviction that there really were 'madmen in authority', in Keynes's deft phrase. At the 1960 Labour Party conference, opposition leader Hugh Gaitskell promised to 'fight and fight and fight again to save the party we love' from the 'pacifists, unilateralists and fellow travellers' who clung to the idea of nuclear disarmament while the Cold War simmered away, but his speech only put more fire in the bellies of those he decried. To many in the party, Gaitskell was on the wrong side of the argument, more so than the Conservative Harold Macmillan, who beat away at the great ideological drums of his party in support of Britain as a world power. It was too soon for the popular consensus to register that Britain was anything but that, though in 1959 Macmillan confessed as much to his diary. 'UK had better give up the struggle and accept, as gracefully as possible, the position of a second-rate power.' A year later a young Dennis Potter put his finger on the national pulse. 'The atmosphere is one of polite decay and immense self-deception. But it *is* our country, the nation in transition, caught between a magnificent past and a sentimental lethargy.'

It is not that Britten had been scared to broach the subject of war before now. As early as 1949 he declared 'the first act of sanity for any nation is to break with war. The first patriotic, sane, morally decent step for the youth – any youth of any nation – is to withhold himself from military service.' There had been the occasional outburst in his music: *Grimes*; the songs he wrote in high fever after Belsen, *The Holy Sonnets of John Donne*; the empty morality in Captain Vere's decision. And there was his idea with Duncan for an artistic apology to the people of Hiroshima in the late 1940s, sadly unfulfilled. But he had not yet addressed these themes unambiguously in his music. On paper he was one of Edward Shils's Establishment figures: cosy with royalty and government, unwilling to bite the hand that awarded him honours and commissions. It is almost as though Britten, like Gaitskell, was so used to being on the wrong side of any political argument that it took him a while to catch up.

But he did catch up as the 1950s progressed, surprised to see his views now shared by such diverse people. Even John Osborne's Jimmy Porter in *Look Back in Anger* was on his side. 'If the big bang does come, and we all get killed off, it won't be in aid of the old-fashioned, grand design. It'll just be for the Brave New-nothing-very-much-thank-you. About as pointless and inglorious as stepping in front of a bus.' So in the late 1950s Britten could appear happily alongside J. B. Priestley, Cecil Day Lewis, Sybil Thorndike, Peggy Ashcroft and a host of other luminaries in a CND gala at Royal Festival Hall. A year later he could donate money for CND's 1960 Aldermaston March, a protest against the Atomic Weapons Research Establishment on the village's outskirts. In 1961 he could lend his name to the Pete Seeger Committee – along with singer Paul Robeson, writer Doris Lessing and playwright Sean O'Casey – in support of the folk singer's appeal against his conviction for contempt of Congress, snared by the House Committee on Un-American Activities. ('DANGEROUS MINSTREL NABBED HERE' the *New York Post* reported sarcastically.)

Thus the commission that came his way in October 1958 could not have been better timed. Britten was asked to write a piece to celebrate Basil Spence's new cathedral in Coventry, to be built alongside the ruins of the old – which had been destroyed in a devastating air raid on 14 November 1940 – and consecrated in 1962. 'The new work they seek could be full length or a substantial 30/40 minutes one: its libretto could be sacred or secular,' he was told. 'The committee will be very pleased if this great occasion could help bring forth an important new work from you ... they will be v. pleased if you would conduct it.' He had been thinking about a big public work for almost two years, telling Mayer in January 1957, 'I am just starting a Mass myself, a rather sad 20th century, European, affair.' And then at the beginning of 1958 he saw the revival of *Peter Grimes* at Covent Garden, the occasion on which he described the piece as evoking 'the worry of 20th century life'. And now this proposed work for Coventry. What if sacred and secular worlds were combined in one piece? And what if through this work he broke with the privileged men and women Shils dismissed with such contempt? He accepted the commission, Wilfred Owen very much on his mind.

In the late 1960s Britten told Sidney Nolan that *War Requiem* was reparation – 'an attempt to modify or to adjust the wrongs of the world or the pains of the world with some dream, with some aesthetic kind of object'. To other friends at the time Britten appeared to have something similar on his mind, something close to Camus's weighty line from *The Plague*: 'It is not rebellion itself which is noble but the demands it makes upon us.' Britten was not interested in just protesting at how bad things had been and could easily be again; he wanted to make things good, to make people change their outlook. To his sister Barbara after the premiere he said, 'aren't those poems wonderful, & how one thinks of that bloody 1914–18 war especially – I hope it'll make people think a bit.'

This was his purpose. But having chosen a liturgical text, he need not have then attacked it. There was enough to occupy him in the Wilfred Owen poems, leaving the religious ritual free to be enacted at face value, not scuttled. Yet Britten thought both Church and State had blood on their hands when it came to war. There were exceptions, of course – the Quakers and Canon Dick Sheppard, and the resistant theologian Dietrich Bonhoeffer and the radical Bishop of Woolwich, both of whom he admired.* But the Church to his mind was a worthy target. In his copy of Owen's poems Britten marked a highly charged section of a letter from Owen to his family. 'Already I have comprehended a light which never will filter into the dogma of any national church: namely, that one of Christ's essential commands was: Passivity at any price! Suffer dishonour and disgrace; but never resort to arms. Be bullied, be outraged, be killed; but do not kill.' This is the core reason Britten chose Owen's poems, or at the very least Owen's war, not the war he himself had lived through. The imagery of government and grandees marching a generation of young men off to their deaths in putrid trenches (the 'tunnel life lived in a troll kingdom', in historian Arthur Marwick's evocative phrase), fully backed by the established church, remained potent. Owen's credo was identical to Britten's, yet the iconography of his war was more savage, more emphatic of the brutal treatment dished out to young men, both those who fought and those who chose not to.

Britten used some lines from the preface to Owen's *Collected Poems* as an epigraph:

> My subject is War, and the pity of War.
> The Poetry is in the pity . . .
> All a poet can do today is warn.

The poetry may well be in the pity, but the warning in *War Requiem* is in Britten's careful juxtaposition of Owen's poems with liturgical text – 'a kind of commentary on the Mass', as he wrote revealingly to

---

* The Bishop controversially argued earlier that year against a supernatural being, stating that 'assertions about God are in the last analysis assertions about Love', while Bonhoeffer was an adventurer-theologian, highly critical of the German Protestant churches' supine relationship with the Nazis who eventually murdered him.

Fischer-Dieskau. Thus the bells that chime through the Introit – 'Requiem aeternam dona eis, Domine' (Grant them eternal rest, O Lord) – are placed next to a brittle Owen poem, 'What passing-bells for these who die as cattle?' In the Dies Irae (Day of wrath), the Latin for 'The trumpet, scattering a wondrous sound through the sepulchres of the regions' is set to resounding brass fanfares, frightening in their sheer power. This is juxtaposed with Owen's weary lines, 'Bugles sang, saddening the evening air / And bugles answered, sorrowful to hear.' The Lacrimosa, in which the penitent is prepared for God's judgement, sits beside Owen's poem about a dead soldier who will surely awake if only he can be moved into the rays of the kindly, healing sun. The Agnus Dei, in which the Somme becomes Calvary and the soldier Christ, and against the choir's still, soft prayer for mercy the tenor enacts the sacrifice Owen wrote about to his family, underlined in Britten's copy: 'But they who love the greater love / Lay down their life; they do not hate.' And mention of Abraham in the Offertorium leads to Owen's trenchant refashioning of the biblical story, 'The parable of the old man and the young':

> Behold,
> A ram, caught in a thicket by its horns,
> Offer the Ram of Pride instead of him.
> But the old man would not so, but slew his son, –
> And half the seed of Europe, one by one.

There are many more such parallels, which Britten scratched into his old schooldays German notebook. And what comes from the two texts, together and in isolation, is a mixture of savagery and blankness, of squalid, muddy slaughter alongside Old Testament judgement and damnation. In his bitter parody of the story of Abraham and Isaac, Owen signalled an Epicurean conceit. 'Is he willing to prevent evil but not able? Then is he impotent. Is he able but not willing? Then is he malevolent. Is he both able and willing? Whence then is evil?' Britten, quoting from his own earlier, venerating setting of the same story in his *Canticle II*, is in complete agreement.

The cogency of *War Requiem*'s language and architecture is the equal of anything Britten conjured out of Owen's poems and the requiem text, equal also to the idea he had of using German, English and Russian soloists to symbolize concord between previously warring nations. (In denying Vishnevskaya permission to be involved, Madame Furtseva asked the soprano, 'But how can you, a Soviet woman, stand next to a German and an Englishman and perform a political work?') Britten had the best of every world to hand: tenor and bass soloists (Pears and Fischer-Dieskau in the premiere) accompanied by a chamber orchestra (the Melos Ensemble, conducted by Britten) in the Owen texts; a large orchestra (the City of Birmingham Symphony Orchestra, conducted by Meredith Davies), a mixed choir and soprano soloist (Heather Harper) for the Mass sections; a boys' choir tucked away with the organ, providing antiphonal commentary in Latin. And though all the musicians play together in the final pages of the work, mostly Britten marshalled his troops with Mahlerian discipline. It is an odd thing to say about a work involving up to three conductors, 200 or so musicians and containing one of the two great primal screams of his output – the lyrical climax of the piece, which is underlined by a grinding, mechanical trudge, equalling in power the murmuring eruption of sailors at the end of *Billy Budd* – that much of the music is so delicate. There is sadness and ugliness as well (again, the grinding gears Bernstein mentioned never quite meshing) and an ironic sweetness in the score's final pages, which Britten denied when asked about it. But it is the delicacy that impresses.

Britten's great achievement here was in composing a work that those so inclined would identify in it the religious traditions it encases, but probe no further – much as they would admire in Coventry Piper's Baptistery Window and Graham Sutherland's large tapestry. In one way it is an unambiguous monument to the war dead, the names of four of whom – all schoolboy friends of Britten's or Pears's – appear on the score's dedication page.* Others, Britten knew, would weep for the unrelenting cruelty the whole work enacts, and still others would attack him for his audacity in trampling on graves. ('Some of my right-wing friends loathed it.') Britten appears to tie it all up in a neat bow, setting the words 'In paradisum deducant te Angeli' (May angels lead you into paradise) immediately after the chilly minutes in which the dead German and English soldiers confront each other, before finally saying with a weary shrug, 'Let us sleep now'. There is no resolution, however, which

---

* One of these, Piers Dunkerley, to whom Britten was so attracted in the 1930s, survived the war but committed suicide in 1959, only a year or so after leaving the Royal Marines, following an argument with his fiancée. He had struggled to find his feet outside the navy, and Britten viewed him as much a casualty of war as the other three dedicatees – Roger Burney, David Gill and Michael Halliday.

Pears insisted was intentional. 'It *isn't* the end, we haven't escaped, we must still think about it, we are not allowed to end in a peaceful dream.'

I 2

Peter Shaffer completed his euphoric, reverential *Time & Tide* review of the 30 May 1962 premiere with an unexpected comment: 'It makes criticism impertinent.' Shaffer was a playwright rather than a music critic per se, though his opinion was shared by many who were. William Mann had done his best to jinx the piece, examining the score and labelling it a masterpiece in *The Times* five days before the premiere. In his review he reiterated his first impression that it was 'the most masterly and nobly imagined work Britten has ever given us', and suggested 'that every performance it is given ought to be a momentous occasion'. *War Requiem* was hostage to such fortune, of course, and there would later be a backlash, not least from those who became a little sick of so many carefully scheduled momentous occasions, the piece hitched to one protest or memorial after another. But the later reception can take nothing away from the actual work and its profound music and message. Even the former Wehrmacht soldier involved in its creation, Fischer-Dieskau, was undone by it, the meeting of the two ghosts in particular. 'I did not know where to hide my face. Dead friends and past suffering arose in my mind.'

Britten was thrilled with it, thrilled with the balance between his old musical language (the large, thick orchestral sonority and strong rhetorical gestures) and the new (a more intimate, subdued approach). Mostly he was pleased with the overall concept – 'the one musical masterwork we possess with overt pacifist meanings', as Tippett described it. In preparing for the premiere there were the expected Trollopian battles between composer and clergy, and the acoustic in Coventry's new cathedral did its best to undermine the performance (as did the poor chorus and the City of Birmingham Symphony Orchestra), but even these factors he quickly put behind him as he attempted to bask in the glow of its reception.

There had now been a series of major works generating enthusiastic critical response – *The Turn of the Screw*, *Nocturne*, *A Midsummer Night's Dream* and the Sonata for cello. Things had turned round since the dark, swampy days of *Gloriana*, in part because Britten had become more careful about his commitments and collaborators. It is also that Britten's new sparser style demanded coherence in musical language and thinking. The projects he pursued in the late 1950s and early 1960s were all startlingly original and near flawless structurally too. Of course his good favour with critics would not last, as he would soon discover. But he had enjoyed an impressive run since his 1953 nadir, and if he continued to swipe at critics hereafter, it is only because it was by then ingrained behaviour.

He was still defensive, suspicious of his recent success. In speeches at Hull University for an honorary doctorate and Aldeburgh's Moot Hall, Grimes's old stamping ground, on receiving the Honorary Freedom of the Borough, Britten spoke of music being in a time of change, a time when artists were using a language few others spoke. 'It is this gulf between the public and the serious artist which has helped to encourage a deep-seated philistinism about the arts, which there is – I hate to admit it – in so many English people.' Perhaps he meant cynicism, for he thought that composers were now writing for themselves, not their public, and that audiences were left alienated and cynical about contemporary art. To distinguish himself from such thinking, he cited his music for young people and talked proudly of his work with his own community for the festival each year. And he laid into Stravinsky ('His judgements of other men's music often seem to me arrogant and ignorant, and they are always changing'), careful all the while not to mention him by name. This mixture of defensiveness and incomprehension remained, and only increased as the 1960s progressed.

13

'The truth is that I have had a very bad year, illness after illness, & I fear my life has got thoroughly disorganised. I think the cause, honestly, is that I gave out a great deal of myself in the War Requiem, & my body has taken revenge!' Severe shoulder pain had forced him to step aside as conductor of all forces in the *War Requiem* premiere; he took on the chamber orchestra instead, initiating a performance tradition of separate conductors he did not originally conceive and the work does not require. The big scores he had conducted in concert and in the recording studio over the previous years, the revised *Billy Budd* among them, had wreaked havoc with his health.* Opera particularly exacerbated the problem, stretching and straining his body as he looked after both stage and pit. Britten was formerly unfazed by his doctor's prohibitions, resignedly telling Solti long before the flare-up, 'I know now that to tackle the preparation and performances of a work of the size of "Billy Budd" is beyond my strength and talents. I am sure I am much more valuable in the stalls . . .' Now there was no escaping it. He had promised Rostropovich a large work for cello and orchestra, but illness, parading doctors and shoulder pain scotched the plan.

The tests and treatments and ensuing cancellations depressed him greatly. A two-week holiday in his beloved Venice in September 1962 – each day marked by a diet of Tiepolo, Bellini and the like – helped lift his mood, but while there he contracted a bug that put paid to any progress in his health. 'I am so dreadfully sorry I'm being such a broken reed at the moment – it is the bloodiest nuisance from every point of view,' he told Pears at the end of October. 'I suppose one can't help having weak spots, and being a jumpy neurotic type – but at least I'm determined now not to be such an infernal nuisance to everyone – including myself, because it isn't fun to feel like the wrong end of a broken down bus for most of the time.' Pears, performing *Grimes* at Covent Garden, responded warmly and revealingly, talking of his shame that Britten should feel the need to write an apology 'when it is I that should be looking after you & loving you, should long ago have thrown my silly career out of the window & come & tried to protect you a bit from worry and tension'. The theme would now run and run, right up to Britten's final months and the sad recriminations following his death.

Slowly he recovered, hunkered down in Aldeburgh reading Firbank and Henry James, sketching ideas for the new Rostropovich piece (what would become the Cello Symphony) – only slightly daunted to be working on such a scale so soon after the exhausting *War Requiem*. Nor was he able to leave *War Requiem* behind: in January 1963 he spent almost a week in London's Kingsway Hall recording it for Decca, directing his huge forces with precision, his voice resounding in the hall as though ordering claret at the Garrick. This time, Vishnevskaya was allowed to

---

* Partly because of the unfussy way he carried himself at the instrument, Britten was still able to play the piano, as he did on a German tour with Pears in November 1962.

participate and she played all sorts of hysterical tricks, somehow thinking she was considered little more than a chorister because of where John Culshaw positioned her, the stereo effects carefully calculated. Her involvement was the result of an unsteady détente between Britten and Madame Furtseva (a consequence of patient correspondence and Britten's ongoing commitment to one of the Soviet Union's most brilliant musicians), which in March 1963, following a snowed-in winter working holiday in Greece and a skiing break in Switzerland (a fall leaving his foot in plaster and a German recital tour cancelled), culminated in Britten's involvement in a Festival of British Musical Art in Moscow and Leningrad.

Even without the Cello Symphony, Britten still took a representative sample of his work to the Soviet Union, including the Sonata for cello, *Serenade*, *Winter Words* and *Sechs Hölderlin-Fragmente*. These were spread over five concerts between 8 and 17 March, and were leavened by some Schubert and Purcell and the *Sea Interludes*, a late replacement for the unfinished work. Britten and Pears's affection for *Serenade* never abated, *Nocturne* curiously never equalling it. It is almost as though they both liked going back to a simpler stage in their lives, to the early days of their love and relationship, before *Grimes* and fame and everything that followed.

Of course the festival was Soviet propaganda intended for Western consumption: see how our artists and musicians are trained and funded and given the use of dachas in Peredelkino or Komarovo. Britten was not interested in this aspect of the festival: he saw the visit solely as a cultural exchange. He did his bit for the cause, posing in Red Square alongside Slava and Galina, Pears and Marion, all in fur hats, the dreamlike St Basil's Cathedral as backdrop.

He did not always step with care through the propaganda minefields. It was perhaps unsurprising that he tripped up, given the things he had recently been saying about the role of composers, performers and audiences in society (and would talk about the following year in Aspen). When in an interview with *Pravda* he was asked a question along this line, he immediately warmed to a well-rehearsed theme. 'One of the principal social obligations of the artist consists of the moulding, education and development of the artistic taste of the people.' Martin Cooper, chief music critic of the *Daily Telegraph* and a fluent Russian speaker, was in the Soviet Union for the festival. He read the interview and wrote a thoughtful article for his own paper in response. Art for *the* people, Cooper argued, bound Britten to the 'full Communist doctrine of art as an instrument of ideological propaganda', and made him a subscriber to Khrushchev's long, hysterical speeches denouncing Western decadence and contemporary art.

Britten felt more persecuted by the onslaught Cooper's argument initiated than by anything the Soviets had thrown at him. He complained to friends about being misinterpreted and certainly the ideological connotation was unintended. Yet Cooper also pushed a wider argument about the approach Western artists should take towards repressive regimes. How was it possible that Britten did not realize the circumstances in which Soviet artists and musicians plied their trade? And would it not have been better if, instead of finishing his interview with professions of solidarity and collusion between the artists and art of two countries, he had voiced the dissent unavailable to his Soviet peers? 'The first duty of artists in the West,' Cooper suggested, 'is to force an awareness and resentment of this straitjacket on Russian artists, since no prisoner will escape if he is unaware of being chained.'

The young Britten would have had his chest prodded by Auden until all the arguments were clear. The forty-nine-year-old Britten drafted an overwrought response, at the invitation of the *Observer*, in which he was determined to see only trees and not much wood. He never completed or published the article, though he reused some of its themes in his Aspen speech. It is an illuminating document. 'One of the most disturbing features of this time is that so many people seem to prefer to read about art rather than to experience it,' he began. 'Perhaps it is easier to read about things than to do them, or is it that having read the critics one knows what to feel without bothering to think?' He was off. He asked whether art should be for everyone or something to which people aspire. ('I do not deny that there is much in the greatest of art that can transcend circumstance, & we would be silly, just because our conditions are different, to give up trying to perform the masterpieces of other ages. But, the communication cannot be complete.') He complained about composers today writing in a language that places barriers between them and those who *do* aspire to know their music. ('Fond as I am of much abstract painting, I cannot get involved with them as with "subject" paintings.') He wrote too about his own music, how he preferred the parable technique in opera to tackling contemporary subjects, and how he wanted to hear songs and operas in a language he understood. And he spoke of the mystery of composing, how once all the planning of a piece is done down to the finest detail, 'everything must give way to the "still, small voice" which is the heaven-sent guide to the next note, the sign of gift or personality, or whatever one wishes to call it, & which is after all the only thing in art which really matters'.

He still skirted around Cooper's key argument and accusation, addressing them obliquely only once. 'Have we, as artists, a social duty? I think we have, or to put it differently, I think we all fundamentally have a wish to take our part in society.' Composers should serve whatever society they are in. It seems a little toothless compared to the Britten of the 1930s icily referring to Shostakovich as 'a member of the Soviet regime, living and apparently revelling in the present conditions' (this was before the composer's long fight with Stalin). It is toothless even compared to what he would say in his Aspen speech: 'In totalitarian regimes, we know that great official pressure is used to bring the artist into line and make him conform to the State's ideology.' And this is perhaps the most revealing undercurrent of the draft article – that it dissents from the Cold War anxiety then swirling around Britain and finds nothing so bad about Soviet communism next to British capitalism.

When in August 1968 troops from five Communist countries invaded Czechoslovakia – a reprise of Soviet actions in Hungary twelve years earlier – Rostropovich the next night performed the Czech Dvořák's Cello Concerto to a Proms audience in Albert Hall, tears pouring down his cheeks. Auden, living just over the border in Austria and reprising the rage he had felt on September 1, 1939, telephoned the *Observer* after the print deadline and dictated a savage poem, which the paper found space for.

> The Ogre does what ogres can,
> Deeds quite impossible for Man,
> But one prize is beyond his reach:
> The Ogre cannot master speech
>
> About a subjugated plain,
> Among its desperate and slain,
> The Ogre stalks with hands on hips,
> While drivel gushes from his lips.

Yet Britten would not even accede to a request from Czech conductor Rafael Kubelik to sign a telegram of protest. He condemned the invasion to friends, bizarrely comparing it to the American 'occupation' of the nearby Bentwaters USAF base, but decided to maintain all cultural links in a hope that it might prove a more effective influence. (More selfishly, he wished to protect his relationship with Rostropovich, much as he once wished to with Auden, en route to Spain.) He later said he made private entreaties on behalf of the Czechs, but did not specify to whom. 'The side of communism which is violent is abhorrent to me. But when one travels to Iron Curtain countries as I have had occasion to do, one is conscious simply of human beings.' It was just a bit woolly.

The irony of Britten articulating these thoughts just then, about artists serving their society, is that in many ways the 1960s would be a decade of retreat for him. The public statement of *War Requiem* was followed by a series of increasingly intimate works, mostly written for his small community in Aldeburgh. Of course the world would sit up and listen, but he was now competing with a far more professional metropolitan arts scene, his voice one of many, and his accent quite different. At the end of the 1960s he would despair that the avant-garde had left him behind, and that his old friend Tippett now held the mantle. It was only partly true. Anyway, it was Britten's decision to pare down his music during the course of the decade, simplifying his thoughts, tearing all the excess away. And it was his decision to build up his own small-town festival rather than appear at major houses and halls in the world's greatest cities. As the 1960s unfolded, the Victorian corsetry restraining British society loosened, in Rab Butler's evocative phrase. When Arthur Marwick looked back thirty years later, he dismissed those who thought the decade merely a 'transient time of ecstasy and excess, fit only for nostalgia or contempt'. It was, he argued, nothing short of a revolution, which 'established the enduring cultural values and social behaviour for the rest of the century' in Britain and beyond. The historian Dominic Sandbrook thinks Marwick and others overstated the speed and extent of social change. But at the very least it was a time of transition, economically and culturally. Britten stepped carefully on the shifting ground.

7

Retreat

Aldeburgh, 1963–1970

I

Britten turned fifty in November 1963 and pleaded vainly with the BBC to hold off celebrations until his seventy-fifth birthday, a milestone he would never reach. He was still lean and fit, but looked his age: his cheekbones were more noticeable, his eyes and face fleshier, hair swatched with grey – Crozier's description of him, in effect. He laughed off the fact that his perfect pitch had sunk a semitone ('I hear the overture to *Meistersinger* in "my" C sharp major instead of C major'), reasoning that it was simple enough to convert it.

Tributes came from everywhere. There were features and broadcasts, articles and interviews. There was a Festschrift edited by his old friend Tony Gishford with contributions from friends and colleagues, including Forster, Sitwell and Plomer. (Crozier turned in a grotesque what-next essay, 'Albert in Later Life', which detailed a career of blackmail, pederasty, pornography and arson for the grocer. Gishford turned it down, further increasing Crozier's bitterness.) There was a Prom concert devoted to Britten's music, including the first British performance of *Cantata misericordium*, a stark, beautiful sibling of *Cantata academica*; composed for the centenary of the International Red Cross, it tenderly tells the parable of the Good Samaritan. The Albert Hall audience cheered him loudly at the end, 'which must have convinced him that his music forms a living and cherished part of the experience of a very wide public', wrote Donald Mitchell in the *Telegraph*. There were testimonials from around the world, including two close to home. 'In the last years your music has come to mean more and more to me,' said Walton through slightly gritted teeth, while Tippett made a typically generous and astute observation: 'Of all the musicians I have met, Britten is the most sheerly musical – music seems to flow out of his mind, out of his body.' There was a new production of *Peter Grimes* at Sadler's Wells, directed by Coleman, and a concert performance of the slighted *Gloriana*, conducted by Bryan Fairfax. 'I can say that when you and I are no longer here,' wrote Rostropovich (through a translator), 'millions of ordinary people will still be celebrating your birthdays – your 125th, 150th and 200th birthdays. I foresee these jubilees and congratulate you in advance – you and your music.'

This time *Gloriana* fared better, though the atmosphere at the Royal Festival Hall shifted from celebration to shock as news of John F. Kennedy's assassination filtered through the crowd; the onstage death of one historic ruler at the opera's close had its tragic parallel in the demise of another only hours earlier. Matters were not helped by the strangely knockabout, low-key circumstances of the performance: it had an impressive cast, appearing for pennies, yet was produced by Fairfax and his new Polyphonia Orchestra independently of Britten and sold relatively few tickets. Britten cobbled together a large guest list and the evening was saved – not least because of the after-party hosted by the Harewoods at Orme Square – though he was bewildered by the occasion and the little traction the opera still seemed to have with audiences. The poison would not be drained from *Gloriana* until the 1966 Sadler's Wells production, which generated a more open and appreciative response.

He was downcast about much of the carry-on, referring to the celebratory performances and tributes as memorial concerts and obituaries. It was part affectation; he remained a modest man and found much of the rejoicing embarrassing, yet secretly he was pleased, of course. Another part was genuine, however, an astute, early sense of a change in the air regarding the public perception of his music, a feeling that would cling to him at the end of the decade. The change was not Britain's alone: Britten had finally returned to his collaboration with Plomer on the Nō play, embarking on a voyage with foreign charts and only a good sense of direction as a guide. Would audiences survive the journey?

In January 1964, immediately following the successful Covent Garden premiere of the revised *Billy Budd* – now in two acts, not four, critics tacitly vindicated, Piper's designs made slightly more abstract, casting and chorus indifferent – Britten decamped to Venice for six weeks to work on the Church Parable, away from the constant distractions and calls on his time. He and Pears took an apartment in the stately, wedding-cake Palazzo Mocenigo right on the Grand Canal. It was full of woodwormed furniture and heavy, dusty curtains, and they were battered by the cruel winter weather and impenetrable fog, but it was ideal for their purpose. At various times they hosted Colin Graham, Marion Harewood and Imogen Holst, spending spare afternoons in galleries (Britten marvelling at the sheer number of masterpieces per yard) and nights in theatres. The Parable slowly took shape.

Time was short – the new work was to be premiered in that year's festival – and Britten was tired, emotionally and physically, worn out from November's birthday celebrations. Moreover, he still did not quite know how to shape it, how to steer it clear of Japanese pastiche. But Venice performed its magic once more: exploring the city's glorious churches, Britten heard choirs singing plainsong and motets, which swirled and echoed around the cavernous buildings. It gave him an idea: what if the piece was less to do with carefully notated and controlled performances and more with the chance sounds and harmonies stemming from a freer notation and livelier acoustic? Since childhood he had been fascinated by what he called the Gothic acoustic, 'where the note reverberates for some time after it is struck or sung, an acoustic which produces a string of notes together, its own form of harmony'. It was a bold notion and not just because he was such an exacting artist; he had to devise a way of writing down on paper the picture he had in mind, simultaneously giving the performers their freedom, and he had to notate something that would change from one acoustic to the next.

To complicate matters, he decided to do without a conductor. Nō plays manage it, he reasoned, but there was something more to his decision than this, something that had frustrated him for years. 'So often you find a really first-class orchestra suffering under a not very gifted or very intelligent or technically developed conductor.' He was trying to make his music foolproof, to hand over all responsibility to the performers. He sought staged chamber music, and that is what he got. Two years after the premiere of *Curlew River*, when instrumentalists were used to following singers and taking their cues from each other's nods or lines, Britten identified in the performances 'a level of seriousness and creativity in the playing which you don't always get when there is a conductor leading', which is certainly true – a bad conductor can always reduce an orchestra to far less than the sum of its parts. It was a controversial idea ('I know conductors are rather cross about this'), though it was in essence just a more polite enactment of almost any of his diary entries from thirty years earlier.

He did not entirely escape the Japanese sounds he had been anxious to avoid. The transitory passage between prologue and drama replicates the wispy instrumental music and dull, thudding percussion of a Nō ensemble. The instruments Britten wrote for are similarly cast: flute, horn, viola, double bass, harp, percussion and chamber organ. But somewhere amid the plainsong that strongly influenced the melodic writing and the self-generated harmonies, he found a distinct voice.

For all the work's freedom, Britten and his director, Colin Graham, were prescriptive about stylization and staging in the new genre. Graham drew up a rule book – literally: a dense architectural manifesto, in which entries and movements are plotted and planned, every tiny gesture detailed, the philosophy of the genre explained. 'Once the spectator becomes geared to the convention his emotions are imperceptibly but passionately involved in a drama doubly distilled by the very economy of its theatrical means. Such involvement can be shattered by a single uncontrolled, weak, or unnecessary gesture.' It reads as terribly pedantic now, sometimes self-important, but it helped them map out the piece as they built it, the equivalent of Britten's early sketch of the *Indomitable* when writing *Billy Budd*.

So in Venice, without Plomer's direct help, Britten worked away at the libretto. He tightened the story of the poor Madwoman searching for her twelve-year-old son. She is taken across Curlew River by a Ferryman (a benign variant of Charon, the ferryman on River Styx) who tells her that people are gathering on the opposite bank at the site of a shrine erected a year earlier, which is said to have healing powers. As the Ferryman's story unfolds the mother becomes more and more agitated, convinced it is her son's shrine, that his abductor has murdered him. Once at the shrine, she joins in the prayers, which are interrupted by the boy's spirit, who appears before her, granting her benediction, assuaging her pain. 'Go your way in peace, mother. / The dead shall rise again / And in that blessed day / We shall meet in heav'n.'

On many levels, Britten, Plomer and Graham were successful in their theatrical revolution. The musical language is startlingly distinct from

Britten's most recent work: it is pared to the bone, delicate solo lines woven together fairly loosely and given their own energy and momentum by the acoustic and sheer chance of each performance. The acting is highly stylized, which mostly serves the music well. The dull-grieved realization by the Madwoman (played by a tenor) that she has discovered her son's tomb, followed by the sudden introduction of his treble voice to the texture – startling amid all the low instruments and male voices – and then her miraculous transformation, is hugely affecting.

Once the parable plays out, however, its message is grace through belief, nothing more. Coming so soon after *War Requiem*'s trenchant attack on religious complacency, it is a hollow tale. In many ways the original play *Sumidagawa* occupies a far stranger and more disturbing territory, since the child's spirit disappears for ever after the brief reunion, leaving no crumb of comfort: the mother is left inconsolable (much like the ending of *The Turn of the Screw*, a sharp deus ex machina that leaves the audience reeling). Plomer stuck to something like this in his original draft: 'What seemed her son is nothing but a mound, / A grassy mound alone beside a road. / Lament for a woman so bereaved, / And give her the only thing we can – our tears.' Yet Britten wanted a happier ending, almost as though he needed to step back from the bleakness of *War Requiem*. So once more he borrowed the clothes, language and imagery of Christianity, either as a disguise or because he knew they would be recognized by others. At the very least they provided him with a vehicle for his bold theatrical experiment.

In terms of the drama, the Christianizing of *Curlew River* is more successful than that of *The Rape of Lucretia*. Even so, it delivers far less of a punch than any of the Parables he had composed for the stage since the mid-1940s. The impact of *Budd* or *Grimes* is far greater than that of any of the Church Parables, mostly because neither of the grand operas involves magic or miracles. Instead we are left with the ghastly, flawed behaviour of human beings, which is all too recognizable. Auden addressed the distinction in the mid-1930s. 'There must always be two kinds of art, escape-art, for man needs escape as he needs food and deep sleep, and parable-art, that art which shall teach man to unlearn hatred and learn love.' With *Curlew River* Britten made escape-art but labelled it parable-art all the same. He was once more identifying himself publicly with the Christian traditions of his upbringing, regardless of his agnosticism in the 1960s and recent attack on the Church in *War Requiem*, a great example of Auden's parable-art.

Robert Tear, who came into Britten's life just then, covering and performing Pears's roles, later suggested that this identification was symptomatic of the composer's narrow philosophical outlook, one Tear found distressingly bourgeois. 'Where Michael Tippett sees religion as a personal and individual quest ... Ben retires to the safe ground of the mass, Anglicanism commenting, if unconsciously, on his intellectual and spiritual quiescence.' Later rejection may have fuelled Tear's criticism, yet that does not make it inaccurate and the fact remains that in *Curlew River* and other works in this decade of seismic social change, Britten was happy in the sounds and smells of the established church. He would soon compose a chilling riposte to such thinking, which only underlined his inconsistency further.

2

The 1964 Aldeburgh Festival was a feast of delicacies rare and bewitching. There was an exhibition of Sidney Nolan paintings inspired by Shakespeare sonnets, and a display of Georg Ehrlich bronzes. Britten had long admired and collected Ehrlich's work, his sketches or statues of boys in particular. More than ten years earlier Ehrlich captured him brilliantly in a slightly irascible bronze – down to the cocked right eyebrow and prominent vein in his forehead. The festival also included the first British performance of the Cello Symphony, which Rostropovich and Britten premiered in the Great Hall of the Moscow Conservatory three months earlier. Khachaturian and Shostakovich sat impassive in the audience, large heroic portraits of Mozart and Tchaikovsky above them, while students lapped it up, thrilled by the work's novelty and the glimpse it afforded them of the outside world.

The great pianist Sviatoslav Richter, whom Rostropovich had introduced to Britten in 1961, was also at the festival, dropping in to give an unscheduled Schubert recital, during which Britten joined him for Schubert's four-handed Variations in A flat, a coolly poised series of miniatures knitted from fairly unpromising material. 'Where else but in Aldeburgh is one likely to stumble inadvertently on the experience of a lifetime?' the *Daily Telegraph* critic wrote. For all the *joie de vivre* of these improvised duet concerts, Richter was uncomfortable with the speed with which Britten put them together. 'If I remember correctly, there were no more than three rehearsals!' he wrote of his recording of a four-handed Mozart sonata with Britten (three really would have been more than enough). And the studio session for Britten's Piano Concerto took place after only one rehearsal, to Richter's dismay. This was all too English for the careful Russian. Yet Britten had never worried over much about rehearsal time with those whose musical instincts he shared or admired.

The Symphony for Cello and Orchestra makes *Curlew River* seem even more improbable. It is a mass of contradictions: gritty yet lyrical; immense yet intimate; sprawling yet tightly packed. It could never have been written like this ten years earlier, so unflashy is the first move-ment's solo writing, so bare the orchestration. Rostropovich had asked for a concerto and instead found himself caught in the middle of a hugely meditative work, a counterpoint to the symphonic argument unfolding around him. The Scherzo brims with the sort of energy and momentum Britten had crafted so well in his fast music of the 1930s and often steered away from subsequently, here occluded in shadows. Cello and orchestra wander together in the Adagio, barely acknowledg-ing the other's existence until Britten conjures a most extraordinary sonority: a high, folksy cello tune, accompanied by whirring strings playing spectral harmonics, offset by a strange, ethereal horn melody. This unexpected, intimate dreamscape is a breathtaking moment. Brit-ten defers to concerto convention by granting his soloist a cadenza at the end of the haunting movement, which, like the Violin Concerto of twenty-four years earlier, melts into a passacaglia, the folksy tune its basis. The movement unfolds with stirring inevitability, the cello a will-ing accomplice. And the last minute or so, grand in sound and gesture, is a throwback to the early 1940s. It is an outstanding piece.

To have heard this work in June in the handsome Blythburgh church – a host of magnificent fifteenth-century carved wooden angels covering the ceiling – and then less than a week later *Curlew River* in Orford church – with its flinty, weather-beaten exterior and worn brasses that miraculously escaped the destructive attention of both Protestants and Puritans – was to encounter two very different Brittens. Martin Cooper, Britten's recent *bête noire*, did not much like the Christian aspect of *Curlew River*, but was enthusiastic about the music and concept. So too the composer's greatest cheer-leader in the 1960s, William Mann in *The Times*, who thought the Church Parable might be 'the start of a new, perhaps the most important stage in Britten's creative life'. Britten had worried about how the piece would be received, much as others in his circle were concerned Pears would be mocked for playing a woman, and was pathetically grateful for the positive critical response. He handed Graham a sheaf of reviews, saying, 'It's all right – you must read them – there's a whole new attitude.' Had he not already noticed how warm the waters had become?

For some critics, however, it was an Indian summer. After Britten's death the perceptive Peter Heyworth wrote in the *Observer* that in the years following the Cello Symphony 'his style grew more sparse and in the process a certain narrowness of range became apparent, especially when his later music is measured against the astonishing promise of the works he wrote before "Peter Grimes"'. (The irony of a critic fondly referring to the works of the 1930s and early 1940s should not be lost.) Even before the decade was over there were those who found disturbing the difference between earlier and later Britten works. Welcoming *The Poet's Echo*, the 1965 song cycle Britten wrote for Vishnevskaya, Desmond Shawe-Taylor expressed his concerns in a review bannered 'Two Aspects of Britten'. 'Those who may have feared that the two church parables and last year's William Blake cycle heralded an increasingly austere period in Britten's work will take heart from these picturesque and lyrical songs.' There was talk that Britten feared the success of *War Requiem*, feared that people were drawn to it for its sentiment rather than its musical qualities and message, and that *Curlew River* was the composer's corrective and challenge. There is not much to support this; *Curlew River* was eight years in the making and was always intended to be an intimate work, with a matching language. The new language did infiltrate other works in the decade, however, and Britten was aware he was pruning his music more and more, trying to live up to Bridge's example, trapped in some ways by the narrow scope of the Church Parables. He taught rarely (Oliver Knussen and Colin Matthews would take on the responsibility of training and mentoring subsequent generations of composers far more assiduously than Britten ever did), but when he looked at the manuscripts of young composers, his advice was invariably that they should strip back the musical language and focus on the still, authentic voice in their head. When another critic wrote after his death that *War Requiem* somehow jinxed him, that the 'steady stripping down of texture in subsequent pieces certainly suggested an artist in search of some more basic self', he misread Britten's motivation. He was absolutely right, however, regarding Britten's aesthetic.

3

A month after the festival Britten was in Aspen, Colorado, receiving the inaugural Aspen Award for services to the humanities. Reactions to '*our* speech', as he termed it to Pears, were subsequently hijacked by the intemperate remarks Britten made about recording, but there was much more to it than this. Having stated that he wanted to be of use to society, a drum he had long been beating, he set out what he expected of society in return. An artist 'demands that his art shall be accepted as an essential part of human activity, and human expression; and that he shall be accepted as a genuine practitioner of that art and consequently of value to the community; reasonably, he demands from society a secure living and a pension when he has worked long enough'. These were modest requirements, he thought, but still far from the reach of most British artists. Reading a copy of the address after the event, Plomer got its measure. 'The whole gist of your speech is that every piece of music is a special communication and becomes a collaboration between composer, executant and auditor. It is so strange that so basic and vital an idea is so seldom made explicit.' Britten called it the 'holy triangle of composer, performer and listener', and considered it an inviolable pact.

On the matter of a secure living, Britten was not speaking for himself, of course. Only three days after receiving the award the *Daily Mail* published a scurrilous article under the highbrow title 'Britten: Master, Composer, Man Against War', which nonetheless occupied itself with more lowbrow concerns. It listed his earnings for the previous year: £53,000 royalties from the *War Requiem* recording in its first fourteen months; £1,000 from the sale of scores; £10,000 ($30,000) from the Aspen Award; £300 for each of the thirty or so recitals he gave outside Aldeburgh each year; and a £1,000 conducting fee. The article's source is unclear and the figures are all over the place: the sale of scores generated far more than £1,000, the *War Requiem* recording far less. (His gross income in 1963–4 was £40,339.*) But the article illustrates both the hype surrounding the recording and a barely concealed sense of incredulity that a contemporary British composer could (and deserved to) earn this sort of money.

There were new pieces on his mind, and a memorial performance of *War Requiem* on 4 August 1964 in sombre recognition of the fiftieth anniversary of the start of the First World War. (It was a televised broadcast from the Proms, Britten conducting the chamber orchestra, Meredith Davies the rest.) Not even Sargent on the podium for the other piece on the programme, Vaughan Williams's Symphony No. 6, could spoil the occasion for Britten. It was art as protest.† With Plomer he kicked around two Bible stories for a second Church Parable – Tobias and the Angel, and the curious episode in the Book of Daniel involving three young Israelites, Ananias, Misael and Azarias. Plomer thought the former too complex, too daunting, attractive as it was. Instead they turned to the three youths who refuse to worship a false idol, are thrust into a fiery furnace by the proud Babylonian King Nebuchadnezzar for their insolence, only to emerge unscathed, an angel having protected them.

Despite all they had established in the genre, progress would still be slow. The EOG was to tour productions of *Lucretia*, *Albert Herring* and *The Turn of the Screw* to the Soviet Union in September and October 1964 – Furtseva purring away in the background, each member of the large company pocketing two roubles per day subsistence (a little under £1) and adhering to stern warnings not to dabble in currency speculation or anti-Communist propaganda – followed by a tour in Western Europe of a number of *War Requiem* performances. But it also became apparent Britten had never recovered from the birthday celebrations of the previous year, let alone all that followed. Some months earlier, his doctors had insisted he take his health more seriously and in this spirit he resolved to make 1965 a sabbatical from all performances and public appearances. Pears vowed to do the same and it was a resolution they both stuck to in their different ways. Yet even with the worst

---

* £670,000 today.
† He would be pleased by the large number of *War Requiem* performances planned throughout the world to commemorate the centenary of the war's beginning.

of the touring behind him and the prospect of the sabbatical year almost within reach, depression plagued him once more. While composing a new work for Rostropovich in November 1964 he wrote a sad, revealing letter to Pears. 'I've been madly low & depressed – you being away mostly I expect, but worried about my work which seems so bad always . . . I *must* get [to be] a better composer some how – but how —— but how —?' He was either suspicious of the music that resulted from his great natural fluency or just depressed.

The First Suite for Cello does not betray a lack of confidence, though in certain ways it does represent a further stylistic retreat. Britten magicks an intimate sound-world, one in which listeners are not invited to participate but almost stumble upon it by accident, overhearing it by chance. There is no more forlorn opening to a work by Britten than the beginning of this suite, but it would be wrong to put this down to his mood; as ever, he (mostly) managed to quarantine the music from his fluctuating emotions. And in some ways he was covering old ground. Each of the Suite's six movements has a name and character – Fuga, Serenata, Bordone, etc. – which are interspersed with the doleful Canto opening the work. Britten's challenge was to interpret these forms on a cello, where only two strings can be sustained at any one time, and where the bigger contrapuntal picture must be created with tricks and illusions. He had Bach's six cello suites as a model, which fleet-footedly skip through a dazzling series of Baroque dances. He also had his own *Lachrymae* to fall back on, which overcomes the contrapuntal limitations of a string instrument with great assurance, the piano filling out the texture when required. Certainly there are nods towards antiquity: in the Bordone, Britten conjures a whole peasant band, replete with droning bass, dull tabors thrumming away and a melody dancing atop. And the Marcia is at once a buttoned-up battlefield call to arms – yet more drums and a gauche stumping tune – and a more lyrical piece, brought to an end with a ghostly bugle call. It is a work of many layers, each delineated and sustained with poise.

Britten would write two more such suites, half fulfilling a joke contract made with Rostropovich – drawn up on a table napkin and signed by the composer – for a body of works to match Bach's literature for the solo cello. They are a tribute to both Rostropovich and Bach, whose music Britten conducted rarely, perhaps even reluctantly, yet with unshowy understanding.

4

Sabbatical or no sabbatical, there were still unpleasant chores to complete. In January 1965 he wrote a short letter to George Harewood, who had recently fathered a child by Patricia Tuckwell. He evoked admiration, affection and gratitude for their long, warm friendship and the great things they had built together. 'All the same, we must face facts, & that it doesn't seem possible, at any rate for the time being, for you to come to our Aldeburgh Festivals. Do you think, therefore, that it makes any sense your continuing to be our President?' Fidelity Cranbrook thought he adopted a prissy and pompous take on the Harewood situation, and there was something disarmingly puritanical in his reaction, never more so than in the 1960s. Reiss thought it was less to do with loyalty towards Marion and more because Britten felt so vulnerable about his own domestic position, looking for more conventional morality in others. The truth lies somewhere in between, but the result was the same: Harewood duly resigned. He thought the request childish, but had seen it coming – at the 1964 Holland Festival he had gone backstage to greet Britten after a concert, only to see him rush out of the stage door with Pears to avoid a meeting. Harewood found out the next day that Britten asked his driver to stop on the way to the port so he could be sick at the roadside, so unsettled was he by the near miss, the potential of confrontation, his nerves playing out in the usual manner. Back in London Britten wrote a terse note to Harewood saying that his behaviour towards Marion rendered their friendship impossible, and formally severed relations in January. (Marion later married the British politician Jeremy Thorpe.)

Although Britten's relationship with the Rostropoviches gave him many of the things he had experienced with the Harewoods, it was a young scholar and critic who now supplied the others. Donald Mitchell was an early Britten cheer-leader a good ten years before Mann assumed the post. In those days Britten thought Mitchell a slightly dotty puppy dog and held mixed feelings about his book with Hans Keller. Yet the seriousness and skill with which Mitchell wrote about Britten's music resulted in an unexpected association between poacher and gamekeeper. As Britten's relationship with Boosey & Hawkes further deteriorated in the years following Stein's death and Gishford's removal, Mitchell was hired by the firm as a part-time liaison officer – holding the hand of one party, gently agitating the other – which lasted until Roth effected his dismissal. This was the final straw. Britten had long battled Roth's supposed antagonism to his music, convinced he considered it inferior to Stravinsky's works of genius. When Britten heard the news of Mitchell's dismissal in February 1964, he told him not to 'worry too much about – & –; I'm sure there'll be some future. I occasionally dream of Faber + Faber – music publishers!' (Mitchell was then advising Faber & Faber on its music books.) It was a throwaway remark, but one made at exactly the time Britten's new contract with Boosey & Hawkes was on his desk awaiting signature.

There is no idea too crazy in advertising, but publishing is a more traditional industry, slow to change and wary of innovation. Nonetheless, Mitchell took the idea to Richard de la Mare, Faber's chairman (and son of Britten's childhood poet Walter), who responded warmly. 'I have no idea how this can be done, but clearly we have to do it.' And do it they did, putting Mitchell in charge of the venture and signing up Britten on the understanding they would together discover and publish the new generation of British composers, something his old house had not done. It was a blow for Britten's publishing firm of thirty years, each party accusing the other of betrayal. As was his wont, Britten saw only one side of the story. Yet on this occasion it was Roth who overplayed his hand. Where else could Britten go, he seemed to say.

The new Faber team lavished attention on Britten and his scores. The rehearsal score of *Curlew River*, in which Holst somehow distilled all the independent musical lines into a coherent map, is a handsome product: oversized, with a striking modern cover designed by Berthold Wolpe and a pocket inside the back flap housing Graham's twenty-page rule book. 'I had never dreamed that published music could again become a delight to the eye & a stimulus to performance,' Britten would tell Mitchell at the end of the decade. 'I am deeply impressed & very very grateful.'

Britten and Mitchell fast became boon companions, the young critic and his sparkly wife Kathleen – a sparrow-sized headmistress with a quick wit and generous personality – increasingly part of the Red House retinue. Mitchell initiated the practice that coloured the last ten years of Britten's life (and some time thereafter) – the revision and publication of his juvenilia and jobbing scores. On trips to Aldeburgh he would encourage Britten to pull out old manuscripts secreted away, his enthusiasm for the early, unpublished works genuine. Britten was pleased with the attention, but also the care with which Mitchell went about his work. He dusted down scores such as *The Sycamore Tree* and *Sweet was the song*, two short yet touching works written in his late teens. He also revised his rather plaintive *A Wealden Trio: The Song of the Women*, Ford Madox Ford's bleak picture of working-class yuletide poverty, composed when Britten was sixteen and now given a dedicatee, the extraordinary Rosamund Strode, who succeeded Holst in 1964 when she decided to devote more time to her father's music. Not all were published straight away, though the de la Mare songs Britten assembled in 1968 were, and boast a dedication to the poet's son, a thank-you present for Faber Music. Britten would famously return to *Paul Bunyan* in his final years, in the grip of illness, nostalgia and regret. And since Britten's death his estate has sanctioned publication of all sorts of juvenilia: String Quartet in F (1928) and a handful of other works for quartet; *Quatre chansons françaises* (1928); *Two Portraits* (1930); and various works for piano.

The quality of the works is not the most important aspect of this practice; some are clearly better than others, and those that are – *Quatre chansons françaises, Quartettino* – have entered the repertory. Of more significance is Britten's interest in this period of his life for the first time since he raided a similar cupboard in 1933, searching for material for *Simple Symphony*, his father dying next door. In the intervening thirty-odd years he had been too interested in progressing as a composer to look backwards. But now, concerned as he was with finding the simplest language in which to express his musical ideas, he found himself intrigued with the sound of his original voice. What was it that had made him write so boldly when he knew so little? 'People sometimes seem to think that, with a number of works now lying behind, one must be bursting with confidence,' he wrote in 1963. 'It is not so at all. I haven't yet achieved the simplicity I should like in my music, and I am enormously aware that I haven't yet come up to the technical standards Bridge set me.'

5

Having dealt with Harewood, Britten and Pears set off on the first leg of their sabbatical travels, six weeks in India with the Hesses. They visited the walled city of Old Delhi, full of crumbling villas and mosques, its streets a jumble of bicycles, cars and cows, and women in colourful saris, their faces friendly ('so remote from stiff, cold old England'). They caught boats across muddy rivers and drove through improvised bazaars. In New Delhi there were policemen in pith helmets to obey, spice markets to visit, rich food, temple dances and incongruous Victorian redbrick buildings to appreciate – England's imperial footprint still strong. They admired Sir Edwin Lutyens's vision for the new city, at the same time despairing at the invidious contrast it formed with the old, racked with poverty as it was. They travelled outside Delhi – to Agra and to Udaipur, then on to the swampy slums and beggary of Bombay and the splendour of Madras, then Ootacamund, high in the hills, then Kanjeveram, with its temples, then Thekaddy, home to the Periyar National Park. They were captivated one night by a chorus of dogs baying at the bright moon, one day by the sheer number of exotic birds they encountered and ticked off in a book, and then by a military band playing Gilbert and Sullivan in the garden of the Governor's House in Madras while they drank tea – a discordant juxtaposition in the young, independent nation. Finally they sought out either ghosts or consolation in the church Pears's father had been christened in more than a hundred years earlier.

Britten brought *Anna Karenina* with him and wrote excitedly to Colin Graham about its operatic prospects. Graham worked away at a draft libretto, later saying that one of Britten's hopes for the opera was to counter the prevailing belief he could not write great love music. It was an odd anxiety, easily contradicted by the lush music Essex sings to Queen Elizabeth, or Lucretia to her husband, or Quint to Miles, or Sid and Nancy to each other. But Britten steered mostly clear of the straightforward relationships that required such passionate music, and anyway preferred to look at such liaisons in a distorting mirror. So it was with *Anna Karenina*. Graham observed that Britten's interest lay not in the central love story but in the contrast between the two couples – the selfish, scandal-hunting Anna and her spoilt Count, and the slow-burning love between Kitty and the philosopher-farmer Levin.

'Anna Karenina' would get further than most of Britten's unwritten operas. It was planned with the fiery Vishnevskaya in mind as Anna, Pears her long-suffering cuckold, Alexei Karenin. The libretto survived rewrites and Rostropovich's interventions; it even survived the Soviet invasion of Czechoslovakia in August, until the Foreign Office told Britten he could not accept a Bolshoi commission for the piece. He decided instead to make a smaller version for Aldeburgh with Heather Harper, an echo of when the creamy Northern Irish soprano took over Vishnevskaya's part in the *War Requiem* premiere at ten days' notice, helped by her perfect pitch. People started talking about the opera, asking him how it was going and when it would be finished. As soon as word was out, companies requested the first European performance, which Britten found dispiriting. Why couldn't he be left in peace to write the thing? Britten interrogated Rosamund Strode. Had she talked about the work with anyone? Could someone have overheard her discussing it? She had not, of course, as Britten would have known, but still he had to ask, hating himself for doing so.

In these circumstances the project was quietly shelved, possibly as much to do with the sheer complexity of the story, the Herculean task of reducing it to a serviceable libretto, as with the public mutterings. Once again an operatic skeleton had missed the moment when it could be given flesh. Mostly Britten's composition process was just as he had explained it to Duncan many years earlier: an idea was mooted and then months or years passed while Britten teased out its problems and potential. Then, when it was ripe, it would be written at speed. This was how *Curlew River*, an extreme example, was composed. But often an idea's time just passed. Either Britten found no solution to the myriad problems in creating opera from an original source, or his enthusiasm waned, or another, more exciting prospect emerged. 'Anna Karenina' missed its window.

6

Back in Aldeburgh, newly appointed by the Queen to the Order of Merit (the UK's highest civil honour, limited to just twenty-four living members at any time), Britten set to work sketching some Blake settings for Fischer-Dieskau that he had promised for the 1965 festival. He told Pears he found little inspiration in writing for other singers, though this was partly for show: he felt guilty about composing songs for someone else, putting on an act for his partner's benefit, which both men pretended to believe. The songs he came up with – brooding, dark and hopeless as they are – drip with inspiration and invention. Britten had known Blake's poetry since the mid-1930s, shortly before he met Auden. He set 'The Sick Rose' in *Serenade* – managing to capture the strange, threatening heart of the poem in glassy, distant string sounds – and returned to him in *A Charm of Lullabies* and *Spring Symphony*. There had also been two single settings in the 1930s, one being 'A Poison Tree', which would have a second outing in the new cycle.

Pears was responsible for creating the text, harvesting words from Blake's *Songs of Experience*, *Auguries of Innocence* and 'Proverbs of Hell' from *The Marriage of Heaven and Hell*. He too had long admired the artist, poet and printmaker: in 1949 he bought Blake's *St Paul and the Viper*, a gorgeous watercolour (*c.* 1803–5), which hung in pride of place over the fireplace in Crag House and was now a cherished part of the collection at the Red House. He took to the three Blake volumes with enthusiasm and skill, buoyed by his surgery on *A Midsummer Night's Dream*.

Blake inhabits a dark world. London is a city of fear and death, full of clap-ridden harlots who pass on syphilis to their young customers and newborns, so that the disease 'blights with plagues the Marriage hearse'. It is a city teeming with soldiers back from imperial errands, wounded in some war or other. It is the home of the little chimneysweep who weeps in the snow while his parents take their misplaced piety to church.

Pears prefaced each song with one of the Proverbs, which is linked thematically to the longer poem that follows. Britten took his cue from Pears, linking them musically as well. Perhaps the most striking of these Proverbs follows Blake's dystopic sketch of London, and leads into the cruelty and religious hypocrisy of 'The Chimney Sweeper': 'Prisons are built with stones of Law, / Brothels with bricks of Religion.' It is Blake at his angry best, a theme he returns to in the final song of the cycle: 'Ev'ry Night and ev'ry Morn / Some to Misery are Born. / Ev'ry Morn and ev'ry Night / Some are Born to sweet delight.' Those miserable creatures condemned to endless night hold on to their religion as surely as their gin, but it makes no material difference to their desperate lives. The critic John Warrack thought that with the cycle Britten had 'here come most fully to terms with the darkness and sense of cruelty that has always stalked his art'. It was a perceptive comment.

Blake was another good match for Britten. He hated the sophistry of the Church of England, but loved Bible stories and images. He was simultaneously a trenchant critic of the Church and, like Christopher Smart, a Holy Fool: visions and condemnations poured out of him in equal measure. In *The Marriage of Heaven and Hell* he writes of the ancient poets who invented gods to explain the surrounding woods and lakes and cities, their explanations sticking over time and giving rise to the priests who enslaved the ignorant with these poetic tales. 'And at length they pronounc'd that the Gods had order'd such things. / Thus men forgot that All deities reside in the human breast.' This is why Auden thought spiritual beliefs should be kept separate from the misery of the established church.

There were other strong Blakean influences on Auden that were no doubt transfused to Britten in the 1930s. Auden described 'The Prolific and the Devourer', a piece he worked on in 1939 without ever completing, as 'just a new Marriage of Heaven and Hell', borrowing his title from the Blake. And when Auden had written the quirky, admonishing poem for Britten three years earlier ('Underneath the abject willow, / Lover, sulk no more; / Act from thought should quickly follow: / What is thinking for?'), he was paraphrasing Blake: 'Prudence is a rich ugly old maid courted by Incapacity. / He who desires but acts not, breeds pestilence.' Of course Auden's religious affiliations changed over time, but his love of Blake remained, and it was Blake whom Britten emulated in these gritty songs. He was more conventional than the poet, of course, and subtler too. But Blake offered Britten a way of engaging with the humanistic aspects of Christianity without requiring either belief or church membership – more successfully, perhaps, than *Curlew River*.

The cycle's dedicatee, Fischer-Dieskau, was grand and fussily arrogant, sternly instructing pianists how to play their accompaniments and remaining uninterested in any reciprocal suggestions (Richter was a rare exception). Britten came to think of him as a school bully. At the first London performance of *Songs and Proverbs of William Blake* Britten was his customarily nervous self. 'Ben touchingly apologised for his bad playing,' Fischer-Dieskau later wrote in his autobiography, which is full of names of great men and women who admired his artistry, 'and I admitted his errors in precision.'* It was an unlikely combination of

---

* 'You've been the crown prince of Lieder for thirty-five years,' Graham Johnson said to Fischer-Dieskau when interviewing him in the early 1990s. '"That's very kind of you to say that, but it's forty-five." I was expecting, "That's very kind of you to say that, but there was always Hermann Prey, there was always . . ." No, "forty-five."'

personalities, great composer and great baritone, each prickly and domineering in his own way, each free of any ability for self-parody. But Fischer-Dieskau was the most famous lieder singer of the era, and possessed a remarkable voice – simultaneously high and mellow, low and gravelly. He would mix a little of his head voice in with his chest voice when singing high, which gave it an intensely lyrical quality and allowed him to float above the stave with ease. All this he had displayed in *War Requiem*, and his sound is in every note of the Blake songs.

The aesthetic of the cycle is that of *Curlew River*. The piano accompaniment often works independently of the vocal line, both parts conjuring great colours and melodies from small cells. The piano writing itself is heavily layered, the two hands working occasionally as if independent. (Graham Johnson rightly observes that often in the cycle the piano sounds as though it is an orchestral reduction.) Britten was always good at colouring words with pianistic flourishes; in the cycle he achieves no less, except that each flourish also suggests a different instrument – a trumpet fanfare here, a glossy string harmonic there. The threatening timpani that rumble under Owen's poem 'Be slowly lifted up, thou long black arm' in *War Requiem* are revived at one point, and there is a reedy old organ accompanying the hymn tune in Britten's setting of 'A Poison Tree' (which relays the perils of anger left to ferment), the composer almost wilfully ignoring the harmonic implications of the melody. The vocal writing is simple: there is none of the peacock's-tail coloratura he still gave Pears, but he honoured Fischer-Dieskau's voice and musicianship in other ways.

They performed the work only a few times together after its premiere in June, but recorded it in December 1965, when Britten's intention to tape the cycle in sequence was trumped by the baritone's detailed plans for the four-hour session. The songs were mapped according to their tessitura, which required Britten to work out of sync and temper. This was no problem technically for him; his opera sessions were constructed in this way, his unerring sense of tempo meaning that there were none of the usual problems when Culshaw sat down in the editing suite. But he did not like working in this manner on a song cycle; more to the point, he did not like ceding control of such things to another artist.

In his autobiography Fischer-Dieskau writes of a rehearsal of ten Schubert songs for his recital with Britten in the 1972 Festival. 'Over and over, when Ben would interrupt himself during rehearsals at his old piano in the wonderful large studio of Red House to think out loud about tempi and techniques, I needed only to keep my ears open to profit from his ideas.' He missed Britten's purpose. As Rostropovich realized in their first play-through of the Cello Sonata, this was Britten's way of correcting a musical point, about which he had either thought long and hard or was instinctively responding to, but which through his hatred of confrontation he was prevented from addressing directly. Rostropovich realized his error when, at their hurried, mostly silent dinner, Britten hummed a phrase exactly how he wanted it played, not how Rostropovich had performed it. And through such instinctive understanding their friendship and musical partnership became much warmer and ultimately more fruitful than anything that could be mustered between Britten and Fischer-Dieskau.

7

The sabbatical, such as it was, continued in August, Britten and Pears travelling to Armenia with the Rostropoviches. Armenia was Shostakovich's idea: Vishnevskaya had worried about what she could possibly feed her guests if they stayed in Moscow, the supply and type of food being what it was. 'Where could I find edible steak for them, and fresh fish?' It seemed an unlikely concern for these most privileged Soviets, who furnished their dacha with aquariums and kitchenware and Irish linen from Harrods, who drove around in a new Mercedes picked up in West Berlin, and who dined in private rooms in local restaurants on caviar, borscht and grilled whole chicken, all washed down with vodka and Turkish coffee. Perhaps Vishnevskaya was concerned more about Britten's digestion than the austere diet on which most Muscovites survived, so after a couple of days at the dacha outside Moscow they travelled to Dilijan, high in the mountains in the northern Armenian province of Tavush.

Guests of the Armenian Composers' Union, they settled in for three weeks of reading, sunbathing, swimming and mushroom picking (Britten leaving their bounty untouched: it was a food he disliked). Their compound was normally reserved for the use of Armenian composers, a number of whom were there with their families, but Rostropovich had pulled all sorts of strings. ('Can one imagine Arthur Bliss, William

Walton and Ben and lots more taking their holidays together on Windermere and entertaining Fischer-Dieskau and Henze for a month?' Pears wrote wryly in his diary. 'Not quite.') They lived on cognac and vodka ('Moscow-mineral-water', they called it) and ate simple food: sturgeon every third meal, stuffed tomatoes, aubergine and fruit. There were picnics and barbecues, informal concerts, speeches and presentations, and ornate protestations of brotherhood in Aldeburgh Deutsch. At the end of the visit a small Britten Festival was planned in Yerevan, the Armenian capital, the thought of which filled the two Englishmen with dread.

The trip was not all borscht and vodka: Britten spent some of his time sketching a new work for Vishnevskaya. At Heathrow he had picked up a Penguin edition of Pushkin's verse and now set about writing her some songs. He chose six poems from their English translation and then had his hosts read them aloud in Russian, meticulously teaching him the pronunciation, which he replicated in a transliteration. He then wrote each song quickly from the transliteration, playing it immediately to Rostropovich, who corrected any slips in prosody. It was not an ideal method, he conceded, but the dedicatees, the cellist and his wife, thought he captured well both the sound of the language and Pushkin's gloomy forebodings. And it demonstrated him working quickly and spontaneously to a different type of inspiration.

Britten later described the cycle as 'a dialogue between the poet and the unresponsiveness of the natural world he describes'. *The Poet's Echo* is more than this, however, snared as it is in a lingering sense of regret or, worse, siege, which drips its way through the piano accompaniment of 'My Heart . . .' ('But now old wounds have started burning / Inflamed by beauty and her fire'). The same feeling is at the core of 'Lines Written during a Sleepless Night', the cycle's concluding song, which purrs away with a sort of hypnotic, enduring stillness, while a nearby clock ticktocks unerringly, insomnia's companion, and the poet is left to make sense of the niggling voices and night noises. 'Do you breathe reproachful murmurs / At my lost and wasted day?'

At the end of the trip Rostropovich insisted they drive to Pushkin's birthplace, Pskov, in north-west Russia close to Estonia. They visited Pushkin's house and museum, with its framed manuscripts and dark pictures on the wall, a small, old piano in the sitting room and ageing clock tower outside. After a simple meal their host asked to hear the Pushkin settings, so they repaired to the sitting room. Vishnevskaya sang the two she knew and Pears hummed his way through the rest. Hardly had Britten begun the final song when the old clock outside began to chime. 'It seemed to strike far more than midnight, to go on all through the song, and afterwards we sat spellbound,' wrote Pears. 'It was the most natural thing to have happened, and yet unique, astonishing, wonderful.'

Graham Johnson has suggested that the opening song, 'Echo', and the fourth song, 'The Nightingale and the Rose', offer a critique of the Soviet government's suppression of dissenting artists. If the howls and thunder rolls and singing maidens all find their quick echo in nature, why is it that the poet, who strives to write for his countrymen from his heart, hears nothing in return? And if the beguiling song of a nightingale cannot enrapture the coldly beautiful rose, how can an artist expect anything more from his public? It was likely that the impetuous Pushkin, who clashed frequently with the government of the day and was exiled to his mother's estate for a time, had in mind a criticism of authority. If Britten did so too, it was well disguised. After several visits, he still thought the Soviet system generous. He appreciated the composers' compound and the supportive approach to culture it represented. 'I wish something similar could happen in England,' he wrote in the *Sunday Telegraph* on his return, 'but I fear that composers are still not taken as seriously here as over there, nor have we English composers quite as much public spirit as our Russian colleagues.' Of course he was unimpressed by a lot of the music he heard on the visit, and Pears was rightly sceptical of the heaps of unplayed manuscripts sanctioned and paid for by the Union of Composers. Yet they were moved by the seriousness with which the Soviets viewed their culture, and this outweighed reservations they may have felt about the political ideology. 'The dangers of too much security are so small compared to those of worrying artists as much as we do. I can't believe an artist is often ruined by too much security, and without it one may frighten off potentially useful creators.'

Britten never publicly addressed the oppressive circumstances in which his friend Shostakovich was then working; instead, he continually averred that any composer worth his salt must work for his own society, the implication being that he must write irrespective of the political system in place. It was not a black-and-white argument for him – the villainous Soviets on one side, laissez-faire Americans on the other, Britain caught somewhere in between. (The invasion of Czecho-slovakia in 1968 would shift sympathy from the Soviet cause.) Indeed the Soviet system greatly influenced his further-evolving thoughts on a composer's relationship with society, which he articulated more and more in this decade.

8

Soon after their return Britten's short, strange work *Voices for Today* received a triple premiere in London, Paris and New York. Commissioned the previous year to mark the twentieth anniversary of the United Nations, Britten only managed to get round to it in the month before they flew to Moscow. It is a slight, episodic piece, but a snug fit for both the occasion and Britten's pacifist convictions. After discussing the commission with Forster, Plomer, Pears and Mitchell, Britten selected texts from fifteen of the 'great peace lovers of history', ranging from Virgil and Sophocles to Christ, Melville and Camus. It is an odd little jigsaw, but evidence that the themes he explored so publicly in *War Requiem* remained in his mind. Despite the implied grandeur of a simultaneous three-country premiere, *Voices for Today* is a relatively gentle work; a more virulent exploration of the same themes would have to wait until *Owen Wingrave*.

Britten sketched some ideas for *The Burning Fiery Furnace*, but his sister Beth's dissolving marriage and refuge in alcohol – Edith's fears borne out – stalled his progress. Regardless of Beth's quandary, however, output had already slowed, especially when compared to his productivity before the sabbatical year. 'I loathe date-lines now,' he told Walter Hussey in late November, '& write ever so slowly.' To Peg Hesse he was even more downcast. 'I know you realise how difficult my life has become; but perhaps you don't realise that the chief new difficulty is at the moment advancing age – how I cannot any more "knock off" things as I could. I have lost much of the confidence of the younger man, & am not nearly so prolific.' This must be taken with a pinch of salt, for he was still producing big works and remained an extremely disciplined composer. But he did now find himself fighting over every note. It was only five years since he had written proudly of the speed with which he composed *A Midsummer Night's Dream* – 'seven months for everything, including the score. This is not up to the speed of Mozart or Verdi, but these days, when the line of musical language is broken, it is much rarer.' The fears of twenty-five years earlier – that he would run out of notes or ideas – had caught up with him. He vowed to conserve his time and energies for composition alone, instead of frittering them away on a draining public life. 'I am determined that my life isn't *over* yet!' he continued to Hesse. 'I have too much to say & to do, & which I, perhaps vainly, think is important. What is *not* important and must be sloughed away as quick as poss., is the extraneous things, the useless honours, the things that others can do (& better), the senseless public life. But it takes time & needs patience.' The festival was the significant exception to this resolution.

Regardless of the brave face they all put on regarding the Jubilee Hall extension – funded to no small degree by an auction at Christie's of manuscripts and artworks by friends of Britten and Pears, Auden, Eliot, Spender, Henry Moore and Alma Mahler-Werfel among them – it remained too small, its acoustic too boxy. The festival simply did not have a venue for large-scale secular works. When he considered the matter in 1954 Britten pursued a conventional theatre, with a proscenium arch and a proper fly system and all the other accoutrements of a working opera house, built from scratch. But his direction had changed, his new dramas housed in a local church. Yet how could the festival evolve without programming larger concert repertory? There was a further consideration, that the festival could not keep pace with demand. In the early days Britten and Pears rounded the corners by paying peppercorn fees, donating their own services, writing the odd cheque, bringing in broadcasting fees, or making claims on their guarantors; none of this disguised the fact that the economics of the enterprise did not add up. They were hostage to the limited number of seats they could sell for any event and altogether too much goodwill. What was needed was a hall seating 800 or 1,000 people which would help balance the books.

Slightly down the hill from the Old Mill, away from the centre of the small village of Snape and tucked next to a fissure of the River Alde, was an old brewer's malt-house. Malting operations had ceased earlier in the year and the new owner was looking to let out some of the empty buildings while it developed grain-storage in others, transporting stock to London and Rotterdam on lumbering barges. Stephen Reiss inspected the sprawling site, which was peppered with Victorian redbrick outhouses and an 'uncommonly impressive group of Early Industrial buildings', according to Pevsner, and found himself drawn to a great barn-like structure near the back of the property. It had an uncharacteristically high roof for a malt-house (they would find out later that this was the work of the pioneering owner of the original business, who designed the building with an eye on better controlling temperatures and economizing the labour involved in handling the grain through gravity), which Reiss thought would fit their needs. The potential acoustic was anyone's guess, though the shoebox shape, brick walls and wooden roof augured well.

After Britten and Pears looked at the building, Reiss contacted the Anglo-Danish engineer Ove Arup, who was then working on Jørn Utzon's inspired but deeply flawed design for an opera house on the site of an old tram depot in Sydney. Arup passed Reiss's letter on to one of his associates, the gnome-like Derek Sugden, a charming man passionate about music, Suffolk and, as chance would have it, the Aldeburgh Festival. Sugden came and inspected the derelict malt-house and was asked how much it would cost to convert it into a concert hall. The building was divided into smaller kilns by a sequence of cross-walls. Its roof had turned to charcoal over the hundred years of malting. And ovens remained deep in the basement, a subterranean cavern straight out of Wagner's Nibelheim. Turning it into a concert hall would be a huge task. Before Sugden had time to scribble some calculations, Britten averred: 'We can't spend a penny more than fifty thousand.' Sugden laughed off such an absurdly low figure; he knew that the Queen Elizabeth Hall, then under construction, would cost around £3 million. When he told Britten that they were looking at more than £100,000, the composer responded, 'Oh, we'll never raise anything like that.'*

It all happened remarkably quickly. Culshaw came and clambered around the old building, trying to grade its potential as a recording venue, finding himself struck by the atmosphere, by the surrounding reeds and the view of Iken church over the marshes. Britten talked acoustics with Sugden ('To give you an idea of the sound I like, I prefer the *War Requiem* in Ely Cathedral, when I can't hear all the words, to the Festival Hall, when I can. I'd like it as *full* as possible, a full sound'), and insisted it was to be a concert hall first and foremost. If it turned out

---

* It ended up costing around £570,000 – £8.5 million today.

to be suitable for opera as well, so be it, but this was not to be a factor in the design. Sugden drew up plans and created a model, photographs of which appeared in the 1966 festival programme book and which leave nothing to the imagination: viewing it today is to picture the concert hall in detail. Funds came from a public appeal and from Decca, the Gulbenkian Trust and the Arts Council.

Throughout the almost two years it took from beginning the project to opening the hall, Britten alternated between vision and caution, stubbornness and acquiescence. When eleven years earlier he had thrown his weight behind a new theatre in Aldeburgh he had thrust it on the town council and the festival committee with little preparation or politicking. He was stung by their rejection. This time he was more astute and though they moved with great speed, Britten took care to consult and enthuse those involved. Reiss was an ideal project manager, somehow fitting it in with his myriad responsibilities.

9

While he made plans and bent ears, Britten was given a medical diagnosis of his stomach problems. His 'tummy' had deteriorated over time, as had Pears's sympathy. The slightest ailment in Pears would leave Britten anxious and concerned, but the tenor could never quite disguise his impatience and crossness over his partner's many illnesses. Britten's stomach laid him low in Armenia, and Pears had administered a string of potions, both mild and wild. But mostly the tenor was happy if work kept him away from Aldeburgh while Britten was unwell.

Now, however, there was an authentic illness to dispel lingering thoughts that Britten's problems were psychosomatic. His doctors diagnosed diverticulitis, where pouches form in the colon, giving rise to a number of symptoms: abdominal pain, nausea, cramping and constipation. By the time Britten went for surgery in February 1966, he had completed the composition sketch of *The Burning Fiery Furnace* and much of the orchestration. He spent three weeks in hospital and recuperated in Aldeburgh, cared for by a nurse, a rehearsal for life at the Red House in his final years. He tottered around the garden, went for slow drives and gradually eased himself back into work on the Church Parable, to be premiered in June. But he was battered by the illness and operation, and found the recovery hard – a break in erratic, alluring Marrakesh notwithstanding. 'I am sorry I have been such a drag on you these last years; with so much to think about, it has been wretched for you to have the extra worry of my tum,' he told Pears in April, revisiting territory traversed in 1962.

Both Graham and Plomer stressed the contemporary political resonances of *The Burning Fiery Furnace*. Graham wrote in his production notes that the 'political aspect of the story, the schism between the Babylonians and the three young Jews, should be continually stressed', a theme Plomer picked up in the festival programme book. 'It may be felt that in this new version the character of Nebuchadnezzar, the cult of "the god of gold", and the resistance movement – ultimately triumphant – of the three young Jewish exiles are not without some relation to our own times.' It was a slightly askew assertion. The three Jewish youths, who are forced to adopt the Babylonian names Shadrach, Meshach and Abednego, praise God when they realize an angel is protecting them in the flames. They recite the Song of the Three Holy Children ('O all ye Works of the Lord, bless ye the Lord'), which has its own life outside this story (not least in *Peter Grimes*) as the Benedicite, part of Anglican and Catholic worship. Nebuchadnezzar, realizing a miraculous intervention has taken place, shifts his allegiance to the God of the Israelites. ('Hear my decree: There is no god except this God, / The God of Shadrach, Meshach and Abednego.') The story, in metaphor and meaning, in its miracle and impotent furnace, could not be further from the European events of 1933–45.

Graham made a further unfortunate claim, that the production's visual presentation 'was drawn from the colours and action in the stained-glass windows at Chartres Cathedral'. He had visited the cathedral with Britten and marvelled at the simple, brilliant iconography and the clarity with which Bible stories were depicted. Annena Stubbs's costumes took their cue from the glorious windows: the three youths were robed in deep blues and shiny golds, while Nebuchadnezzar was cloaked in stunning ochres and roses, his face in a golden mask – a great, gilded scarab, as Graham called him. But production photographs also reveal the inherent stasis of the Chartres windows, with bodies at peculiar angles and hands in exaggerated gestures.

The music is intriguing, more unleashed than that of the earlier Parable. Britten swapped the predecessor's horn for an alto trombone, which thickens the texture and introduces a decadent colour to the orgiastic scene in which the great Babylonian god Merodak is praised. And when the wordless angel sings over the youths' prayers it is a still, shivery moment, which owes something to the soaring treble solo in Allegri's *Miserere*. It is not as taut as its predecessor, however. The boy entertainers at the feast prefigure the *commedia dell'arte* scene in *Death in Venice*, but here, as they ask the sort of riddles that Portia or Princess Turandot pose to their potential suitors, they are almost too much of a good thing. The procession of instrumentalists around the church just prior to the Merodak scene verges on repetitive rather than inventive. For all its imaginative colouring, there is something jarring about the music, Britten invoking in the scene a broad-brushed orientalism in support of Babylonian decadence, in contrast to the pure tunes of the Israelites.

Some critics at the work's premiere appreciated its political resonances, those elements of Auden's 'parable-art'. Jeremy Noble in the *New Statesman* felt sure that Britten and Plomer were attacking nationalism and its 'concomitant evils of conformism, intolerance and racial hatred', while Desmond Shawe-Taylor spoke of its modern relevance. But in fact, once more Britten had been drawn to a parable that deals with the grace and power of the Abrahamic God. Despite Plomer's assertion and Noble's observation, despite the decade in which it was composed, it is the parable's original story that dominates in Britten's version. We are left again with the impression that Britten enjoyed revisiting a childhood story, which he took at face value and retold in his unique way, without quite clarifying in his own mind the implications of the retelling.

10

For the Vienna Boys' Choir Britten composed *The Golden Vanity*, a sort of *Boy's Own* version of *Billy Budd*. He had mooted the idea of a short opera for the choir in October 1964, the boys pleading with him to write something that did not require them to frock up. So Britten composed this vaudeville based on an old English ballad, a dark tale in which a lowly cabin-boy saves the *Golden Vanity* from capture by grog-filled pirates, spiking the hull of their Turkish Galilee until it fills with water and sinks, taking them with it. Safe and jubilant, the captain decides not to honour the reward he promised the boy – a pension of gold and silver and the hand of his pretty young daughter – and leaves him instead to drown in the Lowland Sea. When guilt pricks his conscience he hauls the cabin-boy aboard, but it is too late and he dies on deck. His shipmates wrap him in his hammock, wipe back tears and drop him into the ocean. And those who sail past the spot thereafter will hear the cabin-boy's plaintive cry: 'Oh, messmates take me up for I'm sinking with the tide!'

The Golden Vanity is only twenty minutes long but full of delicious characterizations: the teeth-chattering sailors who think they will be captured, their treasure plundered; the plucky cabin-boy with his clear, ambitious plan and social aspirations; the drowning pirates left to gurgle away below the water-line; the hard-nosed captain, his greed and sense of status clouding his judgement; and the watery piano accompaniment that sets the scene. Like Vere, the captain tortures himself for the rest of his life over his actions. And like the crew of the *Indomitable*, the messmates of the *Golden Vanity* are left wondering why none of them disobeyed their captain and bosun to throw their friend a rope. Even here, in a short work for children, there is a troubling moral about human behaviour. When the work's librettist Colin Graham termed the piece satirical, Britten was having none of it: this was serious stuff.

Neatly Britten went straight from the *Golden Vanity* to the *Indomitable*, dropping in to watch the BBC record *Billy Budd* for television. The film is full of big buckles and suspiciously shiny shoes, and Billy sports a bad wig atop a plain head, but it is still an astonishing achievement for such a young industry. (The film won the Television Opera Award for the year, in an admittedly uncrowded field.) The look of Coleman's careful production is not too far in appearance from the 1962 film adaptation of Melville's book that starred Peter Ustinov as Vere (and director), and a handsome young Terence Stamp as Billy. In the BBC production Charles Mackerras navigated the two studios – one for orchestra, the other for the set and cast – with élan, all sins apparently forgiven. And Pears is terrific as Vere, his creased face betraying the barb in the words he utters in the Epilogue: 'I am an old man now, and my mind can go back in peace . . .' Britten was impressed by the process (the two studios aside) and the outcome, telling Coleman after the event, 'I was certainly made to think furiously about the medium, as it stands now. If we ever do a piece together (& I much hope we do) we must certainly have a long talk about the whole matter well in advance of any actual planning.'

He had his own studio commitments just then: Decca recorded *A Midsummer Night's Dream* in autumn under the composer's baton – out of sequence, Britten's flawless memory for tempo ensuring that no seam was exposed – Pears leaving him to it once he had done Lysander, another tour beckoning. And the Maltings conversion was never far from his mind. When it looked as though the huge amount of timber for the roof could not be sourced and the hall's opening was slipping back as a result, Britten held frosty meetings with Sugden and the local builders contracted for the conversion. He calmly but coolly pointed out the number of people committed to the opening on 2 June the following year, not least Her Majesty the Queen. 'I don't think we can take this discussion any further, Derek. You've just got to finish it on time.'

With Pears away he found himself dwelling on the sort of career the tenor had built for himself, so dependent on aircraft and agents, on performances somewhere in Europe one day and a rehearsal in London the next. Unable to confront Pears on the matter, he took it out instead on young Robert Tear, refusing him permission to enact exactly such a scenario for the EOG. 'This kind of rushed life is one of the curses of music today: a kind of greed to do everything which is physically possible, but it lowers standards, & harms artists, in a sad way.'

They leaped on a plane themselves once Pears returned, travelling to the Soviet Union to spend time with the Rostropoviches over Christmas 1966. It was bitterly cold and the wind tore at their throats. And it was not all play: there were recitals of *Dichterliebe* to an initially dour Leningrad crowd and an enthusiastic Moscow audience. It was in Leningrad, wandering the opulent eighteenth-century halls of the Hermitage, that Britten found himself transfixed by Rembrandt's *The Return of the Prodigal Son*. How different the late painting is from his depiction of Abraham and Isaac. It is full of astonishing details: an overwhelming feeling of compassion on the elderly father's part, gratitude and love on the son's, hollow-eyed hostility from his brother. Here was the subject for the next Church Parable, he would tell Plomer in March 1967. 'For several reasons (which I won't bore you with now) I do want to do it for next year – it would be wonderful to complete the trilogy when one's mind is working in this direction . . .' Following a holiday in the Caribbean in January, which Britten and Pears filled with walks and birdwatching and lazing on warm, golden beaches, composer and librettist saddled up once more for their final collaboration, though neither man knew it. Britten still greatly admired Plomer. 'His writing is succinct and clear and beautifully lyrical; he has a way of putting words together so that they belong to each other absolutely.' And Plomer was a natural, gentle foil to Britten's ideas and impatience.

Somehow, between illnesses and concerts, between grippes and tours to East Germany, he managed to compose a work with which to inaugurate the Maltings. He was remarkably profligate in this specialized area just then, arranging, for the March opening of the Queen Elizabeth Hall, two folk melodies, 'Hankin Booby' and 'Mage on a Cree'. They are downbeat, grim arrangements for wind and drums, which snarl and rattle to the Elizabethan sounds and rhythms Britten explored so deftly in *Gloriana*, a sinister undertone in evidence, as if the composer was unwilling to gift the occasion any joy. This he saved for his own hall and *The Building of the House*. Holst ferreted through *The Whole Book of Psalms* (the metrical Psalter) and mustered the most relevant for the opening of a new concert hall: 'Except the Lord the house doth make, / And thereunto doth set his hand, / What men do build it cannot stand'. She stepped around the inconvenient theological hurdles of the second verse, replacing 'But they whom God doth love and keep / Receive all things with quiet sleep' with 'But they shall thrive whom God doth bless, / Their house shall stand through storm and stress'. The sentiments of this bit of cod King James would be sorely tested in a devastating fire two years later. For his part, Britten borrowed the psalm's melody – a 'High Dutch Tune' according to the Ravenscroft Psalter (a favourite of Bach's) – and gave it to the full choir. It is not a particularly prepossessing tune – too clunky by half – but this worked almost to Britten's advantage, for it sits within an orchestral texture of stunning, breathless virtuosity, the violins stitching it a dazzling backdrop.

Britten and Pears described the Queen Elizabeth Hall to Peg Hesse as 'hideous – a real *studio*, all the works visible, holes for this & that, lights & ventilators all showing – no magic at all. Not like our dear Maltings at Snape which is going on a-pace & looks wonderful.' It certainly did. Sugden and the building foreman Bill Muttitt had somehow found enough timber and slate for the steeply raked roof, enough bricks to match the existing shell and allow it to be raised by three feet, and discovered a local carpenter who would make the 800 wooden chairs.

By the beginning of May the building was almost done. In a touching photograph, Britten, Pears and Sugden look on as one of the carpenters plays his violin in the hall. He is seated on a stool on the Maltings stage, hair brushed back, looking to the world like a member of the Amadeus Quartet; only his apron and bag of tools give him away. The brickwork and roof are visible and most of the seats in place. Britten is rapt by the performance, his mind racing, while Pears and Sugden have huge smiles on their faces. The hall's glorious acoustic – glossy yet precise – was casting its spell for the first time.

II

The opening on 2 June 1967 was an altogether more formal affair. The Queen and Prince Philip lunched with Britten, Pears and some appropriately titled guests at the Red House, all overseen by Barbara. They then drove to Snape, passing by the Old Mill – another Britten rebuilding project, from another lifetime – and into the grounds of the new concert hall. The Queen inspected the auditorium, with its beautiful honeyed timber ceiling and Victorian redbrick walls, and then looked out over the marshy expanse towards Aldeburgh. The audience stood for the national anthem in Britten's arrangement for chorus and orchestra, which starts as a hushed prayer – basses rumbling around the bottom of the texture like Chaliapin – before exploding in riotous jubilation in the second verse, as befits the words: 'O Lord our God arise / Scatter her enemies / And make them fall.' Then followed *The Building of the House* (this was the occasion on which the choir exceeded its brief, singing the opening phrases a semitone sharp) and the works of three other English composers – Frederick Delius, Gustav Holst (conducted by his daughter) and Purcell.

'Weren't the Festival and Benjamin Britten lucky to find such a wonderful place for music!' one charming lady was overheard telling another in an early concert, as though the hall had stood there waiting for them all along. In a sense it had – but how lucky that men with vision had encountered it. Aside from not buying the place outright in the first instance, which led later to some tense negotiations over the lease, they got everything right. They had no trouble filling it either, Reiss engineering it all with energy and proficiency. They extended the festival to twenty-four days, up from twelve, then reduced it to seventeen in 1972, which it remains to this day. There was a fair assortment of Britten works to sample: the Maltings hosted *The Golden Vanity* – the boys in striped jerseys and unconvincing Abraham Lincoln beards – the Piano Concerto, *Spring Symphony, Canticle I, Introduction and Rondo alla Burlesca* and *Mazurka Elegiaca* (performed by Richter and Britten) and a new Colin Graham production of *A Midsummer Night's Dream*, with the young James Bowman and Margaret Price as Oberon and Tytania. Away from Snape there were outings for *A Ceremony of Carols, Six Metamorphoses after Ovid* and *The Burning Fiery Furnace*. There was the music of Britten's heroes too: Bridge, Mozart and Mahler, and a new version of Purcell's *The Fairy Queen*, a nice counterpoint to Britten's own opera on the subject. There were also one-act operas commissioned from Berkeley and Walton, an old debt being repaid to the former, a polite handshake for the latter. And for the first time in over ten years, Britten and Pears performed Schubert's *Die schöne Müllerin*, filling the Maltings when once they would have had to make do with the Jubilee Hall.

Naturally there were those who regretted the festival's expansion, those who thought the intimacy gone, that the town had lost its cultural core. But no musician who had ever struggled with the inadequacies of the Jubilee Hall, and none now in thrall to the glorious acoustic of the Maltings, regretted the change. Britten of course hoped to retain the qualities that had made the festival special; he was also determined it would not become too fashionable, too like Glyndebourne. Yet he knew things would change, not least aesthetically: he anticipated a 'new open-stage technique of opera production' evolving in the Maltings, and he cast his eye over some of the other disused buildings on the site: 'some new need will become apparent, and we'll have to expand some more'. The festival finally had shoes worth filling.

They were captivated by quite another hall later in the year. Following EOG performances in Montreal in September and recitals in New York – their first there in almost twenty years ('A curtain will be drawn over my old enemy New York') – Britten and Pears embarked on a British Council recital tour through South America. They experienced the dull, permanent rain and stunning waterfalls of southern Chile and the religious parades in Guadalajara, replete with brass bands, fireworks and a portable Virgin Mary carried through the streets on a platter.

They visited pyramids in the countryside, those strange, alluring symbols of Mayan civilization. They were overwhelmed by the city of Cuzco, originally the capital of the Inca Empire, and looked on, transfixed, as locals dotted the silver beach of Copacabana at night with candles and flowers in praise of one deity or another. Britten disliked the altitude at times, his heart pumping away ineffectively he thought, and spent some of the trip in bed, throwing back antibiotics and missing an orchestral concert of his music in São Paulo. But in Buenos Aires, in the magical Teatro Colón, they performed Purcell, together with *Michelangelo Sonnets*, *Winter Words* and *Sechs Hölderlin-Fragmente*. Pears whispered his way through the last verse of an unaccompanied encore, 'I wonder as I wander', his sound filling the enormous hall, enhanced by the auditorium's acoustic wizardry.

South America inspired all sorts of ghosts and superstitions. Britten dreamed that the Red House had burned or fallen down, or that he died and left the festival without a leader, or that he was in Vienna on a bus and Schubert asked him to pay his fare. Yet somewhere between the graphic dreams and dreary receptions, between the many concerts and constant travelling, he gave shape in his mind to *The Prodigal Son*. Back in Aldeburgh, after a shattering performance of *War Requiem* in Ypres ('You can imagine one's feelings – especially at the Menin Gate, with the names of 55,000 British soldiers just missing'), he set to work.

Plomer and Britten identified more of Auden's 'parable-art' in this story than in its two predecessors. 'With its unforgettable climax of reward and rejoicing lavished not upon virtuous correctness but upon a sinner,' Plomer wrote in the 1968 programme book, 'this parable celebrates the triumph of forgiveness.' Pears was given the role of Tempter, a Nick Shadow character not present in the biblical version, who entices the boy away from his mundane life tilling his father's land, into all sorts of villainy. He is essentially the Younger Son's inner voice, and the boy himself is a kind of gullible Albert Herring, losing all his money to harlots and gamblers and drunks. Holed up once more in Venice in January 1968 to work on the piece, Britten conjured great lines and colours for the crooks and pimps. As in *The Burning Fiery Furnace*, there is an oriental feeling to this music of abandonment, a slightly troubling association, but there is an attractive lushness to it – not least the trumpet, which riffs away above the texture as though in a smoky jazz club, much as Britten had evoked it almost thirty years earlier in his incidental score to *Johnson over Jordan*. The moment the Tempter reveals his hand is sudden, hard and bitter: 'I have broken up that family / Before your eyes'. The young lad falls first into despair and then gritty resolution, his words tacked to a plaintive viola line.

The climax is not as unforgettable as Plomer claimed, a gilded celebration of a father's forgiveness: 'He was dead, and is alive again, / Was lost, and is found.' This may be because sickness intervened. Britten had filled his time in Venice with the usual visitors and excursions, but it was desperately cold: he traipsed around the city after lunch, eyes streaming, nose red, looking at paintings, and returned to the warm apartment to play through the morning's work on the Palazzo Mocenigo's rickety piano. Pears was there looking after him, allowing him to work uninterrupted each morning, as was Marion, Mary Potter (painting away contentedly), Rosamund Strode and finally Donald Mitchell, a welcome male presence by then, Britten thought. But back in Aldeburgh in February, with Pears on tour in America with Julian Bream, he was put to bed for a week with high temperatures, sweats and delirium. It was more serious than a cold and fever, however. 'They discovered the bug quite soon – our old friend streptococcus back again – but this time finding out an old weakness in the heart, so it had to be stamped on violently, and at once,' he told Mayer. A specialist diagnosed bacterial endocarditis, the inner tissues of the heart inflamed. His heart had been poor in childhood, friends reasoned, perhaps even congenitally defective; he was vulnerable to this sullen reprise. Britten was admitted immediately to Ipswich Hospital and remained for a month, unable to work on the last quarter of *The Prodigal Son*. 'It is sickening that it had to be the most difficult & important bit of the whole work which remained to be done,' he told Plomer at the end of April, but could at least report that the piece was now finished.

He composed the difficult section of the Parable as he slowly recovered, his body pumped full of penicillin, his mood low, time against him. It is something of a damp squib. The music is not quite ecstatic enough, not transformative in any way, which would have underlined the power of the old man's forgiveness – the crux of this piece of 'parable-art'. Even the jealous Elder Son soon joins the party, meekly compliant in the face of his father's authority and generosity, the moment of rebellion and then grace playing for little. 'I *hope* it's all right,' Britten told Plomer, 'worthy of the wonderful subject & you, but under the circumstances

I've done all I can & I hope you & God will forgive any inadequacies (of which I fear there are many).'

Following the premiere of *The Prodigal Son* in June 1968, Peter Heyworth put his finger on what he thought the problem with the three Church Parables. 'Somehow the props ... the village church at twilight, the hooded monks, the plainsong ... finally seem more theatrical than conventional theatre, and the other-worldliness they evoke less a confrontation with the world than a germ-free refuge from it.' The exaggerated physical poses, the single set, the narrative device whereby visiting monks arrive in the local church to tell a story, disrobing and putting on colourful costumes to this end – all of this was strangely artificial. 'In the twenty-four years I knew Benjamin Britten,' Colin Graham later wrote, 'I directed seventeen of his nineteen stage works: of those seventeen I collaborated closely with him on fifteen, including eight of the last nine premieres.' Yet Graham was not a brilliantly imaginative director. He was thoughtful, keen, diligent, but so too was he conservative in his taste and aesthetic, controlling in a sometimes pedantic, superficial way (directing singers to move on this note or that word), and not blessed with a sense of humour. 'The problem with you,' the director Peter Hall once told him, 'is that your style of stage direction is nothing more than superior stage management, and what you need to do is to go out and learn something about style.' This is what critic Tom Sutcliffe meant in his *Times* obituary. 'Graham often claimed to be putting the music first – but did not see the corollary might be that the staging would come some way behind.' Graham's conservative qualities endeared his work to Britten, who appreciated his unquestioning, unfussy loyalty, but his productions were often cold and passionless. They also ensured that their new style of theatre, and the one to come, was half-cocked at best. And once more Britten was directing his energies away from the main stage into works that today are relatively obscure.

12

Britten was featured composer in the Edinburgh Festival in August 1968. Over the two weeks, works old and new were presented: *Spring Symphony*, the Violin Concerto (with Menuhin), *Cantata misericordium* (with Pears and Fischer-Dieskau), *Peter Grimes*, *The Prodigal Son* and *The Burning Fiery Furnace*, the Sonata for cello and two cello suites (Rostropovich admiring the second, which Britten completed a year earlier, even more than the first), *Songs and Proverbs of William Blake*, *War Requiem* (Vishnevskaya), *Sinfonietta*, *Winter Words* and the Piano Concerto (Peter Frankl replacing an indisposed Richter). There was also a performance of *Winterreise*, Britten's playing darkening and deepening with time, Culshaw thought. It was an extraordinary scrapbook of his life: his evolving musical language, his political and artistic obsessions, and the performers who meant so much to him all there, remarkably well preserved.

The weather was Edinburgh-in-August unpredictable, and the Soviet invasion of Czechoslovakia weighed heavily on their minds. But in the largish house they shared with the Mitchells (Britten and Pears in separate rooms) and in various restaurants nearby, they splashed back liberal quantities of Laphroaig and supped on duck, coddled eggs or asparagus soup, toasting friendship and music along the way. Rostropovich would reply, raising his glass to friends of Ben and Peter, 'because the friends declare the man', and they would all toast the 'survival of art despite political and national differences'. Kathleen Mitchell was able to watch both men closely and described Pears as a kind, noble person, immersed in the *Confessions* of St Augustine (approving of his prayer to be 'continent', as he recited it, 'but not yet'), performing every second or third day, and looking after Britten at every turn. 'He is never over fussy or obtrusive, but is ever there, as a guardian angel, alert & responsive.' Despite the attention and enthusiastic audiences, Britten returned to Aldeburgh with relief; this type of music-making, if not necessarily on this scale, was what his own festival offered, and he did not need to travel to Edinburgh for the honour.

There were other opportunities close to hand. The proximity of the Maltings to the Red House meant Britten became interested in recording large-scale works by other composers, which formerly would have detained him in London, sulking in Islington (their base in the capital from 1965), between sessions. Over coming years he put down Bach's *Brandenburg Concertos* and *St John Passion*, Purcell's *The Fairy Queen*, the strange, magical world of Schumann's *Szenen aus Goethes Faust*, and Elgar's *Dream of Gerontius* – Pears a noble old man en route to Purgatory, with promises of greater things to come. ('Remember to keep your eyes closed reverently,' Britten sagely advised when Pears performed the piece in late March 1968.) They are luscious performances that tick along as logically as Britten's own piano recordings, infused with freedom and tenderness, each piece of the puzzle carefully buffed before being put in place.

There was another great opportunity close by. Britten's thoughts about television had fermented ever since the *Billy Budd* screening: with Culshaw's move from Decca to BBC Television in 1967, similar projects were discussed with greater urgency. In September 1967, in the boomy splendour of Long Melford church, Britten recorded Bach's *Christmas Oratorio* for BBC Colour TV. And in the following year's festival Culshaw installed in the Maltings a sling of television cameras, invisible to the paying public, to film an all-Tchaikovsky programme that included the *Romeo and Juliet* overture and Rostropovich performing *Variations on a Rococo Theme*. More than a million people saw the concert on television: Britten was now fully alert to the medium's potential.

Thus in early 1969 the Maltings was transformed into a giant television studio for the filming of *Peter Grimes*. A platform was erected high on scaffolding at the rear of the hall, large enough to house a full orchestra. Beneath it cameras and booms, tracks and cables were put in place. On stage Culshaw and his team recreated Crabbe's Borough as best they could. Britten sat over it all, high on the orchestra platform, as though king of some dark troll world; it was only the second time he ever conducted the piece, he remarked with astonishment to a friend. The set-up was Britten's idea and Culshaw's compromise: it would avoid the split studios common in British opera films and circumvent the Continent's pre-recorded, badly mimed versions. Britten's long-time collaborator Basil Coleman fell victim to the compromise; he simply could not envisage how such a large score could be filmed in this manner and for a while remained outside the constellation.

In his mad scene Pears is a crazed, frightened Magwitch, and absolutely convincing filmed so close, with no footlights to hide behind. Throughout, he sounds radiant, so inside his own voice, so aware of every nuance, every sleight of hand. In 'The Great Bear' he floats above the texture, a dreamy, magnetic visionary. The film was a much bigger undertaking than *Budd* and not everyone came out of it as well as Pears. The whole show wears the traces of its principal compromise: it is neither fish nor fowl, neither great television nor compelling theatre, and was not a success with audiences or critics.

Britten had thought about composing an opera especially for television long before the success or otherwise of the *Grimes* venture was known (*Noye's Fludde* was originally intended for television). His eye was on another Henry James story, 'Owen Wingrave', first published in 1892 in *The Graphic*, 'a superior illustrated weekly newspaper' established to take on the mighty *Illustrated London News*. It is the sort of story he had long been drawn to. A young pacifist soldier decides he can no longer support the military life that has pulsed through his family's veins for generations. General Sir Philip Wingrave mistakes his grandson's courage for weakness and disinherits him, while Owen's haughty fiancée goads him into sleeping in a reputedly haunted room in the house to prove his bravery. Two of his ancestors died in the room, a father who struck and killed his son for not defending family honour in a schoolboy scrap, only to end up the next day dead himself, the cause unknown. Owen accepts the challenge, but is later discovered dead inside the room, without a mark on his body. His fiancée and family are left rehearsing their culpability.

Myfanwy Piper began sketching ideas for the libretto in early 1968, though the project was not publicly announced until March 1969. The *Grimes* filming changed everything: Britten junked much of what Piper had written, certain that a more theatrical form of opera was needed, not a cinematic version doing its best to conform to the generic expectations of television. 'I am convinced – and this comes from my recent television experience – that the audience needs the tunes, it needs the lyricism of the aria and the ensemble, rather than the realistic side of perpetual recitative.' The BBC stumped up £10,000 for the commission – a good amount, if not quite rivalling Stravinky's fee for *The Rake's Progress* – and with the *Grimes* film in the can, the set-up at the Maltings a success as far as the composer was concerned, Britten launched himself on his first major opera since *A Midsummer Night's Dream*. With Piper his collaborator and the theme so close to his heart, he anticipated a smooth run.

Then catastrophe. Late on the opening day of the 1969 festival a farmer's son left the Crown pub in Snape as last orders were called and noticed a dull red halo circling the Maltings, distinct against the black night: the concert hall was on fire. The alarm was raised and bit by bit fire crews and locals spilled onto the grounds to save what they could. Festival personnel were in Aldeburgh at a performance in the Jubilee

Hall and by the time Reiss arrived on site, the roof had crashed to the ground, tiles cracking in flames that spewed high above the building, the noise and destruction ghastly. It was probably the consequence of a carelessly discarded cigarette-end or faulty wiring, not the more sinister conspiracies about arson that emerged in the following days and months. There was nothing Reiss could do, so he made the frantic trip back into Aldeburgh to break the news. Britten took it calmly (far more so than Derek Sugden, who equated it with losing a child), his hyper-practical brain immediately turning to the new venues into which they needed to shoehorn works during the three-week festival – a huge undertaking given how pivotal the Maltings had become in just two years.

In the morning he went with Pears to survey the wreckage, clambering over the site as he had done so happily only a few years earlier, a sober figure in jacket and knitted tie, a worried expression on his face. He encountered a scene from the Blitz: twisted metal limbs, charred wooden beams, shards of tiling flung in all directions over the muddy ground, stage lights still in place but now burned out, bobbies patrolling the shell. Britten's precious Steinway, on which the previous day he had given a towering performance of Schubert's 'Trout' Quintet with members of the Amadeus Quartet and bassist Adrian Beers, was there in the rubble, its frame a misshapen wreck, its casing and honey-coloured soundboard charcoal, like the roof. Yet the walls remained intact, 'these marvellous brick walls . . . which have contributed so much to . . . the beauty of the sound', as Britten told a BBC reporter. And not for a minute did he think the hall would not be rebuilt. People have come 'to love it as we have ourselves. It's become a part of our family.' Sugden joined the two on site, marvelling at their upbeat manner, disarmed though by their determination to start the rebuilding project the next day. 'Exactly as it was?' enquired Sugden. 'Oh yes, exactly,' responded Britten. 'Well, Ben, just one or two little things . . .' added Pears, as was his wont. And then they got on with the festival.

13

As the 1960s drew to a close Britten despaired at how little time he had for everything he needed to do. He seemed invincible in the days and weeks following the disaster at Snape, holding a press conference to announce the Snape Maltings Rebuilding Fund, improvising a new staging for Mozart's *Idomeneo* in Blythburgh church, the singers getting dressed in a hastily erected marquee. But as summer passed, the reality of all the begging letters and gracious acknowledgements he had to write sank in. He signed over the commissioning fee for *Wingrave* to the fund; it was an automatic gesture, one he could afford (his gross income in 1968–9 was a little under £69,000*), yet was generous nonetheless. By October he was back in the studio, recording *The Golden Vanity* and *Children's Crusade*, the same month in which he conducted *Lucretia* at Sadler's Wells; soon after he left with Pears for America and a recital tour that would help fund the rebuilding. There was insurance cover, but he was determined to raise £200,000 or more to effect the greater changes to the site he and Pears had for two years been imagining, determined also to fund an endowment to rid the festival of its perpetual money worries. Then, of course, there were the works to which he was committed – *Owen Wingrave* chief among them – and which he could not allow to be elbowed to one side by his other responsibilities. 'Because after all, one's main job *is* to write music, and one also mustn't sort of get ill by betraying one's real self.' Yet in America he looked dreadful, his face a sullen *Carnevale* mask, his hair thick with grey, appearing every bit as ill as he was determined not to be.

Children's Crusade (and the work that followed it, *Who are these Children?*) occupies a landscape even blacker than that of its stablemate, *The Golden Vanity*. It was composed to mark the fiftieth anniversary of Save the Children Fund, which was celebrated a matter of weeks before the fire. Scored for boys' voices, two pianos, organ and a whole artillery of percussion instruments, *Children's Crusade* is hardly celebratory in character, yet this setting of Brecht was oddly suited to the occasion. Britten had long admired the story and its author, witnessing a performance of *Mutter Courage und ihre Kinder* in Zurich after the war, starring Therese Giehse, which had astonished him.

The ballad tells the sorry tale of fifty-odd Polish children wandering from the wreckage of their villages in the early months of the Second World War, their parents dead, their siblings missing. In parody of adulthood they elect a leader, storm a shack looking for food or shelter, and catch a mangy dog with a plan to eat him, later sending him off with a

* £940,000 today.

pathetic note tied to his neck pleading for help. They fight with rival children, before conducting a trial and a funeral, Protestants, Catholics and Nazis consigning one poor boy to a shallow grave, the cause of death hinted at but not revealed. They trudge through the snow, wearily following their leader who knows no more than they do how to get to peace and safety. 'Had people who cuffed them for stealing / Offered them shelter instead!' But they are offered no shelter and somewhere along the grim pilgrimage they starve to death.

The work is full of the musical language of the Church Parables. The accompaniment seems detached from the angular vocal lines, sounding more like a blacksmith's workshop than an orchestra, a jangling smithy's anvil in the mix. There is the occasional dog bark, and the gang's drummer-boy gets a good beat going until his mates shout him down, but the texture is brittle, the mood unremittingly chilly. Following its premiere in London's St Paul's Cathedral on 19 May 1969, Britten himself called it a grisly work, observing that 'the boys (singing & hitting) made a tremendous impression of passion & sincerity alongside the assinine pomposity of the established church!'

A month or so after Britten finished it, Donald Mitchell gave him Frank Kendon's 1930 memoir *The Small Years*, which recounts a utopian rural childhood in touching detail. 'It is really a most extraordinarily vivid re-living of early childhood, & you are right in thinking that it would mean a lot to me,' Britten responded. 'It is strange how strong a feeling one has for those "small years".' He cited other books that provoked in him such feelings for his childhood, among them *David Copperfield* and *Bevis: The Story of a Boy*, an adventure about a well-to-do lad and his best friend who build rafts and re-enact famous historical battles, both of them on the cusp of adulthood but still captivated by the rough and tumble of adolescence.

It was a long time since Britten had created such happy, confident childhoods in his own works. *Who are these Children?*, the song cycle he composed while plotting the concert hall's rebuilding and scratching at the libretto for *Owen Wingrave*, is no exception. It takes its title from one of the twelve William Soutar lyrics, rhymes and riddles Britten finally settled on for the cycle. In the title poem, impoverished village children look on uncomprehending as landed gentlefolk – the men in scarlet coats, women wearing blood-red lipstick – ride to hunt, impervious to the world at war around them. The children – and those in a later poem who lie dead on the road, victims of enemy bombing, an air-raid siren wailing incessantly if impotently in the piano – are close relatives of the Polish refugees of the earlier work. And when in the later poem Britten sets the line 'The blood of children corrupts the hearts of men', the piano gurgling away in the background, he establishes his credo. 'I become frightfully angry when children are treated badly,' he told a journalist on his American tour only months later, though such feeling was obvious in his works from the past two decades.

Sidney Nolan captured this dark aspect of Britten's work in a series of illustrations for a limited facsimile edition of the *Children's Crusade* composition draft. There is a stark beauty to the pictures, which plot the ultimately futile journey of the children. Their bodies are amorphous, a finger-daub of paint for trousers, their eyes strangely haunting. The pack leader has an old face, the Nazi kid a sinister death mask, the boy in the velvet collar a drawn, sickly mien. And in the final illustration the thin dog limps across the page, the note around its neck ('The dog knows the way'), while the spirits of the dead children float above. They are equally mesmerizing and repellent.

Other spirits haunt the illustrations, for Nolan, like Britten, visited a concentration camp after the war. At the behest of the *Observer*, he travelled to Auschwitz in 1960 to do some drawings, and was overwhelmed by the experience, the camp bearing the weight of so much death. He discussed it with Britten and they forged another bond, this time over the darkest moment in modern European history.

In spring 1970 the EOG toured to Australia to perform the Church Parables in the Adelaide Festival alongside some recitals and concerts. They flew the long journey in fits and starts: Adaban, Bombay, Ceylon, Singapore, Perth then Adelaide, each stop linked on their route map by looping arcs. Despairing at the receptions and anything to do with officialdom, Britten observed that 'this side of Australian life is a nightmare of snobbishness & quasi-Edwardian grand formality'. They thought the Adelaide Festival a hopeless jumble served up to nice but naive audiences, slow in their applause.

The most compelling reason for flying halfway around the globe ('Fill yourself up to the top and get poured onto the plane' was Britten's generic approach to air travel) was not the Adelaide Festival or the recitals in New Zealand, but rather the outback travelling planned with the Australian Nolan and his wife, Cynthia. Peg Hesse, now a widow, joined them on their travels. There were claims on their time in various cities, of course, and they enjoyed a visit to Green Island, a nascent resort on the Great Barrier Reef with an underwater observatory, where they marvelled at the huge coral, lethal stingray and clams the size of a coffee table. But it was the outback that allured them. At Ayers Rock (now Uluru) and other sacred indigenous sites, the friends felt the low hum of millennia-old spirituality, the rock full of significance and folklore (their 'St Peter's Rome', Britten told a young friend). In Alice Springs Britten saw some beautiful Aboriginal boys, gracefully moving against the pink landscape, the heat shimmering around them. 'Isn't that marvellous?' he said to Nolan. By a sacred water hole at Mount Olga (now Kata Tjuta), the silence overwhelming, Britten said, 'Australia hasn't made a sound yet.' It was not meant in the way visiting Europeans usually make the observation, startled by the continent's bush light and silence. These were early days in the Western appreciation of indigenous Australian art and songlines, before Prime Minister Gough Whitlam's attempts at *rapprochement* between white and black Australia; Europeans simply did not know much about the continent's indigenous peoples and history (Australians not much more).

But they felt they knew all too much about their own continent. Britten confided in Nolan during the trip that he thought Western civilization in crisis, its destiny inevitably tragic, and could only admire the Aboriginals who 'had for 40,000 years kept a harmony with the continent and kept a discipline and hadn't gone to war or anything like that'. On a tin plane flying to Cairns, three brandies under their belts, the two talked about collaborating on a ballet based on the indigenous boys they had seen, exploring the harmony these boys had with their land. Britten would contrast them with an English boy of the same age, the teenage Piers Dunkerley on his mind. There would be a tragic ending for the English boy – sad after so much promise and opportunity – and a sort of *Zauberflöte* transformation for the Aboriginal story.

Britten chatted away boyishly, as he had often done when encountering a new story or poem, whether it be Rimbaud or Owen or Crabbe. But as they prepared to land he shrugged off his excitement. 'Well, that's the end of that. When we get back to England I won't be like that any more. My destiny is to be in harness and to die in harness. There won't be any more of that.' And there was not, though Nolan sketched a synopsis for the ballet – detailing dawn light and sand hills and bird-calls and mystical ceremonies – and embarked on a series of exquisite artworks based on their discussion. Britten went as far as mentioning the idea to Covent Garden, but no further.

It was Nolan's second near miss on similar terrain. In 1963 he had attempted to interest Britten in a grand work for the opening of the Sydney Opera House: an opera with his music, Australian author Patrick White's words, and Nolan's designs. In the late 1940s Nolan became captivated with the story of Englishwoman Eliza Fraser, who was aboard her husband's ship when it was wrecked on a coral reef on the north-eastern coast of Australia. Local Aborigines captured them when they landed their leaky longboat on a large sandy island. They were stripped naked and forced into slavery, Captain Fraser hunting with the indigenous men, Eliza digging for roots with the women. The captain was eventually speared, his wife a witness. A motley crew of soldiers and convicts from the mainland, who had heard of her predicament, eventually rescued her. To an Australian, this is the narrative of the country's violent European origins; in one of Nolan's paintings Eliza is a faceless animal, stripped bare, her body wildly contorted, the landscape harsh, unsparing. To Britten, it was an unsympathetic tale. At the best of times he did not like to receive a synopsis on spec, so in the interval of a concert at Melford Hall in mid-September – his fiftieth birthday celebrations around the corner, *Curlew River* as yet unwritten – Britten had wearily told Nolan and White of the myriad projects that would make his involvement impossible. 'Don't you have control of your own life?' White asked tactlessly, which of course killed the proposed collaboration on the spot.

After his return from Australia, Britten asked Nolan for a memento of the country, the ballet idea and the beautiful boys in Alice Springs. In mixed media Nolan created a hunched Aboriginal boy in profile, an arm-like boomerang tracing his torso and calves as though painted on his body in chalky pigment, his shadowy face like those in the *Children's Crusade* illustrations. It is a stunning, haunted work, belonging neither to the tradition of the noble-savage artwork of colonial Australia, nor the watery landscapes of Aboriginal artist Albert Namatjira, nor the indigenous dot-paintings (never portraiture, such are Aboriginal beliefs) that would explode in popularity later in the decade. He sent it to Britten and Pears at the Red House in late 1971, where it still hangs.

True to his word, Britten returned from Australia and immersed himself in *Owen Wingrave*. He enjoyed the thematic overlaps with his earlier Henry James opera – the innocent young protagonists in each, the sudden spectral denouement and hint of remorse to come – but shied away from the earlier work's architectural technique of theme and variations (though both pieces employ twelve-note motifs). For all his thoughts about theatricalizing the televisual conventions, Britten and Piper enjoyed the potential for quick-fire dialogue, rapid fades between characters and scenes, and portraying the passage of time. It is a hybrid work and was thus vulnerable to exactly the compromises of the *Peter Grimes* film. Mitchell later thought many of the *Grimes* problems should have been laid at the feet of Culshaw, whom he considered greatly out of his depth in the visual medium. Culshaw bowed to Britten's demands instead of standing by the experienced Basil Coleman, with his list of legitimate concerns. The film ended up being directed almost by committee. This time round Coleman was barely even considered; Culshaw selected cinematographer Brian Large (who had co-directed the *Grimes* film with Joan Cross), which Britten eventually countered by insisting on splitting the role with Colin Graham, a foil for Large, whose lack of experience with singers concerned the composer. Coleman was understandably hurt – 'we won't & mustn't let an artistic difference of opinion break an old & valuable friendship, will we? must we?' appealed Britten.

The repercussions from this one decision were many, but they had no bearing on the composition of the nuanced *Wingrave*. Piper assembled a good prose libretto from a fairly ordinary shilling ghost story. Britten composed a beguiling score, completing it in August 1970, which he infused not with the musical language of *The Turn of the Screw* but with that of even earlier, seemingly unrelated works. The trudging third interlude, which follows on from Owen's passionate avowal to break the cycle of military death and hollow glory that his family represents (at Agincourt, Lucknow and Waterloo, his father killed by a sabre cut, his fiancée's father and uncle 'slaughtered while the empty banners flew'), is close in spirit to the Passacaglia in *Peter Grimes*, its melody later stripped of ornament for the ballad that opens Act 2. The quasi-funeral march following Owen's disinheriting is related to the marches

Britten wrote in the 1930s and 1940s, giddy on Mahler. The cross-fades between characters, in which individual thoughts about Owen's treachery are articulated, are no more elaborate than the Threnody in *Albert Herring*, where the villagers grieve with Mrs Herring for her missing son; and the score is full of other sounds straight from *Billy Budd*. After the dramatic and musical developments of the 1960s – the threadbare textures and the somewhat artificial theatrical conventions of the Church Parables – *Wingrave* is an unexpected if welcome throwback.

It was not only his desire for set pieces in the film – this 'knife-edged balance between the photograph, the picture . . . and also the musical excitement' – that pushed him in this direction. The opera would be seen by millions of people and he wanted it to be an encapsulation of his lifelong pacifistic convictions – even more so than *War Requiem*, the success of which had caught him by surprise. Here he knew what he was doing. And it is as though in reaching back to his youthful conscience and convictions, imagining himself in Owen's shoes, refusing to participate in the war machine, he was also reaching back to more youthful music. This was the pacifist Britten of *Sinfonia da Requiem* and *Peter Grimes* and *The Holy Sonnets of John Donne*, contemptuous of the opposing argument. It was the boy Britten turning his back on soldiers at London's Hyde Park Barracks, as Owen does when he encounters the Horse Guards early in the opera, imagining them in a bloody battle instead of trotting peacefully through Kensington Gardens. The mundane domestic setting of *Owen Wingrave* somehow made it more authentic than the high ritual of *War Requiem*.

Britten and Piper made a few false steps, some of which remained uncorrected. Sir Philip, with his 'smouldering eye, red-rimmed with the glint of far-off battles', in Owen's words, is a pantomime villain, rattling around in his study and vocal chords. (Colin Matthews thought Sir Philip's clattering lines might even have been intended as a parody of some of Pears's later mannerisms, though this seems uncharacteristically cruel.*) The scene in which he berates his grandson, offstage, his furious, clipped, empty phrases filling the house, makes him seem

---

* This aspect of Pears's singing is what Dudley Moore mercilessly and uncannily parodied in his *Beyond the Fringe* performance of a 'setting by Benjamin Britten of an old English air, "Little Miss Muffett"'. It concludes with a vocal flourish that could be from *Serenade*.

46. Carpenter Len Edwards tests the acoustic of Snape Maltings Concert Hall for the first time, May 1967. Britten is captivated, Pears delighted.

47. The Queen opens the new hall, 2 June 1967.

48. Leaving the
Concertgebouw in
Amsterdam following
the premiere of
Spring Symphony,
14 July 1949.

49. Acknowledging applause
after a performance of *War
Requiem* at the Berlin
Staatsoper, 5 January 1968.

50. The composer's hand: Britten's feathery composition sketch of the opening bars of
A Midsummer Night's Dream.

51. Britten perched high on scaffolding in the Maltings for the filming of *Peter Grimes*, early 1969.

52. Britten and Pears climbing through the wreckage of the Maltings on 8 June 1969, following the calamitous fire after the opening night of the festival.

53. 'The boy, Tadzio, shall inspire me.' Robert Huguenin as Tadzio and Pears as Aschenbach in the first production of *Death in Venice*, the Maltings, June 1973.

54. A frail Britten in the library at the Red House, watched over by his stalwart nurse Rita Thomson, 19 December 1974.

55. Welcoming the Queen Mother, the patron of the Aldeburgh Festival, to lunch in June 1975.

56. On the balcony of the Hotel Danieli during the final trip to Venice, November 1975.

57. Rehearsals for *Phaedra*,
June 1976. Britten and
Janet Baker sit together,
Colin Matthews behind.

58. Baron Britten of Aldeburgh in the County of Suffolk. The garden party
at the Red House on 12 June 1976 to celebrate Britten's life peerage.

59. Britten and Pears in Bergen, July 1976, escaping the stifling English
summer, five months before the composer's death.

ridiculous. All the women are ghastly, bar the sympathetic Mrs Coyle, wife of Owen's military instructor. Owen's fiancée and her mother, and his thin-lipped aunt, speak in awful military clichés. 'Why do you tremble like a boy, the first time in the field?' Kate asks Owen near his and the opera's end. Or Miss Wingrave, observing of Owen's father: 'He laid down his life for Queen and country, something it seems you do not care to do', which is fairly close to what was said in 1941 about Britten in the *Sunday Times*. But these are small points in the face of so much inventiveness, so much sly recapitulation.

The only flaw that cannot be brushed aside is the weak denouement. It has none of the cumulative power of *The Turn of the Screw* or the understated pathos of *Peter Grimes*. It is a little like the climax of *The Prodigal Son*, which passes for nothing and leaves the audience cheated of a showdown. It is not that Britten did not try to set up a cumulative ending: the scene in which Owen is locked in the haunted room plays out gradually over the course of a passacaglia, one that underpins some lyrical vocal lines and virtuosic instrumental obbligatos. But this fizzes out amid Kate's sobbing explanation of what has happened and the arrival of Sir Philip, who pushes open the door to discover Owen's body, the rest of the cast frozen in a postcard pose. Another of Britten's narrators then reprises the Act 2 ballad, and the audience is left furious that the handsome, idealistic visionary cannot hit even one of these immovable cardboard targets.

Pears knew the ending was weak and suggested he utter the words 'My boy!' on arriving outside the room. It did not change much. But the disappointing ending cannot disguise the sheer quality of *Owen Wingrave*. Its natural companion is not *The Turn of the Screw* but *Billy Budd*. Both title characters are fundamentally good people – secular prophets, almost – brought down by social conventions. It does not matter that one is a warrior, the other a pacifist, for *Wingrave* is a land-bound *Budd*, a drawing-room naval battle. Some commentators have argued that it is another coming-out tale, that Owen has identified not solely his beliefs but also his sexuality. There is none of this in the story, however: the opera drips with first-principle hatred of war. Owen's 'peace aria' is an intense and potent declaration: 'In peace I have found my image, I have found myself.' And Britten makes sure none of its purpose is lost: the aria slowly unravels like a spool, the vocal line gripping, the accompaniment made up of *Budd*-like primary chords with a tinkling music-box adornment. It is breathtaking.

All this makes the opera's neglect today so unfortunate. Most probably it was tainted by its first cramped and stilted production. The Maltings, new and improved by the time of the 1970 festival (and opened once more by the Queen, Britten conducting scenes from *Gloriana* with great subtlety, sweat pouring off his puffy cheeks, his head surprisingly buried in the score, Pears an ageing Essex by his side), was again transformed into a giant marionette theatre, Britten in heavy glasses and a sour mood pulling the strings. The filming was a miserable experience. Benjamin Luxon (Owen), Janet Baker (Kate) and Nigel Douglas (Lechmere) all thought they were too old for their parts, especially the unforgiving close-ups, and they had a point: in the James novella these three are in their late teens; in real life they were thirty-three, thirty-seven and forty-one respect-ively. Britten was recovering from a hernia operation and handed rehearsals over to Steuart Bedford. And as with so many of his opera productions outside the aegis of the EOG (and some within), the com-poser fell out with most of his colleagues. The BBC's byzantine workings and relative lack of experience in televising opera infuriated him, though it is just as likely he was cross with himself for rejecting Coleman. Armed with final approval in his contract, Britten insisted on reshooting various scenes, which brought the process to a showdown. Yet even with the reshoots the film looks cluttered, its direction clunky. Britten thought any problems in the perception or structure of the stillborn opera would be solved on stage at Covent Garden a little over two years later, which was not, alas, the case. But by then he had more urgent things on his mind.

Late

8

Der Abschied

Aldeburgh, Horham, 1971–1976

I

'In the history of art,' observed the philosopher Theodor Adorno mischievously, 'late works are the catastrophes.' Not disasters: catastrophes – a spectacular subversion of an artist's oeuvre, all within the context of a sense of mortality overtaking the individual. The final period is necessarily ruptured from the earlier: carefully sculptured works of youth and maturity make way for pieces branded with tears and fissures as proof of a recklessness or powerlessness in the face of inevitable demise. Edward Said thought Adorno viewed Beethoven's late works as a form of exile, a conscious decision by the composer to abandon his easy rapport with audiences, establishing instead a hostile, alienated relationship. Said developed Adorno's idea into a wider argument about artists 'whose work expresses lateness through the peculiarities of its style'. He was intrigued by the 'late style' of Thomas Mann, Jean Genet, C. P. Cavafy and Giuseppe Tomasi di Lampedusa, author of the wondrous novel *The Leopard*. What Said sought was not harmony and resolution, but the intransigence Adorno identified in Beethoven, the 'unresolved contradiction'.

Britten would not normally have had much truck with these ideas. Yet in 1964 he identified just such a trend in Schubert's music, an inexplicable shift in the last year or so of his life, when syphilis was draining him of his health. Arguably the 'richest and most productive eighteen months in our music history', Britten proposed, followed Beethoven's death in March 1827 and culminated in Schubert's demise at the tragically young age of thirty-one in November 1828. It was 'the period in which Franz Schubert wrote his *Winterreise*, the C major Symphony, his last three piano sonatas, the C major String Quintet, as well as a dozen other glorious pieces. The creation of these works in that space of time seems hardly credible; but the standard of inspiration, of magic, is miraculous and past all explanation.' Schubert knew he had never composed better, knew that with Beethoven in his grave the mantle of greatest composer in the world was his alone, and time was short.

Britten had none of Schubert's certainty in the early 1970s, a time of low artistic confidence. Nor did he have Schubert's sense of mortality, his doctors having advised that the penicillin he took in 1968 had done the trick. His music at the beginning of this decade did not represent a rupture with the past. *Owen Wingrave* contains the Church Parables' freedom of rhythmic notation and exploitation of heterophony (the technique in which a melody is played simultaneously with a variant of itself, like a genetic mutation), even if its strongest connection is to the more extrovert works of the 1950s. If there was a marked shift in style in Britten's career it had been in the austere works that followed *War Requiem*, but, aged only fifty when these works began to emerge, and with health and medicine on his side, he was young for a 'late style'.

Lateness is not solely about technique or reaching a specific age, however, but about an urgency that takes over when an artist recognizes his time is soon up. It is the Verdi of the late-bloom *Otello* and *Falstaff*, Beethoven of the *Missa solemnis* (the subject of much of Adorno's theorizing), the elderly Richard Strauss writing works of pain and valediction. And it is Mozart in his final year, producing two extraordinary string quintets, concertos for piano and clarinet, *Die Zauberflöte* and *La clemenza di Tito*, and the incomplete *Requiem*.

Britten was too young to think this way in the 1960s. He was still too young at the beginning of the 1970s, as he went about completing and recording *Owen Wingrave*, despite the various illnesses that clung with grim persistence. 'He must have known that some of the works of the late Sixties, early Seventies were pretty low key and revisiting old ground,' said Colin Matthews, 'but nobody would have dared tell him that.' Nobody needed to, for something shifted in his thinking post-*Wingrave*. 'It's nothing to do with the fact that Ben's written himself out,' a defensive Pears told Graham Johnson, implying that Britten's determination to embark on a new opera immediately after *Wingrave* had, in fact, everything to do with his wondering if he still had a voice.

It was the Britten of 1941 in California, urgently writing down every idea lest he wake up one morning to discover he had nothing further to say.

The new opera had been on his mind for some years, yet it was only in September 1970, temporarily clear of the *Wingrave* fog, that Britten felt able to write to Thomas Mann's son Golo, presuming on their old Brooklyn acquaintanceship and their mutual friends the Hesses. 'I have been longing for ages to make an opera out of Death in Venice, and circumstances, too complicated to go into now, have suddenly made me want to go ahead with it rather quickly. Would you be sympathetic to the idea enough to let me do this?' Mann was sympathetic (his father had always thought if a musical dramatization were ever to be made of *Doktor Faustus*, Britten was the man to do it). At the same time Britten asked Myfanwy Piper if she would be willing to undertake her third libretto for him.

It is impossible to say whether the complicated circumstances Britten wrote of to Mann were connected to his own concerns regarding his compositional voice and power, and it is hard to avoid the impression that he sensed a shift in his own music. Johnson thinks there was something all too prescient about the choice of Mann's novella. It was not so much the subject matter – a distinguished, creatively blocked author dies a degraded and lonely death from cholera when he refuses to leave stinking, infected Venice, desperate not to be parted from the beautiful adolescent boy he loves – though the more salacious aspects of the narrative would raise all sorts of eyebrows in years to come. It was more that Britten did not yet know about the illness that would plague his own final years when he chose the book. So Mann's portrait of a distinguished writer, middle-aged but nonetheless near the end of his life, full of ideas but seemingly unable to give them form, began to take on far more autobiographical parallels than *Peter Grimes* had ever mustered.

It is also possible that Britten sensed the new and narrowing path he now trod was not necessarily solely of his own making. Pears would turn sixty-one in 1971, and there was a feeling his performing career was winding down. On stage at the Maltings in September 1970 they filmed a scenic *Winterreise* for television – Britten hidden from view, Pears in a travel cape looking like an elderly, disoriented Sherlock Holmes wandering Dartmoor in search of the diabolical hound; he could not have seemed more distant from the young, distraught lover of Schubert's cycle. The fact that this film and others like it were made in such numbers and quick succession spoke to Britten and Pears's star power in the 1960s and 1970s, but this particular film, along with the tenor's harrumphing cameo in *Owen Wingrave*, suggest a star on the wane. When later asked about the sense of urgency he felt in composing *Death in Venice*, Britten replied: 'For one thing, it is probably Peter's last major operatic part . . .'

At the end of January 1971 Britten, Pears and the Pipers set off on a driving holiday through France, artist at the wheel, tenor navigating, composer and writer in the back seat plotting the shape of the new opera. They were confident by then that copyright hitches resulting from the exclusivity deal struck between Warner Bros. and Mann's estate over the 1971 Visconti film would eventually be ironed out in their favour, not least because of Golo's solicitous response. They proceeded at speed: Myfanwy knew the drill, knew what Britten required of her personally and artistically. Even so, it was a far more complex undertaking than either of their previous collaborations; it would take some time for the story to be wrestled to the ground, a viable opera scenario extracted.

2

The greater urgency gave rise to a broader impatience. During 1970 Britten had become increasingly frustrated with Reiss, in many ways the architect – or at least engineer – of the Aldeburgh Festival's expansion and success in the 1960s. Reiss had countered Britten's cautiousness and year after year had created a full schedule for the many artists and organizations involved, never more so than after 1967. Throughout the 1960s he raised money for the expansion of the festival's infrastructure. He project-managed the building and rebuilding of the Maltings and oversaw two openings of the hall by the Queen. But by late 1969, in the aftermath of the fire, Britten was already distressed by Reiss's inability to delegate.

> Dear Stephen, you can't be personally responsible for everything – the long-range vision, of course, which you have shown over & over again in

the past, & will in the future – but the details must be looked after by responsible skilled others. Please don't get cross with this. We are all going through a kind of growing crisis, & that on top of all our other jobs is a bit much for everyone!

Too many things were slipping through the cracks. Reiss did not seem to know how to exploit the new premises or finalize a financial agreement with the restaurant, bar and Festival Club. There seemed to be too little advertising, and artist contracts were dispatched too haphazardly. Of course Britten knew every detail, every flaw, in the festival's operation; those around him had learned that it was a fine balance between swamping him with information and keeping him in the dark; wary of his wrath, they mostly erred on the side of the former.

From Reiss's perspective, Britten and Pears were too ambitious too soon. Following the huge success of the Maltings, they were suddenly caught up in their desire to leave a legacy that matched their talents and achievements, determined to build their own monument. They wanted to develop the other decrepit buildings on the site at Snape – one into a school, another into an opera house seating 500, yet another into a gallery housing Nolan's paintings – and could not understand why Reiss dragged his feet: hadn't they rebuilt the Maltings in under a year? Weren't they capable of anything to which they put their hand? In a curious reversal of roles, Reiss urged caution, and as a consequence anger and antagonism brewed away beneath the surface of planning meetings. Reiss wanted things to be how they once were: a cosy chat between the three – over a drink at the Red House or on holiday somewhere – and the decision then put into play. But no one had time for that sort of operation any more and the festival Reiss helped grow now seemed on the verge of devouring him. 'I think we are all of us too involved with the old method to "jump" Stephen into these new methods ourselves,' Britten wrote to the festival's chairman, Fidelity Cranbrook, in late 1970. 'Stephen obviously has too much value & experience to be jettisoned unless he really can't make this jump. But unless something is done quickly I fear we shall all be in the loony bin.'

When Reiss sacked the new caretaker soon after the 1971 festival, a little over a year since he had been brought in to lighten Reiss's load, Britten was furious. Much has been made of the composer's attachment to the man's seventeen-year-old son – not least by Reiss himself, who later, improbably, described the boy as an obvious model for Tadzio in *Death in Venice* – but it was not an issue. Regardless of the documented incompetence of the caretaker, the decision to remove him without consulting Britten was the final straw. At a vicious encounter at the Red House – Pears silent, Britten white-faced and fierce – Reiss was told to leave them. He resigned soon afterwards.

The whole sorry tale became notorious in Aldeburgh, further proof of Britten's hard-nosed behaviour (Cranbrook came close to resigning over it). It is not difficult to understand why the episode was so scandalous, because it was easily the longest successful friendship and relationship in Britten's working life to have been terminated in such a manner. Next to Colin Graham (and disregarding Harewood, who was never an employee), Crozier's collaborative friendship of seven years probably came closest, yet this was less than half the span of Reiss's ties with Britten and the festival. Regardless of its longevity, however, it concluded in circumstances similar to the decline of the relationship with Crozier: by the end, neither Crozier nor Reiss was quite quick or compliant enough for Britten. But Reiss had none of the prickliness which more than anything else sabotaged Crozier's relationship with Britten; given what Reiss had done for the composer since 1955, the end to the friendship seemed doubly treacherous.

For once the dismissal (as it was in effect) was not summary, and for once (Harewood aside) Britten did not hide behind Pears or other bearers of bad or ambiguous tidings. Nor could it be said to have conformed to the warning Reiss had received from Anne Wood, the EOG's manager before him, when he started the job that Britten quickly 'devoured people and spewed out what was left and no use to him'. Nor was it an instance of Britten reinventing the past to suit his own narrative or behaviour, which happened frequently in his adulthood, nor of an immediate, mesmeric enthusiasm for a new friend or collaborator being replaced by a withering silence or cold shoulder once the limitations of the person's work or friendship were revealed. The two had sailed through many worse storms, and each was now direct with the other – Britten cruelly so, Reiss recoiling from the pistol-whipping he received. Each was almost immediately full of regret and sadness. Ironically, it was one of the more adult conclusions to a relationship Britten ever navigated, despite the impatience.

But it was not only Reiss: many stories about Britten's ready cruelty emerged in these years. Robert Tear, having performed the difficult aria 'Ach mein Sinn' for Britten in a recording session of Bach's *St John Passion*, was wearily brushed aside with the words, 'Well, if that's all you can do, you'd better go on doing it.' The pianist Viola Tunnard, who unknown to Britten was suffering from motor neurone disease, which affected her playing in *Idomeneo*, was told: 'You'd better stay, we've tried everybody else and no one is free.' At an infamous Red House dinner, at which Graham Johnson's enthusiasm for *Der Rosenkavalier* inspired him, unwisely, to sing the beginning of the Act 3 trio, 'Marie Theres'! . . .', Britten icily responded: 'I know how it goes, thank you very much, and I don't need you to sing it to me.' He did not even spare loyal Elizabeth Mayer following her stroke in 1967. Britten and Pears were in New York for a few days before travelling to South America and Beata had to ask if they would visit her mother. 'Well, it probably makes no sense to see Elizabeth, you know, she's in hospital,' they demurred. 'You go and see her,' Beata responded furiously, and they visited briefly en route to the airport, dimly aware of their shameful behaviour.

It was all so callous, so unbelievably touchy and selfish, when different words and actions could just as easily have been chosen. These were not occasions on which some social or musical transgression had occurred: it was just the unpleasant, selfish side to Britten's personality breaking free of the self-restraint that normally prevailed, encouraged or enabled by Pears. More and more people walked on eggshells around him. There were a few exceptions. Young composers – such as the brilliant, precocious Oliver Knussen, collecting an autograph from Stravinsky and conducting his first symphony with the London Symphony Orchestra at the age of fifteen – enjoyed an easy rapport with him. And there were young performers who benefited from his largesse, not least Ronan Magill, a teenage pianist with conspicuous talent and a mother determined to help him capitalize on it. But many people got instead the narrowed eyes, the thin lips and waspish comments.

As his behaviour worsened, Pears, Rosamund Strode, Marion, Donald Mitchell, Barbara, Beth, and Bill Servaes, Reiss's replacement, circled the wagons, protecting him as best they could from outside distractions and claims on his time. It was necessary, of course, but it also seemed to reinforce aspects of the changed behaviour. In February 1970 Britten bought Chapel House in the small Suffolk village of

Horham, twenty-three miles north-west of Aldeburgh. It was a detached two-storey cottage with uninterrupted views across the fields. He added a modern sitting room, with floor-to-ceiling windows onto the garden and space for a grand piano. He had a wooden studio installed in the back garden – an inland Suffolk beach hut, in effect. Chapel House was intended as a composing retreat, an escape from Aldeburgh's frantic atmosphere and from the aircraft that buzzed low into the nearby American airbase. It proved its worth in the following years: he composed most of *Owen Wingrave* there and would complete much of *Death in Venice* looking out over the same view. There he relaxed with Pears and the occasional friend, overseen by a village housekeeper who prepared meals and cleaned up after him. It was a retreat into a world before *Grimes*, or perhaps *War Requiem*: a world before he was famous.

3

As the Reiss fiasco slowly unfolded, Britten and Myfanwy Piper worked in fits and starts on *Death in Venice*. A number of key decisions were made as early as May 1971 when, in a taxi crossing Edinburgh, Britten talked freely to Donald Mitchell about the piece. They had settled on only two principals, Aschenbach and a figure of death who disguises himself as a number of different characters, each expediting the distinguished author's downfall; minor characters would come from the chorus. And there would be three levels of narrative: Aschenbach's soliloquies, in which he expresses his hopes and doubts; the beach, on which much of the action occurs; and the activity in Venice, a city with rich Romantic links to death and creativity, from Byron to John Addington Symonds, Wagner to Mann. Britten had not yet determined the constituency of the orchestra, but thought it would be staged in the round at Snape, an idea probably from Colin Graham, who was once more to be entrusted with the premiere.

Piper was working from this skeleton when she came to the Red House for the BBC broadcast of *Owen Wingrave* on 16 May. Britten found the occasion uncomfortable, doubtful that the opera worked 'on the box', critical of how it looked and shuddering as he recalled the unpleasant experience. But at least he could hide in his own house to watch it, avoiding the crush bar and the receptions and speeches and the instant criticisms normally associated with his premieres. Unusually, critics enjoyed what the public did not, *The Times* labelling it the work of a composer 'at the masterly height of his career', Martin Cooper calling it 'unmistakably one of the composer's most powerful utterances'. It was a perceptive take on Britten's return to large-scale opera, despite the flawed performance and constrictive medium. Piper took away more ideas about the new work, which she chipped away at in the following months.

Britten had no such luxury: it was festival time once more and his mind was on Soviet intransigence (Richter and the Borodin Quartet did not appear as scheduled), the premiere of his *Canticle IV*, his own performance of Elgar's *Dream of Gerontius*, and of course the ongoing, underlying tensions with Reiss, his dismissal imminent. *Gerontius* in the Maltings must have been an extraordinary performance, if Britten's recording of it a month later is any indication. It is a tender, introverted, pictorial reading – a radiant Yvonne Minton as the Angel in this instance, as tremulous as the penitent Soul she is escorting from one life to the next. But it is dramatic when it needs to be, full of heavenly voices and snarling horns – Purgatory guarded by Cerberus. Britten builds unerringly to the climax – spending a good fifteen minutes doing so – which blazes forth with intense power. It is an un-treacly reading from this reluctant Elgarian.

The festival included a counterpart for *Gerontius*: Britten's *Canticle IV 'Journey of the Magi'*, a setting of a poem by T. S. Eliot for countertenor, tenor, baritone and piano. It is Eliot's attempt to humanize probably the most famous story ever told, which he does by reuniting the three kings in their old age as they try to recall every detail of their journey to Bethlehem and what they discovered. There are moments of harmony in their recollection ('A cold coming we had of it, / Just the worst time of the year / For a journey' – which Eliot borrowed from Bishop Lancelot Andrewes's 1622 nativity sermon), and moments in which they talk over each other, as though their memories have been jogged, their mood querulous ('Then we came to a tavern with vine-leaves over the lintel, / Six hands at an open door dicing for pieces of silver'). Eliot shies away from describing what they encountered in the stable: 'it was (you may say) satisfactory', the kings mutter repeatedly, understatedly, as if no words could do the scene justice. And the young kings then head home to their heathen kingdoms, changed by the experience, no longer at ease, 'With their alien people clutching their gods', wary of what was to follow in the name of this saviour.

It was the first work of 1971 – composed in ten days in January, just before the trip to France – and though it shares some of the language of the Church Parables, it is a more controlled and opulent work. Of course Britten has fun with the words and images – from the lumbering camel train, which he spells out in the accompaniment, to the clumping passacaglia as the kings near their destination, now on foot. But his best touch is saved for the moment the kings intone 'satisfactory', for here the piano launches on *Magi videntes stellam* (The magi, having seen the star), the plainsong Antiphon chanted before the Magnificat in Vespers on the Feast of the Epiphany. The words may refer to a desert journey, yet Britten invokes a glorious Venetian church, with bells chiming and echoing throughout the washy acoustic, incense filling the space, the chant winding its way above the texture and left floating.

Between the end of the festival and the *Gerontius* recording, a second draft of the *Death in Venice* scenario emerged. While Britten busied himself with other recordings and concerts, including the first complete performance of *Who are these Children?*, Piper wrote the first libretto draft of Act 1. With this in his hand, Britten decamped to Venice in October, Pears and the Pipers at his side. They looked at the city almost with fresh eyes, determined not to miss anything they might appropriate for the opera. They tracked down a gondolier who knew the traditional cries, and in a notebook ('D in V BB Venice 1971' printed on the cover) Britten wrote out the strange animal calls as the Venetian made them, Pears jotting down the words. Britten sketched in the so-called 'Serenissima' theme (a historical name for the city), which he later wove into the score as Aschenbach travels to Venice. He noted down the bells of St Mark's, incorporating them into the opera's delayed overture, a sonic picture of the city in which bells clang away, their ripe overtones written into the score. He sketched the opening of Aschenbach's first soliloquy and notated the expansive theme with which the exquisite view of the beach from Aschenbach's hotel room is revealed. The sketchbook was unusual for Britten; he would often scribble ideas about a libretto, but thematic and harmonic ideas tended to brew in his mind unwritten until he was ready to compose. So too was the 'view theme' a departure from custom, since it originally came to him intact in France when he was in the back of the car talking about the opera with Myfanwy. It was an almost unprecedented example of a musical theme, conceived fully and early in the planning of an opera, lasting the distance.

There was a medical coda to the Venice trip, much as there had been to the one before. Strode remembered Britten at some point saying of his schedule: 'First of all I've got to finish this one, then there's a big work, then an opera, and then I'll be ill.' The stress of finishing and staging an opera would usually send him to bed with one ailment or another, but there was no big work to blame this time: his last major piece was *Owen Wingrave*, completed a full fifteen months earlier. And as haunting and assured as is his Third Suite for Cello, with its incorporation of three Russian folk songs and the Orthodox Hymn for the Departed, and with the spirit of Bach's first solo suite infusing the Barcarola, he had knocked it out in only a week as far back as February.* Yet home from Venice Britten found himself out of sorts. His teeth seemed to be the problem this time, but the illness played out as general poor health. In November he underwent dental surgery, the procedure and the extracted teeth leaving him sore and frustrated, his mood dark. Britten and Piper had a little more time now the premiere had slipped back from September 1972 to June 1973, but it was still a huge undertaking.

Britten composed the opera's first notes some time before Christmas 1971, but it was only in January, while staying with Peg Hesse in Germany, that he made real progress. 'Aschenbach is walking in the suburbs of Munich on a spring evening', the score states at its top, but this is no placid walk in the park: Britten conjures the most extraordinary texture from just two clarinets and two horns – a whirring, claustrophobic, slow passing of time. 'My mind beats on,' Aschenbach sings, 'my mind beats on, and no words come.' Never before had Britten packed so much narrative weight into the opening line of an opera.

There were the usual interruptions: Easter performances at Snape; a damp holiday with Pears in the Ligurian fishing village of Camogli, in which the hours and quarters were marked by the church clock a little too zealously for their taste, though this was more than compensated for by the bands and bonfires on the feast day of the town's patron saint; the Aldeburgh Festival, which included Britten's one-off recital

* It was a consolation prize for Rostropovich, whose public support for the dissident Alexander Solzhenitsyn, following the writer's acceptance of the 1970 Nobel Prize in Literature, detrimentally affected his career for a period of four years.

with Fischer-Dieskau: a meeting of performing equals, each man wary of the other, marking territory, extraordinary music-making emerging as a result; and the recording of Schumann's *Faust* following its festival outing. He resented every intrusion and even on holiday found it impossible to relax, unwilling to put the opera from his mind. As the months passed, the composition sketch materialized. There were problems, of course: the libretto had layers of meaning and metaphor quite distinct from its plot-driven predecessors, and these were dealt with one by one. Pears, visiting Britten at Schloss Wolfsgarten early in 1972, suggested that instead of a treble for the Voice of Apollo, who enters Aschenbach's dreams to warn him against Dionysian excess, Britten should write for a counter-tenor – 'colder, not manly or womanly, & a sound there hasn't been used before'. (This change reunited the three vocalists from *Canticle IV*, James Bowman, Pears and John Shirley-Quirk.) Britten decided that the chorus could describe 'The Games of Apollo', in which Tadzio and his friends compete in a pentathlon, the beautiful boy triumphing. Piper thought these should be danced naked – a touch of classical Greece, she explained – a suggestion Britten toyed with but eventually rejected, concerned that his motive might be misconstrued.

Everything seemed to take more effort. Fischer-Dieskau saw him tottering during and following the festival performance of *Faust*, barely able to speak afterwards. And a choir member noticed his resigned weariness in the recording session for the same piece when the producer announced over the tannoy: 'Take one hundred and thirty-four.' He had trouble climbing stairs, and the tennis matches and meandering walks that had long been an important part of his life were now too difficult to pursue. He escaped to Horham whenever he could, and it was from there that he returned to Aldeburgh in August 1972, responding to a summons from his doctor.

4

Britten was diagnosed with aortic incompetence, a condition where blood leaks through the valve, causing the heart to work overtime to compensate; scar tissue replaces muscle fibre and eventually the heart wears out. Ian Tait had discovered evidence of aortic valve disease when he became Britten's doctor in 1960. Such aortic defects are usually either congenital or develop as a consequence of rheumatic fever in childhood; with no history of the latter, Tait concluded the defect was congenital. In a check-up as long ago as 1938 Britten was told that his heart was healthy, contrary to childhood legend, that there were no congenital problems or coronary repercussions of his infant pneumonia. Tait deemed the diagnosis incorrect. 'Ben would *not* have been considered fit for military service.'

It is possible to manage such a condition for a long time: despite its weakness, Britten's heart had functioned well for more than fifty years. There were symptoms along the way – breathlessness in tennis matches or while clambering around in the high altitudes of South America – but on the whole he managed to lead an active life. The endocarditis in 1968 changed all this, Tait concluded. Penicillin had done its job back then, but Britten's heart was aggravated by the infection and the valve had probably been deteriorating ever since. Thus the physical decline so obvious in footage of Britten at the 1970 festival, his hair grey, his face red and puffy, his eyes closed in either exhaustion or melancholia as the final bars of *Gloriana* are performed offstage. He needed to undergo surgery to replace the leaky valve, sooner rather than later.

Britten was usually good with his doctors. He accepted their expertise and followed their instructions without demur. But not this time: *Death in Venice* took priority over surgery. Tait agreed it was possible to control his condition with drugs so long as Britten cut down on all other commitments and saw a cardiologist as soon as the opera was done. (He refused to see a heart specialist before then, rightly fearing he would be advised to undertake the surgery immediately.) 'I wanted passionately to finish this piece before anything happened,' he told *The Times* at the end of 1974. 'I had to keep going, and then, when I had finished, put myself into the doctors' hands.' There was no shifting him. He responded well to the drugs and on a good day could forget about his condition. But he still found it impossible to climb stairs without wheezing, and a general, dulling tiredness overtook him. 'Ben is writing an evil opera, and it's killing him,' Pears complained somewhat hyperbolically to Nolan.

But only somewhat: both the diagnosis and Britten's obsessive response to it confirmed that this was indeed now his late period. For all the opera's connections with certain works from the 1960s, the recognition that he was very ill, that he would possibly not have so many more days to compose, injected his work with greater urgency and intensity. There is something of Adorno's 'unresolved contradiction' to the piece, a quality that links it with its predecessors, but which at the same time goes out of its way to break with the past, to tread new ground. Colin Matthews, drafted in to prepare the vocal score and soon to help with the orchestration, 'couldn't work out how it was going to work dramatically, even having copied out every note of the music'. This was the reason Britten initially asked the youthful Graham Johnson to undertake the vocal score, the pianist thought: Britten feared showing it to more experienced practitioners, feared their incomprehension or rebuttal, young Stravinskys picking over the bones. Ultimately Johnson's work was deemed insufficient, but his recollection speaks to Britten's paranoia.

It was not only the inherent dramatic problems that alarmed Matthews. 'I thought it was going to be something of a disaster because there was quite a lot of gossip about it at the time. Everybody was worried that he'd chosen a subject that was going to be scandalous and that here for the first time he was admitting to his homosexuality in a way that he hadn't before.' After so many works, so much pervasive conflation between composer and character, here finally was a *roman-à-clef*. Those in Britten's intimate circle hid behind Mann's cloak of respectability, though (especially given the writer's own ambiguous sexuality) this was scarcely an effective disguise.

'Tempting as it was to simplify for the sake of theatrical neatness,' Piper later wrote, 'we decided to keep [Mann's] order with very few omissions or rearrangement.' The respect for Mann works surprisingly well: only occasionally did Britten and Piper find themselves stranded down some inhospitable Venetian alley. Piper noted that they were determined to balance the 'passionate-erotic and the poetic-symbolic' in the original story, which they thought would guard the opera against the more sensational charges levelled at Mann's novella.

Such was the thinking behind the incorporation of Mann's various mythological allusions, from Tadzio as Hermes (the handsome god who, like Gerontius's angel, guides newly departed souls to the afterlife) to the foul, alluring Dionysus who enters Aschenbach's dreams, only to leave him shattered and addicted to his freewheeling cult. Britten and Piper also came up with some smart narrative innovations, not least turning Mann's lightly sketched hotel manager into seven distinct characters, each of whom is the figure of Death in disguise: the Traveller, who entices Aschenbach to Venice instead of his summer house in the clean mountain air; the Elderly Fop, whom Aschenbach encounters en route to Venice, perfumed and giggly, flirting with Italian rough-trade; the Old Gondolier, who rows Aschenbach to the Lido, but suddenly disappears upon arrival, his provenance deeply suspect; the Hotel Manager, who hides from his guests the rumours of a sickness poisoning the city; the Hotel Barber, who blackens Aschenbach's hair and rouges his cheeks to make him appear younger, more attractive to his prey; the Leader of the Players, as sinister as Punch, denying news of a plague; and the Voice of Dionysus, who triumphs over Apollo in Aschenbach's sordid dream.

So too were they inspired in their solution for the beautiful Tadzio, who is mute in Mann: they made him a dancer. But then they decided to make Tadzio's friends and the beach attendants dancers as well, which enabled them 'to organize the children's games in the two beach scenes into ballets'. Had they stopped there it would have been fine, but Britten and Piper seemed determined to load Tadzio with more metaphorical weight than Mann ever thought necessary. So the boys compete in their games, these 'Olympian tales / Of rivalry', the chorus name-checking half the population of Mount Olympus in the (drawn-out) process, Tadzio's victory confirming his godlike status. It is another of Britten's narrative devices, fifteen minutes of staginess that clogs an already long act and would not be missed were it absent. (Sviatoslav Richter likened them to a 'physical education class in a kindergarten, with no feeling of aesthetics of poetry'.)

Another instance is the extended evening scene in the following act where the hotel guests are entertained by a troupe of strolling players performing a repertory of corny traditional songs, acting out the lyrics with forced, marionette gaiety. The guests then join in a laughing song that lasts much longer than is needed for us to notice that neither Aschenbach nor Tadzio is amused by the vulgar comedy. At least here Britten gave them inspired music, taking his cue from Mann's discrepant band of mandolin, guitar, harmonica and fiddle, transforming it into a virtuosic yet unsettling ensemble of street buskers.

But there is so much inspiration that such structural flaws are almost irrelevant. Heinrich Schütz's *St Matthew Passion*, which Pears was enthusiastically performing in these years, inspired the style of recitative

Britten employed for Aschenbach's interior monologues: the pitch specified, the rhythm left to the singer. (Appropriately, Britten's manuscript in
these sections looks like plainsong notation in a medieval psalter.) There
are beach scenes straight from the composer's Lowestoft childhood:
vendors hawking their wares – fruits and pies, fresh fish; garish figures
and young children assuming equality in the water; a string of rowing
boats and beach huts, sandcastles and bathing gowns. There is the
mixture of panic and delirium as Aschenbach pursues Tadzio through
Venice, at one point resting his head against the door of the boy's hotel
room, imagining him doing the same on the other side, breathing in syn-
chronicity. There is the arresting dream sequence that uses everything
from Mann and more: men and women dressed in furs, horns on their
heads, gripping torches or daggers, beating cymbals and drums, howling like dogs. It is one of Britten's great moments of release, which at its
first full rehearsal had the players looking at each other with bewildered
awe: the orchestral texture is thick and ecstatic, the percussion clanks
like a large gamelan ensemble, the chorus moans 'aa-oo' – a wild, ani-
malistic parody of how Aschenbach first hears Tadzio's name sung
alluringly by the same chorus ('Ad-ziù!') – and the writer awakes muttering the same noises himself, ravaged, his demise now inevitable. 'And
in his very soul he tasted the bestial degradation of his fall,' as Mann
puts it.

There is the beautiful, still Phaedrus monologue in which Aschenbach imagines Socrates's wise, learned response to Phaedrus's questions,
piano and harp unified and transformed into something like a lute for
the moment. There is the brilliant, unhinged Gabrieli canzone that
blazes out at the end of the Socratic musings, Britten depicting the sound
swilling around the boomy insides of St Mark's, which sets up the final
scene. And there is the quite awful moment when Aschenbach finally
receives a clear beckon from Tadzio, but is unable to rise; he slumps in
his deckchair, dead from cholera. Tadzio (who has none of the sickly
incandescence of the boy in the novella) continues his walk out to sea –
Hermes escorting Aschenbach's soul to one place or the other – while
the orchestra plays the most exquisite, most Mahlerian, utterance of
Britten's entire output, Aschenbach's and Tadzio's motifs at last meshed
together. It is an overwhelming couple of minutes.

The orchestrating was still to come when, on the last day of 1972,

Britten played through the entire opera to a handful of friends, Colin Graham and the Pipers among them, having completed the great bulk of the composition sketch two weeks earlier. There would be tinkering to come – changes to the serene postlude and the Phaedrus monologue; a final decision about where exactly the two acts would be divided; and a replacement written for one of the Players' songs when Britten discovered the popular tune was still in copyright – but the hard work was done. Those at the New Year's Eve play-through were left stunned by the strange, inspired sound-world conjured by the sickly man at the piano. For all that Britten had eerily come to shadow Aschenbach's character and career, they were in the late stages of their lives completely different artists. Mann's Aschenbach was writing arid work, lacking in joy and distinction. 'His later style gave up the old sheer audacities, the fresh and subtle nuances – it became fixed and exemplary, conservative, formal, even formulated.' Britten, on the other hand, had produced 'either the best or the worst music I've ever written', a work of searing brilliance and originality, his powers undiminished.

5

Once concerts in Bavaria, London and Wolfsgarten were behind him (the latter a celebration for Peg Hesse's sixtieth birthday), and once he had fleshed out the *Death in Venice* sketch into a full orchestral score – Rosamund Strode ruling up the manuscript and pencilling in the vocal parts, Colin Matthews filling in the gaps the composer felt able to leave – Britten kept his promise to his doctor. On 30 March 1973 he attended a consultation with Graham Hayward, a London cardiologist whom Tait had known at St Bartholomew's Hospital. Hayward, a beefy, ex-navy boxer with an imperious manner, was upbeat about Britten's condition, telling him that after surgery and a summer's convalescence he would be as 'good as new – even conducting!' In mid-April Hayward's senior registrar at the National Heart Hospital, Michael Petch, undertook Britten's cardiac catheterization to establish the type of surgery required. Britten complained about the canned music on the ward but was otherwise meek and co-operative. Petch was far less sanguine about the condition of Britten's heart and his prospects for a full recovery, however, despite the huge advances in heart surgery in previous decades, not least the first British transplant operation five years earlier, led by South African surgeon Donald Ross. 'Actually it *is* cheering to realise that 10 years ago they couldn't do these fabulous things,' as Britten told Plomer.

Ross was a pioneering advocate of tissue rather than mechanical valves: biological matter was preferable because the alternative condemned a patient to a life of blood tests and anticoagulants. 'The surgeon must weigh the advantages and disadvantages of the various valves, taking into consideration the patient's age, life style and other relevant factors,' Ross would later write in *Surgery and your Heart*. Hayward did all this, but he got it into his head that Britten was a very heavy drinker (him being an artist and all). Alcohol is incompatible with anticoagulants and so, courtesy of the good results Ross had obtained with autografts, a tissue valve was chosen.

On 2 May Britten returned to the London Clinic and awaited his surgery, to take place five days later at the National Heart Hospital. He was upset about missing rehearsals for *Death in Venice* and the Covent Garden production of *Owen Wingrave*, but was otherwise a normal, scared, obedient patient.

The surgery and mop-up took six hours and was hugely problematic from the outset. The complications were subsequently blamed on a number of factors: the poor condition of Britten's heart; the small stroke he suffered when debris from the old valve entered his bloodstream and lodged in the brain; the length of time it took to restart his heart and remove him from bypass. All of this was true, but the real problem was both more simple and more serious. When Ross cut open Britten's chest and began working on the grossly enlarged heart he discovered the aorta was riddled with tertiary syphilis.

This was suddenly the wrong procedure. Britten's aorta was so distended that it was going to be almost impossible to make the new valve fit the space Ross and his team were about to create. Had he been using a mechanical valve Ross could, in surgery, have picked a better fit for the disfigured aorta, matching the circumference of one with the other. As it was, he had to make do with what was at hand. As Ross tried to stretch the tissue valve to make it fit the syphilitic aorta – stitching it in place where he could otherwise have firmly bound a mechanical valve – an already long operation was made longer, leaving Britten vulnerable to the host of complications that subsequently occurred.

It was known that undiagnosed syphilis was then common, especially among male homosexuals, who often displayed no external symptoms. It was easy enough to overlook the infection in its dormant phase, when the external clues were as slight as a different timbre to a heartbeat, or to mistake the symptoms of this Great Imitator for another disease. 'Only by devotion to habitual suspiciousness and anticipatory watching are the early signs of cardiovascular syphilis detectable,' wrote STD pioneer Dr Maganlal Vora in 1942, a year before penicillin would revolutionize medical care for the infected. 'Inadequate treatment of early syphilis and late treatment are often at the root of cardiovascular syphilis.' It was infinitely worse if the patient in need of the habitual suspiciousness was famous: the stigma was large, so tests were rarely undertaken in the absence of symptoms. Gentlemen of a certain class did not discuss such things. Yet from the 1920s to the 1940s, one in seven of the tests yielded a positive result: the decades of Britten's youth and early adulthood were awash with the disease. Britten's eminence, conventionality and stories of childhood heart problems no doubt deflected any further probing into his medical history by his doctor in 1960 when the first symptoms of aortic valve disease were presented.

Britten certainly had no suspicion he was syphilitic. But it seems likely that as he squirmed and sweated and hallucinated his way through those days in the early months of 1940, only two years after his heart was given the all clear and just as he was about to write his great love song to Pears, *Seven Sonnets of Michelangelo*, his body was reacting not to streptococcal tonsillitis but to syphilis, now in its secondary stage. All the symptoms were there. The sulphonamide with which he had been treated then alleviated some of them but left the syphilis infection untouched. 'In many cases advice is not sought and, even when it is, the true significance of the findings may be missed,' the authors of the paper 'Secondary Syphilis of the Tonsils' later wrote. 'The otolaryngologist especially must be on the alert because he may be the first to see the patient with manifestations in the oral cavity and pharynx and these are the most common extra-genital sites of syphilis.' So it was with Britten. Auden's accusation in 1942 that 'sickness is your substitute for the Bohemian' could not have been more wrong.

In 1940 he would still have had three to five years in which the brand new drug penicillin would cure him ($20 per dose in 1943, which fell to fifty-five cents in 1946 following mass production to treat Allied soldiers). But by 1960 – and certainly by 1973 – nothing could be done: tertiary syphilis is treatable, but after a certain period the damage is done. Penicillin at this late stage can actually make things worse. The antibiotic will kill the spirochete that long ago invaded and enlarged the aorta, living thereafter in symbiosis with its host. But in so doing, the aortic tissues can be rendered hopelessly loose, the valve flapping impotently. It is what is known as the therapeutic paradox, where treatment clears up a specific problem yet actually makes the patient worse. In 1968 Britten was given penicillin for his endocarditis (which can occur in conjunction with syphilis, though the diagnostic tests for each are distinct) and it destroyed the strange organic glue that had kept Britten's syphilitic heart functioning for many years, thereby initiating his slow, desperate decline.

6

Nothing was said publicly (Ross barely said anything in surgery). There was something tragically nineteenth-century to it all – partly because by the 1970s penicillin had so effectively countered syphilitic infection in Western society, partly because of the prevailing Romantic associations between artists and the disease. But there was something contemporary about it too, Ross having to be inside his chest to discover the extent of tissue damage. Further surgery was useless. The discreet veil Ross drew over the operation gave rise to lurid rumours that lingered well past the 1980s – that the anaesthetist was incompetent, the surgeon drunk. But these were baseless. It was nothing more than a tragic chain of events.

Over time Ross felt the burden of his discovery in surgery and the decisions he made in an instant about disclosure. Ten years or so after Britten's death he confided in cardiologist Hywel Davies, a close friend following Davies's referral in the early 1960s of Ross's first heart-transplant patient. Davies thinks Ross told him so as to make the news public – without his fingerprints on it. Davies did not oblige him on this point. At a chance meeting with Ross's assistant surgeon, who was in the operating theatre and watched events unfold, Davies confirmed the diagnosis, but thereafter kept his own counsel.

The disease does not necessarily tell us much about Britten's relationship with Pears, even though he was the likely cause of infection. Pears probably caught syphilis before becoming Britten's lover, remaining one of the many symptom-less sufferers. The personal implications become more complicated if infection occurred after 1939, though there were certainly enough hints during their time together to suggest that while Britten was monogamous (later celibate), Pears, on wet, windy Sundays in dreary hotels around the world, played around. There was Basil Reeve's recollection of Pears haunting gay bars in the late 1930s or early 1940s, the later whispers of Pears's infidelity and Britten's gestures of forgiveness that bordered, curiously, on contrition. There were the many mild tiffs and stronger arguments that seemed too great to have had their origins merely in Pears's thoughtlessness or lack of punctuality. There was Colin Graham's observation that 'Peter was the one who was a naughty boy and always going out on the tiles'. And there were their separate lives – not just separate bedrooms, but, from the mid-1950s, whole parallel lives, pinched together at certain junctures, soon afterwards let go to run separate once more.

Colin Matthews recalls that by the time he was working for Britten 'the relationship was difficult to fathom, as Pears was rarely around. I mean quite honestly you took it for granted that it was a strong relationship, but there was little evidence of it on the surface.' Reiss described their bond more harshly, characterizing Pears as the parent of a gifted and wilful child, giving way in their frequent arguments. 'I felt it essential to their well-being that they had their separate lives and didn't see *too* much of each other.' Rita Thomson, a sparky Scottish nursing sister who looked after Britten at the National Heart Hospital with ready humour and a firm hand and who later became a trusted friend, thought 'Peter was always the one with more outside interests than Ben ever had. I remember Ben saying to me, "I don't mind if Peter has little dalliances as long as he doesn't tell me."' And dally he did. None of this is to negate the extraordinary, loving connection between them both, but it does suggest the bond was unevenly weighted, and that perhaps by the end it was primarily musical, intellectual and historical. They were a good match with guests around a dinner table – Britten witty and charming when happy, Pears alert and emollient when he was not – but Pears sought elsewhere the sexual frisson his partner was unable to provide, while Britten was content to be left alone to compose, secure in the knowledge that he enjoyed a loving, supportive relationship with an artist and friend he admired.

Colin Matthews also identified in Britten an unsophisticated reaction to his own sexuality. He never made gay jokes or inferences, nor did he even use the word 'gay'; he hated Pears's occasional camp behaviour and his one attempt at a more bouffant hairstyle ('You look like an old queen'); he disliked socializing with gay couples, was initially aghast at the idea of wearing checked trousers, and was no doubt sniffy about Colin Graham's easy promiscuity in the 1960s. There was repression, of course, never more so than before the change in law and public opinion. 'I feel that Ben certainly felt guilty [about his homosexuality] and that it was wrong,' said Rita Thomson. But Matthews thought the repression extended to *all* brands of sexuality, not merely his own – hence his overblown, priggish response to Harewood's affair and marriage breakdown. Emotionally he seemed happiest throughout his life when writing chatty, chummy letters to public schoolboys, as though on summer break without enough time to pen a romantic sonnet. It was much as Isherwood described his own relationship with Auden in the 1930s: 'Their friendship was rooted in schoolboy memories and the mood of its sexuality was adolescent.' It was this world – of chaste schoolboy crushes and unsophisticated rapport, of conversations that skimmed across the surface of human interaction, of another person validating his great gifts, of papering over his intense vulnerability – that appealed to him. It was a psychosexual minefield, one that influenced his music to a great extent. But it left Pears, from early in their relationship, looking elsewhere for a sexual life. And in sad irony it left Britten, the more puritanical of the pair, with a sexually transmitted disease that slowly ate away at his heart, his bad behaviour increasing as his health deteriorated.

7

Recovery was desperately slow. Rita Thomson visited when Britten was recuperating in the London Clinic and arrived to see him being served dinner on a large tray – a heavy silver dome covering a two-inch-thick steak – as though supping at the Athenaeum. He was lonely – Pears was busy at Covent Garden with *Owen Wingrave* and only rarely at his bedside – and it was Thomson who three weeks after the operation escorted him back to the Red House. A series of nurses cared for him at home, none too successfully, until the following Easter when Britten lured Thomson to Aldeburgh permanently.

She later recalled Britten's precarious health in the first month and year, how the heart never reduced in size and how the ill-fitting valve was never able to gain in strength. He was two stone overweight, bloated with water: it was only when Michael Petch became his specialist in 1974 and changed his medication that the weight was shifted. He could not stretch out his arms, leaving him unable to work on large manuscripts, and the stroke removed his ability to sense where his right hand was. He could not find his mouth to feed himself without looking, and knowing intuitively where his hand was on a piano was impossible. It should have been a gentle time in which his wounds healed, his drugs were stabilized and his stitches removed. Instead, he needed help washing and shaving, needed to be dressed and helped down stairs. Pears or a nurse would read to him – *The Water Babies*, say, or poetry by Eliot or Burns. At first they clung to the hope that it was just a slow recovery. 'His right arm and leg are still far from perfect functioning,' Pears wrote to Anthony Gishford soon after the operation, 'but they are better – and we are told everything will be alright.' And Britten was determined to exercise himself into good health, taking meandering walks along the neighbouring golf course. But after a year or eighteen months it became obvious to everyone that he was not improving. 'It's no good pretending that this operation has been anything but a failure,' Pears exclaimed to Rosamund Strode at one point.

Pears was merely articulating what the surgeon had kept to himself. 'His [valve] didn't fit perfectly from day one,' Petch later said. 'And it leaked – it leaked more than it should have done, and so there was this continuing extra burden on the heart.' (Petch was never told of the syphilis and today is sceptical of the diagnosis, believing that the tests for endocarditis Britten underwent in 1968 should have revealed any infection.) Late the following year in a cold, grey Aldeburgh, Britten would turn to Thomson and ask: 'Do you think I'm going to get any better?' She didn't. 'Do you think this is as good as it gets?' Well, there would be good days and bad days, she told him. There would be bursts of energy and periods of exhaustion. And there would be people who stimulated him and people who wore him out; sometimes they would be one and the same. He cried a little, yet drew strength from the knowledge. 'I think once he had accepted it, he felt that he must get on with everything, he must get on with his work.'

At least there was no madness in the mix. Although it is clinically possible for neurological damage to occur in conjunction with cardiovascular syphilis, it is uncommon. Britten was no Adrian Leverkühn, the fictional composer who prowls his way through Thomas Mann's *Doktor Faustus*, intentionally contracting syphilis as part of a diabolical pact to transform his evident gifts into greatness. (Mann modelled the compositional style of his diseased genius on Arnold Schoenberg, though his pathology was more Schumann or Schubert.) It is neurosyphilis that is so associated with the strange, brilliant late works of nineteenth- and twentieth-century artists and musicians, Paul Gauguin and Hugo Wolf among them. Though spared encroaching insanity, there was a definite change in Britten's personality. Matthews remembers a much gentler figure after the operation, resolved, determined to compose as much as he could, but without the moody, touchy side that had governed his life and work. A weight was lifted. Matthews's brother David 'put it down to the fact that he [had been] living a kind of over-safe life, and then, of course, the fact that he found out that he was going to die in a few years destroyed all that – and the music of the last years has a more compelling quality because of that'.

The realization made Britten's comments at Aspen about Schubert all the more poignant. There was no neurological connection between the two composers: it seems likely that as Schubert stepped out of the shadow of Beethoven and composed the miraculous, magical works of those last eighteen months, his body wracked with pain, his syphilitic mind was fast deteriorating. Not so with Britten. But there was something compelling about the way both composers recognized their time was almost up and that they had so many ideas to turn into new works while they still could.

This was all ahead of him. First there was the operatic showing of Mann's other great tragic character, Gustav von Aschenbach. Britten was too ill to attend the June premiere of *Death in Venice* in the Maltings, retreating to Horham instead, though he would have gauged its public impact from the reviews. Most critics thought the Games of Apollo too long, Desmond Shawe-Taylor likening the sequence to the

Masque scene in *Gloriana*, not without cause. But so too did they identify in this extraordinary late piece the human and mythological symbolism, and admire the tautness of the score and richness of Britten's musical language. The *Guardian* critic Edward Greenfield commented on the subject matter: 'Benjamin Britten, consistently perverse in his choice of opera subjects, has once again proved the impossible. Thomas Mann's *Death in Venice*, a compressed and intense story, an artist's inner monologue, lacking conversation, lacking plot, has against all the odds become a great opera.' The perceptive Bayan Northcott even noted the opera's strange mixture of fragility and brute strength, its simultaneous links and severance with the past – Adorno's catastrophe, if you like: '*Death in Venice* was composed under the threat of severe illness and it shows signs, both in its subject matter and technique, of having been executed as the last and supreme effort of an artist's final period.' And they all appreciated Pears's astonishing performance as Aschenbach; he was less than a week from his sixty-third birthday, here in a role that kept him on stage for the opera's duration, magically ageing and declining before the audience's eyes.

Part of the opera's success was due to John Piper and Colin Graham, both of whom had somehow caught the work's essence in a production that shied away from literalism ('Britten had been growing away from conventional forms of staging ever since *Gloriana*,' Graham later suggested, not quite accurately), capturing the filmic essence of the opera in quick scene shifts, evocative lighting and a heavy dose of stylization. But they all missed the composer during rehearsals and Graham was not the only one to observe that Britten would have tightened the pentathlon scene had he been there. Following a private performance at Snape in September, where he saw the work for the first time, Britten tinkered with the scene but was still too unwell to manage anything more extensive – either for the Covent Garden performances in October or later showings.

At least he was well enough to attend the London premiere, trying to resume certain aspects of his former life. He sat in a box at Covent Garden, smartly dressed in his favourite velvet smoking jacket, giving every appearance of returning to health. Not long before this he had travelled by car to Wales for a short holiday with Pears. It was on this break that Pears once more displayed the callous side to his personality. When the car broke down they found themselves hurrying to catch a train, Britten carrying the suitcase, struggling to keep up. Thomson thought this was Pears in denial about Britten's illness ('because you can't *see* somebody's heart not being very good'), never asking after his health, maintaining as full a concert schedule as he could muster. There was almost certainly something in this, Pears wishing the pain and illness away. But there was also an element of Pears thinking that Britten was making the whole thing up. Donald Mitchell, watching from the sidelines, thought Pears

> was never willing to accept that Ben was as ill as he was . . . Peter had certainly rather taken the view that there was a lot of hypochondria there in Ben, and he had to be jollied along and encouraged, and life had to go on as normal; and I think that was quite a strong element and I think maybe he was unwilling to admit to himself that Ben was as ill as he was.

And even if Britten was as sick as he said he was, Pears saw no reason to change the habits of a lifetime.

8

The celebrations for Britten's sixtieth birthday were as extravagant as those for his fiftieth. There were performances, a day of broadcasts and a BBC2 documentary. There was a concert at the Royal Albert Hall that showcased the youthful Britten, the composer of *Sinfonia da Requiem* and *Spring Symphony*. 'Now North and South and East and West', runs Auden's contribution to the symphony, 'Those I love lie down to rest; / The moon looks on them all / The healers and the brilliant talkers, / The eccentrics and the silent walkers, / The dumpy and the tall.' Auden had died two months earlier – from heart failure, of all things, which also killed Plomer in the same month – news of which upset Britten greatly. How had such an important friendship been discarded so trivially? Auden had tried on different occasions to effect a reconciliation, as had Spender and other mutual friends, but each time Britten found cause to stay away, leaving Auden with the greatest grief in his life, as he told those close to him. 'Well you see, he was such a bully,' Britten repeatedly justified himself to Spender two years later, aware of the pain he had caused. Britten stayed in Suffolk while the capital celebrated his birthday, which is probably just as well: hearing Auden's words would have set him off once more.

Auden's death left Britten free to fish out *Paul Bunyan* from the cupboard in Aldeburgh housing his 'early horrors'. And this was how he managed to start composing again: revisiting two early works that had languished for more than thirty years. The first was his String Quartet in D, which he composed in mid-1931, an eager seventeen-year-old working with John Ireland and Frank Bridge, singing in the English Madrigal Society, yet to compose his Op. 1. In February 1974 he brushed down the quartet, made a few alterations and the following month invited the Gabrieli String Quartet to give an informal performance, forty-two years almost to the day since its previous outing.

There were plenty more works where this came from, so its revival cannot be attributed solely to nostalgia: there was much for Britten to admire in his younger self. The first movement contains an engrossing, whispery hint of the heterophony that preoccupied him as he got older, while the lyrical second movement slowly unwinds, the harmony shifting steadily, an opulent viola melody embroidered by the other instruments. The revisions to *Paul Bunyan* were similarly minor, though what he was trying to rehabilitate here was more psychological than musical: Britten was revisiting a difficult theatrical and collaborative experience. He was not greatly impressed by some of what he discovered, but Pears was struck by the quality of the music and persuaded his partner to sanction a festival performance. So in June 1974, at the twenty-seventh Aldeburgh Festival, an altogether more distinguished cast than that involved in the premiere assembled on stage at the Maltings to present excerpts from *Bunyan*: Pears, Heather Harper, Janet Baker, John Shirley-Quirk, all accompanied by Steuart Bedford on piano. The audience clapped and smiled at Auden's words and Britten's simple tunes. Pears persuaded Britten to undertake further revisions.

There were other, non-posthumous, attempts at *rapprochement*. 'I do know Ben felt bad about some of the estrangements which had occurred,' Rosamund Strode said. Britten found himself behaving like Queen Elizabeth at the kaleidoscopic end of *Gloriana*, haunted by the people he had betrayed. Harewood, Coleman, Reiss and Isherwood were all welcomed back into his life to differing degrees, though none regained his earlier intimacy. It was all a little late: Britten was mostly too ill to see them, playing out his remorse instead in stilted correspondence. He could still hurt people: Thomson would leave him with his occasional visitors, telling him to behave himself, and would ask afterwards how it went. 'Oh, I was awful,' he would respond sheepishly. But mostly, exhaustion and the gentleness Colin Matthews identified prevailed. He was not performing any more, which is what had always made him so intense, his responses so fast and unforgiving.

The days fell into a simple pattern. He rose late and was bathed and dressed by Thomson, making it downstairs by around 11 a.m. There, he would drink a light lager to take off the edge and settle down to work – perhaps with Rosamund, perhaps on the new works that increasingly occupied him from mid-1974 onward. After lunch he went to bed until four o'clock, when he came downstairs once more to work further or go for a walk. Then dinner and an early night. This plodding scenario was played out in both Aldeburgh and Horham. At Horham he walked in the garden or sat quietly for long stretches, resenting the physiotherapist who kept him from his composing, fending off Thomson's occasional query, 'Can I talk to you or are you working?' Britten was full of ideas. He made plans for a Christmas piece from the same stable as *Noye's Fludde*, which excited him hugely, though it never went far. And in an old Gresham's notebook, alongside schoolboy essays on Shakespeare and Wordsworth, he plotted a 'Sea Symphony', a work he had long contemplated. He listed poems by Beddoes and Wordsworth, Melville and Milton. He even returned to Shelley's 'Dirge', which had launched his sea-music obsession fifty years earlier. In his copy of Melville's 'The Maldive Shark' he scribbled ideas in the margins, his handwriting not much scrappier than before. (His music sketching was shakier, but still legible.)

In these circumstances, in July 1974 he produced an astonishing, febrile coda to the series of canticles he began writing in 1947, *Canticle V 'The Death of Saint Narcissus'*. It was his first new piece since the operation, once more a gift for Pears. And in the same way that the tennis court at the Red House was now dug up so he was not reminded of his frailty, Britten composed for the canticle a harp accompaniment; if he was not going to play the piece, he made sure no other pianist was going to. Osian Ellis had long proved his mettle in recitals with Pears, earning Britten's grateful dedication in his 1969 Suite for Harp, a slight if useful collection of genre pieces.

He professed not to understand T. S. Eliot's youthful poem on which *Canticle V* is based. Eliot blends the stories of the Narcissus of early Christianity with his mythical namesake, and throws in the imagery of

St Sebastian for good measure. Regardless of whether he fully compre-hended Eliot's metaphysical conceits, Britten certainly identified the poem's imagery. Bells toll as the narrator reveals the bloody cloth and limbs of the saint. A trudging unison melody underpins Narcissus's youthful journey towards his faith, the moment when he becomes 'a dancer before God'. And as burning arrows fly through the air and pierce his flesh, the harp whooshes high and loud. There is an unre-strained, muscular lyricism to it all, never more so than in the vocal writing, which leaps about with youthful agility. It is so different from the muted reverence of its immediate predecessor, *Canticle IV*. The scholar Arnold Whittall first drew the neat connection between the young, beautiful Narcissus and Tadzio. Yet in *Canticle V*, protagonist and composer are both insouciant in the face of death.

Pears spent three months away from Britten in autumn 1974, rehears-ing and performing *Death in Venice* at the Metropolitan Opera, which was a big success. Britten was too ill to attend (though he toyed with the idea) and the separation depressed him enormously. It was now that he came to realize his condition would never improve. He decamped to Schloss Wolfsgarten for four weeks, which cheered him a little. There, with manuscript on lap, he sketched *Suite on English Folk Tunes*, a home for the earlier 'Hankin Booby'. Like *Canticle V*, the suite is a vigorous work, but amid the youthful thumping and clumping of the opening movement there are hints of the sage, older composer – a skit-tery violin extemporization, for instance, so much wilder than the band music that spills out of the Boar in *Peter Grimes*. The fourth movement, 'Hunt the Squirrel', sounds like the backdrop to a frenetic ceilidh, replete with a fiendish violin solo that slithers precariously along the fingerboard. Only in the elegiac final movement, an arrangement of the folk song 'Lord Melbourne', does Britten live up to the suite's subtitle, 'A Time There Was', lifted from the opening line of the last song in *Win-ter Words*. As in Mahler's 'Der Tamboursg'sell', there is a wistfulness to the cor anglais solo that meanders through the movement, never putting down roots, barely bothering to resolve itself in cadence. Only here does Britten let his guard down and hint at thoughts of mortality.

On his return from Wolfsgarten Britten wrote his greatest love letter to Pears. In accepting his mortality and likely fate, Britten wanted to record what the relationship meant while still able to do so.

My darling heart (perhaps an unfortunate phrase – but I can't use any other) I feel I must write a squiggle which I couldn't say on the telephone without bursting into those silly tears – I do love you so terribly, & not only glorious you, but your singing. I've just listened to a re-broadcast of Winter Words (something like Sept. '72) and honestly you are the greatest artist that ever was – every nuance, subtle & never overdone – those great words, so sad & wise, painted for one, that heavenly sound you make, full but always coloured for words & music. What have I done to deserve such an artist and man to write for? I had to switch off before the folk songs because I couldn't [take] anything after – 'how long, how long' [the conclusion to the cycle]. How long? only till Dec. 20th – I think I can just bear it

But I love you,
I love you
I love you.
B.

It was the Britten of *Canticle I* – youthful, ecstatic, proud: 'So I my best beloved's am; so he is mine.'

9

At no point did Britten consider stopping. His GP Ian Tait later thought his drive and inspiration had left him, but this is misconceived: he was teeming with ideas. There was no talk now of Britten having written himself out; 'there is life in this poor old dog still', as he told a friend in January 1975. Part of his depression stemmed from how long everything now took to get down on paper, how exhausted he was after only an hour's work. (This was the man who used to orchestrate his big works while holding conversations.) He was less certain, perhaps, less sure about revisions, and for a time he distrusted his ideas. 'I can't pretend the music is very wonderful,' he told his old colleague Reginald Goodall in April, 'but it is fun planning it and trying to write it down.' But he was impossibly self-deprecating, for the series of works he produced in these years puts to rest all questions about his judgement.

Rostropovich, his travel restrictions lifted, was shocked by Britten's appearance in 1974. Photographs at the time show two different Brittens: the first an enfeebled, droopy-eyed, wild-haired old man; the second a glint-eyed, ferocious musician looking at scores, or grinning broadly as he shakes the hands of the crew-members of the *Golden Vanity*, or bowing slightly to the festival's new patron, the Queen Mother, as she arrives at the Red House for lunch. Thomson remembers him chuckling away in early 1975 as he sketched 'A death', the final song of *Sacred and Profane*, his set of eight medieval lyrics for unaccompanied choir, which alternate between reverential and pastoral poems. It was a courageous gesture, for 'A death' skates uncomfortably close to the first of these Brittens. 'When my eyes get misty,' it begins (in modern translation), 'And my ears are full of hissing, / And my nose gets cold, / And my tongue folds, / And my face goes slack, / And my lips blacken, / And my mouth grins, / And my spittle runs'. The whole piece is an extraordinary conglomeration of ideas and styles. There are flashes of the composer of *A Ceremony of Carols*, never more so than in the third piece, 'Lenten is come', with its limping phrases and slow harmony. This is preceded by a sharply observed depiction of madness, the women clucking away repetitively ('Birds in the wood, / The fish in the river'), the men underpinning them with a long, sombre pedal melody ('Much sorrow I live with'). The exquisite, venerating fifth song sounds like something from one of the Venetian churches Britten visited obsessively, a soaring soprano line sitting atop a simple, homophonic hymn. The seventh dips into the madrigals Britten sang as a student, its harmony crunching along, the edges smoothed. And the final song, which recalls *A Boy was Born*, begins with full-throated Pérotin wailings, and ends with Britten humorously dispatching the protagonist to his grave ('For the whole world I don't care one jot').

Without catching his breath Britten produced *A Birthday Hansel*, 'written at the special wish of Her Majesty the Queen for her mother's seventy-fifth birthday, August 4th 1975', as the dedication states. It was the Queen's attempt to lift Britten's spirits and encourage him back to work. This cycle for high voice and harp also belies the circumstances of its composition, for it is yet another touching, youthful-sounding work. Honouring the Queen Mother's Scottish heritage, Britten selected some poems by Robert Burns, which Thomson brought to life by reading them to him, inflecting the words and rhythms with her Scottish accent. They are full of dialect – 'prief' for best-quality cloth; 'sark' for shirt;

'hoggie' for young ewe – which attractively burrs the texture. (A 'hansel' is itself a Scottish word for a gift.) And they are full of Scottish sounds: bagpipe drones in the opening and closing songs; funny little grace notes in the second, Britten here remembering the herring-girls who coloured his childhood; a Scottish reel to conclude the cycle. Mostly the accompaniment sounds like those in his first book of folk-song arrangements – the harmony pivoting from one key to the next, the vocal line feigning nonchalance. And mostly the melodies sound like authentic folk songs, though each is original. There is an introspective, chilly climax to the work, 'The Winter', which evokes in a little under three minutes what takes Schubert almost eighty to do in *Winterreise*. Britten originally followed this with an even darker setting, 'Ae Fond Kiss', whose grim pessimism and sparse textures left the birthday tribute listing somewhat despairingly. The seven remaining songs are linked by harp interludes, and if the bridge between each sometimes creaks a bit, the cycle is no worse for it.

Sacred and Profane was not performed until September 1975, while *A Birthday Hansel* had to wait until the following January for its premiere, when Pears and Osian Ellis performed it at Schloss Elmau in Bavaria, repeating it a few days later at Uphall near Sandringham for its dedicatee. There were also two important Britten premieres in the 1975 Aldeburgh Festival, which made the world think that perhaps Britten was on the mend. As well as the first showings of *Canticle V* and *Suite on English Folk Tunes*, there was something wonderfully defiant about the festival as a whole. *Death in Venice* was revived and the String Quartet in D relaunched. There was a performance of *Six Metamorphoses after Ovid*, its take on the Narcissus legend forming a counterpoint to the new canticle. Theodor Uppman sang the sad aria 'Billy in the Darbies', twenty-four years after creating the role of Budd. There were performances of *Songs and Proverbs of William Blake*, wrested from Fischer-Dieskau by baritone Graham Titus, and *The Poet's Echo*, taken from Vishnevskaya by Pears. Plomer and Auden were honoured, the former earning the 'loving' dedication of *Canticle V* and a celebratory concert, the latter in a lecture by Spender on 'The Young Auden'. (This was probably the occasion on which Britten clothed his regrets about Auden in repeated justifications.)

There was a touch of *The Wizard of Oz* to it all, of the master hidden away conjuring new works at pace, though he relied more than ever on his team of helpers for each new piece – Colin Matthews (on one occasion joined by his brother David after some years away from Aldeburgh), conductor Steuart Bedford, Rosamund Strode and Donald Mitchell. His voice no longer sounded through the Red House or the Maltings, and if audiences had peeked behind the curtain they would have seen Bill Servaes and Rosamund pulling levers and barking commands, not Britten. Or they would notice how Thomson helped preserve Britten's energy by keeping people away and managing the Red House schedule. 'I've lost Ben,' Pears complained to his pupil, the tenor Neil Mackie. 'Rita's taken over.' But Britten craved the professional and personal attention Thomson gave him, and valued the protectiveness and solicitousness that allowed him to continue composing. As with every facet of this very private man's life, his health was nobody else's business, and those outside his circle of intimates knew little about his actual condition.

In the same festival concert in which *Suite on English Folk Tunes* received its premiere, Janet Baker sang Berlioz's *Les Nuits d'été*, her performance displaying a captivating mixture of ecstasy and radiance. Britten was greatly impressed. 'I want to write you a piece like that,' he told her immediately afterwards, and began work a mere week after the festival's end. It is one of his most inspired and brilliant works. Taking a pencil to his copy of Racine's *Phèdre* in Robert Lowell's free translation, Britten drew lines through whole chunks of dialogue with all the energy and precision he had brought to adapting *A Midsummer Night's Dream* all those years ago. He reduced the handful of characters to just one, Phaedra herself, who tells of her lust for her husband Theseus's son, Hippolytus, in an extended monologue. First she addresses her unseen stepson ('See, Prince! Look, this monster, ravenous / for her execution, will not flinch. / I want your sword's spasmodic final inch' – so like the lines excised from *Lucretia*), then her nurse Oenone ('How shall I hide / my thick adulterous passion for this youth, / who has rejected me, and knows the truth?') and finally her husband ('It was I, who lusted for your son with my hot eye').

We lose certain key scenes from the Racine. We do not know that when Phaedra tells Hippolytus of her feelings she believes Theseus may be dead. Nor do we know of Hippolytus's love for Aricia, an Athenian princess. Nor do we see the chilling scene in which Oenone falsely denounces Hippolytus to his father, accusing him of attempting to rape Phaedra, covering for her mistress. And we lose the section in which

Phaedra, in a jealous rage over Aricia, refuses to dispel the lies, which leaves Theseus's curse against his son in place, his death inevitable. But we do get Phaedra's eventual exoneration of the tragic youth after his death, his horses having dashed the chariot against the rocks when startled by the terrifying horned monster that has come to fulfil Theseus's curse. And in real time we watch her life slowly wind down as the poison she has ingested does its work, unable to live with herself for her actions.

> Theseus, I stand before you to absolve
> your noble son. Sire, only this resolve
> upheld me, and made me throw down my knife.
> I've chosen a slower way to end my life –
> Medea's poison; chills already dart
> along my boiling veins and squeeze my heart.
> A cold composure I have never known
> gives me a moment's poise. I stand alone
> and seem to see my outraged husband fade
> and waver into death's dissolving shade.
> My eyes at last give up their light, and see
> the day they've soiled resume its purity.

The music is every bit as inspired as the contraction of the play. Taking his cue from the baroque cantata, Britten divided the work into recitatives, ritornellos and arias. He wrote for a small string orchestra, to which he added percussion and harpsichord. Most of the melodic material derives from the opening violin phrase, which lurches from high above the stave to just below it. Phaedra discloses her love for Hippolytus in strong-boned phrases – big leaps over a courtly accompaniment. Her confession to her husband is punctuated by spiky refashionings of the opening phrase. As poison darts through her veins there is a steady ratcheting up of tension as the strings are layered one on top of the other in long, slow scales. Phaedra's heart flutters and fades away, and after a few motific restatements the piece gently ends. It is an astonishing portrait of a complex, tightly coiled monster, an utterly compelling depiction of desire, betrayal, jealousy, honour and just a touch of madness. It took Britten only a month to compose and he wrote directly into full score, dispensing with the need for a sketch, so certain was he of his voice. Once more Matthews was enlisted to create a vocal score, and at the play-through Britten added the vocal line with his good, left hand, going into octaves at Phaedra's declamation: 'The wife of Theseus loves Hippolytus!'

10

Britten had only just begun work on *Phaedra* when in July 1975 he attended the new production of *Peter Grimes* at Covent Garden. It was a small-budget show directed by Elijah Moshinsky and conducted by Colin Davis, with Canadian Jon Vickers in the title role. Moshinsky stripped down the staging as much as he could, revelling in the Brechtian layers and psychology of the piece, in shadowy lighting and stark imagery, the cast straight from a Bruegel canvas. Writing to Davis, Britten was unexpectedly appreciative of the staging ('I was most impressed by the look of it and if that is economy – I am all for it'), but privately he despaired at certain key aspects, not least Vickers in the title role. 'Why does this man not observe what I wanted? Why does he have to sentimentalize this piece, and sentimentalize that monologue in a shameful way?' Davis's reading of the piece lacked Britten's subtlety; Vickers's indulgent performance, a hulking, wide-browed villain far from Pears's interpretation, was no doubt the source of some of the disapproval.

It is astonishing that this was the first new Covent Garden production of the opera in almost thirty years.* The grumpy, homophobic Vickers thought that, up until then, *Peter Grimes* was esteemed but not enjoyed in England, and that Britten and Pears were too close to the piece to allow it its universal significance. This was obviously untrue, but Moshinsky's expressionistic production and the *Heldentenor* Vickers's performance evidently made many people see the opera anew. The composer lasted only one act – the second – his health and spirits poor. It was his final visit to Covent Garden.

There were other valedictions. In November, with Thomson and the Servaeses, Britten visited Venice for the last time. (His passport had a

---

* In 1953 John Cranko restudied Guthrie's 1947 production, Roger Ramsdell adapting Moiseiwitsch's designs.

little over a year to run, which would just see him out.) As the holiday drew near Britten panicked, inventing reasons to cancel. Thomson stood firm and he finally gave in. When they flew into Venice, with the banking plane offering them a postcard view of La Serenissima, he finally relaxed.

They took rooms in Hotel Danieli, with its cathedral-like lobby, private water entrance for gondolas and stunning view over the piazza from the balconies. Each morning they set out on an excursion, Britten in a wheelchair, red-faced and puffy-cheeked, pushed by Bill Servaes. They travelled in a vaporetto, the craft barely able to clear the low bridges and narrow canals, or so it seemed, revisiting favourite buildings, galleries and churches. Following the morning outing and lunch in a local restaurant, Thomson took Britten back to the hotel for a rest. She would wake him in time to hear the bells threaded through the score of *Death in Venice* and which gave him such lasting delight, throwing the balcony doors open to intensify their impact. The city was cold and wet, much of it flooded, and people were pushed around on carts like medieval players, or made their way through the streets in waders. Britten was frail, but thrilled to be there once more. Home-movie footage shows him sitting out on his balcony high above the flooded piazza, smiling, cold sunlight glinting off the water below; or being spun around in his wheelchair by Thomson, feigning dizziness, mugging to the camera. It was here, with all the sounds and smells around him, that he completed the string quartet begun the previous month.

The String Quartet No. 3 is another extraordinary product of Britten's Indian summer proper, not the one critics identified in the early 1960s. A daring work in many ways – notwithstanding Britten's deprecatory response to it during its composition – its sparse textures somehow managing to sound symphonic. It is full of imaginative ideas: voices in the first movement that do not seem to align, but which generate their own momentum as a result; tiny fragments, toyed with incessantly, finally knitted into something far bigger and more splendid; peasant basses and extemporized fiddle lines in the second movement; a sad, lyrical solo birdsong in the third, high above the stave and never pausing for breath, which is soon joined by a whole chorus of autumn birds, the songs of which Britten had notated at Horham; a burlesque movement that never allows us to find our footing; a sardonic trio section that sounds like an old hurdy-gurdy, the viola scratching away on the wrong side of the bridge, as Britten asked Rosamund to demonstrate; and a final movement, 'La Serenissima', in which a serene, ultimately ecstatic melody plays out over a tramping ground bass derived from the tolling bells of Santa Maria della Salute, a peal rung only once a year that Britten encountered most fortuitously.

It is a work of great calm and resolve, and, in its gently lapping rhythms, its musical quotations from *Death in Venice* and the clanging city itself, the quartet acts as an unexpected coda to the opera. 'One is very conscious of keys when one writes,' Britten had told Janet Baker eight years earlier, confessing that those 'very "southern" keys with lots of flats have got a softness, an indulgence, that the clearer more "northern" D's & C's haven't.' Thus the bright E major – Aschenbach's key – of the final movement is chosen carefully. David Matthews suggests it is even more than this, that in the quiet serenity of the finale there is a continuation of Aschenbach's redemption – redemption that is carefully stitched into the short postlude to *Death in Venice* but which passes so quickly it is easy to miss. 'The finale is a sort of Aschenbach's finale, the sort of piece that he would have written if he were a composer.'

'I want the work to end with a question,' Britten said of the quartet, but in everything else in his life he was tying up loose ends, leaving nothing open or to chance. First the major opera for Pears; then a final canticle; a last orchestral work; one more choral piece; a final song cycle for his life's companion; a cantata for a much admired colleague; and now a final string quartet, his first essay in the genre in thirty years. 'One day, I'll write a string quartet for you,' he told Hans Keller some time after the musicologist's analysis of the second quartet appeared in 1947; here it was at last. (Keller did not initially seem very grateful, though later wrote warmly about the piece to Britten: 'I think it is absolutely stunning, and immeasurably newer than any avant-garde stuff one has heard, even in relatively distinguished circles.') Colin Matthews identifies continuity in the numbered string quartets (via the Cello Symphony); it is as though Britten thought the long period following No. 2 represented unfinished business. The language of the second and third quartets is different, of course, and the links with *Death in Venice* make No. 3 a contemporary work (as does the strong inflection of Shostakovich). But there is a thread running through the quartets. The passacaglia of the third quartet is a good companion for the Chacony of the second, while the late work's subtle formal design makes it a close sibling of the first quartet, Britten's riposte to the critics who thought him too dependent on established forms.

Back from Venice, Britten invited Colin Matthews to work on the new piece, playing it through on the piano while Britten made the necessary changes. They had three sessions together and then, on 17 December, Matthews's brother David joined in for a final play-through. There was a long silence after the wistful passacaglia, which the composer finally broke by asking in a small voice, 'Do you think it's any good?' He looked well, the brothers thought, and in a relaxed mood, but David noticed that his voice was not strong and he needed help walking. Nonetheless, they were both struck by the quartet's great power.

In January 1976, after a Red House Christmas full of people and eating and drinking, the composer holding up rather well, Britten confessed to Oliver Knussen that he was now managing only 'an occasional tiny bit of writing'. But he still could not stop. At Rostropovich's invitation, and in honour of Paul Sacher's seventieth birthday, he wrote a short, grim melody plucked from the letters of his old friend's surname. Rostropovich had invited eleven other composers to come in on the project – Boulez, Dutilleux and Lutosławski among them – and he gave the first performance at Sacher's birthday concert in May. It was a tribute to Sacher, but it was to Rostropovich's incomparable friendship and musical partnership that Britten here bade farewell.

In February he honoured his promise to the viola-player Cecil Aronowitz and recast the piano accompaniment of *Lachrymae* as a pitch-perfect arrangement for string orchestra. It pulses with the dark colours and extraordinary layerings of *Phaedra*, but the winner here is John Dowland, whose melodies Britten embroidered with such skill: the strings sound like a consort of viols, less abrasive than piano, far truer to Britten's original source of inspiration for the work. It was probably intended for that year's festival, though it was not performed until the following year and Britten never heard it.

There were realizations aplenty, now and in the months to come – some William Croft and Jeremiah Clarke, and a set of eight folk-song arrangements for harp and tenor, a number of them collected by Cecil Sharp at the century's beginning. They were transformed by Britten, who grabbed ideas from his arsenal: canons invented from scarcely promising material, a technique he perfected in *The Beggar's Opera* in 1948; unexpected harmony, counterpoint and harmonics, which thrum and plink away on the harp; clever word painting; affecting postludes. The most beautiful of these songs – perhaps the most beautiful of all his many folk-song arrangements – is a sad little Welsh tune, 'Bugeilio'r Gwenith Gwyn'. It tells (in Welsh) the story of a young man's unrequited love, which Britten sets as a lute song, the narrator strumming away as he relays his unhappy tale, Dowland's melancholia thick in the air. The arrangements in this volume are gentler than those made by the young, homesick composer, stuck in America, unwell and frustrated; but they display all the earlier songs' life and invention. And though there is nostalgia at work in these settings, much as there was in the first volume, such arrangements now took up less space on the page and in his mind. They were practical.

The biggest piece of unfinished business was *Paul Bunyan*. Since Auden's death he had picked and prodded at it, unwilling to undertake the wholesale revision he thought it needed. But each new outing – the excerpts performed in the 1974 festival, the broadcast of these in December that year, the first complete transmission on 1 February 1976 – had lessened the unhappy memories of the piece and its librettist and the circumstances of its composition. In preparing *Bunyan* for each outing, Britten brought it closer to the work he wished he had written, and he was struck by how strong he found it. But the 1976 broadcast shattered him, especially the opening to the final Litany. 'The campfire embers are black and cold, / The banjos are broken, the stories are told, / The woods are cut down and the young are grown old.' He broke down crying, this young man grown old, and was comforted by Pears, Auden a heavy unacknowledged presence in the room.

I I

The broadcast and Britten's unleashed emotional reaction to it exorcised the *Bunyan* demons. At Snape in June, attending the final rehearsal for the first production of the operetta in thirty-five years, Britten was unabashedly thrilled with it. Steuart Bedford was once more his arms and ears on the podium, conducting a large, young cast. It was a production of the English Music Theatre Company, which the previous year had grown out of the moribund EOG, directed by Colin Graham. On 4 July the United States would celebrate the 200th anniversary of the Declaration of Independence and the Aldeburgh Festival had some sport with this important slice of history. The programme book included an article entitled 'Happy Birthday, America' and a reproduction of Archibald MacNeal Willard's famous painting *The Spirit of '76*, in which a wild-eyed drummer, flanked by a fife player and one of Mahler's drummer-boys, marches across a reeking landscape, the Betsy Ross flag visible behind him. It was almost as though Britten did not quite trust the operetta to stand on its own feet, and jumped at the smokescreen the Independence Day celebrations provided. What was *Bunyan* if not a celebration of America's folkloric origins?

There was no disguising Britten's physical decline. Many at the premiere of *Phaedra* on 16 June could not reconcile the composer of such a virile work with the feeble man unsteadily acknowledging applause from the directors' box. 'I just couldn't believe that the man who had written it was in that condition,' said George Malcolm. A 1941 photograph reproduced in the programme book of a handsome young Britten sitting next to Auden (who looks at his friend with warmth and admiration) only underlined the tragic shift. So too did Auden's words from beyond the grave, courtesy of the poet's *New York Times* article of 1941, which was also reproduced in the programme book. In it Auden talks confidently of mythology and machines, of nature and politics, and of Bunyan himself: 'his dreams have all the naive swaggering optimism of the nineteenth century; he is as Victorian as New York.' How long it seemed since these two artists had stomped around the 'great hotel' together, Britten despairing at its unruliness.

Photographs of a rehearsal in June for *Phaedra* show Britten examining his score, looking every inch the Britten of old (a garish paisley shirt under his jacket replacing his traditional collar and tie – whether as a concession to the decade or his health is unclear). He revelled in Baker's performance and Bedford's understanding of the music and it shows in his sharp eyes and lively face, though there was arguably too much nobility in Baker's characterization, when what is needed is a mix of wide-eyed madness and icy control. He is a dynamic figure, too, in photographs of a rehearsal at Snape of another poignant nod to Auden, the first festival performance of *Our Hunting Fathers* (the wild 'Messalina' movement striking Britten as 'a bit over the top', as he told Colin Matthews). Sitting in the front row between André Previn and soprano Elisabeth Söderström (Thomson a reassuring, shadowy figure in the background), Britten scrunches up his face in concentration, checking notes against a full score. In these instances he was dealing with musicians he had chosen and admired and trusted, and there was none of the performance anxiety that had so blighted his concert career. By evening, though, he was drained of the little energy he had.

Britten managed an occasional good night. On 9 June, not quite a week into the twenty-ninth Aldeburgh Festival, Isherwood and his partner Don Bachardy dined with Britten and Pears at the Red House, Britten bursting into tears at the sight of his old friend. The dinner – a greatly diminished echo of another farewell they had shared in America in 1942 – was intended as a coda to a lunch Pears had enjoyed with Isherwood and Bachardy in America the previous November, where they discussed the absent Britten. Isherwood wrote up the lunch in detail in his diary.

> He seemed just the same as ever, only rather magnificently older. Don said he liked Peter better than anyone he's met for a long time. And I was so happy to be able to end this apparent feud. I only say 'apparent' because Peter maintained that there was never any bad feelings on Ben's part against me, only against Wystan. But Ben did refuse to see me, when I wanted to introduce Don to him in England. I think Peter was just covering up for Ben.

On 12 June a handful of Britten's friends gathered in the garden of the Red House for an informal drinks party, after the announcement that morning in *The Times* that Britten was now a life peer, a final gesture from queen to composer: he was now to be known as Baron Britten of Aldeburgh, in the County of Suffolk. Harewood was not alone in thinking it a 'curiously unnecessary honour', yet Mitchell thought it went some way to restoring his self-confidence. 'No one remembers me, I'm forgotten, I'm not seen out of Aldeburgh,' Mitchell remembered him saying over and over in these last months. But at the party, in a wheelchair and the same paisley shirt, Britten smiled and talked and sipped his wine. His sister Barbara stood close by, looking prematurely funereal. Mitchell chatted amiably to him, as did Fidelity Cranbrook, who for years had helped steer the festival through the mire of local hostility. And as the final guests departed, Pears wheeled Britten back into the house, the two somehow separated from their friends, alone together.

They escaped the drought and the heat wave (the hottest British summer on record) to stay in a stately late-nineteenth-century hotel overlooking a fjord some miles south of Bergen, home of Grieg. They took short excursions on the water, enjoying the fresh air and food, but it was as hot there as at home and Britten's brave face sometimes slipped. 'I should so love to think that you enjoyed some of the time in Norway,' Pears wrote on their return, once more on the road, 'but I'm afraid you didn't, and can only just hope that in retrospect when you're back at dear Horham, they may not seem so painful & that some few things may appear rather lovely.'

Despite the heat, in Norway Britten began work on a new piece for Rostropovich and the National Symphony Orchestra, as vibrant as anything written the previous year. It was to be a setting of Edith Sitwell's poem 'Praise We Great Men', written at Britten's behest in 1959 for a Royal Festival Hall celebration of coinciding Purcell and Handel anniversaries. 'The ideal would be a poem, in praise of Purcell and Handel, or in praise of praising great men of art (which I feel these days is getting rarer & rarer),' he wrote ominously at the time. Sitwell recited it at the concert and Britten was soon talking about a setting. But other projects intervened and it was only now that he returned to her stately lines.

> Praise we great men
> From all the hearths and homes of men, from hives
> Of honey-making lives.
> Praise with our music those
> Who bring the morning light
> To the hearts of men, those households of high heaven!

How fitting that Britten should turn to this so near the end of his life. Nothing in the completed fragment betrays his illness: he evokes a scented world of small chiming clocks, with radiant, shimmering strings, slow-moving harmonies, and a warm horn chorale, above which a tenor soloist sings the words, 'Praise we the just'. The fragment contains Billy Budd's woodwind stutterings and has moments of great tenderness that recall the optimistic prairie works of the early 1940s – Walt Whitman's 'vast something'. Its structure evokes the muscular *Cantata academica*, a world away from the austere Church Parables.

Back from Bergen, Britten put his sketch to one side to complete a work intended to mark a visit to Ipswich the following July by the

Queen on the occasion of her Silver Jubilee. Written for young people to sing (optional tenors) and play, *Welcome Ode* mines the ground occupied by *Spring Symphony* and, in its original ad lib scoring, Psalm 150. Haymakers, rakers, reapers and mowers – all represented by a growling, bawdy trombone solo – are instructed to put down their tools and enjoy the sunny holiday (by no means a given in Ipswich). An orchestral jig of astonishing vitality bursts with Gaelic inflexions, and as well as paying respectful honour to 'our brave queen', there is a setting of Henry Fielding's 'Ode to the New Year' ('This is a day; 'tis one to ten / Our sons will never see again'), with its hints of Shakespeare's great St Crispin's Day speech. Colin Matthews orchestrated the piece from the composition sketch, submitting sections to Britten as he finished them. Their final session on it together was in early October, when they arranged to meet a month later to work on *Praise We Great Men*.

Most of the music from this late period is so ensnared in the narrative of decline that engulfed Britten in these final years that its undiminished vigour is often unrecognized. The scores conform on every page to Britten's resolution in the 1960s to strip back his music to its bare essentials, Bridge's stern example ever on his mind. But there is also a warmth that is not always so apparent in the scores of the previous decade; there is a distillation of the colours and virtuosity of his early works that in the 1960s he attempted to leave behind. Instead of decline, then, these were years of unfettered brilliance, of inspiration at every turn and of notebooks brimming with plans and ideas. It is as Pears had written about Schubert's last songs only a few years earlier: 'Schubert never stopped till the end came.' And this is the perplexing, unanswerable question surrounding Britten's illness. Had his heart been uninfected by syphilis, he probably would not have needed surgery. Without surgery, would he have gone on composing for years with the skill, vision and youthfulness exhibited in these late works, or was it only his clattery old heart and the portents of mortality that so focused his mind?

12

He urged the Amadeus Quartet to learn his String Quartet No. 3 quickly, fearful that he would never hear it performed on the instruments for which it was intended. In late September the quartet came to rehearse with him at the Red House, a little under three months before the scheduled premiere. The players were full of questions about this unusual, deeply personal work. How is it meant to sound here? Did you have *this* in mind? Britten worked with them in detail. They were struck by his precision, by how he knew exactly what he wanted from each of them and had crafted the music according to the personality of each player. When they reached the slow movement Britten addressed the first violinist, Norbert Brainin: 'Now Norbert, I want to speak to you about this fingering.' Keller's criticism was quickly dispatched. And after a stab at the passacaglia, Britten told cellist Martin Lovett of the sound he was meant to be creating; when they picked up their bows once more the great toll of the Santa Maria della Salute bells filled the library, stunning them all.

He wrote an optimistic letter to Basil Coleman, his handwriting almost normal. Coleman was to direct a ten-part adaptation of *Anna Karenina* for BBC television, to be screened the following year, and Britten enthused about the book, his own near miss with Tolstoy on his mind. 'Will you have a day or two free to spend with us at Xmas?' he added. 'Like last year? We both (& Rita) hope so, very much. All goes well here, except that Peter, having a few days off, is really too tired to profit by them. But he is very resilient. *Do* try & come to see us at Xmas – only us, of course! Lots of love, Ben.' If I make such plans, I'll still be here to see them through, he seemed to be saying.

In October he attended a 'concert party' at the Jubilee Hall, which was transformed into a cabaret club for the occasion. The following year's festival would be the thirtieth, but it was clear Britten would not be alive for the celebrations, so Pears brought them forward. It was all light fare: Pears and Jenni Wake-Walker pounded away at Grainger's four-handed arrangement of Gershwin's 'Embraceable You', fighting over pedals as they went; and a Whiffenpoofs-type ensemble from Cambridge performed *a cappella* arrangements. But there were also some deeply touching moments. Accompanied by Graham Johnson, Pears sang three of Britten's *Cabaret Songs* alongside 'Miss Otis Regrets', and even if only two people in the hall could picture the booze and squalor of February House, or the calm sanctuary of the Mayers' house on Long Island, it in no way undermined the resonance. Pears then sang 'I'll see you again', the gentle waltz from Noel Coward's *Bitter Sweet*.

I'll see you again whenever spring breaks through again.
Time may lie heavy between, but what has been, is past forgetting.
This sweet memory across the years will come to me.
Though my world may go awry, in my heart 'twill ever lie,
Just the echo of a sigh, goodbye.

Everyone then toasted the next thirty years, after which Britten quietly slipped away into the night.

His health deteriorated rapidly thereafter. He cancelled his appointment with Colin Matthews in early November, the one where they were going to plot the remainder of *Praise We Great Men*, leaving only a tantalizing torso instead of the great work that was emerging. And when the Amadeus Quartet rang to check on their next rehearsal, planned for 19 November, Britten brushed them off. 'Just tell them from me they know it,' he told Thomson, who had taken the call. For his sixty-third birthday, after a terrible night of fitful sleep and oxygen from a tank, he decided he wanted a champagne party at the Red House with some of his favourite friends. Thomson and Pears assembled Britten's sisters, Peg Hesse (who was in town), the Servaeses, Holst and Mary Potter, and they drank champagne downstairs, going up to his bedroom one at a time to see him and say their final goodbyes. They each had ten minutes or so with him, trying not to be mawkish or awkward, before leaving the room with a wave or a smile. Britten was calm and direct with each: 'If this is it, and I am sure it is, I want to go. I can't bear to go on any longer not being able to do all the things I used to do,' he told Beth. He refused morphine in these weeks, despite the pain and nausea, and his mind was clear.

A few days after the champagne party, Pears wrote to Britten's other great love, from another era, Wulff Scherchen, thanking him for his birthday wishes.

Dearest Wulff,

Ben was so touched to have your letter. He is slowly fading, taking his time, uncomfortable but not in great pain, calm and loving all the time, drowsier each day but surprising us too with sudden questions. All there, as one says –

My love to you,
Peter

Barbara saw him one last time as he slowly faded. 'Sorry, old thing,' he shrugged at her, as calm and loving as Pears said, now just that bit weaker.

On Friday, 3 December Michael Petch came to stay. After a good dinner with Pears, the wine flowing, Petch checked in on his patient once more. 'Goodnight, Mike,' Britten whispered as he made his retreat. Britten's breathing deteriorated in the early hours of the morning. The night nurse, Susie Walton, sensing the end was imminent, rang the bell to summon Thomson from her exhausted sleep, which took several attempts. She eventually entered the room at 4.15 a.m., arriving just in time to watch Britten die in Pears's arms.

Despite his gradual decline, it was too shocking. Thomson and Pears fell to their knees and stayed there a long time, unbearably distraught. Walton began the necessary clean-up, and because it was a bitterly cold night, a severe, snow-like frost on the ground, she saw that a fire was lit downstairs. Petch was woken a little before dawn and came along the corridor, sadly redundant; he left the Red House as it slowly came to life, driving Walton back home. On his return he stopped to watch the sunrise over the dour, shingly beach on which Britten had often composed his thoughts and music. Two days later Britten's death was registered. In the column marked 'Cause of death' was written 'Congestive Cardiac Failure; Aortic Incompetence' – all of which was true, but only a small part of the story.

The funeral was held on 7 December. On its way to Aldeburgh parish church the hearse drove along the High Street, which was lined by sombre villagers. Grim-faced friends and family made their way into the church grounds, where the crew from the lifeboat formed a guard of honour. In parody of the Lowestoft childhood photographs of the 'four Bs', Bobby, Beth and Barbara filed into the church, looking far older than their years. Pears followed, his hand clutching Thomson's, his face stricken, and then a bereft-looking Rostropovich.

The Bishop of St Edmundsbury and Ipswich, Leslie Brown, had visited Britten in his final months, providing him with spiritual comfort. In these sessions Britten spoke to him nostalgically about his untroubled belief in Christ as a boy and how sad he was to have lost such simple faith. 'I do not believe that Ben could be dishonest,' the Bishop told the congregation. 'He believed deeply in a Reality which works in us and through us and is the source of goodness and beauty, joy and love. He was sometimes troubled because he was not sure if he could give the name of God to that Reality.' He was describing the Britten of *Death in Venice* and *Billy Budd*, but he also captured the twenty-something Britten who wrote of Mahler's 'Der Abschied' (Farewell): 'It is cruel, you know, that music should be so beautiful. It has the beauty of loneliness & of pain: of strength & freedom.' The Bishop added the touching words, 'Ben will like the sound of the trumpets, though he will find it difficult to believe that they are sounding for him.' The choir sang the sixteen-year-old Britten's *A Hymn to the Virgin*, his simple yet affecting anthem, so sure in its faith and musical vision, and the bell-ringers pealed away noisily, earning Holst's enthusiastic approval. He was buried in the churchyard, lowered into his grave by five or six men as Pears looked on, distressed, the surrounding trees leafless, the grave lined with rushes from marshes at the Maltings.

13

'My dearest darling,' Pears had written two years earlier from New York, in response to Britten's outpouring of love and emotion.

> No one has ever ever had a lovelier letter than the one which came from you today – You say things which turn my heart over with love and pride, and I love you for every single word you write. But you know, Love is blind – and what your dear eyes do not see is that it is *you* who have given *me* everything, right from the beginning, from yourself in Grand Rapids! through Grimes & Serenade & Michelangelo and Canticles – one thing after another, right up to this great Aschenbach – I am here as your mouthpiece and I live in your music – And I can never be thankful enough to you and to Fate for all the heavenly joy we have had together for 35 years.
>
> My darling, I love you – P.

Few of those close to Pears thought him an easy man to read; his personality often seemed not quite in focus. Thomson, who stayed on at the Red House at Pears's invitation, thought he spent his entire life telling people what they wanted to hear. 'I am no longer quite sure if what I'm telling is truth or invention,' he wrote to Britten a month before his death following an American radio interview. 'It doesn't matter very much anyway, does it?' Incapable of arguing, allergic to confrontation, Pears was in many ways the ideal foil to Britten's sulks and rages and dark moods. He would deflect him effortlessly when it came to music or art or casting: 'No, no, no, no: that's too dreary. It's not what we want, Ben. Let's get somebody else.' It could be another singer or director or the pianist Gerald Moore; it did not seem to matter. But Pears never called Britten out on his more outrageous behaviour; worse, he almost seemed to enable it, as people had been doing for Britten since he was a child.

'Ben's love for Peter never wavered,' said Thomson. Over time Pears came to find the responsibilities of his relationship with this glass-jawed, needy, brilliant man stifling. So he developed the career and lifestyle that allowed him his independence, all the while fulfilling a vital role in Britten's life, and Britten in his. He was deeply upset by his partner's death. Part of this was bereavement, part of it guilt: he was away so often in the final years and months, teaching and performing, helping to promote the school at Snape that would now become such an important part of his life, and the self-recrimination was evident.

But so too was there a sense of release. 'I mean you're released from this exhilarating and inspiring and ecstatic relationship,' said Mitchell, 'but which has always been partly at the cost of your own ego. Well now here was an opportunity for the Pears ego to expand without constraint.' Graham Johnson often saw him in tears after Britten's death, including once during a recital, when Pears abruptly walked off stage and wept in the wings, having sung the last song Schubert ever wrote, 'Taubenpost', which is full of longing and despair. 'I think he felt guilty about aspects of his relationship. I think he knew he hadn't been the perfect friend,' Johnson said. 'He felt in a sense he hadn't been worthy of Britten's love. He felt that Britten had been more loving towards him than he had been towards Britten.'

John Tooley, who achieved the impossible by keeping relations between Britten and Covent Garden on an (almost) even keel, thought the imbalance inevitable due to Britten's psychological make-up, not Pears's opaque personality.

They found a lot of happiness together, because they shared many things, but there always seemed to me to be a bit of Ben that was so locked away within himself, and incapable of being released, that you sometimes wondered whether in fact he was really going to achieve what was within him to have in pleasure, and fulfilment, and satisfaction as a human being. I don't think that he ever got that.

Pears went on almost as before, determined to prove he was his own man, not a Chester Kallman figure, caught in Auden's shadow. So he tried just that bit harder: he thought of the roles he should now sing – Florestan, the heroic political prisoner in Beethoven's *Fidelio*, not at all his voice – and the concerts he must perform, and the master-classes he must give. This pattern began immediately after the funeral of his lover of thirty-seven years, when Pears hitched a ride back to London with Rostropovich, en route to Cardiff, where he was to sing *Saint Nicolas* the following day.

A stroke at the end of 1980 slowed him down, but only slightly. It was the day after he filmed excerpts from *Death in Venice* for *A Time There Was*, his over-rouged, tired face betraying perplexity as he fluffed take after take. 'I'm sorry, I just can't get it,' he apologized as he called for a score. Pears continued to lecture and teach and proselytize, and helped turn the school at the Maltings into what it is today: a superb centre of music-making at the highest level. He was kind and generous, bullheaded and frustrating, his continued direction of the Aldeburgh Festival displaying all these qualities. He did not view the festival as a memorial to Britten. In fact, Mitchell remembers his reluctance to programme Britten's music, shrugging his shoulders at those who hinted that perhaps it was a nice idea, saying, 'Well honestly,' exasperated at the suggestion or implication. 'There'd be these early stages of planning and there wouldn't be a single Britten work or Britten project or Britten proposal in it, and you know we had to bring Britten back into it, and isn't that odd?'

In *The Swimming Pool Library*, novelist Alan Hollinghurst captures Pears well in the last years of his life, placing him at a 1983 Covent Garden performance of *Billy Budd*, seeing the same John Piper set on which he had created Captain Vere over thirty years earlier. 'Pears was shuffling very slowly along the aisle towards the front of the stalls, supported by a man on either side. Most of the bland audience showed no recognition of who he was, though occasionally someone would stare, or look away hurriedly from the singer's stroke-slackened but beautiful white-crested head.' As the interval concludes and the lights go down, the narrator's grandfather comments: 'I don't give him long.' But he lived another three years, dying in April 1986 of coronary thrombosis,* leaving behind a remarkable legacy: recordings, roles, institutions, performing traditions and a prominent place in the history of English music, both in his own right and in the life of one of its greatest composers.

14

Pears was right about what Britten had given him, the great roles from Grimes to Aschenbach, extraordinary works from *Michelangelo Sonnets* to the final canticle. Even beyond the works themselves, though, Britten's gift was to change the way music is thought about and presented in his country of birth, shifting it far closer to the Continental model of training and performance he admired in his youth and thought lacking in more slapdash Britain. Some of the composer's obituaries were a little mealy-mouthed on this point, though the *Daily Telegraph* got it just right: 'Benjamin Britten, the truly towering talent of his age.' Britten would have made no such claim on his own behalf. 'All of us – the public, critics, and composers themselves – spend far too much time worrying about whether a work is a shattering masterpiece,' he said ten years before his death. 'Let us not be so self-conscious. Maybe in thirty years' time very few works that are well known today will still be played, but does that matter so much? Surely out of the works that are written some good will come, even if it is not now; and these will lead on to people who are better than ourselves.'

Much good did come from the revolution he precipitated. But he would be astounded to see how many of his works are played today. And if he did not warm to the manner in which many of the operas are now staged, he would at least approve of how subsequent generations have identified the message and meaning in his works, the universal ideas positioned in the most local of settings. Even those who crowded Westminster Abbey for his memorial service on 10 March 1977 – Pears reciting Smart's madhouse poem 'Rejoice in the Lamb' – could not have

* Coronary thrombosis is commonplace in patients with aortic syphilis, but is not diagnostically conclusive on its own.

predicted the continuing resonance of his music.* He was the twentieth century's consummate musician, but he was also the spoilt child Forster once identified, who stamped his foot until he got his way, ruthlessly dispatching those who obstructed him. In so doing, he produced a body of works and performances that was unrivalled in the twentieth century and is unlikely to be surpassed any time soon.

---

* Britten earned just over £100,000 in 1974–5 (equivalent to £700,000 today) and his probate wealth was £1,664,714 (£10 million), over £300,000 more than Laurence Olivier's thirteen years later. In the calendar year 2011 his estate earned £1,512,222 in royalties, with no signs of diminishing. The money is spent on the festival, school and archive, on commissions, subsidies and promotions, and on causes close to Britten's heart.

Notes

ABBREVIATIONS

ATTW   *A Time There Was: A Profile of Benjamin Britten*, film by Tony Palmer (London Weekend Television, 1980), a transcript and out-takes are kept at the Britten–Pears Library

BOM   Paul Kildea (ed.), *Britten on Music* (Oxford, 2008)

BPL   The collections of The Britten–Pears Library, Aldeburgh, Suffolk

CGIH   Christopher Grogan (ed.), *Imogen Holst: A Life in Music*, revised edition (Woodbridge, 2010)

D   Britten's diary, BPL; or John Evans (ed.), *Journeying Boy: The Diaries of the Young Benjamin Britten 1928–1938* (London, 2009)

HCBB   Humphrey Carpenter, *Benjamin Britten: A Biography* (London, 1992)

JBBC   John Bridcut, *Britten's Children* (London, 2006)

L1   Donald Mitchell and Philip Reed (eds.), *Letters from a Life: The Selected Letters and Diaries of Benjamin Britten 1913–1976*, vol. 1: *1923–1939* (London, 1991); these letters are annotated in detail and these annotations are quoted throughout this book

L2   Donald Mitchell and Philip Reed (eds.), *Letters from a Life: The Selected Letters and Diaries of Benjamin Britten 1913–1976*, vol. 2: *1939–1945* (London, 1991)

L3   Donald Mitchell, Philip Reed and Mervyn Cooke (eds.), *Letters from a Life: The Selected Letters of Benjamin Britten 1913–1976*, vol. 3: *1946–1951* (London, 2004)

L4   Philip Reed, Mervyn Cooke and Donald Mitchell (eds.), *Letters from a Life: The Selected Letters of Benjamin Britten 1913–1976*, vol. 4: *1952–1957* (Woodbridge, 2008)

L5   Philip Reed and Mervyn Cooke (eds.), *Letters from a Life: The Selected Letters of Benjamin Britten 1913–1976*, vol. 5: *1958–1965* (Woodbridge, 2010)

L6   Philip Reed and Mervyn Cooke (eds.), *Letters from a Life: The Selected Letters of Benjamin Britten 1913–1976*, vol. 6: *1966–1976* (Woodbridge, 2012)

MBB   Beth Welford, *My Brother Ben* (Abbotsbrook, 1986)
NBB   Eric Crozier, Notes on Benjamin Britten (unpublished, 1966)
PKSB   Paul Kildea, *Selling Britten: Music and the Market Place* (Oxford, 2002)

PROLOGUE: THE ART OF DISSENT

p. 1   '*All art*': James Baldwin, 'The Precarious Vogue of Ingmar Bergman', *Esquire* (Apr. 1960), republished as 'The Northern Protestant', in Toni Morrison (ed.), *James Baldwin: Collected Essays* (New York, 1998), p. 246.

p. 1   '*city of the dead*': Author's transcription of BBC broadcast, 14 June 1940.

p. 1   '*their finest*': Hansard, HC Deb., vol. 362, col. 61, 18 June 1940.

p. 1   '*whether British*': Hansard, HC Deb., vol. 361, col. 1361, 13 June 1940.

p. 2   '*Is my*': Ibid.

p. 2   '*He is*': Peter Pears, 'Neither a Hero nor a Villain', *Radio Times* (8 Mar. 1946), in Philip Brett (ed.), *Benjamin Britten: Peter Grimes*, Cambridge Opera Handbooks (Cambridge, 1983), p. 152.

p. 3   '*a subject*': 'Opera's New Face', *Time* (16 Feb. 1948), p. 66.

p. 3   '*a middle-class*': George Orwell, *The Road to Wigan Pier* (London, 1937), p. 163.

p. 3   '*A central*': Murray Schafer, *British Composers in Interview* (London, 1963), BOM, p. 226.

p. 4   '*heavily repressed*': Hans Keller, 'The Musical Character', in Donald Mitchell and Hans Keller (eds.), *Benjamin Britten: A Commentary on his Works from a Group of Specialists* (London, 1952), p. 350.

p. 4   '*It has*': Andrew Porter, programme note for 1971 New York Opera production of *Albert Herring*, in Brett, *Peter Grimes*, p. 195.

p. 4   '*predominantly negative*': Brett, 'Postscript', ibid., p. 192.

p. 4   '*The more*': Peter Pears to Britten [1 Mar. 1944], L 2, p. 1189.

p. 5   '*try to talk*': D, 2 Aug. 1935.

p. 6   '*It is*': Britten to Princess Margaret of Hesse, 20 Jan. 1958, L 5, p. 14.

p. 7   '*By the time*': Edmund Wilson, 'London in Midsummer', in his *Europe without Baedeker* (New York, 1947), pp. 186–91.

p. 7   '*It's an encouraging*': Britten to Princess Margaret of Hesse, 20 Jan. 1958, L 5, p. 14.

p. 8   '*Very warm-hearted*': John Lindsay interviewed by Donald Mitchell, 10 July 1990, BPL.

p. 8   '*No man*': Ronald Duncan, *Working with Britten: A Personal Memoir* (Welcombe, 1981), p. 145.

p. 8   '*A mother's*': NBB.

p. 8   '*that he*': Humphrey Maud interviewed by Donald Mitchell, 11 Sept. 1998, BPL.

p. 8   '*The atmosphere*': Stephen Spender interviewed by Donald Mitchell, 27 Oct. 1990, BPL.

p. 8   '*Well Ben*': As relayed by Spender, ibid.

p. 8   '*To be*': Alan Blyth, *Remembering Britten* (London, 1981), p. 136.

p. 8   '*I think*': Michael Tippett, 'Obituary', *Listener* (16 Dec. 1976), in Blyth, *Remembering Britten*, p. 70.

p. 8   '*Pope*': Robert Tear, *Tear Here* (London, 1990), pp. 137–8.

p. 9   '*an atmosphere*': Ibid., p. 104.

p. 9   '*a lasting*': Blyth, *Remembering Britten*, p. 74.

p. 9   '*a little*': Paul Campion and Rosy Runciman, *Glyndebourne Recorded* (London, 1994), p. 37.

p. 9   '*Monty Slater*': NBB.

p. 9   '*future Professor*': NBB.

p. 10   '*He has*': Eric Crozier to Nancy Evans [?July 1949], L3, p. 521.

p. 10   '*obviously very*': Marion Thorpe interviewed by Michael Oliver, 1996, BPL.

p. 10   '*wonderful*': Ibid.

p. 10   '*He needed*': Rosamund Strode interviewed by the author, 7 May 2009.

p. 10   '*came in*': Imogen Holst's diary, 20 Jan. 1953, CGIH, p. 237.

p. 10   '*I must say*': Donald Mitchell interviewed by the author, 22 Oct. 2008.

p. 10   '*For public*': NBB.

p. 11   '*It sounds*': Marion Thorpe interviewed by Michael Oliver, 1996, BPL.

p. 11   '*His neck*': NBB.

p. 12   '*It always*': Tippett, 'Obituary', p. 70.

p. 12   '*It seems*': Ibid., pp. 70–71.

p. 13   '*The artist*': Anton Chekhov to Aleksei Suvorin, 30 May 1888, in Avrahm Yarmolinsky (ed.), *Letters of Anton Chekhov* (New York, 1973), p. 71.

p. 14   '*When you*': ATTW.

p. 14   '*Britten's artistic*': Philip Brett, 'The Britten Era' (1997), PKSB, p. 6.

CHAPTER 1. BOYHOOD: SUFFOLK, 1913–1930

p. 19   '*Suffolk*': Britten, 'Freeman of Lowestoft', *Tempo*, 21 (Autumn 1951), BOM, p. 108.

p. 19   '*Some of you*': Ibid, p. 110.

p. 21   '*Hark!*': George Crabbe, 'The Borough', in Norma Dalrymple-Champneys (ed.), *George Crabbe: The Complete Poetical Works*, vol. 1 (Oxford, 1988), p. 367.

p. 21   '*When he*': E. M. Forster, 'George Crabbe: The Poet and the Man', *Listener* (29 May 1941), in Philip Brett (ed.), *Benjamin Britten: Peter Grimes*, Cambridge Opera Handbooks (Cambridge, 1983), p. 3.

p. 22   '*Where hang*': Crabbe, 'The Borough', p. 361.

p. 23   '*Especially at*': W. G. Sebald, *The Rings of Saturn* (London, 1998), p. 159.

p. 23   '*rows of*': Ibid., p. 42.

p. 23   '*When the*': MBB, p. 23.

p. 24   '*singing*': Britten, 'England and the Folk-Art Problem', *Modern Music*, 18/2 (Jan.–Feb. 1941), BOM, p. 32.

p. 24   '*admitted periodically*': MBB, p. 17.

p. 25   '*utterly absurd*': Basil Reeve interviewed by Jennifer Doctor and the author, June 1999, BPL.

p. 25   '*attractively ugly*': NBB.

p. 26   '*I took*': Marjorie Britten, quoted in HCBB, pp. 24–5.

p. 26   '*He was*': John Pounder interviewed by Donald Mitchell, 24 June 1989, BPL; Basil Reeve interviewed by Mitchell, 3 Oct. 1986, BPL.

p. 26   '*that his*': NBB.

p. 26   '*His father*': NBB.

p. 27   '*He never*': Basil Reeve interviewed by Donald Mitchell, 3 Oct. 1986, BPL.

p. 27   '*security*': Thomas Sewell to Britten, Feb. 1948, L 1, p. 83.

p. 27   '*Personally*': Ibid.

p. 27   '*My dear*': R. V. Britten to Britten, 11 July 1933, L 1, p. 310.

p. 28   '*The mother*': John Pounder, interviewed by Donald Mitchell, 24 June 1989, BPL.

p. 28   '*I liked*': John Alston interviewed by Donald Mitchell and Philip Reed, 21 June 1988, BPL.

p. 28   '*she ran*': Basil Reeve interviewed by the author, 3 July 2009.

p. 28   '*I don't*': Basil Reeve interviewed by Donald Mitchell, 3 Oct. 1986, BPL.

p. 28   '*It's very*': ATTW.

p. 28   '*He certainly*': ATTW.

p. 28   '*You know*': Basil Reeve interviewed by Donald Mitchell, 3 Oct. 1986, BPL.

p. 29   '*I suspect*': Ibid.

p. 29   '*I never*': John Alston interviewed by Donald Mitchell and Philip Reed, 21 June 1988, BPL.

p. 31   '*Lift your*': MBB, p. 44.

p. 31   '*little wonder*': D, 31 Dec. 1933.

p. 31   '*the rules*': Hermione Lee, *Virginia Woolf* (London, 1996), p. 146.

p. 32   *For the first*: MBB, p. 30.

p. 33   '*threatening roar*': Imogen Holst, *Britten* (London, 1970), p. 13.

p. 35   '*I do feel*': Britten, prefatory note, *Tit for Tat*, BOM, p. 356.

p. 35   '*It's because*': Imogen Holst's diary, 8 Feb. 1953, CGIH, p. 243.

p. 36   *'a lovely'*: Eric Crozier and Nancy Evans, 'After Long Pursuit', unpublished typescript, BPL.

p. 36   *'last twelve'*: Elizabeth David, *Italian Food* (London, 1977), p. 30.

p. 37   *'I do not'*: Sybille Bedford, *Quicksands: A Memoir* (London, 2005), p. 61.

p. 37   *'she was'*: Charles Dickens, *Great Expectations* (Harmondsworth, 1965), p. 74.

p. 37   *'I can never'*: Britten to Ethel Astle, 2 Aug. 1942, L 2, pp. 1069–70.

p. 38   *'The [prep] school'*: Alec Waugh, *Public School Life: Boys Parents Masters* (London, 1922), p. 21.

p. 38   *'I can remember'*: *Guardian* (7 June 1971), HCBB, p. 10.

p. 38   *'his contacts'*: Britten, sleeve-note to Decca recording, LW 5163 (1955), BOM, p. 358.

p. 38   *'He wasn't'*: HCBB, p. 10.

p. 39   *'he worked'*: Britten, sleeve-note to Decca recording, LW 5163.

p. 39   *'Such a'*: Holst, *Britten*, p. 20.

p. 39   *'Edward Benjamin'*: John Bridcut, *Britten* (London, 2010), pp. 195–219.

p. 40   *'I have'*: Britten, speech on receiving honorary degree at Hull University, *London Magazine*, 3 (Oct. 1963), BOM, p. 214.

p. 40   *'I do'*: Michael Kennedy, *Portrait of Walton* (Oxford, 1989), p. 131.

p. 41   *'Between the'*: Murray Schafer, *British Composers in Interview* (London, 1963), BOM, p. 228.

p. 42   *'I remember'*: Britten, 'The Artist and his Medium: Composer and Listener', BBC Schools Home Service, broadcast 18 Oct. 1946, BOM, pp. 61–2.

p. 43   *'He has only'*: R. V. Britten to The British Broadcasting Company, Ltd. [before 14 July 1926], L 1, p. 86.

p. 43   *'The outlook'*: Charles Macpherson to Mrs Kennard, 14 Dec. 1926, L 1, p. 90.

p. 43   *'although I'*: Britten, 'The Artist and his Medium', p. 62.

p. 44   *'As a'*: Britten, 'Britten Looking Back', *Sunday Telegraph* (17 Nov. 1963), BOM, p. 250.

p. 45   *'So you are'*: Holst, *Britten*, pp. 22–5.

p. 45   *'not only'*: Earl of Harewood, 'The Man', in Donald Mitchell and Hans Keller (eds.), *Benjamin Britten: A Commentary on his Works from a Group of Specialists* (London, 1952), p. 6.

p. 45   *'The English'*: Stephen Spender, 'Afterword: Looking Back', in his *World within World* (London, 2001), pp. 376–7.

p. 46   *'I remember'*: Britten, 'Britten Looking Back', p. 250.

p. 46   *'I heard'*: Ibid., p. 253.

p. 47   *'Mr Greatorex'*: Britten to Mrs Britten, 23 Sept. 1928, L 1, p. 96.

p. 47   *'flimsy technick'*: Ibid.

p. 48   'I owe': W. H. Auden, 'The Liberal Fascist', in Edward Mendelson (ed.), *The English Auden* (London, 1986), p. 323.

p. 48   'Is Greatorex': Spender, 'Greatorex', *Grasshopper* (1955), L1, p. 223.

p. 48   'modern idiom': *The Gresham*, 12 (Oct. 1928–July 1930), L1, p. 123.

p. 49   'Go and': D, 31 July 1928.

p. 49   'He told': NBB.

p. 49   'having been': NBB.

p. 49   'He talked': Beata Sauerlander interviewed by Christopher Headington, June 1988, BPL.

p. 50   'In the opinion': L1, p. 403.

p. 50   'Well I': Britten interviewed by Joseph Cooper, *The Composer Speaks*, BBC General Overseas Service, broadcast 7 July 1957, BOM, p. 147.

p. 50   'I believe': Humphrey Carpenter, *W. H. Auden: A Biography* (Oxford, 1992), p. 25.

p. 51   'It meant': Ibid., pp. 25–6.

p. 51   'I think': D, 6 Dec. 1929. Britten's misspellings are mostly reproduced without comment.

p. 51   'I have': Britten to Mrs Britten, 18 Mar. 1929, L1, p. 110.

p. 51   'All the': D, 4 Feb. 1929.

p. 52   'I am': D, 20 Nov. 1929.

p. 53   *In preparing*: Colin Matthews, foreword to Britten, *Quartettino*, Faber Music (London, 1983).

p. 53   *Footnote*: Britten, 'Britten Looking Back', p. 250.

p. 54   'If I': D, 13 Aug. 1930.

p. 54   'it is no': *The Gresham* (7 June 1930), HCBB, pp. 31–2.

p. 55   'it is terribly': D, 27 Dec. 1930.

p. 56   'Everything was': Basil Reeve interviewed by Donald Mitchell, 3 Oct. 1986, BPL.

p. 57   'I am terribly': D, 27 July 1930.

CHAPTER 2. APPRENTICESHIP: LONDON, SUFFOLK, 1930–1939

p. 58   'I've lived': Britten interviewed by the Earl of Harewood, *People Today*, BBC Home Service, broadcast 23 June 1960, BOM, p. 178.

p. 58   'I hate': Murray Schafer, *British Composers in Interview* (London, 1963), BOM, p. 223.

p. 59   'Royal Opera': Edward Dent, *A Theatre for Everybody* (London and New York, 1945), p. 137.

p. 59   'foreign men': Britten to his parents, 24 Sept. 1930, L1, p. 140.

p. 59   'Thank you': Ibid.

p. 59   *'I was'*: Britten interviewed by Charles Reid, 'Back to Britain with Britten', *High Fidelity Magazine* (Dec. 1959), BOM, p. 171.

p. 59   *'conservatory dignitary'*: Cyril Ehrlich, *The Music Profession in Britain since the Eighteenth Century* (Oxford, 1988), p. 223. Ehrlich is paraphrasing the observations of Sydney Harrison.

p. 60   *'little more'*: Ibid., p. 228.

p. 60   *'he can'*: Stephen Potter's diary, 12 Oct. 1952, CGIH, p. 194.

p. 60   *'My struggle'*: Britten interviewed by Charles Reid, 'Back to Britain with Britten', p. 171.

p. 60   *'very clever'*: Remo Lauricella interviewed by Donald Mitchell, 1987, BPL.

p. 60   *'how highly'*: Hugh Allen to Britten's parents, 3 Aug. 1931, L1, p. 197.

p. 61   *'Without'*: Britten, 'Britten Looking Back', *Sunday Telegraph* (17 Nov. 1963), BOM, p. 252.

p. 62   *'quite drunk'*: D, 22 Oct. 1931.

p. 63   *Ireland scholar*: Bruce Phillips interviewed by the author, 24 Apr. 2009; Phillips to the author, 27 Sept. 2009.

p. 63   *'If I'*: Frank Bridge to Britten, 13 Aug. 1930, L1, p. 133.

p. 63   *'very beautiful'*: D, 2 Oct. 1930; 17 Sept. 1931.

p. 64   *'magnificent'*: D, 10 Feb. 1932.

p. 64   *'He is'*: D, 16 Oct. 1930.

p. 64   *'so talented'*: Remo Lauricella interviewed by Donald Mitchell, 1987, BPL.

p. 64   *'I think'*: Frank Bridge to Britten, 13 Aug. 1930, L1, p. 133.

p. 64   *'let him'*: John Ireland [to ?], 23 Mar. 1954, L1, p. 146.

p. 65   *'I feel'*: D, 12 July 1937.

p. 66   *'Sometimes he'*: *New York Times* (13 July 1939), L2, p. 686.

p. 67   *'I do not'*: John Ireland [to ?], 23 Mar. 1954, L1, p. 146.

p. 67   *'Everyone was'*: Quoted in Noel Annan, *Our Age* (London, 1990), p. 154.

p. 68   *'Practise &'*: D, 9 Feb. 1931.

p. 68   *'so far'*: D, 27 Oct. 1931.

p. 69   *'Ben can't'*: L1, p. 104.

p. 69   *'I had'*: Britten, 'Britten Looking Back', p. 253.

p. 69   *'one didn't'*: L1, p. 288.

p. 69   *'cold fish'*: HCBB, p. 35.

p. 69   *'Now, do'*: Charles Mackerras interviewed by Richard Jarman, 21 Apr. 2009, BPL.

p. 70   *'terrible execrable conductor'*: D, 4 Nov. 1931.

p. 70   *'despicable . . . old-fashioned'*: D, 10 Sept. 1931; 22 Sept. 1931.

p. 70   *'unscholastic . . . 60 strings'*: D, 18 Nov. 1931; 25 Nov. 1931.

p. 70   *'I cannot'*: D, 25 Feb. 1932.

p. 70   *'dull'*: D, 21 Oct. 1931.

p. 70   '*absolute vandal ... lack of detail*': D, 11 Aug. 1934; 30 Sept. 1932.

p. 70   '*Henry J. Wood*': D, 13 Aug. 1935.

p. 70   '*disgraceful ... Listen to ... vandal*': D, 11 May 1932; 24 Nov. 1932; 14 Oct. 1937.

p. 71   '*When F.B.*': D, 16 Jan. 1935.

p. 71   '*F.B. conducts*': D, 11 Feb. 1932.

p. 72   '*This work*': D, 17 Feb. 1932.

p. 74   '*She is*': D, 19 Aug. 1932.

p. 74   '*marvellous*': D, 23 May 1932.

p. 74   '*the best*': D, 11 Mar. 1932.

p. 74   '*v. good*': D, 11 Apr. 1932.

p. 75   '*so as*': D, 4 Nov. 1932.

p. 75   '*The radio-gram*': *Gramophone* (Jan. 1934), p. 59.

p. 76   '*Anne did*': D, 11 Dec. 1933.

p. 76   '*I remember*': L 1, p. 420.

p. 77   '*Remarkable*': D, 28 Jan. 1931.

p. 78   'Oedipus Rex *demonstrated*': Britten, 'Soviet Opera at B.B.C.: Shostakowitch's "Lady Macbeth"', *World Film News*, 1/1 (Apr. 1936), BOM, p. 17.

p. 78   '*Of course*': Ralph Vaughan Williams to Ivor Atkins [1932], L 1, p. 259.

p. 78   '*It is*': Claude Debussy to Igor Stravinsky, 9 Nov. 1913, in Igor Stravinsky and Robert Craft, *Conversations with Igor Stravinsky* (New York, 1959), p. 55.

p. 79   '*At about*': Britten, 'Britten Looking Back', p. 251.

p. 79   '*astounding*': D, 13 Feb. 1933; 8 Mar. 1933.

p. 79   '*leave England*': Schafer, *British Composers in Interview*, p. 224.

p. 80   '*I am going*': Britten, 'Britten Looking Back', p. 252.

p. 80   '*The insinuation*': Reid, 'Back to Britain with Britten', p. 172.

p. 80   '*It might*': Earl of Harewood, 'The Man', in Donald Mitchell and Hans Keller (eds.), *Benjamin Britten: A Commentary on his Works from a Group of Specialists* (London, 1952), p. 3.

p. 81   '*it's my*': D, 30 Apr. 1937; for comment on *Les Illuminations*, see Britten to Ralph Hawkes, 19 Oct. 1939, L 2, p. 711.

p. 81   '*I did*': Britten interviewed by Joseph Cooper, 'The Composer Speaks', BBC General Overseas Service, broadcast 7 July 1957, BOM, p. 148.

p. 81   '*No; not really*': Britten interviewed by John Amis, BBC Transcription Service, recorded 19 Dec. 1964, BOM, p. 273.

p. 82   '*had an*': Barrie Gavin, *A Tenor Man's Story*, Central Television, broadcast 1985, L 1, p. 222.

p. 82   '*This magic*': Britten, 'On Receiving the First Aspen Award', 31 July 1964, BOM, pp. 260–61.

p. 83   '*there will*': W. R. Anderson, 'Wireless Notes', *Musical Times* (Nov. 1934), p. 991, PKSB, p. 43.

p. 83   *'You were'*: Reid, 'Back to Britain with Britten', p. 172.

p. 84   *'Let us see'*: D, 31 Dec. 1933.

p. 86   *'He who'*: John Reith, 'Memorandum of Information on the Scope and Conduct of the Broadcasting Service' (1925), in Paddy Scannell and David Cardiff, *A Social History of British Broadcasting*, vol. 1: *1922–1939* (Oxford, 1991), p. 7.

p. 87   *'I do'*: PKSB, p. 19.

p. 87   *'I have had'*: Britten to Leslie Woodgate, 28 Feb. 1934, L 1, p. 329.

p. 87   *'Here modern'*: Ferruccio Bonavia, in *Daily Telegraph* (24 Feb. 1934), L 1, p. 329.

p. 87   *'The only'*: Britten, 'Variations on a Critical Theme', *Opera*, 3/3 (Mar. 1952), pp. 144–6, BOM, p. 115.

p. 88   *'The B.B.C.'*: Jennifer Doctor, *The BBC and Ultra-Modern Music, 1922–1936: Shaping a Nation's Tastes* (Cambridge, 1999), p. 189.

p. 88   *'To Benjamin Britten'*: Britten, 'On Receiving the First Aspen Award', p. 255.

p. 88   *'If I say'*: Ibid., p. 261.

p. 89   *'Italian Parrys'*: D, 2 Apr. 1934.

p. 90   *'dangers'*: Edward J. Dent to Herbert Thompson, 4 Apr. 1934, in Lewis Foreman, *From Parry to Britten: British Music in Letters 1900–1945* (London, 1987), p. 172.

p. 90   *Footnote: The Times* (9 Apr. 1934), L 1, p. 337.

p. 91   *'Look at'*: JBBC, p. 57.

p. 91   *'Come today'*: Telegram to Britten, 7 Apr. 1934, L 1, p. 334.

p. 92   *'Goodbye'*: MBB, p. 75.

p. 92   *'A great'*: D, 9 Apr. 1934.

p. 93   *'He was'*: Helen Wallace, 'Musical marriage that Soared – and Soured', *Daily Telegraph* (26 Apr. 2007).

p. 94   *'The general opinion'*: Wilfred Ridgway to Hubert Foss, 23 Jan. 1935, PKSB, p. 29.

p. 94   *'I incline'*: Hubert Foss to Humphrey Milford, undated [late June 1934], PKSB, p. 27.

p. 94   *'it may'*: Hubert Foss to Humphrey Milford, 2 June 1933, HCBB, p. 62.

p. 94   *'I am afraid'*: Hubert Foss to Britten, 29 Apr. 1932, HCBB, p. 24.

p. 95   *'When Benjamin Britten'*: Britten, sleeve-note to Decca recording, LW 5163, BOM, p. 358.

p. 97   *Mother and son*: R. L. Bidwell, *Currency Conversion Tables: A Hundred Years of Change* (London, 1970), p. 22.

p. 97   *'I felt so sorry'*: Britten to Grace Williams, 8 Nov. 1934, L 1, p. 354.

p. 97   *'BAD'*: Ibid., pp. 353–4.

p. 97   *'Don't be'*: Britten to Arthur Benjamin, 4 Nov. 1934, L 1, p. 351.

p. 97   *'glorious score'*: D, 7 Nov. 1934.

p. 98   '*as if*': Britten to Grace Williams, 8 Nov. 1934, L 1, p. 354.

p. 98   '*prodigious*': Ehrlich, *The Music Profession in Britain,* p. 207.

p. 98   '*R.V.W.*': Britten to Grace Williams, 16 Jan. 1935, L 1, pp. 363–4.

p. 98   '*beautiful music*': Quoted in Michael Kennedy, *Adrian Boult* (London, 1987), p. 158.

p. 98   '*All five*': Doctor, *The BBC and Ultra-Modern Music*, p. 194.

p. 99   *Footnote*: D, 2 May 1935.

p. 100   '*It is the most*': Evelyn Waugh, *Vile Bodies* (London, 1953), p. 144.

p. 101   '*leftwing propaganda*': William Coldstream interviewed by Donald Mitchell, 18 Nov. 1978, L 1, p. 392.

p. 101   '*a certain*': D, 27 Apr. 1935.

p. 102   '*I don't*': Questionnaire from Jay Leyda [Dec. 1940], L 2, p. 897.

p. 102   '*I had to work*': Britten, 'The Artist and his Medium: Composer and Listener', BBC Schools Home Service, broadcast 18 Oct. 1946, BOM, p. 63.

p. 102   '*I spend*': D, 1 May 1935.

p. 103   '*an ordinary*': William Coldstream interviewed by Donald Mitchell, 18 Nov. 1978, L 1, p. 392.

p. 103   '*mentally precocious*': W. H. Auden, 'The Liberal Fascist', in Edward Mendelson (ed.), *The English Auden* (London, 1986), p. 322.

p. 103   '*He looked*': Humphrey Carpenter, *W. H. Auden: A Biography* (Oxford, 1992), p. 183.

p. 103   '*If his face*': Alastair Smart, 'Hockney: The Biography by Christopher Simon Sykes', *Daily Telegraph* (13 Dec. 2011).

p. 104   '*It may well be*': Basil Wright, private communication, 1948, L 1, p. 379.

p. 105   '*I think*': 'Benjamin Britten: Musician of the Year in Conversation with John Warrack', *Musical America*, 84 (Dec. 1964), BOM, p. 265.

p. 105   '*A prep-school*': Humphrey Carpenter, *The Brideshead Generation* (London, 1989), p. 132.

p. 105   '*Don't be*': Edward Mendelson, *Early Auden* (London, 1999), p. 281.

p. 105   '*Auden is*': D, 5 July 1935.

p. 106   '*Of course*': Britten to Marjorie Fass, 24 Oct. 1935, L 1, p. 378.

p. 106   '*a Kensington . . . tolerated*': D, 23 Oct. 1935; 5 Sept. 1935.

p. 106   '*Letters after*': D, 2 Aug. 1935.

p. 106   '*Fascism*': R. Palme Dutt, *Fascism and Social Revolution* (London, 1934), p. 94.

p. 106   '*strong opposition*': Britten to Marjorie Fass, 24 Oct. 1935, L 1, p. 378.

p. 106   '*The International*': D, 7 Mar. 1936.

p. 107   '*a grand*': D, 28 Nov. 1936.

p. 107   '*I always*': D, 17 Sept. 1935.

p. 107   '*I do not easily*': Britten, speech on receiving honorary degree at Hull University, *London Magazine*, 3 (Oct. 1963), BOM, p. 214.

p. 108   '*I am a*': Britten interviewed by the Arts Council of Great Britain, 5 July 1950, BOM, p. 101.

p. 108   '*I have no*': Britten to Imogen Holst, 21 Oct. 1943, L 2, p. 1162.

p. 109   '*Gramophone*': 'Interview with Charles Osborne', *London Magazine*, 3 (Oct. 1963), BOM, p. 246.

p. 110   '*Acts of*': W. H. Auden, 'Negroes', in Mendelson, *The English Auden*, pp. 292–3.

p. 111   '*It is doubtful*': W. H. Auden, '*Documentary Film. By Paul Rotha*', *Listener* (19 Feb. 1936), ibid., p. 355.

p. 112   '*The fifteen*': Britten to Grace Williams, 16 Jan. 1935, L 1, p. 364.

p. 113   '*It was*': Reid, 'Back to Britain with Britten', p. 172.

p. 114   '*firm of*': Britten to Marjorie Fass, 24 Oct. 1935, L 1, p. 379.

p. 114   '*by continually*': Michael Sidnell, *Dances of Death* (London, 1984), p. 50.

p. 114   '*a slim*': Robert Medley, *Drawn from the Life: A Memoir* (London, 1983), pp. 162–3.

p. 114   '*authentic*': Sidnell, *Dances of Death*, p. 155.

p. 114   '*thirties homosexual*': Brett, '*Peter Grimes*: The Growth of the Libretto', in Paul Banks (ed.), *The Making of Peter Grimes*, vol. 2: *Notes and Commentaries* (Woodbridge, 1996), p. 62.

p. 115   '*that he*': Christopher Isherwood, *Christopher and his Kind: 1929–1939* (London, 1977), p. 72.

p. 115   '*I feel*': Britten to Marjorie Fass, 30 Dec. 1935, L 1, p. 391.

p. 116   '*1936 finds*': D, 1 Jan. 1936.

p. 116   '*it makes*': D, 7 Apr. 1936.

p. 117   '*I am getting*': D, 15 Apr. 1936.

p. 117   '*Underneath*': Mendelson, *The English Auden*, p. 160.

p. 118   '*A thing*': Lennox Berkeley to Britten, 29 Apr. 1937, L 1, p. 490.

p. 118   '*We talk*': D, 2 Jan. 1936.

p. 119   '*I had always*': Britten interviewed by the Earl of Harewood, BOM, p. 179.

p. 119   '*Really this*': D, 20 Jan. 1936.

p. 120   '*To live*': Ralph Fox, *Lenin: A Biography* (London, 1933), p. 123.

p. 121   '*if it*': L 1, pp. 448–9.

p. 121   '*As in*': *Daily Telegraph* (26 Feb. 1936), L 1, p. 371.

p. 121   '*a little more*': D, 25 Feb. 1936.

p. 121   '*I feel*': D, 26 Feb. 1936.

p. 121   '*he doesn't*': D, 30 Apr. 1937.

p. 122   '*It isn't*': D, 2 Mar. 1936.

p. 122   '*It is*': D, 24 Apr. 1936.

p. 122   '*a disbanded*': Britten to John Pounder, 21 Apr. 1936, L 1, p. 422.

p. 123   '*Life is*': D, 5 June 1936.

p. 123   '*avowed*': D, 30 July 1936.

p. 124   '*queerness*': D, 4 Apr. 1937.

p. 124   '*Christian*': MBB, p. 101.

p. 125   '*I lose*': D, 31 Jan. 1937.

p. 125   '*We were*': Carpenter, *W. H. Auden*, p. 188.

p. 126   'F6 *was*': Ibid., p. 195.

p. 126   '*English ruling*': Spender, 'The Left Wing Orthodoxy', *New Verse*, 31–2 (Autumn 1938), in Patrick Deane (ed.), *History in our Hands* (London, 1998), p. 222.

p. 126   '*I am not*': W. H. Auden to E. R. Dodds, 8 Dec. 1936, in Carpenter, *W. H. Auden*, p. 207.

p. 127   '*It is really*': Spender, 'The Left Wing Orthodoxy', p. 222.

p. 127   '*Wystan*': Britten to John Pounder, 2 Jan. 1937, L 1, p. 465.

p. 127   '*It is terribly*': D, 8 Jan. 1937.

p. 127   '*The Spanish*': George Orwell, 'Why I Write', *Gangrel* (Summer 1946), p. 8.

p. 127   '*offered*': Carpenter, *W. H. Auden*, p. 206.

p. 127   '*It would*': D, 10 Dec. 1936.

p. 128   '*However with*': D, 1 Jan. 1937.

p. 128   '*the logical*': Randall Swingler, editorial, *Left Review* (April 1938), in Deane, *History in our Hands*, p. 109.

p. 128   '*But what*': Britten to Mrs Britten, 28 July 1936, L 1, p. 436.

p. 128   '*It is also*': Britten to John Pounder, 2 Jan. 1937, L 1, p. 465.

p. 131   '*It is cruel*': Britten to Henry Boys [postmarked 29 June 1937], L 1, p. 493.

p. 131   '*had an especially*': Britten, 'How a Musical Work Originates', *Listener* (30 July 1942), BOM, p. 42.

p. 132   '*I listened*': D, 6 May 1931.

p. 133   '*Thank you*': Frank Bridge to Britten, 16 Mar. 1938, L 1, p. 503.

p. 133   '*I think*': Peter Pears to Britten, 27 Aug. 1937, L 1, p. 507.

p. 134   '*He's a dear*': D, 8 Sept. 1937.

p. 134   '*He gives*': D, 25 June 1937.

p. 134   '*Very pleasant*': D, 3 July 1937.

p. 136   '*Bridge hated*': Britten, 'Britten Looking Back', p. 252.

p. 136   '*never again*': Marjorie Fass to Daphne Oliver [n.d.], HCBB, p. 114.

p. 136   '*The thing*': Ibid.

p. 136   '*I know*': Ibid., pp. 114–15.

p. 137   '*he makes*': D, 10 Sept. 1937.

p. 137   '*he is*': D, 11 Apr. 1937.

p. 137   '*running*': Pears to Britten [after 30 May and before 5 June 1938], L 1, p. 559.

p. 138   '*I do*': Britten to Wulff Scherchen [25 June 1938], L 1, pp. 562–3.

p. 138   *Footnote*: Christopher Isherwood, *Lost Years: A Memoir 1945–1951* (London, 2000), p. 59.

p. 139   '*pleasant*': Wulff Scherchen to Britten, 26 June 1938, L 1, p. 564.

p. 140   '*any station*': Britten to Ralph Hawkes, 5 May 1938, L 1, p. 555.

p. 140   '*certainly sounds*': Britten to Ralph Hawkes, 6 Aug. 1938, L 1, p. 574.

p. 140   '*This is*': William McNaught, *Musical Times* (Sept. 1938), L 1, p. 578.

p. 140   '*concerto is*': W. H. Haddon Squire, *Christian Science Monitor* (Aug. 1938), L1, p. 578.

p. 141   '*Mr Britten*': Ferruccio Bonavia, *Daily Telegraph* (19 Aug. 1938), L1, p. 577.

p. 141   '*Britten's Variations*': *Musical Times* (July 1938), L1, p. 561.

p. 141   '*Mr Britten's*': *Observer* (10 Oct. 1937), L1, p. 515.

p. 141   '*I expect*': Marjorie Fass to Daphne Oliver, 19 Aug. 1938, L1, pp. 576–7.

p. 142   '*overrun*': Ehrlich, *The Music Profession in Britain*, p. 221.

p. 142   '*foreign artists*': Ibid.

p. 143   '*And what*': W. H. Auden to Britten [n.d.], L1, p. 575.

p. 144   '*I love you*': JBBC, p. 68.

p. 144   '*Oh my darling*': Wulff Scherchen to Britten, 6 Dec. 1938, JBBC, p. 71.

p. 144   '*lost to*': Wulff Scherchen, 'Lost to the worlds', JBBC, p. 75.

p. 145   '*Good-night*': Britten to Wulff Scherchen, 22 Jan. 1939, JBBC, p. 81.

p. 145   '*a German*': William Coldstream's notebook, 17 Jan. 1939, L2, p. 1337.

p. 145   '*To my friend*': HCBB, p. 90.

p. 145   '*I got*': Britten to Aaron Copland, 8 May 1939, L2, p. 634.

p. 145   '*Much love*': Britten to Wulff Scherchen, 16 May 1939, JBBC, p. 91.

p. 146   '*Hedli, what*': Britten to Hedli Anderson [?Oct. 1939], L2, p. 720.

p. 146   '*One had*': Britten interviewed by Reid, 'Back to Britain with Britten', p. 172.

p. 147   '*You see*': Britten to Wulff Scherchen, 22 Apr. 1939, JBBC, p. 87.

p. 147   '*After Munich*': Britten interviewed by Reid, 'Back to Britain with Britten', pp. 172–3.

p. 147   '*For the duration*': Peter Conrad, *Modern Times, Modern Places* (London, 1999), p. 501.

p. 147   '*how long*': Walter Benjamin's diary, Oct. 1938, in Evelyn Juers, *House of Exile* (Artarmon, 2008), pp. 232–3.

p. 147   '*Think of*': D, 13 Mar. 1938.

p. 147   '*But I*': Britten to Basil Wright, 1 Sept. 1938, L1, pp. 581–2.

p. 148   '*I have*': Cyril Connolly to Noël Blakiston, in Paul Fussell, *Abroad: British Literary Travelling Between the Wars* (Oxford, 1980), p. 16.

p. 148   '*spiritual fogs*': Britten, 'An English Composer Sees America' [draft], *Tempo* (American edn.), 1/2 (Apr. 1940), BOM, p. 24.

p. 149   '*So that*': Frank Bridge to Britten [29 Apr. 1939], L2, p. 632.

CHAPTER 3. EXILE: AMERICA, ENGLAND, 1939–1945

p. 150   '*What a*': Britten to Wulff Scherchen, 1–3 May 1939, BPL.

p. 151   '*I've come*': Britten to Aaron Copland, 8 May 1939, L2, p. 634.

p. 151   '*I beg*': Ralph Hawkes to Britten, 29 Aug. 1939, L2, p. 695.

p. 151   *'management'*: Britten to Ralph Hawkes, 3 June 1939, L 2, p. 650.

p. 152   *'The work'*: Britten interviewed by the Earl of Harewood, *People Today*, BBC Home Service, broadcast 23 June 1960, BOM, p. 181.

p. 152   *'I think'*: Britten interviewed by Donald Mitchell, 'Mapreading', Feb. 1969, BOM, p. 324.

p. 152   *'The composer'*: Britten interviewed by the Earl of Harewood, BOM, p. 181.

p. 153   *'I shall'*: Peter Pears to Britten, 9 Jan. 1940, L 2, p. 759.

p. 153   *'it is* you': Peter Pears to Britten [postmarked 21 Nov. 1974], L 1, p. 60.

p. 153   *'I love'*: Britten to Wulff Scherchen, 9 June 1939, BPL.

p. 153   *'No more'*: Britten to Wulff Scherchen, 27 June 1939, BPL.

p. 153   *'I have'*: Wulff Scherchen to Britten, 30 May 1939, BPL.

p. 154   *'I'm afraid'*: Britten to Enid Slater, 7 Nov. 1939, L 2, p. 724.

p. 154   *'O – if'*: Britten to Wulff Scherchen, 8 Dec. 1939, BPL.

p. 154   *'I'm terribly'*: Peter Pears to Britten, 9 Jan. 1940, L 2, p. 759.

p. 154   *'I ought'*: Britten to Donald Mitchell, 7 Oct. 1963, L 5, p. 507.

p. 155   *'If he'*: Marjorie Fass to Daphne Oliver, 22 Aug. 1938, L 1, p. 557.

p. 156   *'I might'*: Britten to Beth Welford, 25 June 1939, L 2, p. 671.

p. 156   *'I am'*: Ibid.

p. 157   *'Wystan'*: Britten to Kit Welford, 4 Apr. 1940, L 2, p. 794.

p. 157   *'nervous breakdown'*: L 1, p. 42.

p. 157   *'one of'*: Britten to Enid Slater, 7 Nov. 1939, L 2, p. 724.

p. 158   *'My mother'*: Michael Mayer interviewed by Donald Mitchell, 22 June 1988, BPL.

p. 158   *'War is'*: Evelyn Juers, *House of Exile* (Artarmon, 2008), p. 263.

p. 159   *'Waves'*: W. H. Auden, 'September 1, 1939', in Edward Mendelson (ed.), *The English Auden* (London, 1986), p. 245.

p. 159   *'London and'*: Mollie Panter-Downes, 'Letter from London', *New Yorker* (9 Sept. 1939), p. 28.

p. 160   *'I'm making'*: Britten interviewed by William King, *New York Sun* (27 Apr. 1940), L 2, p. 705.

p. 160   *'I'm glad'*: Lennox Berkeley to Britten, 21 Apr. 1940, L 2, p. 705.

p. 160   *'I've got'*: Britten to Beth Welford, 15 Mar. 1940, L 2, p. 795.

p. 160   *'His tonsils'*: Peter Pears to Beth Welford, 20 Feb. 1940, MBB, p. 132.

p. 160   *'he had a long'*: Ibid., p. 131.

p. 160   *'Dr Mayer'*: Ibid., p. 134.

p. 161   *'But everyone'*: Ibid., p. 132.

p. 161   *'Outwardly'*: Britten interviewed by Charles Reid, 'Back to Britain with Britten', *High Fidelity Magazine* (Dec. 1959), BOM, p. 173.

p. 161   *'I find'*: Britten to Beth and Kit Welford, 30 June 1940, L 2, p. 823.

p. 161   *'The literary'*: Isherwood's diary, 20 Jan. 1940, in Catherine Bucknell (ed.), *Christopher Isherwood Diaries*, vol. 1: *1939–1960* (London, 1996), p. 83.

p. 161   *'If I'*: Ibid., p. 84.

p. 161   *'ambitious young'*: Cyril Connolly, 'Comment', *Horizon* (Feb. 1940), p. 69.

p. 161   *'four of our'*: Quoted in P. N. Furbank, *E. M. Forster: A Life*, vol. 2 (London, 1978), p. 238.

p. 162   *'What I'*: Evelyn Waugh, *Put Out More Flags* (Harmondsworth, 1954), p. 39.

p. 162   *'He's been'*: William King, *New York Sun*, 9 Dec. 1940, in Peter Stansky and William Abrahams, *London's Burning: Life, Death & Art in the Second World War* (London, 1994), p. 139.

p. 162   *'There is'*: Ralph Hawkes to Britten, 26 Sept. 1940, L 2, p. 870.

p. 162   *'Whatever struggle'*: Britten, 'An English Composer Sees America', *Tempo* (American edn.), 1/2 (Apr. 1940), BOM, p. 24.

p. 163   *'I am'*: Britten, 'Au Revoir to the U.S.A.', *Modern Music*, 19/2 (Jan.–Feb. 1942), BOM, p. 36.

p. 164   *'the honest'*: W. H. Auden, 'The Public v. the Late Mr William Butler Yeats', *Partisan Review* (Spring 1939), in Mendelson, *The English Auden*, p. 393.

p. 165   *'The Irish'*: Britten to Kit Welford, 4 Apr. 1940, L 2, p. 793.

p. 165   *'The things that'*: Ibid.

p. 165   *'Ten cents'*: Albert Goldberg interviewed by Donald Mitchell, 1989, L 2, p. 766.

p. 166   *'They're fed up'*: Britten to Kit Welford, 4 Apr. 1940, L 2, p. 793.

p. 166   *'In some'*: Ibid.

p. 166   *'enjoy the'*: Juers, *House of Exile*, p. 294.

p. 166   *'What one'*: Britten to Kit Welford, 4 Apr. 1940, L 2, p. 793.

p. 166   *'You see'*: Ibid., p. 794.

p. 167   *'I had'*: Britten to Beth Welford, 21 Jan. 1940, L 2, p. 769.

p. 167   *'By-the-way'*: Britten to Albert Goldberg, 29 Apr. 1940, L 2, p. 806.

p. 167   *Footnote*: Elizabeth Mayer to Albert Goldberg, 7 May 1940, L 2, p. 809.

p. 168   *'Since my'*: Britten to Lennox Berkeley [8 Sept. 1939], L 2, p. 752. This is dated incorrectly in L 2.

p. 168   *'Frankly, he'*: *New York World-Telegram* (29 Mar. 1940), L 2, p. 790.

p. 168   *'Let me'*: Imogen Holst's diary, 11 Feb. 1953, CGIH, p. 245.

p. 170   *'I get'*: Edward Mendelson, *Later Auden* (London, 1999), p. xviii.

p. 170   *'Mr Benjamin Britten's'*: Prince Konoye to Director of the Cultural Bureau, Japanese Foreign Office [n.d.], L 2, p. 881.

p. 171   *'First movement'*: Beata Sauerlander interviewed for ATTW.

p. 171   *'year-long party'*: Sherill Tippins, *February House* (London, 2005), p. xii.

p. 172   *'all that'*: Denis de Rougemont interviewed, L 2, p. 864.

p. 172   *'Everytime we'*: Britten to Beth and Kit Welford, 30 June 1940, L 2, p. 822.

p. 172   *'the way the'*: Louis MacNeice, *The Strings are False* (London, 1965), p. 35.

p. 173   *'he and I'*: Paul Bowles to Donald Mitchell, 8 Dec. 1982, L 2, p. 865.

p. 174   '*complaining*': Wulff Scherchen to Donald Mitchell, 1989, L 2, p. 801.

p. 174   '*sudden craze*': Britten to Enid Slater, 7 Apr. 1940, L 2, p. 799.

p. 174   '*My will*': Michelangelo, Sonnet XXX, trans. Elizabeth Mayer and Peter Pears.

p. 175   '*a post*': Britten to Albert Goldberg, 20 Dec. 1940, L 2, p. 893.

p. 176   '*In the beginning*': Imogen Holst interviewed by Donald Mitchell, 22 June 1977, BPL.

p. 176   '*Later on*': Britten to Douglas Moore, 24 June 1941, L 2, p. 946.

p. 177   '*any concert*': Britten to Elizabeth Sprague Coolidge, 20 Jan. 1941, L 2, p. 905.

p. 178   '*New York*': Britten to Enid Slater, 17 June 1941, L 2, p. 944.

p. 178   *Footnote*: Robert Stradling and Meirion Hughes, *The English Musical Renaissance 1860–1940* (London and New York, 1993), p. 174.

p. 178   '*Bunyan*': *New York Sun* (27 Apr. 1940), L 2, p. 709.

p. 179   '*In the plot*': Olin Downes, in *New York Times* (6 May 1941), L 2, p. 915.

p. 180   '*The result*': Unpublished tribute to Britten, probably on his fiftieth birthday, in Donald Mitchell and John Evans (comps.), *Pictures from a Life* (London, 1978), plate 113.

p. 180   '*cool-headed*': John Fuller to the author, 16 Sept. 2009.

p. 181   '*I mean*': Stephen Spender interviewed by Donald Mitchell, 27 Oct. 1990, BPL.

p. 181   '*Today I*': François Truffaut, *Hitchcock* (London, 1986), p. 84.

p. 181   '*Jo?*': Robert Douglas-Fairhurst, *Becoming Dickens: The Invention of a Novelist* (London, 2011), p. 36.

p. 181   '*I am*': 'Interview with Charles Osborne', *London Magazine*, 3 (Oct. 1963), BOM, p. 248.

p. 182   '*Here one*': Britten, 'Some Notes on Forster and Music', in Oliver Stallybrass (ed.), *Aspects of E. M. Forster* (London, 1969), pp. 81–6.

p. 183   '*At the moment*': Britten to Wulff Scherchen, 9 Sept. 1941, L 2, p. 977.

p. 183   '*Money*': Britten to Wulff Scherchen, 9 Sept. 1941, L 2, p. 977.

p. 183   *Footnote*: Britten to Erwin Stein, 10 May 1944, L 2, p. 1197. Given the even-handed assessment, it is not possible that Britten was referring here to Malcolm Sargent, as Donald Mitchell and Philip Reed suggest. *New York Herald Tribune* (31 Mar. 1941), L 2, p. 911.

p. 184   '*California is*': Quoted in Peter Conrad, *Modern Times, Modern Places* (London, 1999), p. 526.

p. 184   '*it was in California*': Britten, 'On Receiving the First Aspen Award', 30 July 1964, BOM, p. 262.

p. 184   '*Even when*': E. M. Forster, 'George Crabbe: The Poet and the Man', in Philip Brett (ed.), *Benjamin Britten: Peter Grimes*, Cambridge Opera Handbooks (Cambridge, 1983), p. 4.

p. 184   '*We've just*': Britten to Elizabeth Mayer, 29 July 1941, L 2, p. 961.

p. 184   'the Sea calls': Brett, *Peter Grimes*, p. 50.

p. 185   'by the time': Ibid., p. 35.

p. 185   'I'm sorry': Christopher Isherwood to Britten, 18 Feb. 1942, L 3, p. 92.

p. 186   'The Britten': Edith Sitwell to Colin Hampton, 3 Nov. 1943, L 3, p. 544.

p. 186   'selfish': Britten to Beth Welford, 4 Nov. 1941, L 2, p. 992.

p. 186   'I'm afraid': Ibid., p. 993.

p. 187   'My recollection': Britten to Joe Cole, 18 Aug. 1972, L 2, p. 985.

p. 187   'He wanted': David Rothman interviewed by Donald Mitchell for ATTW, L 2, p. 999.

p. 187   'Ben to Southold': Elizabeth Mayer's diary, 6 [*recte* 8] Nov. 1941.

p. 187   'discussed the': Caroline Seebohm, 'Conscripts to an Age', unpublished, quoted in L 2, p. 980.

p. 187   'I am': Britten to Elizabeth Sprague Coolidge, 18 Oct. 1941, L 2, p. 987.

p. 188   'It is not': E. R. Lewis, letter to the editor, *Musical Times* (June 1941); editor's response, *Musical Times* (Aug. 1941), L 2, pp. 870–71.

p. 188   'the Battle': George Baker, *Sunday Times* (15 June 1941), in Mervyn Cooke (ed.), *The Cambridge Companion to Benjamin Britten* (Cambridge, 1999), p. 3.

p. 188   'Yer pays': Britten to Albert Goldberg, 20 Oct. 1941, L 2, p. 988.

p. 188   'You'll never': Eric Crozier, 'Recollections of Britten's Years at the Old Mill, Snape, Suffolk (1939–47)', BBC Radio 3, broadcast 18 June 1993, BPL.

p. 189   'One of': Britten, Introduction to Sadler's Wells Opera Guide, *Peter Grimes* (London, 1945), BOM, p. 50.

p. 190   'it was something': Britten interviewed by Joseph Cooper, 'The Composer Speaks', BBC General Overseas Service, broadcast 7 July 1957, BOM, p. 150.

p. 190   'Parry's national': Britten, 'England and the Folk-Art Problem', *Modern Music*, 18/2 (Jan.–Feb. 1941), BOM, p. 31.

p. 192   'I was': Bobby Rothman interviewed by Donald Mitchell, 23 Oct. 1992, BPL.

p. 192   'Bobby': Ibid.

p. 192   'He was *very fond*': Ibid.

p. 192   *Footnote*: Walter Isaacson, *Einstein: His Life and Universe* (New York, 2007), p. 624.

p. 193   'Benjy': HCBB, p. 163.

p. 194   'To Benjamin': Christopher Isherwood's diary, 16 Jan. 1942, Bucknell, *Christopher Isherwood Diaries*, vol. 1, p. 206.

p. 194   'I found': Virgil Thomson, in *New York Herald-Tribune* (23 Dec. 1941), L 2, p. 1011.

p. 194   'I really': Britten to Elizabeth Sprague Coolidge, 6 Jan. 1942, L 2, p. 1013.

p. 194   'I knew': John Waterhouse, 'Soirée Musicale', *Birmingham Post* (18 Nov. 1963), L 3, p. 76.

p. 195   'He just': John Lindsay interviewed by Donald Mitchell, 10 July 1990, BPL.

p. 195   'What an': Britten to Peggy Brosa, 15 Feb. 1942, L 2, p. 1018.

p. 195   'It makes': Britten to Kit Welford, 1 Mar. 1942, L 2, p. 1021.

p. 196   'If he': *Time* (16 Jan. 1948), L 2, p. 1019.

p. 196   'Ben was': Peter Pears to Humphrey Carpenter, 18 Apr. 1980, BPL.

p. 196   Footnote: Pears's Exit Permit Application, 5 Feb. 1942, BPL.

p. 197   'Goodness': W. H. Auden to Britten [31 Jan. 1942], L 2, p. 1015.

p. 197   'To set': W. H. Auden, 'New Year Letter', in his *Collected Longer Poems* (London, 1968), pp. 80–81.

p. 197   'Your attraction': W. H. Auden to Britten [31 Jan. 1942], L 2, pp. 1015–16.

p. 198   'No amount': Alan Bennett, *The Habit of Art* (London, 2009), p. 67.

p. 198   'I think': 'Benjamin Britten: Musician of the year in conversation with John Warrack', *Musical America*, 84 (Dec. 1964), BOM, p. 266.

p. 199   'in art': Britten to Kit Welford, 1 Mar. 1942, L 2, p. 1021.

p. 199   'The end': Mitchell and Evans, *Pictures from a Life*, plate 160.

p. 199   'We are': Britten to Elizabeth Mayer, 25 Mar. 1942, L 2, p. 1026.

p. 199   'Particularly against': Evelyn Waugh, *Vile Bodies* (London, 1953), p. 24.

p. 200   'I'm having': D, 19 Jan. 1935.

p. 200   Footnote: Remo Lauricella interviewed by Donald Mitchell, 1987, BPL.

p. 201   'perhaps he': Peter Pears to Humphrey Carpenter, 18 Apr. 1980, BPL.

p. 201   'This cannot': Pears to Elizabeth Mayer, 19 Apr. 1942, L 2, p. 1032.

p. 202   'For a': Britten to Beata Wachstein (née Mayer), 6 June 1942, L 2, p. 1062.

p. 202   'People stumble': Joseph Grigg, in *Spectator* (26 June 1942).

p. 202   'All the excitement': Britten to Elizabeth Mayer, 4 May 1942, L 2, p. 1037.

p. 203   'a pound': J. R. Ackerley, *My Father and Myself* (London, 1992), p. 135.

p. 203   'a paved': Quoted in Gregory Woods, *Articulate Flesh: Male Homo-Eroticism and Modern Poetry* (New Haven, 1987), p. 55.

p. 203   'great haunter': Basil Reeve interviewed by the author, 3 July 2009.

p. 203   'Peter sang': Britten to Elizabeth Mayer, 17 May 1942, L 2, p. 1050.

p. 204   'He has': Britten to Elizabeth Mayer, 4 May 1942, L 2, p. 1037.

p. 204   'Since I': Britten, Statement to the Local Tribunal for the Registration of Conscientious Objectors, 4 May 1942, L 2, p. 1046.

p. 205   'I do': Report on Britten's Local Tribunal, 28 May 1942, L 2, p. 1046.

p. 205   'I hate': Ethel Bridge to Appellate Tribunal [n.d.], L 2, p. 1049.

p. 205   'I could': Britten, Appeal to the Appellate Tribunal [June 1942], L 2, p. 1058.

p. 205   'one of': Britten to Elizabeth Mayer, 30 Sept. 1942, L 2, p. 1088.

p. 206   '*without conditions*': Clerk to the Appellate Tribunal to Britten, 19 Aug. 1942, L 3, p. 94.

p. 206   '*Local Tribunal*': Ibid.

p. 206   '*His religious*': Eric Walter White, *Benjamin Britten: His Life and Operas* (London, 1970), p. 91.

p. 206   '*He was*': Alan Blyth, *Remembering Britten* (London, 1981), p. 22.

p. 206   '*I'm not*': Murray Perahia interviewed by Donald Mitchell, Autumn 2000, BPL.

p. 206   *one recent study*: Graham Elliot, *Benjamin Britten: The Spiritual Dimension* (Oxford, 2005).

p. 207   *Donald Mitchell's*: Earl of Harewood, *The Tongs and the Bones* (London, 1981), p. 86.

p. 207   '*What he*': Donald Mitchell interviewed by the author, 22 Oct. 2008.

p. 207   '*We are*': Michael Tippett, 'Obituary', *Listener* (16 Dec. 1976), in Blyth, *Remembering Britten*, p. 67.

p. 207   '*I am not*': Peter Pears, ATTW.

p. 208   '*I don't*': Peter Pears to Britten, 24 May 1942, L 2, p. 1054.

p. 208   '*Why the*': Britten to Peter Pears, 1 June 1942, L 2, p. 1055.

p. 209   '*I am still*': Britten to Peter Pears, 23 Nov. 1942, L 2, p. 1103.

p. 209   '*I wonder*': Britten to Beata Wachstein, 6 June 1942, L 2, p. 1063.

p. 209   '*I don't care*': Britten to Peter Pears, 12 June 1942, L 2, p. 1064.

p. 209   '*a fishing*': Britten to Bobby Rothman, 24 June 1942, L 2, pp. 1068–9.

p. 209   '*five-year*': Robert Hewison, *Under Siege* (London, 1979), p. 56.

p. 210   '*Britten has*': J. A. Westrup, 'The Virtuosity of Benjamin Britten', *Listener* (16 July 1942), L 1, p. 530.

p. 210   '*Up till*': William Glock, in *Observer* (26 July 1942), L 2, p. 1074.

p. 210   '*Our reactions*': Edward Sackville-West, in *New Statesman and Nation* (1 Aug. 1942).

p. 210   '*the possibility*': Quoted in Hewison, *Under Siege*, p. 176.

p. 211   '*surface brilliance*': Edward Sackville-West, 'Music: Some Aspects of the Contemporary Problem', *Horizon* (July 1944), L 2, p. 1119.

p. 211   '*the finest*': Edward Sackville-West, in *New Statesman and Nation* (3 Oct. 1942), L 2, p. 1077.

p. 212   '*the musicians*': Stephen Spender, *World within World* (London, 2001), p. 314.

p. 212   '*How squalid*': Quoted in Hewison, *Under Siege*, p. 169.

p. 213   '*her unspoken*': John Lehmann, *I am my Brother* (London, 1960), p. 281.

p. 214   '*she & Wood*': D, 9 Nov. 1932.

p. 214   '*the besotted*': Gerald Moore, *Am I Too Loud?* (Harmondsworth, 1962), p. 107.

p. 214   '*All that*': Spender, *World within World*, p. 156.

p. 215   '*because people*': Ibid., p. 313.

p. 215   'There was': Ibid.

p. 217   'impossible': Britten to Peter Pears, 25 Sept. 1942, L 2, p. 1080.

p. 217   'I'm too': Ibid.

p. 217   'Sophie's at it': Britten to Peter Pears [after 28 Oct. and before 2 Nov. 1944], L 2, p. 1230.

p. 218   'You know': Peter Pears to Britten [early Dec. 1942], L 2, p. 1108.

p. 218   'the opera': Britten to Elizabeth Mayer, 30 Sept. 1942, L 2, p. 1089.

p. 219   'I was impressed': Quoted in Brett, Peter Grimes, p. 29.

p. 219   'It is': Britten to Elizabeth Mayer, 5 June 1942, L 2, p. 1059.

p. 220   'knowledge of': Montagu Slater, 'The Purpose of a Left Review', Left Review, 1/9 (June 1935), p. 364.

p. 220   'In writing': Britten, Introduction to Sadler's Wells Opera Guide, Peter Grimes.

p. 220   'a nice': Britten to Peter Pears, 12 June 1942, L 2, p. 1065.

p. 220   'This treaty': The Times (12 June 1942), p. 1.

p. 221   'there are': Britten to Peter Pears, 11 Mar. 1943, L 2, p. 1124.

p. 221   'I see': Ibid.

p. 221   'no reasons': Britten to Erwin Stein, 12 Mar. 1943, L 2, p. 1130.

p. 222   'You're not': Montagu Slater, Peter Grimes and Other Poems (London, 1946), p. 53.

p. 222   'We are': Britten to Ronald Duncan, 24 Feb. 1945, L 2, p. 1243.

p. 223   'to pick': Britten to Ralph Hawkes, 9 Mar. 1943, L 2, p. 1121.

p. 223   'Beyond these': Ralph Hawkes to Britten, 28 June 1943, BPL.

p. 224   'That is': Peter Pears to Britten Oct. 1944, L 2, p. 1228.

p. 225   'he is': Britten to David Rothman, 7 May 1943, L 2, p. 1148.

p. 226   'appreciate its': Britten, 'Verdi – A Symposium', Opera, 2/3 (Feb. 1951), BOM, p. 102.

p. 226   'what a': Britten to Peter Pears, 21 Mar. 1943, L 2, p. 1133.

p. 227   'chance for': Britten interviewed by Donald Mitchell, 'Mapreading', BOM, p. 325.

p. 227   'as flexibly': Britten to Elizabeth Mayer, 8 Dec. 1943, L 2, p. 1172.

p. 228   'Five years': Observer (24 Oct. 1943), L 2, pp. 1175–6.

p. 229   'I still': Helen Wallace, Boosey & Hawkes: The Publishing Story (London, 2007), p. 49.

p. 229   'It is': Britten to Elizabeth Mayer, 6 Apr. 1943, L 2, p. 1144.

p. 230   'think of': Britten to Peter Pears, 11 Mar. 1943, L 2, p. 1124.

p. 230   'Hamburg': Daily Telegraph (21 Oct. 1943), in Stan Winer, Between the Lies (London, 2004), p. 64.

p. 230   'We gave': Spender, World within World, p. 321.

p. 230   'Knowing how': Britten to Bobby Rothman, 12 Jan. 1944, L 2, p. 1183.

p. 231   'aggressive pacifism': Blyth, Remembering Britten, p. 90.

p. 231   'how he': Eric Gordon, Mark the Music: The Life and Work of Marc Blitzstein (New York, 1989), L 2, p. 1176.

p. 231   'I have': Britten to Elizabeth Mayer, 8 Dec. 1943, L 2, p. 1172.

p. 231   'Incidentally': John Amis, Amiscellany: My Life, My Music (London, 1986), p. 174.

p. 232   'the one': Bennett, The Habit of Art, p. 49.

p. 232   'I want': Tippett, 'Obituary', p. 70.

p. 233   'It is also': Britten to Imogen Holst, 21 Oct. 1943, L 2, p. 1162.

p. 234   'corporate antagonism': Edward Downes, Peter Grimes Symposium, 15 June 1995, BPL.

p. 234   'Oh, couple': John Lindsay interviewed by Donald Mitchell, 10 July 1990, BPL.

p. 234   'very off-colour': Tony Scotland, Lennox & Freda (Wilby, 2010), p. 322.

p. 234   'Kenneth Green': Peter Pears to Elizabeth Mayer, 6 Aug. 1944, L 2, p. 1216.

p. 235   Footnote: Hubert Foss, 'Britten and "Peter Grimes"', Listener (27 Sept. 1945), p. 361.

p. 236   'P.G. is': Peter Pears to Britten [1 Mar. 1944], L 2, p. 1189.

p. 236   'Ben came': HCBB, p. 214.

p. 236   'the view': Britten to Elizabeth Mayer, 13 May 1944, L 2, p. 1200.

p. 236   'My bloody': Britten to Peter Pears, 12 June 1944, L 2, p. 1203.

p. 237   'Work with': Peter Pears to Britten [8/9 Nov. 1944], L 2, p. 1234.

p. 238   'I can't': Britten to Erwin Stein, 12 Mar. 1943, L 2, p. 1131.

p. 238   'The L.P.O.': Britten to Peter Pears, 20 Nov. 1944, L 2, p. 1236.

p. 239   'I suppose': Eric Crozier and Nancy Evans, 'After Long Pursuit', unpublished typescript, BPL.

p. 240   'I have': Britten to Mary Behrend, 10 Feb. 1945, L 2, p. 1241.

p. 241   'Our collaboration': Eric Crozier and Nancy Evans, 'After Long Pursuit', Opera Quarterly, 10/4 (1994), pp. 15–16.

p. 241   'I hope': Eric Crozier, 'Notes on the Production of Benjamin Britten's "Peter Grimes"', in Paul Banks (ed.), The Making of Peter Grimes, vol. 2: Notes and Commentaries (Woodbridge, 1996), p. 7.

p. 242   'convince our': Ibid.

p. 242   'quarrelsomeness': PKSB, p. 75.

p. 243   'It is': Tippett, 'Obituary', p. 70.

p. 243   'Affectionate': Tyrone Guthrie to Joan Cross, 7 June 1945, in Banks, The Making of Peter Grimes, vol. 2, p. 45.

CHAPTER 4. REHABILITATION: ENGLAND, 1945–1951

p. 248   'This opera': Edmund Wilson, Europe without Baedeker (New York, 1947), pp. 161–2.

p. 248   'It is an': Scott Goddard, in News Chronicle (8 June 1945), L 2, p. 1256.

p. 249   'I'm an': Edward Dent, A Theatre for Everybody (London and New York, 1945), p. 98.

p. 249   '*I am passionately*': 'Conversation with Benjamin Britten', *Tempo*, 1/6 (Feb. 1944), BOM, p. 43.

p. 250   '*There was*': Joan Cross, in *The Times* (1 June 1985), in Paul Banks (ed.), *The Making of Peter Grimes*, vol. 2: *Notes and Commentaries* (Woodbridge, 1996), p. 46.

p. 251   '*little more*': Eric Crozier, 'Lucretia – 1946', in Crozier (ed.), *The Rape of Lucretia* (London, 1948), p. 56.

p. 251   '*It became*': Scott Goddard, *British Music of our Time* (Harmondsworth, 1946), L 2, p. 1264.

p. 252   '*I think*': Britten to Imogen Holst, 26 June 1945, L 2, p. 1268.

p. 252   '*Mr Churchill's*': *Peace News* (27 July 1945), BOM, p. 48.

p. 253   '*Politicians*': Murray Schafer, *British Composers in Interview* (London, 1963), BOM, p. 226.

p. 253   '*Not only*': Britten and Peter Pears, programme note for recital on 8 Dec. 1949, BOM, p. 83.

p. 254   '*This day*': Author's transcription of BBC radio broadcast, 19 Apr. 1945.

p. 254   '*Men and women*': Yehudi Menuhin, *Unfinished Journey* (London, 1977), pp. 178–9.

p. 255   '*I IMPLORE*': Drusilla Modjeska, 'The Multiple Lives of a Muse: Carolyn Burke's "Lee Miller"', *The Monthly* (Mar. 2006).

p. 255   '*stench*': Ibid.

p. 255   '*We gave*': Schafer, *British Composers in Interview*, p. 231.

p. 255   '*that the experience*': ATTW.

p. 255   *Footnote*: Anita Lasker to her aunt, 30 July 1945, L 2, p. 1274.

p. 256   '*Auden got*': Schafer, *British Composers in Interview*, p. 224.

p. 256   '*The theme*': Ibid.

p. 257   '*If you*': Britten to Montagu Slater, 28 Aug. 1945, L 2, p. 1279.

p. 258   '*he'd go*': John Lindsay interviewed by Donald Mitchell, 10 July 1990, BPL.

p. 258   '*I've been*': Ronald Duncan, *Benjamin Britten: A Personal Memoir* (London, 1979), p. 59.

p. 258   '*Well you*': John Lindsay interviewed by Donald Mitchell, 10 July 1990, BPL.

p. 259   '*suggested that*': HCBB, p. 225.

p. 260   '*What is*': Olin Downes, in *New York Times* (6 May 1941), L 2, p. 915.

p. 260   '*a kind*': Quoted in Nouritza Matossian, *Jannis Xenakis* (Paris, 1981), p. 52.

p. 261   '*Henry Purcell*': Britten, *250th Anniversary of the Death of Henry Purcell* (1945), BOM, p. 52.

p. 261   '*This is going*': D, 13 Oct. 1936.

p. 261   '*those very*': Britten, *250th Anniversary of the Death of Henry Purcell*, p. 52.

p. 261   'cold': Britten, 'On Realizing the Continuo in Purcell's Songs', in Imogen Holst (ed.), *Henry Purcell 1659–1695: Essays on his Music* (London, 1959), p. 8.

p. 262   'I'm so': Britten to Mary Behrend, 3 Dec. 1945, L 2, p. 1285.

p. 263   'That's the': JBBC, p. 25.

p. 263   'I'm hoping': Britten to Ralph Hawkes, 19 Dec. 1945, L 2, p. 1286

p. 264   'don't be too': Ibid.

p. 264   'is easily': HCBB, p. 151.

p. 264   'I wonder': Britten to Ralph Hawkes, 19 Dec. 1945, L 2, p. 1286.

p. 264   'It is': Britten to Peter Pears, 24 Jan. 1946, L 3, p. 139.

p. 266   'the whole': PKSB, p. 76.

p. 267   *Footnote: Neue Zürcher Zeitung und Schweizerisches Handelsblatt* (3 June 1946), L 3, p. 198.

p. 268   'Peter & I': Britten to Ralph Hawkes, 4 Feb. 1946, L 3, p. 145.

p. 268   'he was': Elizabeth Mayer to Britten, 7 Feb. 1946, L 3, p. 208.

p. 269   'Don't be': Edward Dent to Britten, 27 Feb. 1946, L 3, p. 169.

p. 269   'Thank you': Britten to Edward Dent, 14 Mar. 1946, L 3, p. 169.

p. 269   'that in': Arthur Benjamin to Britten [?Aug.] 1946, L 3, p. 146.

p. 270   'Peter Grimes': Peter Grimes, reader's report, 10 May 1945, British Library, Lord Chamberlain Plays Correspondence, 6286.

p. 270   'moral perceptions': Eric Crozier and Nancy Evans, 'After Long Pursuit', unpublished typescript, BPL.

p. 270   'Physically': The Rape of Lucretia, reader's report, 16 Feb. 1946, British Library, Lord Chamberlain Plays Correspondence, 6878.

p. 271   'a hymn': Duncan, *Benjamin Britten*, pp. 60, 68.

p. 271   *Footnote*: Lord Chamberlain's office to Wauna Paul, 5 Sept. 1961, British Library, Lord Chamberlain Plays Correspondence, Lady Chatterley, 1960/1010. Lord Chamberlain's office to Gerald Raffles, 10 June 1958, British Library, Lord Chamberlain Plays Correspondence, A Taste of Honey, 1958/1017.

p. 272   'The composer': Britten, 'Foreword', in Crozier, *The Rape of Lucretia*, p. 8.

p. 273   'If she': HCBB, p. 235.

p. 273   'looked for': HCBB, p. 261.

p. 273   'If Britten': Tom Rosenthal interviewed by the author, 3 Aug. 2011.

p. 274   'Britten took': Myfanwy Piper, 'Writing for Britten', in David Herbert (ed.), *The Operas of Benjamin Britten* (London, 1989), p. 14.

p. 274   'Homosexuality': NBB.

p. 275   'The old': Montagu Slater to Britten, 3 Dec. 1944, in Banks, *The Making of Peter Grimes*, p. 40.

p. 275   'I can't': Joan Cross interviewed by Elizabeth Sweeting, 29 Oct. 1985, BPL.

p. 275   'I knew': HCBB, p. 237.

p. 276   'do not': David Kynaston, *Austerity Britain: 1945–51* (London, 2008), p. 176.

p. 277   *'it must'*: Britten to Ralph Hawkes, 30 June 1946, L 3, p. 199.

p. 277   *'what had'*: Ernest Newman, in *Sunday Times* (21 July 1946), L 3, p. 217.

p. 277   *'If you're'*: HCBB, p. 239.

p. 277   *'the dramatic'*: Michael Tippett to Britten, 11 July 1946, L 3, p. 223.

p. 277   *'Tell me'*: MBB, p. 189.

p. 277   *Footnote*: Bruno Monsaingeon (ed.), *Sviatoslav Richter: Notebooks and Conversations* (Princeton, 2002), p. 187.

p. 278   *'I wouldn't'*: Eric Crozier interviewed by Humphrey Burton, 10 June 1991, L 3, p. 209.

p. 278   *'One day'*: Britten to Elizabeth Mayer, 18 Dec. 1946, L 3, p. 267.

p. 279   *'There's no'*: *Time* (19 Aug. 1946), in Humphrey Burton, *Leonard Bernstein* (London, 1994), p. 152.

p. 279   *'It was'*: NBB.

p. 280   *'I now'*: Duncan, *Benjamin Britten*, p. 85.

p. 280   *'Ben and I'*: Ibid., p. 81.

p. 281   *'It was'*: Etienne Amyot to George Barnes, 2 July 1946, BBC Written Archive Centre, Composer File, Benjamin Britten, file 1b, 1945–50.

p. 281   *'My own'*: Britten to Edward Sackville-West, 23 Aug. 1946, L 3, p. 239.

p. 281   *'I have'*: Britten to Imogen Holst, 22 Aug. 1946, L 3, p. 237.

p. 281   *'Our friendship'*: Eric Crozier and Nancy Evans, 'After Long Pursuit', unpublished typescript, BPL.

p. 281   *Footnote*: Britten, 'Verdi – A Symposium', *Opera*, 2/3 (Feb. 1951), BOM, p. 103.

p. 282   *'Eric'*: L 3, p. 248.

p. 282   *'Britten's music'*: Steuart Wilson memo, 2 Dec. 1946, Arts Council England, PKSB, p. 86.

p. 282   *'If there'*: Britten, Eric Crozier and John Piper interviewed by James McKechnie, BBC Third Programme, broadcast 19 June 1947, BOM, p. 70.

p. 282   *'We believe'*: Announcement of the formation of the English Opera Group, L 3, p. 243.

p. 284   *'It must'*: *New York Times* (6 Jan. 1949), L 3, p. 479.

p. 285   *'I like'*: Britten to Grace Williams, 11 Mar. 1949, L 3, p. 495.

p. 285   *'I can'*: David Webster to Britten, 15 Nov. 1946, L 3, p. 203.

p. 285   *'a symphony'*: Ralph Hawkes to Britten, 14 Mar. 1946, L 3, p. 237.

p. 286   *'Mr Benjamin'*: Arts Council Advisory Panel on Music, minutes, 30 Oct. 1947, Arts Council England.

p. 286   *Footnote*: Ernst Roth, *The Business of Music: Reflections of a Music Publisher* (London, 1969), p. 229.

p. 287   *'There were'*: Ibid., 28 Oct. 1946.

p. 289   *'The Stock Exchange'*: George Orwell, *The Lion and the Unicorn* (London, 1941), quoted in Kynaston, *Austerity Britain*, p. 173.

p. 289   *'The great'*: Ibid., p. 186.

p. 289   *'Now I'*: Eric Crozier to Nancy Evans [n.d.], L 3, p. 277.

p. 289   '*Lady Bracknell*': Joan Cross interviewed by Elizabeth Sweeting, 29 Oct. 1985, BPL.

p. 289   '*His setting*': Eric Crozier to Nancy Evans [Dec. 1949], L3, p. 251.

p. 290   '*Was it*': Guy de Maupassant, 'Le Rosier de Madame Husson', in *Boule de Suif and Other Stories*, trans. Marjorie Laurie (Harmondsworth, 1940), p. 174.

p. 291   '*decently squiffy*': Albert Herring, reader's report [May 1947], British Library, Lord Chamberlain Plays Correspondence, 1947/16.

p. 291   '*a shyness*': Charles Stuart, 'Maupassant Reversed', *Observer* (22 June 1947); see also Clifford Hindley, 'Not the Marrying Kind: Britten's *Albert Herring*', *Cambridge Opera Journal*, 6/2 (1994), p. 159.

p. 291   '*We've fallen*': Britten to Jean Redcliffe-Maud, 8 Jan. 1947, L3, p. 271.

p. 292   '*wallpaper*': Christopher Isherwood, *Lost Years: A Memoir 1945–1951* (London, 2000), p. 86.

p. 292   '*I guess*': Kynaston, *Austerity Britain*, p. 249.

p. 292   '*kind of*': John Lehmann, *The Ample Proposition* (London, 1966), in Kynaston, *Austerity Britain*, p. 192.

p. 293   '*A married*': Cyril Connolly, *Ideas and Places* (London, 1953), pp. 118–19.

p. 293   '*Well, why*': HCBB, p. 240.

p. 294   '*Since Napoleon*': Concert programme, 18 Apr. 1947, L3, p. 291.

p. 294   '*I have*': Laura Cumming, 'Picasso: Peace and Freedom', *Observer* (23 May 2010).

p. 295   '*the characters*': Janet Baker, 'Working with Britten', in Herbert, *The Operas of Benjamin Britten*, p. 1.

p. 295   '*Ben and*': HCBB, pp. 251–2.

p. 295   '*This isn't*': Eric Crozier, 'Staging First Productions 1', in Herbert, *The Operas of Benjamin Britten*, p. 29.

p. 295   '*In Mr Britten*': Ernest Newman, 'Mr Britten and *Albert Herring* – I', *Sunday Times* (29 June 1947), L3, p. 296.

p. 296   '*Incidentally*': Britten to Erwin Stein, 8 Aug. 1947, L3, p. 306.

p. 296   '*Far from*': Frederick Goldbeck, 'Comment l'esprit vient à un Parsifal de sous-préfecture', *Le Figaro* (2 Aug. 1947), L3, p. 309.

p. 296   '*Eh bien?*': Eric Crozier and Nancy Evans, 'After Long Pursuit', *Opera Quarterly*, 10/4 (1994), p. 10.

p. 297   '*there was*': Eric Crozier, 1948 Aldeburgh Festival programme book, PKSB, p. 148.

p. 297   '*Why not*': Ibid.

p. 298   '*And let*': 'The Arts Council: Its Policy and Hopes', *Listener* (12 July 1945), PKSB, p. 152.

p. 298   '*The walls*': Britten to Peter Pears [between 4 and 11 Sept. 1947], L3, p. 322.

p. 299   '*it reminded*': Britten to Peter Pears [21 Mar. 1948], L3, p. 386.

p. 299   *'Don't be'*: Britten to Peter Pears [early Dec. 1947], L 3, p. 341.

p. 301   *'I'm up'*: Britten to Ronald Duncan [after 9 Nov. 1947], L 3, p. 330.

p. 302   *'This British'*: Montague Haltrecht, *The Quiet Showman: Sir David Webster and the Royal Opera House* (London, 1975), p. 102.

p. 302   *'we have'*: Britten, 'An Opera is Planned', BBC Third Programme, broadcast 19 June 1947, BOM, p. 73.

p. 302   *'I think'*: Britten to Mary Behrend [?10 Nov. 1947], L 3, p. 333.

p. 302   *'The dear'*: Britten to Lennox Berkeley [*c.* 15 Nov. 1947], L 3, p. 335.

p. 302   Footnote: Earl of Harewood, *The Tongs and the Bones* (London, 1981), p. 151.

p. 303   *'Ben often'*: Colin Graham interviewed by Keith Grant, 1988, BPL.

p. 303   *'You look'*: HCBB, p. 267.

p. 304   *'We don't'*: John Piper, 'The Design of Lucretia', in Crozier, *The Rape of Lucretia*, p. 69.

p. 304   *'Well yes'*: Myfanwy Piper interviewed by Michael Oliver, 1997, BPL.

p. 304   *'Whatever he'*: Britten to Myfanwy Piper, 16 May 1954, L 4, p. 243.

p. 304   Footnote: John Piper, 'Designing for Britten', in Herbert, *The Operas of Benjamin Britten*, p. 6.

p. 304   Footnote: Piper, 'The Design of Lucretia', p. 71.

p. 305   *'shades of'*: Piper, 'Designing for Britten', p. 7.

p. 305   *'of all'*: Basil Coleman interviewed by William Kerley, 28 May 2004, BPL.

p. 306   *'friendly until'*: Tanya Moiseiwitsch interviewed by John Drummond, 20 Apr. 1993, BPL.

p. 306   *This was Piper's*: Alexandra Harris, *Romantic Moderns: English Writers, Artists and the Imagination from Virginia Woolf to John Piper* (London, 2010).

p. 307   *'When I'*: Piper, 'The Design of Lucretia', p. 67.

p. 307   *'They were'*: John and Myfanwy Piper interviewed by Elizabeth Sweeting, 6 Sept. 1986, BPL.

p. 307   *'fear of'*: Myfanwy Piper interviewed by Michael Oliver, 1997, BPL.

p. 307   *'I saw'*: Britten to Myfanwy Piper, 3 Jan. 1954, L 4, p. 206.

p. 307   *'The first'*: Edward Dent to Britten, 27 Feb. 1946, L 3, p. 188.

p. 307   Footnote: John Piper to Britten, 26 Nov. 1950, in Frances Spalding, *John Piper, Myfanwy Piper: Lives in Art* (Oxford, 2009), p. 313.

p. 308   *'The Covent'*: Britten to Henry Boys, 24 Nov. 1947, L 3, p. 338.

p. 308   *'But anyhow'*: Britten to Mary Behrend [?10 Nov. 1947], L 3, p. 333.

p. 309   *'Anyone, anywhere'*: Britten, 'On Receiving the First Aspen Award', 30 July 1964, BOM, p. 261.

p. 309   *'rackety'*: Michael Channon, *Repeated Takes* (London, 1995), p. 81.

p. 309   *'Benjamin Britten'*: Stephen Williams, 'Britten the Too-Brilliant', *Lantern* (Sept. 1947), PKSB, p. 213.

p. 309   *'Britten is'*: in *Penguin Music Magazine* (May 1947), PKSB, p. 213.

p. 311   'I came': Kynaston, *Austerity Britain*, p. 200.

p. 311   'go down': Adrian Ball (ed.), *Food of Love* (London, 1971), pp. 24–5.

p. 311   'Yes, writing's': Britten to Peter Pears, 18 Dec. 1947, L3, p. 344.

p. 312   'for 20': Britten to Ronald Duncan [mid-Jan. 1948], L3, p. 351.

p. 313   'that old': Peter Pears to Britten, 22 Mar. 1948, L3, p. 387.

p. 313   'Deep down': Britten to Walter Hussey, 22 Mar. 1948, L3, p. 388.

p. 313   'e.g. every': Britten to Ralph Hawkes, 27 Feb. 1948, L3, p. 373.

p. 313   'If only I had': MBB, p. 191.

p. 313   It was not: 'Opera's New Face', *Time* (16 Feb. 1948), L3, p. 372.

p. 313   'So the': Olin Downes, 'Opera by Britten in Premiere Here', *New York Times* (13 Feb. 1948), L3, p. 376.

p. 313   'It is fantastic': Britten to Ralph Hawkes, 27 Feb. 1948, L3, pp. 373–4.

p. 315   'I feel': Britten, *The Beggar's Opera*, programme note, May 1948, BOM, p. 374.

p. 315   'I believe': Herbert Murrill to Lindsay Wellington, 30 July 1951, PKSB, p. 93.

p. 315   'of people': Tyrone Guthrie, *The Beggar's Opera*, programme note, May 1948, L3, p. 393.

p. 316   'It would': in *Evening News* (19 Sept. 1948), PKSB, p. 97.

p. 316   'natural unsuitability': Edward Sackville-West, in *New Statesman and Nation* (5 June 1948), L3, p. 401.

p. 316   'Where are': Tanya Moiseiwitsch interviewed by John Drummond, 20 Apr. 1993, BPL.

p. 316   'sea-port': Quoted by E. M. Forster, in *Listener* (24 June 1948), HCBB, p. 256.

p. 317   'It is': E. M. Forster, 'George Crabbe: The Poet and the Man', in Philip Brett (ed.), *Benjamin Britten: Peter Grimes*, Cambridge Opera Handbooks (Cambridge, 1983), p. 3.

p. 317   'There were': Fidelity Cranbrook interviewed by Pam Wheeler, 3 Feb. 1988, BPL.

p. 318   'I should': Brett, *Peter Grimes*, p. 20.

p. 318   'The church': NBB.

p. 319   'the great': Joan Cross interviewed by Elizabeth Sweeting, 29 Oct. 1985, BPL.

p. 319   'You must never': HCBB, p. 269.

p. 319   'Of course': Harewood, *The Tongs and the Bones*, p. 83.

p. 319   'in the sense': Earl of Harewood, 1948 Aldeburgh Festival programme book, HCBB, p. 268.

p. 320   'It is not': Britten interviewed by the Earl of Harewood, *People Today*, BBC Home Service, broadcast 23 June 1960, BOM, p. 177.

p. 320   'may feel': Earl of Harewood, 1948 Aldeburgh Festival programme book, HCBB, p. 268.

p. 320   'People were': Graham Johnson interviewed by the author, 4 Nov. 2010.

p. 321   'I'm crotchety': Britten to Piers Dunkerley, 23 Dec. 1948, L 3, p. 470.

p. 322   'only those': Eric Crozier to Eric Walter White, 21 Feb. 1949, PKSB, pp. 98–9.

p. 323   'Some people': Schafer, British Composers in Interview, p. 230.

p. 323   'I am': Britten to David Webster, 27 Oct. 1948, L 3, pp. 436–7.

p. 323   'It is': Britten to Peter Pears [mid-Dec. 1948], L 3, p. 469.

p. 324   'Perhaps after': Britten to Peter Pears [after 19 Feb. 1949], L 3, p. 490.

p. 324   'so very': Britten to Peter Pears [28 Oct. 1948], L 3, p. 442.

p. 324   'You know': Basil Douglas interviewed by Donald Mitchell, 16 Nov. 1987, BPL.

p. 324   'Well, John': John Tooley interviewed by Michael Oliver, 1997, BPL.

p. 325   'see us': E. M. Forster to Christopher Isherwood, 10 July 1939, in Wendy Moffat, E. M. Forster: A New Life (London, 2010), p. 248.

p. 325   'get a': Ibid., p. 48.

p. 325   'if I': E. M. Forster, Two Cheers for Democracy, quoted ibid., p. 248.

p. 325   'He is': Stephen Spender, World within World (London, 2001), p. 183.

p. 325   'Unluckily': E. M. Forster to Eric Crozier, 24 Oct. 1948, in Philip Reed, 'From First Thoughts to First Night', in Mervyn Cooke and Philip Reed (eds.), Benjamin Britten: Billy Budd, Cambridge Opera Handbooks (Cambridge, 1993), p. 45.

p. 325   'comedy must': Crozier, 'Staging First Productions 1', p. 31.

p. 325   'I want': E. M. Forster to Britten, 20 Dec. 1948, in Cooke and Reed, Billy Budd, p. 46.

p. 326   'Melville': E. M. Forster, Aspects of the Novel (London, 1993), p. 98.

p. 326   'Now, it': 'Discussion on Billy Budd', BBC Third Programme, broadcast 12 Nov. 1960, BOM, p. 197.

p. 327   'I am an': Forster's first draft, Billy Budd, Prologue, L 3, p. 482.

p. 327   'Peter's taking': Britten to Ronald Duncan, 19 Jan. 1949, L 3, p. 484.

p. 328   'I am feeling': Britten to Elizabeth Mayer, 7 Feb. 1949, L 3, p. 489.

p. 328   'Lovely as': Britten to Peter Pears [2 Mar. 1949], L 3, p. 491.

p. 329   'Morgan': Eric Crozier to Nancy Evans, 4 Mar. 1949, L 3, p. 497.

p. 329   'A prose': 'Discussion on Billy Budd', p. 204.

p. 329   'small but': E. M. Forster to Britten, 16 Jan. 1959, L 5, p. 98.

p. 329   'I found': Britten, 'Some Notes on Forster and Music', in Oliver Stallybrass (ed.), Aspects of E. M. Forster (London, 1969), BOM, p. 319.

p. 329   'Something is': Eric Crozier to Nancy Evans [5 Mar. 1949], L 3, p. 497.

p. 330   'I like': Britten to Peter Pears [before 18 Mar. 1949], L 3, p. 496.

p. 330   'a symphony': Britten, 'A Note on the Spring Symphony', Music Survey, 2 (Spring 1950), BOM, p. 374.

p. 330   'It is in': Ibid.

p. 330   It was an odd: See Edward Mendelson, Early Auden (London, 1999), pp. 164–72.

p. 331   '70 little': Britten to Edward Sackville-West, 27 July 1949, L 3, p. 535.

p. 331   *'It is as though'*: Desmond Shawe-Taylor, in *New Statesman and Nation* (23 July 1949), L3, p. 528.

p. 331   *'I have no'*: Britten to Elizabeth Mayer, 9 Jan. 1949, L3, p. 478.

p. 331   *'the author's'*: [Martin Cooper], in *Times Literary Supplement* (19 Feb. 1949), L3, p. 505.

p. 332   *Footnote*: Ernest Newman, in *Sunday Times* (9 Dec. 1951), L3, p. 697.

p. 332   *'the old'*: Igor Stravinsky to Lincoln Kirstein, 25 Aug. 1950, in Stephen Walsh, *Stravinsky: The Second Exile* (London, 2006), p. 260.

p. 332   *'I have seldom'*: Eric Crozier to Nancy Evans, 7 Apr. 1949, L3, p. 506.

p. 333   *'Of course'*: Shawe-Taylor, in *New Statesman and Nation* (23 July 1949), L3, p. 518.

p. 334   *'I have known'*: Eric Crozier to Nancy Evans [?July 1949], L3, p. 521.

p. 334   *'But if'*: Britten to Ralph Hawkes, 29 May 1949 [sent after 19 June], L3, p. 513.

p. 334   *'Eric really'*: Basil Douglas interviewed by Donald Mitchell, 16 Nov. 1987, BPL.

p. 335   *'We can't'*: Britten to Eric Crozier [late June 1949], L3, p. 520.

p. 335   *'as though'*: Eric Crozier to Nancy Evans, 15 Aug. 1949, L3, p. 537.

p. 335   *'I do not'*: Eric Crozier to Nancy Evans, 22 Aug. 1949, L3, p. 537.

p. 335   *Footnote*: Billy Budd, reader's report, 12 Dec. 1951, British Library, Lord Chamberlain Plays Correspondence, 3611.

p. 336   *'This town'*: Britten to Elizabeth Sweeting [11 Nov. 1949], L3, p. 554.

p. 336   *'beastly'*: Britten to Lesley Bedford [Dec. 1949], L3, p. 556.

p. 338   *'not what'*: Imogen Holst's diary, 4 Mar. 1953, CGIH, p. 255.

p. 338   *'Britten himself'*: Igor Stravinsky to Nicolas Nabokov, 15 Dec. 1949, in Walsh, *Stravinsky: The Second Exile*, p. 252.

p. 338   *'Britten is'*: Ibid., p. 620.

p. 338   *'everything but'*: Humphrey Carpenter, *W. H. Auden: A Biography* (Oxford, 1992), p. 370.

p. 339   *'he cant'*: W. H. Auden to Elizabeth Mayer [Sept. 1951], ibid.

p. 339   *'Kleenex'*: Igor Stravinsky, *Themes and Conclusions* (London, 1972), pp. 26–7.

p. 339   *'In this'*: Isherwood, *Lost Years*, p. 213.

p. 339   *'I still'*: Ibid., p. 214.

p. 339   *'It is'*: Christopher Isherwood to Britten, 15 Dec. 1949, L3, p. 558.

p. 340   *Footnote*: James Lawrie to Basil Douglas, 9 Nov. 1951, BPL.

p. 342   *'What I'*: Britten to Ralph Downes, 11 Nov. 1948, L3, p. 463.

p. 342   *'shockingly low'*: Arts Council Opera and Ballet Sub-Committee, minutes, 5 July 1950, BOM, pp. 86–101.

p. 342   *'Great music'*: Britten, introduction to Boyd Neel, *The Story of an Orchestra* (London, 1950), BOM, p. 85.

p. 343   *'I regret'*: Britten to Howard Roberts, 31 Jan. 1951, L3, p. 639.

p. 343   *'Oh my'*: Fidelity Cranbrook interviewed by Pam Wheeler, 3 Feb. 1988, BPL.

p. 343   *Footnote*: BOM, p. 97.

p. 344   *'As well'*: Basil Coleman, 'Staging First Productions 2', in Herbert, *The Operas of Benjamin Britten*, p. 35.

p. 344   *'would sort'*: David Matthews interviewed by Michael Oliver, 1997, BPL.

p. 344   *'He has'*: E. M. Forster to Bob Buckingham, 23 Apr. 1950, L 3, p. 588.

p. 346   *'I want'*: E. M. Forster to Britten [early Dec. 1950], in Mary Lago and P. N. Furbank (eds.), *Selected Letters of E. M. Forster*, vol. 2: *1921–1970* (London, 1985), p. 242.

p. 346   *'like some'*: Eric Crozier and Nancy Evans, 'After Long Pursuit', unpublished typescript, BPL.

p. 346   *'I am'*: E. M. Forster's diary, 31 Dec. 1950, in Philip Gardner (ed.), *The Journals and Diaries of E. M. Forster* (London, 2011), vol. 2, p. 112.

p. 347   *'lovable'*: E. M. Forster to Britten, 20 Dec. 1948, in Lago and Furbank, *Selected Letters of E. M. Forster*, vol. 2, p. 235.

p. 347   *'Beyond'*: Herman Melville, *Billy Budd, Sailor and Other Stories* (London, 1986), p. 366.

p. 347   *'the horrible'*: Melville, *Billy Budd, Sailor*, p. vii.

p. 347   *Footnote*: Sidney Nolan interviewed by Donald Mitchell, 11 June 1990, BPL.

p. 348   *'We felt'*: 'Discussion on *Billy Budd*', p. 206.

p. 348   *'for my'*: Ibid., p. 207.

p. 348   *'in an'*: Richard Holmes, *Coleridge: Darker Reflections* (London, 1999), p. 11.

p. 349   *Footnote*: Letter to the author, 23 June 2012.

p. 349   *Footnote*: *The Sopranos*, Series 4, episode 12.

p. 350   *'It is'*: Britten to Marion Harewood, 22 Oct. 1950, L 3, p. 620.

p. 350   *'I hope'*: Britten to Albert Goldberg, 23 Oct. 1950, L 3, p. 621.

p. 351   *'I wish'*: Ian Kemp (ed.), *Michael Tippett: A Symposium on his 60th Birthday* (London, 1965), p. 30.

p. 352   *'Until such'*: Britten, in *The Times* (8 May 1951), BOM, pp. 106–7.

p. 353   *'Really the'*: Britten to Eric Walter White, 22 Aug. 1951, L 3, p. 674.

p. 353   *'I feel'*: Britten to the Harewoods, 2 Oct. 1951, L 3, p. 681.

p. 353   *'He doesn't'*: Britten to Erwin Stein, 9 Sept. 1951, L 3, p. 677.

p. 353   *'I was very'*: Basil Douglas interviewed by Donald Mitchell, 16 Nov. 1987, BPL.

p. 353   *Footnote*: W. H. Auden, 'Some Reflections on Opera as a Medium', *Tempo*, 20 (Summer 1951), p. 9.

p. 354   *'I think'*: Basil Coleman interviewed by William Kerley, 28 May 2004, BPL.

p. 355   *'WISHING YOU'*: W. H. Auden and Igor Stravinsky, telegram to Britten, 1 Dec. 1951, BPL.

p. 355   *'one of'*: Eric Crozier and Nancy Evans, 'After Long Pursuit', unpublished typescript, BPL.

p. 355   '*One always*': in *Evening News* (3 Dec. 1951), PKSB, p. 130.
p. 355   '*the result*': Britten to E. M. Forster, 30 Dec. 1958, L 5, p. 97.

CHAPTER 5. ESTABLISHMENT: ENGLAND, 1952–1955

p. 356   '*This. Is.*': Author's transcription of BBC radio broadcast, 6 Feb. 1952.
p. 356   '*may in*': Herman Melville, *Billy Budd, Sailor and Other Stories* (London, 1986), p. 367.
p. 357   '*What with*': E. M. Forster to Britten, 30 Sept. 1948, in Mary Lago and P. N. Furbank (eds.), *Selected Letters of E. M. Forster*, vol. 2: *1921–1970* (London, 1985), p. 233.
p. 358   '*Yes, that's*': HCBB, p. 305.
p. 358   '*special selfish*': Britten, 'Three Premieres', in Neville Cardus (ed.), *Kathleen Ferrier: A Memoir* (London, 1954), p. 61.
p. 359   '*It's the perfect*': Earl of Harewood, *The Tongs and the Bones* (London, 1981), p. 134.
p. 359   '*Here is*': Ralph Vaughan Williams, *National Music and Other Essays* (Oxford, 1972), pp. 72–3.
p. 361   '*long and*': Clarendon, 'L'Œuvre du XXe siècle', *Le Figaro* (28 May 1952), in Mark Carroll, *Music and Ideology in Cold War Europe* (Cambridge, 2003), p. 20.
p. 361   '*Auden's just*': William Walton to Christopher Hassall, 10 June 1952, L 4, p. 66.
p. 362   '*just folk*': Robert Hewison, '"Happy Were He": Benjamin Britten and the *Gloriana* Story', in Paul Banks (ed.), *Britten's Gloriana* (Woodbridge, 1993), p. 13.
p. 362   '*the traces*': Lytton Strachey, *Elizabeth and Essex* (London, 2000), p. 25.
p. 363   '*a quite*': Britten to William Plomer, 24 July 1952, L 4, p. 76.
p. 363   '*I like*': William Plomer to Britten, 2 Aug. 1952, L 4, p. 81.
p. 363   '*The fierce*': Strachey, *Elizabeth and Essex*, p. 16.
p. 364   '*tidy up*': Rosamund Strode interviewed by the author, 7 May 2009.
p. 364   '*I wonder*': William Plomer to Britten [Oct. 1952], L 4, p. 92.
p. 365   '*The orchestra*': Memorandum from David Webster (1952), Benjamin Britten correspondence, Royal Opera House, Covent Garden.
p. 365   '*two little*': Britten to Basil Coleman, 6 Oct. 1952, L 4, p. 90.
p. 365   '*Anyhow you*': Britten to David Webster, 20 Nov. 1952, L 4, p. 97.
p. 365   *Footnote*: David Webster to Viscount Waverley, 25 July 1952, PKSB, p. 135.
p. 365   *Footnote*: Royal Opera House, Covent Garden, Board Meeting, minutes, 1950–1956, 25 Sept. 1952.
p. 366   '*if it*': Imogen Holst's diary, 4 Apr. 1953, CGIH, p. 261.
p. 366   '*the labels*': Ronald Duncan, *Benjamin Britten: A Personal Memoir* (London, 1979), pp. 109–10.

p. 367   '*We were*': Imogen Holst's diary, 29 Sept. 1952, CGIH, p. 186.

p. 368   '*Good old*': Holst's diary, 7 Oct. 1952, CGIH, p. 190.

p. 368   '*because he*': Ibid.

p. 368   '*if only*': Holst's diary, 7 Dec. 1952, CGIH, p. 223.

p. 368   '*What do*': Holst's diary, 10 Oct. 1952, CGIH, p. 194.

p. 368   '*Sibelius*': Holst's diary, 2 Dec. 1952, CGIH, p. 218.

p. 369   '*how wretched*': Holst's diary, 11 Dec. 1952, CGIH, p. 224.

p. 369   '*well I must*': Holst's diary, 13 Jan. 1953, CGIH, p. 233.

p. 369   '*Then at*': Holst's diary, 2 Dec. 1952, CGIH, p. 217.

p. 369   '*The Opera*': Britten to Princess Margaret of Hesse, 11 Dec. 1952, L4, p. 111.

p. 370   '*Historical operas*': Gloriana, reader's report, 29 May 1953, British Library, Lord Chamberlain Plays Correspondence, 5620.

p. 371   '*You know*': Donald Mitchell, 'The Paradox of *Gloriana*: Simple and Difficult', in Banks, *Britten's Gloriana*, p. 67.

p. 371   '*Queen Salote*': *Royal Opera Night*, British Pathé, June 1953.

p. 372   '*one of the*': Harewood, *The Tongs and the Bones*, p. 138.

p. 372   '*Clap, damn*': Peter Alexander, *William Plomer: A Biography* (Oxford, 1990), p. 278.

p. 373   '*Dickie and*': Noel Coward's diary, 12 June 1953, in Graham Payne and Sheridan Morley (eds.), *The Noel Coward Diaries* (London, 1982), p. 214.

p. 373   '*But make*': Britten to Mary Behrend, 1 Dec. 1953, L4, p. 197.

p. 374   '*Under the*': Strachey, *Elizabeth and Essex*, p. 201.

p. 374   '*The work*': Britten to Elizabeth Mayer, 30 Aug. 1953, L4, p. 177.

p. 374   *Footnote*: Selina Hastings, *The Secret Lives of Somerset Maugham* (London, 2009), p. 115.

p. 375   '*Even the*': Beverly Baxter, 'The One Sour Note of the Coronation', *Maclean's Magazine* (1 Sept. 1953), PKSB, p. 214.

p. 375   '*Public resentment*': Marie Stopes, in *The Times* (20 June 1953), L4, p. 160.

p. 375   '*an almost*': Martin Cooper, in *Spectator* (19 June 1953), L4, p. 161.

p. 375   '*B.B. has*': Walton to Christopher Hassall [1952], L4, p. 107.

p. 376   '*entertained absurd*': Michael Tippett, *Those Twentieth Century Blues* (London, 1992), p. 214.

p. 376   '*There are*': Ibid., p. 215.

p. 376   '*maze of*': John Ireland to Britten, 26 Aug. 1954, L4, p. 268.

p. 376   '*The influence*': In *People* (24 July 1955), p. 7.

p. 376   '*Homosexuals are*': Ibid.

p. 377   '*I think*': Peter Hennessy, *Having It So Good: Britain in the Fifties* (London, 2007), p. 171.

p. 377   '*the latest*': John Deane Porter, 'Isn't It about Time Someone Said This ... Plainly and Frankly?' *Daily Express* (9 Apr. 1959), p. 8.

p. 378   'Scotland Yard': Percy Elland to Lord Beaverbrook, 15 Jan. 1954, L 3, p. 604.

p. 378   'The secrets': Edward Shils, *The Torment of Secrecy*, quoted in Hennessy, *Having It So Good*, p. 170.

p. 378   *Footnote*: Peter Wildblood, *Against the Law* (London, 1955), p. 35.

p. 379   'If homosexuality': E. M. Forster, 'A Magistrate's Figures', *New Statesman and Nation* (31 Oct. 1953), p. 509.

p. 379   'There were several': Rupert Croft-Cooke, *The Verdict of You All* (London, 1955), p. 145.

p. 379   'How to': Wendy Moffat, *E. M. Forster: A New Life* (London, 2010), p. 306.

p. 379   'The subject': Lord Clarendon to Laurence Olivier [1951], in *Guardian* (26 Aug. 2008).

p. 380   'understand why': Coward's diary, 17 Feb. 1957, in Payne and Morley, *The Noel Coward Diaries*, p. 349.

p. 381   'The fact': Britten to Elizabeth Mayer, 30 Aug. 1953, L 4, p. 177.

p. 381   'But – there': Ibid.

p. 381   *Pears delivered*: Harewood, *The Tongs and the Bones*, p. 138.

p. 381   'On the whole': William Plomer to Britten, 23 July 1953, L 4, p. 166.

p. 381   'It shut': Harewood, *The Tongs and the Bones*, p. 148.

p. 382   'influence of': Ibid., p. 138.

p. 382   'I would have': John Bridcut, *Britten* (London, 2010), p. 157.

p. 382   *Montagu Slater*: Philip Brett (ed.), *Benjamin Britten: Peter Grimes*, Cambridge Opera Handbooks (Cambridge, 1983), p. 30.

p. 382   'What a': Imogen Holst's diary, 2 Dec. 1952, CGIH, p. 217.

p. 382   'Ben's lack': Lincoln Kirstein interviewed by Nicholas Jenkins, *W. H. Auden Society Newsletter*, 7 (Oct. 1991), HCBB, p. 327.

p. 383   'Outside the': Edward Shils, 'The Intellectuals:– (1) Great Britain', *Encounter*, 4/4 (Apr. 1955), p. 16.

p. 385   'I suppose': Imogen Holst's diary, 18 June 1953, CGIH, p. 273.

p. 385   *Footnote*: W. H. Auden to Elizabeth Mayer, 16 July 1953, L 4, p. 164.

p. 386   'he gets': Stephen Potter's diary, 13 Dec. 1953, CGIH, p. 319.

p. 386   'I don't': Imogen Holst's diary, 11 Aug. 1953, CGIH, p. 287.

p. 386   'very dear': *Evening News* (11 Dec. 1953).

p. 387   'It is': Britten to Erwin Stein, 1 Jan. 1954, L 4, p. 199.

p. 388   'simplicity and': Ibid., p. 200.

p. 388   'wonderful, impressive': D, 1 June 1932.

p. 389   'The servants': F. O. Matthiessen and Kenneth Murdock (eds.), *The Notebooks of Henry James* (New York, 1947).

p. 389   'The children are bad': Quoted in Patricia Howard (ed.), *Benjamin Britten: The Turn of the Screw*, Cambridge Opera Handbooks (Cambridge, 1985), p. 2.

p. 389   'gingerly': Harewood, *The Tongs and the Bones*, p. 139.

p. 390   '*Hello, Maud*': Nancy Cunard, 'Black Man and White Ladyship' (Toulon, 1931), in Lawrence Rainey (ed.), *Modernism: An Anthology* (London, 2005), p. 767.

p. 390   '*She is*': Britten to Basil Coleman, 29 May 1954, L4, p. 248.

p. 391   '*Only make*': Henry James, *The Art of the Novel* (New York, 1948), p. 176.

p. 391   '*I don't*': Myfanwy Piper to Patricia Howard, 22 Feb. 1982, in Howard, *The Turn of the Screw*, p. 23.

p. 391   '*it seemed*': Imogen Holst, *Britten* (London, 1970), p. 54.

p. 391   *Footnote*: Quoted in Kate Summerscale, *The Suspicions of Mr Whicher or The Murder at Road Hill House* (London, 2009), p. 146.

p. 393   '*Turning and*': W. B. Yeats, 'The Second Coming', in *The Collected Poems of W. B. Yeats* (London, 1939), pp. 210–11.

p. 394   '*What is*': Myfanwy Piper, 'Writing for Britten', in David Herbert (ed.), *The Operas of Benjamin Britten* (London, 1989), p. 12.

p. 394   '*I think*': 'Discussion on *Billy Budd*', BBC Third Programme, broadcast 12 Nov. 1960, BOM, p. 197.

p. 394   '*The point*': ATTW.

p. 395   '*never aware*': *Guardian* (7 June 1971), HCBB, p. 536.

p. 395   '*That is*': Colin Matthews interviewed by Michael Oliver, 9 Jan. 1997, BPL.

p. 396   '*not really*': 'Discussion on *Billy Budd*', p. 197.

p. 396   '*left the*': Britten to Neil Saunders, 28 June 1955, L4, p. 301.

p. 396   '*The imagination*': Wilfred Owen to Susan Owen, 28 Sept. 1911, in Harold Owen and John Bell (eds.), *Wilfred Owen: Collected Letters* (Oxford, 1967), p. 88.

p. 397   '*I feel*': 'Discussion on *Billy Budd*', p. 196.

p. 399   '*It started*': David Hemmings interviewed by Tom Sutcliffe, 2000, L4, p. 226.

p. 399   '*the composer's*': *L'Express* (25 Sept. 1954), HCBB, p. 360.

p. 400   '*the most*': John Ireland to Charles Markes, 1954, L4, p. 268.

p. 400   '*Ben's behaviour*': JBBC, p. 197.

p. 401   '*nearly catastrophic*': HCBB, p. 357.

p. 401   '*Was he*': HCBB, p. 357.

p. 402   '*Ben came*': HCBB, p. 350.

p. 402   '*One could*': HCBB, p. 343.

p. 402   '*furiously jealous*': David Hemmings, *Blow-Up and Other Exaggerations*, L4, p. 224.

p. 402   '*And as*': Duncan, *Benjamin Britten*, p. 126.

p. 402   *Footnote*: Imogen Holst's diary, 8 Feb. 1953, CGIH, pp. 243–4.

p. 403   '*What am*': Colin Matthews to the author, 1 June 2011.

p. 403   '*I don't know. I've*': HCBB, p. 431.

p. 403   '*In the*': Peter Pears to Britten, 7 July 1976, BPL.

p. 404   *'Slava'*: Imogen Holst interviewed by Donald Mitchell, 22 June 1977, BPL.

p. 404   *'Peter is'*: Ibid.

p. 404   *'have dragged'*: Imogen Holst's diary, 3 July 1953, CGIH, p. 276.

p. 404   *'found the'*: Holst's diary, 6 Apr. 1953, CGIH, p. 261.

p. 404   *Footnote*: John Lindsay interviewed by Donald Mitchell, 10 July 1990, BPL.

p. 405   *'It's often'*: HCBB, p. 354.

p. 405   *'Her features'*: Stephen Spender, *World within World* (London, 2001), p. 316.

p. 405   *'The trouble'*: Elizabeth Salter and Allanah Harper (eds.), *Edith Sitwell: Fire of the Mind: An Anthology* (London, 1976), p. 176.

p. 405   *'courage & light'*: Britten to Edith Sitwell, 27 Sept. 1954, L 4, p. 289.

p. 406   *'What a'*: Britten to William Plomer, 8 Nov. 1954, L 4, p. 302.

p. 406   *'I am so haunted'*: Edith Sitwell to Britten, 26 Apr. 1955, L 4, p. 316.

p. 406   *'I must confess'*: Britten to Edith Sitwell, 28 Apr. 1955, L 4, p. 316.

p. 407   *'I don't see'*: Britten to Erwin Stein, 12 Jan. 1955, L 4, p. 306.

p. 408   *'I do'*: Ernst Roth to Britten, 10 Aug. 1953, L 4, p. 203.

CHAPTER 6. PROSPERITY: THE FAR EAST, ENGLAND, 1955–1963

p. 410   *'Sung all'*: Michael Flanders and Donald Swann, 'A Guide to Britten', L 4, p. 322.

p. 410   *'curiously attractive'*: Britten to Imogen Holst, 1 Dec. 1955, L 4, p. 353.

p. 410   *'jangled'*: Peter Pears to Mary Potter, 1 Dec. 1955, L 4, p. 356.

p. 411   *'Although'*: Britten to Roger Duncan, 26 Dec. 1955, L 4, p. 377.

p. 411   *'Like everything'*: Britten to Mary Potter, 23 Dec. 1955, L 4, p. 374.

p. 411   *'One is'*: Peter Pears, 'Far East Diary (1955–56)', in Philip Reed (ed.), *The Travel Diaries of Peter Pears 1936–1978* (Woodbridge, 1999), p. 35.

p. 412   *'they are'*: Britten to Erwin and Sophie Stein [n.d.], L 4, p. 388.

p. 412   *'CONFIDENT'*: Britten telegram to Ninette de Valois, 23 Jan. 1956, L 4, p. 391.

p. 412   *Footnote*: Britten to Basil Douglas, 22 Dec. 1955, L 4, p. 371.

p. 414   *'The slim'*: Prince Ludwig of Hesse, *Ausflug Ost* (Darmstadt, 1956), quoted in Reed, *The Travel Diaries of Peter Pears*, p. 50.

p. 414   *'the Yellow'*: Britten to Roger Duncan, 8 Feb. 1956, L 4, p. 404.

p. 415   *'It is'*: Britten to Roger Duncan, 21 Feb. 1956, L 4, p. 408.

p. 415   *'among the'*: Britten, 'To the Music Lovers of Japan', NHK broadcast 1 Jan. 1958, BOM, pp. 156–7.

p. 415   *'It all'*: Britten, 'Curlew River', 1964 Aldeburgh Festival programme book, BOM, p. 382.

p. 415   *'We've flown'*: Britten to Roger Duncan, 11 Mar. 1956, L 4, pp. 425–6.

p. 416   *'Let me'*: Colin Graham interviewed by Donald Mitchell, 3 Mar. 1992, BPL.

p. 416   *'That b. Ballet'*: Britten to Prince Ludwig of Hesse, 7 Nov. 1956, L 4, p. 471.

p. 418   *'I never'*: Britten to William Plomer, 25 Jan. 1957, L 4, p. 479.

p. 419   *'I thought'*: Elizabeth Mayer to Britten [postmarked 1 Nov. 1957], L 4, p. 558.

p. 419   *'Indonesian (?)'*: Donald Mitchell, in *Musical Times*, 98 (Feb. 1957), L 4, p. 485.

p. 419   *'Once again'*: Felix Aprahamian, in *Sunday Times* (6 Jan. 1957), L 4, p. 485.

p. 419   *'In every'*: Britten to Elizabeth Mayer, 13 Jan. 1957, L 4, p. 495.

p. 419   *'However, in'*: Britten to James Lawrie, 16 Jan. 1957, L 4, p. 500.

p. 420   *Yet even*: PKSB, p. 115.

p. 420   *'We are'*: Basil Douglas to Britten, 3 Dec. 1955, in Maureen Garnham, *As I Saw It: Basil Douglas, Benjamin Britten and the English Opera Group 1955–1957* (London, 1998), p. 62.

p. 421   *'What one'*: 'Benjamin Britten Talks to Edmund Tracey', *Sadler's Wells Magazine* (Autumn 1966), BOM, p. 293.

p. 422   *'I like'*: Ibid., p. 294.

p. 423   *'I get'*: Britten to Ronald Duncan, 3 Feb. 1957, L 4, p. 509.

p. 424   *'it might'*: Britten to Leslie Boosey, 10 Sept. 1957, L 4, p. 534.

p. 425   *'The notes'*: Peter Pears to the Hesses [23 Aug. 1957], L 4, p. 549.

p. 425   *'As Erwin'*: Ibid.

p. 425   *'One is'*: Britten, 'Dennis Brain 1921–1957', *Tempo*, 46 (Winter 1958), BOM, p. 159.

p. 425   *'Neither of'*: Peter Pears to the Hesses, 4 Sept. 1957, L 4, p. 554.

p. 427   *'alas, away'*: Britten to Edith Sitwell, 3 Mar. 1959, L 5, p. 124.

p. 427   *'A perfectly'*: Britten to Anthony Gishford, 8 Apr. 1957, L 4, p. 521.

p. 428   *'It won't'*: Britten to Marion Harewood, 20 Aug. 1958, L 5, pp. 62–3.

p. 429   *'a tremendous'*: Britten to Princess Margaret of Hesse, 11 Aug. 1958, L 5, p. 65.

p. 430   *'But night'*: Britten interviewed by Donald Mitchell, 'Mapreading', Feb. 1969, BOM, p. 325.

p. 430   *'MY HAPPINESS'*: Alma Mahler-Werfel telegram to Britten, 7 May 1959, L 5, p. 136.

p. 431   *'How few'*: Mstislav Rostropovich, 'Dear Ben', in Anthony Gishford (ed.), *Tribute to Benjamin Britten on his Fiftieth Birthday* (London, 1963), p. 16.

p. 432   *'I have'*: Britten to Peter Gould, 12 Mar. 1959, L 5, p. 80.

p. 432   *'It had'*: Britten to Rudolf Schwarz, 21 Oct. 1957, L 4, p. 457.

p. 432   *'Neither wind'*: Nicholas Kenyon, *The BBC Symphony Orchestra: The First Fifty Years 1930–1980* (London, 1981), p. 254.

p. 432   *'Pears has'*: Britten, 'Britten and Pears', *Audio Record Review* (Dec. 1967), BOM, p. 310.

p. 433   *'The notes'*: Artur Schnabel, in *Chicago Daily News* (11 June 1958).

p. 434   *'whatever we'*: William Glock, 'Four New English Operas', *Encounter*, 19 (Apr. 1955), p. 51.

p. 435   *'Because I'*: HCBB, p. 385.

p. 435   *'When suddenly'*: Ibid.

p. 436   *'keep your'*: Jenni Wake-Walker (ed.), *Time & Concord: Aldeburgh Festival Recollections* (Saxmundham, 1997), p. 41.

p. 437   *'all the'*: Decca advertisement, 1959 Aldeburgh Festival programme book, L 5, p. 67.

p. 437   *'I know'*: Muriel James to Britten, 6 Sept. 1965, PKSB, p. 229.

p. 437   *'As you'*: Britten to Ernst Roth, 13 Jan. 1963, PKSB, p. 226.

p. 438   *Terence Rattigan's*: Michael Darlow, *Terrence Rattigan: The Man and his Work* (London, 2010), p. 542.

p. 438   *'I feel'*: Britten to Sophie Stein, 20 July 1958, L 5, p. 60.

p. 439   *'deprived this'*: Earl of Harewood, 'In Memoriam: Erwin Stein 1885–1958', in Gishford, *Tribute to Benjamin Britten*, p. 160.

p. 439   *'It is'*: Desmond Shawe-Taylor, in *Sunday Times* (1 Feb. 1959), L 5, p. 103.

p. 439   *'whole choir'*: Britten to George Malcolm, 5 Jan. 1959, L 5, p. 103.

p. 441   *'expand with'*: Mervyn Cooke, *Britten and the Far East: Asian Influences in the Music of Benjamin Britten* (Woodbridge, 1998), p. 145.

p. 441   *'Why shouldn't'*: Peter Pears to Britten, 16 Feb. 1959, L 5, p. 116.

p. 441   *'Wystan looking'*: Peter Pears to Britten, 12 Feb. 1959, L 5, p. 112.

p. 442   *'what is one'*: Britten to Peter Pears, 17 Feb. 1959, L 5, p. 110.

p. 442   *'Lord Theseus'*: Myfanwy Piper, draft Prologue, L 5, p. 163.

p. 443   *'a fascinating'*: Britten to William Plomer, 24 Aug. 1959, L 5, p. 171.

p. 443   *'I can'*: Britten, BBC broadcast, 24 June 1960, BOM, p. 191.

p. 443   *'very different'*: Britten, 'A New Britten Opera', *Observer* (5 June 1960), BOM, p. 188.

p. 444   *'You use'*: W. H. Auden, *Lectures on Shakespeare* (Princeton, 2000), p. 56.

p. 444   *'Lucia has'*: Britten to Peter Pears, 27 Feb. 1959, L 5, p. 119.

p. 445   *'I think'*: Britten interviewed by the Earl of Harewood, *People Today*, BBC Home Service, broadcast 23 June 1960, BOM, p. 176.

p. 445   *'Ben was'*: Stephen Reiss to Christopher Headington, 24 June 1990, BPL.

p. 445   *'Ultimately, it'*: Britten, 'A New Britten Opera', p. 189.

p. 445   *'If it'*: Ibid.

p. 445   *Footnote*: John Copley interviewed by the author, 3 June 2011.

p. 446   *'It was a'*: Britten to Marjorie Fass, 28 July 1960, HCBB, p. 397.

p. 446   *'I was'*: Peter Pears to Britten, 17 Dec. 1959, L 5, p. 201.

p. 447   *'Shakespeare'*: Britten, BBC broadcast, 25 June 1960, BOM, p. 190.

p. 447   'That Britten': Desmond Shawe-Taylor, 'Britten's "Dream" Opera', *Sunday Times* (12 June 1960), L 5, p. 231.

p. 447   'The local': 'A Great New English Opera', *The Times* (17 June 1960), L 5, p. 233.

p. 447   'the latter': Britten to Peter Pears [11 Mar. 1960], L 5, p. 209.

p. 447   'I wish': Britten to Roger Duncan, 13 Apr. 1960, L 5, p. 223.

p. 448   'I must': Britten to John Cranko [draft], 1 Aug. 1960, L 5, pp. 242–3.

p. 448   'From the': Galina Vishnevskaya, *Galina: A Russian Story* (London, 1984), p. 364.

p. 450   'He had': Britten to Galina Vishnevskaya, 1 Apr. 1961, L 5, p. 324.

p. 450   'I was': HCBB, p. 402.

p. 450   'Often he': William Mann, in *The Times* (10 July 1961), L 5, p. 301.

p. 450   'astonishingly full': William Mann, in *The Times* (5 July 1961), HCBB, p. 402.

p. 450   *Footnote*: John Bridcut, *Rostropovich: The Genius of the Cello* (BBC Four, 2011).

p. 452   'madmen': John Maynard Keynes, *The General Theory of Employment, Interest and Money* (London, 1936), chapter 24, V.

p. 452   'fight and': Peter Hennessy, *Having It So Good: Britain in the Fifties* (London, 2007), p. 527.

p. 452   'UK had': Macmillan's diary, 26 July 1959, ibid., p. 576.

p. 452   'The atmosphere': Dennis Potter, *The Glittering Coffin* (London, 1960), p. 33.

p. 452   'the first': Britten and Peter Pears, programme note, 8 Dec. 1949, BOM, p. 83.

p. 452   'If the': John Osborne, *Look Back in Anger* (Genoa, 1994), p. 142.

p. 453   *In 1961*: David King Dunaway, *How Can I Keep from Singing: Pete Seeger* (New York, 1981), p. 209.

p. 453   'The new': John Lowe to Britten, 7 Oct. 1958, in Mervyn Cooke, *Britten: War Requiem*, Cambridge Music Handbooks (Cambridge, 1996), p. 21.

p. 453   'I am': Britten to Elizabeth Mayer, 13 Jan. 1957, L 4, p. 496.

p. 453   'an attempt': Sidney Nolan interviewed by Donald Mitchell, 11 June 1990, BPL.

p. 453   'It is': Albert Camus, *The Plague*, in James Christian, *Philosophy: An Introduction to the Art of Wondering* (Belmont, Calif., 2005), p. 92.

p. 454   'aren't those': Britten to Barbara Britten [?June 1962], L 5, p. 407.

p. 454   'Already I': Wilfred Owen to Susan Owen [*c.* 16 May 1917], in Harold Owen and John Bell (eds.), *Wilfred Owen: Collected Letters* (Oxford, 1967), p. 461.

p. 454   'tunnel life': Arthur Marwick, *The Deluge: British Society and the First World War* (London, 1965), p. 80.

p. 454   *'a kind'*: Britten to Dietrich Fischer-Dieskau, 16 Feb. 1961, L 5, p. 313.

p. 454   *Footnote*: John Robinson, *Honest to God* (London, 1963), p. 105.

p. 455   *'Is he'*: Christopher Hitchens, *God is Not Great* (London, 2007), p. 268.

p. 456   *'But how'*: Vishnevskaya, *Galina*, p. 366.

p. 456   *'Some of'*: 'Interview with Charles Osborne', *London Magazine*, 3 (3 Oct. 1963), BOM, p. 249.

p. 457   *'It* isn't *the end'*: Christopher Headington, *Peter Pears: A Biography* (London, 1992), p. 322.

p. 457   *'It makes'*: Peter Shaffer, in *Time & Tide* (7 June 1962), L 5, p. 407.

p. 457   *'the most'*: William Mann, in *The Times* (31 May 1962), L 5, p. 404.

p. 457   *'I did'*: Dietrich Fischer-Dieskau, *Echoes of a Lifetime* (London, 1989), p. 258.

p. 457   *'the one'*: Michael Tippett, Britten obituary, *Pacifist*, 15/3 (Jan. 1977), L 5, p. 409.

p. 458   *'It is'*: Britten, speech on being granted Freedom of Borough of Aldeburgh, 22 Oct. 1962, BOM, p. 218.

p. 458   *'His judgements'*: Britten, in *London Magazine*, 3 (Oct. 1963), BOM, p. 215.

p. 458   *'The truth'*: Britten to Paul Sacher, 13 Jan. 1963, L 5, p. 465.

p. 459   *'I know now'*: Britten to Georg Solti, 25 Oct. 1961, L 5, p. 354.

p. 459   *'I am'*: Britten to Peter Pears, 29 Oct. 1962, L 5, p. 445.

p. 459   *'when it'*: Peter Pears to Britten [?30 Oct. 1962], L 5, p. 445.

p. 460   *'One of'*: 'The Artist – to the People', *Pravda* (18 Mar. 1963), BOM, p. 233.

p. 461   *'full Communist'*: Martin Cooper, 'For People – or "the People"', *Daily Telegraph* (30 Mar. 1963), BOM, p. 234.

p. 461   *'The first'*: Ibid., p. 235.

p. 461   *'One of the'*: Britten, draft of unpublished *Observer* article [1963], BOM, p. 236.

p. 461   *'I do not'*: Ibid., p. 237.

p. 461   *'Fond as'*: Ibid., p. 239.

p. 462   *'everything must'*: Ibid., p. 240.

p. 462   *'Have we'*: Ibid., p. 237.

p. 462   *'a member'*: Britten, draft of 'Soviet Opera at B.B.C.: Shostakowitch's "Lady Macbeth"', *World Film News*, 1/1 (Apr. 1936), BOM, p. 18.

p. 462   *'In totalitarian'*: Britten, 'On Receiving the First Aspen Award', 30 July 1964, BOM, p. 258.

p. 463   *'The side'*: Murray Schafer, *British Composers in Interview* (London, 1963), BOM, p. 226.

p. 463   *'transient time'*: Arthur Marwick, *The Sixties: Cultural Revolution in Britain, France, Italy, and the United States, c.1958–c.1974* (Oxford, 1998), p. 806.

p. 463   *The historian Dominic*: Dominic Sandbrook, *White Heat: A History of Britain in the Swinging Sixties* (London, 2006).

CHAPTER 7. RETREAT: ALDEBURGH, 1963–1970

p. 464   '*I hear*': Murray Schafer, *British Composers in Interview* (London, 1963), BOM, p. 232.

p. 464   '*which must*': Donald Mitchell, in *Daily Telegraph* (13 Sept. 1963), HCBB, p. 420.

p. 464   '*In the*': William Walton to Britten, 23 Nov. 1963, L 5, p. 538.

p. 465   '*of all the*': Michael Tippett, in *Observer* (17 Nov. 1963), HCBB, p. 420.

p. 465   '*I can*': Mstislav Rostropovich, 'Dear Ben', in Anthony Gishford (ed.), *Tribute to Benjamin Britten on his Fiftieth Birthday* (London, 1963), pp. 14–15.

p. 466   '*where the*': 'Benjamin Britten Talks to Edmund Tracey', *Sadler's Wells Magazine* (Autumn 1966), BOM, p. 294.

p. 466   '*So often*': Ibid.

p. 466   '*a level*': Ibid.

p. 467   '*Once the*': Colin Graham, *Production Notes and Remarks on the Style of Performing Curlew River* (London, 1965), p. 3.

p. 468   '*What seemed*': Mervyn Cooke, *Britten and the Far East: Asian Influences in the Music of Benjamin Britten* (Woodbridge, 1998), p. 140.

p. 468   '*There must*': Edward Mendelson, *Later Auden* (London, 1999), p. xvii.

p. 469   '*Where Michael*': Robert Tear, *Tear Here* (London, 1990), p. 107.

p. 469   '*Where else*': *Daily Telegraph* (20 June 1964), HCBB, p. 432.

p. 470   '*If I*': Bruno Monsaingeon (ed.), *Sviatoslav Richter: Notebooks and Conversations* (Princeton, 2002), pp. 299, 285.

p. 471   '*the start*': William Mann, in *The Times* (15 June 1964), L 5, p. 584.

p. 471   '*It's all*': Colin Graham interviewed by Keith Grant, 1988, BPL.

p. 471   '*his style*': Peter Heyworth, 'Putting our Music on the Map', *Observer* (5 Dec. 1976).

p. 471   '*Those who*': Desmond Shawe-Taylor, 'Two Aspects of Britten', *Sunday Times* (24 July 1966).

p. 472   '*steady stripping*': Bayan Northcott, 'The Anguish of Benjamin Britten', *Sunday Telegraph* (5 Dec. 1976).

p. 472   '*demands that*': Britten, 'On Receiving the First Aspen Award', 30 July 1964, BOM, p. 259.

p. 472   '*The whole*': William Plomer to Britten, 16 Oct. 1964, L 5, p. 604.

p. 472   '*holy triangle*': Britten, 'On Receiving the First Aspen Award', p. 261.

p. 474   '*I've been*': Britten to Peter Pears, 17 Nov. 1964, L 5, p. 614.

p. 475   '*All the*': Britten to Earl of Harewood, 15 Jan. 1965, L 5, p. 630.

p. 476   *'worry too much'*: Britten to Donald Mitchell, 5 Feb. 1964, L 5, p. 552.

p. 476   *'I have no'*: David Wright, *Faber Music: The First 25 Years 1965–1990* (London, 1990), p. 5.

p. 476   *'I had'*: Britten to Donald Mitchell, 12 Sept. 1969, L 6, p. 308.

p. 477   *'People sometimes'*: Britten, 'Britten Looking Back', *Sunday Telegraph* (17 Nov. 1963), BOM, p. 253.

p. 478   *'so remote'*: Britten to John Newton, 19 Jan. 1965, L 5, pp. 633–4.

p. 480   *'here come'*: John Warrack, in *Daily Telegraph* (27 June 1965), HCBB, p. 449.

p. 481   *'And at'*: William Blake, 'Proverbs of Hell', in *The Marriage of Heaven and Hell* (Oxford, 1975), plate 11.

p. 481   *'just a new'*: W. H. Auden to Mrs A. E. Dodds [May 1939], in Humphrey Carpenter, *W. H. Auden: A Biography* (Oxford, 1992), p. 267.

p. 481   *'Prudence is'*: Blake, 'Proverbs of Hell', plate 7.

p. 481   *'Ben touchingly'*: Dietrich Fischer-Dieskau, *Echoes of a Lifetime* (London, 1989), p. 262.

p. 481   *Footnote*: Graham Johnson interviewed by the author, 4 Nov. 2010.

p. 482   *'Over and'*: Fischer-Dieskau, *Echoes of a Lifetime*, p. 272.

p. 483   *'Where could'*: Galina Vishnevskaya, *Galina: A Russian Story* (London, 1984), p. 369.

p. 483   *'Can one'*: Peter Pears's diary, 12 Aug. 1965, in Philip Reed (ed.), *The Travel Diaries of Peter Pears 1936–1978* (Woodbridge, 1999), p. 107.

p. 485   *'a dialogue'*: Britten, 'A Composer in Russia', *Sunday Telegraph* (24 Oct. 1965), BOM, p. 282.

p. 485   *'It seemed'*: Pears's diary [Aug. 1965], in Reed, *The Travel Diaries of Peter Pears*, p. 133.

p. 485   *'I wish'*: Britten, 'A Composer in Russia', p. 282.

p. 485   *'The dangers'*: Ibid.

p. 486   *'great peace'*: Britten to Donald Mitchell, 10 May 1965, L 5, p. 672.

p. 486   *'I loathe'*: Britten to Walter Hussey, 24 Nov. 1965, BPL.

p. 486   *'I know'*: Britten to Princess Margaret of Hesse, 6 Jan. 1966, L 6, p. 000.

p. 487   *'seven months'*: Britten, 'A New Britten Opera', *Observer* (5 June 1960), BOM, p. 187.

p. 487   *'I am determined'*: Britten to Princess Margaret of Hesse, 6 Jan. 1966, L 6, p. 9.

p. 488   *'uncommonly impressive'*: Nikolaus Pevsner, *The Buildings of England: Suffolk* (Harmondsworth, 1961), p. 389.

p. 488   *'We can't'*: HCBB, p. 456.

p. 488   *'To give'*: Ibid.

p. 490   *'I am'*: Britten to Peter Pears, 3 Apr. 1966, L 6, p. 23.

p. 490   *'political aspect'*: Colin Graham, 'Production Notes', *The Burning Fiery Furnace* (London, 1983), p. 201.

p. 490   *'It may'*: William Plomer, in 1966 Aldeburgh Festival programme book, p. 11.

p. 491   *'was drawn'*: Graham, 'Production Notes'.

p. 491   *'concomitant'*: Jeremy Noble, in *New Statesman and Nation* (17 June 1966), HCBB, p. 462.

p. 492   *'I was'*: Britten to Basil Coleman, 12 Sept. 1966, L 6, p. 68.

p. 493   *'I don't'*: HCBB, p. 468.

p. 493   *'This kind'*: Britten to Robert Tear, 22 Dec. 1966, L 6, p. 87.

p. 493   *'For several'*: Britten to William Plomer, 17 Mar. 1967, L 6, p. 100.

p. 494   *'His writing'*: 'Benjamin Britten Talks to Edmund Tracey', p. 295.

p. 494   *'hideous'*: Britten to Princess Margaret of Hesse, 18 Feb. 1967, L 6, p. 93.

p. 495   *'Weren't the'*: Jenni Wake-Walker (ed.), *Time & Concord: Aldeburgh Festival Recollections* (Saxmundham, 1997), p. 89.

p. 496   *'new open-stage'*: Harold Rosenthal, 'Britten on Aldeburgh and the Future', *Opera*, 18 (Autumn 1967), BOM, pp. 313, 314.

p. 496   *'A curtain'*: Britten to Rosamund Strode, 24 Sept. 1967, L 6, p. 146.

p. 497   *'You can'*: Britten to William Plomer, 10 Nov. 1967, L 6, p. 150.

p. 497   *'With its'*: William Plomer, 1968 Aldeburgh Festival programme book, p. 29.

p. 498   *'They discovered'*: Britten to Elizabeth Mayer, 27 Mar. 1968, L 6, pp. 211–12.

p. 498   *'It is sickening'*: Britten to William Plomer, 29 Apr. 1968, L 6, p. 216.

p. 498   *'I hope its'*: Ibid.

p. 499   *'Somehow'*: Peter Heyworth, in *Observer* (16 June 1968), HCBB, p. 482.

p. 499   *'In the twenty-four'*: Colin Graham, 'Staging First Productions 3', in David Herbert (ed.), *The Operas of Benjamin Britten* (London, 1989), p. 44.

p. 499   *'The problem'*: Colin Graham interviewed by Donald Mitchell, 3 Mar. 1992, BPL.

p. 499   *'Graham often'*: Tom Sutcliffe, 'Colin Graham', *The Times* (9 Apr. 2007).

p. 500   *'because the friends'*: Kathleen Mitchell, 'Edinburgh Diary 1968', in Philip Reed (ed.), *On Mahler and Britten* (Woodbridge, 1995), p. 204.

p. 500   *'He is'*: Ibid., p. 202.

p. 500   *'Remember to'*: Britten to Peter Pears [between 26 and 29 Mar. 1968], L 6, p. 209.

p. 502   *'I am convinced'*: Britten interviewed by Donald Mitchell, 'Mapreading', Feb. 1969, BOM, pp. 322–3.

p. 503   *'these marvellous'*: Britten interviewed by the BBC, 8 June 1969, BOM, p. 335.

p. 503   *'to love'*: Ibid., p. 336.

p. 503   *'Exactly as'*: HCBB, p. 492.

p. 504   *'Because after all'*: Britten interviewed by John Tusa for BBC Television, 1 Jan. 1970, BOM, p. 342.

p. 505   '*the boys*': Britten to William Plomer, 22 May 1969, L6, p. 282.

p. 505   '*It is really*': Britten to Donald Mitchell, 28 Dec. 1968, L6, p. 250.

p. 506   '*I become*': *New York Times* (16 Nov. 1969), HCBB, p. 498.

p. 506   '*this side*': Britten to Donald Mitchell, 20 Mar. 1970, L6, p. 341.

p. 506   '*Fill yourself*': Reed, *The Travel Diaries of Peter Pears*, p. 183.

p. 507   '*St Peter's*': Britten to Ronan Magill, 5 Apr. 1970, L6, p. 353.

p. 507   '*Isn't that*': Sidney Nolan interviewed by Donald Mitchell, 11 June 1990, BPL.

p. 507   '*Australia hasn't*': Ibid.

p. 507   '*had for*': Ibid.

p. 507   '*Well, that's*': Ibid.

p. 508   '*Don't you*': David Marr, *Patrick White: A Life* (London, 1991), p. 426.

p. 509   '*we won't*': Britten to Basil Coleman [postmarked 4 Aug. 1969], L6, p. 296.

p. 510   '*knife-edged*': Britten interviewed by Donald Mitchell, 'Mapreading', p. 321.

CHAPTER 8. *DER ABSCHIED*: ALDEBURGH, HORHAM, 1971–1976

p. 515   '*In the history*': Theodor Adorno, 'Late Style in Beethoven', tr. Susan Gillespie, in his *Essays on Music* (Berkeley, Calif., 2002), p. 567.

p. 515   '*whose work*': Edward Said, *On Late Style* (London, 2006), p. xii.

p. 515   '*unresolved contradiction*': Ibid., p. 7.

p. 515   '*richest and most*': Britten, 'On Receiving the First Aspen Award', 30 July 1964, BOM, p. 260.

p. 516   '*He must*': Colin Matthews interviewed by Michael Oliver, 9 Jan. 1997, BPL.

p. 516   '*It's nothing*': Graham Johnson interviewed by the author, 4 Nov. 2010.

p. 517   '*I have*': Britten to Golo Mann, 8 Sept. 1970, L6, p. 383.

p. 518   '*For one*': Alan Blyth, 'Britten Returns to Composing', *The Times* (30 Dec. 1974), in Donald Mitchell (ed.), *Benjamin Britten: Death in Venice*, Cambridge Opera Handbooks (Cambridge, 1987), p. 26.

p. 518   '*Dear Stephen*': Britten to Stephen Reiss, 17 Oct. 1969, L6, p. 312.

p. 519   '*I think*': Britten to Fidelity Cranbrook [draft], 9 Sept. 1970, BPL.

p. 520   '*devoured people*': HCBB, p. 528.

p. 521   '*Well, if*': Robert Tear, *Tear Here* (London, 1990), p. 104.

p. 521   '*You'd better*': Ibid.

p. 521   '*I know*': HCBB, p. 518.

p. 521   '*Well, it*': HCBB, p. 477.

p. 523   '*at the masterly*': William Mann, in *The Times* (15 May 1971).

p. 523   '*unmistakably*': Martin Cooper, in *Daily Telegraph* (17 May 1971), HCBB, p. 519.

p. 525   *'First of all'*: Rosamund Strode interviewed by David Matthews, 2 Feb. 2004, BPL.

p. 525   *Footnote*: Britten to Paul Sacher, 7 May 1971, L 6, p. 417.

p. 526   *'colder, not'*: Britten to Myfanwy Piper, 6 Feb. 1972, L 6, p. 491.

p. 527   *'Ben would'*: HCBB, p. 542.

p. 527   *'I wanted'*: *The Times* (30 Dec. 1974).

p. 527   *'Ben is'*: HCBB, p. 546.

p. 528   *'couldn't work out'*: Colin Matthews interviewed by the author, 3 Nov. 2010.

p. 528   *'I thought'*: Colin Matthews interviewed by Michael Oliver, 9 Jan. 1997, BPL.

p. 528   *'Tempting as'*: Myfanwy Piper, 'The Libretto', in Mitchell, *Death in Venice*, p. 47.

p. 528   *'passionate-erotic'*: Ibid.

p. 529   *'to organize'*: Ibid.

p. 529   *'physical education'*: Bruno Monsaingeon (ed.), *Sviatoslav Richter: Notebooks and Conversations* (Princeton, 2002), p. 217.

p. 530   *'And in'*: Thomas Mann, *Death in Venice*, trans. H. T. Lowe-Porter (Harmondsworth, 1971), p. 76.

p. 531   *'His later'*: Ibid., p. 18.

p. 531   *'either the'*: Britten to Frederick Ashton, 21 Oct. 1972, L 6, p. 528.

p. 531   *'good as'*: Britten to Ray Minshull, 3 Apr. 1973, BPL.

p. 532   *'Actually it'*: Britten to William Plomer [postmarked 19 Apr. 1973], BPL.

p. 532   *'The surgeon'*: Donald Ross and Barbara Hyams, *Surgery and your Heart* (Beaconsfield, 1982), p. 44.

p. 533   *'Only by devotion'*: M. P. Vora, 'Cardiovascular Syphilis', *Medical Bulletin*, 10/19 (3 Oct. 1942), p. 444.

p. 533   *'In many'*: E. A. Baarsma, B. Kazzaz and K. I. Soei, 'Secondary Syphilis of the Tonsils', *Journal of Laryngology and Otology*, 99 (June 1985), p. 601.

p. 534   *Davies thinks*: Hywel Davies interviewed by the author, 22 Nov. 2011.

p. 535   *'Peter was the one'*: Colin Graham interviewed by Donald Mitchell, 3 Mar. 1992, BPL.

p. 535   *'the relationship'*: Colin Matthews interviewed by the author, 3 Nov. 2010.

p. 535   *'I felt'*: Stephen Reiss to Christopher Headington, 24 June 1990, BPL.

p. 535   *'Peter was always'*: Rita Thomson interviewed by Colin Matthews, 12 Dec. 2003, BPL.

p. 536   *'You look'*: Ibid.

p. 536   *'I feel'*: Ibid.

p. 536   *'Their friendship'*: Christopher Isherwood, *Christopher and his Kind* (London, 1977), p. 197.

p. 537   'His right': Peter Pears to Anthony Gishford [17 May 1973], L6, p. 560.

p. 537   'It's no': HCBB, p. 561.

p. 537   'His [valve] didn't': Michael Petch interviewed by Stephen Lock, 15 Apr. 2009, BPL.

p. 537   Petch was: Michael Petch interviewed by the author, 20 July 2011.

p. 538   'I think': Rita Thomson interviewed by Colin Matthews, 12 Dec. 2003, BPL.

p. 538   'put it': David Matthews interviewed by Michael Oliver, 1997, BPL.

p. 539   'Benjamin Britten, consistently': Edward Greenfield, in Guardian (18 June 1973), in Mitchell, Death in Venice, p. 198.

p. 539   'Death in Venice was composed': Bayan Northcott, New Statesman (22 June 1973), ibid., p. 203.

p. 539   'Britten had': Graham, 'Staging First Productions 3', in David Herbert (ed.), The Operas of Benjamin Britten (London, 1989), p. 56.

p. 540   'because you': Rita Thomson interviewed by Colin Matthews, 12 Dec. 2003, BPL.

p. 540   'was never': Christopher Headington interviewed by Donald Mitchell, 22 Nov. 1990, BPL.

p. 540   'Well you see': Natasha Spender interviewed by Donald Mitchell, 27 Oct. 1990, BPL.

p. 541   'I do know': HCBB, p. 566.

p. 542   'Oh, I was': Rita Thomson interviewed by Colin Matthews, 12 Dec. 2003, BPL.

p. 542   'Can I': Ibid.

p. 544   'My darling': Britten to Peter Pears, 17 Nov. 1974, L6, p. 645.

p. 544   'there is': Britten to Hans Heinsheimer, 21 Jan. 1975, L6, p. 664.

p. 544   'I can't': Britten to Reginald Goodall, 21 Apr. 1975, L6, p. 673.

p. 547   'I've lost': HCBB, p. 569.

p. 547   'I want to': HCBB, p. 573.

p. 549   'I was most': Britten to Colin Davis, 14 July 1975, BPL.

p. 549   'Why does': John Tooley interviewed by Michael Oliver, 1997, BPL.

p. 551   'One is': Britten to Janet Baker, 3 Jan. 1967, L6, p. 7.

p. 551   'The finale': David Matthews interviewed by Michael Oliver, 1997, BPL.

p. 551   'I want the work': Colin Matthews, 'Working Notes', in Alan Blyth Remembering Britten (London, 1981), p. 179.

p. 551   'One day': David Matthews, Britten (London, 2003), p. 152.

p. 551   'I think it is': Hans Keller to Britten, 5 Mar. 1976, L6, p. 668.

p. 552   'Do you': David Matthews interviewed by Michael Oliver, 1997, BPL.

p. 552   'an occasional': Britten to Oliver Knussen, 21 Jan. 1976, L6, p. 702.

p. 554   'I just': HCBB, p. 578.

p. 554   'his dreams': W. H. Auden, 'Paul Bunyan', New York Times (4 May 1941), in 1976 Aldeburgh Festival programme book, p. 12.

p. 554   'a bit over': Colin Matthews interviewed by the author, 9 Dec. 2011.

p. 555   *'He seemed'*: Christopher Isherwood, *Liberation, Diaries*, vol. 3: *1970–1983* (London, 2012), p. 486.

p. 555   *'curiously unnecessary'*: Earl of Harewood, *The Tongs and the Bones* (London, 1981), p. 147.

p. 555   *'No one'*: HCBB, p. 580.

p. 556   *'I should'*: Peter Pears to Britten, 7 July 1976, BPL.

p. 556   *'The ideal'*: Britten to Edith Sitwell, 3 Mar. 1959, L 5, p. 124.

p. 557   *'Schubert never'*: Peter Pears, 'Schubert's Last Songs', 1970 Aldeburgh Festival programme book, p. 24.

p. 558   *'Now Norbert'*: Rita Thomson interviewed by Colin Matthews, 12 Dec. 2003, BPL.

p. 558   *And after*: Ibid.

p. 558   *'Will you have'*: Britten to Basil Coleman, 27 Sept. 1976, L 6, p. 729.

p. 559   *'Just tell'*: Rita Thomson interviewed by Colin Matthews, 12 Dec. 2003, BPL.

p. 559   *'If this'*: MBB, p. 199.

p. 559   *'Dearest Wulff'*: Peter Pears to John Woolford (Wulff Scherchen) [postmarked 25 Nov. 1976], L 6, p. 732.

p. 560   *'Sorry, old'*: Barbara Britten interviewed for ATTW.

p. 560   *'Congestive Cardiac'*: Britten's death certificate, 6 Dec. 1976, BPL.

p. 560   *'I do not believe'*: MBB, p. 200.

p. 561   *'Ben will like'*: HCBB, p. 585.

p. 561   *'My dearest'*: Peter Pears to Britten [postmarked 21 Nov. 1974], L 1, pp. 60–61.

p. 561   *'I am no longer'*: Peter Pears to Britten, 4 Nov. 1976, BPL.

p. 562   *'No, no'*: Graham Johnson interviewed by the author, 4 Nov. 2010.

p. 562   *'Ben's love'*: Rita Thomson interviewed by Colin Matthews, 12 Dec. 2003, BPL.

p. 562   *'I mean'*: Christopher Headington interviewed by Donald Mitchell, 22 Nov. 1990, BPL.

p. 562   *'I think'*: Graham Johnson interviewed by the author, 4 Nov. 2010.

p. 562   *'They found'*: John Tooley interviewed by Michael Oliver, 1997, BPL.

p. 563   *'I'm sorry'*: ATTW out-takes.

p. 563   *'Well honestly'*: Christopher Headington interviewed by Donald Mitchell, 22 Nov. 1990, BPL.

p. 563   *'Pears was'*: Alan Hollinghurst, *The Swimming Pool Library* (London, 1988), p. 122.

p. 564   *'Benjamin Britten'*: Britten obituary, *Daily Telegraph* (6 Dec. 1976).

p. 564   *'All of us'*: 'Benjamin Britten Talks to Edmund Tracey', *Sadler's Wells Magazine* (Autumn 1966), BOM, p. 298.

Picture Credits

6 Will R. Rose; 11 Enid Slater; 18 The Cecil Beaton Studio Archive at Sotheby's; 20 Angus McBean Photograph (MS Thr 581). Copyright © Harvard Theatre Collection, Houghton Library, Harvard University; 21 George Rodger, copyright © Getty Images; 22 Copyright © Getty Images; 23 Kurt Hutton, copyright © Getty Images; 24 Kurt Hutton, copyright © Getty Images; 25 Ford Jenkins A.I.B.P.; 26 Kurt Hutton, copyright © Getty Images; 27 Kurt Hutton, copyright © Getty Images; 29 Erich Auerbach, copyright © Getty Images; 30 Denis de Marney, copyright © Getty Images; 32 Houston Rogers, copyright © Victoria & Albert Museum, London; 33 Kurt Hutton; 34 Kurt Hutton; 36 Copyright © Brian Seed/Lebrecht Music & Arts; 37 Erich Auerbach, copyright © Getty Images; 38 Copyright © Brian Seed/Lebrecht Music & Arts; 39 Erich Auerbach, copyright © Getty Images; 42 Marion Thorpe; 43 Nigel Luckhurst; 44 Nigel Luckhurst; 45 Copyright © Brian Seed/Lebrecht Music & Arts; 46 Arthur Sidey, copyright © Mirrorpix; 47 Copyright © Brian Seed/Lebrecht Music & Arts; 49 Maria Schone; 50 Copyright © The British Library Board (Add 60605, f.2). Copyright © 1960 by Hawkes & Son (London) Ltd. Reproduced by permission of Boosey & Hawkes Music Publishers Ltd; 52 Copyright © Clive Strutt; 53 Nigel Luckhurst; 54 Edward Morgan; 55 Nigel Luckhurst; 56 William Serveas; 57 Nigel Luckhurst; 58 Nigel Luckhurst; 59 Hans H. Rowe.

All other photographs courtesy of the Britten–Pears Library, Aldeburgh.

Index

MacNeice, Louis – *cont.*
    BB 216; *The Dark Tower* 216,
    263; *Letters from Iceland* (with
    Auden) 145
McPhee, Colin 412, 413–14
Macpherson, Charles 43
McVicar, Sir David 272
Madras 478
Madrigal Society *see* English Madrigal
    Society
Magill, Ronan 521
Magnificat (unfinished) 97
Mahler, Gustav 44, 93, 123, 130*n*,
    286, 287, 496; BB compared
    with 15, 34, 43–4, 115, 155,
    169, 211, 330; influence on BB
    120, 131, 168, 308, 428–9, 432,
    439; 'Der Abschied' 131, 561;
    Des Knaben Wunderhorn 308,
    428–9, 543; *Das Lied von der
    Erde* 131, 169–70, 298, 299,
    330; symphonies 167*n*, 258,
    330, 430
Mahler-Werfel, Alma 166, 430, 487
Mahony, Francis 110
Malaysian national anthem (rejected)
    423–4
Malcolm, George 433, 439, 554
Manchester 266
Manchester Guardian (newspaper) 98,
    129; *see also Guardian*
Mandikian, Arda 399
Mann, Golo 166, 173, 517, 518
Mann, Heinrich 166; *Ein ernstes
    Leben* 219
Mann, Thomas 105, 515, 522; diary
    68; emigration 147; sexuality
    528; *Death in Venice* 517, 518,
    528, 529, 530, 539; *Doktor
    Faustus* 517, 538
Mann, William 450, 457, 471, 475
Mannheim 368*n*

Mansfield, Katherine 148
Mansfield Park (proposed opera
    version) 279–80, 396
Margaret, Princess 319, 372
Margaret, Princess of Hesse and the
    Rhine ('Peg'): background and
    marriage 387; BB stays with
    387, 415, 416, 525, 526, 531,
    543; correspondence with BB
    6, 7, 369, 425, 429, 486,
    494; friendship with BB 273,
    360, 382, 424, 517; last
    meeting with BB 559; travels
    with BB 382, 412, 414, 449,
    477–8, 506–7
Maribor 410
Marlowe, Christopher, *Doctor
    Faustus* 406
Marrakesh 490
marriage, BB's views on 404
Martinů, Bohuslav 93, 163
Marwick, Arthur 454, 463
Marx, Karl 107, 111
Marx Brothers 73, 112, 279
Mary, Princess Royal and Countess of
    Harewood 382
Mary, Queen 277
Mascagni, Pietro, *Cavalleria rusticana*
    97
Masefield, John 40
Massenet, Jules 269; *Manon* 294, 359
Masterman, Charles 33
Mata Hari 74, 102
Matinées musicales 177
Matisse, Henri 287
Matter of Life and Death, A (film)
    284
Matthews, Colin: assistant to BB 53,
    395, 547; and String Quartet
    No. 3 552; teaching 471; views
    on BB 510, 516, 528, 535, 536,
    538, 542, 551; and *Death in*